THE
BEST PLAYS
OF 1965-1966

EDITED BY OTIS L. GUERNSEY JR.

Illustrated with photographs and
with drawings by HIRSCHFELD

DODD, MEAD & COMPANY

NEW YORK • TORONTO

66-17967

EDITOR'S NOTE

IN THE index to this volume there are more than 5,000 names of people in and around the theater in New York, across the country and across the seas. The subject of *The Best Plays of 1965-66* is one whole year of their never-failing creativity and productivity; one year of theater expressed in facts, in statistics, in essays evaluating this work from the outside and from the inside, and, first hand, in ten representations of the work itself. Augmentations of the coverage this year include a one-page summary of the off-Broadway season to match the one-page summary of the Broadway season, both appearing in sections of the report on "The Season in New York." The Directory of Professional Regional Theater has expanded and will continue to expand in parallel with the growth of the cross-country theater movement. One of the Best Plays —*Superman*—is represented in a triple combination of text, photographs and drawings. Among this volume's essayists are the authors of Best Plays presenting their views on their own work, on the theater as a whole and on its modern mid-19th century sociological context; and guest experts on many aspects of the living stage, from acting and directing to criticizing and teaching.

The subject of the theater in 1965-66 is as great in size as it is greatly fascinating, and no individual or small group could possibly assemble all the facts and views offered here. Like previous volumes in this series, *The Best Plays of 1965-66* is the work of more than a hundred willing hands, including all those named in the press departments of the shows produced on and off Broadway, and many unnamed members of the producers' staffs. This is their book in thousands of ways, in thousands of exact answers to exacting questions. This book has also benefitted materially from the skillful and diligent attentions of Jonathan Dodd of Dodd, Mead & Company; of Rue Canvin of the New York *Herald Tribune* (off-Broadway productions and Shakespeare festivals); of Elizabeth Rivers of The Dramatists Guild (prizes, publications and necrology); of Ella A. Mallin of ANTA (Directory of Professional Regional Theater); of Ossia Trilling (London and Paris seasons). It also owes much of its substantive value to my wife's patient help in checking the pages.

For all these indispensable contributions; to all the Best Play authors and essayists listed in the Table of Contents; to the designers for their sketches and to the photographers for their photos; to Al Hirschfeld for his penetrating caricatures (he conceals the name of his daughter Nina in these drawings like a rebus puzzle, and her name is imbedded, too, in the type of this volume; she made her Broadway stage debut this season in the chorus of a musical); to George Freedley and the Theater Collection; to Hobe Morrison and *Variety,* and to all others who helped in great and small ways, I offer my own sincere thanks as a down payment on the massive future gratitude which, I predict, will accrue to their work from those who will use and enjoy *The Best Plays of 1965-66*.

OTIS L. GUERNSEY JR.

June 1, 1966

CONTENTS

PHOTOGRAPHS FOLLOW PAGE 348

EDITOR'S NOTE vii

SUMMARIES OF THE SEASONS 1
 The Season in New York 3
  One-page summary of the Broadway Season 4
  One-page summary of the off-Broadway Season 30
 The Season Around the United States 42
  Introduction 42
  Boston 45
  Chicago 48
  Dallas 49
  Houston and Seattle 51
  Los Angeles 52
  Minneapolis 57
  Philadelphia and Pittsburgh 62
  San Francisco 65
  Washington, D. C. 67
  A Directory of Professional Regional Theater 70
 The Shakespeare Festivals 90
 The Season in London 102
  Highlights of the London Season 109
  Highlights of the Paris Season 114

THE TEN BEST PLAYS 119
 Generation 121
 The Royal Hunt of the Sun 146
 Hogan's Goat 169
 Man of La Mancha 195
 Inadmissible Evidence 221
 It's a Bird It's a Plane It's SUPERMAN 242
 Cactus Flower 245
 The Persecution and Assassination of Jean-Paul Marat as Performed

ix

by the Inmates of the Asylum of Charenton Under the Direction of the
Marquis de Sade   269
Philadelphia, Here I Come!   301
The Lion in Winter   324

A GRAPHIC GLANCE BY HIRSCHFELD   349

PLAYS PRODUCED IN THE UNITED STATES   363
Plays Produced on Broadway   365
Plays Produced off Broadway   415
Cast Replacements and Touring Companies   439
A Selected List of Plays First Produced Outside New York City   443

FACTS AND FIGURES   447
Long Runs on Broadway   449
Long Runs off Broadway   450
Drama Critics Circle Voting 1965-66   451
New York Drama Critics Circle Awards   452
Pulitzer Prize Winners   453
Additional Prizes and Awards 1965-66   454
1965-66 Publications of Recently Produced Plays   457
Original Cast Albums of New York Shows   458
The Best Plays, 1894-1965   458
Necrology   469

INDEX   472

Drawings by HIRSCHFELD

Bob Holiday (as Superman), Michael O'Sullivan, Linda Lavin and
Jack Cassidy in "It's a Bird   It's a Plane   It's SUPERMAN"   17

Laurence Naismith, Ivor Emmanuel, Shani Wallis and Tessie O'Shea in
"A Time for Singing"   19

Alan Webb, Tony Randall and Thelma Ritter in "U T B U" (Unhealthy
to Be Unpleasant)   23

David Carradine (as Atahuallpa) and Christopher Plummer (as Pizzaro) in "The Royal Hunt of the Sun"   149

Irving Jacobson (as Sancho), Richard Kiley (as Don Quixote) and Joan Diener (as Aldonza) in "Man of La Mancha"   199

Zohra Lampert, Sam Levene and Estelle Winwood in "Nathan Weinstein, Mystic, Connecticut"   350

Julie Harris and Charles Nelson Reilly in "Skyscraper"   351

Roland Culver, Edward Atienza, Vivien Leigh, John Gielgud, Jennifer Hilary, Ethel Griffies, John Merivale and Paula Laurence in the revival of "Ivanov"   352-353

Zoe Caldwell, Kate Reid and Margaret Leighton in "Slapstick Tragedy"   354

Louis Gossett and Menasha Skulnik in "The Zulu and the Zayda"   355

Beatrice Arthur, Angela Lansbury and Jane Connell in "Mame"   356-357

Michael Kermoyan, Irra Petina, Constance Towers and Lillian Gish in "Anya"   358

Val Bisoglio, Mitchell Ryan, Robert Duval and Lee Remick in "Wait Until Dark"   359

Edward Winter, Robert Symonds, Elizabeth Huddle, Glenn Mazen, Beatrice Manley, Paul Mann and Brock Peters in "The Caucasian Chalk Circle"   360-361

Helen Gallagher, Gwen Verdon and Thelma Oliver in "Sweet Charity"   362

Anne Jeffreys, Alfred Drake and Lee Venora in the revival of "Kismet"   369

Betty Linton and Billy De Wolfe in the revival of "How to Succeed in Business Without Really Trying"   407

Ethel Merman and Harry Bellaver in the revival of "Annie Get Your Gun"   413

Lotte Goslar and Menasha Skulnik in "The Zulu and the Zayda."   355

SUMMARIES
OF THE
SEASONS

THE SEASON IN NEW YORK

By Otis L. Guernsey Jr.

". . . THE THEATER was in strong hands, many of them in their first grasp of Broadway, with still more strong hands reaching."

That's the way our New York report ended in last year's *Best Plays* volume. As things turned out, it was prophetic. The new, 1965-66 theater season in New York was nowhere; it was headed for a disaster appalling in its unmitigated totality of mediocrity, when a funny thing happened—the new-reaching hands caught, took hold and gripped firm. When old hands faltered, scripts from brand new sources arrived in time to save the season.

In 1965-66 the playwriting "establishment" failed the theater on Broadway and off; yet in this same period audiences were treated to several fine musicals, two poetic dramas, a comedy mostly in verse disguised as prose, two hot comedies and other delectations. Where did they come from? You might as well say the stork brought them. Of the ten Best Plays in this volume, *eight* were either playwriting debuts in some sense or new territory for old practitioners, as follows: *Generation* was William Goodhart's first script produced on any stage; the book of *Man of La Mancha* was Dale Wasserman's first Broadway musical and Mitch Leigh's first Broadway score; *Cactus Flower* was Abe Burrows' first non-musical playwriting credit; *The Persecution and Assassination of Marat as Performed by the Inmates of the Asylum of Charenton Under the Direction of the Marquis de Sade* was Peter Weiss's American stage debut and *Philadelphia, Here I Come!* was Brian Friel's; *The Lion in Winter* was James Goldman's first Broadway effort solo, without a collaborator; the book of *"It's a Bird It's a Plane It's SUPERMAN"* was the professional playwriting debut of David Newman and Robert Benton, and *Hogan's Goat* was William Alfred's first professional production.

Of 1965-66's Best Plays, only John Osborne's *Inadmissible Evidence* and Peter Shaffer's *The Royal Hunt of the Sun* came from expected sources. Elsewhere, great expectations failed to materialize; the likes of Jerome Chodorov William Hanley, Alan Jay Lerner, Mary Drayton, Neil Simon, William Inge, Jack Richardson, George Abbott, Robert Dhery, Jerome Weidman and, yes, Edward Albee and Tennessee Williams, fell far short of their best—some of them spectacularly far short. So many so very talented playwrights failed on so many levels that except for the miracle of the neophytes the 1965-66 season would have left the New York stage on its hands and knees.

Any Broadway season is constructed from equal parts of talent, effort, hope and cash. The first varies from year to year with the winds of artistic chance.

3

The 1965-66 Season on Broadway

PLAYS (25)

Mrs. Dally
A Very Rich Woman
GENERATION
Minor Miracle
The Impossible Years
Postmark Zero
Mating Dance
Xmas in Las Vegas
The Zulu and the Zayda (with music)
The Playroom
Me and Thee
CACTUS FLOWER
Utbu
Malcolm
The Wayward Stork
The Great Indoors
Wait Until Dark
Slapstick Tragedy
Nathan Weinstein, Mystic, Connecticut
First One Asleep, Whistle
Where's Daddy?
THE LION IN WINTER
3 Bags Full
Happily Never After
The Best Laid Plans

MUSICALS (11)

Drat! The Cat!
On a Clear Day You Can See Forever
Skyscraper
MAN OF LA MANCHA
Anya
The Yearling
Sweet Charity
Pousse-Café
A Time for Singing
Mame

REVIVALS (16)

South Pacific
The Music Man
Kismet
Carousel
The Saint of Bleecker Street
Street Scene
The Consul
Danton's Death
The Country Wife
You Can't Take It With You
Oklahoma
How to Succeed in Business Without Really Trying
Ivanov
The Most Happy Fella
Where's Charley?
Annie Get Your Gun

FOREIGN PLAYS IN ENGLISH (14)

Oliver (musical; return engagement)
Pickwick (musical)
Entertaining Mr. Sloane
The Right Honourable Gentleman
The Condemned of Altona
The Caucasian Chalk Circle
THE ROYAL HUNT OF THE SUN
The Devils
INADMISSIBLE EVIDENCE
La Grosse Valise (musical)
MARAT/SADE
PHILADELPHIA, HERE I COME!
Hostile Witness
Wait a Minim! (revue)

SPECIALTIES (4)

The World of Charles Aznavour
Marcel Marceau
Bunraku (puppet theater)
Mark Twain Tonight!

PRODUCTIONS BY FOREIGN LANGUAGE TROUPES (6)

The Comédie Française
L'Avare
Le Cid
La Reine Morte
Un Fil a la Patte
Bavarian State Theater
Woyzeck and Die Mitschuldigen
Die Ratten

HOLDOVER SHOW WHICH BECAME A HIT DURING 1965-66

The Roar of the Greasepaint—The Smell of the Crowd

Categorized above are all the plays listed in the "Plays Produced on Broadway" section of this volume.

Plays listed in CAPITAL LETTERS have been designated Best Plays of 1965-66 in this volume.

Plays listed in bold face type were classified as hits in *Variety's* annual list of hits and flops as of June 22, 1966.

Plays listed in *italics* were still running on May 31, 1966.

The last three flow more steadily, and they did so in 1965-66 as in previous years. Effort and hope (and money) went into a grand total of 76 shows this season, as compared with 81 last year and 75 the year before. Of these, 49 were new (counting new foreign plays in English). 1965-66 brought in the same number of new American plays—25—as in 1964-65 and one more musical—11. If you look for centers of gravity in the production list (see the one-page chart of the 1965-66 season accompanying this chapter) you will notice immediately that foreign authors had very much more than their share of success on both the top and second levels. And, among the 25 new American playscripts there continued an alarming preponderance of comedy over drama.

In the matter of money, *Variety* estimates that Broadway grossed a ring-tailed all-time-record $53,862,187, topping last year's record by more than three million. The number of playing weeks in 1965-66 (if ten shows play ten weeks, that's 100 playing weeks) reached 1,295—the second highest in theater history, second only to 1947-48's 1,325 and exceeding last season by 45 playing weeks. The record gross was attained with a top ticket price which broke the old sawbuck barrier ($9.90) and kept on inching upward: $11.90 for *On a Clear Day You Can See Forever* . . . $12 for *Superman* . . . ?

Of course, that $53,862,187 wasn't all profit—far from it. In 1965-66, average production costs had risen to $500,000 for a musical and $160,000 for a straight play (from $300,000 and $80,000 in the 1950s). There were five shows that were mounted but folded before their Broadway openings, and they cost their backers more than $750,000 (two of these, *Venus Is* and *The Office* folded in New York during previews). Five big musicals—*Drat! The Cat! Anya, The Yearling, La Grosse Valise* and *Pousse-Café*—died for $2,010,000. And that's not all. Seven of the holdover musicals from the 1964-65 season closed during 1965-66 at an estimated loss of $2,310,000.

On the other hand, *Fiddler on the Roof* holding over from 1964-65 has already earned an estimated $1,250,000, not including a film sale, and is still moving out. The fabulous *Hello, Dolly!* has long since passed the $3,000,000 mark. The arrival of *Sweet Charity* made it three high-grossers running concurrently on Broadway for Neil Simon. The other two, held over from past seasons, were *Barefoot in the Park* and *The Odd Couple*. The week of February 16 (just for instance) the total gross of Simon's three Broadway productions was $153,733. These are the kind of figures which, even in the midst of losses, keep hope and effort alive and money available to place scripts under option for next year.

What kind of a season was it? Well, the new playwrights saved it from disaster, but not from its share of failures. In a broad sense it was a failure of American playwriting. Our authors came up with what, in my opinion, were the two best scripts of the year—*Hogan's Goat* and *Man of La Mancha*—but allowed the foreign authors to steal the bulk of the show both on and off Broadway, particularly over there on the dramatic, or "serious" side of the theatrical balance.

The list of skilled and popular performers whose vehicles died under them includes Ruth Gordon, Arlene Francis, Harry Secombe, Lee Tracy, Van

Johnson, Tom Ewell, Jason Robards, Anne Bancroft, Lillian Gish, David Wayne, Victor Spinetti, Tony Randall, Robert Cummings, Curt Jurgens, Margaret Leighton, Sam Levene, Betty Field, Hiram Sherman, Theodore Bikel and Paul Ford. Lincoln Center Repertory fared poorly (artistically, not financially) at the Vivian Beaumont Theater under the direction of Jules Irving and Herbert Blau. On and off Broadway during the season there were four one-performance flops and several no-performance flops—plays that got as far as previews in New York but closed before their first night.

Black comedies darker than *Marat/Sade* fared almost as badly as sex comedies less adroit than *Cactus Flower*. Bear in mind, though—bear firmly in mind—that the important information conveyed in that sentence is not the fact of the several failures but the fact of the two successes. In a television documentary about Broadway a scene showed a bulldozer levelling masses of junked scenery on the Jersey Meadows, together with the comment that Broadway's major product is failure. This is a glaring fallacy, of course; but it's typical of a certain strain of criticism designed to be self-serving rather than public-serving, intended to make a mess that the critic can stamp around in and leave footprints calling attention to himself. Broadway's major product is fabulously successful shows that survive for years on the stages of the world, including our own regional theater stages. Broadway's major product is success, and its failures are merely a form of artistic waste; awkward and unsightly and even greater in bulk than the product itself, but of no more importance than a slag heap created by a gold mine.

John F. Wharton, who is consultant-director of the Legitimate Theater Industry Exploratory Commission, said that he has found a delightful and exciting new way to experience the theater. Ignoring the thud of flopping shows, he listens instead for the sound of success—the soaring melodies, the compelling language of good dramas, the relaxed laughter of good comedy. Did he hear such enjoyable sounds in 1965-66? He certainly did, and on a very broad scale from farce to drama. Mr. Wharton's attitude tells a clear truth about the theater, clear of the rubbish that often collects around it and obscures it. The truth is that if our theater brings forth exciting and entertaining shows, then it is serving its purpose no matter what other distressing things happen. Let those who get their kicks from the morbid contemplation of ugliness concentrate upon Broadway's slag heap of failure; I am for Mr. Wharton. 1965-66 brought forth its share of successes, and I prefer to scrutinize *them*. The quintessential truth is that there *was* a *Man of La Mancha,* a *Cactus Flower,* a *Hogan's Goat,* a *Marat/Sade* in New York this season—and lots more to make this an exciting year on and off Broadway. That is to say: whatever its failures, its degree of productivity or its "average," the 1965-66 season provided a group of shows that no theatergoer would want to have missed, or could ever forget.

The Hits

The word "hit" is used often and loosely as a synonym for "popular" or "successful"; but in its tight commercial-theater meaning a "hit" is a show that took in enough money at the box office to get off the nut. There are as many forms of success in the theater as in any other human activity, and they will be duly considered hereinunder. But in this section the word "hit" is used only in its pure fiscal sense of a show that paid back its cost before May 31, 1966. As of that date, the last day of the season as recorded in this *Best Plays* volume, there were ten hits among the season's 76 productions (according to a *Variety* estimate), as follows:

Pickwick	*Marat/Sade*
Generation	*Wait Until Dark*
The Impossible Years	*Cactus Flower*
You Can't Take It With You	*Mark Twain Tonight!*
Inadmissible Evidence	*The World of Charles Aznavour*

There was no American musical hit as of May 31, 1966. Shows which kept on running after that date must be conceded a chance to become hits as they continue onward into 1966-67. As of the season's end, those shows whose chances to pay off looked certain were *Man of La Mancha,** *Sweet Charity* and *Mame.*

As usual, there were some special cases on the hit list. This year (as last year, with Victor Borge and Maurice Chevalier) there were two solo shows: Charles Aznavour with a repertory of songs, most of them in the French language; and *Mark Twain Tonight!,* Hal Holbrook's virtuoso performance of Mark Twain on the lecture platform, to which Holbrook has added new material since his first New York appearance off Broadway in 1959. This was his Mark Twain's Broadway debut in a limited engagement which became a triumph and received a special citation from the New York Drama Critics Circle. Another special case is the British musical *Pickwick,* with Harry Secombe, a popular grand opera tenor and musical comedy star, making his American debut as Charles Dickens' orotund traveller, philosopher and clubman. Imported to America after 18 months in London, *Pickwick* like Secombe himself was cheery, in good voice, but trying too hard to be droll, on too unsophisticated a level. The show was at its best in the quicksilver performance of Anton Rodgers as the rascally Mr. Jingle. *Pickwick* didn't do well on Broadway, but it didn't have to; David Merrick recouped its cost on a road tour before it ever faced Broadway's critics.

For some, the most satisfying kind of a hit may be the big-grossing Broadway musical with ice more than $25 thick on the tickets and a fat movie sale in the offing. For the genuine theater buff, though, the most satisfying hit is the one that coincides with artistic excellence. So it is a particular pleasure to note that four of this year's Best Plays achieved hit status at the box office: *Generation, Inadmissible Evidence, Marat/Sade* and *Cactus Flower.*

William Goodhart's *Generation* starred Henry Fonda as an advertising executive whose daughter has married a Greenwich Village photographer (married yesterday and the baby expected tomorrow). She and her devoted but

* Soon after the season's end (as reported by *Variety* on June 22, 1966, in its annual list of hits and flops) both *Man of La Mancha* and the revival of *Ivanov* formally achieved hit status.

arrogantly individualistic husband are determined to share the adventure of childbirth, without the help of doctors, in their studio-loft (designed by George Jenkins as the prototype of the militantly Bohemian pad: brick walls, exposed pipes, makeshift furniture). This comedy earned its place on the hit list and the Best Plays list not only by its expertise of timing in Fonda's smooth performance, or the lumpy humor of A. Larry Haines in the supporting role of a doctor brought in against the patient's will; it earned its place not just with gags about a man in a gray flannel suit confronting a beatnik son-in-law who sometimes likes to wear his wife's beads. Exploring the gulf between the generations, it finds and scrutinizes one of the real issues in today's running dispute between 20 and 40-year-olds.

Many of the most irritating contemporary youthful extravagancies are aimed (consciously or unconsciously) to penetrate and ridicule the false pretenses, the hypocrisies and mendacities of the previous generation, particularly in areas of moral and ethical judgment. Now, it isn't merely the father-in-law's preoccupation with making money in the advertising business that sets off the fireworks in *Generation*. What sends up the rockets is the father-in-law's pretense, even to himself, that he is not *really* like other advertising men but is "boring from within" to set higher standards of taste. It isn't his self-interest, but his euphemism, that invites scorn. It is this mendacity, the fact that he's kidding himself and others, this wanting to have his advertising cake and eat it too, that calls down the derision of his son-in-law (who may be kidding *himself* just a little, thinking that he's self-sufficient).

William Inge tried to work this same territory, this no-man's-land between the generations, in *Where's Daddy?*, also about a young married couple expecting a baby in the outrageous environment of a New York pad. Inge's play carried as many jokes under its arm as *Generation,* on somewhat the same general subject, but without a strong theme. It merely multiplied the character gags: the mother (Betty Field) who has decided to blink at nothing, however outrageous; a benign foster-father (Hiram Sherman); a hip Negro couple living next door. *Where's Daddy?* must be the kind of play people mean when they say that a Broadway season consists in "nothing but comedies." Inge's play was a nothing-but-comedy, whereas Goodhart's *Generation* went right to the heart of a very sensitive matter with almost every laugh.

The next (chronologically) of the Best Plays on the hit list was John Osborne's *Inadmissible Evidence,* which, taken together with *The Royal Hunt of the Sun, Marat/Sade* and *Philadelphia, Here I Come!*—all of them Best Plays which will be considered here as a group, though only two achieved formal hit status—brings up two subjects at once. The first and most problematical is the serious plight of serious plays in the Broadway theater. The second and more immediate is the prominence of foreign authors on Broadway in 1965-66.

Recent signs like the economic struggle for survival waged across two seasons (and finally won) by *The Subject Was Roses,* the failure last year of *Tiny Alice* and the continuing overwhelming preponderance of comedies on the production list, have led most observers to believe that the audience for so-called "serious" drama on Broadway is shrinking. (By "serious" I do not mean Sophoclean-serious, I mean serious on balance; scripts billed as "plays" rather than "comedies" and not played primarily for laughs. The borderline case is *Marat/Sade*.) Most dramatic scripts can't seem to get a grip on the audience, and it has been suggested that this alarming condition prevails simply because the plays haven't been strong enough. The scripts, it is argued, haven't managed to take a firm hold on the audience because they haven't managed to take a firm hold on their subject matter in our wildly upheaving, neurotic, stressful era.

This answer may be the right one. Maybe it *is* the plays and not the audience; because, this season, along came three on-balance-serious scripts from Europe (not counting *Marat/Sade*) which *did* find ways to harness the extremely complicated and powerful emotional forces of today; enough to attract an audience and run in glory and respect through the season, if not get off the nut at the box office. The first was Peter Shaffer's *The Royal Hunt of the Sun,* a spectacular confrontation both physically and philosophically between the Conquistador leader Pizarro and the great Inca Atahuallpa. This was a pageant of staging effects by John Dexter, costume and scenic effects (including a twelve-foot sunburst) by Michael Annals and setpiece language effects by Shaffer. David Carradine's physically stylized performance of the Inca man-God Atahuallpa became more and more effective as events approached closer and closer to Atahuallpa's murder. Here Pizarro, disillusioned with life's realities and admiring the Inca so much that he half-believes in his divinity (as Atahuallpa half-believes in Pizarro's divinity), puts Atahuallpa to death in the fervent hope that the Inca's father the Sun-God will revive him at dawn. In this murder Pizarro hopes to find the means for conquering death after a life time spent hating and fearing it. His last hope dies with the Inca's mortality.

Shaffer's play started slowly. It lumbered toward its climax through the bitter musings of Pizarro (Christopher Plummer) and the ironic reminiscences of a narrator (George Rose) about the adventures of the band of Conquistadors. But it built to an electrifying conclusion as Pizarro kills his Indian friend in an attempt to challenge death itself.

Another European on-balance-serious script that was good enough to attract audiences—and even to become a hit—was John Osborne's *Inadmissible Evidence*. It concerned itself with the corrosiveness of the mid-20th century. It studies and prods, prods and studies a middle-aged lawyer who senses that life is rolling over him, kicking down his values, placing him on trial for unavoidable errors of judgment, crushing him and moving on past him to a bright future he will never share. The lawyer positively festers onstage. His guilts and fears materialize in a dream trial and in rejections by those he loves and in devastating self-criticism. Each effort he makes to alleviate his condition by scratching at it makes it worse and loses him another friend, or another pound of self-respect, until he is all used up.

Osborne's script is a character revelation in thoughts spoken out loud; a form of theater that could be called a controlled tantrum. What's happening is, one man is coming apart, and the sound of it is piteous. The play vibrates, not with events, but with Osborne's gift for expression. It reaches its height of panicky emotion, not in any confrontation, but in a great overflowing of envy and admiration as the lawyer tries to explain himself one last time, reaching out for sympathy, to his teen-aged daughter (his long speech to her appears in its entirety in the synopsis of *Inadmissible Evidence* in the Best Plays section of this volume). And Nicol Williamson gave the season's best male straight-play performance as the lawyer. Nothing less than the best would have been adequate for a role so demanding that it required a gifted alternate, James Patterson, to play the matinee performances.

Inadmissible Evidence never ventures into way-out absurdism, but its tantrum construction is a far-out form of theater. Is a radical structure, then, the secret of success for modern dramatic material? Is a distortion of conventional form, touched up with a lick or two of sensation (as in a scene with a homosexual client in *Inadmissible Evidence* and the drooling madmen of *Marat/Sade*) necessary to the success of "serious" theater on Broadway?

No. A third European Best Play of 1965-66 (with a good chance of achieving hit status), Brian Friel's *Philadelphia, Here I Come!,* was conventional in structure and almost unfailingly modest in subject matter; yet it was the most powerful, the most poignant playscript of all the imports. As it begins, a young Irishman, son of a respected shop-owner in a small town, is going to his aunt's in Philadelphia to live and work. He hopes that his unresponsive father, whom he loves in spite of his callow mockery of the old man, will show some sign of regret at his departure. That's all it is: a simple little father-and-son emotional estrangement which tears the feelings right out of your chest with the clarity and purity of its expression. It can be argued that, technically, *Philadelphia, Here I Come!* is a comedy; yet its subject and treatment are as severe as any drama could wish to be.

Philadelphia, Here I Come! has one eccentricity: the young man, Gar, is written to be played by two actors, one of whom represents Gar's external self and the other his secret thoughts—a device which cannot be said to be very new or very radical. Otherwise, there was very little mannerism in the concept or performance of this play. It isn't even written in the darlin' language of most scripts which are exported by the Dublin theater. This is a dour, North-of-Ireland work, spare and muscular in speech, weighing the words intended to describe a father and son who cannot reach each other in words, or by any other means. The play was fully realized in Hilton Edwards' fine staging, and it was brilliantly performed by a company in which the outstanding work was done by Mairin D. O'Sullivan as the elderly housekeeper who loves Gar and his father as she scolds them; and by Eamon Kelly as the inscrutible parent.

The urge to label Peter Weiss's *Marat/Sade* as a "serious" hit is strong but should be denied; *Marat/Sade* is a Best Play and certainly was a hit and won the New York Drama Critics award for the best foreign play of 1965-66 (in very strong competition), but it probably should be labeled a comedy despite its horrendous goings-on. The image on its advertising posters was holding out the masque of tragedy—but the masque of comedy was grinning underneath. It has been called a "black *Hellzapoppin.*" It was funny as a crutch, cheerful as a sick joke, a gargoyle play which enacted Marat's assassination (but that's not what it is really *about*) as staged by the Marquis de Sade and his group of amateur actors recruited from the drooling, crawling, gurgling, moaning, grimacing inmates of the madhouse at Charenton in France in the Napoleonic era. This script plays a strange game without much volleying. Instead, it is a series of brilliant vignettes, of historic poses presented almost as tableaux, pausing in the middle of each stroke to admire the form. Marat is seen as a single-minded, even bloody-minded man of the people and opposing him is the cynical, sensual, inner-seeking Marquis de Sade. Marat devotes himself to externals, to the people and revolution, to natural science, while de Sade believes only in self and in exploring every avenue of sensation. Their debate on inwardness vs. outwardness was never resolved in *The Persecution and Assassination of Marat as Performed by the Inmates of the Asylum of Charenton Under the Direction of the Marquis de Sade* (to give the play its full title for a change). But this debate was the inner circle of a show formed in concentric circles of ironic images and madmen's ravings.

As with many modern German scripts, Weiss's *Marat/Sade* has a built-in message about spreading and sharing guilt (i.e.: every civilization has its blood bath; the French had their "final solution" to the problem of the aristocrats—the guillotine—and followed it promptly with Napoleon's bloody and militaristic activities; *that's* what this play is about). But the message in this case is buried in vivid externals. There was shock value even in the costumes designed by Gunilla Palmstierna-Weiss (the playwright's wife). Peter Brook staged his madhouse scenes in a key of horrible fascination, in a *danse macabre* whose few formal paces among the spastic gestures and stampings were choreographed by Malcolm Goddard. This imported *Marat/Sade*—in an English version by Geoffrey Skelton adapted in verse by Adrian Mitchell—was one of the Royal Shakespeare Company's modern-play projects, so its cast was uniformly excellent, with a particular citation to Ian Richardson in the pivotal role of a paronoiac patient playing Marat and crying to the mob from his tin bathtub. (It should be emphasized that this show was acted on three levels: first, of madmen; second, of madmen playing historical figures amateurishly; third, of the historical figures fully realized.) During the New York engagement various members of the acting company stated publicly that the effort of performing *Marat/Sade* was almost too great, and that they would be glad when its limited engagement was ended. This complaint sounded strange to American ears: an actor who found his part so demanding that he wished his hit show would close? It sounded like a publicity gimmick because there is no real Broadway parallel to these performers' situation. They are members of a permanent repertory company, and they would go on acting, go on functioning after this too-exacting production closed. Some day, we hope, American actors will have complaints like that.

To make it on Broadway a serious play doesn't necessarily have to be perverted, or violent, or absurd, or camp, or existential enough, it just has to be *strong* enough to grip a contemporary audience with either a universal conflict (extrovert vs. introvert, father vs. son, civilized evil vs. savage evil, etc.) or an exceptionally timely one (modern man having the rug pulled out from under him). To succeed on Broadway, apparently, a serious play should have a strong underweave of black laughter—of sarcasm and irony—to indicate that this whole business of suffering may best be taken, after all, as a colossal joke. But as *Philadelphia, Here I Come!, Inadmissible Evidence, The Royal Hunt of the Sun* and *Hogan's Goat* off Broadway and maybe even *Marat/Sade* demonstrated this season, a script can tip its balance onto the dramatic side and still acquire eager listeners. It may be harder to write a strong drama in this era of cool, but once written it has an audience.

There's no doubt that our theatrical brethren from across the seas took more than their share of the New York stage in 1965-66; and they did it in depth, all the way from the front-and-center Broadway hit position to the dimmest recesses of off-Broadway. From Europe, in addition to the abovementioned shows, came *Wait a Minim!, Entertaining Mr. Sloane, The Right Honourable Gentleman, The Devils, Hostile Witness, Live Like Pigs, The Trigon* and *Serjeant Musgrave's Dance,* of which more later. Only a year ago, when European works of the highest repute were flopping one after another in New York, the best foreign work tasted thin and watery in comparison to Brodway scripts like *Tiny Alice* or *The Odd Couple.* Even though the European absurdists—Ionesco, Beckett, Pinter—have changed the shape of the American theater permanently with the powerful wrench of their inventiveness, the year-ago crop of European scripts—by the likes of Anouilh, Duerrenmatt, Iris Murdoch, Bill Naughton, Arnold Wesker, Enid Bagnold, even Brecht—found a cold welcome here. But in 1965-66 it was different. Foreign authors dominated the New York stage, not with gimmicks or existentialist sick jokes, but with good, solid scripts. Without the foreign plays, the season would have been unusually skimpy during a temporary lull in American playwrighting. Thanks to them, it was a round and full experience of theatergoing.

The fourth Best Play to make the hit list was *Cactus Flower,* the comedy smash which Abe Burrows adapted from a Paris (Europeans again!) hit entitled *Fleur de Cactus* by the comedy-writing team of Pierre Barillet and Jean-Pierre Gredy. It had the unmistakable look of a French farce in romantic convolutions in which the single theme of sexual attraction was played and replayed in as many variations as a Bach fugue. But everything else in it was 100 per cent Americanized and Burrows-ized: the successful young Park Avenue dentist, a philanderer in his boyish, clean-cut American way; his lanky and overly-efficient nurse who slowly develops into a long-stemmed American beauty as depicted in glorious living color and perfect comedy sense by Lauren Bacall; the luscious Greenwich Village good-time girl with a heart as big as all outdoors; plus an entertaining assortment of patients, rivals and night club types.

"*Cactus Flower* is maybe the first that has traveled this well since *Tovarich,*" Burrows commented of his work, and he believes a major reason for its success here is that he localized it so thoroughly that New York audiences identified with it perfectly. The characters, the jokes, the staging were all as Broadway as Abe Burrows; which is to say, they succeeded in creating uproarious laughter without really trying, with verbal and situation gags trained up to the easy manner and deep penetration of wit.

Another comedy on the hit list was *The Impossible Years,* the Broadway playwriting debut of Bob Fisher and Arthur Marx. In it, Alan King played a successful psychiatrist, a child-care expert, who can't manage his own teen-aged daughter. King is an actor-comedian, a caricaturist and monologist, who is accustomed to grabbing audiences and making them laugh, all by himself in some night club. He has a special gift of projecting both the underdog who may get up at any moment and win and the top dog whose position is shaky. Small wonder that he found the routine comic relationships of *The Impossible Years* adequate to his purpose of spending the season on Broadway. But no small admiration is due him for a splendid performance which put his play into the hit column.

Still another comedy hit was the Association of Producing Artists revival of *You Can't Take It With You.* In recent seasons APA repertory has been offered off Broadway by the Phoenix Theater with great distinction. Now, in moving to Broadway with a single production, the APA-Phoenix continued its success story, with an acting company that has developed into an ensemble (in *You Can't Take It With You* their star performer, Rosemary Harris, played the minor role of the ingenue) and with the Moss Hart-George S. Kaufman humor fully realized in Ellis Rabb's direction. The 30-year-old script about an eccentric family devoted to individualistic expression and yet inviting all comers to join in their zestful pursuit of happiness (except for the income tax man) proved to be even more appealing to modern audiences than scores of scripts written the day before yesterday.

The special dramatic category of thrillers was well represented on Broadway this season, and one of them made the hit list: Frederick Knott's *Wait Until Dark,* with Lee Remick as a blind girl victimized by a deadly insect of a villain (Robert Duvall) who has reason to believe that heroin is secreted somewhere in her apartment. In a climatic scene, as the plot thickened in a hushed theater, with the killer stalking the blind girl on a pitch-black-dark stage, there occurred a surprise that made the audience cry out aloud. The logic of *Wait Until Dark* was somewhat less than relentless in places, but a thriller has to get a pretty good grip on an audience to make it yelp.

These were the lucky ten hits—one melodrama; five comedies including one very black and one very old: a drama, a musical and two specialty shows. There were eleven hits the year before, but only one of last year's holdovers *(The Roar of the Greasepaint—The Smell of the Crowd)* achieved hit status in 1965-66, whose holdovers into 1966-67 will almost certainly do better. Comedy predominated, but there *was* a drama among the hits, and nothing shabby or shoddy was supported. The Broadway playgoer didn't support *everything* that was good, but this ideal condition never comes true. In every season, in addition to the shows that distinguish themselves with respectable runs without actually making it as hits, there are two or more shows which are well worth an audience's time and money but which for various reasons, sometimes mysterious, don't catch on as they should. For example, in 1965-66 *A Very Rich Woman, The Lion in Winter* and *3 Bags Full* folded after short runs. These three comedies had most of what it takes to make a hit on Broadway. In other words, they had the most to lose by failure; and in their failure the theater and the theatergoers lost the most, too.

Successful and Otherwise

"Success, as I see it, is a result, not a goal," Flaubert said, and he ought to have been speaking of Broadway. The goal on Broadway is always the same: to attract an audience and run. Success on Broadway is a different matter; sometimes it coincides with reaching the goal, and sometimes not. It can be achieved in many forms by players and plays which do *not* reach the goal of popular support in a long run. For example, two of the season's performing bests, by two girls named Harris—Rosemary in *The Lion in Winter* and Barbara in *On a Clear Day You Can See Forever*—came in shows which fell short of attaining hit status. Among the most interesting visual impressions of 1965-66 were William Ritman's blackened junkyard surroundings for the one-room set of *Entertaining Mr. Sloane* (seen for only 13 performances) and Will Steven Armstrong's captivating art nouveau stylization of a Madison Avenue town house in *3 Bags Full* (seen only 33 times).

The ultimate form of theater success (we insist) is selection as a Best Play in this volume. This selection was made with the script itself as the primary consideration, for the reason that the script is the very spirit of the theater: it is not only the quintessence of the theater's present, it is also most of what endures into the future. The Best Plays are the best scripts, giving as little weight to comparative production values as is humanly possible, and with no regard whatever to a play's type (comedy, musical or drama) origin (on or off Broadway) or degree of success at the box office. The Best Plays of 1965-66 were these (an asterisk with the performance number means the play was still running on June 1, 1966), in the order in which they opened:

Generation (hit; 269* perfs.)	*Cactus Flower* (hit; 199* perfs.)
The Royal Hunt of the Sun (247* perfs.)	*Marat/Sade* (hit; 144 perfs.)
Hogan's Goat (off B'way; 221* perfs.)	*Philadelphia, Here I Come!* (119* perfs.)
Man of La Mancha (216* perfs.)	*The Lion in Winter* (92 perfs.)
Inadmissible Evidence (hit; 166 perfs.)	*Superman* (75* perfs.)

Technically there were no American musical hits as of the end of 1965-66, but certainly wonderful *Man of La Mancha,* the musical play about Cervantes and his Don Quixote, would grace any season. It started slowly on the road to success, downtown at the ANTA Washington Square Theater (this musical has sometimes been called an off-Broadway show because of its geographical location, but it is not; its contracts with the authors, the actors, etc., are Broadway contracts). Even with good reviews it took a while for audiences to find it tucked away in its corner of the city. But finally they did, and *Man* *of La Mancha* became a hot ticket.* Among its many prizes and citations was the New York Drama Critics Circle award for the best musical of the season.

Man of La Mancha was produced by Albert W. Selden and Hal James, and it was one of those happy special cases in which many creative elements clustered into a solid success phenomenon. It had the best male performance in a musical in Richard Kiley's stringy, bony and finally heart-rending Don Quixote. It had top-notch singing support from Ray Middleton, Joan Diener and Robert Rounseville in a production staged with unfailing excitement by Albert Marre in the problematical area of the theater's thrust stage. Howard Bay's setting presented the play perfectly with an open-stage platform and a few props to represent plays-within-plays (Cervantes is in prison telling the story of Don Quixote to his fellow-prisoners and acting it out as he tells it). The set was versatile enough to contain the far-ranging imagined adventures of the knight of La Mancha and his squire Sancho Panza—all this without any cumbersome moving-about of scenery except for a ladder which descended into the prison set, ominously, to admit Inquisition characters. The musical had the best costumes (by Howard Bay and Patton Campbell), the best music and lyrics (by Mitch Leigh and Joe Darion), the best choreography (Jack Cole's) including the brutal rape of a serving-wench by lusty Muleteers, expressed in dance.

Man of La Mancha is an achievement of overall excellence, and in addition it opposes every modern theatrical fad and fashion except the fad of setting things to music. In recent years a trend has crept in like a trader rat to rob our drama of the bright things like anger and tragedy, leaving in their place dull despair and self-pity as though these were equal in emotion merely because they are equal in weight. *Man of La Mancha* treads heavily on this rat. It is musical drama that brought tears to the eyes of many in its audience; yet, lo and behold, it is theater of hope, drama of endurance, in angry revolt against all forms of despair. Don Quixote's dreams and knightly poses transcend any motive of mendacity; they achieve near-tragic stature in a hero whose goal is "To bear with unbearable sorrow, To fight the unbeatable foe"—and you can't get any farther from despair and surrender than that.

The Cervantes-Don Quixote character of *Man of La Mancha* is brother to the pipe dreamers of Eugene O'Neill's *The Iceman Cometh;* cousin to Willy Loman in *Death of a Salesman.* The show was out of (and, I think, above) its theatrical time in 1966 in the same way that Don Quixote was above *his* time in the 16th century. It may be, even, that some of the knight's aspirations are wholly incomprehensible, even as comic exaggerations, to the generation coming along. When the Mitch Leigh-Joe Darion song number "The Quest" was first recorded on a record for popular circulation, a line of the lyric expressing Don Quixote's ideals was changed from "To love, pure and chaste, from afar" to "To be better far than you are." Love like that they have never imagined, but being better they dig; especially in its meaning of being better off in a materialistic society.

No, the 1960s have no welcome mat out for plays of ideal and aspiration

* According to a *Variety* estimate, it achieved formal hit status before the end of June, 1966.

and courage; they are a time for plays about characters sitting in garbage cans complaining about what went wrong. If *Man of La Mancha* can't reverse the gravitation, maybe it can help to start a trend of its own. In his introduction to the synopsis of his musical in the Best Plays section of this volume, Dale Wasserman declares he knew he was working against the grain of the modern theater when he selected and organized the Cervantes-Don Quixote material. He was so admirably successful that maybe he will jog others out of the blue monotony of neurotic cynicism into an occasional appreciation of the human spirit in a larger-than-life phase.

Musically speaking, the season's first success was announced in the challenging trumpets of *Man of La Mancha;* then it rested on its laurels and made do with fair-to-middling shows until the last weeks, when it roused to the fanfare of *Superman* and *Mame.* Meanwhile, audiences subsisted on *Sweet Charity* and the musical musings of a couple of crazy, mixed-up kids named Harris. In Alan Jay Lerner's *On a Clear Day You Can See Forever* Barbara Harris was just loaded with ESP (and talent, in an enchanting performance) as a lass who can read thoughts, make plants obey her orders to grow and, under hypnosis by a handsome psychiatrist, remember her previous incarnation. In *Skyscraper,* based on Elmer Rice's *Dream Girl,* Julie Harris is a dreamer whose romantic fantasies are acted out as she tries to choose among the men in her life, at the same time preventing the high-rise brigands next door from swallowing her little old New York house into their shiny new skyscraper project. There was a lot of handsome production designed by Robert Randolph in *Skyscraper* and a good tune in *On a Clear Day,* but it was the performing rather than the material that filled out these shows. The same was true of *Sweet Charity* even though it was Neil Simon himself who wrote the musical's book, based on the Italian movie *Nights of Cabiria.* In *Sweet Charity* (which opened at the refurbished Palace and brought that storied theater back to the legitimate stage), Simon's book about a dance hall hostess doesn't glitter as sharply as his two hit comedies that were concurrent with it, *Barefoot in the Park* and *The Odd Couple.* But an appealing song and dance performance by Gwen Verdon put the show over, with an important assist from Bob Fosse's choreography and staging.

Then Superman arrived in the nick of time to lift the season out of its musical lethargy. If our musical theater cannot create its own original material (and this year it cannibalized a comic strip, the novels *Don Quixote, Auntie Mame, The Yearling, How Green Was My Valley* and *Pickwick,* the movie *Nights of Cabiria* and the plays *Dream Girl* and *Anastasia*), then the next best thing is to find that the very choice of material adapted is a major part of the fun. So it was with the show whose official title was *"It's a Bird It's a Plane It's SUPERMAN,"* quotes and all, a Best Play, devoted faithfully and extremely cleverly to the comic strip on which it was based. It was not camped, but played as straight as possible in a good laugh at our secret longing for a hero who could solve all problems, defeat all enemies. The joke is not on Superman, as it is on TV's Batman. The joke is right where it should be—on us and our childish instincts. When something goes wrong in Metropolis, Clark Kent is there to fix it—meek Clark Kent, reporter on the *Daily Planet,* scorned

BOB HOLIDAY (AS SUPERMAN), MICHAEL O'SULLIVAN, LINDA LAVIN AND
JACK CASSIDY IN "IT'S A BIRD IT'S A PLANE IT'S SUPERMAN"

as an underdog by his fellow-reporter Lois Lane until presto! he strips off his
sober clothes and stands revealed, muscles bulging in his blue and red cape
costume, the Superman of Lois's dreams. He is impersonated to the pen-and-
ink life by Bob Holiday and directed in dead-pan style by Harold Prince
(Superman is a straight man). This Man of Steel faces a foeman worthy of
his invincible and indestructible mettle: a mad scientist, a gangling, thread-
paper comic strip villain played by Michael O'Sullivan, who is furious because
he's never won a Nobel Prize. He plots to draw attention to himself by de-
stroying indestructible Superman. How? Physically Superman is invulnerable,

but psychologically he is not; like mere mortals he needs to be loved, to have his good works appreciated. Taking dead aim at this vulnerable spot, the mad scientist pursues our hero through the musical's two lively acts; through an excellent, faintly rocky score by Charles Strouse and Lee Adams, waiting for him to alight from his flights through the air over Metropolis (by means, we assume, of a contraption of invisible wires); and finally penetrating Clark Kent's disguise with the help of a slippery newshawk played by Jack Cassidy.

The mad scientist nearly stages the upset of the century, but Superman wins out in the end (phew!). As a good guy, Superman is so square that it's too much to expect for him to be likeable. He is, though; this Superman is almost human. What is he but a knight-errant of the space age who can "fight the unbeatable foe" and win, who *can* "reach the unreachable star?" Superman is Don Quixote's dream come true; and Don Quixote's dream, though it may be laughable, is never ridiculous. The same goes for Superman in his welcome arrival in a stage version.

Following close upon the flowing cape of Superman was another musical whose heroine would no doubt have invited the Man of Steel to cocktails to feel his muscles—*Mame,* the life-loving subject of Patrick Dennis's novel *Auntie Mame* who (as Rosalind Russell) has already appeared in a play and a movie. Now (as Angela Lansbury) she appears in a musical version, sweeping all before her so that she may bring up her beloved nephew Patrick in the style to which he should be accustomed. He must learn to mix martinis, to tango in a speakeasy and, of course, to get along in a progressive school at which the little boys run around naked with the little girls. In wealth and in Depression, in foxhunting Georgia and in snobbish suburbia, Miss Lansbury's Mame was always equal to and a little bit ahead of the demands placed on her by a strenuous and all-embracing life, and so was the actress in her role. It was a delight to meet Mame's friends, too: Beatrice Arthur as a contralto musical comedy star ready at any moment to strike a heavy blow for her best friend or *against* her; Jane Connell as the mousy secretary who is sent forth to have some fun and comes back sadder, wiser and pregnant. It's also a pleasure to report that Jerry Herman's score is typical Jerry Herman: it bounces with singable songs for performers who want to expend a lot of energy, and his lyrics blend with the flow of the book adapted by Jerome Lawrence and Robert E. Lee from their own play. The William and Jean Eckart scenery and Robert Mackintosh costumes were both handsome and efficient, chic as could be but never overblown except for deliberate effect. *Mame,* the last new show of the year, put a real exclamation point on the 1965-66 season.

It's highly probable that *Mame* will achieve hit status; and so will *Sweet Charity* and *Man of La Mancha;* and so, very likely, will *Wait a Minim!* This revue from South Africa has been touring its own country and the world for more than four years; yet its young performers were still sassy and boisterous and proud of their material. The show was paced briskly by director-producer Leon Gluckman through efficient scenery made of sliding panels designed by Gluckman and Frank Rembach. A program note stated, "Coming from South Africa, where the political climate is hot and angry, it is inevitable that *Wait a Minim!* should have a point of view." This point of view punctuated the

LAURENCE NAISMITH, IVOR EMMANUEL, SHANI WALLIS AND TESSIE O'SHEA
IN "A TIME FOR SINGING"

show in a repeated pantomime in which a white man makes friendly overtures
to a Negro, then fires at him point-blank with a pistol. But as a whole the
show had little to do with anger and much to do with melody and folk humor,
with songs collected mostly from Africa but lightly salted with Asian and
European numbers. The versatile young company not only performed all the
satirical sketches, dances and songs but also played their own musical instruments—which in the case of *Wait a Minim!* was no mean accomplishment.
Andrew Tracey played seventeen instruments onstage, including a sousaphone
and a Chopi timbala (whatever that is); Paul Tracey played thirteen and
Nigel Pegram ten.

Another musical, *A Time for Singing,* put forward Tessie O'Shea as the
wife and mother of the coal-mining Morgans in an adaptation of Richard
Llewellyn's *How Green Was My Valley.* Miss O'Shea has a friendly way with
a song and a comedy line—which is more than could be said for her vehicle.
It was a bulky but not very agile show—lots of good voices and songs, lots of

romantic and sociological problems in the book, attractive and serviceable scenery by Ming Cho Lee, but not much beauty or inspiration, inner or outer, when all was said and done from its happy-family opening to its somber mine-accident conclusion. The built-in values of *How Green Was My Valley* did little to rescue *A Time for Singing;* nor could the built-in values of a book based on the play *Anastasia* and a score based on Rachmaninoff's music rescue *Anya;* nor could *La Grosse Valise,* with its built-in values of Robert Dhery humor, repeat the success of Dhery's previous revue from Paris, *La Plume de Ma Tante.* This was a season when very few sure-fire ideas worked out, and most reliable sources dried up, in musicals as well as elsewhere in the theater.

Turning to comedy, James Goldman's *The Lion in Winter,* about a roaring, clawing family gathering of Plantagenets and Capets in frosty Chinon at Christmas time, 1183, had only a short run—but this was the only respect in which it was the least of the Best Plays. It is a semi-historical, semi-dramatic comedy about succession to the crown of England. Henry II and his queen, Eleanor of Aquitaine, whom he holds imprisoned because of her several rebellions against him, have three sons: Richard (later King Richard the Lion-Hearted), Geoffrey and John (later King John who accepted the Magna Carta). All three sons are scheming for the crown in a day when primogeniture did not determine the succession. The script has hidden claws; it is printed out as prose, but much of it speaks and reads as pentameter. Its savage humor is offered in stylish irony by Rosemary Harris as Eleanor the scorned and scorning queen who plots keenly against her husband Henry for love of watching him suffer, and who is ready to eat him or love him, either one, alive and whole. Miss Harris's portrayal of Eleanor was realized in such depth that at one performance, as she delivered Eleanor's line about being able to express despair with a smile, the audience broke into applause of her acting. Robert Preston's performance, too, was among the season's best; a stylish, bearded, bristling lion of a Henry II who walks like a king and schemes like a Borgia but can't quite bring himself to destroy his own troublesome young. Outstanding supporting performances under Noel Willman's superior direction were given by Suzanne Grossmann as Alais the king's mistress and Christopher Walken as young King Philip of France. Will Steven Armstrong's costumes and scenery suggested the period without weighing down the actors or the play in ornament. His single set of pillars and arches, for example, represented all the many rooms of Chinon from bedroom to wine cellar, without shifting scenery, merely by moving in props like a tapestry or a table.

The failure of *The Lion in Winter* to attract a large enough audience to support it even modestly is one of those Broadway mysteries to which so many emphatic solutions are offered in sidewalk discussions. It was a period play, which is risky, but it was also a comedy, which is not. The deliberate use of anachronism in the script (wrapping up Christmas presents, etc.) has troubled some observers; others have praised it for helping modern audiences to identify closely with the characters. The powerful New York *Times* drama critic damned it with a who-cares attitude toward its subject matter, but plays have succeeded before over the dead body of *Times* opinion and will again. At the other end of the scale, Walter Kerr of the New York *Herald Tribune* praised

Miss Harris's Eleanor as one of the ten or twelve best performances anyone might be likely to see in a lifetime of theatergoing, and many other journalists and show folk spread the good word about *The Lion in Winter* with the zeal of prophets. So why should *Lion* have failed? How could it have failed? No one knows for sure, but it is an outstanding script which must certainly have a long life before it in future productions. To its four producers—Eugene V. Wolsk, Walter A. Hyman, Alan King (in his second major contribution to this Broadway season) and Emanuel Azenberg—all credit for putting it on. To the Broadway theater, shame for its failure.

Elsewhere in comedy it was a rose-colored year. This season there was no special magic in the color black, even when laid on in great splashes. The blackest script played as a joke was *Entertaining Mr. Sloane,* the Broadway debut of its British author, Joe Orton. This was a play about a murderer who thinks he has found sanctuary with a family living in a house surrounded by a junkyard; but he finds that he is no match for this family, and the price of his security is to serve as lover to the middle-aged lady of the house *and* to her brother, both of whom enjoy being roughly handled. *Mr. Sloane* was relentlessly well acted by Dudley Sutton as the hapless murderer, Sheila Hancock and Lee Montague as his predators and George Turner as their whining father—but it seemed relentlessly forbidding.

The blackest American script of consequence was Edward Albee's short-lived adaptation of James Purdy's novel *Malcolm,* produced by Theater 1966. It was a low-camp charade of shining innocence eroded and degraded in the tale of a symbolically pure fifteen-year-old who vacates a symbolic golden throne to enter the world, where he is corrupted by friendship, luxury, art and love and destroyed in an orgiastic marriage with a pop singer. Estelle Parsons played a prostitute as the most overblown, slatternly, anti-feminine symbol to be invented for the stage in a long time, and Ruth White was outstanding as an all-consuming matron. But *Malcolm* succeeded only in proving that a little bit of camp goes a long way in the theater, and a lot of it was more than this play could bear. Like *Mr. Sloane, Malcolm* left an impression that was strong but unfavorable.

No, sick jokes didn't do especially well this season, even in the old reliable form of a clique for murdering the wrong sort of people in *UTBU,* a short-lived Tony Randall vehicle. Those who believe that the theater has a welcome mat out for neurotic sensationalism are thinking of a different time and place than Broadway in 1965-66. Here and now we had gentle comedies about a nice old Jewish grandpa and a friendly young Zulu; about a likeable old capitalist and family man juggling bags of diamonds with the parlormaid in his New York town house; about a rich Boston widow whose children are scheming to take her money away from her. The latter comedy was *A Very Rich Woman,* adapted by Ruth Gordon from a French script and played richly by her under the direction of her husband, Garson Kanin, with strong support from Ethel Griffies, Ernest Truex and Raymond Walburn as caricatures of the old Boston school, and with Diana Muldaur attractively in attendance as a nurse at the clinic in which the avaricious daughters imprison their indomitable mother. This play was acted as it was written, with relish, and it deserved a more enthusiastic response than it got.

So did Jerome Chodorov's *3 Bags Full,* in which Paul Ford played the abovementioned gent with the diamonds, bedeviled by his servants, his family and his business associate until he has no alternative but to stare out at the audience in an open-mouthed but silent plea for sympathy, in helpless resignation. Ford's performance was a show in itself, as was the art nouveau styling of Armstrong's setting and Freddy Wittop's costumes. *3 Bags Full* could have occupied a large place in the season, and it left a big hole when it closed. The other warm frivolity—*The Zulu and the Zayda*—lasted through most of the season with its story of a Jewish family living in South Africa and hiring a young Zulu (Louis Gossett) to look after their zayda, or grandfather (Menasha Skulnik), to keep him out of trouble. This script was the Broadway writing debut of the actor Howard Da Silva (in collaboration with Felix Leon). It concerned itself warm-heartedly—but fairly obviously—with interracial harmony, and it benefitted greatly from its production values: Dore Schary's gentle touch in the staging, the sets by William and Jean Eckart and eleven Harold Rome song numbers scattered through the play.

Sex was a highly successful subject for comedy—but only once, in *Cactus Flower.* In other plays indentifying themselves as comedies in the author's credit line ("A New Comedy by . . ."), sex was a flop this season—a one-performance flop in the cases of *Mating Dance* and *Me and Thee.* Jokes about artificial insemination (in *The Wayward Stork*) and marital and pre-marital relations (in *Happily Never After*) failed to get much of a laugh. To wrap up the subject of comedy on Broadway in 1965-66, some character ideas in plays which missed the mark were a horse-playing priest in *Minor Miracle,* a retired civil servant coping with a neurotic daughter in *Nathan Weinstein, Mystic, Connecticut* and a playwright posing as a beatnik in *The Best Laid Plans.*

In drama, the very best offerings were the plays described in the previous section, plus off-Broadway's *Hogan's Goat.* Next best were the thrillers, showing off (again) a foreign author in his (again) Broadway debut. This was Jack Roffey and his *Hostile Witness,* a coolly British cat-and-mouse game with a famous solicitor, played by Ray Milland, framed for murder and placed on trial before a wryly solemn judge (played in a memorably amusing vignette by Melville Cooper), and saved only at the very last second after every possibility of suspense had been squeezed dry under Reginald Denham's direction. More lurid games were played in the American thrillers: Frederick Knott's *Wait Until Dark,* described in the section on hits; and Mary Drayton's *The Playroom,* about a clique of pot-smoking teen-agers who kidnap a tot for spite and find that they may have to murder their victim in order to escape punishment for abducting her. *Wait Until Dark* succeeded in finding an audience for its screams-in-the-dark melodrama; *The Playroom* did not and closed early, although it was a script of quite considerable substance and just missed being one of the season's best.

Elsewhere in drama, the interesting failures were European, the sad disappointments, alas! American. Of course, American scripts on Broadway are usually raw and new, while European scripts were tested before being im-

ALAN WEBB, TONY RANDALL AND THELMA RITTER IN "U T B U"
(UNHEALTHY TO BE UNPLEASANT)

ported—somebody loved them enough to bring them over here. The late John
Whiting's *The Devils,* based on Aldous Huxley's book, arrived in an excellent
production by Alexander H. Cohen, in the magnificence of a lofty setting by
Rouben Ter-Arutunian, and in the promise of bravura performing by Anne
Bancroft and Jason Robards in the grim story of a nun who hallucinates night-
time visits from a handsome, libertine priest. She sends him to the gallows
when she reveals publicly the supposed possession of herself and her sisters
by this sacerdotal devil. Under the direction of Michael Cacoyannis, *The
Devils* was less inward-searching than outwardly melodramatic (until scenes
of the priest's growing self-knowledge in his painful demise), with Shepperd
Strudwick alone finding the right key in which to perform, in his role of a
disapproving bishop.

Michael Dyne's *The Right Honourable Gentleman* was also a point of some
dramatic interest in the season, with its careful acting-out of a real Victorian
political scandal. It was most expertly stylized under Frith Banbury's direction,
with Charles D. Gray playing Sir Charles Dilke, whose reputation was destroyed in a messy divorce case just as eventual leadership of the party (Gladstone's) in Parliament seemed within his grasp. This was a good job expertly

done but perhaps just a bit creaky in its theatrical joints as it played out its mannered expose.

A most conspicuous event was the seven-performance disappointment of the two Tennessee Williams one-acters, character portraits of aging and distressed women played by Margaret Leighton and Kate Reid under the portmanteau title *Slapstick Tragedy*. The news was bad for younger playwrights, too. William Hanley's full-length reworking of his one-acter *Mrs. Dally,* about a middle-aged woman's loneliness and frustration both in marriage and in a love affair with a young man, didn't quite fill out, even though Arlene Francis and Ralph Meeker were in excellent form as the married couple trying to console each other for what went wrong with their marriage. Jack Richardson missed with *Xmas in Las Vegas* (a cloud silver-lined with the fact that now, at least, we don't have to absorb that ugly abbreviation "Xmas" into the roster of enduring American play titles). *Postmark Zero* failed to dramatize successfully the World War II emotions of Stalingrad in letters from its participants; *The Great Indoors* grappled with problems of bias without accomplishment; and *First One Asleep, Whistle* closed after only one performance of its emotional problem of an unmarried mother and her 7-year-old daughter.

In revivals, a British production of Chekhov's *Ivanov*—the first major Broadway production of this play in modern times—brought John Gielgud and Vivian Leigh to New York for a limited engagement; theirs was a prime star attraction, if not exactly a Chekhovian triumph either from a standpoint of the play itself or its staging. Marcel Marceau returned to New York with his pantomime programs, including the Bip sketches and other routines which have retained all their charm and poignancy in the ten-year interval since their first presentation in New York, in 1955 off Broadway at the Phoenix Theater (Marceau appeared at the City Center, so that unlike his countryman, Charles Aznavour, Marceau's solo show wasn't under consideration for *Variety's* hit list; City Center shows never are). And not everything that happens in the theater district can be classified as a show to be recorded formally as "produced on Broadway." Among subsidiary activities was Vittorio Gassman's one-performance acting concert entitled *Game of Heroes,* the evening of February 21 at Lincoln Center. Then there was the visit of burlesque to the Times Square area in the spring, at the Hudson Theater, in a three-a-day form with programs changed weekly in the best grind-house tradition.

Individual successes of acting, direction, scene design, music and lyric writing, choreography, etc., have been mentioned along with their shows in this report. But there is an individual whose contribution to the American theater is so wide and *continuous* that he's in a class of achievement by himself. This season he (or his Arts Foundation) produced *Marat/Sade, Inadmissible Evidence* and *Philadelphia, Here I Come!;* he produced *Cactus Flower;* he produced *Pickwick* and the return engagement of *Oliver;* and just to avoid actually defying the gods (chutzpah, yes; hubris, no) he also co-produced a musical that folded out of town, *Hot September*. When he was not doing all this he was doing something else like annoying the *Times* drama critic. I refer of course to David Merrick, the man of this and every recent theater year. Merrick has elevated and enriched the American theater with his courage, taste and healthy avarice, and in turn it has quite properly elevated and enriched him. He livens things up generally, and it's a pleasure to have him around, not only for profit but also for fun.

It should be noted, too, that the scene designers provided an unusually interesting visual spectacle this season. It is almost an offense to pick out a "best" from among their outstanding work because only minor details of personal preference can make a distinction. The most conspicuous of the 1965-66 scenic successes were Howard's Bay's *Man of La Mancha,* the best design yet for that difficult stage downtown at ANTA Washington Square Theater; Jo Mielziner's *Danton's Death,* a first-time design for the new Vivian Beaumont Theater, and his *The Playroom;* Will Steven Armstrong's art nouveau *3 Bags Full* and his adaptable *The Lion in Winter;* Robert Randolph's *Skyscraper* and *Sweet Charity* and *Anya* AND *Superman;* Rouben Ter-Arutunian's *The Devils;* Michael Annals' *The Royal Hunt of the Sun;* William and Jean Eckart's *Mame,* and Ming Cho Lee's *A Time for Singing.*

Elsewhere on the roster of individual successes, it was a hell of a good year for performers named Harris—Rosemary, Barbara and Julie—and for performers named O'Sullivan—Mairin D. and Michael. For Lovelady Powell, it must have been an intensely frustrating year—she was in *two* shows that were mounted for Broadway but never made it.

The absolute peak of the 1965-66 season? It was the emotional crescendo of Don Quixote's refusal to surrender to unbeatable death and his defeat by it in *Man of La Mancha.* And here are the *Best Plays* editor's personal choices for the very bests of the 1965-66 season in various categories:

Plays

PLAY: *Hogan's Goat*

ACTOR: Nicol Williamson in *Inadmissible Evidence*

ACTRESS: Rosemary Harris in *The Lion in Winter*

SUPPORTING ACTOR: David Carradine in *The Royal Hunt of the Sun*

SUPPORTING ACTRESS: Mairin D. O'Sullivan in *Philadelphia, Here I Come!*

DIRECTOR: Peter Brook, *Marat/Sade, Etc.*

SCENERY: Jo Mielziner, *Danton's Death, The Playroom*

COSTUMES: Gunilla Palmstierna-Weiss, *Marat/Sade, Etc.*

CHOREOGRAPHY: Malcolm Goddard, *Marat/Sade, Etc.*

Musicals

MUSICAL: *Man of La Mancha*

ACTOR: Richard Kiley in *Man of La Mancha*

ACTRESS: Barbara Harris in *On a Clear Day You Can See Forever*

SUPPORTING ACTOR: Michael O'Sullivan in *Superman, Etc.*

SUPPORTING ACTRESS: Beatrice Arthur in *Mame.*

DIRECTOR: Albert Marre, *Man of La Mancha*

SCENERY: Howard Bay, *Man of La Mancha*

COSTUMES: Howard Bay and Patton Campbell, *Man of La Mancha*

CHOREOGRAPHY: Jack Cole, *Man of La Mancha*

MUSIC AND LYRICS: Mitch Leigh and Joe Darion, *Man of La Mancha*

The Repertory Caper

The effort to establish in New York City a subsidized resident repertory company within the Lincoln Center organization entered its second phase during the season of 1965-66. Following the two previous seasons downtown at ANTA Washington Square Theater under the direction of Robert Whitehead and Elia Kazan, the company was delivered over to the direction of Herbert Blau and Jules Irving and moved to its permanent home at the Vivian Beaumont Theater in Lincoln Center, where four productions were presented. The Messrs. Blau and Irving, recruited from the regional theater in San Francisco, where they had been operating a resident company called the Actor's Playhouse, inherited many problems from the old regime: dissension at the top, dissatisfaction in the company, deficit at the box office. They also inherited a certain amount of distinction from the two-year production record which included two *new* Best Plays (by Arthur Miller) and a couple of creditable revivals along with a couple of flops.

In their first season, Blau and Irving may have made long strides toward solving some of the problems. They filled out the acting company with a score of their own people from San Francisco. The audience for their subscription period of performances exceeded 92 per cent of capacity, and at season's end approximately 50 per cent had renewed their subscriptions for next season— and they brought their four productions in for less than the estimated $600,000 deficit which, in a subsidized operation, is presumably anticipated and underwritten.

But Blau and Irving were not able in 1965-66 to add to the sum of the Repertory Company of Lincoln Center's distinction. Blau's staging of *Danton's Death* and *The Condemned of Altona* and Irving's of *The Caucasian Chalk Circle* had nowhere near the excitement, the sense of reaching out for new patterns of stagecraft, as was evident in, say, Kazan's staging of his least popular result, *The Changeling*. And the new group of Lincoln Center Repertory actors isn't yet equal to the challenge of a strong rendering of a difficult play (I say *yet* because it isn't fair to make a judgment of a new company after only one season in a strange new theater).

The Lincoln Center season's major distinction was its new environment and its stage designs. The Vivian Beaumont Theater (which finally cost $9,700,-000) is austerely beautiful, a highly efficient machine for putting on plays, with a machine's functional beauty. Outside, it has clean, squared lines of glass and travertine. Inside, its upholstery is bright red plush to stir the senses, and its walls and ceiling are a very dark brown so that they seem to disappear as the stage receives its lighting for the play. The stage itself is adaptable for radical thrust arrangements or proscenium openings of various sizes, and the auditorium seats 1,140 for proscenium-style plays and 1,083 when seats are removed to accommodate a thrust stage. The theater was designed by the late Eero Saarinen with Jo Mielziner. Mielziner's were the first sets to be used there, for *Danton's Death,* in a grand display of his and the theater's virtuosity, with a geometrical background of lines coming to a point in the distance, and with setpieces of scenery moved on and offstage, thrust forward and pulled back, comprising the major visual excitement and freedom of motion in an otherwise heavy and turgid play.

Attempting to evaluate the Kazan-Whitehead administration in last year's volume, I pointed out that although they had scored some very great successes they had not been able to lead the group into starting the process of *becoming;* into progress toward a definable repertory goal. The Messrs. Blau and Irving, for all the lack of distinction in their individual productions, *have* begun such a progress. Their goal, if I understand it correctly, is to create a theater of loud involvement, with plays that have the "size" to fill their stage with modern social and emotional significance. This goal was exemplified in their choice of plays for Lincoln Center Repertory in 1965-66: *Danton's Death,* a ranting 19th century German play about the French Revolution and its tyranny disguised as public good; *The Country Wife,* a breather for the company, which had done it in San Francisco; *The Condemned of Altona,* another of those plays about widening the circle of German war and atrocity guilt, this one the American premiere of a 1959 Sartre script; and *The Caucasian Chalk Circle,* the New York premiere of an episodic Brecht work arranging human symbols (Chinese humans, each wearing his symbolic personality openly, in masks designed by James Hart Stearns) in the familiar message about the triumph of the honest peasant over wicked authority.

Certainly the first and last of these plays served what I understand to be the present purpose of Lincoln Center Rep. They were big enough to fill the Beaumont's stage, and loud enough to be heard clearly. But at the same time they were dull enough to be ignored easily. This was theater of harangue, and it raised doubt that its goal is worthwhile as compared, say, with a goal of perfecting an American repertory company in the ensemble presentation of a principally American repertory of plays. Blau and Irving chose *no* American play for their opening year's repertory (and, as of this volume's press time, *no* American play for 1966-67). This very absence of American plays from the Lincoln Center Repertory schedule was conspicuous, particularly as compared with the Kazan-Whitehead record. It's still too early to make any conclusive judgments about the aims and achievements of the new directors, but the question "Why no American plays?", aimed at an American repertory company, can only be answered by stimulating productions of plays from other sources. No such thing happened at the Vivian Beaumont in 1965-66. *The Caucasian Chalk Circle* was well enough received to be held over for additional performances beyond its scheduled time, but it was the best of a very unstimulating lot.

It's no secret that while Lincoln Center Repertory has been fiddling, the Association of Producing Artists-Phoenix repertory has been burning with a bright blue flame of theater energy, bringing plays to New York which they mounted originally in Ann Arbor, Mich., under the sponsorship of the University of Michigan Professional Theater Program. Ellis Rabb is APA-Phoenix's director and his wife, Rosemary Harris, is its star performer. After a couple of seasons off Broadway, APA moved to Broadway this season; not in repertory but with a single production, a revival of the comedy *You Can't*

Take It With You, a 30-year-old American script by a couple of commercial-theater fellows named Hart and Kaufman. Its success all year long in Broadway competition, and the success on Broadway last year of another group's revival of Tennessee Williams' *The Glass Menagerie* for 175 performances, leaves no doubt that there is plenty of juice in the body of American plays, plus a large New York audience for them when they are skillfully restaged. APA has announced its intention of playing a whole season on Broadway in 1966-67 in a repertory of seven plays including *You Can't Take It With You* and another work entitled *We Comrades Three* adapted from the writings of Walt Whitman. While Lincoln Center is still deep in the experimental state after three years of experiment, APA is emerging as a full-blown Broadway fact.

The season's activity included visits from foreign troupes showing us what results may be achieved within the repertory system. The *Marat/Sade* brought to Broadway by David Merrick was a production by the Royal Shakespeare Company, a repertory group which is rooted in the performing traditions of its own country's greatest literary treasure and is employing these skills, stretching these artistic muscles, in productions of new scripts (see Joseph Papp's article in the Shakespeare section of this volume). The Comédie Française, polished like an old stone in the river of centuries, visited New York with Molière's *L'Avare,* Corneille's *Le Cid,* de Montherlant's *La Reine Morte* and Feydeau's *Un Fil a la Patte.* The Bavarian State Theater contrasted Büchner's *Woyzeck* with Goethe's *The Accomplice* on one program and offered Hauptmann's *Die Ratten* on another. The Japanese were represented by their Bunraku in an attractive repertory of puppet theater.

Off Broadway, the American Savoyards continued to offer Gilbert and Sullivan productions in seasons of repertory; and, musically speaking at least, the American stage heritage is living theater in New York. Three groups devote themselves to presenting again and again the great musical hits of the Broadway past. New York City Opera, a repertory company with guest stars, this year staged *The Saint of Bleecker Street, The Consul* and *Street Scene.* New York City Center Light Opera's one-by-one revivals in 1965-66 were *South Pacific, The Music Man* and *Oklahoma!,* together with a spring schedule of four Frank Loesser musicals: *How to Succeed in Business Without Really Trying, The Most Happy Fella* and *Where's Charley?,* to be followed by *Guys and Dolls* June 8. The Music Theater of Lincoln Center's one-at-a-time musicals, lavishly revived under the guidance of Richard Rodgers, were *Kismet* with Alfred Drake in his original role of Hajj, *Carousel* with John Raitt in his original role of Billy Bigelow and, on the last day of the season, *Annie Get Your Gun* with Ethel Merman in her original role of Annie Oakley.

This wealth of musical production is all to the good; now we need comparable showcases for our Broadway straight-play heritage, not instead of musical production, but to match it. New York is a city where a very rich man may walk up a street with a very poor man and turn into their doors at homes which are side by side. The extreme condition of each points up the extreme condition of the other, by contrast, and this same relationship exists between the two genres of American stage works. Our musicals are richly displayed, year after year, in revival and in repertory, while our straight plays subsist mainly upon spare print on the library shelves; unfleshed. Yet their potential for entertainment is so rich (sample a few in past *Best Plays* volumes) that an improvement in their condition is bound to take place. They are a principal support of the regional theater in revivals in dozens of playhouses from coast to coast, and in several cases they have had a second success off Broadway, sometimes an even greater success than in their first run. It seems inevitable that the American straight-play backlog will find an outlet for major production in New York; if not by Lincoln Center Repertory, then by APA-Phoenix Repertory or by some other group; and the sooner the better, or the day may come when a foreign troupe arrives here with American plays in repertory to show us how it should and could be done.

Off Broadway

There was apparent shrinkage off Broadway in 1965-66, blamed almost universally on rising production costs. This season there were 66 shows as compared with 75 a year ago. There were nine fewer shows, but one of them, William Alfred's *Hogan's Goat,* was the best straight playscript of the year in any part of the New York theater, in my opinion. There were fewer shows but more activity in what has become known as off-off-Broadway: the Cafe La Mama, the Judson Poets' Theater, etc. There were fewer shows, but production of *new* playscripts held up pretty well (31 as compared with 33 last year), with most of the numerical drop-off taking place in the musical and revival categories.

There were no new Pinter, Becket, Genet or Ionesco plays and no clear evidence of any mould-breakers coming along behind them. Even Theater 1965-1966 marked time with *Krapp's Last Tape* and *The Zoo Story* and a revival of Beckett's *Happy Days* presented first in French, with Madeleine Renaud, and then in English, with Ruth White. The intellectual environment which produced the most interesting new playwright of the off-Broadway year was neither Houston Street nor King's Road, but Harvard. The season as a whole was overbalanced on the conventional side, no doubt about that.

The shining example of this off-Broadway year was *Hogan's Goat,* the first professional production of its author, William Alfred, a Harvard professor. His play is a verse drama about the first-generation Irish community in Brooklyn in 1890, zeroing in on a young political leader whose consuming ambition drives him to destruction. It is clearly a Best Play of the season, and under close scrutiny I find it to be the very best play of 1965-66. Measured against its closest competition, it is not as sharp-pointed as *Philadelphia, Here I Come!,* but it is broader in scope and richer in expression. It is not as inventive as *Marat/Sade* (the New York Drama Critics Circle choice) or *Inadmissible Evidence* but it is their equal in expression and their superior in construction and cohesion. It is a period play (like *Marat/Sade*) but its examination of a human being's drive to emerge from the ruck in defiance of all rules and risks is extremely pertinent to our modern population-swelling, status-seeking, amoral society.

The 1965-66 Season off Broadway

PLAYS (24)

Friends and Enemies
Swim Low Little Goldfish
The World of Ray Bradbury
Play That on Your Old Piano
Good Day and The Exhaustion of Our Son's Love
Kill the One-Eyed Man
HOGAN'S GOAT
Happy Ending and Day of Absence
Bugs and Veronica
An Impudent Wolf
The Parasite
The Pocket Watch
Rooms
Jonah
The Coop
Laughwind
Monopoly
Ludlow Fair and The Madness of Lady Bright
6 From La Mama (two programs of one-act plays)
The Journey of the Fifth Horse
Bohikee Creek
Fitz and Biscuit
Big Man

MUSICALS (3)

Hotel Passionato
Great Scot!
Hooray! It's a Glorious Day . . . and all that

REVUES (6)

The Game Is Up (cabaret)
Pick a Number XV (cabaret)
Just for Openers (cabaret)
New Cole Porter Revue (cabaret)
The Mad Show (cabaret)
Return of Second City (cabaret)

REVIVALS (17)

Krapp's Last Tape and The Zoo Story
New York Shakespeare Love's Labor's Lost
Coriolanus
Troilus and Cressida
American Savoyards
The Yeomen of the Guard
Ruddigore
The Pirates of Penzance
Princess Ida
The Trojan Women (return engagement)
Happy Days (also performed in French)
Miss Julie and The Stronger
Medea
The White Devil
Winterset
Phèdre
The Deadly Game
When We Dead Awaken

FOREIGN PLAYS IN ENGLISH (7)

Troubled Waters
Live Like Pigs
The Trigon
Serjeant Musgrave's Dance
The World of Gunter Grass
Sunset
The Butterfly Dream

SPECIALTIES (6)

Mardi Gras (outdoor musical)
Leonard Bernstein's Theater Songs
An Evening's Frost
Woman
The Bernard Shaw Story
Half Horse Half Alligator

PRODUCTIONS BY FOREIGN-LANGUAGE TROUPES (3)

Hello Charlie (Yiddish musical)
The Fifth Commandment (Yiddish musical)
Who Do I Deserve This? (German revue)

Categorized above are all the plays listed in the "Plays Produced off Broadway" section of this volume.
Play listed in CAPITAL LETTERS has been designated a Best Play of 1965-66 in this volume.
Plays listed in *italics* were still running on May 31, 1966.

Hogan's Goat is a fine play with a universal theme set in a background of American history—and if that sounds like an ideal qualification for the Pulitzer Prize, so much the more embarrassing. Once again in 1965-66, as in 1962-63 and 1963-64, the Pulitzer Prize givers withheld their award for theater. Trying to figure out no-award motives leads only to confusion; for example, when no award is given, is it because the prize is too important for the play? Does the prize go only to plays that are so obviously great and lasting that they will add to the luster of the prize—or is the prize intended to add to the luster of the play which, whatever its secondary faults, is the best of its season? Is a *Hogan's Goat* (for example) supposed to encourage the Pulitzer Prize and add to its distinction, or vice versa? I think we should get this all straight, somehow. Next time the Pulitzer Prize is offered perhaps the winning play-wright should give some thought to whether he, in his turn, will *allow* the Pulitzer committee to distinguish itself with the great name of his play.

The Pulitzer Prize or any other prize is worth nothing until it is given away. It is material junk until the act of its bestowal—*then* and only then it becomes something of value in encouragement for the recipient. While we are on the subject of awards, the New York Drama Critics Circle choices—*Marat/Sade* as best play and *Man of La Mancha* as best musical—were made by a new point system of voting for first, second and third choices instead, as in the past, by a plurality of first choices. Under the old system a play could win by getting the votes of only a minority of the critics, but at least it was somebody's pick as the very best work of the year. Under the new system, a second-rate play could win, theoretically, by piling up a majority of second- and third-place points on the subsequent, graded ballots.

Hogan's Goat attracted only two third-place choices in the Critics' voting (see its breakdown in detail in the awards section of this volume), a fact upon which time will no doubt make the most eloquent comment. As for the play itself, the goat of the title is one Matthew Stanton, immigrant and sometime fancy-boy of Agnes Hogan, a full-blooded creature who dies as the play be-gins (Alfred plans to dramatize the Agnes-Matt story one of these years). Hogan's Goat, as Stanton was once called to his chagrin, is now married to a woman whose indrawn nature is somewhat too delicate to endure the rough-and-tumble of Brooklyn politics. The Stantons have married secretly, in Lon-don, outside the Catholic Church; and this state of affairs is to them a guilty secret. The incumbent Mayor of Brooklyn is a crooked old wolf with long yellow teeth (this is the meatiest role, played by Tom Ahearne with seemingly total conviction that dishonesty is neither the best nor the worst but the only workable policy). As he maneuvers to snatch this office of Mayor from the old wolf, Stanton walks a tightrope between the Church's and the voters' anathema. He is destroyed as any tragic hero should be, totally, "down on my knees and all the world a desert," by his own temper, his own sinful past, his own overwhelming ambition.

Hogan's Goat was first produced by The American Place Theater, the group that has adapted St. Clements Church on West 46th Street for theater ex-perimentation. Last year American Place produced Robert Lowell's *The Old Glory* including *Benito Cereno*, another poetic drama. Alfred's poetry is more theatrical than Lowell's; it is real spoken *language,* rich in the character and characteristics of the Irish community. Like Lowell's play, Alfred's ran its course at St. Clements and then was moved to another off-Broadway theater to make way for American Place's subscription program of three more productions. Its season which had begun so well with the year's best playscript continued with creditable work: *Jonah,* a play by Paul Goodman about facing commitments, with the Biblical character adopting a Yiddish accent; *The Journey of the Fifth Horse,* by Ronald Ribman based on a Turgenev story, which won an Obie Award; and *Doubles and Opposites,* a program of one-acters (and when one of the three didn't pan out, they dropped it and substituted some movie shorts).

If there were such a thing as a bandwagon off Broadway, it would be cut into two or three small, hinged segments. The program of one-acters, tightly connected or deliberately unconnected and contrasting, *is* off Broadway. American Place does them; Theater 1966 does them; Albee, Jones, Pinter and Ionesco made their New York stage reputations with them; of 1965-66's new-play programs off Broadway, fourteen were evenings of one-acters. Two of these were programs of experimental plays brought from off-off-Broadway's Cafe La Mama into more formal off-Broadway display for first-nighters and critics (who weren't especially impressed). Among 1965-66's single-playwright programs of one-acters were those of Arkady Leokum, Ray Bradbury, Douglas Turner Ward, John White, Stanley Mann, Jerome Kass, Lanford Wilson, Robert Unger and Maxime Furlaud.

A season ago, LeRoi Jones' one-acter *The Toilet* emerged from one of these programs as a Best Play of its year. There was no such outstanding short work in 1965-66, but Jerome Kass's *Monopoly* was an especially interesting program of four intensely personal vignettes: a girl going to her first high school dance, a husband made to play dog for his wife, a middle-aged student in love with her young teacher, and an unhappy evening of Monopoly with two couples suffering emotional upheavals. Mr. Kass's proccupation is with human beings, not symbols, and he presents them with such understanding—such sympathy without excuses for their shortcomings—that his *Monopoly* was both a promise fulfilled and a promise of even better to come.

Ray Bradbury's evening of science-fiction one-acters deserved more attention than it received from New York audiences. Bradbury's technique is to comment on the present by projecting its characteristics into the future in immense blowups, exaggerations which might logically occur with the passage of time. For example, the villain of one of the short plays in *The World of Ray Bradbury* was a glorified TV apparatus that trapped and consumed its viewers—which is what may really happen some day if we fail to appreciate an entertainment phenomenon like Bradbury's imaginative view of externals, eloquently realized in this production by Eldon Elder's sets. Another deserving program that fared better was the actor Douglas Turner Ward's playwriting debut with the satirical sketches *Happy Ending* and *Day of Absence.* The first was a cynical joke about the valuable perquisites to be obtained in domestic service; the second was a Stepin Fetchit-like portrait of white Southern citizens who wake up one morning to find that all their town's Negroes have disappeared. Also, Arkady Leokum's *Friends* and *Enemies* commented force-fully on man's mistreatment of man in the relations between a meek waiter and a difficult customer, and a meek teacher and his tormenting pupil.

In some ways off Broadway always has been, and is becoming more and more, a Little Broadway. A conspicuous parallel in 1965-66 was the invasion by noteworthy foreign scripts. Certainly one of the most interesting new play-wrights presented to New York audiences this season was John Arden, whose professional New York theater debut took place with the importation last summer of his *Live Like Pigs,* about a noisy, slovenly British family moving into a sedate housing project. A second, even more provocative Arden script followed in March: *Serjeant Musgrave's Dance,* a moody expression of pac-ifism set in Victorian days to let it speak for itself without contemporary bias. The script is paced like a dead march as it moves slowly toward its climax, with John Colicos as the "serjeant" who brings home a rotting corpse from the colonial wars to show the complacent citizenry what war *is.* Its slowness in coming to the point weakened the very suspense for which it strove so carefully, but it was a powerful play nevertheless.

Arthur Cantor's production and direction of *The Trigon* by James Broom Lynne was another high point of the season off Broadway. This was a British script about the fragile pretenses of two young men sharing a flat and the at-tentions of a girl; pretenses which are smashed cruelly, deliberately, by a stranger who seduces the girl and forces the two young men to look at them-selves under the varnish. The relationships were most skillfully developed in Arthur Cantor's direction and in the acting, particularly in that of Jeremy Geidt in one of the season's top performances as the more effete of the young men. Another Cantor contribution to the off-Broadway year was the produc-tion of *The World of Gunter Grass,* selections in English from the work of the German novelist, adapted and staged by Dennis Rosa on a small but versatile set designed by Richard Seger.

There were some foreign failures, too. A translation of the Russian play *Sunset,* by Isaac Babel, didn't live up to expectations, nor did an adaptation of Ugo Betti's *Troubled Waters.* An adaptation of the classical Chinese *The Butterfly Dream* was merely a theatrical curio. And there was an adaptation of a Scandinavian script, *Break-Up,* that folded during previews, *before* open-ing night, just like an ill-starred Broadway venture.

The off-Broadway season's musical highlight was *The Mad Show,* a caper based on the comic viewpoint of *Mad Magazine,* conceived and staged by Steve Vinaver. The writing—a zany grab-bag of comments, portraits and sick jokes was another theater writing debut, that of Larry Siegel and Stan Hart, with Mary Rodgers supplying a spirited score played on piano and percussion. *The Mad Show* was a revue with comic-strip characters. Some of them, like Little Orphan Annie, were cut out of cardboard and stationed around the stage in some of the scenes. Others, like the members of a TV-crazed family or a group of football announcers, were portrayed by a small group of young and energetic actors. Stationary or in motion, it was fun—*Mad* fun.

The revue form seems to work as well in the off-Broadway context as the program of one-acters. Chicago's talented Second City returned with new material. In the cabarets, there was a new edition of Julius Monk's review at Plaza 9; another collection of Cole Porter songs, revisited; a new edition of *The Game Is Up* by Rod Warren, who also put on still another cabaret revue called *Just for Openers*. The phenomenally long run of *The Fantasticks* to the contrary (at season's end it had reached 2,538 performances and was still going strong), it seems to be the book musical that finds hard going off Broadway. Three tried this year and all failed: *Hotel Passionato* (sex and sin in hotel rooms), *Great Scot* (the life and times of the poet Robert Burns) and *Hooray! It's a Glorious Day . . . and all that* (love in a business office).

The flair and imagination of off Broadway's young stage artists enhanced a number of revivals in 1965-66, as in every previous season. The American Savoyards and the New York Shakespeare Festival were exploring their subjects as usual. There was a return engagement of *The Trojan Women* as staged by Michael Cacoyannis. There were revivals of Strindberg, Ibsen, Racine (in a new English version of *Phèdre* by William Packard), Maxwell Anderson (in a disappointing *Winterset*) and of James Yaffe's stage adaptation of Duerrenmatt's novel *The Deadly Game*. Gloria Foster gave an outstanding performance in the title role of Robinson Jeffers' *Medea*. Another standout was the Circle-in-the-Square production of *The White Devil*, John Webster's Elizabethan horror drama of seven murders staged by Jack Landau in modern dress.

The season's specialties included a program of Leonard Bernstein's theater songs and a program of Robert Frost's poetry and prose produced in the University of Michigan Professional Theater Program (same sponsorship as APA) and brought here for 132 performances. There were solo shows by Gale Sondergaard, Bramwell Fletcher and William Mooney. There were two shows produced for Yiddish-speaking audiences, and there was a German-language revue.

Then there was what is now being called off-off-Broadway: the beehive of experimental play production put on, usually, without such formalities as Equity contracts, daily performance schedules or invitations to be seen by critics. In the listings in this volume, "Broadway" is the collection of shows with Broadway union contracts, plus major repertory and visiting groups; "off-Broadway" is the collection of regularly-scheduled professional productions whose union contracts recognize their non-Broadway status with concessions. Presumably, "off-off-Broadway" is any stage activity farther out than that, but in truth it is almost impossible to define or to grasp statistically —which, I am told, is part of its charm. The word used was "relaxed"; off-off-Broadway is relaxed, proud of it and suspicious of any attempt at regimentation, or even of definition. The most frequently-cited centers of its effort (I mean, where the *action* is) are two coffee houses: the Cafe La Mama, where experimenting theater artists put on a new play each week, once in a long while holding one over for a second week, and the Caffe Cino operating at about the same frequency. The Judson Poets' Theater puts on about five plays a year, at irregular intervals. The New Dramatists put on workshop productions of scripts of the member-playwrights for invited audiences at their newly-acquired headquarters. The New Theater's Monday Night Play Series offered this season experimental productions of scripts like John Osborne's *A Subject of Scandal and Concern,* John Arden's *The Waters of Babylon* and Arnold Wesker's *The Kitchen* staged by Jack Gelber (even off-off-Broadway, foreign playwrights are getting into the act). At Lincoln Center, the little Forum Theater in the basement of the Vivian Beaumont was being used experimentally, for invited audiences. Then there is the Albee-Barr-Wilder (Theater 1966) New Playwrights Unit Workshop for experimental production, some of whose more interesting scripts have been transferred from the workshop to the Cherry Lane Theater for a formal off-Broadway presentation. This group has received a Rockefeller grant of $197,000 (of which $65,000 is to be matched) under the name Albarwild, for the purpose of presenting deserving off-off-Broadway scripts at the Cherry Lane. There is the IASTA workshop and the ANTA matinees. Being formally organized and sponsored, the last named half dozen groups are not quite perfectly relaxed, but they can't be ignored even in a short glance at off-off-Broadway.

As conservatism set into the off-Broadway year in choice of plays and manner of production, the fringe activity increased. The moral of this 1965-66 theater story is that the process of ferment is persistent within the very lively New York stage. Many of those sparking bubbles at the top, on the starry stages of Broadway, are the end result of continuous yeasty ferment of imagination down on the bottom, where you can hardly see it taking place. Luckily for our theater, this process of generation persists no matter what sort of context is provided or withheld, or how many doors are closed against it. It persists in spite of rising costs and with or without subsidy; with the blessing of the theater establishment or in the face of its disapproval; if not on Broadway, then off; if not off Broadway then off-off-Broadway, wherever that happens to be.

Offstage

Offstage, 1965-66 was a year in which the Federal government dipped its toe into arts subsidy; a year in which drama critics were diminished (in number), criticized (by playwrights), changed (by the *Times*) and needled (by David Merrick); a year of strikes and rising costs and *Hello, Dolly!* in Vietnam.

In June, 1965, President Johnson signed the first bill setting up a program of Federal aid to the arts at a ceremony attended by many persons of national prominence in the arts (Arthur Miller refused his invitation in protest against foreign policy). This bill set up Federal arts-subsidy machinery which, like most government undertakings, sounds like a Rube Goldberg structure. Here is how the bureau pyramids: Congress established a National Foundation on the Arts and Humanities. Within this are two groups with the responsibility to disburse funds: the National Endowment for the Arts and the National Endowment for the Humanities. The Endowment chairmen (arts, Roger L. Stevens; humanities, Henry Allen Moe) are appointed by the President of the United States for four-year terms. Within each Endowment is a National

Council composed of volunteers prominent in American arts who help the Endowment chairmen decide where the money is to go.

The National Endowment for the Arts received $5,000,000 on July 1, 1965. This has been spread around with the help of the National Council on the Arts, and there will be another $4,000,000 next year. In addition, $2,000,000 has been set aside to match funds for arts enterprises. Last year's grants to the theater, directly or indirectly, were as follows:

$40,000 matching grant to American P.E.N. to help meet administrative costs of an International P.E.N. Congress in New York.

$103,000 grants-in-aid to choreographers.

$7,000 grant to American Educational Theater Association to study children's theater at the secondary school level.

$30,000 to ANTA to help non-profit theaters by establishing regional offices in St. Louis and San Francisco.

$300,000 allocated to a plan to create a theater laboratory for professional singers, dancers and actors under Jerome Robbins' direction.

$750,000 to help resident professional theaters develop artistically.

$500,000 to assemble three highly professional theater companies to improve secondary-school instruction in dramatic literature and to give free performances for students.

$250,000 to help playwrights in their productions of ten new plays in regional and university theaters. This program has been entitled the Playwrights Experimental Theater.

$200,000 in grants-in-aid to creative writers to complete work in progress.

At the very end of the 1965-66 season it was announced by Roger L. Stevens that $660,000 had been granted to sixteen resident repertory theaters, bringing 1965-66 Endowment grants which might in some way be of use to the theater to a total of $2,840,000. The sixteen grants were $160,000 in matching funds to William Ball's American Conservatory Theater; $125,000 in matching funds to APA-Phoenix; and lesser, non-matching grants to Actors Theater (Louisville, Ky.), Actor's Workshop (San Francisco), Arizona Repertory Theater (Phoenix), Center Stage (Baltimore), Charles Playhouse (Boston), Cleveland Play House, Dallas Theater Center, Front Street Theater (Memphis), Hartford, Conn. Stage Company, Long Wharf Theater (New Haven), Olney, Md. Theater, Seattle Repertory Theater, Theater Company of Boston, Inc. and Theater of the Living Arts (Philadelphia).

It was a rough year for the critics. The number of daily-paper first-night New York critics dropped from six to five with the merger of the *Herald Tribune,* the *World-Telegram and Sun* and the *Journal-American* into a single operating unit publishing one morning, one afternoon and one Sunday paper. John McClain was the odd man out, at his own request; Norman Nadel remained as drama critic of the merged evening papers. Walter Kerr remained at his morning paper post.

The playwrights' own privately-circulated journal, *The Dramatists Guild Quarterly* (of which this writer is the editor), looked closely at the work of the contemporary drama critics and rated it in various categories, in a poll conducted by the *Quarterly* among those playwrights, librettists, composers and lyricists whose work had been reviewed on or off Broadway during the 1964-65 season just past. In answer to the question, "Which critic wrote the most perceptive review of your 1964-65 work?" the dramatists picked Howard Taubman of the *Times,* Richard Watts Jr. of the *Post* and Walter Kerr of the *Herald Tribune,* in that order, by one-vote margins. Kerr was voted the critic whom the playwrights most enjoyed reading by two to one over his nearest rival (Watts), and Kerr also was the two-to-one choice as the critic who best understands playwriting, with Robert Brustein of the *New Republic* second and Richard Gilman of *Newsweek* third.

A substitution of major critics took place when Stanley Kauffmann took Howard Taubman's place on the *Times,* with Taubman moving on to roving, at-large comment on all the arts. Even before the season began the *Times* let it be known that Taubman intended to relinquish his post. At the opening night of the first new play, *Mrs. Dally* on Sept. 22, all eyes were on the *Times'* critic's seats to discover who would be sitting there. It was still Howard Taubman (and pretty soon he was the only *Times* man sitting in free seats on opening night, as the paper ordered all its arts department employees and executives off the first-night list; they now attend second nights unless they buy their own first-night tickets). But by Jan. 1 the *Times* had found its new man—Kauffmann, theater critic for the local educational TV station (WNTA, Channel 13), and movie critic of the *New Republic.* The first show he reviewed for the *Times* was the short-lived comedy *UTBU* whose title is an abbreviation for a murder organization called "Unhealthy To Be Unpleasant."

The critics were under continuous fire from David Merrick (he gives them no rest). In June he castigated the Messrs. Kerr and Taubman for their reviews of *The Roar of the Greasepaint—The Smell of the Crowd.* During the tryout run of *Cactus Flower* in Philadelphia, Merrick harassed a TV interviewer (Tom Snyder) sampling public opinion after a performance, in the following manner: Merrick and Harvey D. Sabinson, the show's press agent, joined those being questioned and, unrecognized by Snyder, told him on the air that the show was the greatest; then they gave the signal for another press agent, Robert Ullman, to cut the power line (which in fact he did), blacking out the TV program. In London, where Mary Martin's international touring company of *Hello, Dolly!* was received with less than enthusiasm by the London critics, Merrick advertised a rave review which Bernard Levin (at that time the *Daily Mail* critic) had written after seeing the New York *Dolly* a year or so previously. And, later on in a speech in Washington, D.C., Merrick delivered his Sunday punch against the London critics by declaring them worse than the New York critics.

Merrick's most conspicuous involvement with the business of play reviewing concerned Stanley Kauffmann and was triggered by the paid preview issue, which itself triggered more than one controversy this season. Paid previews came under new scrutiny after the late Dorothy Kilgallen reviewed a Broadway preview performance of *Skyscraper* in her *Journal-American* column on the grounds that it was a paid public performance and that her pre-opening night review could be evaluated by her readers as an appraisal of a not-quite-finished product in the same way as a *Variety* review of a show in its tryout tour. Many journalists agreed with her and applauded; most show folk did not.

Soon afterwards, as the *Times's* new critic Stanley Kauffmann settled into his routine, it became apparent that he and his newspaper were going to institute a new policy of covering the theater on the last paid preview before opening night. They reasoned that a work of art requiring as much time and effort as a professional play production deserves a more studied evaluation in the morning-paper review than can be given by a critic who has only about 80 minutes to write his notice in order to make the late editions of his paper on the night of the opening (and of course no morning paper wants to postpone running the review for a day; this would give the evening paper critics the first say on a show). The *Times's* modus operandi was to ask permission of a play's producer to review the preview; then if it was refused the paper would buy preview tickets for its critic and inform the producer that the critic was attending that performance. The other two morning papers—the *Herald Tribune* and the *Daily News*—were invited by the *Times* to join in this policy, but their critics declined, both preferring to offer their readers the immediate white-hot reaction even at the expense of that final literary polish which might be possible with more time ("I might even write worse," John Chapman disagreed).

When David Merrick was asked for his views on the preview-reviewing controversy, he said he didn't care what performance the critics attended, they wouldn't understand what they saw anyway. But when the final-preview tickets to Merrick's production of *Philadelphia, Here I Come!* arrived at the *Times* they were accompanied by a note "At your peril!" Coincidentally with Kauffmann's arrival at the Helen Hayes Theater to cover *Philadelphia,* it was discovered that the theater had "a rat in the generator." The lights went out, the performance was cancelled and the entire audience was given its money back and sent home. There was no show for Kauffmann to see and review.

Kauffmann had insisted from the beginning of the controversy that he was able to meet the stiff deadline if necessary, but he preferred the 24-hour review-at-leisure. Many theater folk were unkind enough to suggest that there never *really* was any rat in any generator; that Merrick went to considerable expense (and the innocent-bystanding preview audience to some inconvenience) to find out whether Kauffmann could meet the 80-minute deadline. Cancellation of this *Philadelphia* preview caused Kauffmann to review this show on opening night, and *Hostile Witness,* too, because *Witness's* last preview took place the night *Philadelphia* opened. And so now we know. Kauffmann *can* review in 80 minutes if he must (but when he finally saw *Philadelphia* he didn't much like it).

The critics troubled the theater by their absence as well as by their presence in 1965-66. There were two newspaper strikes, the first coinciding with the opening of the season. It began Sept. 16 and lasted twenty-four days, so that for the first two new plays, *Mrs. Dally* and *A Very Rich Woman,* there were only two reviews, by Kerr and Watts, whose papers weren't involved in the strike. *Generation* stayed out of town long enough so that all the critics were back on the job in time to review it when it finally opened.

The second strike, against the newly-merged *World Journal Tribune,* began April 24 and lasted through the end of the season, so that critics on these papers missed reviewing *Mame* and *A Time for Singing* and *The World of Gunter Grass* off Broadway. The absentees were sorely missed. Capable as the remaining critics may have been, the very smallness of their number (three: *Post, News, Times*) greatly increased that uneasy feeling in the New York theater that too much is riding on the judgments of too few.

The old tradition of "the show must go on" is more and more difficult to maintain in the face of complex modern catastrophes. On November 9 the lights went out—all the way out in the memorable East Coast power failure. Most shows managed to get back into business the following evening. Then the New York City transit strike of subway and bus workers on January 1 closed a production or two off Broadway for its duration. The Broadway shows stuck it out with two or three hits still playing to capacity but with others suffering for want of audiences.

On the cheerful side of 1965-66 there was the fabulous continuing career of the musical *Hello, Dolly!* whose three productions were often grossing together more than $300,000 weekly around the country and around the world. The New York company, with Ginger Rogers, was one of the hits that kept selling out even during the transit strike. The national company, starring Carol Channing, set the following records out West: all-time record week's legitimate theater gross $295,025 (for ten performances, seven evenings and three matinees at a $9-$3 scale) and the all-time record legitimate theater gross for a regular eight-performance week, $198,774. The international company, starring Mary Martin, played Tokyo, where Miss Martin brought down the house with a special rendition, "Hello, Tokyo!". Then, when scheduled engagements in Moscow and Leningrad were cancelled by the Russian authorities, David Merrick took this company to Korea, Okinawa and finally to Bien Hoa in Vietnam, where it was performed for the troops and President Johnson wired Miss Martin: "You are making your President and all of Texas proud of you." The final stop for this company was London, where it opened December 2 at the Drury Lane.

The pricing and handling of theater tickets came often under discussion during the season, mostly centered upon the legally high-priced ticket rather than upon scalping—although there were reports in April of ice building up. Federal restrictions on the sale of theater tickets were repealed as of January 1, and efforts are continuing to have state and local restrictions relaxed, too. John F. Wharton recommended to the Legitimate Theater Industry Exploratory Commission that the theater work out a flexible-pricing policy in which last-minute tickets to the hits could be sold for as much as the traffic would bear up to $25. He also suggested that prices be lowered at mixed-review shows to stimulate sales, particularly among young audiences. In Wharton's opinion, the present rigid-price system fails to satisfy the affluent buyer unless he resorts to the black market, and it caters to the least desirable of the theater's customers, the one who wants last-minute cheap tickets to a hit and won't support a worthy flop. Wharton questioned the system in an article in Playbill: "Theater tickets are a perishable commodity. A Saturday night ticket is in great demand at 8 p.m. that night; at 11 p.m. it is worth nothing. A farmer who brings to market the only strawberries available that day will be paid everything the market will bear, and no one complains. Yet when the same principle is applied to theater tickets, outraged cries of 'black market' and 'robbery' go up. Why?"

For his musical *Superman,* Harold Prince edged the top tickets up to $12 and reduced his least expensive locations to $2. Tickets at both these prices sold well. The $9 and $3 locations sold last.

In housing, Broadway had a brief shortage of small, non-musical theaters at the peak of the season, but it was no great problem. New York gained the Vivian Beaumont (described in the section on repertory) and a refurbished Palace which was bought by James and Joseph Nederlander of Detroit. It was restored to some of its old glamor by Ralph Alswang (he stripped away the layers of "renovation" and uncovered ironwork and marble and a sculptured ceiling), and it was returned to legitimate theater use with the opening of *Sweet Charity.* The 54th Street Theater was renamed the George Abbott. Efforts to save the old Metropolitan Opera House were continuing as the season ended, with the opera company scheduled to begin performances in its new Lincoln Center home in the fall of 1966. Around the country these were some of the new theaters and/or cultural centers being constructed and planned during 1965-66: Theater Atlanta (Ga.); Saratoga (N.Y.) Performing Arts Center; 1,700-seat theater in La Jolla, Calif.; Studio Arena Theater, Buffalo; Scott Theater, Ft. Worth (Tex.); Cole Porter Theater, Los Angeles; Mechanic Theater, Baltimore; Houston (Tex.) Music Theater; Newark (N.J.) State College Theater for the Performing Arts; two Theater Group theaters at Los Angeles; Samaret (N.J.) Performing Arts Center; and of course the John F. Kennedy Center for the Performing Arts in Washington, D.C.

With theater interest growing in the hinterlands, Martin Tahse organized the American Musical Theater Club. Tahse will produce musicals to play in theaters across the country to a subscription audience which he hopes will reach 300,000 by 1968. Also anticipating decentralization of the theater was Robert Brustein, newly appointed chairman of Yale Drama School. Brustein's announced intention is to train his students for a repertory-regional theater career. And in the meantime the Broadway scripts were sustaining the theater everywhere in America: *Mary, Mary, Never Too Late* and *Who's Afraid of Virginia Woolf?* led in stock production popularity, with *A Funny Thing Happened on the Way to the Forum, The Music Man* and *The Sound of Music* in the music theaters; among amateur producers the most popular were *Our Town, The Miracle Worker, Take Her, She's Mine, Arsenic and Old Lace, Mary, Mary* and *Harvey.*

Just before the season ended Arthur Cantor, one of three executors of the estate of the late Billy Rose, formed a plan which will give hinterland theater a regular Broadway showcase. It is his intention to operate the Billy Rose Theater on West 41st Street as a Billy Rose International Festival of visiting productions, from abroad and from around the United States, for four-week engagements. This could provide a Broadway viewing for outstanding regional Theater productions like APA's *You Can't Take It With You* or Theater Group's *The Deputy,* which toured other cities this season. Mr. Cantor plans to open the Billy Rose International Festival in October 1967.

The 1965-66 New York theater revels now are ended; they took place with subsidy and fiscal reorganization under continuous discussion, while Broadway (and off Broadway) continued to get along as an old established permanent floating crap game of individual judgment and risk. There were problems and disappointments, but those who look to decentralization as the hope of the American theater of the future are looking for a short way home that leads over a cliff. The regional theater's playscripts are not *really* brought by the stork or even by the Rockefeller Foundation or the National Foundation on the Arts, they are gestated the hard way in New York. To change the metaphor a little, the regional theater is nursing lustily on Broadway and is a long, long way from being weaned. If New York goes dry, the regional theater must starve or worse; and by worse, I mean Ibsen and Chekhov.

Fortunately for *all* theater in America, Broadway continues to discharge its creative responsibility, even as it bears the weight of its own excesses. It is deceptively strong; it has no secret weaknesses, its weaknesses are all on the surface for any detracter to see. It is its strength that is hidden, like the power of a magnet. Every September the New York theater turns itself on and draws to itself every alloy of playwriting creativity until its minimum needs are filled. Even in a year like 1965-66, when usually reliable sources found themselves at a loss for the right words, the necessary inspiration took place. Somehow, the magnet drew in a musical based on a TV play, a verse drama from Harvard, a British repertory production of a German play, an adaptation of a French farce, just to name a few. Any one of these would have distinguished any season, and certainly they will distinguish future seasons in the regional theater and elsewhere, even in places where the taste and energy of the source is deprecated as the very plays that came from it are being revived.

This curious power of the New York stage may be magic; or it may be only the availability of a theater-oriented audience and the facilities to put on plays—in comfortable theaters and in uncomfortable ones; in coffee houses, in parks, in the streets. No. On second thought, it must be magic. The 1965-66 revels were summoned out of air, out of the thin air where fledglings fly, by some wizardry of inspiration. Most have served their purpose and are destined to vanish; but some are magically equipped to last on and on in new productions and fresh interpretations all over the country, all over the world and some, maybe, down through the years.

○
○
○

THE SEASON AROUND THE UNITED STATES

with

A DIRECTORY OF PROFESSIONAL REGIONAL THEATER

Compiled by the American National Theater and Academy

○
○
○

INTRODUCTION

By Ella A. Malin

Director of Information and Publications,
National Theater Service, ANTA

IN A scant five years, professional regional theater has developed into a force in American cultural life. The 1961 edition of *Best Plays* lists five groups: Arena Stage (Washington, D. C.), The Charles Playhouse (Boston), the Actor's Workshop (San Francisco) and in Texas, the Dallas Theater Center and the Alley Theater (Houston). In 1966 there are thirty-three groups in twenty states and thirty cities. Seven states and the District of Columbia have more than one; three cities (Boston, Washington, and St. Paul-Minneapolis) each have two. Four universities (Carnegie Tech, UCLA, Michigan and Stanford) have provided homes for outstanding companies. The Professional Theater Program (University of Michigan) presented productions by both the APA-Phoenix and the American Conservatory Theater (organized by William Ball and jointly sponsored by the Pittsburgh Playhouse and Carnegie Tech from July 1965 to January 1966).

These theaters were responsible for presenting more than 200 plays of which about twenty were new plays or American premieres. Forty-eight plays were produced by more than one theater. *Tartuffe, You Can't Take It With You, The Typists* and *The Tiger,* and *Twelfth Night* were the most popular, playing at six theaters each during the season. Other leading contenders were

42

Who's Afraid of Virginia Woolf? The Birthday Party, Major Barbara, Galileo, The Private Ear and *The Public Eye,* and *The Cocktail Party,* which received three or four productions apiece. Shakespeare, Shaw, Goldoni, and Ibsen were leaders among the classics, but Noel Coward, O'Neill, Beckett, Albee, Anouilh, Wilder, Miller and Schisgal followed close behind. From off-Broadway came *The Knack, The Firebugs, The Blood Knot, The Fantasticks, The Amorous Flea, Oh, Dad, Poor Dad, Etc., Riverwind, The Balcony, Little Mary Sunshine* and *In White America.* The English premiere of Ionesco's *The Pedestrian in the Air* was given at Chicago's Goodman Theater; Arena House (Harrisburg, Pa.) premiered a new musical, *My Wife and I,* as its final production; Theater Saint Paul ended its season with an original revue and a new play by its playwright-in-residence, Barry Pritchard. The Actor's Workshop tested three new productions at its Encore Theater. Arena Stage produced Loring Mandel's *Project Immortality.* APA introduced *Herakles* by Archibald MacLeish during Michigan's Professional Theater Program. The outlets for new plays obviously grow as the professional resident theaters multiply.

Their contribution to the employment of theater personnel is equally impressive. At a fast count, 125 directors guided hundreds of actors in both classical and modern repertory (with the exception of Chicago's Goodman Memorial Theater and the Dallas Theater Center, all groups dealt with here employ professional Equity companies). A huge number of technicians, designers, managers and other theater staff is employed at a time when employment in the New York theater, the road and summer theaters is dwindling.

At least five more theaters are preparing to launch their first season; the universities are increasingly playing a role in the proliferation of theater companies and affiliations with resident theater programs. New York University under the leadership of Dean Robert Corrigan and Professor Theodore Hoffman (both of whom have been head of Carnegie Tech's program) and the Yale School of Drama headed by a critic, Robert Brustein, are preparing full-scale training and production programs for the fall of 1966. Cornell University will be associated with the Ithaca Theater Festival programmed for 1967 and Boston University has formed an effective affiliation with the Berkshire Theater Festival in Stockbridge this summer. Other universities plan professional theater programs next winter.

During this period of phenomenal growth, there have been, however, some unexpected shifts and changes. Last season, Sir Tyrone Guthrie turned the artistic reins of his Minneapolis team over to Douglas Campbell, the associate artistic director. The season showed its first deficit and in 1966 Oliver Rea, president and co-founder, resigned before the new season was underway. The administrative and artistic direction are now in the hands of Mr. Campbell and Peter Zeisler, both of whom helped establish the theater. Last year Theater Saint Paul, one of the soundest community theaters, became a professional resident theater. Now its future is uncertain. Stuart Vaughan, artistic director of the Seattle Repertory Theater, left before the current season was over. William Bushnell and Douglas Seale took over Center Stage in Baltimore from its founder, Edward Golden Jr. San Francisco's Herbert Blau and Jules Irving, and a company of twenty, left the Actor's Workshop and took up residence at New York's Vivian Beaumont Theater amidst applause and controversy. Their replacements in San Franisco, artistic director John Hancock and manager Ken Kitch, have been highly praised for the quality of their work and of the new actors they have added to the company. Now they seem to be settling into a new and successful era for the Actor's Workshop.

Aside from financial problems and personnel changes, artistic criticism of resident theaters is sharper and deeper. The theater writers and critics have been swinging around the country to attend performances at the major resident theaters. Now that the novelty has worn off, they as well as the local critics are making sterner demands and talking about standards. One of the chief complaints seems to be about the actor. There is a feeling that the emphasis, for the most part, is on the physical production rather than on the acting company. American actors are considered not to be trained for the flexibility required in a repertory company. There are hints that some reasons other than training may prevent a theater from getting and keeping versatile and experienced performers: reasons involving salaries, the lack of stimulation and recreation, and the demand for instant success.

In March 1965, twenty-six of the professional resident companies, including Repertory Theater of Lincoln Center, The American Shakespeare Festival and the Oregon Shakespeare Festival formed the League of Resident Theaters. Peter Zeisler of the Tyrone Guthrie Theater was elected president, Thomas Fichandler (Arena Stage) is vice-president and William Bushnell (Center Stage) is secretary. In addition to the primary goal of establishing standard repertory contracts and serving as a negotiating agency with Actors Equity, the League wants the resident professional theater to create an identity within its community. Whether or not this will be an aid in raising and maintaining high standards is a question. But it does serve to emphasize the permanency of the resident professional theater movement.

Among the heartening factors is the slow but growing acceptance of theater as a permanent cultural institution worthy of community support in much the same way as museums, libraries and symphony orchestras. Despite opposition over many years, the National Foundation on the Arts and Humanities was signed into federal law September 29, 1965, and has already allocated $600,000 of government monies to support resident professional theaters. With new support from foundations and the National Council on the Arts, the American National Theater and Academy has developed four new Regional Administrator posts to advance and coordinate theater activities around the country. Individual states, also stimulated by government subsidy, are establishing new arts councils at a rapid rate, and it is expected that theater across the country will be greatly encouraged by their organized efforts. One thing is certain: continuing government subsidy is closer to reality than at any time since the government-sponsored Federal Theater was created as a make-work project. The large foundations—Ford, Rockefeller and Old Dominion—have also given extensive sums of money to development programs for theater. Lesser-known and smaller foundations are now beginning to add their support.

Community contributions to theater are also increasing in some areas, and the development of new audiences in the United States—through continuity of exposure, new school curricula and productions of plays that have, up to now, only been available in the metropolitan cities—will strengthen and enlarge theater as a whole. It is hoped that the resident professional theater movement will enrich the experience and extend the scope not only of the audience but also the actor, the playwright, the director and all theater practitioners.

BOSTON

By Elliot Norton

Drama critic, Boston *Record American* and *Sunday Advertiser*

ALTHOUGH they produced no dramas of towering significance and no performances likely to remain forever fixed in the memory, the commercial theaters of Boston presented during the season of 1965-'66 a certain number of productions of some merit and at least a few which, for good reasons or sometimes for no discernible reason, won widespread popular support.

Most of these shows were new, presented here in tryout for New York. All were, of course, unperfected when they arrived and some were still in that condition when they left, or limped out of town. A few—the Henry Fonda comedy, *Generation,* was one—would not get all their newly rewritten scenes until after Boston, during the "previews" that precede Broadway's first nights.

Of the musicals, the most popular was *Mame,* which came in at the end of the season and immediately sold out to the walls. The most unsuccessful was *Hot September,* which, arriving here early in the fall, lasted for four weeks only and was then closed down for good; it could not be rescued for Broadway.

Of the plays without music, the most prosperous newcomer was *The Impossible Years,* with Alan King and the best, perhaps, was the Irish import *Philadelphia, Here I Come! The Devils* by John Whiting, brought here from England by Alexander H. Cohen, had more substance, more dramatic potential, than any of the others, but didn't work out on the stage; in Boston, in any case (she was not well, and this must be taken into consideration) Anne Bancroft just wasn't up to the role of the neurotic nun. Disappointing, too, was the revival of *Ivanov,* which despite the smooth, sure acting of Sir John Gielgud, seemed static and, in the end, tedious.

Of the "road shows," which is to say plays that have been previously tested and are produced here in "national" companies, the most interesting in many ways was a production of *The Deputy* which was originated in Los Angeles last summer by the Theater Group of the University of California at Los Angeles, under the direction of Gordon Davidson, and brought here to open a tour which could not include New York because there it had already been produced, withal badly. This production was essentially the same in the text as that which Herman Shumlin staged on Broadway, but it differed in spirit, and despite certain weak spots it was better acted. The Shumlin show emphasized the failure of Pope Pius XII to confront Hitler bluntly, placing the burden squarely on the pontiff's shoulders. The Los Angeles *Deputy* shifted the onus just a little to make all men who sit silent in the face of barbarism guilty and responsible. This is a more reasonable interpretation and a stronger one.

Also in from the road, *Luv* brought laughter to Boston, and *The Subject Was Roses* contributed its thoughtful study of family clashes which cut deep into the lives of parents and children.

Meanwhile, back at the Charles Playhouse on Warrenton Street and in the small theater of the Hotel Touraine, our resident "regional" theaters were producing a share of interesting dramas, some very well acted and directed, some disappointing.

By and large, this was a productive season for the Charles company, which has been gaining artistic strength along with an increasing number of patrons. Like The Theater Company of Boston, Inc., the Charles organization operates under a number of significant handicaps. One of these is practical but not self-evident. In the course of each season, we get in Boston most of the best of the going plays of the commercial theater and many of the best actors and actresses of the world. Unlike other regional theaters, ours must present on their stages players to compete with these visiting stars. Conceivably, inferior performances may be overlooked in some other outposts of the drama, but not here.

The Charles Playhouse got around this problem here twice during the semester of 1965-'66 by bringing in stars from Canada, each time with notable success. Eric House appeared with the resident company in *Poor Bitos* and made that curiously fascinating drama viable. Later, Tony Van Bridge gave a solid and stimulating title performance in Brecht's *Galileo* and lifted many of the supporting players a level or two higher. Later, at the end of the season, the Charles managed without guest artists to produce *The Typists* and *The Tiger* of Murray Schisgal with considerable credit. Lynn Milgrim, whose work has been generally and consistently effective, took both women's roles in these oddball dramas, with distinction. In *The Tiger,* Edward Zang supported her nobly; in *The Typists,* Lawrence Pressman was somewhat less inspired, yet capable. What makes this encouraging is that both the men acted maturely, shunning some of the unfortunate comic tricks with which they, like so many players in these "resident" theaters, had previously wooed the younger and less sophisticated members of the audience. They let the author have his way; they let him make the jokes.

This would seem to mean that the Charles company, with its tenth season coming up, is ready to undertake a new series of dramas with more professional effectiveness. The years of floundering may be ended. Now, one hopes, there will be a great forward movement, with fine plays uniformly well acted. The prospects are good.

The Charles, which operates in a three-quarters-round playhouse fashioned eight years ago from an old night club on Warrenton Street, accommodates about 500 people, not enough to make a fortune but a good many more than the Theater Company of Boston, Inc., can accommodate. The Theater Company began operations three seasons ago in a playhouse crowded into one room of the Hotel Bostonian, a tiny place with ninety-five seats. How the producers got scenery on the stage sometimes seemed a mystery; they got the actors on and off through the audience.

When they were told suddenly last summer to vacate their tiny theater, because the hotel had been sold and a school was to move in almost at once, the mentors of the Theater Company were hard put to it to find a new location. Eventually, they made arrangements to convert what had been a dining room of the Hotel Touraine, at the corner of Tremont and Boylston Streets. This proved advantageous. If their new playhouse is somewhat less elaborate, shall we say, than the Tyrone Guthrie Theater of Minneapolis, it is at least more accessible and it has nearly three times as many seats as did the miniature theater in the Bostonian.

As they have from the beginning, the actors and actresses of this company concentrated during the first season in their new location largely on new plays, or plays new to Boston, most of them in the general tradition of the avant garde. Once during the year, in a production of *Measure for Measure,* they undertook a classic, with dire results. Although many of their players are very competent and some are gifted, they lack the training, the posture, the style for Shakespeare. They were defeated by *Measure for Measure.*

They recovered quickly, however, from the setback. At the end of the year, in a Festival of New American Plays, they did some very interesting things. This Festival was made possible by a grant from the Rockefeller Foundation, whose directors contributed something over $10,000, a sum which might seem ludicrous on Broadway but which looms large with the Theater Company, whose directors become slightly dazed—figuratively speaking—at the mere mention of "so much money."

What these same mentors did with that money and the other funds which they had to scrape up in Boston was commendable. Not all the plays they presented were masterpieces of dramaturgy. One or two were gratuitously ugly, after the sick fashion of some of the avant gardesman. But each one had a measure of merit; each was given a fair hearing in terms of acting and direction, and each gave the authors, the actors and the audience an opportunity to break a little fresh ground in the continuing and seemingly endless battle to get the truth about mankind into dramas which are seriously intended.

Perhaps the best of these plays, none of which had ever been done on the stage before, were *A Rat's Mass,* by Adrienne Kennedy, and *Frank Merriwell's Last Race,* by Geoffrey Bush, an ill-assorted pair. Miss Kennedy, author in the past of *The Funny House of a Negro* has a dark vision, morbid and perhaps cynical, but she is able to create a mood and to suggest with a poet's instinct some of the horror that may underlie the lives of children—Negro children—who, in her play, are betrayed into evil by the sly diabolism of a thoroughly evil and utterly disarming white child. Mr. Bush, a Bostonian, has a much different approach. His turn is for pure farce with a hint of satire. His touch is light, his vision fresh. Possibly because they are required to do so many somber dramas, the Theater Company actors played *Frank Merriwell's*

Last Race with a jaunty sense of joy, filling the Hotel Touraine with the sound of laughter.

By and large, and especially because of that courageous adventure with untested dramas, the Theater Company of Boston, Inc. had a good year. That they made no money with their program is not to be wondered at; that they were able to survive is partly to the credit of the Rockefeller Foundation, but mostly to their own indomitable courage and competence. They are not merely enthusiasts; they are talented.

The Boston theater season was more or less enriched by certain other enterprises—as for example Winterfest. This is an annual presentation of all the arts and entertainments in February at the War Memorial Auditorium by a newly organized and potentialy influential non-profit group called the Cultural Foundation of Boston, Inc. In a makeshift theater of the Memorial Auditorium, a place not ideal for drama, the Foundation presented productions by the Theater Company and the Charles Playhouse, and also dramas by two companies from the world beyond Boston: The Karamu Players of Cleveland, an integrated troupe, offered a curiously interesting version of Pinter's *The Birthday Party,* and the two-years-old Trinity Square Playhouse of Providence, R. I., produced *A Long Day's Journey Into Night.*

In nearby Waltham, Brandeis University introduced a professional company onto the campus, presenting two plays with Equity casts for students and for anyone else who wanted to come. With Morris Carnovsky, now Adjunct Professor of Theater Arts, as star and director, too, the company offered *Volpone* and later *King Lear* and, hopefully, established a new college tradition for professional performances of the classics.

CHICAGO

By Glenna Syse

Drama critic, Chicago *Sun-Times*

One weekend last March provided a fitting example of the irony of the Chicago theatrical scene. Under the auspices of the Theater Communications Group, created by the Ford Foundation, twenty-eight artistic directors from the nation's professional, resident theaters gathered here to audition a select group of eighty drama students from hither and yon. The irony—not one of the twenty-directors represented a Chicago theater. Reason? Simple. Chicago does not yet have a professional, resident theater (our Goodman Memorial Theater is non-Equity).

Chicago is a hub of theatrical activity, but it stands still while the wheel moves. Good intentions, committee meetings and surveys abound, but we continue to play it by ear—and the tune is a familiar refrain. One can honestly say the hottest conversational gambit in the Chicago theater for the year was who would take over for Carol Channing in *Hello, Dolly!* when she left for a movie assignment. The lively guessing game nominated everyone from

Tuesday Weld to Bette Davis. Meanwhile, they were doing Shakespeare, Shaw and Sartre in Podunk.

One experimental but healthy growth has already apparently withered. The University of Chicago, with the help of a small grant from the Rockefeller Foundation, recruited John Reich of Goodman Memorial Theater to direct a professional production of Molière's *The Misanthrope* in the university's small but handsome Law School auditorium. Reich cast George Grizzard and Barbara Baxley in the leads and gathered a strong local crew around them. The result had style and taste. But in spite of plaudits and prodding from press and public, the university has, at this writing, decided to bank, not fan the fire. Likely it will wait until it has the funds to build a bigger theater.

Meanwhile, the trend at the Goodman continued along the lines of adventuresome programming. *The Cocktail Party* was a stiff affair, largely due to the stentorian delivery by guest star Robert Flemyng. And *The Winter's Tale* was tedious and guileless.

The booking triumph at Goodman was *The Pedestrian in the Air* by Eugene Ionesco, who is not really mad, just crazy like a fox. A rambunctious show with lots of wile behind its caprice, it was deliciously led by Alvin Epstein, an uncommonly good actor. There was nothing mawkish, maudlin or overblown in Jerome Kilty's *Dylan* as he gave the title role a quiet, impudent portrayal. And Morris Carnovsky, a frequent Goodman guest, lent his seasoned style to Brecht's *Galileo,* directed by Howard Da Silva, whose contribution was highly touted but disappointing.

In other areas, Alvina Krause, who taught many a future star in a long career at Northwestern University, presented a three-month season at the Harper Theater. Her young and earnest company presented Pirandello's *Six Characters in Search of an Author,* Duerrenmatt's *The Physicists* and Shaw's *Too True To Be Good.* The best thing the troupe did was announce its aims as modest.

Three other notes: Michael Miller, the director of Hull House's Parkway Community Theater in a Negro community, is making a name for himself. His Sponono was sheer excitement. Second, Chicago finally had a show that was vastly superior to the Broadway production—the touring West Coast production of *The Deputy.* And you should know, perhaps, that David Merrick came to town and said he had no complaints about Chicago drama critics. Then he beamed like a barracuda and said, "Everything I've told you is lies."

DALLAS

By Gynter Quill

Drama critic, Waco *Tribune-Herald*

DALLAS kindled few big fires this season in the year-long survey from the classics to the avant garde at the Theater Center and the gamut from Berlin to

Tom Jones-Harvey Schmidt at the Summer Musicals, all of them homemade. Still, with an artistic level that was generally high at both theaters, it was a respectable season if not a rewarding one.

One of the Theater Center's handsomest productions in its six seasons was *The Tempest,* designed by Danish artist Bjorn Wiinblad with rich, bright hues and striking lines, robes and masks and feathered headpieces that gave it a magical dream quality, and staged by manging director Paul Baker with grace of movement. It had some surfeit of foolish antics and the usual unsolved problem of what to do about Caliban, but Shakespeare's poetic oddity was anything but earthbound. It had in Michael O'Sullivan a Prospero of some majesty and excellent, resonant voice; in Elizabeth Lumpkin a Miranda of winsome naivete, and in Mike Dendy a Gonzalo of statesmanlike wisdom and urbanity.

Jean Kerr's witty battle of the sexes, *Mary, Mary,* was one of the season's most likable offerings, with Anna Paul Schaefer and Randolph Tallman. Mike Dendy, David Pursley and Ken Latimer, three stalwarts of the repertory company, were the scientists in Duerrenmatt's *The Physicists* and almost lost the show to Ella-Mae Brainard as the scheming doctor in charge of the asylum. *Rashomon* had the feel of Japan and the flavor of antiquity in Duk Hyung Yoo's setting, but the fun was more in the puzzle of who did what than in any emotional engagement. *You Can't Take It With You,* proving its perdurability, was fun all the way, even with casting that aged some young people and made some older ones young.

And there was an experimental staged reading of a play by Clifford Sage and Hal Lewis, *Creep Past the Mountain Lion,* based upon a novel by Jewel Gibson, with Rex Ingram as a parson who wonders if the "unwritten law" protecting family honor is for the Negro as well as for the white man. Peggy Wood added a generous touch of artistry as a matriarchal Hecuba who makes herself and the Trojan women the "gods of Troy" in Jay Dratler's new study of the Trojan War, *The Golden Warriors,* half-read and half-acted on a bare stage.

On the intimate lower-level Down Center Stage there was a spirited production by Ryland Merkey of John Jennings' musical *Riverwind* and some strong theater in his staging of Pinter's *The Birthday Party.* There was style and conviction in Bob Baca's direction of Lorca's *The House of Bernarda Alba* and a broad-winking look, via Warren Hammack's production, at the romantic merry-go-round of Schnitzler's *La Ronde.* Winding up the season was *The Amorous Flea,* a rollicking musical version of Molière's *School for Wives.*

Returning in repertory were Arthur Kopit's *Oh, Dad etc.* moved upstairs from Down Center, Sheridan's *The Rivals* and, for the fifth season with almost the same cast, *Julius Caesar.*

This year, there was no touring Carol Burnett show to rescue the Summer Musicals' season financially, even if it was a better year artistically. Two weeks before the opening, Mary Martin's box office record-breaking touring *Hello, Dolly!,* observers wailed, siphoned off enough entertainment money to have made the difference between black and red. So, for the first time since managing director Tom Hughes' initial season five years ago, the Summer Musicals lost money.

The opening production, a low *High Spirits,* with Agnes Moorehead and Iva Withers, helped that happen. But one more like the mid-season *The King and I,* boosted tremendously by Ann Blyth and settings by Peter Wolf (perhaps the most stunning that show has ever had), would have tipped the balance the other way. The year was the sixth highest grosser in twenty-four seasons.

None of the season's other four came close to the success of *The King and I,* but the enterprise got a gentle lift with the spoofing of Elvis Presleyism and teenagers by Rose Marie and Roger Smith in *Bye Bye Birdie.* It was propelled higher by one of the Musicals' favorites, *Annie Get Your Gun,* which hasn't missed in four engagements. The sharpshooter this time was Patti Page in her first book show anywhere, right on target with the Berlin music but a little off the mark with her acting.

Coming on the heels of *The King and I, 110 in the Shade* was a frost, for neither the tune version of *The Rainmaker* nor the rest of the company nor the cash receipts came up to the warmth of Dorothy Collins as the plain Lizzie. Patrice Munsel was a red-hot Kate and George Wallace a virile shrew-tamer in the finale, a cheerfully saucy *Kiss Me Kate.* It gave the management cause to cheer, too, as the all-around best production of the season and a solid success with the ticket buyers.

Margaret Rodgers shared the billing with Tom Hughes this year as co-producer. Others on their team were Jack Lee as musical director, John Sharpe as choreographer, H. R. Poindexter as production manager and Peter Wolf as designer.

HOUSTON and SEATTLE

By William Goyen

Playwright, novelist and essayist

IN HOUSTON, The 1965-66 season at the Alley Theater was an abbreviated one because of the building plans and problems relating to the great new theater in downtown Houston. Only five plays were presented: *The Devil's Disciple, Ah, Wilderness! Right You Are If You Think You Are, You Can't Take it With You,* and *Duel of Angels.* The season played to 94 per cent capacity, and the resounding hit which caused talk and acclaim was Hart and Kaufman's *You Can't Take it With You* directed by William Hardy. Miss Vance planned and scheduled the play last year—before the successful revival of it by the APA in New York. The Alley gave the play new brilliance and freshness, and audience and critics remarked the simplicity and spontaneity of the staging.

Meanwhile, snags and delays in building the massive and monumental new Houston theater for the Alley players only enhanced excitement over the opening date, now announced as October 19, 1966. The opening presentation had not yet been decided upon at season's end. The new theater will not be fully used by the Alley until the fall of 1967. The 1966-67 Season will be played in the old Alley Theater. The 1965-66 Season, the Alley's eighteenth season, ended during the second week in May.

IN SEATTLE, the Seattle Repertory Theater opened its third and most successful season with three plays in three days: *Julius Caesar, Long Day's Journey Into Night,* and *The Importance of Being Earnest.* Stuart Vaughan, artistic director of the Seattle theater directed and appeared in *Caesar* and *Earnest. Long Day's Journey* was directed by Pirie McDonald. There followed revivals from the past season's repertory, *Ah, Wilderness!* and *The Cherry Orchard,* both directed by Mr. Vaughan, *Heartbreak House* directed by Mr. Vaughan, and *Galileo* directed by Pirie McDonald.

Mr. Vaughan's uncompromising and brilliant career in Seattle was cut short by the sudden termination of his contract in January, 1966, clearly brought about by tension between the ambitions of his Board of Directors and his own philosophy. Many felt that Mr. Vaughan's dismissal trumpeted the first warnings of serious competition between regional theater boards and artistic directors in the U. S. Pirie McDonald, Mr. Vaughan's assistant director, followed in the artistic director's place. The irony of the situation was that the third season in Seattle was the most financially and artistically successful of all. Vaughan's *Caesar,* played in modern dress, caused the most attention and controversy. His *Earnest* was considered by local critics to be somewhat precious, though handsome and brittly elegant.

LOS ANGELES: TWO VIEWS

Producer's View by Worley Thorne

Producer, Los Angeles and Broadway

"A PLAY," says Kenneth Tynan, "is basically a means of spending two hours in the dark without being bored."

By this definition *Any Wednesday* is not very much of a play. Neither is *Mary, Mary* much. Within most of us, *most of us,* I submit, they bore . . . really bore.

Sex without sex . . . risque without being risque. Naughty in the most infantile way, they do not get to our feelings. And we rarely think of them afterwards.

It is the complete inner boredom of such "hits" which must take a large share of the blame for the decline of the Broadway Theater, which now has but one theater for each three which existed 35 years ago. The conditions which breed these vapid plays include high costs and "critic"-columnists writing for the entertainment of millions who rarely go to the theater but like to divert themselves on the subway and the New York Central by reading of the foibles of theater folk.

Yet most theater today is Broadway-dominated. It has little urgency, little relevance. This is the trap set for Los Angeles and other theatrical centers in our country.

We live in a world at ferment. A war in Vietnam, racial injustice, riots, anxiety over mental health, police brutality, world-wide poverty, extremism, people seething everywhere, the crush of megalopolis; and, ironically, knowledge doubles every fifteen years.

But the "hit" Broadway theater seeks to compete with television by coming out of molds similar to, yet producing no comedy better than, *Dick Van Dyke* or *Bewitched,* good shows we get free from television.

On those Broadway boards it is nearly impossible for a drama to survive. Witness *Slow Dance on the Killing Ground* last season, which died prematurely with almost unanimous rave reviews; and *Conversation At Midnight* by Edna St. Vincent Millay, with several rave reviews and several pans, but dialogue which contains greatness, in a brief run. My wife, actress Susan Davis, and I produced the latter play. Because this play did not make money in New York it is considered a "failure" and may be little performed elsewhere. A dramatic edition has not been published (although Millay's original dialogues are in print).

The challenge is being taken up by Los Angeles and so-called "regional" theaters growing healthily around the country. As New York declines, Los Angeles during the current and forthcoming season will have built *four* new proscenium theaters averaging about 2,000 seats each. The past several seasons have also seen the birth of three new arena theaters of approximately 3,000 seats each, one of which has several times converted to thrust-style staging for drama by removing one-third of its seats (Valley Music Theater).

The raw materials are here in abundance: the nation's greatest concentration of actors, writers and directors. (If this sounds exaggerated, speak to someone who has had the opportunity of seeing a half-dozen plays in New York, followed by a trip to Los Angeles and a half-dozen plays here and ask him to compare, for example, the level of acting). The Los Angeles theaters cannot or will not get by with the slender leftovers of Broadway. They choose their play material from the best the world has to offer; old and, increasingly, new.

We first produced *Conversation At Midnight* in Los Angeles. It ran through much of the 1961-62 season. Brilliantly directed by Robert Gist, it had an equally exciting, creative cast: Eduard Franz, James Coburn, Jack Albertson, Sandy Kenyon and Hal England. Audiences could not forget it; people came back two, three, four, five . . . eight times to see the play; not only the "intellectuals" and students we expected to come, but housewives, cab-drivers, retired people with ordinary educations. The play had something to say to each of them which made them want to come back.

This kind of theater will not be replaced by television. It will not be attended merely because the club is having a theater party for some good cause; or just to serve one's time dutifully "for culture," like taking milk of magnesia because it's prescribed. This kind of theater we do not want to shake off the minute the curtain goes down. New plays are being produced in the smaller-capacity houses at a startling rate in Los Angeles, some good, some as bad as *P.S. I Love You;* most with more promise than anything immediate. Nevertheless there *is* promise: a place for writers, actors and directors to find out what theater is all about. With few exceptions, happily, these writers work out of their own needs rather than the New York formulas.

As decentralization of the theater, already a fact, becomes fully recognized in the national consciousness, more and more touring companies will emanate regularly from theatrical centers, Los Angeles foremost . . . bypassing New York except perhaps as another stop on the way. In fact, this activity has started, as far back as *Don Juan in Hell.* This season there was the Theater Group production of *The Deputy,* directed by Gordon Davidson, which had a lengthy national tour.

The question for Los Angeles is: will it develop the kind of theater which deeply involves and enlarges audiences, under a system of criticism and economics designed to allow it to flourish? Or will it simply become the new Broadway?

Critic's View by Dale Olson

Drama critic, *Daily Variety*

WHEREAS seasons in the past have found Los Angeles dependent on imported theater in the areas of important activity, the current year indicates the city is beginning to come into its own as a source of stage material for the entire country. Unlike those cities where specialized so-called "regional theater" organizations are the major focus, Los Angeles today is in the midst of an expansion of its audience, its production interest and its creative abundance that is making the city into one of the important centers of general legitimate theater activity.

There are those who choose to call the expansion a "cultural boom," but the term is inappropriate. This vast, constantly-growing Western metropolis has always had a considerable portion of culture. The big change is that it is now being recognized by the rest of the world. Strangely enough, it took material substance to bring about this recognition. Since the opening of the Music Center in December, 1964, with its immediate acceptance by the artists of the world, a new sense of personal pride has developed in the people of Los Angeles. It has been evidenced in an enormous growth in attendance for all public-performance events and has made a particular mark on the theater. The 3,300-seat Dorothy Chandler Pavilion, named after the chief sponsor of the entire project, is already in full use. By the fall of 1967 there also will be a 2,100-seat Howard Ahmanson Theater, for legitimate productions, and a 750-seat Mark Taper Forum, for lectures, concert readings and smaller theatrical events.

Theater Group, the UCLA Extension-sponsored project now going into its eighth season using campus auditoria, has been selected as the resident theater company for the Music Center complex. With the opening of the Ahmanson

Theater, Theater Group, then to be known as Theater Group of Los Angeles, will begin its first season as Los Angeles' own resident company. Started by John Houseman, who is no longer affiliated, and Dean Abbot Kaplan of UCLA, Theater Group came about at a turning point in national attention to Los Angeles theater and rode the crest of that wave to achieve its own particular significance among new, nationally prominent organizations. The group has made a secure niche for itself playing to sellout seasons on subscription and single ticket sales. With the financial support and organization of the Music Center staff, operated through a Performing Arts Council of which Lyle Dye Jr. is executive director, the potential of Theater Group appears limitless.

Pasadena Playhouse, now in its 50th year as a leading acting school and a production organization of considerable importance, struck forth under a rejuvenation program this season that met with varying reactions. The Playhouse has long been in a state of financial strain, its quality lacking and its energies drying. After a first season of the first fully professional resident theater company ever to be formed in Los Angeles, the enormity of the Playhouse financial status was revealed. Dr. C. Lowell Lees, formerly of the University of Utah, resigned his post as president of the Playhouse, and prominent local citizens are even now engaged in a fund-raising campaign to keep the doors open. The Playhouse is more than $500,000 in debt and the eventuality of an announced second resident theater season is in question. Nevertheless, the thirteen-member company of actors, each carefully selected and well-equipped, proved interesting in its infancy, and a 43 per cent attendance level for the first season indicates interest and sufficient reason to continue.

James A. Doolittle, President of the Greek Theater Association which operates both the summer outdoor theater of its name and the Huntington Hartford Theater in Hollywood, has been stalwart in building local production. Since taking over the Hartford, a beautiful 997-seat house which had lain almost dormant since its opening several years before, Doolittle was able to increase audiences so rapidly he brought in more than $1,000,000 in ticket sales in the first year of operation. The Theater Guild has been so impressed with this success it now considers Los Angeles one of the choice cities in its American subscription program.

What is more important than the success Doolittle has achieved with touring productions is the success that has also come with productions he staged here, last season with *Rattle of a Simple Man,* co-starring Tammy Grimes and John Astin, and *Incident At Vichy,* with Joseph Wiseman and Jean Pierre Aumont. Eli Wallach and Anne Jackson, after two years away from the production, were persuaded by Doolittle to repeat their original work in Schisgal's *The Tiger* and *The Typists,* to enormous accolades.

One major effort made this year by Doolittle failed. The producer revived Eugene O'Neill's *Anna Christie,* with Carroll Baker starring and Jack Garfein directing. The cast also included James Whitmore, Hermione Baddeley and Albert Salmi, all excellent actors. There were hauntingly handsome sets by Peter Larkin in an obviously expensive production. It met with disastrous results. The play is dated. Garfein's direction was dull, without flair and lacking in any sensitivity. Miss Baker's performance was equally mechanical, dull, with no vocal levels, and she drew very likely the worst critical assault experienced by an actress in the community. But the play was done, and on a high commercial level; and that is a chance that might not have been taken a few years ago.

Edwin Lester, whose Los Angeles Civic Light Opera Co. also is a resident company of the Music Center and a backbone of local theater for 29 years, this season presented *The Great Waltz* with a new book. He has scheduled *The Student Prince* for next season. Each of his productions comes in at the $400,000 budget level.

Actors Equity Association, under its Coast head, Lee Harris, and the West Coast Advisory Board, has agreed on an unusual new contract with the Actors Theater Repertory Company, headed by Rudy Solari and Corey Allen. The producing organization has associated with the Beverly Hills School District for a season of commercial theater production on a profit-participation basis. The entire company of thirty actors will work on the basis of participation.

Little theater appears to be growing from "little" to the same status as off Broadway in New York. Where the Players Ring at one time was the major success, there has been a burst of other productivity. John Rust maintained a lengthy run at both the Players Ring Gallery and the Ivar Theater with *Who's Afraid of Virginia Woolf?*, co-starring himself with Ruth Warrick, and continued with *Tiny Alice,* a West Coast premiere starring Signe Hasso. The delightful musical farce, *The Amorous Flea,* with much of its New York cast, ran twenty-one weeks at the Las Palmas, and Sidney Michaels' *Dylan* met with considerable success at the Stage Society.

It hasn't all been cakes and ale. There have been dismal flops, like the world premiere this season of Seeleg Lester's *Belial* at the Coronet Theater and an ambitious musical, *What This Country Needs,* that lasted less than a week at the Music Box. There also was an ill-produced presentation of *Blues For Mister Charlie,* the James Baldwin play, at the Lindy Opera House, that ran down the curtain after a few days' run. Paddy Chayefsky's film script of *The Goddess* was adapted by Casey Bishop for stage production in a showcase group and later presented again by another workshop—both dismally. And Lawrence Parke came up with an original, *The Outcasts,* which also fared badly.

But American National Theater and Academy, for so long virtually inactive in local production, came up with a series of excellent professional productions aimed at touring throughout the state. John Kerr and Kate Drain Lawson headed the project. And the California Arts Commission set touring productions of Adrienne Marden's presentation of *The Rivalry* and Judith Anderson's *Medea* for small communities throughout the state. Showcase groups, the invitational companies of actors formed to showcase professional performers to film and television buyers of talent, found themselves restricted by the new Equity ruling allowing only nine performances, but some like the Angels Company, Theater 40 (a new group now devoted exclusively to training and experience in Shakespeare, shaky but building in its work) continued their struggles. Equity Library Theater West, after a prior season of lackluster work, reorganized and is attempting to better itself. A new opera workshop, under the direction of Kenneth Gale, presented a striking production of Menotti's *The Consul.*

The musical stock theaters, a year ago riding the crest of the business, began to slow up. Material is getting scarce. But Nick Mayo, Randolph Hale and Art Linkletter stepped out of the usual in-the-round format, limiting their capacity by changing to a thrust stage, but also expanding their impact on local theater with productions of Judith Anderson in *Medea,* Maurice Evans in *Dial M for Murder,* and Charlton Heston in *A Man for All Seasons,* as they had the previous season with Shirley Booth and Sidney Blackmer in *Come Back, Little Sheba.* Also noteworthy was their in-the-round presentation of Ethel Merman and Russell Nype in *Call Me Madam.* They proved their type of theater doesn't have to be limited to musical shows, and they have a growing audience. Sammy Lewis and Danny Dare with their Melodyland and Carousel Theaters also continue to bring in suburban crowds.

Los Angeles is pleased at its theater season's successes. It isn't important that some presentations have failed; it *is* important that producers are gaining momentum, chances are being taken and theater has come alive. It's just the start. As Harold Prince said on a recent visit, "There is no reason why an important musical or drama can't run here for six months." He's right. There are movements to give that a chance, too. Among them is the planning of a new Cole Porter Theater in the Century City Alcoa project, to run shows simultaneously with their runs in New York. Theatrically, Los Angeles is on the move and aiming to provide a large and vital portion of the country's theater.

MINNEAPOLIS

By Hume Cronyn

Broadway and motion picture star, who played the title roles in *Richard III* and *The Miser* and Epihodov in *The Cherry Orchard* at the Tyrone Guthrie Theater during the season of 1965.

I LEFT Minneapolis late in November, 1965, at the end of our second season there. My wife (Jessica Tandy) and I had been members of the initial company in 1963, so that in the past three years we have spent nearly 18 months at the Tyrone Guthrie Theater. As theatrical engagements go it was a long one. That we formed opinions of this theater's accomplishments and failings was inevitable; but whether I can report them objectively is open to question. Contrary to popular assumption, passages of time and distance do not necessarily make for either clarification or objectivity. They may simply confirm one's prejudice. This is one of the disappointing enigmas of professional criticism. The theater reviewer writing against a horrifyingly immediate deadline is often more accurate and perceptive than the critic whose work allows for considered deliberation. Immediacy seems to admit some touch of humility that on deliberation is not to be allowed. Judgments must be absolute and preferably Olympian. My judgments are not even secure, let alone absolute; and my opinions, at best, are based on educated prejudice.

It is the actor's nature at the end of a long season to have collected and cherished as many complaints as a G.I. at the end of a long war. The experiences are not altogether dissimilar. Being no exception to the general rule, I must acknowledge at once that my single, overwhelming reaction to our two seasons in Minnesota is admiration for the Tyrone Guthrie Theater's success: not its artistic success, which will be disputed, nor its business success, which will be patronized, but its overall success as an effective institution for the professional presentation of a classic repertory. The choice of plays is always argued, the direction disputed, the performances discussed—only constructively of course—but when all the sharpshooting is done the theater remains, a continuing and developing civic asset where, four years ago, there was only a hole in the ground.

This aspect of the theater as a functioning and, to use an industrial phrase, almost "wholly integrated" organization, is generally overlooked or taken for granted, as though a theater should come "on stream" like a new factory allowing only for the inevitable "start-up costs" and a few "technical bugs" which have been anticipated and allowed for in the budget. I don't suggest that the Tyrone Guthrie Theater was built solely as a model of operating efficiency—plays are presented there as well. But I do suggest that Peter Zeisler, our patron saint Dr. Guthrie, Oliver Rea and Tanya Moiseiwitsch deserve enormous credit for accomplishments not often recognized.

The Minnesota Theater Company's program lists 130 individuals, excluding volunteers and members of the Board, actively engaged in its operations. (I don't happen to think it's nearly enough, but I will get to that later.) Many of these people are specialists and most are rugged individualists. Although assembling the necessary skills and achieving the necessary collaboration to get the curtain up without public screams of anguish may be a dull consideration, it is a vastly important one.

In the season of 1965 the Minnesota Theater Company presented five plays in repertory: *Richard III, The Way of the World, The Cherry Orchard, The Caucasian Chalk Circle,* and a revival production of its first season's popular success, *The Miser.* The overall season was 39 weeks, the playing Season— including three weeks of school performances—was 31 weeks. The acting company consisted of thirty-two actors, six of whom were McKnight Fellowship students. Local extras were employed in all productions. "Artistic," design, and musical direction involved six directors under the leadership of Dr. Guthrie, while Oliver Rea and Peter Zeisler as managing directors headed a production staff of sixty-four and an administrative staff of twenty-six. The production and operating budgets combined to something over $1,000,000 and, according to a recent press release, there was a reported deficit in 1965 (the first deficit experienced) of $82,000.

The season of 1966 had its official opening on May 31 and will be of approximately the same length as the previous one. The following plays have been announced: *The Skin of Our Teeth, The Dance of Death, As You Like It, The Doctor's Dilemma* and *S/S Glencairn*. Douglas Campbell takes over from Tyrone Guthrie as the artistic director, but it is expected that Dr. Guthrie will direct at least one production during the season. So much for vital statistics concerning the Minnesota Theater Company as they have been announced.

I once had a new and gifted author look me straight in the eye and ask me, quite solemnly, to define the values of experience. The enquiry left me speechless, which in my case is a difficult response to achieve. It was a question he would not have dreamed of asking his dentist. The business of forging a repertory company takes time (while the Minnesota Theater Company was in its third season, England's Royal Shakespeare Company played its 107th), and precedented formulas may be less applicable than in other professions. A certain amount of stumbling is inevitable. "Artistic direction," no matter how talented, cannot solve the problems by itself. A standard can be invited but not imposed. We learn by doing, often by failing.

The failure that may be avoidable is the formation—or at least the continuance—of a company unequipped to attempt Shakespeare, Sheridan, Molière, Chekhov and Tennessee Williams. I do not underestimate the difficulties involved. First, there are a limited number of American actors of the required versatility—a much abused word but an unavoidable requirement of repertory. It is a company that must be cast, not a play. Second, there is the wage scale which is generally too low to attract actors who have wives or husbands, children or leases or who have been so improvident as to commit themselves to anything other than a part. My wife and I enjoy all these indulgences—but then, as Herman Shumlin pointed out last year (in one of those articles in defense of Broadway), we are millionaires and therefore exceptions ("Dear Herman, thank you—and from your mouth to God's ear."). I dare say there were similar exceptions in Minneapolis such as Mr. and Mrs. Cromwell, Mr. and Mrs. Flanders, Mr. and Mrs. Richardson, and Mr. and Mrs. Zeisler. I congratulate them all.

The third difficulty is the passionate advocacy or disparagement of Broadway on the one hand and of the regional theater on the other: "'The New York theater is dead" vs. "who wants to get buried in the boondocks?" Why must it be either/or? Obviously, the two must become more closely related. The regional theater needs the support and stimulation of New York's theater artists; and a day will come when repertory companies other than Michigan's APA—which has avoided the "regional" stigma—may appear with honor in New York. I don't know of a so-called regional production to date that can match the brilliance of the *best* of Broadway, but conversely there is no continuity of effort or standard in New York (and has not been since the days of The Group Theater) that can match the best the regional theater has to offer.

During early crises at New York's Lincoln Center, when it became obvious that a new theater was not going to be born free, fresh and glowing, like Primavera on her clam shell, there was much argument about what was the fundamental failure. A frequent suggestion was the contamination of Broadway. Kazan's reputation had been made there and Robert Whitehead was an established and successful producer in the commercial theater. Alas and alack, what else could be expected. Oh, for new brooms, brave new worlds and Robert Brustein.

Now, among the authors Mr. Whitehead had produced in New York prior to his Lincoln Center commitment were the following: Euripedes (Jeffers' adaptation), Dostoyevsky (Ackland adaptation), Shakespeare, Marlowe, Gertrude Stein, T.S. Eliot, Shaw, O'Neill, Williams, Miller, Odets, Inge, McCullers, Anouilh, Robert Bolt and Thornton Wilder—hardly a shabby record or a crassly commercial one. Perhaps repertory or regional theaters can suffer more disastrous influences than the taint of commercial experience. It is interesting to read that Helen Hayes has joined the APA. Miss Hayes has had a long association with Broadway and is a ranking member of the theater establishment. (Anyone who has survived 25 years in the theater may qualify for that epithet. I do.) It will be fascinating to see whether this new association marks The Decline and Corruption of the APA as Precipitated by Miss Helen Hayes under the Direction of Ellis Rabb. I wouldn't bet on it. Rather, I'd suggest that her presence will strengthen the company in a variety of ways, the least of them being commercial and the most significant the example and challenge she should pose for the company and its directors.

The APA is already "an actors' company" which, in my opinion, gives it its greatest strength. Exceptions admitted, the best repertory companies have generally been actors' companies; by that I mean groups in which the primary dependence and emphasis is on the performance of the acting company in relation to the *content* of the play, as opposed to its physical form or style. I don't think the Minnesota Theater Company comes under that definition; and this is not meant as a reflection on its acting company. There are a number of expert and experienced actors at the Tyrone Guthrie Theater and an equal number of promising ones. What I am suggesting is an imbalance at present.

The Minnesota Theater Company suffered the initial blessing of a brilliant, original and positive artistic director. Its theater is named after him and is created in his own image. Without Tyrone Guthrie it would probably not exist. As he bestrides our narrow theatrical world like a colossus, there is no need to labor his talents. The trick is not to drown in them.

The Guthrie Theater is a director's and designer's theater. In only three seasons it has evolved a trade mark of production. There are beautiful costumes, striking choreographic effects, choral responses, musical interludes, magnificent properties and a good deal of dim lighting. There is also a prevalent public opinion that the thrust stage with its minimal scenery, demands all the dressing it can get, as though some law of compensation was required. If so, it is a far cry from "two boards and a passion."

Can a relatively new company be expected to generate great emotion, to catch the conscience of its audience, to bring the inner life of the play to bear and to hold without every possible external support? Perhaps not, but it must attempt it or fall back on embroidery.

What is the future of the Minnesota Theater Company? Much will depend on evolving policy and the goals it sets for itself. At the moment, I believe, it trembles in the balance between an opulent, regional, stock-repertory company on the one hand and a really important national repertory company on the other. If the latter isn't a reasonable ambition, what's a heaven for?

"Regional" is a word I dislike, though I use it repeatedly out of laziness. The word connotes insularity and suggests immediate limitations. The Minnesota Theater Company has to get out of Minnesota—further out than what is locally referred to as "the five-State Area." I don't mean it must *leave* Minnesota but that it must meet the challenge of comparisons, face new audiences, experience other theaters and provide the company with the stimulation of a different environment.

The professional acting company must be enlarged. Twenty-six actors plus six McKnight Fellowship students, no matter how gifted, should not be expected to carry a season of five plays over 30 weeks, rehearsing for the best part of five months into the bargain. Actors playing big parts in a classical repertory do not give good performances when they play six and occasionally seven times a week.

Even more important, a continuing attempt has to be made to challenge, stimulate and develop the company as a whole—in every department. There is a comforting but dangerous tendency everywhere to settle for known quantities, the amiable and familiar co-worker. There is also the reassuring rationale that "the company must be held together", and that growth is only possible under such circumstances. This is an arguable matter of degree. Carried to an extreme, the Auld Lang Syne principle can make for arrested development.

"This is our thing, Cosa Nostra, we like it that way and mind your own business"—Admirable for the Mafia, perhaps, but less satisfying to a theater's audience and stultifying to the development of the acting company.

Development is not always a matter of money, but money helps. Large companies cost money. Training programs, touring, workshops and better wages all cost money. Yet the Minnesota Theater Company had a loss of $82,000 last year and the Lincoln Center management has already announced a probable deficit of $500,000. And they will continue to lose money. It's a harsh world. The concept of the theater as a cultural asset, an institution not less significant than a public library, art gallery, symphony orchestra or the Metropolitan Opera comes hard. There seems to be an American tendency to build impressive theaters, spend a great deal on physical productions and expect companies of equal magnificence to materialize on cue. I wonder whether the Guggenheim and Hartford art galleries brought such a response from American painters?

I have considerable sympathy for the dedicated Boards of Directors who have agonized and exhausted themselves in an initial effort to raise the funds necessary to open a theater, only to be faced in mid-season by an artistic director behaving like Oliver Twist. Perhaps the allocation of available money—never easily available—has to be reconsidered to the sacrifice of outward and visible signs, in the hope of an inward, and temporarily invisible, grace.

The Minnesota Theater Company *has* a training program, *has* toured (briefly), *has* a workshop (of sorts), and is only commencing its fourth year of operation. Under these circumstances my emphasis may be misplaced. And, in the coming season, this theater will also sponsor a symposium on dramatic criticism—or, at least, this was in the committee stage last fall.

I have been asked specifically to comment on the relationship between the Minnesota Theater Company and the communities of Minneapolis and St. Paul. I doubt that their theater pleases *everybody,* but the support and hospitality offered the company could hardly be better. What may be lacking is the opportunity to take what the community has to offer. The schedule of regular rehearsals, understudy rehearsals, classes and performances is such that a day or night off almost always means retreat and collapse. The actors' hours make conventional socializing difficult. Repertory is supposedly far more stimulating than the long-run play, and so it should be, but much depends on the work load and the environment. How to bring the company more closely in touch with all that Minneapolis has to offer, how to reconcile the actors' weird and infrequent hours of leisure with what's available in the way of public entertainment, recreation or, more stimulating than either, conversation entirely unrelated to the theater and all its ferment, is not easy. I only know that halfway through a 40-week season the lack is felt and can hardly be blamed on the Minneapolitans.

These, however, are minor problems. It is the work that counts. If I appear critical in that regard, I hope it may be put down to enthusiasm for an ideal— no matter how Utopian. Even at this distance I should like to be considered a member of the Minnesota Theater Company only temporarily shelved. Certainly I am most grateful to it for the opportunities offered me and the experience, sometimes painful, always enriching, that is provided.

I believe that the repertory system, properly supported, properly developed, holds the best of all hopes for the American theater; the hope for better actors, directors, designers, all theater crafts; the hope for better service to the playwright and the eventual development of new ones. That hope will only become a promise with time, the nourishment of talent and our continuing reach. We may exceed our grasp in these beginnings—but there is no alternative other than mediocrity.

PHILADELPHIA and PITTSBURGH

By Ernest Schier

Drama critic, *The Bulletin*

IN PHILADELPHIA there were questions that had to be answered. Was Theater of the Living Arts here to stay? Would the quality of the work improve? Were the actors committed to the idea of a new theater—or would they head back to New York to be embalmed in the prosperity of daytime television?

Did Philadelphia—burial ground and springboard for pre-Broadway try-outs—want a professional resident company?

Yes, yes, yes and yes again. The 7,500 subscriptions of the first season, won by pleading and badgering over a non-stop round of cocktails and canapes, moved up to 8,500 (while the ATS-Theater Guild series dipped to below 8,000). A significant statistic: Living Arts' audience is predominantly under the age of 40.

The two housewives who conceived and nurtured Living Arts unselfishly withdrew from active roles (they are Celia Loverman and Jean Goldman, hallowed be their names). Thomas T. Fleming, young (37) and energetic took over the top job as president of the Board. Fleming fought the fussy fire department to a standstill, bought the building next door and converted it into a smoking lounge and directed himself to raising funds and planning for the future.

The shifts and changes left Andre Gregory, the talented artistic director, free to concentrate in the second year on his area. Key members of the company, including David Hurst, Ron Leibman, Lois Smith, Jerome Dempsey and Sally Kirkland, returned to form a solid acting nucleus (and will be back for a third season). It might also be noted that the specter of cultural piracy has been raised. Anthony Zerbe, Gene Gross and Arnette Jens, all with tours of duty with Washington's Arena Stage, have joined Theater of the Living Arts.

The second season of Theater of the Living Arts has been an improvement over the first. Gregory, showing more confidence, has been less nervous, less ostentatious and less patronizing in his work. (Horrible example from last year: in the premiere production of *Galileo* each scene was introduced three times—sung from a box over the stage, announced pontifically and heralded by a placard.) This season's opening production of *Uncle Vanya* from a crisp translation by Alex Szogyi, was an effective exercise in controlled mood. Hurst's Vanya seemed erratic and, in the final, heartbreaking scene, Flora Elkins (Sonya) and Hurst were somewhat mechanically exact. But the company succeeded in producing a redeeming sense of compassion for Chekhov's study of wasted lives.

Uncle Vanya was received well and followed by two popular successes, *The Critic* (bravely paired with Arnold Weinstein's *They,* directed by George Sherman) and Gregory's own stimulating production of *Poor Bitos,* with George Bartenieff in the title role and Anthony Zerbe as Maxim Saint-Just.

The twin bill of *The Stronger* and *Miss Julie*—Living Arts' fourth production—fared badly on opening night. In the curtain raiser, Flora Elkins showed promise of bringing a distinctive style to the stage, but suffered from jitters. Lois Smith and Anthony Zerbe tackled *Miss Julie* and were quite helpless to cope with director Sherman's significant-pause technique.

Living Arts rounded out the season with Saul Bellow's *The Last Analysis*.

Unquestionably, Living Arts has taken great strides in its second season. The standards are high, the physical productions on the thrust stage are impressive and Gregory and his alternate director Sherman seem intent on finding fresh ways of interpreting classics and some of the more significant new plays. The problems are familiar ones: money (of course), getting good actors and keeping them, developing a style, doing something about stage speech (ethnic and regional echoes are heard throughout the company) and developing an audience. A new theater will be needed to replace the current 500-seat theater (a converted movie house in an inconvenient, rundown section of the city), but that's a future problem.

National recognition has come early to Living Arts. Much has been written about its rapid growth, and while this is satisfying to the artistic company as well as the board of directors, there is no way of determining whether it will help or hinder the group. Living Arts has an audience of approximately 15,000 for each production. It is an impressive beginning. More impressive is the local recognition that along with the Art Museum and the Philadelphia Orchestra, the community wants and will support a theater of its own that is prepared to make a permanent contribution to the intellectual and cultural life of Philadelphia.

On the pre-Broadway front, there was a marked improvement too. There was nowhere to go but up after the disaster called 1964-65.

That busy importer David Merrick arranged the American premieres of John Osborne's jolting drama *Inadmissible Evidence* and the persuasive Irish comedy, *Philadelphia, Here I Come!* Also, we had Abe Burrows' boulevard comedy, *Cactus Flower.*

Best new pre-Broadway musical was *Sweet Charity* with Gwen Verdon. Music Theater of Lincoln Center sent a brace of pleasant revivals in *Carousel* and *Kismet,* while Harold Prince tried out *"It's a Bird It's a Plane It's SUPERMAN."*

There were the usual number of chrome-plated musicals and witless sex comedies. They all blur together in one shapeless lump: *The Wayward Stork, Me and Thee, Drat! The Cat!, UTBU, The Best Laid Plans, Bascom Barlow* (retitled *3 Bags Full* for Broadway) and *This Winter's Hobby.* Two reputable writers who failed were Jack Richardson with *Xmas in Las Vegas* and Reginald Rose with *The Porcelain Year.*

Eva Le Gallienne led the National Repertory Theater into Philadelphia for its annual visit, with three plays: *The Madwoman of Chaillot, The Rivals* and *The Trojan Women.* As productions they were only moderately successful, and again the NRT failed to attract large-sized audiences.

A resident Philadelphia theater called Society Hill Playhouse operates Wednesday through Saturday. The company pursues the most modern of moderns and tries to encourage new writers. Performances are on the level of enthusiastic amateurs. This year the company offered Arthur Kopit's *Chamber Music* and *Dutchman* by LeRoi Jones as a double bill; a new farce by Paul Alelyunas titled *What's-His-Name the Analyst;* John Arden's *The Waters of Babylon,* and a full-length play by local writer Frank Freda, *Momma, Look at Bang Bang!*

Expanding to take over a small, improvised theater previously operated by another local group, Society Hill had greater success in presenting the first local production of *The Sign in Sidney Brustein's Window* and *The Glass Menagerie.*

IN PITTSBURGH, at the other end of the state, the joint effort by the Pittsburgh Playhouse and Carnegie Tech to establish a resident theater began well and ended with bruised feelings on both sides when artistic director William Ball abruptly resigned.

Financial disagreement partly accounted for the dispute between Ball and the sponsoring organizations. The total subsidy ran to $426,000. The box office produced only $142,000 of this.

At the core of the dispute were opposing philosophies. Ball conceived of something called a "visitational theater" that would travel around the country. The Playhouse, under Richard Hoover, wanted a permanent group for Pittsburgh.

Ball opened his first show July 15. The production of *Tartuffe* was warmly received and ran for thirty-eight performances. Repertory was quickly introduced in the two Playhouse theaters (350 and 550 seats) with productions of *Tiny Alice, Six Characters in Search of an Author* and *Antigone.*

Before his departure in mid-December, Ball turned out a total of eleven productions. According to Playhouse general manager Hoover, there was never any dissatisfaction, and indeed only admiration and respect, for Ball's artistic efforts. Since his departure, Hoover has continued the flow of productions at the Playhouse, jobbing actors and hiring individual directors for each show. He's willing to try again to get a permanent theater going and is in the process of trying to find somebody who will stay.

SAN FRANCISCO

By Paine Knickerbocker

Drama critic, San Francisco *Chronicle*

THE FIRST YEAR of the Actor's Workshop under the leadership of John Hancock and Ken Kitch was a struggle but suggests great promise. The company was faced with a major financial crisis in late December and weathered that, securing $40,000 from the city's Hotel Tax Fund, and $70,000 from private sources. Its Board of Directors now reflects a wider representation of the community, and such new actors as Alfred Leberfeld, Barton Heyman, and Abe Vigoda, who were imported to supplant those who had gone with Jules Irving and Herbert Blau to Lincoln Center Repertory, have revealed considerable talent.

But of course the primary test is the productions themselves. Hancock persuaded Tennessee Williams to come out and work with the company for its initial presentation, but his rewriting was not sufficient to make an exciting play of *The Milk Train Doesn't Stop Here Anymore*. However, Hancock's direction, the theatricality of the production, and the cast—headed by Winifred Mann and Robert Benson—which Kitch and Hancock assembled indicated that in spite of last season's departures, the Workshop was still a lively organization. The American premiere of Brecht's *Edward II* brought Eric Bentley out to help prepare the production, and also provided an electrifying performance by Heyman in the title role.

Although all the plays were not as triumphant as these first two, the season was a success, and the final production of *A Midsummer Night's Dream* alone was enough to justify it. Similar to the interpretation Jan Kott proposes in *Shakespeare: Our Contemporary,* this bold and imaginative concept was far removed from the lyric fantasy to which we have become conditioned. The Workshop appears to be in good hands, and happily it is now making a greater use of other resident players.

Several local companies did not survive. The Cathedral Civic Theater, headed by Rachmael ben Avram, which performed behind the altar in Grace Cathedral, folded, as did the International Repertory Theater, and the Hyatt Music Theater, a 2500-seat theater-in-the-round, in Burlingame.

Stronger than in several years are The Playhouse and The Interplayers, which appear to be flourishing under new, vigorous managements. The San Francisco Mime Troupe, under the aegis of R. G. Davis, maintained its impudent voice, being particularly successful with its satiric Minstrel Show, and Jack Aranson founded the City Theater, which enjoyed a long run with a most persuasive *Dylan*. The Committee, founded in 1963, continued to make its amusing, audacious, and pertinent comment.

Late in the season, the Actor's Workshop presented Brecht's *A Man's a Man* at the Encore. Directed by Marc Estrin, it was based on John Hancock's production off Broadway several years ago, and was an immediate hit. The significance of the 1925 play in the light of the Vietnam situation was emphasized by Sergeant Bloody Five wearing a green beret.

Ben Bagley brought *The Decline and Fall of the Entire World as Seen Through the Eyes of Cole Porter* to the Little Fox, an elegant little jewel box of a theater admirably suited to the production which combined the best of two presentations off Broadway, and included the original collage paintings by Shirley Kaplan. Harold Lang, Fay DeWitt, Nagle Jackson, Bobo Lewis and Sybil Scotford were in its cast. And as these paragraphs are being written, a new musical called *Little Pete* after an actual Chinese highbinder who was active in Chinatown vice before the earthquake, was being planned for a June opening by producers Doug Von Koss and Lee Von Rahau, who will direct. In its cast are Lisa Lu, Jack Hill, George Ede, Anthony Smith and Estrellita Rania. The book and music are by Paul and Frankie Johnson and the musical arrangements by Tony Musante.

Hopes for a much-needed new theater in San Francisco appear rosy, so that within a few years, if it can endure, the Workshop may finally have the home it merits. At present it operates in two theaters, neither one satisfactory: the major productions are staged in the Marines, on its second floor; the experimental plays in the Encore which is much smaller.

WASHINGTON

By Leo Brady

Professor, Dept. of Speech and Drama, Catholic University

MOST of the new plays in Washington exist in manuscript form at the Library of Congress copyright office where some 3,000 were registered in 1965, but three originals were given first performances last season in the nation's capital (not counting those that pass through the National Theater on the way to New York) and at least two more were promised at the tag-end of the season.

Arena Stage was responsible for two of them: Loring Mandel's *Project Immortality* and Howard Sackler's *Mr. Welk and Jersey Jim*. Mandel's play got a solid production, but its theme (should a genius let posterity pick his brains with a tape-recorder?) ran like a parallel line alongside the scenes that were supposed to embody it. In spite of Dana Elcar's muscular portrait of the genius, complete with corny European sense of humor, the play was quick with words but slow with action and expired long before the main character did. Sackler's short play shared a bill with Ionesco and Pinter, somewhat in their vein but not their class: a two-man vaudeville turn with wet jokes, a Grand Guignol ending, and little distinction.

T. J. Spencer's *Jonah* had its premiere in the more modest confines of the Catholic University Theater and led one visiting reviewer to remark that it was the *Jonah* New York should have had (instead of Paul Goodman's), a provincial view rejected by cosmopolitan Washingtonians. Out of the Old Testament material, Spencer made a jovially irreverent comedy, with a broad wink at contemporary life, and presented himself as a witty and imaginative writer. His scenes were more theatrical than Mandel's, though both writers preferred the verbal to the dramatic.

The Washington Theater Club announced a topical satire on the city entitled *Spread Eagle* for late in the season, but otherwise confined itself to living up to its billing as Washington's off-Broadway theater (it is really off-16th Street) by introducing Schisgal's *The Typists* and *The Tiger*, Hanley's *Slow Dance on the Killing Ground*, and Pinter's *The Birthday Party*. Davey Marlin-Jones staged the Pinter play with perhaps too heavy a hand on squeezed-out significance, but John Hillerman gave a finely controlled performance as Stanley. This group is organized as a club and you have to buy a membership (one dollar) before you buy a ticket. The 145 seats are arranged around a rectangle, and the entrance to the auditorium is at stage left: if you're late, you walk right into the play. (At Arena, as at Lincoln Center, you must wait in the lobby until the first interval—these days liturgy is more fiercely observed in the theater than in church.)

Olney Theater will have done three new plays in the last three summers when it introduces Hugh Leonard's *Stephen D* in July under the direction of

James Waring. This theater on the outskirts had its best summer in years in 1965, with a profit on every play, even *Tartuffe* and *Waiting for Godot*.

With 16,000 subscribers, Arena's box office never bleeds, but *Saint Joan* and *Serjeant Musgrave's Dance* were its biggest winners. The Arden play had the distinction of drawing the heaviest protest mail in the resident theater's history, not because of the anti-war sentiments but because of some lusty highjinks under a blanket. *Oh What a Lovely War,* new to the area, will close out the season in the round. This theater, which annually has a playwright in residence, hopes to do more to nurture original drama in the future.

The National's new plays were, of course, temporary tenants and not of native origin. *Luv* and *Cactus Flower* were predictably popular, and *The Subject Was Roses* and *Hostile Witness* won healthy responses. The John Gielgud-Vivien Leigh *Ivanov* played to standing room for two weeks, proving again the local interest in prestige productions, even though the highly-skilled company gave one of those British performances which creates the impression that the actors have stopped off at the theater to run through the play on their way to something really important—like tea at the Embassy.

Georgetown University did an evening of short plays written by students, and Catholic University did its annual musical comedy, but these are staples of the local cultural scene, like the Shakespearean readings at the Library of Congress and the visits of eminent overseas companies, such as that of the Comédie Française to Lisner Auditorium, where they made Molière and Corneille glow.

Culture and traffic, the two hottest items in Washington after poverty and Viet Nam, came into conflict on the banks of the Potomac, where work was begun on the Kennedy Center. Government workers driving to the office had to detour or get mud on their tires. They hope the completed building won't add to their annoyance, since theatrical construction in the area is not notable for its excellence. Howard University's Ira Aldridge Theater has poor sightlines and a cramped backstage. The new theater in Maryland University's Arts Center has a high movie-house ceiling which gobbles up sound, though its backstage provisions are good. George Washington University's Lisner Auditorium is too vast out front even for the Washington Opera Society, and too limited backstage for a troupe of marionettes, but one of its wartime defects is being remedied with the installation of an air-conditioning system. It would be logical for the Opera group and at least one of the local ballet companies to call the Kennedy Center home, but rumors say that the plans provide for no storage space or proper rehearsal room, and there is fear that the huge memorial complex will do nothing more than perform the function— on an expanded scale—now carried on by the National, Lisner and Constitution Hall.

If there is any moral to be drawn from the season, it is that good new plays (scarce as they are) are easier to find than superior actors. Arena's company was constantly taking raps from the reviewers for the low quality of its performance (and its direction, too, for that matter), and the criticism reminded students that the same plight prevails at the Lincoln Center in New York: style in the costuming, flair in the mounting, the last word in sound equipment, luxury in the auditorium—and then the play begins and disenchantment flows over all. Conscious of this defect, Zelda Fichandler at Arena, under a grant from the Rockefeller Foundation, set up classes in voice, movement, and acting technique. But the problem may go deeper than training. Top flight actors seem to feel about resident companies the way Willie Mays might feel about sand-lot baseball, even though the analogy is by no means exact. Foundation grants have alleviated the financial problem, but actors would still apparently rather be sorry in New York than safe in Washington. Maybe acting is at a low ebb because histrionic talent is being drawn these days into other fields, such as politics and protest. (Imagine Dirksen as Dogberry, or Adam Clayton Powell as Othello, or the draft-card burners as Billy Budds.)

Some mention ought to be made of Arena Stage's program—the paper one, that is, handed out by ushers. It is beautifully edited and designed, equivalent to and in many instances superior to *The Playbill,* though this may be just another dispiriting example of the byproduct being more impressive than the main item.

A DIRECTORY OF
PROFESSIONAL REGIONAL THEATER

Professional 1965-66 programs and repertory productions by leading resident companies around the United States (excluding Broadway, off Broadway, touring New York shows, summer theaters and Shakespeare festivals) are listed in alphabetical order of their locations. This directory was compiled by the American National Theater and Academy (ANTA) for *The Best Plays of 1965-66*. Figures in parentheses following titles give number of performances. Date given is opening date. Plus sign (+) indicates play still running June 1, 1966, with no limited number of performances.

ABINGDON, VA.

Barter Theater: Main Theater

THE HAPPIEST MILLIONAIRE (20). By Kyle Crichton. June 8, 1965. Director, Clinton Atkinson; scenery, Eve Lyon; lighting, Albin Aukerlund; costumes, Lucille Baillie. With Jack Cowles, Guy Bongiovanni, Lang Scruggs, Robert Foley, Jo Henderson.

THE THREEPENNY OPERA (20). Musical by Bertolt Brecht; based on John Gay's *Beggar's Opera;* English adaptation, Marc Blitzstein; music, Kurt Weill. June 22, 1965. Director, Clinton Atkinson; scenery, Eve Lyon; lighting, Albin Aukerlund; costumes, Lucille Baillie; musical director, Elizabeth C. Cummings. With Liz Ingleson, Michael Norell, John Randolph Jones, John Riordan, Jo Henderson.

HAY FEVER (20). By Noel Coward. July 6, 1965. Director, Robert Porterfield; scenery, Eve Lyon; lighting, Albin Aukerlund; costumes, Lucille Baillie. With Sophia D'Arcy, David Birney, Liz Ingleson, Robert Foley.

TARTUFFE (12). By Molière; English translation by Richard Wilbur. July 27, 1965. Director, Clinton Atkinson; scenery, Eve Lyon; lighting, Albin Aukerlund; costumes, Anthony Eikenbary. With Liz Ingleson, Clinton Atkinson, Robert Foley, Michael Norell.

LEADER OF THE PACK (8). By Sherman Ewing. August 24, 1965. Director, Clinton Atkinson; scenery, Eve Lyon; lighting, Albin Aukerlund. With Liz Ingleson, Michelle Black, Salem Ludwig.

NEVER TOO LATE (16). By Sumner Arthur Long. September 7, 1965. Director, Clinton Atkinson; scenery and lighting, Albin Aukerlund. With Carolyn Cowles, Michael Norell, Liz Ingleson, Jerry Chase.

THE KNACK (15). By Ann Jellicoe. September 21, 1965. Director, Clinton Atkinson; lighting, Albin Aukerlund. With Guy Bongiovanni, Jack Cowles, David Birney, Jean Birney.

TWELFTH NIGHT (21). By William Shakespeare. April 15, 1966. Director, Ira Zuckerman; scenery, Lynn Pecktal; lighting, Albin Aukerlund; costumes, Karin Bacon. With Robert Summers, David Sabin, Peter Blaxill, James Cahill, Jane Lowry, Nancy Reardon, Rhoda B. Carrol.

YOU CAN'T TAKE IT WITH YOU (10). By Moss Hart and George S. Kaufman. April 28, 1966. Director, Ira Zuckerman; scenery, William J. Wall; lighting, Albin Aukerlund; costumes, Karin Bacon. With Nancy Reardon, Joseph Stern, Doris Gregory, James Cahill.

Barter Theater: Festival Playhouse

WHO'S AFRAID OF VIRGINIA WOOLF? (10). By Edward Albee. June 29, 1965. Director, Clinton Atkinson; lighting, Albin Aukerlund. With Libby Lyman, Edd K. Gasper, Jo Henderson, Jack Cowles.

AN EVENING OF MAN vs. WOMAN or WOMAN vs. MAN (12). By George Bernard Shaw. July 13, 1965. Director, Peter W. Culman; scenery, Eve Lyon; lighting, Albin Aukerlund; costumes, Lucille Baillie. With Robert Foley, Pat Echeverria.

WAITING FOR GODOT (8). By Samuel Beckett. July 27, 1965. Director, Jerry Chase; lighting, Albin Aukerlund; costumes, Lucille

Baillie. With John Riordan, John Glover, Gaetano Bongiovanni, John Randolph Jones, Lyman Packer.

PICTURES IN THE HALLWAY (6). By Sean O'Casey. July 30, 1965. Director, Jack Cowles; lighting, Albin Aukerlund. With David Birney, Mac McLaughlin, Jerry Chase, Pat Echeverria, Paul Ruben, Nancy Langhorne.

THE PRIVATE EAR and THE PUBLIC EYE (3). By Peter Shaffer. August 10, 1965. Directors, Lamont Palmer and Clinton Atkinson; scenery, Eve Lyon; lighting, Albin Aukerlund; costumes, Lucille Baillie. With John Glover, John Riordan, Michelle Black, David Birney, John Randolph Jones, Malie Bruton.

ANN ARBOR, MICH.

Association of Producing Artists (APA)—Phoenix Repertory (in University of Michigan Professional Theater Program)

YOU CAN'T TAKE IT WITH YOU (14). By Moss Hart and George S. Kaufman. September 29, 1965. Director, Ellis Rabb; scenery and lighting, James Tilton; costumes, Nancy Potts.

THE WILD DUCK (14). By Henrik Ibsen; adapted by Eva Le Gallienne. October 6,

1965. Director, Stephen Porter; scenery and lighting, James Tilton; costumes, Nancy Potts.

HERAKLES (14). By Archibald MacLeish (premiere). October 27, 1965. Director, Alan Schneider; scenery and lighting, James Tilton; costumes, Nancy Potts.

PERFORMER	"YOU CAN'T TAKE IT WITH YOU"	"THE WILD DUCK"	"HERAKLES"
Claribel Baird	Olga		
Joseph Bird	Mr. De Pinna	Relling	
Patricia Conolly			Miss Parfit
Clayton Corzatte	Tony Kirky	Gregers Werle	
Keene Curtis	Boris Kolenkhov	Molvik; The Bald Gentleman	The Guide
Gordon Gould	Ed	Pettersen	
Jennifer Harmon	Essie	Hedwig Ekdal	Little Hodd
Rosemary Harris	Alice		Megara
Betty Miller	Mrs. Kirby	Gina Ekdal	Xenoclea
Donald Moffat	Martin Vanderhof	Hjalmar Ekdal	
Nat Simmons	Donald		
Dee Victor	Penelope Sycamore	Mrs. Sorby	Mrs. Hoadley
Sydney Walker	Paul Sycamore	Old Ekdal	Herakles
Paulette Waters	Rheba		
Richard Woods	Mr. Kirby	Mr. Werle	
Robert Einenkel		Jensen	
Joel Kramer		The Fat Gentleman	
Diana Linders	Gay Wellington		
Stephen Wyman	Henderson	Graaberg	

American Conservatory Theater (in University of Michigan Professional Theater Program)

TINY ALICE (15). By Edward Albee. January 11, 1966. Director, William Ball; designer, Mark Negin; lighting, Jules Fisher. With DeAnn Mears, Ray Reinhardt, Harry Frazier, Paul Shenar, Anthony Teague and Al Alu.

TARTUFFE (15). By Molière; translated by Richard Wilbur. January 24, 1966. Director, William Ball; scenery, Mark Negin; lighting, Jules Fisher; costumes, Jane Greenwood. With Rene Auberjonois, John Carpenter, DeAnn Mears, Barbara Caruso, Robin Gammell, Charles Siebert.

There were also performances of BEYOND THE FRINGE by Alan Bennett, Peter Cook, Jonathan Miller and Dudley Moore; director, Hugh Alexander; lighting, Steven Cohen; costumes, David Toser; with Hugh Alexander, Rene Auberjonois, Robin Gammell, Charles Siebert;

and ENDGAME by Samuel Beckett; director, Edward Payson Call; scenery, Stuart Wurtzel; lighting, Steven Cohen; costumes, David Toser; with Rene Auberjonois, Robin Gammell, Jay Doyle, Joan Croyden.

UNIVERSITY OF MICHIGAN'S PROFESSIONAL THEATER PROGRAM also included limited engagements of ABSENCE OF A CELLO by Ira Wallach, THE SUBJECT WAS ROSES by Frank D. Gilroy, Euripides' THE TROJAN WOMEN translated by Edith Hamilton and BAREFOOT IN THE PARK by Neil Simon.

ATLANTA

Pocket Theater

HAY FEVER (16). By Noel Coward. September 30, 1965. Director, Mitzi Hyman; designer, Luis Maza. With Jane Higgins, Elton Drake, Muriel Moore, Jan Albrecht, David Warfield.

FAREWELL, FAREWELL EUGENE (14). By John Vari and Roger Ackland. October 28, 1965. Director, Mitzi Hyman; designer, Luis Maza. With Doris Blass, Betty Anderson, Jack Jackson, Ann Geer, Doris Bucher.

THE REHEARSAL (15). By Jean Anouilh; translated by Lucienne Hill. December 2, 1965. Director, Mitzi Hyman; designer, Luis Maza. With Jane Albrecht, Malcolm Brush, John Phipps, Gloria Maloof, Dick Boudoin.

CANDIDA (16). By George Bernard Shaw. January 6, 1966. Director, Richard C. Munroe; designer, Luis Maza. With Mitzi Hyman, Fred Chappell, John Barlett.

THE DUMBWAITER and THE COLLECTION (15). By Harold Pinter. February 3, 1966. Directors Doris Bucher and Richard C. Monroe; designer, Luis Maza. With Art Pellman, Ed Stafford, Tom Chadwick, Dan Satacroce, Lisa English, John McDorman.

THE NIGHT OF THE IGUANA (16). By Tennessee Williams. March 17, 1966. Director, Richard C. Munroe; scenery and costumes, Luis Maza; lighting, Charles Walker. With Muriel Moore, John McDorman, Mitzi Hyman, Gus Mann.

HEDDA GABLER (12). By Henrik Ibsen; translated by William Archer. April 21, 1966. Director, Mitzi Hyman; designer, Luis Maza. With Dorothy McConkey Poulos, Art Pellman, Tom Chadwick, Pat McGuire.

BALTIMORE

Center Stage

CAESAR AND CLEOPATRA (34). By George Bernard Shaw. October 28, 1965. Director, Douglas Seale; scenery, Douglas W. Schmidt; lighting, Mark Rodgers; costumes, Scott Bushnell. With Douglas Seale, Sharon Laughlin, Juanita Bethea, Donald Symington.

THE TAVERN (35). By George M. Cohan. December 2, 1965. Director, John Marley; scenery, Whitney LeBlanc; lighting, Mark Rodgers; costumes, Georgia Ryther. With James Cromwell, William McKereghan, Sharon Laughlin, Ed Preble, Leslie Paul, Donald Symington.

ARDELE (33). By Jean Anouilh; translated by Lucienne Hill. January 6, 1966. Director, Douglas Seale; scenery and lighting, Mark Rodgers; costumes, Scott Bushnell. With Douglas Seale, Ellen Darrel Tovatt, Sharon Laughlin, Jeffrey Hildner, Patricia Falkenhain, Donald Symington.

THE BIRTHDAY PARTY (35). By Harold Pinter. February 10, 1966. Director, Brooks

Jones; scenery and lighting, Mark Rodgers; costumes, Scott Bushnell. With Ed Preble, Kate Wilkinson, John Schuck, Ellen Darrel Tovatt, William McKereghan, Patrick Tovatt.

THE DAYS BETWEEN (33). By Robert Anderson (professional premiere). March 17, 1966. Director, Douglas Seale; scenery and lighting, Mark Rodgers; costumes, Georgia Ryther. With Sharon Laughlin, Elizabeth Thurman, John Schuck, Jeffrey Hildner, Burke Byrnes, Donald Symington.

THE CHINESE WALL (34). By Max Frisch; translated by James Rosenberg; adapted by Douglas Seale. April 21, 1966. Director, Douglas Seale; scenery and lighting, Mark Rodgers; costumes, Scott Bushnell; choreographer, Zenaide Trigg. With Donald Symington, John Schuck, Ellen Darrel Tovatt, Burke Byrnes, Elizabeth Thurman, Jordan Singer.

AS YOU LIKE IT (48). By William Shakespeare. May 26, 1966. Director, Douglas Seale; scenery and lighting, Mark Rodgers; costumes, Georgia Ryther. With Center Stage Company.

BOSTON (See article on its season)

Charles Playhouse

THE MISER (48). By Molière. September 29, 1965. Director, Michael Murray; scenery and costumes, William D. Roberts; lighting, Hugh E. Lester, With Peggy Pope, John Devlin, Lucy Martin, Lawrence Pressman, Terrence Currier.

POOR BITOS (40). By Jean Anouilh; translated by Lucienne Hill. November 10, 1965. Director, Michael Murray; scenery and costumes, William D. Roberts; lighting, Hugh E. Lester. With Eric House, Harvey Solin, Robert Gaus, Lawrence Pressman.

MAJOR BARBARA (40). By George Bernard Shaw. December 15, 1965. Director, Louis Criss; scenery and costumes, William D. Roberts; lighting, Hugh E. Lester. With Michael Moriarty, Ronald Bishop, Terrence Currier.

GALILEO (48). By Bertolt Brecht; English version by Charles Laughton. January 19, 1966. Director, Michael Murray; scenery and costumes, William D. Roberts; lighting, Hugh E. Lester; music, Newton Wayland. With Tony Van Bridge, Paul Millikin, Lynn Milgrim, Robert Gaus, Terrence Currier, Edward Zang, Ronald Bishop, Lawrence Pressman.

THE INSPECTOR GENERAL (40). By Nikolai Gogol; translated by Thomas J. Butler. March 2, 1966. Director, Michael Murray; scenery and costumes, William D. Roberts; lighting, Hugh E. Lester. With Gwyllum Evans, Edward Zang, Brendan Burke, Joe Hardy, Maureen Fitzgerald, Lynn Milgrim.

THE TYPISTS and THE TIGER (48). By Murray Schisgal. April 6, 1966. Director, Michael Murray; scenery and costumes, William D. Roberts; lighting, Hugh E. Lester. With Lynn Milgrim, Edward Zang, Lawrence Pressman.

Theater Company of Boston, Inc.

THE LUNCH HOUR by John Mortimer; and ACT WITHOUT WORDS I and PLAY by Samuel Beckett (23). October 20, 1965. Director, David Wheeler; scenery, Robert Allen; lighting, Alan A. Melad. With Paul Benedict, Lisa Richards, Josephine Lane, Mark Epstein, Naomi Thornton, Ted Kazanoff.

YES IS FOR A VERY YOUNG MAN (30). By Gertrude Stein. November 11, 1965. Director, David Wheeler; scenery, Robert Allen; lighting, Alan A. Melad; costumes, Linda Faiola. With Lisa Richards, Burris De Benning, Paul Benedict, Bronia Stefan, Mark Epstein.

MEASURE FOR MEASURE (29). By William Shakespeare. December 9, 1965. Director, David Wheeler; scenery, Alexander Pertzoff; lighting, Dennis Parichy; costumes, Olga Pertzoff and Linda Faiola. With Barry Primus, R. Scott Thomas, Paul Benedict, Judy London, Avra Petrides, Mark Epstein.

THE FEAR AND MISERY OF THE THIRD REICH (30). By Bertolt Brecht; translated by Kenneth Tigar and Clayton Koelb. January 6, 1966. Director, David Wheeler; lighting, David Tyndall; costumes, Susan Howarth. With Paul Benedict, Mark Epstein, Ted Kazanoff, Naomi Thornton.

THE BIRTHDAY PARTY (30). By Harold Pinter, February 3, 1966. Director, David Wheeler; scenery, Robert Allen; lighting, Mark Krause and David Tyndall; costumes, Ann Marie Butler. With Mark Epstein, Josephine Lane, Paul Benedict.

THE INFANTRY (22). By Andy and Dave Lewis. March 3, 1966. Director, Andy Lewis; scenery, Robert Allen; lighting, Mark Krause. With Lee Kissman, Burris De Benning, Joe Jamrog, Mark Epstein.

FRANK MERRIWELL'S LAST RACE by Geoffrey Bush, directed by Timothy Affleck; ICARUS'S MOTHER by Sam Shepard, directed by Paul Benedict; SERVANTS OF THE PEOPLE by Lawrence Ferlinghetti, an event (19). March 24, 1966. Scenery, Robert Allen; lighting, Mark Krause; costumes, William Gile. With Paul Benedict, Don Barshay, Blythe Danner, Larry Bryggman, Gustave Johnson, Judy London, Burris De Benning.

THE SERVICE FOR JOSEPH AXMINSTER by George Dennison, directed by Timothy Affleck and A RAT'S MASS by Adrienne Kennedy, directed by David Wheeler (16). April 12, 1966. Scenery, Robert Allen; lighting, Archambault; costumes, William Gile. With Paul Benedict, Edward Finnegan, Warren Finnerty, Josephine Lane, James Spruill, Nadine Turner, Blythe Danner.

A Festival of New American Plays: THE WAX MUSEUM by John Hawkes, directed by David Wheeler and THE INVESTIGATION by Rosalyn Drexler, directed by Paul

Benedict (14). April 28, 1966. Scenery, Robert Allen; lighting, Allan Melad; costumes, William Gile. With Naomi Thornton, Blythe Danner, Jerome Raphel, Joseph Hindy.

Modern Irish Festival: CATHLEEN NI HOULIHAN by W. B. Yeats and EASTER 1916 by Michael MacLiammoir (excerpts from *The Masque of Dublin*), directed by Frank Cassidy; IVY DAY by Mary Manning (based on James Joyce's *The Dubliners*), directed by Paul Benedict (8). May 9, 1966. Scenery and lighting, David Shaver; costumes,

Leslie Shaver. With Terence Currier, Bronia Stefan, Paul Benedict, Joseph Mahar, Edward Finnegan, Jerome Raphel.

THE WAY OUT OF THE WAY IN (14+). Topical revue by Patricia Cumming, Geoffrey Bush, Marjorie Taubenhaus, Peter Felsenthal and others. May 18, 1966. Directors, David Wheeler and Timothy Affleck; scenery, Robert Allen; technician, Alan Melad. With Paul Benedict, Marilyn Chris, Blythe Banner, Joseph Mahar, Barry Primus. Presented cabaret style at the Hotel Bradford Roof.

BUFFALO

Studio Arena Theater

A MOON FOR THE MISBEGOTTEN (15). By Eugene O'Neill. October 7, 1965. Director, José Quintero; scenery, Robert Motley; lighting, David Zierk; costumes, Duane Andersen. With Colleen Dewhurst, James Daly, John O'Shaughnessy, Lou Frizzell, John O'Leary.

OH WHAT A LOVELY WAR (16). Musical revue; Joan Littlewood's Theater Workshop Group Production. October 28, 1965. Director, Edward Parone; musical director, William Cox; designer, Robert Motley (using costumes, sets, slides and props from the original London production); lighting, David Zierk. With Carol Arthur, Gaye Glaeser, Jamie Ross and company and orchestra.

THE ROSE TATTOO (25). By Tennessee Williams. November 18, 1965. Director, Milton Katselas; scenery, Robert Motley; lighting, David Zierk; costumes, Sandra Williamson. With Olympia Dukakis, Joseph Mascolo, Margot Bennett, John Strasberg, Peggy Pope.

THE FIREBUGS (17). By Max Frisch. January 6, 1966. Director, Kim Swados; scenery and lighting, Mr. Swados; costumes, Duane Andersen. With Louis Guss, Barbara Stanton, Reginald Miles, David Margulies, Betty Lutes, Kenneth McMillan.

IRMA LA DOUCE (27). Musical with book

and lyrics by Alexandre Breffort; English version, Julian More, David Heneker, Monty Norman; music, Marguerite Monnot. January 27, 1966. Director, Neal Du Brock; scenery and costumes, Duane Andersen; lighting, David Zierk; musical numbers staged by Eric Kelly; musical direction, William Cox. With Arline Woods, Horace Guittard, Kenneth McMillan, George Di Cenzo, Joseph della Sorte.

A MAN FOR ALL SEASONS (26). By Robert Bolt. February 24, 1966. Director, Hy Kalus; scenery, Thomas Watson; lighting, David Zierk; costumes, Esther Kling. With Lester Rawlins, Kenneth McMillan, Betty Lutes, Sally Rubin.

THE LITTLE FOXES (19). By Lillian Hellman. March 24, 1966. Director, Edward Parone; scenery, Neal Du Brock; lighting, David Zierk; costumes, Duane Andersen. With Colleen Dewhurst, Bette Henritze, Stewart Bradley, Morgan Paull, Gerald Richards.

YOU CAN'T TAKE IT WITH YOU (26). By Moss Hart and George S. Kaufman. April 14, 1966. Director, Hy Kalus; scenery, and costumes, John Boyt; lighting, David Zierk. With Paula Trueman, Russell Gold, Gina Petrushka, Robert W. Stewart, Eugene R. Wood, Jessica Rains.

CHICAGO (See article on its season)

Goodman Memorial Theater

THE COCKTAIL PARTY (23) By T.S. Eliot. October 22, 1965. Director, John Reich; scenery, Richard Kent Wilcox; lighting, G. E. Naselius. With Robert Flemyng, Brenda Forbes, David R. Sage, Nancy Evans-Leonard, William Pappas, Gretchen Pappas.

THE WINTER'S TALE (23). By William Shakespeare. November 26, 1965. Director,

Bella Itkin; scenery, James Maronek; lighting, G. E. Naselius; costumes, Uta Olson; choreography, Frances Allis. With Leo Ciceri, Ryan Ballew, Robert Leonard, Ragnhild Nygaard, Jo Ann Berk.

THE PEDESTRIAN IN THE AIR (23). By Eugene Ionesco; translated by Donald Watson (English premiere). January 7, 1966. Director, Joseph Slowik; scenery, Richard Kent Wilcox; lighting, G. E. Naselius; costumes, D. Hudson Sheffield. With Alvin Epstein, Nancy Evans Leonard, Robert Leonard, Suzanne Larson, Timur Bastug, William Pappas.

DYLAN (23). By Sidney Michaels. February 18, 1966. Director, Charles McGaw; scenery, George Pettit; lighting, G. E. Naselius; costumes, Uta Olson. With Jerome Kilty, Gretchen Pappas, William Pappas.

THE SKIN OF OUR TEETH (23). By Thornton Wilder. March 25, 1966. Director,

Patrick Henry; scenery, Richard Kent Wilcox; lighting, G. E. Naselius; costumes, Kurt Wilhelm. With Edward Binns, Eugenie Leontovich, Beverly Younger.

GALILEO (23). By Bertolt Brecht; translated from final Berlin version by Desmond Vesey. May 6, 1966. Director, Howard Da Silva; scenery, James Maronek with staff of Adler Planetarium; lighting, G. E. Naselius; costumes, D. Hudson Sheffield; music by Hanns Eisler with new ballad by Bill Mathieu. With Morris Carnovsky, Maurice Copeland, Jeff Harris, Gretchen Pappas.

CINCINNATI

Playhouse in the Park

SUMMER OF THE SEVENTEENTH DOLL (20). By Ray Lawler. June 9, 1965. Director, David Hooks; scenery, Douglas W. Schmidt; lighting, Keith Brown; costumes, Caley Summers. With Paddy Croft, Karen Austin, Estelle Parsons.

SHE STOOPS TO CONQUER (21). By Oliver Goldsmith. June 30, 1965. Director, Douglas Seale; scenery, Douglas W. Schmidt; lighting, Keith Brown; costumes, Caley Summers. With Margaretta Warwick, Douglas Seale, Estelle Parsons, Sharon Laughlin, Donald Symington.

THE BLOOD KNOT (20). By Athol Fugard. July 21, 1965. Director, Brooks Jones; scenery, Keith Brown; lighting, Douglas W. Schmidt; costumes, Caley Summers. With Philip Hanson, Andre Womble.

THE GLASS MENAGERIE (20). By Ten-

nessee Williams. August 11, 1965. Director, David Hooks; scenery, Douglas W. Schmidt; lighting, Keith Brown; costumes, Caley Summers. With Patrick Tovatt, Eugenia Rawls, Sharon Laughlin, Max Jacobs.

THE FANTASTICKS (16). Musical suggested by Edmond Rostand's *Les Romantiques;* words by Tom Jones; music, Harvey L. Schmidt. September 1, 1965. Directors, Brooks Jones and Ty McConnell; scenery, Douglas W. Schmidt; musical director, Steven Smith. With Jack Davison, Alice Cannon, Ty McConnell, David Hooks, John A. Coe.

MAN AND SUPERMAN (23). By George Bernard Shaw. April 6, 1966. Director, David Hooks; scenery, Douglas W. Schmidt; lighting, Joe Pacitti; costumes, Caley Summers. With John Scanlan, Charles Cioffi, Mariclare Costello, Ann Whiteside, Jonathon Wood, Roscoe Lee Browne.

CLEVELAND

Cleveland Play House: Euclid-77th Theater

TARTUFFE (26). By Molière; translation by Richard Wilbur. October 6, 1965. Director, William Woodman; scenery, Paul Rodgers; costumes, Phyllis Kress. With Russell Collins, Judith Adams, Michele Ackerman, Edith Owen, Peter Bartlett, Robert Allman, Richard Oberlin.

CARVED IN SNOW (22). By Milton Geiger. November 10, 1965. Director, William Woodman; scenery, Paul Rodgers; costumes, Martha Braun. With Philip Kerr, Richard Oberlin, Peter Bartlett, Susan McArthur, Richard Halverson.

NEVER TOO LATE (32). By Sumner Arthur Long. December 10, 1965. Director, Kirk Willis; scenery, Paul Rodgers; costumes, Edith

Owen. With William Paterson, Vivienne Stotter, Philip Kerr, Patricia Elliott, Richard Oberlin.

POOR RICHARD (26). By Jean Kerr. January 26, 1966. Director, Kirk Willis; scenery, Barbara Fisher; costumes, Martha Braun. With William Paterson, Susan Sullivan, Philip Kerr, Allen Leatherman, Carmie Amata.

THE AMOROUS FLEA (26). March 2, 1966. Musical with book by Jerry Devine, based on Molière's *School for Wives;* music and lyrics by Bruce Montgomery. Director, Kirk Willis; musical director, Donna Renton; scenery, Mary McGinness; costumes, Martha Braun. With Richard Oberlin, Richard Halverson, Bob Moak, Mary Shelley, Michele Ackerman.

TWELFTH NIGHT (4 public; 44 school). By William Shakespeare. March 23, 1966. Director, Kirk Willis; scenery, Paul Rodgers; costumes, Phyllis Kress. With Myrna Kaye, Richard Oberlin, Mary Shelley, Richard Halverson, Susan Sullivan, Robert Allman, Peter Bartlett.

Cleveland Play House: Drury Theater

THE BALLAD OF THE SAD CAFE (26). By Edward Albee, adapted from Carson McCullers' novella. October 20, 1965. Director, William Woodman; scenery and lighting, Paul Rodgers; costumes, Martha Braun; music by Tadd Browne. With Clarence Kavanaugh, Jo-Ann Pinnell, Richard Grom.

UNCLE VANYA (6). By Anton Chekhov. November 24, 1965. Director, Robert Snook; scenery, Paul Rodgers; costumes, Edith Owen. With Allen Leatherman, Susan Sullivan, Patricia Elliott, Robert Snook.

ANTIGONE (6). By Jean Anouilh; adapted by Lewis Galantière. December 1, 1965. Director, Robert Snook; scenery, Paul Rodgers; costumes, Edith Owen. With Patricia Elliott, Vaughn Leatherman, June Gibbons, Susan Sullivan, Larry Tarrant.

YOU CAN'T TAKE IT WITH YOU (22). By Moss Hart and George S. Kaufman. December 15, 1965. Director, Kirk Willis; scenery, Paul Rodgers; costumes, Phyllis Kress. With Dorothy Paxton, Robert Snook, Allen Leatherman, Myrna Kaye, Peter Bartlett.

OUR TOWN (27). By Thornton Wilder. April 13, 1966. Director, Kirk Willis; scenery, Paul Rodgers; costumes, Martha Braun. With Robert Snook, Dorothy Paxton, Janet Downs, Robert Allman, William Howey, Susan Sullivan, Bob Moak.

DYLAN (21). By Sidney Michaels. January 19, 1966. Director, William Woodman; scenery, Paul Rodgers; costumes, Edith Owen. With Patricia Elliott, Richard Oberlin, Larry Tarrant.

YOU NEVER CAN TELL (26). By George Bernard Shaw. February 16, 1966. Director, William Woodman; scenery and lighting, Paul Rodgers; costumes, Phyllis Kress. With Charles Keating, Susan Stirling, Peter Bartlett, Edith Owen, Susan Sullivan, Robert Snook.

WHO's AFRAID OF VIRGINIA WOOLF? (21). By Edward Albee. March 16, 1966. Director, Kirk Willis; scenery, Paul Rodgers; costumes, Edith Owen. With JoAnn Finnell, William Paterson, Catherine Heiser, Larry Tarrant.

THE ABSENCE OF A CELLO (22). By Ira Wallach. April 20, 1966. Director, Robert Snook; scenery, Paul Rodgers; costumes, Phyllis Kress. With Edith Owen, William Paterson, Judith Adams, Vaughn McBride.

Cleveland Play House: Brooks Theater

SLOW DANCE ON THE KILLING GROUND (57). By William Hanley. October 27, 1965. Director, Kirk Willis; scenery, Mary McGinness; costumes, Edith Owen. With Kirk Willis, Andre Womble, Mary Shelley.

DALLAS (See article on its season)

Dallas Theater Center: Kalita Humphreys Theater

MARY, MARY (47). By Jean Kerr. June 11, 1965. Director, Warren Hammack; scenery, David Gibson; lighting, Robyn Baker Flatt and Mona Pursley; costumes, Sally Netzel. With Randolph Tallman, Anna Paul Schaefer.

THE MARRIAGE-GO-ROUND (25). By Leslie Stevens. August 20, 1965. Director, Lynn Trammell; scenery, David Gibson; lighting, Anna Paul Schaefer and Frank Schaefer; costumes, Cinda Siler. With Barnett Shaw, Anna Gonyaw, Sigrid Thor, Mike Dendy.

THE TEMPEST (34). By William Shakespeare. October 14, 1965. Director, Paul Baker and Ken Latimer; scenery, Bjorn Wiinblad;

lighting, David Gibson; costumes, Charlote Cole. With Michael O'Sullivan, Barry Hope, Elizabeth Lumpkin, Randolph Tallman, Ryland Merkey, Mike Dendy.

THE RIVALS (14). By Richard Brinsley Sheridan. November 26, 1965. Director and designer, Robin Lovejoy; lighting, Sally Netzel; costumes, Lavonia Shaw. With Louise Mosley, Patti O'Donnell Wilcox, Ronald Wilcox, Drexel H. Riley, Preston Jones.

OH, DAD, POOR DAD, MAMMA'S HUNG YOU IN THE CLOSET AND I'M FEELIN' SO SAD (6). By Arthur Kopit. December 7, 1965. Director, Ryland Merkey; scenery and costumes, David Pursley; lighting, Bob Baca. With Mary Sue Fridge Jones, Gary Moore, Cecile Guidote, David Pursley.

PETER PAN (17). Musical version of the play by Sir James M. Barrie; lyrics by Carolyn Leigh, Betty Comden, Adolph Green; music by Mark Charlap and Jule Styne. December 17, 1965. Director, Ruth Byers; musical director, Beatrice Gaspar; choreography, Garveth Osterhaus; scenery, David Gibson; lighting, Robyn Baker Flatt; costumes, Charlote Cole. With Betsy Lumpkin, Gene Leggett, Jerry Turner, Penny Metropulos.

JULIUS CAESAR (13). By William Shakespeare. January 6, 1966. Director, Warren Hammack; designer, Mary Sue Fridge Jones; lighting, David Gibson. With Mike Dendy, Patti O'Donnell Wilcox, Robert Frost, Preston Jones, Warren Hammack.

THE PHYSICISTS (21). By Friedrich Duerrenmatt; adapted by James Kirkup. January 20, 1966. Director, Paul Baker; scenery, Nancy Levinson; lighting, Gary Moore; costumes, Marta Cole. With David Pursley, Ella-Mae Brainard, Ken Latimer.

CREEP PAST THE MOUNTAIN LION (3). By Hal Lewis and Clifford Sage; based on a novel by Jewel Gibson. February 7, 1966. Director, Preston Jones; scenery, David Pursley; lighting, Gary Moore; costumes, Michael Bennett. With Rex Ingram.

YOU CAN'T TAKE IT WITH YOU (20). By Moss Hart and George S. Kaufman. February 17, 1966. Director, Ken Latimer; scenery and costumes, Charlote Cole; lighting, Ruthanne Cozine; costumes, Kathleen Benke. With Sandra Moore, Anna Gonyaw, Ryland Merkey, James Nelson Harrell.

THE HOUSE OF BERNARDA ALBA (1). By Frederico Garcia Lorca. March 10, 1966. Director, Bob Baca; designer, Richard Slocum; lighting, Kathleen Benke. With Anna Paul Rogers, Charlote Cole, Judith Davis, Barbara Gilstrap, Roberta Rude, Kathleen Benke, Pat Miller, Zarin Engineer, Claudette Gardner.

RASHOMON (22). By Fay and Michael Kanin; based on stories by Ryunosuke Akutagawa. March 18, 1966. Director, Buddy Smith and Duk Hyung Yoo; scenery and lighting, Duk Hyung Yoo. With Warren Hammack, Ronald Wilcox, Thomas Nichols, Robyn Baker Flatt.

THE AMOROUS FLEA (26). Musical by Jerry Devine, based on Molière's School for Wives. May 5, 1966. Director, Anna Paul Rogers; designer and costumes, David Pursley; lighting, Matt Tracy and Marilyn Markley. With David Pursley, Linda Giese, Penny Metropulos, Edward Herrmann, Thomas Nichols, Richard Jenkins.

THE GOLDEN WARRIORS (13). By Jay Dratler; based on the legend of the fall of Troy. May 10, 1966. Director, Paul Baker; scenery, Nancy Levinson. With Peggy Wood.

WHO'S GOT THE POT? (13). By Plautus; adapted by Richard Slocum from The Pot of Gold. May 26, 1966. Director, Robyn Baker Flatt; scenery, David Gibson.

Dark Night Readings of New Scripts: SIMON (1). By Sally Netzel. July 11, 1965. Director, Fritz Lennon. THE DEMENTED ZARZUELA (1). By Carl Gabler. Director, Sally Netzel. WELTY REVISITED (1). By Mike Dendy. February 27, 1966. Director, Victor Fichtner.

Dallas Theater Center: Down Center Stage Theater

THE TYPISTS and THE TIGER (9). By Murray Schisgal. June 17, 1965. Director, Frank Schaefer; scenery, Richard Slocum; lighting, Ruthanne Cozine. With Patti O'Donnell Wilcox, Henry Carter.

RIVERWIND (35). Musical with book, music and lyrics by John Jennings. July 8, 1965. Director, Ryland Merkey; scenery, Nancy Levinson; lighting, Sally Netzel; costumes, Anna Paul Schaefer; musical director, Beatrice Gaspar; choreography, Sue Sellors Finley. With Cinda Siler, Allen Robertson, Linda Martinsen, Patti O'Donnell Wilcox, Michael Bennett, Louise Mosley, Barry Hope.

LA RONDE (27). By Arthur Schnitzler. October 21, 1965. Director, Warren Hammack; designer, Mary Sue Fridge Jones. With Ashley Simmons, Don Humphreys, Zarin Engineer, Victor Fichtner, Betty June Lary, Bob Burrus, Alexis Munro, Bob Baca, Mona Pursley, Allen Robertson.

THE BIRTHDAY PARTY (26). By Harold Pinter. November, 1965. Director, Ryland Merkey; scenery, David Gibson; costumes, Zarin Engineer. With Jacque Thomas, Cambell Thomas, Warren Hammack, Ashley Simmons, Joel Plotkin, Bob Burrus.

SENSE AND NONSENSE (7). February 18, 1966. Directors, Robyn Baker Flatt, Barbara Le Brun; scenery, Richard Slocum. With Dallas Theater Center's Mime Group.

HARRISBURG

Arena House Theater

STOP THE WORLD—I WANT TO GET OFF (28). Musical with book, music and lyrics by Leslie Bricusse and Anthony Newley. September 25, 1965. Director, Tom Ross Prather; designer, Howard Crampton-Smith; musical director-choreographer, Joe Bousard. With Stuart Howard, Celia Howard, Royce Lenelle, Rosalind Sorbello, Scott Russell.

PICNIC (21). By William Inge. October 20, 1965. Director and designer, Tom Ross Prather; lighting, Howard Crampton-Smith. With Eddie Jones, Joyce Devlin, Royce Lenelle, Stuart Howard, Charmian Sorbello, Ed Van Nuys, Dorothy Erskine, Celia Howard.

WHO'S AFRAID OF VIRGINIA WOOLF? (22). By Edward Albee. November 10, 1965. Director, Tom Ross Prather; designer, Howard Crampton-Smith. With Bruce Hall, Vanda Barra, Eddie Jones, Joyce Devlin.

MY THREE ANGELS (21). By Sam and Bella Spewack. December 8, 1965. Director and designer, Tom Ross Prather; lighting, Howard Crampton-Smith. With Robert R. Wait, Bruce Hall, Eddie Jones.

CATCH ME IF YOU CAN (21). By Jack Weinstock and Willie Gilbert; based on a French play by Robert Thomas. December 30, 1965. Director, Tom Ross Prather; designer, Chuck Rice; lighting, Howard Crampton-Smith. With Bruce Hall, Robert R. Wait, Charmian Sorbello, Barbara Miner.

THE TYPISTS and THE TIGER (21). By Murray Schisgal. January 19, 1966. Director, Tom Ross Prather; designer, Howard Crampton-Smith. With Celia Howard, Robert R. Wait, Bob Larkin.

NEVER TOO LATE (37). By Sumner Arthur Long. February 9, 1966. Director and designer, Tom Ross Prather; lighting, Howard Crampton-Smith. With Bruce Hall, Marina Kate, Robert R. Wait, Marilynn Maltby, Lynn Baxter.

RASHOMON (14). By Fay and Michael Kanin; based on stories by Ryunosuke Akutagawa. March 17, 1966. Director and designer, Tom Ross Prather; lighting, Howard Crampton-Smith. With Kurt Garfield, Mary Tahmin, Ronald Coralian.

POOR RICHARD (21). By Jean Kerr. March 30, 1966. Director and designer, Tom Ross Prather; lighting, Howard Crampton-Smith. With Ronald Coralian, Angela Williams, Ed Van Nuys, Howard Crampton-Smith, Phyllis Vanier.

MY WIFE AND I (21). Musical with book and music by Bill Mahoney (premiere). April 20, 1966. Director and designer, Tom Ross Prather; lighting, Howard Crampton-Smith; costumes, Mary Mulholland; musical director and choreographer, Joe Bousard. With Bruce Hill, Helon Blount, Robert R. Wait, Carol-Leigh Jensen, Ron Leath.

HARTFORD, CONN.

Hartford Stage Company

CAT ON A HOT TIN ROOF (28). By Tennessee Williams. October 22, 1965. Director, Jacques Cartier; scenery and costumes, Edward Graczyk, II; lighting, Stephen Hendrickson. With Anne Lynn, Dennis Longwell, Elizabeth Lawrence, Ann Driscoll, David Ford.

TARTUFFE (28). By Molière. November 19, 1965. Director, Paul Weidner; scenery and costumes, Edward Graczyk, II; lighting, Peter Hunt. With David Ford, Charles Kimbrough, Anne Lynn, Henry Thomas.

MAJOR BARBARA (28). By George Bernard Shaw. December 17, 1965. Director, Jacques Cartier; scenery and costumes, Edward Graczyk, II; lighting, Peter Hunt. With Anne Lynn, Henry Thomas, David Ford, Charles Kimbrough.

HEDDA GABLER (28). By Henrik Ibsen; translated by William Archer. January 14, 1966. Director, Jacques Cartier; scenery and costumes, Paul Weidner; lighting, Peter Hunt. With Charles Kimbrough, Jane MacLeod, Anne Lynn, David Ford.

THE IMPORTANCE OF BEING EARNEST (28). By Oscar Wilde. February 11, 1966. Director, Mel Shapiro; scenery and costumes, John Conklin; lighting, Peter Hunt. With Paul Weidner, Henry Thomas, Elizabeth Lawrence, Anne Lynn, Jane MacLeod.

THE BALCONY (28). By Jean Genet. March 11, 1966. Director, Jacques Cartier; scenery and costumes, John Conklin; lighting, Peter Hunt. With Mara Lane, Henry Thomas, Elizabeth Lawrence, Charles Kimbrough.

TWELFTH NIGHT (28). By William Shakespeare. April 8, 1966. Director, Paul Weidner; scenery and costumes, John Conklin; lighting, Peter Hunt. With Angela D'Ambrosia, Jane MacLeod, Henry Thomas, Elizabeth Lawrence, Charles Kimbrough, David Ford, Richard Lynch.

WHO'S AFRAID OF VIRGINIA WOOLF? (28). By Edward Albee. May 6, 1966. Scenery and costumes, John Conklin; lighting, Peter

Hunt. With Elizabeth Lawrence, Clement Fowler, Charles Kimbrough, Mara Lane.

HOUSTON (See article on its season)

Alley Theater

THE DEVIL'S DISCIPLE (42). By George Bernard Shaw. October 13, 1965. Director, John Wylie; designer, Paul Owen. With Bettye Fitzpatrick, William Hardy, Jerry Hardin, Barry Snider, Tom Toner.

AH, WILDERNESS! (42). By Eugene O'Neill. November 24, 1965. Director, Joseph Ruskin; designer, Paul Owen. With Audrey Ward, John Wylie, Tom Toner, George Anderson, Linda Brown.

RIGHT YOU ARE IF YOU THINK YOU ARE (42). By Luigi Pirandello; translated by Eric Bentley. January 5, 1966. Director, Nina Vance; designer, Paul Owen. With Joseph

Ruskin, Lorraine Meyer, Beth Sanford, Lillian Evans, Jerry Hardin.

YOU CAN'T TAKE IT WITH YOU (42). By Moss Hart and George S. Kaufman. February 16, 1966. Director, William Hardy; designer Paul Owen. With Virginia Payne, Jeanette Clift, Jerry Hardin, Tom Toner.

DUEL OF ANGELS (42). By Jean Giraudoux; translated by Christopher Fry; adapted by Nina Vance and John Wylie. March 30, 1966. Director, Nina Vance; designer, Paul Owen. With Lillian Evans, Dale Helward, Jeannette Clift.

LOS ANGELES (See articles on its season)

Theater Group-UCLA

I RISE IN FLAMES, CRIED THE PHOENIX by Tennessee Williams; THE LOVER by Harold Pinter; WINDOWS (premiere) by Murray Schisgal (26). June 4, 1965. Director, Alfred Ryder; scenery, Joseph A. Rubino; lighting, Myles Harmon; costumes, Minal Mittelman. With Alfred Ryder, Nina Foch, Joyce Van Patten.

ROBERT FROST: Promises To Keep (35). By Philip Abbott. July 7, 1965. Directors, Philip Abbott and John McLiam; scenery, Jim Freiburger; lighting, Myles Harmon; costumes, Michael Travis; music, Naomi Caryl Hirshhorn; arranged and played by Hal Lynch. With Philip Abbott, Sandy Kenyon, Gail Kobe, John McLiam, James O'Reare.

THE DEPUTY (52). By Rolf Hochhuth; adapted by Jerome Rothenberg. August 13, 1965. Director, Gordon Davidson; scenery, costumes and lighting, Peter Wexler. With

Robert Brown, Philip Bourneuf, Alan Napier, Mark Richman.

YEATS & COMPANY; The Prose, Poetry & Plays of W.B. Yeats (37). Adapted by Paul Shyre. October 23, 1965. Director, Paul Shyre; lighting, Arvid Nelson; costumes, Dorothy Jeakins; music, Salli Terri. With John Crowther, Patricia Cutts, Brendan Dillon, Will Kuluva, Diana Maddox, Murray Matheson, Helene Winston.

OH WHAT A LOVELY WAR (32). Musical revue by Joan Littlewood. January 19, 1966. Director, Edward Parone; musical director, Samuel Matlovsky; scenery, Jim Freiburger; lighting, Myles Harmon; (costumes, slides and props from the original London Production). With Susan Browning, Mary Donovan, Lola Fisher, Mitzi Hoag, Maria Lennard, George Backman, Christopher Cary, Peter Church.

LOUISVILLE, KY.

Actors Theater

THE IMPORTANCE OF BEING EARNEST (28). By Oscar Wilde. October 14, 1965. Director, James Dyas; scenery, Robert Soule; lighting, Richard Mix; costumes, Elaine Goodrow. With Bryan E. Clark, Jack Johnson, Kathryn Wheeler, Patricia Stewart, Sally Douglass.

THE PUBLIC EYE by Peter Shaffer and NO EXIT by Jean Paul Sartre (28). November

11, 1965. Director, Ken Costigan; settings, Robert Soule; lighting, Richard Mix; costumes, Elaine Goodrow. With J. S. Johnson, John Seitz, Marguerite Tarrant, Patricia Stewart.

PRIVATE LIVES (28). By Noel Coward. December 2, 1965. Director, James Dyas; scenery, Robert Soule; lighting, Richard Mix; costumes, Elaine Goodrow. With Sally Douglass,

Bryan Clark, John Seitz, Patricia Stewart, Sheila Harlan.

WAITING FOR GODOT (28). By Samuel Beckett. December 30, 1965. Director, Richard Block; scenery, Robert Soule; lighting, Richard Mix; costumes, Elaine Goodrow. With J. S. Johnson, John Seitz, David Semonin, Grant Sheehan, Marc Clark.

A DOLL'S HOUSE (28). By Henrik Ibsen. January 20, 1966. Director, Richard Block; scenery, Brooke Karzen; lighting, Richard Mix; costumes, Lucile Paris. With Patricia Stewart, Grant Sheehan, J. S. Johnson, Mitzi Friedlander, John Seitz.

SCHOOL FOR WIVES (28). By Molière. February 17, 1966. Director, Richard Block;

scenery, Robert Soule; lighting, Richard Mix, costumes, Lucile Paris. With Ned Beatty, Grant Sheehan, Patricia Squires, Paul Watson, Bryan Clark.

DEATH OF A SALESMAN (28). By Arthur Miller. March 10, 1966. Director, Tom Gruenewald; scenery, Robert Soule; lighting, Richard Mix; costumes, Lucile Paris. With Ned Beatty, Jo Deodato, Paul Watson, Grant Sheehan, Jack Collard, Charles Kissinger.

THE TAVERN (28). By George M. Cohan. April 7, 1966. Director, Richard Block; scenery, Robert Soule; lighting, Richard Mix; costumes, Lucile Paris. With Grant Sheehan, Ned Beatty, Patricia Stewart, J. S. Johnson, Sally Douglass.

MEMPHIS

Front Street Theater

THE KING AND I (26). Musical with book and lyrics by Oscar Hammerstein 2d; music by Richard Rodgers. September 23, 1965. Director, George Touliatos; scenery, David Maverick Lane; costumes, Don Fibiger; choral director, Sara Beth Causey; choreography, Meryl Sargent. With Evelyne Anderson, Tom Carson, George Touliatos, Dorothy Johnson.

THE GLASS MENAGERIE (26). By Tennessee Williams. October 28, 1965. Direction and lighting, George Touliatos; scenery, Francis Gassner; costumes, Don Fibiger; With Tom Carson, Madge West, Sheila Larken, Michael Norell.

THE COCKTAIL PARTY (26). By T.S. Eliot. November 25, 1965. Direction, scenery and lighting, George Touliatos; costumes, Don Fibiger. With Michael Norell, Sheila Larken, Barry Fuller.

THE TAVERN (24). By George M. Cohan. December 23, 1965. Director, James Dyas; scenery and lighting, Jim Tilton; costumes, Don Fibiger. With Liz Ingleson, Michael Norell, Tom Carson, Sheila Larken, Barry Fuller.

THE BALLAD OF THE SAD CAFE (26).

By Edward Albee; adapted from Carson McCullers' novella. January 20, 1966. Direction and lighting, Curt Reis; scenery, Richard Wilcox; costumes, Don Fibiger. With Gil Rogers, Polly Holliday, Richard Grom, Don Hayes.

GUYS AND DOLLS (26). Musical based on a story and characters by Damon Runyon; book by Jo Swerling and Abe Burrows; music and lyrics by Frank Loesser. February 17, 1966. Director, James Dyas; dances and productions, Nelle Fisher; scenery, James Tilton; lighting, Lynn LePelley; costumes, Don Fibiger. With Rhonda Oglesby, Ronn Carroll, Polly Holliday, Ted Brown, Gil Rogers.

BECKET (26). By Jean Anouilh; translated by Lucienne Hill. March 17, 1966. Director, William Woodman; scenery, Richard Wilcox; lighting, Lynn LePelley; costumes, Don Fibiger. With William Shust, Gil Rogers, Polly Holiday, Liz Ingleson.

ANTONY AND CLEOPATRA (26). By William Shakespeare. April 4, 1966. Director, William Woodman; scenery, Richard Wilcox; lighting, Lynn LePelley; costumes, Don Fibiger. With Rita Gam, Gil Rogers, Don Hayes, John Seitz.

MILWAUKEE

Milwaukee Repertory Theater

SAINT JOAN (22). By George Bernard Shaw. October 28, 1965. Director, Philip Minor; scenery and lighting, Charles Dox Jr.; costumes, John Lehmeyer; music, Richard Cumming. With Mary Doyle, Stefan Gierasch, Russell Gold, Clinton Kimbrough, Nicholas Martin.

THE DIARY OF A SCOUNDREL (22). By Alexander Ostrovsky; English version by Rodney Ackland. November 18, 1965. Director, Stephen Porter; scenery and lighting, Charles Dox Jr.; costumes, John Lehmeyer. With Anne Francine, Stefan Gierasch, Jeanne Helminiak, Kenneth Hill, Clinton Kimbrough, Virginia

Payne, Pamela Payton-Wright, Roger M. Steffens.

THE TIME OF YOUR LIFE (22). By William Saroyan. December 9, 1965. Director, Tom Brennan; scenery and lighting, Charles Dox Jr.; costumes, John Lehmeyer. With Ronnie Claire Edwards, Stefan Gierasch, Tom Lacy, Nicholas Martin.

MOTHER COURAGE (22). By Bertolt Brecht; English version by Eric Bentley. January 13, 1966. Director, Adrian Hall; scenery and lighting, Charles Dox Jr.; costumes, John Lehmeyer. With Anne Francine, Stefan Gierasch, Clinton Kimbrough, Pamela Payton-Wright.

THE SERVANT OF TWO MASTERS (22). By Carlo Goldoni; adapted by John A. McQuiggan. February 3, 1966. Director, John A. McQuiggan; scenery and lighting, Charles Dox Jr.; costumes, John Lehmeyer; choreog-

raphy, Jerry Grasse. With Robert J. Colonna, Mary Doyle, James Gallery, Kenneth Hill, Tom Lacy, Pamela Payton-Wright.

HENRY IV, PART ONE (22). By William Shakespeare. February 24, 1966. Director, Stephen Porter; scenery and lighting, Charles Dox Jr.; costumes, John Lehmeyer. With Jeanne Feurstenau, James Gallery, Donald Gantry, Stefan Gierasch, June Kasel, Clinton Kimbrough.

THE GLASS MENAGERIE (22). By Tennessee Williams. March 17, 1966. Director, John A. McQuiggan; scenery and lighting, Charles Dox Jr.; costumes, John Lehmeyer. With Mary Doyle, Stefan Gierasch, Sada Thompson, Ralph Williams.

ANATOL (22). By Tom Jones; based on the play by Arthur Schnitzler. April 14, 1966. Music, Offenbach and Richard Cumming. Repeated from previous season.

MINNEAPOLIS (See article on its season)

Tyrone Guthrie Theater

RICHARD III (51). By William Shakespeare. May 10 *; 1965. Director, Tyrone Guthrie; designer, Lewis Brown; music, Herbert Pilhofer.

THE WAY OF THE WORLD (52). By William Congreve. May 11 *, 1965. Director, Douglas Campbell; designer, Tanya Moiseiwitsch.

THE CHERRY ORCHARD (48). By Anton Chekhov; translated by Tyrone Guthrie and Leonid Kipnis. June 15, 1965. Director, Tyrone Guthrie; designer, Tanya Moiseiwitsch.

THE CAUCASIAN CHALK CIRCLE (35). By Bertolt Brecht; English version by Eric Bentley. August 3, 1965. Director, Edward Payson Call; designer, Lewis Brown. With Paul Ballantyne, Ruth Nelson, Zoe Caldwell, John Cromwell, Jessica Tandy, Lee Richardson, Helen Harrelson, Ken Ruta and members of the company in multiple roles.

THE MISER (20). By Molière; translated by George Graveley. September 7, 1965. Director, Edward Payson Call; designer, Tanya Moiseiwitsch.

PERFORMER	"RICHARD III"	"THE WAY OF THE WORLD"	"THE CHERRY ORCHARD"	"THE MISER"
Paul Ballantyne	Derby	Sir Willful	Pishchik	
Earl Boen	Canterbury	Coachman	Guest	Spanish Captain
Graham Brown	Ratcliff	Waitwill		Simon
Zoe Caldwell		Millamant		Frosine
Kristina Callahan		Mincing	Anya	Dame Claude
John Cappelletti	Rivers	Chocolate House Keeper	Guest	Lawyer
Charles Cioffi				Lawyer
John Cromwell	Brockenburg			
Hume Cronyn	Richard		Epihodov	Harpagon
Niki Flacks		Peg	Guest	Prop Girl
Ed Flanders		Petulant	Yasha	Jacques
Kenneth Frankel	Lord Grey	Servant	Guest	La Merluche
Ellen Geer	Lady Anne	Mrs. Fainall	Dunyasha	Mariane
Helen Harrelson	Elizabeth	Foible		
James Horswill	Vaughan			Lawyer

* The Tyrone Guthrie Theater's programs are presented as a repertory unit, so we list their season as a whole instead of adhering to our own seasonal chronology which is June 1, 1965-May 31, 1966.

PERFORMER	"RICHARD III"	"THE WAY OF THE WORLD"	"THE CHERRY ORCHARD"	"THE MISER"
James Lawless	Tyrrel	John		Lawyer
John Lewin	Norfolk			Anselme
John MacKay	Hastings			Don Pedro
Sandy McCallum			Firs	Prop Man
Evie McElroy		Betty		
Robert Milli	Edward IV	Mirabell		La Fleche
Ruth Nelson	Duchess of York		Charlotta	
Robert Pastene	Buckingham	Fainall	Gayev	Commissioner
Lee Richardson	Henry Tudor		Lopahin	Valere
Ken Ruta	Clarence	Witwould	Trofimov	
Thomas Slater	Dorset			Cleante
Alvah Stanley	Catesby		Tramp	Prop Man; Brindavoine
Jessica Tandy		Lady Wishfort	Ranevskaya	
Donald West	Bishop of Ely	Grenadier		Clerk
Ann Whiteside		Prologue		Prop Girl
Nancy Wickwire	Queen Margaret	Mistress Marwood	Varya	Elise

MORRISTOWN, N.J.

Morris Repertory Theater

ROMEO AND JULIET (40). By William Shakespeare. October 29, 1965. Director, Michael Sisk; designer, Peter Wingate. With Michael McCarthy, Victor Raider-Wexler, Paulene Reynolds, Howard Green, Thea Ruth.

GALILEO (26). By Bertolt Brecht; English version by Charles Laughton. November 6, 1965. Director, Michael Sisk; designer, Peter Wingate; songs, John Corigliano. With Drew Eliah, Roderick Nash, John Birrell, Joan Force, Thea Ruth.

WHAT A LOVELY DAY (11). By Michel de Ghelderode; English version of *Pantagleize* by Samuel Draper and Michael Sisk. December 3, 1965. Director, Michael Sisk; scenery and lighting, Peter Wingate and Milton Duke; costumes, Micki Koob. With Ian Wilder, Michael Del Medico, Joan Force.

WAKEFIELD CYCLE OF MYSTERY PLAYS (8). December 26, 1965. Director, Michael Sisk; scenery and costumes, Henry Heymann; lighting, Milton Duke; music, John

Corigliano. With Michael McCarthy, Howard Green, Margery Shaw.

SAINT JOAN (28). By George Bernard Shaw. February 4, 1966. Director, Michael Sisk; scenery and lighting, Milton Duke; costumes, Henry Heymann. With Margery Shaw, Howard Green, Roderick Nash, Victor Raider-Wexler.

UNDER MILK WOOD (12). By Dylan Thomas. February 25, 1966. Director, Michael Sisk.

THE TIME OF YOUR LIFE (14). By William Saroyan. March 11, 1966. Director, Michael Sisk; scenery and lighting, Vincent Piacentini. With Thea Ruth, Victor Raider-Wexler, Peter Berger, Howard Green, Ian Wilder.

THE TRAGEDY OF TRAGEDIES: *The Life and Death of Tom Thumb the Great* (7). By Henry Fielding. April 13, 1966. Director, Michael Sisk; music, John Corigliano. With Michael Del Medico, Ian Wilder, Norton Wettstern, Joan Force, Paulene Reynolds.

NEW HAVEN

Long Wharf Theater

THE CRUCIBLE (14). By Arthur Miller. July 6, 1965. Director, Jon Jory; scenery and lighting, David Hager; costumes, Rosemary Ingham. With William Swetland, Leslie Cass, Sally Noble, Walter Rhodes, Vaughn McBride.

THE HOSTAGE (14). By Brendan Behan. July 20, 1965. Director, Jon Jory; scenery and

lighting, David Hager; costumes, Rosemary Ingham. With Tom Toner, Leslie Cass, Frank Wicks, Walter Rhodes, Margaret Cowles.

LITTLE MARY SUNSHINE (14). By Rick Besoyan. August 3, 1965. Directors, Jon Jory and Frank Wicks; scenery and lighting, David Hager; costumes by Rosemary Ingham; music director, Donna Brunsma. With Vaughn Mc-

Bride, Ted Pugh, John Minto, Sally Noble, Jo Ann Finnell.

THE PRIVATE EAR and THE PUBLIC EYE (14). By Peter Shaffer. August 17, 1965. Director, David Hager; scenery Allen D. Cook; lighting, Sean Kernan; costumes, Rosemary Ingham. With Walter Rhodes, Ted Pugh, Sally Noble, Robert Snook, Don Draper, Leslie Cass.

THE PLOUGH AND THE STARS (25). By Sean O'Casey. October 22, 1965. Director, Jon Jory; scenery and lighting, David Hager; costumes, Rosemary Ingham. With Gladden Schrock, Margaret Cowles, Alek Primrose, Eda Reiss Merin, William Swetland.

VOLPONE (25). By Ben Jonson; adapted by Stefan Zweig. November 19, 1965. Director, Jon Jory; scenery and lighting, David Hager; costumes, Rosemary Ingham. With David Spielberg, Alek Primrose, Sally Noble.

THE PIRATES OF PENZANCE (25). Operetta by Gilbert & Sullivan. December 17, 1965. Director, Frank Wicks; music director, Gordon C. Stewart; scenery and lighting, David Hager; costumes, Alec Sutherland. With Howard Clausen, Jo Ann Finnell, Gladden Schrock, Sally Noble, Gilda G. Moore, Margaret Cowles, Donna Curtis, Ted Pugh.

THE TROJAN WOMEN (25). By Euripides; translated by Edith Hamilton. January 14,

1966. Director, Jon Jory; scenery, Grady Larkins; lighting, David Hager; costumes, Rosemary Ingham. With Eda Reiss Merin, Dimitra Steris, Leslie Cass, Michael McGuire, Adale O'Brien.

HAY FEVER (25). By Noel Coward. February 11, 1966. Director and scenery, David Hager; lighting, Ron Wallace; costumes, Rosemary Ingham. With Marie Masters, Ted Pugh, Jan Farrand, William Swetland, Michael McGuire.

UNCLE VANYA (25). By Anton Chekhov; adapted by Robert Snook. March 11, 1966. Director, Jon Jory; scenery, David Hager; lighting, Ron Wallace and Ron Abbott; costumes, Rosemary Ingham. With William Swetland, Leslie Cass, Sally Noble, Michael McGuire, Gladden Schrock, David Spielberg.

THE RIVALS (25). By Richard Brinsley Sheridan. April 8, 1966. Director, Jon Jory; scenery, David Hager; lighting, Ron Abbott; costumes, Rosemary Ingham. With Niki Flacks, Etain O'Malley, Jean Barker, William Swetland, Ted Pugh.

LONG DAY'S JOURNEY INTO NIGHT (23). By Eugene O'Neill. May 6, 1966. Director, Arvin Brown; scenery, David Hager; lighting, Ron Wallace; costumes, Rosemary Ingham. With Leslie Cass, Mildred Dunnock, Edward Grover, Michael Higgins, Frank Langella.

PASADENA

Pasadena Playhouse

TWO FABLES IN PERVERSITY (28). THE SHOEMAKER'S PRODIGIOUS WIFE by Federico Garcia Lorca; translated by James Graham-Jujan and Richard L. O'Connell and THE FIREBUGS by Max Frisch; translated by Mordecai Gorelik. September 23, 1965. Director, G. Lowell Lees; scenery and costumes, John Naccarato; lighting, William W. Young. With Claude Woolman, Joyce Dotson, Paul Birch, Arthur Peterson, Henry Darrow, Louise Arthur, Jacques Denbeaux.

PEER GYNT (28). By Henrik Ibsen; adapted by C. Lowell Lees. October 21, 1965. Director, C. Lowell Lees; scenery and costumes, John Naccarato; lighting, William W. Young; music, James Prigmore; choreography, Jean Pyatt. With Monte Markham, Gillian Tomlin, Louise Arthur, Claude Woolman.

THE DEVIL'S DISCIPLE (28). By George Bernard Shaw. November 18, 1965. Director, Stuart Margolin; scenery and costumes, John Naccarato; lighting, William W. Young. With

Claude Woolman, Macksene Rux, Bill Erwin, Judith Lowry, Richard Lupino, Joyce Dotson.

LOVE FOR LOVE (28). By William Congreve. December 16, 1965. Director, Claude Woolman; scenery and costumes, John Naccarato; lighting, William W. Young; music, James Prigmore; choreography, Jean Pyatt. With Bill Erwin; Henry Darrow, Stuart Margolin, Cheri Kohler, Richard Lupino, Louise Arthur, Joyce Dotson.

RICHARD III (28). By William Shakespeare. January 20, 1966. Director, C. Lowell Lees; scenery and costumes, John Naccarato; lighting, William W. Young, With Claude Woolman, Richard Lupino, Gillian Tomlin, Louise Arthur.

DARK OF THE MOON (28). By Howard Richardson and William Berney. February 17, 1966. Director, Charles Rome Smith; scenery and costumes, John Naccarato; lighting, William W. Young. With Henry Darrow, Gillian Tomlin, Stuart Margolin, Murray MacLeod.

PHILADELPHIA (See article on its season)

Theater of the Living Arts

UNCLE VANYA (40). By Anton Chekhov; translated by Alex Szogyi. November 16, 1965. Director, Andre Gregory; scenery and lighting, Neil Jampolis; costumes, Domingo Rodriguez. With Gene Gross, Lois Smith, Flora Elkins, Sylvia Gassell, David Hurst, Ron Leibman, Jerome Dempsey, Miriam Phillips.

THEY by Arnold Weinstein and THE CRITIC by Richard Brinsley Sheridan. (40). December 28, 1965. Director, George Sherman; scenery and lighting, Karl Eigsti. With Tom Brannum, Flora Elkins, Ed Crowley, Jonathan Frid, Jerome Dempsey, Sylvia Gassell, Anthony Zerbe.

POOR BITOS (40). By Jean Anouilh. February 8, 1966. Director, Andre Gregory; scenery and lighting, Eugene Lee; costumes, Adam Sage. With George Bartenieff, Anthony Zerbe, Merwin Goldsmith, Ed Crowley, Jonathan Frid, Sally Kirkland.

THE STRONGER and MISS JULIE (40). By August Strindberg; translated by Alex Szogyi and Arvid Paulson. March 22, 1966. Director, George Sherman; scenery and lighting, Eugene Lee; costumes, Adam Sage. With Flora Elkins, Arnette Jens, Lois Smith, Anthony Zerbe.

THE LAST ANALYSIS (40). By Saul Bellow. Director, George Sherman; scenery and costumes, Fred Voepel; lighting, Eugene Lee. With David Hurst, Jerome Dempsey, Sylvia Gassell, Miriam Phillips.

PITTSBURGH (See article on its season)

American Conservatory Theater

TARTUFFE (48). By Molière; translated by Richard Wilbur. July 15, 1965. Director, William Ball; scenery, Mark Negin; lighting, Jules Fisher; costumes, Jane Greenwood.

TINY ALICE (37). By Edward Albee. July 21, 1965. Director, William Ball; scenery and costumes, Mark Negin; lighting, Jules Fisher.

SIX CHARACTERS IN SEARCH OF AN AUTHOR (27). By Luigi Pirandello; translated by Paul Avila Mayer. July 28, 1965. Director, William Ball; scenery, Mark Negin and Stuart Wurtzel; lighting, Jules Fisher.

ANTIGONE (19). By Jean Anouilh; translated by Lewis Galantière. August 1, 1965. Director, Jan Harnick; scenery and costumes, Mark Negin; lighting, Jules Fisher.

THE ROSE TATTOO (17). By Tennessee Williams. August 6, 1965. Director, William Francisco; scenery and costumes, Mark Negin; lighting, Jules Fisher.

NOAH (10). By Andre Obey; translated by Arthur Wilmart. August 19, 1965. Director, William Young; scenery, Thomas P. Struthers; lighting, Jules Fisher; costumes, David Toser.

IN WHITE AMERICA (14). By Martin Duberman. August 31, 1965. Director, Harold Stone; scenery and lighting, William Matthews.

KING LEAR (24). By William Shakespeare. September 3, 1965. Director, William Ball; scenery and costumes, Mark Negin; lighting, Carol Rubinstein.

THE SERVANT OF TWO MASTERS (16). By Carlo Goldoni; translated by Edward J. Dant. September 9, 1965. Director, William Francisco; scenery and costumes, Hudson Sheffield; lighting, William Matthews.

THE DEVIL'S DISCIPLE (13). By George Bernard Shaw. October 9, 1965. Director, Harold Stone; scenery, Stuart Wurtzel; lighting, William Nelson; costumes, David Toser.

THE APOLLO OF BELLAC (6). By Jean Giraudoux; translated by William Ball. October 16, 1965. Director, Rene Auberjonois; scenery, Stuart Wurtzel; lighting, S. Leonard Auerbach; costumes, Gail Singer.

DEATH OF A SALESMAN (15). By Arthur Miller. October 28, 1965. Director, Allen Fletcher; scenery, Thomas P. Struthers; lighting, Carol Rubinstein; costumes, David Toser.

BEYOND THE FRINGE (33). Musical revue by Alan Bennett, Peter Cook, Jonathan Miller and Dudley Moore. December 5, 1965. Director, Hugh Alexander; scenery, Thomas P. Struthers; lighting, Steven Cohen; costumes, David Toser.

ENDGAME (2). By Samuel Beckett. January 28, 1966. Director Edward Payson Call; scenery, Stuart Wurtzel; lighting, Steven Cohen; costumes, David Toser.

The acting company of the American Conservatory Theater: Hugh Alexander, Rene Auberjonois, Barbara Barrie, Barbara Baxley, Roberts Blossom, Jacqueline Brookes, Barbara Caruso, Ludi Claire, Joan Croydon, David Cryer, Richard A. Dysart, Clement Fowler, Harry Frazier, Robin Gammell, Hal Holbrook, David Hurst, Scott Hylands, Poppy Lagos, Lorna Lewis, Laurence Luckinbill, David Margulies, DeAnn Mears, Judith Mihalyi, Michael O'Sullivan, Ray Reinhardt, Carol Rossen, Paul Shenar, Charles Siebert, Robin Strasser, Anthony "Scooter" Teague, Carol Teitel, Sada Thompson, Lee Wallace, Janis Young.

PRINCETON, N.J.

McCarter Theater

MOTHER COURAGE AND HER CHILDREN (9). By Bertolt Brecht; English version by Eric Bentley. October 8, 1965. Director, Morton Siegel; scenery, Clyde W. Blakeley and Barbara Miller; lighting, Clyde W. Blakeley and Jeannean Babcock; music, John Duffy. With Judy London, Charlotte Glenn, Ralph Drischell.

CORIOLANUS (11). By William Shakespeare. October 15, 1965. Director, Arthur W. Lithgow; scenery, Clyde W. Blakeley, and Barbara Miller; lighting, Clyde W. Blakeley and Jeannean Babcock; costumes, C. Morton Cliff. With Larry Linville, Mario Siletti, David Byrd, Ruby Holbrook.

MAJOR BARBARA (11). By George Bernard Shaw. October 29, 1965. Director, Mario Siletti; scenery, Clyde W. Blakeley and Barbara Miller; lighting, Jeannean Babcock; costumes, Charles Blackburn. With Ruby Holbrook, Ann Gee Byrd, Gregory Abels, David Byrd, Emery Battis.

AN ENEMY OF THE PEOPLE (9). By Henrik Ibsen. November 13, 1965. Director, Arthur W. Lithgow; scenery, Clyde W. Blakeley and Myles Smith; lighting, Jeannean Babcock; costumes, Charles Blackburn. With Ralph Drischell, Ann Gee Byrd, Edward Stevelingson.

LADY WINDERMERE'S FAN (17). By Oscar Wilde. February 18, 1966. Director, Mario Siletti; scenery, Barbara C. Miller; lighting, Clyde W. Blakeley; costumes, Charles Blackburn. With Charlotte Glenn, Gordon Clark, Gregory Abels, David Byrd, Ruby Holbrook.

A MIDSUMMER NIGHT'S DREAM (21). By William Shakespeare. February 25, 1966. Director, Jan Moerel; scenery and lighting, Clyde W. Blakeley; costumes, Charles Blackburn. With Gordon Clark, Anne Gee Byrd, Arthur W. Lithgow, David Byrd, Ruby Holbrook.

BOX & COX by John Madison Morton; director, Arthur W. Lithgow and MISS JULIE by August Strindberg; translated by Arvid Paulson; director, Donald Moffat (13). March 11, 1966. Scenery, Barbara C. Miller; lighting, Clyde W. Blakeley; costumes, Charles Blackburn. With Eve Johnson, Tony Musants, Anne Murray.

CANDIDA (12). By George Bernard Shaw. March 25, 1966. Director, Mario Siletti; scenery and lighting, Myles Smith; costumes, Charles Blackburn. With Anne Gee Byrd, Gregory Abels.

ARRAH-NA-POGUE (8). By Dion Boucicault. April 1, 1966. Director, Arthur W. Lithgow; scenery, Barbara C. Miller; lighting, Clyde W. Blakeley; costumes, Charles Blackburn. With James Tripp, Anne Gee Byrd, Mario Siletti.

PROVIDENCE, R.I.

Trinity Square Playhouse

THE CRUCIBLE (22). By Arthur Miller. October 11, 1965. Director, Adrian Hall; scenery, David Christian; lighting, Michael Tschudin; costumes, Rosemary Ingham. With Richard Kneeland, Patricia Echeverria, Sylvia Soares, Robert van Hooten, Flair Bogan.

TARTUFFE (23). By Molière; English version by Richard Wilbur. Director, Adrian Hall; scenery, John Braden; lighting, Michael Tschudin; costumes, Sunny B. Warner. With Richard Kennedy, Barbara Orson, David Christian, Richard Kneeland, Robert van Hooten.

THE BALCONY (19). By Jean Genet. December 9, 1965. Director, Adrian Hall; scenery and costumes, John Braden; lighting, Michael Tschudin. With Robert van Hooten, Barbara Orson, Ellen Brecher, Gene Rousseau, James O. Barnhill, Richard Kennedy.

TWELFTH NIGHT (38). By William Shakespeare. January 6, 1966. Director, Stephen

Porter; scenery, John Braden; costumes, Sunny B. Warner. With Barbara Orson, Katherine Helmond, Marguerite Lenert, Richard Kneeland, Robert van Hooten, Richard Kennedy and Kevin Mitchell.

LONG DAY'S JOURNEY INTO NIGHT (23). By Eugene O'Neill. February 3, 1966. Director, Adrian Hall; scenery, Michael Scott; lighting, Michael Tschudin. With Richard Kennedy, Marguerite Lenert, Richard Kneeland, William Cain, Katherine Helmond.

THE ETERNAL HUSBAND (22). By Gabriel Gladstone; dramatized from Dostoyev-sky's novelette (world premiere). March 3, 1966. Director, Adrian Hall; scenery, Michael Scott; lighting, Barry Kearsley; costumes, Sunny B. Warner. With Vincent Gardenia, William Cain, Katherine Helmond, Richard Kennedy, Richard Kneeland and Marguerite Lenert.

THE PLAYBOY OF THE WESTERN WORLD (24). By J. M. Synge. March 31, 1966. Director, Philip Minor; scenery, Stewart Brecher; lighting, Jody Briggs; costumes, Ellen Brecher. With William Neary, Richard Kennedy, Katherine Helmond, Marguerite Lenert, Robert Moberly and Gene Rousseau.

SAINT PAUL

Theater Saint Paul

SHE LOVES ME (37). Musical based on a play by Miklos Laszlo; book, Joseph Masteroff; lyrics, Sheldon Harnick; music, Jerry Bock. October 16, 1965. Director and musical director, Tom Roland; scenery, Robert D. Emeott; lighting, Dan Goodwin; costumes, Sara Gage; choreography, Tom Roland. With Gerald Hjert, Janice Rittmaster, Jim Weston, Zoaunne Henriot, Gary Gage, Scott Johnson, Tom Roland.

THE TYPISTS and THE TIGER (20). By Murray Schisgal. October 28, 1965. Director, Rex Henriot; scenery, Robert D. Emeott; lighting, Dan Goodwin; costumes, Sara Gage. With Zoaunne Henriot, Tom Roland.

ANDROCLES AND THE LION (19). By George Bernard Shaw. January 6, 1966. Director, Rex Henriot; scenery and costumes, Robert D. Emeott; lighting, Dan Goodwin. With Sandy McCallum, Gary Gage, Tom Roland, Sally Pritchard, Gary Reineke, Frank E. Bumb Jr.

THE PHYSICISTS (15). By Friedrich Duerrenmatt; translated by James Kirkup. Director, Rex Henriot; scenery, Robert D. Emeott; lighting, Frank E. Bumb Jr.; costumes, Sara Gage. With Zoaunne Henriot, Gerald Hjert, Alan Peabody, Gary Gage.

TURN A DEAF EAR (19). By Tom Roland (original revue). March 3, 1966. Director and choreographer, Tom Roland; scenery, Robert D. Emeott; lighting, Frank E. Bumb Jr.; costumes, Sara Gage. With Tom Roland, Gerald Hjert, Zoaunne Henriot, Gary Gage, Mary Marshall.

VISIONS OF SUGAR PLUMS (14). By Barry Pritchard (premiere). March 31, 1966. Director, Rex Henriot; scenery, Robert D. Emeott; lighting, Frank E. Bumb Jr.; costumes, Sara Gage. With Bernie McInerney, Gerald Hjert, Gary Gage, Zoaunne Henriot, Tom Roland.

SAN FRANCISCO (See article on its season)

Actor's Workshop: Marines Theater

THE HISTORY OF THE LAMENTABLE REIGN OF EDWARD THE SECOND (27). By Bertolt Brecht; English version by Eric Bentley. October 22, 1965. Director, John Hancock; scenery, Ian Strasfogel; lighting, Donald Childs. With Barton Heyman, Winifred Mann, Robert Skundberg, Alfred Leberfeld, Abe Vigoda, Joe Brotherton, Robert Benson.

THE LAST ANALYSIS (26). By Saul Bellow. November 26, 1965. Director, John Hancock; scenery, William Stewart Jones; lighting, Jim Rynning. With Abe Vigoda, Maurice Argent, Alfred Leberfeld, Winifred Mann, Tom Tarpey, Rhoda Gemignani, Fanny Lubritsky.

DON JUAN (26). By Molière; translated by Robert Goldsby. December 31, 1965. Director, Tom Gruenewald; scenery, Joan Larkey. With Anthony Smith, Barton Heyman, Rhoda Gemignani, George Hitchcock, Robert Benson, David O. Stiers, Alfred Leberfeld, Abe Vigoda.

THE FATHER (27). By August Strindberg; translated by Michael Meyer. February 4, 1966. Director, John Hancock; scenery, Robert LaVigne; lighting, Rynning & Leake. With Joseph Miksak, Rhoda Gemignani, Alfred Leberfeld, David O. Stiers, Fanny Lubritsky.

A MIDSUMMER NIGHT'S DREAM (26). By William Shakespeare. March 11, 1966. Di-

rector, John Hancock; scenery, Jim Dine; lighting, Al Jutzi. With George Hitchcock, Abe Vigoda, C. David Colson, David O. Steirs, Rhoda Gemignani, Robert Benson, Barton Heyman, Alfred Leberfeld, Winifred Mann, Daniel Ades.

Actor's Workshop: Encore Theater

THE MILK TRAIN DOESN'T STOP HERE ANYMORE (47). By Tennessee Williams. July 23, 1965. Director, John Hancock; scenery, Warren Travis; lighting, Ken Margolis and J. Thompson Poynter. With Winifred Mann, Robert Benson, Sally Kemp, Joyce Lancaster, Robert Skundberg.

THE CAGE (5). By Rick Cluchey. December 11, 1965. Director, Ken Kitch; scenery, Donald J. Childs. With Barton Hayman, Daniel Ades, Robert Benson, Lindsay Moller, Aaron Friedley Jr., Gary Capshow.

POINT CONCEPTION (5). By Michael McQuire. December 12, 1965. Director, Ken Margolis; scenery, Donald J. Childs; lighting, F. Leon Leake. With George Hitchcock, Billie Dixon, Kathleen Heflin, Joyce Lancaster.

THE EMPIRE BUILDERS (28). By Boris Vian; translated by Simon Watson Taylor. February 18, 1966. Director, Marc Estrin; scenery, Carl Worth. With Michael Linenthal, Jane Steckl, Celeste Sarlatte, Marshall Efron, Robert Skundberg.

SEATTLE (See article on its season)

Seattle Repertory Theater

JULIUS CAESAR (29). By William Shakespeare. October 25, 1965. Director, Stuart Vaughan; scenery, Samuel Ball; lighting, Richard Nelson; costumes, Allan Granstrom.

LONG DAY'S JOURNEY INTO NIGHT (30). By Eugene O'Neill. October 26, 1965. Director, Pirie MacDonald; scenery, Samuel Ball; lighting, Richard Nelson; costumes, Allan Granstrom.

THE IMPORTANCE OF BEING EARNEST (31). By Oscar Wilde. October 27, 1965. Director, Stuart Vaughan; scenery, Samuel Ball, lighting, Richard Nelson; costumes, Allan Granstrom.

AH, WILDERNESS! (9). By Eugene O'Neill. November 17, 1965. (Repeated from 1964-65 season).

HEARTBREAK HOUSE (30). By George Bernard Shaw. January 5, 1966. Director, Stuart Vaughan; scenery, Samuel Ball; lighting, Richard E. Nelson; costumes, Allan Granstrom.

THE CHERRY ORCHARD (11). By Anton Chekhov. January 19, 1966. (Repeated from 1964-65 season).

GALILEO (28). By Bertolt Brecht; English version by Charles Laughton. March 2, 1966. Director, Pirie MacDonald; scenery, Samuel Ball; lighting, Richard Nelson and Robert Krahl; costumes, Allan Granstrom.

TWELFTH NIGHT (4). March 27, 1966 and **HAMLET** (5), March 31, 1966; by William Shakespeare. (Repeated from 1964-65 season).

PERFORMER	"JULIUS CAESAR"	"LONG DAY'S JOURNEY INTO NIGHT"	"THE IMPORTANCE OF BEING EARNEST"	"HEARTBREAK HOUSE"
Ray Clary	Decius Brutus; Messala			
Gordon Coffey	Marullus; Artemidorus			
Glenn O. Diehl	Carpenter; Citizen; Ligarius			
Kay Doubleday			Gwendolyn	Ellie Dunn
Jonathan Farwell	Marc Antony		John Worthing	Hector
Pauline Flanagan	Portia		Lady Bracknell	Hesione
Anne Gerety		Mary Tyrone		
John Gilbert	Octavius	Edmund Tyrone	Arthur	
Elizabeth MacDonald		Cathleen		

PERFORMER	"JULIUS CAESAR"	"LONG DAY'S JOURNEY INTO NIGHT"	"THE IMPORTANCE OF BEING EARNEST"	"HEARTBREAK HOUSE"
William Myers	Julius Caesar	James Tyrone		Boss Mangan
Stillman Moss	Flavius; Lepidus			
William Newman	A Cobbler; A Citizen; Popilius; Lucilius			
Don Perkins	Pindarus	James Tyrone Jr.		
Nina Polan	Calpurnia		Miss Prism	Lady Utterword
Archie Smith	Cassius		Rev. Chausable	Shotover
Anne Thompson			Cecily	
George Vogel	Casca		Lane	Mazzini Dunn
Stuart Vaughan	Brutus		Algernon	
Bernard Frawley			Merriman	
Maureen Frawley				Nurse Guiness
Jack Smith			1st Footman	
Michael Goodman			2nd Footman	

GALILEO

Informer	Ray Clary	Doge; Old Cardinal	William Newman
Cardinal Bellarmin	Gordon Coffey	Virginia Galilei	Nina Polan
Matti	Glenn O. Diehl	Federzoni	Archie Smith
1st Lady	Kay Doubleday	Cardinal Barberini	George Vogel
Andrea Sartti	Jonathan Farwell	Priuli	Bernard Frawley
Mrs. Sartti	Anne Gerety	Senator	Jack Smith
Cardinal Inquisitor;		Marsili	Michael Goodwin
Mathematician	John Gilbert	Andrea Sarti (as a boy)	Bruce McLean
Sagredo	William Myers	Galileo Galilei	Thomas Hill
Senator;			
Cardinal Chamberlain	Stillman Moss		

STANFORD, CALIF.

Stanford Repertory Theater

THAT SCOUNDREL SCAPIN (10). By Molière; translated by Donald Sutherland. October 27, 1965. Director, Erik Vos; scenery, Richard L. Hay; lighting, Paul Landry; costumes, Douglas A. Russell. With Jerome Raphel, Gerald Hiken, Carol Androsky, Paul E. Richards, Jane Hoffman.

THE SKIN OF OUR TEETH (16). By Thornton Wilder. December 1, 1965. Director, Mel Shapiro; scenery, Richard L. Hay; lighting, Paul Landry; costumes, Robert McFarland. With Barbara Cason, Jane Hoffman, Harold Gould, Paul E. Richards, Donald Patterson, Ruth Silveira, Carol Androsky.

THE CHAIRS by Eugene Ionesco; translated by Donald M. Allen; directed by Mel Shapiro and THE QUESTIONS (premiere) by John Hawkes; directed by Robert Loper (5).

January 13, 1966. Scenery and costumes, Warren Travis; lighting, Carol Markley. With Jane Hoffman, Paul E. Richards. Stephen D. Newman, Glenn Cannon and Carol Androsky.

ALL'S WELL THAT ENDS WELL (16). By William Shakespeare. March 31, 1966. Director, William Sharp; scenery, Robert McFarland; lighting, Paul Landry; costumes, Jeanne Shultz Davidson. With John Hellweg, Ruth Silveira, Jane Hoffman, Gerald Hiken, Jerome Raphel, Susan Leich.

THE GOOD WOMAN OF SETZUAN (10). By Bertolt Brecht; English version by Eric Bentley. May 11, 1966. Director, Mel Shapiro; scenery, Richard L. Hay; lighting, Paul Landry; costumes, Richard L. Hay. With Gerald Hiken, Jeanne Paynter, Ruth Hunt, Paul Richards, Jane Hoffman.

WASHINGTON, D.C. (See article on its season)

Washington Theater Club

SLOW DANCE ON THE KILLING GROUND (31). By William Hanley. October 13, 1965. Director, Paul Melton; scenery, James Parker; lighting, Clifford Ammon. With John Hillerman, Billy Dee Williams, Sue Lawless.

U.S.A. (41). By Paul Shyre and John Dos Passos; based on the novel by Mr. Dos Passos. November 10, 1965. Director, Davey Marlin-Jones; scenery and costumes, James Parker; lighting, Clifford Ammon. With John Hillerman, Sue Lawless, Jane Singer, John Barrett, Clifford Ammon, Melinda Miller.

ERNEST IN LOVE (40). Musical based on Oscar Wilde's The Importance of Being Earnest; book and lyrics, Anne Croswell; music, Lee Pockriss. December 21, 1965. Director, Davey Marlin-Jones; musical director, Douglas Finney; costumes and scenery, James Parker; lighting, Jeremiah Greenwood. With John Hillerman, Melinda Miller, Sue Lawless, Martin Cassidy, Jane Singer.

ROMEO AND JEANETTE (31). By Jean Anouilh; translated by Miriam John. January 27, 1966. Director, Davey Marlin-Jones; scenery, and costumes, James Parker; lighting, Jere Greenwood. With Melinda Miller, Marie Carroll, Martin J. Cassidy, John Hillerman, William Damon, Jane Singer, Jere Greenwood.

THE TYPISTS and THE TIGER (31). By Murray Schisgal. February 24, 1966. Director, Clifford V. Ammon; scenery, James Parker; lighting, Jere Greenwood. With Sue Lawless, William Damon, Melinda Miller, Ralph Strait.

THE BIRTHDAY PARTY (31). By Harold Pinter. March 24, 1966. Director, Davey Marlin-Jones; scenery and costumes, James Parker; lighting, Clifford Ammon. With William Damon, Sue Lawless, John Hillerman, Melinda Miller, Ralph Strait, Jere Greenwood.

ECCENTRICITIES OF A NIGHTINGALE (31). By Tennessee Williams. April 20, 1966. Director, Davey Marlin-Jones; scenery and costumes, James Parker; lighting, Jere Greenwood. With Melinda Miller, Ralph Strait, Sue Lawless, Raymond Thorne, Betty Parker.

SPREAD EAGLE (15). Original musical revue by Sue Lawless, Russell Baker, E.Y. Harburg and others. May 19, 1966. Music, Dennis Jelalian, Lee Wing, Jay Brower. Director, Davey Marlin-Jones; scenery and costumes, James Parker; with the company.

Arena Stage

SAINT JOAN (33). By George Bernard Shaw. October 28, 1965. Director, Edwin Sherin; scenery, Robin Wagner; lighting, Leo Gallenstein; costumes, Marianna Elliott; music, Charles Gross. With Jane Alexander, Dana Elcar, Anthony Holland, Stephen Joyce.

THE SKIN OF OUR TEETH (33). By Thornton Wilder. December 2, 1965. Director, Zelda Fichandler; scenery, Robin Wagner; lighting, Leo Gallenstein; costumes, Marianna Elliott. With Doris Belack, Dana Elcar, Dorothea Hammond, Janet Sarno.

PROJECT IMMORTALITY (33). By Loring Mandel (premiere). January 6, 1966. Director, Edwin Sherin; scenery, Robin Wagner; lighting, Martin Aronstein; costumes, M. A. Eigsti. With Ted D'Arms, George Ebeling, Dana Elcar, Dorothea Hammond, Lauri Peters, Jon Voight.

THE THREE SISTERS (33). By Anton Chekhov; translated by Stark Young. February 10, 1966. Director, Zelda Fichandler; scenery, Karl Eigsti; lighting, Leo Gallenstein; costumes, M. A. Eigsti. With Jane Alexander, Margaret Cowles, Ted D'Arms, George Ebeling, Dana Elcar, Dorothea Hammond, Janet Sarno.

SERJEANT MUSGRAVE'S DANCE (33). By John Arden. March 17, 1966. Director, Edwin Sherin; scenery, Robin Wagner; lighting, Jules Fisher; costumes, Nancy Potts. With Conrad Bromberg, Ted D'Arms, Robert Foxworth, James Kenny, George Reinholt, Richard Venture.

MR. WELK AND JERSEY JIM by Howard Sackler and THE LESSON by Eugene Ionesco; directed by Edwin Sherin and THE COLLECTION by Harold Pinter; directed by Dana Elcar (33). April 21, 1966. Scenery, Karl Eigsti; lighting, William Eggleston; costumes, M. A. Eigsti. With Richard Venture, Robert Prosky, Jane Alexander, James Kenny, George Ebeling, Janet Sarno.

Oh What a Lovely War is to be the final production of the Arena Stage season, opening June 3.

O
O
O

THE SHAKESPEARE FESTIVALS

O
O
O

INTRODUCTION

By Joseph Papp

Producer of the New York Shakespeare Festival

IT WOULD have amazed William Shakespeare to realize that performances of his plays are responsible for the creation of subsidized repertory theaters throughout the United States. It is also possible that Mr. Shakespeare, as a private entrepreneur, would be somewhat disdainful of theaters that cannot survive through box office receipts. The writing profession in his day was highly competitive and only top-rate dramatists, he amongst them, were able to make a living.

Shakespeare's economic operation, in a certain sense, has had more to do with Broadway than with the non-commercial festivals and burgeoning theaters which are producing his plays in quantity. The parallel is mainly in the area of free enterprise, an economic situation in which the decisive role is played by the ticket buyer. Although the ticket buyer still has an economic role to play in all theater operations open to the public, the difference between Shakespeare's audience and the Broadway audience is extraordinary. The average Elizabethan seeking entertainment in Shakespeare's day had several choices—the ale house, the whore house, the bear-baiting ring, the cock-fighting yard and the playhouse. Of all of these, the playhouse was probably the least expensive; the duly recorded admission to the Globe Theater was one penny. While bear-baiting is not a popular pastime in the United States and cock-fighting is limited to an occasional match raided by the police, the other forms of diversion mentioned above still have a popular following. While drinking and wenching have the same relative place in the standard of living, the price of the theater ticket has risen by several hundred per cent, and it is also obvious that the product has declined in most instances. Another factor that cannot be discounted in this picture is the appearance of film and television, by far the cheapest form of entertainment.

The stage, aside from the real estate interest which monopolizes the field in New York, is one of the last of the "open-market" phenomena. While many of us like to call it an art, it is also a handicraft, and therefore the product is expensive. The alienation of a popular audience from the theater today can be

90

attributed to many factors, it can be debated, but the fact of its high cost out of all proportion to an individual's or a family's budget cannot be questioned. The Federal Theater in the 1930s gave ample demonstration that it was possible to reach new audiences for every form of theater if the price of the ticket did not represent a barrier to admission.

Shakespeare apparently has more immediate understandability to the mass than Beckett, Pinter, Genet or John Arden, so he will continue to draw, and in fact probably outdraw, modern playwrights. Several years ago the Royal Shakespeare Company's West End season, which included plays of Beckett and Pinter, was losing money, but their summer Shakespeare at Stratford-upon-Avon made it up. The free enterprise system at the Globe Theater is being replaced by the socialistic concept of subsidy in the new permanent theaters now coming up. While Shakespeare in his time attracted a wide audience within the private enterprise system, the same system today excludes the popular audience, and Broadway is patronized by the small, more affluent section of our society. To remedy this situation in the new repertory theaters, there is no alternative but to obtain subsidy, if the objective of these theaters is to reach a new audience. Subsidy makes it possible to keep the price of tickets down. Subsidy also makes possible one of the key artistic facets of Shakespeare productions, something that existed in his own time—a permanent acting company. A permanent company also becomes the basis for attracting new playwrights who will write for that group of players.

The sense of democracy that we attribute to Shakespeare, in spite of his plays that deal with the problems of kings and princes, must inevitably stem from the mass audience to which these plays were addressed. This factor accounts in great part for the popular success of American Shakespeare in the 20th century, as well as the following he had during Colonial days. There was nothing anachronistic in an actor dressed in the royal purple speaking some of the most exalted lines in the English language to a hard-handed, roughly dressed audience of frontiersmen. The rise of the professional festival companies in the United States during the last ten years and the increasing audience belie the notion that Shakespeare is highbrow. The probability is that the sophisticate today would turn his nose up at another production of *As You Like It* or *A Midsummer Night's Dream,* whereas great sections of the so-called average audience will find deep sources of pleasure in these plays.

It should not be considered ironic, therefore, to find Shakespeare today returning to his mass base, away from the intelligentsia, and breaking through the limitations imposed by university productions. Most of the professional repertory companies springing up around the country have their roots in Shakespeare. The Association of Producing Artists (APA), one of the most successful of these companies, is headed by Ellis Rabb, whose background is steeped in Shakespearean acting and production. The Tyrone Guthrie Theater at Minneapolis materialized through the efforts of Mr. Guthrie, whose influence in Shakespearean production is widespread. The theater in Seattle evolved through the efforts and leadership of director Stuart Vaughan, whose major work in Shakespeare was performed with the New York Shakespeare Festival in New York City. William Ball, director of the American Conservatory Theater, is another prime example of a "Shakespearean" becoming a significant theatrical force on a national basis. Today, wherever in the United States we find a permanent company, we are bound to find actors, directors and technicians who have cut their teeth on Shakespeare.

The challenge of dealing with poetry and richly drawn human characters is provided by the plays of William Shakespeare. With the international theater moving away from naturalism and in the direction of more abstract and poetic concepts, Shakespeare's plays, over 300 years old, help lay the groundwork for performing in modern repertory. The best example of this in the English-speaking world is The Royal Shakespeare Company, led by the triumvirate, Peter Hall, Peter Brook and Michel Saint-Denis. This company, one of the finest in the world, was founded on Shakespeare, and through his stimulation branched out into significant contemporary drama. Shakespeare still remains the basis of their outstanding work. The company in Stratford, Ontario, originally established by Tyrone Guthrie and followed by the brilliant leadership of Michael Langham, is another example of a Shakespeare-based company having its life source in his work and moving into contemporary productions. Of the two professional American Shakespeare festivals, Stratford, Conn. and the New York Shakespeare Festival, only the latter has acquired a permanent home for winter operations where it will produce modern plays and classics having contemporary significance.

It appears that the creative people who lead these festival companies cannot be sustained on a steady Shakespeare diet and have the need to become a part of the more immediate thinking of the day. It is not merely an artistic question—that of seeking different styles of theater—so much as it is a drive to fulfill theater's historic role in society. Every major theatrical company made its primary contribution when it developed and introduced new plays and playwrights, and any theater person today worth his salt instinctively pursues this goal. The vitality of a Shakespeare production in any age depends on the vitality of the theater of that period. It also depends very much on the thinking and mood of the particular country in which it is produced. When the modern theater is alive and swimming, Shakespeare plays are infused with that spirit and become part of the age.

Not having an outlet for its contemporary comment (until the recent acquisition of year-round quarters), the New York Shakespeare Festival has been drawn in the last two years to the darker and more subtle of Shakespeare's plays. In 1965, *Coriolanus* and *Troilus and Cressida* were produced. In the summer of 1966, *All's Well That Ends Well, Measure for Measure, Richard III* and *Macbeth* will make up the Festival's season. The "problem" plays are attractive because of their greater psychological complexity and thus the potential of a greater appeal to the modern audience than they have had in the past. Also, with the absence of great classic actors, these plays are found to be much more suitable for a repertory company, principally because of the lack of starring roles. These plays are therefore, in a real sense, plays for the ensemble rather than star vehicles.

Shakespeare is the best attraction for reaching the broadest audience because of the humanistic content of the plays, and because of their realism and verbal richness. His plays are providing the basis for the theater of the future. Yet we can say with some degree of assurance that Shakespeare festivals, as we have known them, are on their way out, or at least, on their way to being transformed into new entities which include the plays of Shakespeare, but not exclusively. Shakespeare festivals will continue in New York and elsewhere as the theater movement grows in this country, and Shakespeare's appeal to the masses will continue to serve as the basis for a more democratic theater. As with the New York Shakespeare Festival, the Bard's plays will be produced to attract fresh audiences of all ages, and in the process great numbers will subsequently be educated to become a new and vital audience for the contemporary theater.

Canadian Shakespeare Festival (129). Repertory of three plays by William Shakespeare and one by Anton Chekhov. **Henry IV, Part One** (June 14, 1965; 39): directed by Stuart Burge; designed by Desmond Heeley; music by John Cook. **Falstaff (Henry IV, Part Two)** (June 15, 1965; 30): directed by Stuart Burge; designed by Desmond Heeley; music by John Cook. **Julius Caesar** (June 16, 1965; 45): directed by Douglas Campbell; designed by Leslie Hurry. Anton Chekhov's **The Cherry Orchard** (July 26, 1965; 15): translated by Tyrone Guthrie and Leonid Kipnis; directed by John Hirsch; designed by Brian Jackson; music by Louis Applebaum. Produced by the Stratford Shakespearean Festival at the Festival Theater, Stratford, Ontario, Canada. (Closed October 2, 1965).

PERFORMER	"HENRY IV, PART ONE"	"FALSTAFF"	"JULIUS CAESAR"	"THE CHERRY ORCHARD"
Claude Bede	Blunt	Warwick; Biddulph	Cicero	
Mervyn Blake	Northumberland; Sheriff	Northumberland; Silence		Pishchik
Douglas Campbell	Hotspur			Lopahin
Eric Christmas	Bardolph	Bardolph	Popilius Lena	
Leo Ciceri	King Henry IV	King Henry IV	Marullus; Messala	
Patrick Crean	Traveller	Morton	Flavius; Officer	
Peter Donat		Pistol	Cassius	
Bruno Gerussi	Vernon; Gadshill		Marcus Antonius	Yasha
Max Helpmann	Westmoreland	Westmoreland	Casca	
Martha Henry	Lady Percy	Lady Percy		Dunyasha
Roland Hewgill		Hastings; Davy	Publius; Poet; Volumnius	
Henry Hovencamp		Surrey	Cinna; Clitus	
William Hutt		Shallow	Brutus	Gayev
Frances Hyland		Doll Tearsheet	Calpurnia	Varya
J.C. Juliani	Lancaster; Peto	Lancaster; Peto	Trebonius; Lucilius	
Al Kozlik	Ostler	Fang; Feeble	Soothsayer; Varro	Station Master
Heath Lamberts	Poins	Poins; Wart	Lucius	
Dan McDonald		Gloucester	Decius Brutus; Titinius	A Passer-by
Paul Massie	Mortimer; Vintner	Clarence; Travers	Octavius	
Richard Monette		Harcourt	Dardanius	

PERFORMER	"HENRY IV, PART ONE"	"FALSTAFF"	"JULIUS CAESAR"	"THE CHERRY ORCHARD"
William Needles	Worcester	Chief Justice; Mouldy		Epidohov
Briain Petchey	Servant	Snare; Shadow	Artemidorus; Pindarus	Post Office Clerk
Kenneth Pogue	2d Carrier	Mowbray	Lepidus; Servant	
Leon Pownall	Messenger	Gower	Servant; Young Cato	
Douglas Rain	Prince Hal	Prince Hal		
Kate Reid			Portia	Lyuba
Susan Ringwood				Anya
Edward Rudney		Coleville	Cimber; Strato	
Mary Savidge	Mistress Quickly	Mistress Quickly		Charlotta
Joseph Shaw	Chamberlain; Scroop	Scroop	Julius Caesar	
Powys Thomas	Owen Glendower		Ligarius; Poet Cinna	Firs
Tony van Bridge	Falstaff	Falstaff		
Hugh Webster	Douglas; 1st Carrier		A Cobbler	Petya

Others: David Anderson, Larry Aubrey, Guy Bannerman, Benedict Campbell, Peter Cheyne, Tim Davisson, Maureen Fitzgerald, Mike Fletcher, Mark Gilliland, Lewis Gordon, Ken James, Joan Karasevich, Krysia Jarmicki, Karen Madsen, Janet Murray, Michael O'Regan, David Pape, Donna Peerless, Gregory Reid, Gordon Thomson.

American Shakespeare Festival (112). Repertory of four plays by William Shakespeare. **Coriolanus** (June 19, 1965; 25): directed by Allen Fletcher; scenery and costumes by Will Steven Armstrong; lighting by Tharon Musser; music by Conrad Susa. **Romeo and Juliet** (June 20, 1965; 28): directed by Allen Fletcher; scenery by Will Steven Armstrong; lighting by Tharon Musser; costumes by Ann Roth; music by Conrad Susa; choreography by William Burdick. **The Taming of the Shrew** (June 22, 1965; 26): original production concept by Don Driver; directed by Joseph Anthony; scenery by William Pitkin; lighting by Tharon Musser; costumes by Hal George; songs and music by John Duffy. **King Lear** (June 23, 1965; 33): directed by Allen Fletcher; scenery and costumes by Will Steven Armstrong; lighting by Tharon Musser; music by Conrad Susa. Produced by the American Shakespeare Festival Theater and Academy, Stratford, Conn. (Closed September 12, 1965).

NOTE: *Romeo and Juliet* opened March 8, 1965 for 45 school performances; *Coriolanus* opened April 29, 1965 for 15 school performances; *The Taming of the Shrew* opened March 16, 1965 for 46 school performances; *King Lear* opened June 9, 1965 for one school performance.

PERFORMER	"CORIOLANUS"	"ROMEO AND JULIET"	"THE TAMING OF THE SHREW"	"KING LEAR"
Vincent Aurelia	Young Marcius			
Robert Benedict	Roman Officer; Volscian Lt.	Chorus; (Romeo)	Lucentio	King of France
DeVeren Bookwalter	Messenger	Paris; (Montague Servant)	(Lucentio)	Burgundy
Philip Bosco	Coriolanus			
Geneva Bugbee	(Virgilia)	(Juliet)	Bianca	
Morris Carnovsky				King Lear
John Carpenter	(Agrippa); Senator	Montague	Vincentio	Knight

PERFORMER	"CORIOLANUS"	"ROMEO AND JULIET"	"THE TAMING OF THE SHREW"	"KING LEAR"
John Cunning-ham	Tullus Aufidius	Mercutio	Petruchio	Edmund
Ruby Dee			Katherina	Cordelia
Todd Drexel	(Roman Generals); Volscian Lord	Escalus	Hortensio	French Captain
Rex Everhart	Junius Brutus		Grumio	
Lillian Gish		Nurse		
Ted Graeber	Volscian Lt.; Citizen	Tybalt	A Tailor	Oswald
David Grimm	Roman Officer; Servant	Peter	Curtis; (Gremio)	Servant
Patricia Hamilton	Valeria	Lady Capulet	(Katherina)	Goneril
Mary Hara	(Volumnia)	Lady Montague; (Nurse)	Widow	Regan
Patrick Hines	Agrippa	Friar Laurence		Gloucester
Dennis Jones	Citizen; Servant; Volscian Guard	(Benvolio); Apothecary	(Tranio)	Knight
Stephen Joyce	(Coriolanus)			Edgar
Richard Kuss	Titus Lartius	Gregory; Friar John		Knight; Herald
Aline MacMahon	Volumnia			
Richard Mathews	(Junius Brutus); Citizen	(Tybalt); (Mercutio)		Fool
Richard Morse	Citizen	Balthasar; (Paris)	Tranio	Knight
Edwin Owens	Aedile	Abram	(Minola)	Knight
Roy Poole				Kent
Thomas Ruisinger	(Velutus); Servant; Volscian Lord	(Friar Laurence)	Minola	Old Man
Terence Scammell	Volscian Lt.	Romeo		
Nick Smith	Volscian Guard; (1st Citizen)	Sampson; Chief Officer; (Capulet)	(Hortensio); Pedant	Officer
Josef Sommer	Cominius	Capulet		Albany
Theodore Sorel	1st Citizen	Benvolio	Biondello	Cornwall
Maria Tucci	Virgilia	Juliet		
Frederic Warriner	Velutus		Gremio	

(Parentheses indicate roles in which the actor alternates)

Others: Dennis Aarons, Stephen Bernstein, Lawrence Block, Olivia Cole, Dimo Condos, Jacqueline Coslow, Robert Cremonini, Mona Feit, James Haire, John Hamilton, Linda Kampley, Michael Parish, Marvin Reedy, Jack Rice, Roger Robinson, Stanley Soble, Julius Sulmonetti, David Thompson, William Vines, Norton Wettstein.

New York Shakespeare Festival (69). Season of three plays by William Shakespeare. **Love's Labor's Lost** (June 9, 1965; 23. Closed July 3, 1965): directed by Gerald Freedman; scenery by Ming Cho Lee; lighting by Martin Aronstein; costumes by Theoni V. Aldredge; songs and music by John Morris. **Coriolanus** (July 7, 1965; 23. Closed July 31): directed by Gladys Vaughan; scenery by Ming Cho Lee; lighting by Martin Aronstein; costumes by Theoni V. Aldredge and Ray Diffen; music by David Amram. **Troilus and Cressida** (August 4, 1965; 23. Closed August 28, 1965): directed by Joseph Papp; scenery by Ming Cho Lee; lighting by Martin Aronstein; costumes by Theoni V. Aldredge; music by David Amram. Produced by Joseph Papp in cooperation with the City of New York at the Delacorte Theater, Central Park, New York City.

LOVE'S LABOR'S LOST

Ferdinand ....James Ray
Longaville ....Michael Moriarty
Dumaine ....William Bogert
Berowne ....Richard Jordan
Anthony Dull ....Dan Durning
Costard ....Joseph Bova
Don Adriano De Armado ......Paul Stevens
Moth ....John Pleshette
Jaquenetta ....Alexandra Berlin
Boyet ....Tom Aldredge
Princess of France ....Jane White
Maria ....Nancy Reardon
Katharine ....Margaret Linn
Rosaline ....Rae Allen
A Forester ....Robert Burgess
Sir Nathaniel ....Gerald E. McGonagill
Holofernes ....Robert Ronan
Marcade ....Oliver Dixon
Singer ....Keith Baker
Dancer ....Gerald Teijelo
Lady in Waiting ....Betty Hellman

Understudies: Mr. Ray—William Bogert; Misses White, Allen—Betty Hellman.

Others: Keith Baker, Robert Burgess, Burke Byrnes, Oliver Dixon, John Hoffmeister, Peter Jacob, Bruce Monette, John Vidette.

Festival Line Singers: Alexander Demas, Carole Demas, Debby Kooperman, Paula Lani Rosen, Jonathan David Rosen.

CORIOLANUS

1st Citizen ....Morris Erby
2nd Citizen ....Brad Sullivan
Menenius Agrippa ....Staats Cotsworth
Caius Marcius Coriolanus .....Robert Burr
Roman Senator ....Leonard Hicks
Cominius ....Michael McGuire
Titus Lartius ....Herbert Nelson
Sicinius Velutus ....Alan Ansara
Junius Brutus ....James Earl Jones
Volscian Senator ....Seymour Penzner
Tullus Aufidius ....Mitchell Ryan
Volumnia ....Jane White
Virgilia ....Kate Sullivan
Valeria ....Marcie Hubert
Lieutenant to Aufidius ....Beeson Carroll
1st Roman Officer ....Ed Setrakian
2nd Roman Officer ....James Antonio
1st Roman Citizen ....Leonard Jackson
2nd Roman Citizen ....Morris Erby
3rd Roman Citizen ....Douglas Turner
Patrician ....Humbert Alan Astredo
Aedile ....Maury Cooper
Nicanor ....Ed Setrakian
Adrian ....Humbert Alan Astredo
1st Servingman ....Maury Cooper
2nd Servingman ....James Antonio
3rd Servingman ....William Devane
1st Volscian Watch ....M. M. Streicher
2nd Volscian Watch ....Beeson Carroll
Young Marcius ....Robert Benson
Ross Burr

Understudies: Mr. Cotsworth—Seymour Penzner; Misses White, Sullivan—Marcie Hubert; Master Burr—Edward Britton Burr.

Others: James Arnold, Robert Burgess, Burke Byrnes, Festus Collier, Oliver Dixon, John Genke, Alec Healy, Laura Hicks, John Hoffmeister, Anna Horsford, James Howard, Peter Jacob, Leonard Jackson, Ronald Johnson, Philip Kroopf, George McGrath, George Muschamp, Nat Simmons, John L. Starrs, John Vidette, Lisle Wilson, Peter Yoshida.

Festival Line Singers: Alex Demas, Carole Demas, Thomas Ludlow, Jonathan Rosen, Paula Rosen.

TROILUS AND CRESSIDA

Priam ....Leonard Hicks
Hector ....Paul Stevens
Troilus ....Richard Jordan
Paris ....Humbert Alan Astredo
Deiphobus ....Peter Jacob
Helenus ....Michael Moriarty
Margarelon ....James Howard
Aeneas ....Jack Ryland
Antenor ....Morris Erby
Calchas ....John Hetherington
Pandarus ....Frank Schofield
Agamemnon ....Gerald E. McGonagill
Menelaus ....Michael McGuire
Achilles ....John Vernon
Ajax ....James Earl Jones
Ulysses ....Roscoe Lee Browne
Nestor ....Tom Aldredge
Diomedes ....Al Freeman, Jr.
Patroclus ....Bill Gunn
Thersites ....Joseph Bova
Helen ....Jane White
Cassandra ....Tobi Weinberg
Andromache ....Chase Crosley
Cressida ....Flora Elkins
Alexander ....Seymour Penzner
Servant to Troilus ....James Arnold
Servant to Paris ....Robert Ronan
Servant to Diomedes ....Peter Yoshida
Myrmidon ....Ronald Johnson

Understudies: Mr. Hicks—John Hetherington; Mr. Stevens—Leonard Hicks; Mr. Jordan—Michael Moriarty; Mr. Schofield—Robert Ronan; Messrs. Jones, Freeman—Morris Erby; Mr. Browne—Michael McGuire; Misses White, Elkins, Crosley, Weinberg—Betty Hellman.

Others: Burke Byrnes, Festus Collier, Oliver Dixon, John Genke, Alex Healy, John Hoffmeister, Leonard Jackson, Philip Kroopf, George McGrath, George Muschamp, Nat Simmons, John Starr, John Vidette, Lisle Wilson.

Musicians: Andrew J. Baron, Richard Berg, Henry J. Nowak.

Festival Line Singers: Alex Demas, Carole Demas, Jonathan Rosen, Paula Rosen.

Mobile Theater—New York Shakespeare Festival. Three mobile productions of plays by William Shakespeare on tours of the five boroughs of New York City. **King Henry V** (June 26, 1965; 25. Closed August 21, 1965): directed by Joseph Papp; scenery, Ming Cho Lee; lighting, Martin Aronstein; costumes, Sonia Lowenstein; music, David Amram. **The Taming of the Shrew** (June 27, 1965; 26. Closed August 22, 1965): directed by Joseph Papp; scenery, Ming Cho Lee, lighting, Martin Aronstein; costumes, Theoni V. Aldredge; music, David Amram; choreography, Anthony Weber. **Romeo and Juliet** in the Spanish language (August 25, 1965; 12. Closed September 6, 1965): directed by Osvaldo Riofrancos; translated by Pablo Neruda; scenery and costumes, Jose Varona; lighting, Larry Metzler; music, Francisco de Madina. All three productions produced by Joseph Papp in cooperation with the City of New York; Delacorte Mobile Theater designed by Ming Cho Lee; press, Merle Debuskey, Seymour Krawitz.

KING HENRY V

Chorus ....Roy Shuman
King Henry V ....Robert Hooks
Duke of Exeter ....Drew Eliot
Earl of Westmoreland ......Richard Nettum
Archbishop of Canterbury ....Wayne Wilson
Duke of Orleans ....Norman MacDonald
Bardolph ....John Tyranos
Nym ....William Duell
Pistol ....Charles Durning
Mistress Quickly ....Terri Turner
Duke of Bedford ......Jon Renn McDonald
Lord Scroop ....Arthur Berwick
Earl of Cambridge ....Ray Stubbs
Sir Thomas Grey ....Howard Honig
Charles VI ....Lance Cunard
Lewis ....Frank Groseclose
Constable of France ....Albert Quinton
Montjoy ....Bill Fletcher
Fluellen ....George Stauch
Gower ....Joseph Palmieri
Governor of Harfleur ...Norman MacDonald
Katharine ....Ellen Holly
Alice ....Lynn Hamilton
Duke of Britaine ....Howard Honig
Rambures ....Jack Gianino
Sir Thomas Erpingham ......Wayne Wilson
Duke of Gloucester ....Joe Miller
Alexander Court ....Patrick Gorman
John Bates ....Ray Stubbs
Michael Williams ....Ernie McClintock
Earl of Salisbury ....Richard Marshall

THE TAMING OF THE SHREW

Grumio ....Charles Durning
Petruchio ....Roy Shuman
Hostess of a tavern ....Gladys Riddle
Townswoman ....Lynn Hamilton
Policeman ....Harold Miller
Duke Charles ....Drew Eliot

First Lord ....Bill Fletcher
Second Lord ....Richard Nettum
Bartholomew ....Bill Egan
Lucentio ....Richard Marshall
Tranio ....Jack Gianino
Biondello ....William Duell
Hortensio ....George Stauch
Gremio ....Lance Cunard
Baptista ....Albert Quinton
Katherina (Kate) ....Ellen Holly
Bianca ....Terri Turner
Curtis ....Frank Groseclose
Madcap Haberdasher ....Arthur Berwick
Madcap Tailor ....Ray Stubbs
Bill Collector ....Norman MacDonald
Vincentio ....Wayne Wilson
Widow ....Lynn Hamilton

ROMEO AND JULIET

Singers
  Baritone ....Alfredo Geroldo
  Soprano ....Ann Collins
Musician ....Eddie Alvarez
Peter Sampson ....Ramón Pabón
Gregory ....Antonio Flores
Abram ....Pascual Blanco
Balthasar ....Félix E. Fernández
Benvolio ....Carlos E. Davis
Tybalt ....José Ocasio
Capulet ....Alfonso Manosalvas
Lady Capulet ....Jana Klenburg
Montague ....Gonzalo Madurga
Lady Montague ....Pilar Buchanan
Prince of Verona ....Lázaro Pérez
Romeo ....Frank Ramirez
Paris ....Mario R. Cueto
Nurse to Juliet ....Norma Iris Pagán
Juliet ....Diana Aróstegui
Mercutio ....Claudio Garcia Satur
Friar Laurence ....Osvaldo Riofrancos

National Shakespeare Festival (90). Repertory of three plays by William Shakespeare. **The Merry Wives of Windsor** (June 15, 1965; 43): directed by Mel Shapiro; scenery and costumes, Peggy Kellner; music and songs, Conrad Susa; lighting, Daniel Dugan. **King Henry VIII** (June 23, 1965; 38): directed by Philip Minor; scenery, Peggy Kellner; costumes, Douglas Russell; music and songs, Conrad Susa; lighting, Daniel Dugan. **Coriolanus** (July 13, 1965; 29): directed by Milton Katselas; scenery and costumes, Peggy Kellner; music and songs, Conrad Susa; lighting, Daniel Dugan. Produced by the San Diego National Shakespeare Festival at the Old Globe Theater, San Diego, Calif., in its sixteenth season. (Closed September 12, 1965)

PERFORMER	"THE MERRY WIVES OF WINDSOR"	"KING HENRY VIII"	"CORIOLANUS"
Ramon Bieri	Ford	King Henry VIII	Tullus Aufidius
Jacqueline Brookes	Mistress Page	Queen Katharine	Volumnia
Robert Colonna		Cardinal Campeius	Servant
Jackie Coslow	Anne Page	Anne Bullen	Virgilia
Terrence Evans	Host	Norfolk	1st Citizen
Alan Fudge	Servant	Cranmer	Lieutenant
Janice Fuller	Mistress Quickly	Patience	
James Gallery	Page	Surveyor; Porter	Titus Lartius
Donald Gantry	Fenton	Surrey	
Will Geer	Sir John Falstaff		Cominius
Nathan S. Haas	William Page		Young Marcius
Joseph J. Krysiak	Nym	Sergeant-at-Arms	Citizen
Leroy Logan	Servant	Cromwell	Volscian Senator
Nicholas Martin	Abraham Slender	Prologue; Gentleman; Porter's Man	
Wayne Maunder	Policeman	Lovell	Aedile
Philip Minor	Pistol		Velutus
Michael Montel		Capucius	Senator
Robert Moriarty	Jack Rugby	Gentleman	
Stephen D. Newman	Bardolph	Griffith	Citizen
Patricia O'Connell	Mistress Ford	Old Lady	Valeria
Michael O'Sullivan	Shallow	Wolsey	Agrippa
Jerome Raphel	Doctor Caius	Buckingham	Junius Brutus
Matthew Raymond Sinor			(Young Marcius)
Byron Smith	Robin	Page	
Alan Stambusky		Lord Chamberlain	Servant; Senator
James Storm		Gardiner	Messenger
Robert Teuscher	Simple	Lord Sands	Volscian Senator
Marshall Wright		Guildford	
Anthony Zerbe	Sir Hugh Evans	Suffolk	Coriolanus

(Parentheses indicate role in which the actor alternates)

Oregon Shakespeare Festival (45). Repertory of four plays by William Shakespeare. **Much Ado About Nothing** (July 26, 1965; 12): directed by James Moll. **Macbeth** (July 27, 1965; 11): directed by Richard D. Risso. **The Winter's Tale** (July 28, 1965; 11): directed by Hugh C. Evans. **King Henry VI, Part Two** (July 29, 1965; 11): directed by Edward S. Brubaker. Presented by the Oregon Shakespearean Festival at Ashland, Ore., in its 25th anniversary season. (Closed September 11, 1965.)

NOTE: Ben Johnson's *Volpone* was also presented for three performances on August 31, September 5 and 10, 1965.

PERFORMER	"MUCH ADO ABOUT NOTHING"	"MACBETH"	"THE WINTER'S TALE"	"KING HENRY VI, PART TWO"
Jim Baker		Macbeth	Old Shepherd	
Robert Breuler	Dogberry	Menteith; Old Man	Gaoler	Horner
Edward S. Brubaker		Soldier	Camillo	
Les Carlson	Claudio	Seyton; Murderer	Dion	Simpcox; Smith
Gretchen Corbett		Witch	Perdita	
John Scott Goodhue	Antonio's Son	Apparition; Soldier	Cleomenes	Michael
Jo Firestone Gorman		Witch	Mopsa	Wife to Simpcox
Rick Hamilton			Florizel	
Dan Hays		Soldier	A Bear	George Bevis
Susan Hooper	Hero	Lady in Waiting	2d Lady	Margaret
Nagle Jackson	Benedick		Autolycus	Hume; Lieutenant
Zoe Kamitses	Beatrice	Lady Macbeth	Paulina	
Enid Kent		Lady Macduff	Hermione	
Bonda Lewis	Ursula	Gentlewoman	1st Lady	Eleanor
Bob Locke	Balthasar	Donalbain		Dick
Robert Page	Friar Francis	Duncan	Lord	Vaux; Humphrey Stafford
Shirley Patton	Margaret			
Ray Keith Pond	Don Pedro	Malcolm	Leontes	Gloucester
Herman Poppe		Siward	Mariner	Buckingham
Douglas Richardson		Lennox	1st Lord	Lord Say
Richard D. Risso				Beaufort
William Roberts	Don John	Macduff	Polixenes	
Baker Salsbury	Leonato	Ross	Archidamus	Richard Plantagenet
William Shephard	Verges	Young Siward	Page	Warwick
David Shookhoff		Fleance		
Mara Stahl			Emilia	Margery Jordain
Milton Tarver		Caithness; Murderer	Time	Suffolk
Victor Walston			Mamillius	
Misha Williams	Conrade	Witch		Asmath; Whitmore
Laird Williamson		Banquo	2d Lord	King Henry VI
Rachel Anne Zimmerman			Dorcas	

Producing director, Angus L. Bowmer; designer, Richard L. Hay; music director, W. Bernard Windt; choreography, Shirlee Dodge; costumes, Jack A. Byers; lighting, Robert Brand.

The Royal Shakespeare Theater (310). Repertory of five plays by William Shakespeare and one by Christopher Marlowe. **Love's Labor's Lost** (April 7, 1965; 54). Directed by John Barton; designed by Sally Jacobs. **The Merchant of Venice** (April 15, 1965; 79). Directed by Clifford Williams; scenery, Ralph Koltai; costumes, Nadine Baylis. **The Comedy of Errors** (May 19, 1965; 41). Directed by Clifford Williams; scenery and lighting, John Wyckham, Clifford Williams; costumes, Anthony Powell. **Timon of Athens** (July 1, 1965; 52). Directed by John Schlesinger; designed by Ralph Koltai. **Hamlet** (August 19, 1965; 49). Directed by Peter Hall; scenery, John Bury; costumes, John Bury in collaboration with Ann Curtis. Also **The Jew of Malta** (April 14, 1965; 35) by Christopher Marlowe. Directed by Clifford Williams; designed by Ralph Koltai; costumes in association with Nadine Baylis. Produced by The Royal Shakespeare Company at Stratford-on-Avon, England. (Repertory closed December 11, 1965).

PERFORMER	"THE MERCHANT OF VENICE"	"THE COMEDY OF ERRORS"	"LOVE'S LABOR'S LOST"	"THE JEW OF MALTA"
Katharine Barker	Jessica		Maria	Abigail
Donald Burton	Arragon	Solinus		Selim Calymath
Patsy Byrne	Nerissa		Jaquenetta	Bellamira
Tony Church			Holofernes	Machiavel; Ferneze
John Corvin	Solanio	2d Merchant		Martin Del Bosco
Jeffery Dench	Gratiano	Angelo		1st Knight
Susan Engel		Adriana		
Peter Geddis	Salerio	Pinch		Lodowick
Jonathan Hales		Balthazar		2d Jew
Stephen Hancock	Old Gobbo			
Glenda Jackson			(Princess of France)	
Charles Kay	Launcelot Gobbo	Antipholus of Ephesus	Ferdinand	
James Laurenson		Messenger	Longaville	1st Basso
Stanley Lebor	Morocco		Mercade	1st Jew; Messenger
Robert Lloyd		Dromio of Ephesus		
Brewster Mason			Boyet	
Peter McEnery	Bassanio			Ithamore
Tina Packer		Luciana	(Princess of France)	
Michael Pennington			Dumaine	Mathias
Eric Porter	Shylock			Barabas
Ian Richardson		Antipholus of Syracuse		
William Squire	Antonio		Don Adriano	
Janet Suzman	Portia		Rosaline	
Charles Thomas	Lorenzo		Berowne	
Madoline Thomas		Aemilia		Katherine
David Waller	Duke		Dull	Barnadine
Timothy West	Tubal		Sir Nathaniel	Pilia- Borza
Michael Williams		Aegeon		
		Dromio of Syracuse		
Tim Wylton	Balthasar		Costard	Jacomo

(Parentheses indicate role in which the actor alternates)

PERFORMER	"HAMLET"	"TIMON OF ATHENS"
John Bell	Rosencrantz	
Donald Burton	Horatio	Old Athenian; 2d Senator
Tony Church	Polonius	Flavius
John Corvin	Captain	1st Senator
Jeffery Dench	Marcellus; Ambassador	Head of Senate; Banker
Peter Geddis	Barnardo	Caphis
David Kane		Lieutenant
John Kane	2d Gravedigger	
Charles Kay	Player Queen; Osric	Poet
James Laurenson	Guildenstern	Lucilius
Stanley Lebor	Lucianus	Lord Ventidius
Patrick McGee	Ghost	

PERFORMER	"HAMLET"	"TIMON OF ATHENS"
Brewster Mason	Claudius	Alcibiades
Michael Pennington	Fortinbras	
Paul Rogers		Apemantus
Paul Scofield		Timon
Elizabeth Spriggs	Gertrude	Phrynia
William Squire	Player King	
Janet Suzman	Ophelia	Timandra
Charles Thomas	Laertes	
David Waller	Voltemand; 1st Grave-	Lord Lucullus
	digger	
David Warner	Hamlet	
Timothy West		Lord Lucius
Tim Wylton	Reynaldo; Prologue	Servilius

Others: Laurie Asprey, Murray Brown, John Challis, Robert Grange, Bruce Condell, Robin Culver, Timothy Darwen, William Dysart, Terrence Greenidge, John Gulliver, Marshall Jones, Richard Moore, Sylvester Morand, Cliff Norgate, Robert Walker, John Watts, Alan Tucker, Pall Starr, Pamela Buchner, Jessica Claridge, Roger Jones, Helen Weir, Malcolm McDowell, David Kane, Ted Valentine, Philip Meredith, David Quilter.

O
O
O

THE SEASON IN LONDON

O   By *John Russell Taylor*
O   Author of *Anger and After; A Guide to the New British Drama*
O

SINCE ALL years in the theater are liable to be the worst ever until one stops to put general impressions in order and back them up with chapter and verse, one should perhaps take pause at an initial impression that this particular year has really, all in all, been rather a *good* one. Would a bit of checking and totting up prove this idea to be as inaccurate as gloomier snap judgments usually are? After due consideration, I think not, though needless to say there has been no lack of querulous voices announcing, yet again, that the New Drama in Britain was dead, that traditional standards, especially of acting, were in drastic decline, that London theater was becoming, to its detriment, a mere subsidiary of Broadway, and so on.

Let us work backwards through the charges. First, the supposed domination of the West End by Broadway. This, on investigation, proves to be one of those sweeping statements based on a very small number of spectacular successes; really, when you come down to it, only four: *Hello, Dolly!* and *Funny Girl,* which join *The Sound of Music,* still running over here, among the most unshiftable musicals in London, and *The Owl and the Pussycat* and *Barefoot in the Park,* which have established themselves as likely comedy hits. Beyond that, there is very little: *Any Wednesday,* which flopped; short-lived revivals of *The Glass Menagerie* and *Oh Dad, Poor Dad, etc.* in the West End; the addition of *The Crucible* to the National Theater's repertory; and the currently successful presentation of *Incident at Vichy* with a star-studded cast. Those are about all anyone can instance in substantiation of the view that Broadway is taking over. And of course when it comes down to it no one passionately objects to any of them. We still incline to believe that Broadway will always outdo us in the musical—though *Oliver, Robert and Elizabeth* and several others are around the West End to contest the assumption. It is possible to have two minds about the comedies or even about *Incident at Vichy,* which received a decidedly mixed press, but they can hardly be instanced as examples of the United States palming off its old rubbish on us. The only pity—and it can hardly be blamed on the plays we *have* seen over here—is that we still have not seen so many of what sound from a distance the more interesting works of the younger and more enterprising American dramatists. But then the situation is much the same with current European drama: apart from original-language productions by visiting companies, the only notable London productions of modern European drama have been short runs of Anouilh's *The Cavern* and of Camus's *Caligula,* some readings of Peter Weiss's *The Investigation* by the Royal Shakespeare Company, and the same company's not very successful rendering of Brecht's *Puntila.*

So much for the debits in our acquaintance with contemporary drama from outside Britain. Elsewhere the prospect is far brighter. Stick-in-the-muds continue to grumble about acting standards, and especially about the rarity of London appearances by the acknowledged greats of the British stage. True enough, it seems some time since we saw Peggy Ashcroft, and we have not seen Edith Evans on the West End stage this year, while Sybil Thorndike, though present, can hardly be said to be stretching her talents in, say, a revival of *Arsenic and Old Lace,* however well she does it. On the other hand, Laurence Olivier is always with us at the National Theater; John Gielgud has given us his version of Chekhov's *Ivanov,* with much distinction if not perhaps any great excitement; Donald Wolfit turned up recently as Mr. Barrett in *Robert and Elizabeth;* and both Paul Scofield and Alec Guinness have been reclaimed for our delectation here, Scofield with *The Government Inspector* and *Timon of Athens* for the Royal Shakespeare Company and Guinness in the already mentioned production of *Incident at Vichy,* which has depended heavily on his personal prestige to pull it through. Moreover, there has been no lack of distinguished work at the National Theater, and of glittering revivals elsewhere to uphold the reputation of British actors in the classics.

Of course there are occasional blots on the picture: it has been very noticeable, especially in the present rash of Shaw revivals, that too many of our younger actors just cannot achieve the style necessary to say the more extravagantly literate lines of our classic comedians as though they meant them, let alone as though they might be capable of framing them for themselves. This apart, the year has been vintage for those who prefer their dramatic entertainment, shall we say, with a bloom on it, but with little further back than the 1880s. After Shakespeare/Marlowe in 1964 there has been, understandably, an almost closed season for Elizabethan and Jacobean drama. The Royal Court put on a rather embarrassed and slap-happy production of Middleton's *A Chaste Maid in Cheapside,* failing altogether to find a proper style in which to play it; the Royal Shakespeare had *Timon* as a vehicle for Scofield, and the National countered with yet another *Hamlet,* intended, like the National's opening production, to be a controversial showcase for a leading younger actor—this time David Warner, somewhat depressing and perverse, hopefully publicized as "an angry young Hamlet." The Restoration and 18th century were represented by *Love for Love,* which was added to the National Theater's repertory on their trip to Moscow; productions of *Samson Agonistes,* with Michael Redgrave, and the Isaac Bickerstaff/Charles Dibdin ballad opera *Lionel and Clarissa,* both introduced at the first Guildford Festival under Redgrave's direction, were not transferred to London, the Festival being represented in the West End solely by Emlyn Williams' new version of *A Month in the Country* with Redgrave, Ingrid Bergman and Williams.

Once advanced into the 19th century, however, the revivals really proliferate. Pinero has been creeping back into the repertory, and this last year has seen a serviceable version of his farce *Dandy Dick* at the Mermaid and particularly a beautifully stylish version of *Trelawny of the Wells,* Pinero's nostalgic evocation of the theater of his youth, at the National Theater. Wilde, who could hardly be left out of the revival list, has been represented by a patchy production of *An Ideal Husband,* and Maugham, likely no doubt to be the object of renewed interest as a result of his death, has had West End showings for a vintage comedy, *The Circle,* which came up as fresh as ever, and *The Sacred Flame,* a once-famously controversial, now merely rather dated, "strong drama." But the real sensation of the year has been the sudden, quite unexpected revival of interest in Shaw. It began, really, in Edinburgh, the most unlikely place of all, with a new production, glitteringly cast to be sure, of one of those long-despised later plays which even Shavians tend to skate rapidly over, *Too True to Be Good.* To everybody's surprise this turned out to be not only bearable, but positively entertaining, at least for a couple of acts. A week later the Mermaid backed up this startling insight with *Fanny's First Play,* and in the month or two following these were joined by *Man and Superman, You Never Can Tell* and *The Philanderer,* with more on the way.

For myself, I find the craze, or at least the superlatives which have been thrown about during it, rather exaggerated: the deficiencies of the plays simply as plays are as marked as ever, the characters as likely as ever to degenerate into Shavian glove-puppets, the construction to waver and falter. The last act of *Too True to Be Good* is one of the dullest Shaw ever wrote, *You Never Can Tell* is wilfully ramshackle, *Man and Superman* overdoes all the stuff about the Life Force, and only *The Philanderer* emerges enhanced from the ordeal of revival. On the other hand, the plays do provide showy parts for actors, and the casts assembled have been among the most distinguished to shine on the West End stage for some time. Ralph Richardson in *You Never Can Tell,* Alan Badel and Sian Phillips in *Man and Superman,* Alastair Sim in *Too True to Be Good* have all given performances remarkable enough to dispose audiences to overlook the faults of the plays which housed them. And, beyond this, there is undoubtedly a growing taste among London audiences for good talk and intelligent, sophisticated comedy. This the Shaw revivals have fed and encouraged; and after the prevalence in the last few years of a sort of theater which was primarily anti-dialogue and anti-literary, such a pendulum-swing of taste was only to be expected. Now that it has occurred, though, we may perhaps hope that it will be answered with something better than a selection of the shakier works of Shaw. After all, there is much Restoration comedy that remains unfamiliar, and there are many contemporaries of Shaw whose plays deserve renewed attention quite as much: witness the surprise success of the English Stage Company's production of Granville Barker's *The Voysey Inheritance* at the Royal Court, which began as a pious anniversary gesture towards the theater's earlier great days in the 1900s, and turned into a major triumph with critics and audiences.

And, of course, there is always the possibility that new plays may supply something in keeping with this new, or renewed demand from audiences. Not, naturally, that one would want a stick to beat our modern dramatists, though a number of critics have seized it with that end in view. The theater is, or should be, big enough to accommodate all tastes: John Osborne as well as Noel Coward, Ann Jellicoe as well as Somerset Maugham. But it has been a legitimate grouse in past years that the "New Drama" (as we persist in calling it, a full ten years after *Look Back in Anger*) has tended to keep apart from what you might call popular middle-brow theater. It may have, and often has, brought new audiences into the theater, but it has seldom made much impression on the old audiences: suburbanites who like to "do a show" every now and then, preferably a thriller, comedy or musical; people who come up in coach parties from the North and West. These have been catered to with an ever-dwindling number of old-world entertainments featuring aging but still loved stars. This year the top entrants in this class have been *Charlie Girl,* a smooth, dim musical starring Anna Neagle for nostalgia and Joe Brown, a young but conservative pop star, to provide a few teenage kicks, and *Alibi for a Judge,* a desperately haphazard legal comedy by Henry Cecil and several assistants which has turned into a major hit, I suppose, entirely on the television popularity of its star Andrew Cruikshank, who plays a sort of Scottish homespun Doctor Gillespie in an endless BBC series.

Several other attempts to hit this mark have failed spectacularly, notably the latest Lionel Bart musical *Twang!,* a would-be romp about Robin Hood which cost a bomb, shed director Joan Littlewood and several cast members en route to London, and sank with all hands after a few ignominious weeks. On a slightly higher level of aspiration, most of our dramatic elder statesmen have been absent from the London scene this year. Terence Rattigan's latest play, *Nelson: A Portrait in Miniature,* was not for the theater at all, but for television. J.B. Priestley has been away from the stage for years, though his adaptation with Iris Murdoch of the latter's novel *A Severed Head* continued its long run through most of the year. But another absentee, Noel Coward, did make a spirited comeback with three plays, one full-length and a double bill, under the general title of *Suite in Three Keys.* The most substantial of them, the full-length *A Song at Twilight,* proved to be one of his subtlest and most immaculately fashioned works, concerning the place of homosexuality in the life of a grand old man of literature, and providing in the process three excellent acting roles—for Coward himself, Lilli Palmer and Irene Worth— and a stunning first-act curtain.

While this play, making use as it does of one of the freedoms gained for British theater by the New Dramatists (ten years ago no play dealing directly with homosexuality would have been licensed for performance), might be construed as something of a gesture of reconciliation towards the New Drama from the other side, moves from the New Drama itself have not been lacking. Several New Dramatists have adapted works from the classical repertory: John Osborne has made over Lope de Vega into *A Bond Honoured* for the National Theater, and John Mortimer has done the same for Feydeau with *A Flea in Her Ear;* John Arden has written a new version of *Fidelio* for Sadler's Wells. But more significantly, there have been this year a number of successors to last year's hit *Entertaining Mr. Sloane,* the first unashamedly commercial play in a 1960s idiom. A couple of years ago one could draw a clear line between "New Drama" and the rest; now it is often impossible to be sure.

The most obvious example of this, and one of the biggest hits of the year, is Frank Marcus's comedy *The Killing of Sister George.* This is based, quite simply, on a lesbian triangle: "George," an aging actress who has become a national figure playing the lovable, crusty old heroine of a daily radio soap-opera, discovers that her character is about to be written out of the series, and at the same time has the difficult, rather infantile young woman with whom she lives filched from her by a suave lady executive from the BBC. Very funny, and sharp, and sad, with three magnificent performances from Beryl Reid, Eileen Atkins and Lally Bowers. But New Drama or old, who can say? Obviously the play could not have been written if all that has happened since *Look Back* had not happened, but at the same time it has found a ready audience among the older-fashioned sort of playgoer who generally turns tail and runs at the mention of anything new, difficult, and very probably not quite nice. Almost exactly the same is true of Pauline Macaulay's *The Creeper,* which brought Eric Portman back to the West End after too long an absence, and dealt in similarly popular terms with a vaguely homosexual set-up involving various parasites and would-be parasites around a rich older man. Comedies like the Willis Hall/Keith Waterhouse *Say Who You Are,* Roger Milner's *How's the World Treating You?,* Bill Naughton's *Spring and Port Wine,* and Roger Longrigg's *The Platinum Cat,* or dramas like Bill McIl-wraith's *The Anniversary* and Donald Howarth's *A Lily in Little India* all live, one way or another, in the same no-man's-land, and the first three of them, at least, very successfullly. Ann Jellicoe's latest play *Shelley,* one of the first three to be presented under the new post-George Devine regime at the Royal Court, actually suffered in critical and public estimation because it was so simple, direct and straightforward: whatever we expected from the unpredictable author of *The Sport of My Mad Mother* and *The Knack,* it was certainly not a semi-documentary account of the life of Shelley, however well done (and in this case it was very well done indeed).

There still remains, though, quite a number of plays which, whatever their success with the public, are still unmistakably part of the advance guard of the British theater, and these would be quite sufficient—even if we leave out of account the borderline cases I have just mentioned—to contradict any too-hasty obituaries of the New British Drama. The two main signs of health in an artistic movement, I take it, are that its original leaders continue active and developing, and that a reasonable amount of new talent continues to be recruited. Both these conditions are at present being fulfilled. Surprisingly few of the early notables have fallen by the wayside or turned exclusively to media other than drama. There have been, certainly, occasional disappointments: Robert Bolt has done nothing in the theater since the arty misfire of *Gentle Jack* except to rework an old radio script, *The Thwarting of Baron Bolligrew,* as a Christmas children's show for the Royal Shakespeare Company, and Charles Wood's next produced play after his prize-winning triple bill *Cockade,* a satirical farce called *Meals on Wheels* at the Royal Court, proved to be an unfunny, self-indulgent piece of pseudo-intellectual slapstick which found hardly a single critic to defend it.

But against these should be set major new plays by virtually every major figure in the New Drama. Harold Pinter's *The Homecoming,* his first full-length play since *The Caretaker,* is arguably his masterpiece, certainly the most utterly confident and assured in its effect of all his plays. It works, as far as anything can work, in "pure" dramatic terms, defying all attempts to foist on to it some pat formulation of what it is "about"; it is about six people of one family, in one room, no more and no less. Never has Pinter's ear been more finely attuned to the smallest nuances of conversational English, his action more hypnotically holding. And the Royal Shakespeare Company gave it an almost impeccable performance, directed by the Company's director Peter Hall with the sharpness and precision which have seemed sadly lacking in a number of his own recent productions. John Arden too has been seen at somewhere near his very considerable best in the National Theater's production of *Armstrong's Last Goodnight* (as well as an overdue revival of *Serjeant Musgrave's Dance* at the Royal Court). *Armstrong's Last Goodnight* is superficially daunting, in that it is written in a brilliant recreation of early Renaissance Scots, but the ear rapidly becomes acclimatized, and the confrontation of the violent warlord Armstrong and the devious but humane courtier Lindsay (commandingly played by Albert Finney and Robert Stephens respectively) is so dramatically absorbing that the play has got through without undue difficulty to many theatergoers who in the past have tended to find Arden altogether too complicated to be grasped with pleasure. In this it has no doubt been aided by the success of Arden's other new play this year, *Left-Handed Liberty,* specially commissioned by the City of London and performed at the Mermaid to mark the 750th anniversary of Magna Carta. One never expects very much of such occasional pieces, but Arden's play, while working no doubt on a rather lower level of intensity than *Armstrong's Last Goodnight,* turned out to be an intelligent, provocative, anti-heroic view of the great event, really more of a psychological study of King John than anything else, and a gripping piece of theater. Though Arden remains the least easy to pin down of all our newer dramatists, it does really seem this year that he may at last have managed to break though to that wider public comprehension and acceptance that have so long eluded him.

The latest works of other founding fathers of the New Drama may perhaps be dealt with more briefly. Peter Shaffer provided the National Theater with a masterly piece of high farce in *Black Comedy,* a long one-acter based on the shatteringly simple notion of reversing light values, so that when the characters can see light we cannot, but as soon as their electricity is cut off we can see everything that is happening as clear as day. While John Osborne's much-admired *Inadmissible Evidence* continued its run in the West End, an ambitious new play, *A Patriot for Me,* opened at the Royal Court after a much-publicized tangle with our stage censor. It is a lengthy historical drama about political and homosexual intrigues in the pre-1914 Hapsburg army, centered on the mysterious figure of the spy Redl; it divided critics, being extravagantly admired by many and disliked by a few (including myself) because it seemed, like Osborne's other historical plays, to lose the urgency and passionate rhetoric of his best subjective dramas without gaining any corresponding advantages in organization or rounded characterization. Arnold Wesker tried to break new ground with an intimate two-character play *The Four Seasons,* dealing with the whole course of a love affair, but failed to manage with conviction the highly literary style he apparently found necessary to make his rather obscure point about it. The play for all its faults, however, was not really so bad as everybody said, and his other new play, *Their Very Own and Golden City,* at the Royal Court, should restore him to the field of social drama and significant action in which up to now he has always been most at home. N.F. Simpson returned to the theater after some years' absence with a new absurdist farce, *The Cresta Run,* at the Royal Court. This time the nominal subject was spies, and hardly anybody liked it; I didn't like it either, but then as I have never yet quite seen what other people see in Simpson's plays this came as no great surprise to me. Finally, Alun Owen had a considerable success with a double bill, *The Game,* at the Dublin Festival, but promises that it would appear forthwith in London have not yet been honored; meanwhile, we were at long last given a chance to see his drama of academic life in a Welsh college, *A Little Winter Love,* and it proved such an accomplished piece of dramatic thinking, upheld by all Owen's old resources of vivid dramatic speech and racily immediate characterization, that it was difficult to imagine why no commercial management had snapped it up, leaving it to an enterprising fringe group of advanced sympathies to put it on.

But what of the new talents? Here again the last year has been encouraging. It would be expecting too much, no doubt, to suppose that a new Pinter, Arden or Osborne might spring fully armed upon the scene, and certainly nothing of the sort has happened. But there have been a number of stage debuts, London debuts, or debuts absolutely, that have given every reason to hope for great things forthcoming. The most spectacular appearance of a first stage play was *Ride a Cock Horse,* by David Mercer, already a highly valued television writer. This benefitted greatly at the box-office, and I think lost something critically, from the powerful advocacy of Peter O'Toole in the leading role: Mercer's long and highly charged study of a self-made intellectual's decline into neurotic infantilism, while unmistakably school-of-Osborne, carried a powerful theatrical charge which augurs well for his future in the theater. Edward Bond's *Saved,* another much-publicized victim of our censor's somewhat narrow-minded view of what is and is not fit for adult theatergoers to see, was a rather different matter. Its main controversial scenes, particularly one in which a group of hooligans stone a baby to death and smear it with excrement, were in fact the least convincingly written and the most awkwardly played; but elsewhere there was real subtlety and observation in the story of a rather dumb young man's hopeless passion for an empty-headed girl and his relations with her strange and difficult family. Keith Johnstone's *The Performing Giant,* another play introduced at the Royal Court, was a very strange symbolic comedy-drama about a giant who allows himself to be explored and exploited by pot-holers, the whole thing, apparently, being intended as an allegory of adolescence. Still, it had real qualities, though it was overshadowed by its companion in the bill, David Creegan's *Transcending,* which compressed with striking sureness and theatrical flair enough plot material for a five-act melodrama (or a Feydeau farce) into little over half an hour of cool hilarity. Other plays by new or newish dramatists which elicited rave notices from some and anyway made us aware of considerable potential if not always fully realized talents were Paul Ableman's *Green Julia,* David

Halliwell's *Little Malcolm and His Struggle against the Eunuchs* and John McGrath's *While Guarding the Bofors Gun.* Two dramatists who arrived belatedly but welcome in London were David Perry with his double bill of eccentric comedies *Stuff and Nonsense* and David Campton with his long one-acter about the aftermath of nuclear destruction (among other things) *Little Brother, Little Sister.*

Even this necessarily summary and abbreviated list does not exhaust the interesting material seen on the London stage during the last twelve months, but at least it should give some little idea of the riches and variety still to be found in what many commentators continue to insist has been a bad year. And meanwhile the National Theater and the Royal Shakespeare Company go from strength to strength, despite a certain amount of in-fighting about subsidies; the Royal Court settles into its new routine under William Gaskill after the retirement and deeply mourned death of George Devine, the man who did most to start the New Drama and keep it going at its most difficult time; and West End managers, while of course wringing their hands and shedding crocodile tears about the parlous state of commercial theater, still continue to put on an endless stream of new productions and presumably make enough money from the hits to make it worth their while to continue. So, yes, I suppose you might say that this has been a bad year in the sense that it was not as good as might be hoped (but what year ever is?) and a good year in that it certainly has not been as bad as might have been feared. In the words of a diplomatic school report, "could do better with a little encouragement, but very satisfactory all-round performance." Enough, anyway, to keep us happy and waiting for further developments.

Highlights of the London Season

Compiled by Ossia Trilling

OUTSTANDING LONDON PERFORMANCES

JOHN GIELGUD as Ivanov in *Ivanov*	PAUL SCOFIELD as Khlestakov in *The Government Inspector*	ALEC GUINNESS as Von Berg in *Incident at Vichy*
DAVID WARNER as Hamlet in *Hamlet*	MICHAEL REDGRAVE as Rakitin in *A Month in the Country*	RALPH RICHARDSON as Waiter in *You Never Can Tell*
IRENE WORTH in three roles in *Suite in Three Keys*	ALBERT FINNEY in two roles in *A Flea in Her Ear*	IAN McKELLEN as Andrew Cobham in *Their Very Own and Golden City*
ROBERT STEPHENS as Sir David Lindsay in *Armstrong's Last Goodnight*	PETER O'TOOLE as Peter in *Ride a Cock Horse*	VANESSA REDGRAVE as Jean Brodie in *The Prime of Miss Jean Brodie*
ALAN BADEL as John Tanner in *Man and Superman*	IAIN CUTHBERTSON as Serjeant Musgrave in *Serjeant Musgrave's Dance*	BERYL REID as June Buckridge in *The Killing of Sister George*

OUTSTANDING DIRECTORS

PETER HALL
The Government Inspector

MICHAEL ELLIOTT
Miss Julie

WILLIAM GASKILL
Saved

OUTSTANDING SCENE DESIGNERS

MALCOLM PRIDE
On the Level

JOHN BURY
Hamlet

RENÉ ALLIO
*Armstrong's Last
Goodnight*

OUTSTANDING NEW ENGLISH PLAYS
(D)—Playwright's London debut

THE HOMECOMING by Harold Pinter. A way-out family and its sexual urges. With Ian Holm, Paul Rogers, Vivien Merchant. (91)

LEFT-HANDED LIBERTY by John Arden. The story of King John and the Magna Carta. With Patrick Wymark, Robert Eddison, Sonia Dresdel. (27)

THE KILLING OF SISTER GEORGE by Frank Marcus. An unruly radio star is written out of a popular serial. With Beryl Reid, Eileen Atkins. (400+)

A PATRIOT FOR ME by John Osborne. The downfall of a Russian spy. With Maximilian Schell, George Devine. (53)

GREEN JULIA by Paul Ableman. (D) The vicissitudes of two university men. With Jonathan Lynn, Philip Manikum.

ARMSTRONG'S LAST GOODNIGHT by John Arden. How the English king's envoy bests an undisciplined 16th-century Scottish border chieftain. With Albert Finney, Robert Stephens. (25)

SAVED by Edward Bond. The link between sexual laxity and abnormal violence. With Gwen Nelson, Barbara Ferris, Ronald Pickup. (24)

A LILY IN LITTLE INDIA by Donald Howarth. A mother's boy's unavailing efforts to establish independence. With Ian McKellen, Jill Bennett, Jessie Evans. (113)

BLACK COMEDY by Peter Shaffer. Strangely visible goings-on in the dark. With Louise Purnell, Robert Stephens, Albert Finney. (16+)

SUITE IN THREE KEYS, a trilogy comprising one full-length play *(A Song at Twilight)* and two short ones *(Shadows of the Evening* and *Come Into the Garden Maud)* by Noel Coward. An old man's view of life's complications: a homosexual celebrity's past catches up with him; a dying man caught between two women; a henpecked American tycoon chooses freedom. With Noel Coward, Irene Worth, Lilli Palmer. (29+) and (25+)

THE ANNIVERSARY by Bill McIlwraith. (D) A martinet widow tries in vain to keep her hold on her rebellious children. With Mona Washbourne, Michael Crawford, June Ritchie. (47+)

ALLERGY by Cecil P. Taylor. Triangle drama with psychosomatic obstacles. With Gordon Whiting, Kate Binchy, Roy Hanlon. (22)

THEIR VERY OWN AND GOLDEN CITY by Arnold Wesker. The career of an idealist trapped into compromise by realities. With Ian McKellen, Sebastian Shaw, Ann Firbank. (13+)

INTERESTING LIMITED RUNS OF NEW BRITISH PLAYS

A LITTLE WINTER LOVE by Alun Owen. Rumpus on a Welsh campus. With Paul Maxwell, David McKail, Kenneth Farrington. (13)

RIDE A COCK HORSE by David Mercer. (D) Three women in the life of a working-class provincial writer. With Peter O'Toole, Sian Phillips, Barbara Jefford, Wendy Craig. (45)

FOUR THOUSAND BRASS HALFPENNIES by Bernard Miles. Musical based on

Dryden's *Amphitryon*. With Esmond Knight, Timothy Bateson. (39)

THE WORLD'S BABY by Michael Hastings. A mid-20th-century misfit. With Vanessa Redgrave. (1)

HAPPY DAYS ARE HERE AGAIN by Cecil P. Taylor. (D) Criminal responsibility viewed allegorically through a Marxist lens. With John Barrard, Bernard Goldman. (16)

THE FOUR SEASONS by Arnold Wesker. The flowering and decay of a love affair. With Diane Cilento, Alan Bates. (22)

SOMETHING NASTY IN THE WOOD-SHED by Adrian Rendle. Musical based on *Cold Comfort Farm*. With Patricia Kerry, Richard Curnock. (24)

SHELLEY by Ann Jellicoe. A new view of the poet's life. With Ronald Pickup, Frances Cuka. (19)

THE CRESTA RUN by N.F. Simpson. Absurdist send-up of M.I.5. With Avril Elgar, Sebastian Shaw. (20)

TWANG! by Lionel Bart. Ill-starred musical about Robin Hood that defeated even Joan Littlewood. With James Booth, Bernard Bresslaw, Barbara Windsor. (46)

THE THWARTING OF BARON BOLLI-GREW by Robert Bolt. Fairy-tale for children about a bold dragon and a bolder baron. With Leo McKern, John Normington. (27)

SATURDAY NIGHT AND SUNDAY MORNING by David Duffield. Dramatization of Alan Sillitoe's novel. With Tom Bell, June Ritchie, Joan Heal. (40)

LITTLE MALCOLM AND HIS STRUGGLE WITH THE EUNUCHS by David Halliwell. (D) An art student's revolt grows into a fascist putsch. With John Hurt, Susan Ashworth. (20)

A SMASHING DAY by Alan Plater. (D) An adolescent is hooked by the wrong girl. With Hywel Bennett, Barbara Barnett. (26)

THE PERFORMING GIANT by Keith Johnstone and TRANSCENDING by David Cregan. Surrealist allegory of growing up, and traditional theater satirised, make up a double bill. With Bernard Gallagher, Roddy Maude-Roxby. (11)

POPULAR ATTRACTIONS

THE CIRCLE by W. Somerset Maugham. Revival of a celebrated Maugham drama. With Evelyn Laye, Frank Lawton. (48)

AS YOU LIKE IT by William Shapespeare. Open-air version in delightful Regent's Park. With Gary Raymond, Ann Morrish, Edward Atienza. (85)

THE CREEPER by Pauline Macaulay. Homicidal mania in an epicene millionaire's entourage. With Eric Portman, Peter Blythe. (205)

ALIBI FOR A JUDGE by Felicity Douglas and Henry Cecil, with Basil Dawson. Adapted from Henry Cecil's novel about a peccant judge. With Andrew Cruikshank, Amanda Grinling. (336+)

PASSION FLOWER HOTEL by Wolf Mankowitz. Musical of Rosalind Erskine novel about teenagers' innocuous sex-games. With Karin Fernald, Nicky Henson. (150)

THARK by Ben Travers. Revival of a famous "Aldwych" farce. With Peter Cushing, Alec McCowen. (86)

DANDY DICK by Arthur Wing Pinero. Revival of the 1887 farce. With Robert Eddison, Sonia Dresdel. (67)

TOO TRUE TO BE GOOD by George Bernard Shaw. Revival of the comedy. With Alistair Sim, Kenneth Haigh, George Cole. (149)

FANNY'S FIRST PLAY by George Bernard Shaw. Revival of Shaw's famous theatrical critique. With Robert Eddison, Gwendolyn Watts, Denise Coffey. (67)

SAY WHO YOU ARE by Keith Waterhouse and Willis Hall. Matrimonial farce with an up-to-date attack. With Ian Carmichael, Jan Holden, Patrick Cargill, Dilys Laye. (260+)

LOVE FOR LOVE by Congreve. Revival of famous restoration comedy. With Laurence Olivier, John Stride, Lynn Redgrave. (37)

SPRING AND PORT WINE by Bill Naughton. Hard-hearted working-class dad's heart melted by family cunning. With Alfred Marks, Ruth Dunning. (249+)

TRELAWNEY OF THE WELLS by Arthur Wing Pinero. Revival of Pinero's backstage comedy. With Robert Stephens, Louise Purnell. (30+)

AN IDEAL HUSBAND by Oscar Wilde. Star-studded revival of Wilde comedy of manners. With Margaret Lockwood, Richard Todd. (189+)

CHARLIE GIRL by Ross Taylor, Hugh and Margaret Williams, and Ray Cooney. Musical alliance between bigshots and mods. With Joe Brown, Anna Neagle, Christine Holmes. (190+)

HAMLET by William Shakespeare. Transfer of Peter Hall's successful Stratford production. With David Warner, Janet Suzman, Brewster Mason, Elizabeth Spriggs. (39)

SERJEANT MUSGRAVE'S DANCE by John Arden. Revival of Arden's early anti-military play. With Iain Cuthbertson, Frances Cuka. (45)

MAN AND SUPERMAN by George Bernard Shaw. Revival of famous "Life Force" comedy. With Alan Badel, Sian Phillips, David Robinson, Zena Walker. (163+)

YOU NEVER CAN TELL by George Bernard Shaw. Revival of famous anti-bourgeois shocker. With Ralph Richardson, Harry Andrews, Judy Campbell, Keith Baxter. (159+)

ON THE WAGON by Bernard Miles. One-man show by famous rustic comedian. With Bernard Miles. (47)

A CHASTE MAID AT CHEAPSIDE by Thomas Middleton. Revival of Jacobean bawdy comedy. With Barbara Ferris, Sebastian Shaw. (25)

THE PHILANDERER by George Bernard Shaw. Revival of the comedy about the Shavian "New Woman." With Derek Godfrey, Jane Arden. (37)

HOW'S THE WORLD TREATING YOU? by Roger Milner. (D) How comic can failure be? With Patricia Routledge, Peter Bayliss. (140)

THE MATCHGIRLS by Bill Owen. Wild musical about a historic strike. With Vivienne Martin, Marion Grimaldi, Gerard Hely. (105+)

THE VOYSEY INHERITANCE by Harley Granville-Barker. Revival of famous 60-year-old Royal Court hit. With Sebastian Shaw, John Castle, Avril Elgar. (28+)

ON THE LEVEL by Ronald Millar. Zany musical exploiting a real-life school-examination scandal. With Barrie Ingham, Angela Richards. (48+)

JUNO AND THE PAYCOCK by Sean O'Casey. Olivier's production retrieves Abbey Players' 1964 flop. With Colin Blakeley, Frank Finlay, Joyce Redman. (12+)

A FRIEND INDEED by William Douglas Home. High jinks among adulterous diplomats. With David Hutcheson, David Tomlinson, Jane Baxter, Elizabeth Sellars. (39+)

THE PRIME OF MISS JEAN BRODIE by Jay Presson Allen. Based on Muriel Spark's novel of the unconventional and seemingly innocent Scots schoolmarm. With Vanessa Redgrave, Vickery Turner, William Squire. (30+)

COME SPY WITH ME by Bryan Blackburn. A spy and his crazy disguises. With Danny la Rue, Barbara Windsor. (1+)

SOME AMERICAN PLAYS PRODUCED IN LONDON

THIS PROPERTY IS CONDEMNED in a double-bill with PASSACAGLIA or THE GREAT SOCIETY by James Paul Dey (D). The stifling effects of American suburbia on the imagination. With Murray Kash, Sarah Moffatt. (3)

ANY WEDNESDAY. With Dennis Price, Amanda Barrie. (173)

THE OVERDOG by Albert Bermel. (D) Far-out skit on Herod. With Derek Godfrey, Betty Marsden. (12)

OH DAD, POOR DAD, ETC. New production of Kopit's absurdist comedy. With Hermione Gingold, Murray Melvin. (53)

THE AMEN CORNER. With Claudia McNeil. (22)

BAREFOOT IN THE PARK. With Daniel Massey, Mildred Natwick. (217+)

HELLO, DOLLY! With Mary Martin (later Dora Bryan). (208+)

THE GLASS MENAGERIE. With Gwen Ffrangcon-Davies, Anna Massey. (44)

THE PASTIME OF MONSIEUR ROBERT by Howard Sackler. (D) A de Sade-like French revolutionary has his entourage enact his sexual fantasies out for him. With Julian Glover, Ann Lynn, Susan Engel. (21)

INCIDENT AT VICHY. With Alec Guinness, Anthony Quayle. (93)

ARSENIC AND OLD LACE. With Sybil Thorndike, Athene Seyler, Lewis Casson. (145+)

THE OWL AND THE PUSSYCAT. With Diana Sands. (103+)

FUNNY GIRL. With Barbra Streisand (later Lisa Shane). (55+)

THE BELLOW PLAYS, comprising *Out From Under, Orange Souffle* and *The Wen.* (D). *Out From Under* is a world premiere about the frustrations of a suburbanite in a parking lot. With Miriam Karlin, Harry Towb. (6)

SOME FOREIGN PLAYS PRODUCED IN LONDON

PATENT PENDING by Wim van Leer. (D) Should the Germans who made the gas chambers be brought to book? With Basil Sydney, William Dexter. (25)

PUNTILA by Bertold Brecht. With Roy Dotrice, Patrick Magee. (39)

THE WILY WIDOW by Goldoni. With Mic Rollason, Richard Howard. (17)

BERLINER ENSEMBLE SEASON with *Arturo Ui* (5), *Coriolanus* (6), *Die Dreigroschenoper* (7), and *Die Tage der Commune* (3).

THE PROFESSOR by Hal Porter. (D) Australian traveller's tale from S.E. Asia. With Joss Ackland, Yoko Tani. (32)

THE MARRIAGE OF MISTER MISSISSIPPI by Friedrich Duerrenmatt. With Lillias Walker, Alfred Burke. (21)

THE ROAD by Wole Soyinka. (D) Nigerian drama of truck-drivers' hardships. With Bari Johnson, Rudolf Walker, Horace James. (12)

THE CITY and A PAINTING ON WOOD by Ingmar Bergman. Nicholas Hawtrey, Sylvia Coleridge. (6)

A MONTH IN THE COUNTRY by Turgenev. With Michael Redgrave, Ingrid Bergman. (172)

THÉÂTRE DU NOUVEAU MONDE season with *Klondyke* (3) and *L'Ecole des Femmes* (4).

MAN BETTER MAN by Errol Hill. With Errol Jones. (4)

IVANOV by Chekhov. With John Gielgud, Claire Bloom, Yvonne Mitchell. (124)

EASTER by Strindberg. With Meg Wynn Owen. (21)

THE INVESTIGATION by Peter Weiss. With Roy Dotrice, Glenda Jackson. (6)

THE CAVERN by Jean Anouilh. With Siobhan McKenna, Griffith Jones. (36)

MARAT/SADE by Peter Weiss. Revival prior to New York tour. (9)

THE GULLS by Alain-René Le Sage (free version of *Turcaret*, by Basil Ashmore). With Lloyd Lamble, Bob Monkhouse, Frankie Day. (9)

THE BIRDWATCHER by Georges Feydeau. With Prunella Scales, Michael Bates. (21)

THE GOVERNMENT INSPECTOR by Nikolai Gogol. With Paul Scofield, Paul Rogers. (31)

A FLEA IN HER EAR by Georges Feydeau (free version of *La Puce à l'Oreille*, by John Mortimer). With Geraldine MacEwen, Albert Finney, Edward Hardwicke, Roger Stephens. (21)

THE BEAVER COAT by Gerhart Hauptmann. With Peggy Mount. (63)

MISS JULIE by August Strindberg. With Maggie Smith, Albert Finney. (16)

WORLD THEATER SEASON, with Czech National Theater in *The Insect Play* (8), I Giovani in *Six Characters in Search of an Author* (8) and *The Rules of the Game* (7), Greek National Theater in *Hecuba* (6), *Oedipus Rex* (4) and *Oedipus Coloneus* (4), Polish Popular Theater in *The Wedding* (4), *Crime and Punishment* (8) and *The Colombus Boys* (4), and Leningrad Gorki Theater in *The Idiot* (12) and *Grandma, Uncle Iliko, Hilarion and I* (4).

THE MISER and THE IMAGINARY INVALID by Molière. With Bernard Miles, Duncan MacRae. (67)

THE GAIETY OF NATIONS by Alan Seymour. (D) Vietnamese resent both Chinese and American patronage. With Gordon Whiting, Roy Hanlon. (22)

TANGO by Slawomir Mrozek. With Trevor Nunn, Robert Eddison. (7+)

Highlights of the Paris Season

OUTSTANDING PERFORMANCES

MADELEINE RENAUD
as The Mother in
Days in the Trees

ROBERT HIRSCH
as Jean in
Hunger and Thirst

EDWIGE FEUILLÈRE
as Aurelia in
The Madwoman of Chaillot

MICHELINE BOURDET
as Hortense in
The Prince Disguised

A. M. JULIEN
as Castel-Bénac in
Topaze

PIERRE FRESNAY
as "I" in
The Fixed Idea

MICHEL SIMON
as Rockefeller in
Wind in the Sassafras Trees

GABRIEL CATTAND
as The Lieutenant in
The Screens

GEORGES WILSON
as Matamore in
The Comic Illusion

MARIE BELL
as Madame Princesse in
Madame Princesse

JACQUES FABBRI
as Myusov in
I Want to See Myusov

PIERRE MONDY
as M. Petypon in
The Girl from Maxim's

GERMAINE MONTERO
as Bernarda in
The House of Bernarda Alba

PHILIPPE AVRON
as Prince Myshkin in
The Idiot

DELPHINE SEYRIG
as Sarah in
The Lover

OUTSTANDING DIRECTORS

ANDRÉ BARSACQ
The Idiot

JACQUES CHARON
The Girl From Maxim's

GUY RÉTORÉ
Measure for Measure

OUTSTANDING DESIGNERS

JACQUES NOEL
Hunger and Thirst

JACQUES DUPONT
The Prince Disguised

ANDRÉ MASON
Numantia

OUTSTANDING NEW FRENCH PLAYS
(D)—Playwright's Paris debut

LE REPOS DU SEPTIÈME JOUR (Rest on the Seventh Day) by Paul Claudel. Hitherto unperformed philosophically esoteric play by the late author about the redemption of an ancient Emperor of China. With Maria Casarès, Fernand Ledoux.

LES EAUX ET FORÊTS (Waters and Forests) by Marguerite Duras. An inter-monologue-type drama for three strangers thrown together by an accident. With Claire Deluc, René Erouk.

NUMANCE (Numantia) by Jean Cau, based on Cervantes' book. The dying struggle of a Spanish city besieged by the Romans and preferring destruction to enslavement. With Jean-Pierre Bernard, Annie Bertin, Guy Moigne.

LE HASARD DU COIN DU FEU (The Risks of a Hearth-Corner) by Jean Vilar, adapted from a "dialogue" by Crébillon the Younger about the adventures of an 18th-century amorous playboy. With Jean Vilar, Cathérine Rouvel, Jean-Pierre Cassel.

DU VENT DANS LES BRANCHES DE SASSAFRAS (Wind in the Sassafras Trees) by René de Obaldia. A hilarious parody of a typical American Western. With Michel Simon, Rita Renoir.

LE GOÛTER DES GÉNÉRAUX (The Generals' Tea-Party) by Boris Vian. The late dramatist's hitherto unperformed satire of the dangerous absurdity of the military mind. With André Thorent, Francis Lax, Henriette Conte.

DES JOURNÉES ENTIÈRES DANS LES ARBRES (Whole Days in the Trees) by Marguerite Duras. A rich mother returns from the colonies and embarks on a futile scheme to make something of her worthless son. With Madeleine Renaud, Jean Desailly.

CHANT PUBLIC DEVANT DEUX CHAISES ÉLECTRIQUES (Public Song in Front of Two Electric Chairs) by Armand Gatti. Five acting troupes separated by time and place re-enact the passion of Sacco and Vanzetti. With Pia Colombo, Pierre Meyrand.

L'IDÉE FIXE (The Fixed Idea) by Paul Valéry. Stage version of the late author's literary dialogue in which two intellectuals exchange confidences on a Mediterranean holiday. With Pierre Fresnay, Julien Bertheau.

LA SOIF ET LA FAIM (Hunger and Thirst) by Eugène Ionesco. Ionesco's Everyman, Jean, leaves wife and family in search of an unknown ideal and ends up in a devilish embarrassment. With Robert Hirsch, Annie Ducaux, Jacques Eyser.

LA PROMENADE DU DIMANCHE (Sunday Morning Outing) by Georges Michel. Unconcerned about dangers that threaten mankind, an ostrich-like family attempts to brainwash a rebellious grandson and is left unperturbed even after his accidental death. With Alain Le Mottet, Rosette Zucchelli.

LES PARAVENTS (The Screens) by Jean Genet. A highly formalized and scabrously poetic evocation of the Algerian War of Independence and its fatal effect on patriot and colonizer alike. With Madeleine Renaud, Jean-Louis Barrault, Maria Casarès.

INTERESTING LIMITED RUNS OF NEW FRENCH PLAYS

MONSIEUR ALEXANDRE by Jean Cosmos. The rise and fall of a modern Volpone. With Pierre Hatet, André Haber, Jean Turpin.

COPAINS-CLOPANT (Clackety Pals) by Christian Kursner. A singer upsets the plans of a group of vacationers. With Christian Kursner, Chantal Simon.

LES BAS FONDS DE LA SOCIÉTÉ (Society's Lower Depths) by Henry Mounier. Black humour à la française. With Cathérine Pasteau, André Daguenet.

EL GRECO by Luc Vilsen. The clashes of the Spanish painter with the Inquisition. With Jean-Pierre Bernard, Hélène Sauvaneix.

LE SACRISTAIN BOSSU (The Hunchbacked Beadle) by Elie-Georges Berreby. A priest's conscience and a challenge thereto. With Marc de Georgi, Mireille Perry.

LA MUSICA by Marguerite Duras. A duologue for a couple whose marriage is on the rocks. With Claire Deluc, René Erouk.

POURQUOI PAS VAMOS? (Why Not Vamos?) by Georges Conchon. (D) An exiled South American dictator is recalled, with dreadful results. With Jacques Monod, Jean Le Poulain, Jacques Dufilho.

L'OPÉRA DU MONDE (The World's Opera) by Jacques Audiberti. Posthumous drama of a salesgirl and her post-atomic song. With Emmanuèle Riva.

EULOGE DE COURDOUE (Eulogy of Cordova) by Maurice Clavel. The second thoughts of St. Euloge. With Daniel Sarky, Elia Clermont.

LA CONVERSATION by Claude Mauriac. (D) Duras-like drama about 60 years in the life of a couple. With Reine Courtois, Nicolas Bataille.

VA ET VIENT (Come and Go) by Samuel Beckett. Private confidences of three women in limbo. With Madeleine Renaud, Simone Valère, Annie Bertin.

LA LACUNE (The Omission) by Eugène Ionesco. An eminent Academician's moral downfall on discovering a fatal error—his formal failure to graduate. With Pierre Bertin, Madeleine Renaud, Jean Desailly.

UN ENVOYÉ SPÉCIAL (A Special Envoy) by Jean Escoffier. (D) A journalist reports on his own father, who is a priest, their shared mistress and other experiences. With Jacques Harden.

LE COSMONAUTE AGRICOLE (The Cosmonaut Turned Farmer) and EDOUARD ET AGRIPPINE by René de Obaldia. Two of the author's "Impromptus" about a skyfarer who takes to the rustic life, and an elderly couple faced with the unexpected. With Pierre Baton, Roland Bertin, Josine Comellas.

LES IDOLES (The Idols) by Marc'O. Musical satire on show biz and the pop-singer racket. With Michèle Moretti, Bulle Ogier, Philippe Bruneau.

DIVINE FARCE by Jacques Gripari. An anti-religious satirical cabaret. With Christian Bouillette, Philippe Prince, Maurice Travail.

NOS FEMMES (Our Womenfolk) by Pierre-Alain Jolivet. (D) A 20th century satirical version of The Eumenides. With an anonymous cast.

LES BOUQUINISTES (The Bookstall Keepers) by Antoine Tudal. (D) Two quayside bookstall keepers decide too late to deal with a suspicious nearby angler. With Max Bozzoni, Michel Vitold.

POPULAR ATTRACTIONS

LES TEMPS DIFFICILES (Hard Times) by Edouard Bourdet. Comédie Française's revival of famous inter-war comedy. With Louis Seigner, Louise Conte.

DEUX ANGES SONT VENUES (Came Two Angels) by Albert Husson. Musical version of Husson's hit comedy *La Cuisine des Anges* (My Three Angels). With Roger Pierre, Jean-Marc Thibault, Evelyne Dandry.

SECRETISSIMO (Top Secret) by Marc Camoletti. A famous star caught in a spy scandal. With Danielle Darrieux, Jacques Duby, Jean Parédès.

LES ASSASSINS ASSOCIÉS (Murder Inc.) by Robert Thomas. Three country burghers plot to get rid of their wives. With Denise Grey, Henri Guisol.

MADAME PRINCESSE by Félicien Marceau. Two crooks, he young, she not so young, are thrown together and discover that cooperation pays dividends. With Marie Bell, Jean-Claude Brialy, Barbara Sommers.

RODOGUNE by Corneille. Comédie Française's new production of famous classic. With Simon Eire, Louise Conte.

LES SÉQUESTRÉS D'ALTONA (The Condemned of Altona) by Jean-Paul Sartre. Revival of famous drama of war guilt with original cast. With Serge Reggiani, Claude Dauphin.

CACHE-CACHE (Hide and Seek) by Henri de Monaghan. How a lawyer-dramatist chooses his characters. With Robert Murzeau, Maria-Rosa Rodriguez.

PEPSIE by Pierre-Edmond Victor (real name Pierette Bruno). To the dismay of his wife, a husband is helped in his career by a cabaret-hostess. With Pierette Bruno, Guy Tréjean, Angelo Bardi.

LA FOLLE DE CHAILLOT (The Madwoman of Chaillot) by Jean Giraudoux. Revival of Giraudoux' famous satire on capitalism. With Edwige Feuillère, Michel de Ré.

TA FEMME NOUS TROMPE (Your Wife's Unfaithful to Us) by Alexandre Breffort. The trials of an absurdist dramatist. With Maria Pacôme, Jean Tissier.

LA CALÈCHE (The Carriage) by Jean Giono. Revival of Giono's romantic tale of the rivalry of two enemies, in Napoleonic times, concerning a beautiful singer. With Pierre Vaneck, Pierre Brasseur, Maria Mauban.

L'ILLUSION COMIQUE (The Comic Illusion) by Corneille. Revival of Corneille's rare comedy drama of a father reunited with his lost son by sorcery. With Georges Riquier, Lucien Raimbourg, Georges Wilson, Loleh Bellon.

LA DAME DE CHEZ MAXIM'S (The Girl From Maxim's) by Feydeau. Revival of the famous farce about a cocotte entangled in a respectable family's plans to marry off the son and heir. With Zizi Jeanmaire, Pierre Mondy, Claude Gensac.

LA MAMMA by André Roussin. Revival of hit adaptation of Brancati's *Bel Antonio*. With Elvire Popesco.

LES JUSTES (The Righteous Ones) by Albert Camus. Revival of Camus' political thriller. With Danièle Delorme.

EN ATTENDANT GODOT (Waiting for Godot) by Samuel Beckett. Comic revival of Beckett's philosophical farce. With Jacques Serres, Jo Doumerg.

CE SOIR À SAMARCANDE (Tonight in Samarkand) by Jacques Deval. Revival of Deval's drama about the inescapability of death. With René Davy, Claudine Coster, Geneviève Page.

LE PRINCE TRAVESTI (The Prince Disguised) by Marivaux. Comédie Française's revival of a neglected comedy of a noble suitor for a countess's hand intercepted by an old flame. With Geneviève Casile, Micheline Boudet, Jacques Toja.

LA FIN DU MONDE (The World's End) by Sacha Guitry. Revival of Guitry's 1935 hit about a landlord's bid to revive his ruined fortunes. With Fernand Gravet, Denise Grey.

L'OEUF À LA COQUE (The Boiled Egg) by Marcel Franck. An aging widower takes a young wife. With Pierre Destailles, Jacqueline Jefford.

TOPAZE by Marcel Pagnol. Revival of 1928 comedy about an earnest schoolteacher with a civic conscience who takes over a crooked business. With Jacques Ardouin, Dominique Blanchar, A.M. Julien.

SOME AMERICAN PLAYS PRODUCED IN PARIS

ABSENCE OF A CELLO. With Eléonore Hirt, Michel Lonsdale, Marie Daems.

SUDDENLY LAST SUMMER. With Silvia Monfort.

OUR TOWN. With Fabrice Rouleau.

LUV. With Laurent Terzieff, Bernard Noël, Pascale de Boysson.

THE DUTCHMAN and THE SLAVE (played alternately in French and English). With Chantal Darget, Med Hondo, Gaby Sylvia and with Ruth Breuer, Joanne Alkalaitis.

NO, NO, NANETTE. With Cathy Albert.

JANUS. With Marie Dubois, Dominique Paturel.

THE OWL AND THE PUSSYCAT. With Magali Noël, Jean-Pierre Cassel.

THE CAINE MUTINY. With Jean Mercure.

THE DAY THE WHORES CAME OUT TO PLAY TENNIS. With the Egrégore Company of Montreal.

THE ANDERSONVILLE TRIAL. With Raymond Pellegrin, William Sabatier, Raymond Rouleau.

TELEMACHUS CLAY in English. With Ruth Brever, Alex Rebor.

SOME OTHER FOREIGN PLAYS PRODUCED IN PARIS

THEATER OF NATIONS SEASON included prizewinning Zeffirelli productions of Shakespeare's *Romeo and Juliet* and Verga's *La Lupa.*

AGNES BERNAUER by Hebbel. With Corinne Marchand. Later revived with Jacques Dumesnil, Tania Torrens.

THE CHANGELING by Middleton and Rowley. With Maryvonne Schiltz, Dominique Vilar.

THE TRAGEDY OF KING CRISTOPHE by Aimé Césaire. With the Toucan Company.

CAVIAR AND LENTILS by Scarnaci. With Rosy Varte, Madeleine Damien.

THE BOY FRIEND by Sandy Wilson. With Micheline Presle.

ANTONY AND CLEOPATRA by William Shakespeare. With Jacques Dacqmine, Maria Mauban, A.M. Julien.

THE LOVER and THE COLLECTION by Harold Pinter. With Delphine Seyrig, Michel Bouquet, Jean Rochefort.

DON JUAN IN HELL by George Bernard Shaw. With Pierre Brasseur, Martine Sarcey, Paul Meurisse, Jacques Dumesnil.

THE DAY OF THE TORTOISE by Garinei & Giovannini. With Annie Girardot, Philippe Nicaud.

THE CHERRY ORCHARD by Anton Chekhov. With Suzanne Flon, Pierre Tabard.

YVONNE, PRINCESS OF BURGUNDY by Witold Gombrowicz. With company of *Théâtre de Bourgogne.*

THE NIGHT-TRAIN by Herbert Reinecker. With Gabriel Cattand, Yves Vincent.

THE ZYKOVS by Gorki. With Danielle Ajoret, Toni Taffin.

THE KNIGHT OF THE BURNING PESTLE by Beaumont & Fletcher. With Jean-Baptiste Thierrée, Michèle Moretti.

A MIDSUMMER NIGHT'S DREAM by William Shakespeare. Jean-Paul Roussillon, Bernard Dhéran, Denise Noël.

THE WOMAN HORSE by Bertil Schütt. With Françoise Arnaud, André Lacombe.

I WANT TO SEE MYUSOV by Valentin Katayev. With Jacques Fabbri.

ORESTES by Alfieri. With Jean-Pierre Miquel.

ELECTRA by Sophocles. With Silvia Monfort.

DOCTOR GLASS by Hans Weigel. With Darry Cowl, Marie-France Mignal.

THE PROVINCIAL LADY by Turgenev. With Simone Valère.

THE IDIOT by Dostoevsky, adapted by André Barsacq. With Philippe Avron, Charles Denner, Cathérine Sellers.

THE TWO VENETIAN TWINS by Goldoni. With Dominique Houdart.

MISS JULIE by Strindberg. With Cathérine Pasteau, Jean-Claude Bouillaud.

THE STRONGER by Strindberg. With Fabiène Mai, Lise Donluca.

THE PENDULUM by Aldo Nicolaj. With Danielle Rocca, Jacques d'Aubrac.

OUT OF BOUNDS by Arthur Watkyn. With Michel Serrault, Henri Crémieux.

WOYZECK by Georg Büchner. With Wolfgang Mehring, Rosita Fernandez.

THE GOOD SOLDIER SCHWEIK by Milan Ketel, after Hasek. With Paul le Person.

STRIP-TEASE, KAROL and ON THE HIGH SEAS, three plays by Slawomir Mrożek. With Yves Robert.

PURPLE DUST by Sean O'Casey. With Georges Wilson, Pascal Mazzotti, Judith Magre.

MEASURE FOR MEASURE by William Shakespeare. With Gabrile Cattand, Nita Klein.

THE HYPOTHESIS by Robert Pinget. With Pierre Chabert.

THE GREAT CEREMONIAL by Fernando Arrabal. With Jean Negroni, Maria Machado.

PLUTUS by Aristophanes. With Roger Crouzet.

LIFE'S A DREAM by Calderon. With Spanish-speaking company of *Teatro Espagnol*, Madrid.

GEORGE DILLON by John Osborne and Anthony Creighton. With Gilberte Géniat, Yves-Marc Gilbert.

HOW A FILM SCENARIO IS BORN by Cesare Zavattini. With the company of the *Centro Dramatique de l'Est*.

DEIRDRE OF THE SORROWS by J.M. Synge. With the company of the *Grenier de Vilbert*.

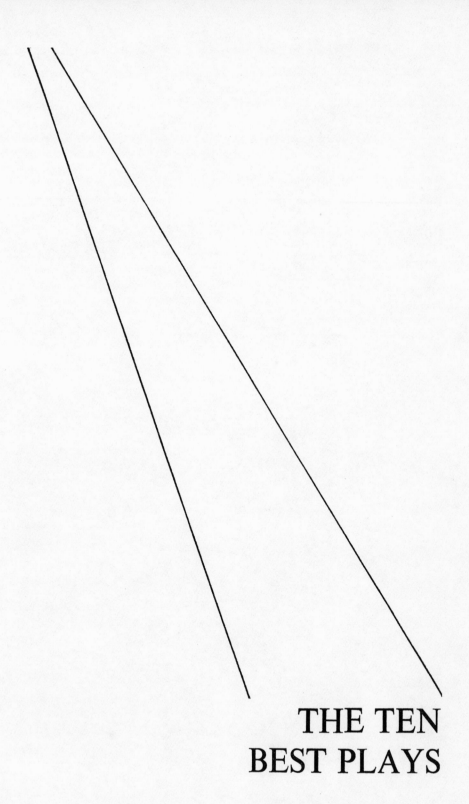

THE TEN
BEST PLAYS

GENERATION

A Play in Three Acts

BY WILLIAM GOODHART

Cast and credits appear on page 374

WILLIAM GOODHART was born and educated in New Haven, Conn. After his graduation from high school he entered Yale University, where his undergraduate career was interrupted by Army service in World War II. He went back to Yale and soon transferred to that university's graduate school of drama. He studied playwriting and design and after Yale Drama School he earned his living as a scenic artist and designer before he was able to concentrate upon writing. Generation *is the third of three scripts by Mr. Goodhart. Its appearance on Broadway is his first production of any kind.*

Mr. Goodhart is married and has three daughters. He lives in New York City, where he is now working on a new play after having finished a screenplay of Walker Percy's novel The Moviegoer.

INTRODUCTION BY THE PLAYWRIGHT

The great advantage of writing a preface is that it gives the playwright an opportunity—however forlorn—to gather up the ideas, insights, and other pet "values" he couldn't get into his play, and at least pile them up alongside it. There is also the opportunity to air his complaints. As for myself, I have such large, untidy collections in both categories that great self-discipline will be required, but I shall attempt, nevertheless, to limit myself to one complaint and try to relate it to its corresponding lost "value."

The objection that seems most worthy of discussion at this point is the inhibiting effect of our reigning Broadway theatrical style, Characterological Naturalism I call it this because what I'm concerned with is not a manner of staging, but an approach to character. It doesn't matter how abstract the setting or how spotty the lighting; if the characters are measured by a ruler that is exactly life size, and an average sized life at that, the result is a deadly Naturalism. It has all but suffocated our serious drama—or sent it reeling to the other extreme in the Absurdist manner—and it is well on the way to reducing satiric comedy to gagged-up impotence, for the Joke is the only un-natural dialogic convention acceptable today. But even then, although the audience manages to absorb jokes without breaking their involvement with the characters, the idea expressed in the joke is taken in its most superficial context, and what may have started out as social satire is received as mere entertainment.

Naturalism has reigned so long, and its effect is so insidious, that simple adherence to it stylistically is often mistaken for artistic integrity. I made this mistake myself and lost an important value. The original impetus to write *Generation* came from conversations with a friend who had seen a great deal of combat in Korea. I realized that his disillusion was different from other post-war disillusions I had known and read about. The young man in my play was originally a Korean veteran, and there used to be a scene in the first act in which he and the father watched an old war movie on TV and got into a violent argument about it. Unfortunately, it took years to get the play produced on Broadway, and as time passed the character in the play got older and older in real time. In order to have seen combat in Korea, he would have to be at least 33 by the time the play opened. This would have made him a different kind of character than I wanted, for he probably would have been nursing a sense of injustice for fifteen years and so crippling himself with self-pity that he would have been incapable of the forthright action required by the play. I could have frozen the time of the play at, say, 1960, but that would have made too big an issue of it. Or I could have made him a Viet Nam veteran, but that, although correct for the character, would have seemed like trying to exploit the newspaper headlines. I suppose I should have said, "Who counts?" and not worried about the age, but in a Naturalistic theater, *everybody* counts. That's one reason why Naturalism has lasted so long, it's so easy for everybody to be an expert. Well, anyway, I made the character younger and had him talk about an older brother who was a Korean veteran, but that didn't play naturally enough or something, and it got lost somewhere between New Haven and Boston, a typical sacrifice to the God of Naturalism.

The great danger of cutting something like this is that the values the lines contained are somehow retained in one's own mind even though they are no longer there for the audience. I didn't realize until later that I had lost much of the background support for the young man. It is apparently not generally realized that the Korean war also had a disillusioning effect upon those who were only teenagers at the time. It was the first time in history that the American good guys didn't beat the hell out of the baddies, and the film fans were really shaken up by it. Who ever heard of a John Wayne movie ending in a stalemate? It was enough to make you lose faith in *all* American institutions —and many decent young men did. I'm over-simplifing, of course, but we are conditioned by movies and TV from childhood, and the ideal of justice prevailing, which was made mandatory by the Production Code, is as much a part of us as the bone calcium from all that homogenized milk we drank. The disillusions of the Korean war, and the daily reports of corruptions in high places, obviously had a great deal to do with the social alienation, beatism, and the search for "cool" as a refuge from further disappointments that was so common among the moral and decent youth of the 1950s. The loss of one's faith in institutions is a profound loss that leaves one drifting and anxious as a motherless child.

When the rebels of the previous generation lost faith in an institution, they got together and tried to replace it with another institution which they were sure would work much better. They consequently find it very difficult to imagine what it's like not to believe in *any* institutions, and not even to share the Rationalistic philosophy on which institutions of all sorts are based. A World War II veteran, such as the father in my play, knows that collective action works because he still carries with him the heartening memory of *their* collective triumph over evil, and it gives him a subtle but very real sense of well-being. Unfortunately, World War II was the last time that important events worked out the way they're supposed to; Korea was a frustrating stalemate, the Russians are ahead in space, Viet Nam is a mess, the good guys haven't been winning lately.

To those over 35, these are just temporary reverses, but to anyone much younger, this is all they have known, and to many of them national pride seems to be just another advertising claim. Victory in World War II doesn't mean any more to them than victories in any previous wars. If they think of it at all, it's in terms of a movie star pulling out a grenade pin with his teeth, blowing up an eighty-ton tank with the tiny grenade, and thus saving a rifle squad made up of one representative of each minority group. In other words, the supportive values of one generation have simply not been passed down successfully to the next. A false idealization has intervened which has rendered it meaningless to a generation particularly sensitive to such distortions. I don't mean to put the blame on Hollywood, I just happen to be fascinated by this aspect of the matter; examples of similar failures by parents, teachers and statesmen are only too evident. One reason for this failure is that the older generation has lost faith too, not as much, perhaps, but enough. They can't admit this, of course, and the hypocrisy this engenders has cost them the respect of their children. This is particularly true of those clear-eyed young men who are determined to maintain their own personal integrity at all costs. Their desperate efforts are generally misunderstood, and they often seem to be splitting hairs too fine to be seen by others, but the maintainance of any sort of integrity in this society is a complex and often absurd undertaking. I like to feel, however, that this younger generation's disgust with a phony, idealized reality will lead to a more meaningful confrontation with an existential reality, for both generations.

I tried to show all this in my play, but I got hung up on the phony reality of Characterological Naturalism, and as I was thrashing around in that frantic goldfish bowl of tryouts and previews, trying to wrap up the whole mess in a fresh, natural-sounding, two-line joke, in character—the curtain went up.

WILLIAM GOODHART

Time: The present

Place: The studio-loft-apartment of Walter Owen in Lower
   Manhattan

ACT I

SYNOPSIS: Late one Saturday afternoon, the sun pours in through plate glass windows facing the street along the right wall of an L-shaped loft atop an old industrial building on Broome Street in New York City. This loft has been turned by hard work and imagination, but with little money, into an attractive photography studio and living area. The walls have been stripped down to their brick, and the furniture is simple and spare. A door at the toe of the L, downstage left, opens to the stairway. A couple of lights and a roll of no-seam paper at the top of the L, upstage right, indicate the professional use to which the area sometimes adapts itself.

> *At curtain rise, Walter Owen enters the front door carrying a suitcase. He is 30, rather intense, slightly long hair, and he wears a sweater under the jacket of his dark suit. He wears something unusual, however: a woman's necklace made of small pieces of bright blue glass. It is a beautiful necklace, and he doesn't seem to be self-conscious about wearing it. Jim Bolton enters behind Walter. He is 47, has a silvery crew-cut, but is vigorous and hearty. He is very well dressed in a suit and topcoat. As Walter stoops to put down the suitcase, his necklace swings out quite obviously, and he absently holds it back. Bolton tries to keep his eyes off of it, but it is clearly a factor in the rather strained atmosphere that exists between them.*

WALTER *(looking around the apartment):* Doris? . . . Doris? *(Crosses up left to the bathroom door, which is closed.)* Doris, your father is here! *(Hearing no response, he looks in.)* Hmn . . . *(He moves into the studio area.)*

BOLTON: Isn't she here?

> *He looks around at the apartment, seeming unaware of the fact that he is holding two dollar bills in his hand.*

WALTER: She must be down at the grocery store getting something for dinner.

BOLTON: Oh, well, I planned to take you uptown for a sort of belated wedding dinner, or something.

WALTER: You don't want to eat here?

BOLTON: Oh, certainly, certainly! I, uh, I didn't know Doris could cook.

WALTER: I taught her how.

BOLTON: *(glancing at the necklace):* Oh. *(Becomes aware of the money in his hand.)* Listen, will you please take this cab fare?!

But Walter will have none of it. Bolton suggests they have a drink, but to Walter's embarrassment he has none of *that* in the house, either. Bolton tries to ease the situation by asking his son-in-law to call him "Jim," but Walter is waiting to see what name turns up naturally.

Bolton seizes the opportunity while Walter is putting away his coat to sneak the two dollars onto the table. He notes the expense in a little book. Bolton makes an effort at small talk.

BOLTON: . . . nice big place you have here. I see what you mean about space. *(Crosses to the window.)* I suppose this, uh, industrial area isn't any rougher than other neighborhoods, and, uh, once you get used to the idea of living in a loft building, and the smell of that hallway, then you, uh, have all this space . . . Now that I think of it, isn't it against the law to live in a loft building?

WALTER: I'm an A.I.R. . . . Artist In Residence. It's a special Building Department permit for artists to live in their studios.

BOLTON: I thought you were a photographer?

WALTER: Well, there *is* an Art of Photography, you know . . . at least that's my story, and I'm, uh, stuck with it.

Bolton wonders where Doris can be. Doris's mother hasn't been told yet about the marriage (she has social aspirations and might be upset). But Bolton has always prided himself on his broad-mindedness, his closeness to Doris. He is glad she got married to a nice young fellow. The only thing is, "I never imagined the bridegroom would be wearing a blue necklace. . . ."

WALTER: . . . uh, well, of course I didn't wear it at the wedding.

BOLTON: Oh, well, *that's* good.

WALTER: Naturally, I wore my *pearls* then.

> *Bolton stares.*

No, I'm only kidding.

BOLTON: This is just a joke then, huh?

WALTER *(fingering the beads):* Well, uh, no, not really. I like these, actually. I came across all these great little pieces of blue glass—a friend of mine is a glass-blower—and I made this necklace for Doris.

BOLTON: Does she ever get to wear it?

WALTER: Sure, this is the first time I've ever worn it.

BOLTON: You mean you're wearing it in *my* honor?

WALTER: In a way, but not really. When I was getting up this morning, it was on the bureau, and the light was really beautiful on it. So I said to Dorry, "Boy, this necklace is really great; I think I'll wear it today." She laughed and said, "Why not? All the primitive warriors wear them." So I decided to wear it today. I mean, if my masculinity depends on not wearing a little string of glass beads, well, you know, forget it. But *then,* we remembered that you were coming in today, and so here I am, up two minutes, and already I'm caught up in this ridiculous dilemma. I told her, if she had put her damn jewelry away at night, this wouldn't have happened!

Smiles at his own unreasonableness.

BOLTON: Well, you seem to have solved your dilemma.

WALTER: Well, having *felt* that I wanted to wear it, I had to be true to myself and wear it.

BOLTON: I see, true to yourself, yes, very good . . .

Bolton sided with Doris against her mother when Doris wanted to come to New York, and he boasts that he himself has "a touch of the beatnik." Walter disavows any connection with beatniks, he and Doris are just themselves.

Walter continues to refuse reimbursement for the taxi fare, even though Bolton, winking, indicates that it will be written off as a tax-deductible business expense.

> *Doris Owen enters the front door. She is an attractive girl of 25, with a serene, intelligent face. She is wearing Walter's raincoat, which is too big for her, and carrying a bag of groceries.*

Doris embraces her father. She takes off the raincoat and stands proudly before him.

BOLTON *(as if she might not have noticed):* You're going to have a baby!

DORIS: I know.

BOLTON: When?!

DORIS: Oh, anytime now . . .

BOLTON: Well, uh, why didn't you call me before, when you first got married?

DORIS: I did.

BOLTON: You did. Yesterday. You just got married yesterday?

DORIS: No, no, we've been married since Tuesday.

They wanted to wait until after the baby was born, but they were so much in love that they threw caution to the winds and got married before the birth.

Bolton wonders what Doris's mother will think—what their friends will think.

BOLTON *(he sits, rubbing his stomach):* Ooh. That bitch of an ulcer has just been *waiting* for something like this to happen! I can see those rows of yoghurt containers already! Oh-h!

DORIS: Oh, come on, Daddy, you've never had any respect for those people, why bother with them now?

BOLTON: I *have* to bother with them. I *live* with them. They're all over me! . . . Oh, sure, this is just a lark for you. What do your friends care how long you've been married. They're probably too stoned to count anyway.

WALTER *(who has been listening with growing irritation):* Now wait a minute, it's not our fault if you're hung up in Chicago.

BOLTON: I am not hung up in Chicago!

WALTER: If you can't enjoy your daughter's child, you're hung up *somewhere!*

BOLTON: Godammit, I *am* enjoying it! *(Turning to Doris.)* I am! *(Turning back to Walter.)* It's just that I don't like to have a lot of smug jerks snickering behind my back! *(Turning back to Doris.)* And I really think it's very inconsiderate of you, Doris, to embarrass your mother and I socially like this.

WALTER: Well, I'm sorry our child is a cause of social embarrassment to you. I'll speak to him about it. *(Cups his hands and shouts down at the baby.)* Hey, you, did you hear that?! You're a cause of social embarrassment! Your Grandfather hates you!

Bolton protests, he will love the baby, only . . . it would have been better if it had been born nine months later. Walter, consistently antagonistic, argues that a later child would be a different child (this one was conceived while watching TV). "The point is," he tells his father-in-law, "you can't wish for a later birth without wishing this child dead, and how do you know he won't develop a cure for the atom bomb?"

Walter suggests that the child could be put in an orphanage for several years, they could hide its existence from Chicago until a final big scene . . . finally Bolton realizes he is being kidded. Doris sends Walter out for yoghurt and confronts her father alone.

Doris comments that Walter and her father are a lot alike, they both take things very seriously.

BOLTON: Don't ask me what I think of him, because I'll only say something I'll regret later.

DORIS: You haven't exactly been at your best either, you know. You don't care *that* much what people in Chicago will say.

BOLTON: I know, I know. But there's something about him . . . ! Oh, hell, it's not just him . . . *All* you kids act so damn superior! It's like . . . well, it's like your whole generation *knows something* I don't know about.

DORIS: . . . *This* is my generation.

BOLTON: What do you mean?

DORIS: Oh, I was just thinking that generation originally meant giving birth and all, so this is my generation, and I'm your generation, and you're . . .

BOLTON: Never mind! It's trouble enough already!

Doris tells her father Walter considers it an honor that she is going to have his baby, and Doris loves Walter. Gradually Bolton is getting ready to accept this status quo, but he is worried about what his hypercritical wife will think.

DORIS: I'm so glad mother and I won't be fighting any more.

BOLTON: What's the matter? Why won't you be fighting?

DORIS: What's there to fight about? I have everything I want now. And when she gets to know Walter . . .

BOLTON: *This* is all you want?!

> She nods.

You mean to tell me that after all those goddam schools, all you want is this rotten old, broken-down, rat-infested . . .

DORIS: We're getting a dog that's practically a Scotty. They're wonderful ratters.

BOLTON: My God, you mean it *is* rat-infested?

DORIS: Well, just a little.

Bolton refers to Walter as a beatnik, and in her turn Doris denies this description. Walter is no beatnik, his parents were respectable folk (they were older and are now dead).

Bolton tries to cheer himself up with thoughts of giving Doris and Walter a nice fat wedding present, but it seems there is nothing the young couple really needs. They are self-sufficient. Walter made all the furniture himself.

BOLTON: . . . He's a carpenter too huh?

DORIS (*coming out with some glasses*): Oh, he can do almost anything like that. Everything we have is hand made. Walter hates anything machine made. See these glasses? A friend of ours made them.

BOLTON (*eyeing the irregularly shaped goblets dubiously, takes one*): Yeah, they look uh, hand-made all right.

> Bolton puts the glass down on the table, but he can't get it to stand
> upright, and is afraid to let go of it.

I can't get this glass to stand up.

DORIS: Oh, yes, well that one you have to lean against something.

> She leans it against something.

It's all right when it's half full.

BOLTON: Say, listen, how about if I just give you money, and you buy whatever you want.

> Doris hesitates again.

Now don't tell me he prints his own money!

> Doris laughs, but doesn't indicate acceptance.

What's the matter? You must need money!

DORIS: We don't need money. Walter does very well. He has a nice little photographic business going. I'll show you some of his work after dinner.

It seems they want nothing that Bolton can give them. He changes the subject and wants to know what the doctor has to say about the birth. At this point *Doris* changes the subject; she hopes their first dinner together will be a pleasant one.

Walter comes back. A customer met him on the street and paid him unexpectedly, so he has brought home half a gallon of wine. He fills the glasses.

WALTER: . . . See! The label was copyrighted in 1959, an excellent year!
He and Doris laugh.

BOLTON: I'll drink a toast to the baby, anyway.
They all get set for the toast. Bolton raises his glass.
Well, to the Little Stranger . . . *(Then to Walter.)* and to the Big Stranger . . .
(Then to Doris.) and to the . . . Sudden Stranger. *(He drinks deeply.)*

Bolton goes to wash up for supper, and Doris and Walter exchange a few fast comments. Walter decides Bolton is "hostile." They are keeping a secret from him, and it is Walter who will decide whether or not they will tell him later.

It will ease the tension, Doris believes, if Walter takes off the necklace during dinner. Walter does so, but when Bolton comes back and remarks "What happened to the primitive warrior?" Walter wants to put the necklace right back on.

Doris diverts Walter's attention by asking him to take pictures of her father. Walter gets set for candids. He arms himself with a camera and instructs his father-in-law to act normally. Bolton, of course, becomes more and more self-conscious as Walter does a couple of practise flashes.

Doris serves Bolton a potato-chips-and-yoghurt dip, and Walter maneuvers to get a picture of him with his mouth full. Despite Bolton's evasions, and to Bolton's dismay, he manages to do it.

Doris is proud of Walter's work and wants to show her father how good a photographer Walter is. She shows Bolton a book of Walter's photographs with poetry.

BOLTON *(reading the title):* "Eleven Kinds of Petulant Whines"! Yours or other people's?

WALTER: Both.

DORIS *(reading from the book):*
All the mating cries are shrill
In this, our summer fester-ville
Of Love . . .
For we are the sallow men, tinted with Tanfastic,
For we are the callow men, bristling with bombastic,

For we are the marshmallow men, peter bog soldiers
Drastic . . .
Bolton looks up, baffled.
Isn't that a riot! He has another funny one about impotence in here too . . .
And there's one that's supposed to be me when Walter first met me . . . it's
about this girl who is *outraged* by the fact that even though she loves and
understands J.D. Salinger, she still might get killed by the atom bomb . . .
She is looking for it in the book and comes across another.
Oh, wait! Here's another one of my favorites . . . we made a song out of this.
I'll sing it for you. Listen . . . *(To Walter.)* Gimme a thing on that geetar,
podner!

WALTER: For what? "Impo-tenting Tonight"?

DORIS: "Pianola"

WALTER: Oh, Dorrie . . .

DORIS: Come on, this is supposed to be a party, isn't it? Gee whiz! What
a couple of stiffs I'm stuck with!

WALTER *(reluctantly getting down the guitar):* What is it, "C"?

DORIS: Yes.

> *Walter strikes the key note, and Doris hums a little to get the pitch
> and then launches into the following in an old Al Jolson piano roll
> style, with a touch of rock and roll. Sings.*

I put my IBM card in that ole pianola,
And it played out my whole life song!
I never knew-ew-ew-ew I was a rock and roller,
Till that melody came along (Yeah, yeah, yeah!)
My Rorschach was swinging,
My I.Q. was sweet,
My Conformity Index had a ricky-tick beat,
When I put my IBM card in that ole pianola,
And it played out my whole life,
It played out my whole life,
It played out my whole life song! (Yeah, yeah-yeah yeah!)

BOLTON *(amused and pleased):* Hey! Hey, take it easy there!
He laughs and returns to the book.

Bolton is really impressed with Walter's work. He offers to use his influence
in the advertising world to throw photographic business Walter's way. Politely, Walter turns down Bolton's offer of help (Walter wants to make his
own way) and this is of course rubs salt in Bolton's wounded feelings. Bolton
strikes back with a comment that any photographer "can do this kind of stuff."

WALTER: But do they *do* it?

BOLTON *(sarcastically):* Well, there's one chimpanzee that . . .

WALTER: No, I mean, have you personally ever seen any of these guys'
pictures like this . . .
Flips open his book for Bolton to see one of the pictures.

BOLTON *(glancing at the picture):* When a man is flying all over the place, making two or three hundred thousand a year, he doesn't have time to hang around waiting for some neurotic tuba player to throw up!

WALTER: Well, I'm relieved to hear that. I wouldn't want any of those guys horning in on *my* racket. No pun intended.

DORIS *(coming back to try to smooth things):* Well, maybe later on, Daddy . . .

But it's too late; they are heading for an inevitable collision. Bolton accuses Walter of having a stereotype image of advertising, and Walter counter-accuses Bolton of having a stereotype image of beatniks (though Doris again disclaims any kinship with beatniks).

WALTER: Do you believe in the Golden Rule?

BOLTON *(uncomfortable with the camera on him):* Yes . . .

WALTER *(lowering the camera):* Well, I don't want to do ads unto others, because I *hate* it when others do ads unto me.

    Doris laughs.

BOLTON: Well, I hate those hard-sell ads myself. Who doesn't! The kind of thing I'm talking about is when you take a clearly superior product, like most of my accounts, and then build a very tasteful campaign, simply explaining *beautifully* the virtues of the product.

WALTER: That's the kind I hate the most! That's the kind, the really dangerous kind that can *ruin* you! They can hook you right into the rat race! Boy, I can just see myself buying a nice new Chevvy, driving out of the showroom happy as a clam, putting on the radio, and Bang! A *Buick* commercial comes on and ruins my Chevvy! You guys are after us night and day with that stuff! You never let anyone *cherish* anything!

BOLTON: That happens to be what holds our whole economy together!

WALTER: I know it and it's horrible! The whole system is so *horrible!*

Doris comes between them. Bolton, calming down, declares he's moving away from direct selling into public relations and industrial accounts. He shows Walter a company pamphlet he has just written, and of which he is rather proud. Walter reads it.

WALTER: My God, listen to this! *(He reads to Doris.)* "So strong was his devotion to the Company, that he didn't have a single absence in the thirty-two years from the day of his employment as stock-boy, to the day of his self-defenestration as president!" Self-defenestration!

DORIS: What does it mean?

WALTER: It means that after thirty-two years of perfect attendance, he jumped out the window!

Even Doris objects to this euphemism, but Bolton defends it as preserving the company image even though it's "fudging a little." Bolton feels that he deserves a modicum of respect, if only because he's a decent person—with a good army record. Walter scoffs at military heroism (he has done his two years and he has a brother who suffered the frustrating experience of wartime military service).

Bolton muses about Madison Avenue having replaced Wall Street as the principal target of scorn. He confesses that he really wanted to be a doctor. This triggers Walter, who despises doctors and says so loudly and clearly.

BOLTON: You don't have any respect for anybody, do you?

WALTER: Yeah, you should have been a doctor, you're just the type. I can just see you as the head of some huge hospital combine that's just about ready to take over the whole government, and you're out making your traditional annual house-call, you're in this beaten-up old horse and buggy, and they got this machine blowing fake snow on you. It's a kind of semi-religious, patriotic parade ceremony. And you're going along, sprinkling LSD25 on the delirious crowd, which is being held back by your uniformed male nurses with their electrified Caducesei. Bzzt-bzzt! Bzzt-bzzt! Yeah, you'd make a marvelous Doctor Dictator.

BOLTON (indignantly): I happen to be for socialized medicine!

WALTER: Oh, beautiful, beautiful! Throw out their rotten institution, and stick in your rotten institution—they're all the same dopey bureaucrats and power-mad crooks hiding behind you Public Relations guys!

BOLTON: Goddamit, if you don't believe in anything, what the hell's the idea marrying my daughter and starting a family!?

WALTER: Because that's the only thing I'm sure of! It's obvious that we're supposed to pair off like this, a man and a woman, that's the way we're *made!* And that's why I distrust any group bigger than two: we're not made *that* way!

BOLTON (crossing angrily to Doris at the stove): You've married an Anarchist, you know that, don't you?!

DORIS (cooking desperately): I know, Daddy, but can't we have a nice dinner anyway?

While Walter tosses the salad, Bolton rants and raves that Walter and his ilk are destroyers, while he, Bolton, is trying to repair, to make things better. If so, Walter argues, then it is hypocritical to cheat on the income tax.

Doris asks them to sit down and tells her father calmly that they aren't rejecting *him,* they're only rejecting his offer of money. But Bolton can't ignore his daughter financially, and he judges maybe that was part of Walter's plan.

BOLTON: . . . You *know* I'll keep after you until I force you into the System! And then you can enjoy being rich without feeling guilty! You married my daughter so you'd be *forced* into the System!

WALTER: I will not be forced into the System under any circumstances!

BOLTON: You're in it already! Like those Holy Men who vow not to kill anything, and with every breath, they kill millions of living organisms in the air! You couldn't *exist* without the System, the water, gas, electric, even the doctors! Your child will fall into their hands like everybody else's!

WALTER: No, it won't! Because I'm delivering it right here myself! (He catches himself.) Oh, dammit, I told him!

DORIS: Oh, don't worry, darling, he won't say anything.

BOLTON *(recovering his voice): Won't say anything?!*

DORIS *(sharply):* Daddy, if you do anything to spoil this, I'll never speak to you again! I mean that!

BOLTON: Do you actually expect me to stand by and let you do an insane thing like that?!

DORIS *(smiling at him):* No, don't stand by—boil water!

She tugs him down. Stunned, he sits slowly, as Doris beams happily over their nice dinner. Curtain.

ACT II

At curtain rise Bolton is alone on the stage with a window open. He leans out and calls down to a friend on the street. He signals the way up to the loft.

Stan Herman enters. He is about the same age as Bolton, but cheerful, laconic and relaxed.

STAN *(fondly):* Jim! How are ya, buddy!

BOLTON *(upset, quickly closes the door):* Why did you come down here in that big Caddy, and with MD plates, yet?

STAN *(taken aback):* It's my car.

BOLTON: But I told you, I don't want anyone to know you're a doctor!

STAN: I thought you were kidding! I have to drive a big Caddy with MD plates; what do you think all that Latin on a doctor's diploma says?

Doris and Walter have gone to a hootenanny, giving Bolton the chance to tell his troubles to his obstetrician-friend, Stan Herman (who feels that Bolton should calm down; things aren't so bad; after all Walter and Doris got married).

Stan advises against a home delivery and wants to examine Doris in his office; Bolton, still overwrought, makes Stan realize that he has no control over the situation. Still Stan refuses to panic. Childbirth is a natural and normal function, even in odd circumstances.

Stan judges that once the delivery starts Walter will holler for help. But Bolton, with grudging respect, doubts that Walter is the kind to "chicken out." Stan looks over the medical textbooks which Walter has studied. He approves.

STAN: . . . "DeLee's Obstetrics." Boy, this takes me back.

BOLTON: I *thought* it looked old! Completely out of date, huh?

STAN: Well, not really. Female anatomy hasn't changed much lately. *(His attention is caught by a piece of paper used as a bookmark.)* Hmn . . . Say, does this boy seem particularly depressed or morbid?

BOLTON: No . . . why?

STAN: Well, he has rather an odd note scribbled on here. "Said the president to his V.P., I'll push you and you push me, on that Great Self-Defenestration Day."

BOLTON: Oh, that son of a . . . !

Bolton wants to know what boiling water is used for at delivery time and can hardly believe it is only used for washing everything (and maybe making instant coffee). They discuss going out to a bar to have a drink, but Bolton can't leave the apartment. He has asked a young lawyer from his agency to stop by. The lawyer used to date Doris, but that's not the reason he has been asked over; he may be needed if Bolton decides to take legal action to save his daughter.

Bolton is so upset that Stan suspects he had a falling-out with his son-in-law. No, Bolton insists, he didn't mind arguing with Walter, even about advertising. . . .

STAN: Advertising! You argued about advertising?!
BOLTON: Yeah.
STAN: How?! You mean he's *for* it?
BOLTON: No, he *hates* it!
STAN: Well, so do you, don't you?
BOLTON: Sure, but he won't grant me that! He doesn't believe I'm trying to improve things from within!
STAN: Oh. Are you?
BOLTON: Certainly! It's just that, uh, well, you know how it is. . . .

Stan is amused by Bolton's pretense. Organized liberal boring-from-within is 1940s thinking, says Stan, it's out of date in this era of young swingers who use Saran Wrap for contraceptives (it doesn't work too well, Stan admits). And hating advertising is also out of date, it's 1950s thinking. Today, you hate the telephone company and treat advertising with amused contempt.

Bolton is tired of amused contempt, and of trying to be understanding. He's angry. He must help prevent his daughter's death, even if anything that goes wrong is blamed on "my defective boiled water."

Stan warns Bolton that his daughter wants a beautiful experience as well as a mechanical birth, but Bolton can think only of the dangers.

BOLTON (pressing hard): She could die right there in that room, couldn't she?
STAN (reluctantly): Yes.
BOLTON: Then why are you for it?
STAN (uncomfortably): I'm not, Jim, I'm *not*. But this baby is probably the most important event of her life so far, and now that I see how committed they are, the psychological momentum they've generated with all these preparations, I realize that if you lose control of yourself, and mess things up, she will never forgive you. I know you told me that before, but you don't really believe it. Well, you'd better believe it. Pregnant young women, I know about —*she will never forgive you!*

The doorbell rings. Thinking that it must be the newlyweds returning, Bolton urges Stan to try not to look so much like a doctor. Stan turns his lapels inward and tries to look like a hipster.

Bolton opens the door. It is only Winston (Winn) Garand, a good-looking, deferential young lawyer from the ad agency. Winn takes Stan for a hipster, but Bolton introduces him as "Dr. Herman." Stan's feelings are hurt that his disguise was blown, but he perks up when he finds that Winn has brought along a bottle of Scotch.

Winn explains to Bolton, painstakingly and in spite of joking by Stan, that Bolton has no legal right to interfere with his daughter's plans about the baby. Bolton, frustrated, even draws the tilting glass when Stan pours the drinks. He feels there must be *something* he can do. But legally there is nothing. The System seems to be all on Walter's side.

Well . . . Winn advises, there is a judge who owes the agency a favor. Maybe this judge could return the favor and have the unborn child declared a Ward of the Court and have Doris ordered into a hospital.

BOLTON: Yes. Well, uh, of course, they wouldn't like that . . .

WINN: Under the circumstances, sir, that would hardly be a factor.

BOLTON: No, no, I suppose not. What I mean is, well, uh, you see in that case the baby would really be, uh, *literally* taken by the System, I mean, with a vengeance . . .

WINN: What system?

BOLTON: Well, uh, *The* System. The Establishment, the Government and uh all that. I mean, that's my only objection . . .

WINN (pleasantly): Oh, I see. I didn't realize you objected to the System.

BOLTON: Well, I don't! I don't! In fact, uh, isn't this judge out of line a bit?

WINN (reassuringly): Oh, don't worry, sir, there's no problem fudging that, it's quite standard.

BOLTON: I see, well, it's very comforting to know he's ready to, uh, do that. Very comforting. Thank you, Winn, for, uh, it. (He looks acutely uncomfortable.) Uh, what do you think, Stan?

> Drink in hand, Stan has been upstage idly leafing through Walter's book of poems. Now he picks up the book.

STAN (blandly): Well, I'll just let the Frame-ee speak for himself. (Reads.)
The Soul of Man,
Despite his pride,
Is rather odd,
A toy balloon
Blown up by God,
Or, strictly speaking,
The air inside,
And *that* is leaking.
He raises his glass to toast.
To poets and young lovers, wherever you are! . . .

They're good for business, Stan adds. Bolton, on the defensive, protests that he hasn't made up his mind yet what action to take.

Stan is for talking to Walter; letting him put on a surgeon's gown and assist at the delivery, if he wants to play doctor. Bolton convinces Stan that the problem goes deeper than that. Walter *hates* doctors.

Bolton toys with the judge strategy. Winn makes him see that if they are going to use the judge it must be done suddenly and without warning.

A patient telephones Stan (he has left this number for emergencies) and Stan disposes of the problem. Meanwhile, Bolton is thinking: maybe the best way to subdue a rebel is to make him rich. If he can only persuade some editor to praise Walter's book and make much of him. . . . "Once he starts worrying about needing a haircut, he's finished!"

Bolton will arrange to have *Cutlass Magazine* express interest in Walter's book (Bolton's agency buys *Cutlass*'s center ad spread).

WINN: Uh, sir, I wouldn't advise getting the agency any more involved than it is now.

BOLTON: Than it is *now?!*

WINN: Well, sir, since *you* are involved, the agency is involved, and scandal is so insidious that . . .

BOLTON: Scandal!

WINN *(as pleasant as ever):* Well, sir, if this effort with *Cutlass* should fail, and it *does* seem like a very long shot, then with effective legal action postponed until Tuesday, there is the very real possibility of a serious obstetrical accident, and the newspapers might not suppress it properly because of its entertainment value—you know, a child conceived out of wedlock, beatniks refusing medical aid until it's too late, prominent Chicago advertising man accomplice before the fact—and the nature of your institutional accounts is such that . . .

BOLTON *(who has been grimly dialing the phone during the above speech):* I *know* the nature of my institutional accounts. *(Into phone.)* Hello, Ozzie, this is Jim Bolton . . . Fine, Oz, how are you, pal? I'm in town and I need some *personal* help . . . No, no, no girls. My, uh, son-in-law, I guess you'd call him, has written a book of some great sort of beatnik poetry with pictures . . . yeah, drug on the market, yes . . . well, sometimes your center spread is a drug on the market too, Oz . . . Well, this doesn't *feel* like me either, but I'm in a bad thing here . . . Well, I want to take one of your editors to dinner . . . Who? . . . Have him down here by seven o'clock tonight . . . Tonight, Oz, *tonight* . . .

Stan will have dinner with them, pretending to be just an old Army buddy of Bolton's (which in fact he was)—but in the meantime he has some errands to do, and he leaves, not before characterizing Winn lightly as "a polite sonofabitch."

Winn reports that they have investigated Walter and found a good service record (but no combat like Stan and Bolton) and no trouble with the police. Winn is a very efficient operative.

Offstage, Doris and Walter are heard singing "On that Great Self-Defenestration Day," coming closer. They sing two verses and then burst into the apartment, ignoring Bolton and Winn as they sing the final verse.

WALTER & DORIS *(sing):*
> On that Great Self-Defenestration Day,
> On that Great Self-Defenestration Day,
> We'll be happy as we can be,
> With the System gone, we'll all be free!
> On that Great Self-Defenestration Day-e-e-e-e-ah-a-a-a-a!

> *At the end of the song, Walter's voice slides into the fading scream of a falling man, as he tilts forward and falls into Doris's arms. They laugh happily.*

BOLTON *(enraged, he bursts out as soon as they stop singing):* Oh, yeah? Well, what about the Supreme Court?!

DORIS: Oh, Daddy! Please don't . . .

BOLTON: Let him answer! They're an institution, aren't they?!

WALTER: So?

BOLTON *(pointing his finger triumphantly):* You *admire* what they've done for integration! Admit it! Hah! Hah!

WALTER: I can tell you one thing, if one of *them* ever sells out, you can just. . . .

Bolton and Walter have locked horns again; meanwhile, Doris sees Winn, and the two greet each other. Doris tries to introduce Winn to her husband. Bolton is throwing UNICEF at Walter as still another benevolent institution.

Winn greets Walter cordially, congratulating him on his marriage, like a good loser. But Walter takes an instant dislike to Winn, who then picks up his briefcase and heads for a graceful exit. On the way out, Winn tells Bolton that he has been transferred from the legal department to public relations. His account, Bolton learns as he sees him out, is the agency itself (which disturbs Bolton because it might mean Winn is here as an agency fixer, not just as a subordinate).

During Bolton's brief absence, Doris has a labor pain. They are five minutes apart now, and Walter wants to get ready.

As Bolton returns, Doris identifies Winn as one of her family's list of Eligible Suitors. Bolton identifies him as part of a scheme to get Walter's book published. Instinctively, Walter shies away from the thought of receiving help from "an organization creep carrying an attache case on a Sunday afternoon."

BOLTON: Oh, come on now, Walter, that's Fifties thinking. The fashionable attitude today is amused contempt.

> *Walter is somewhat taken aback. Bolton presses his advantage.*
You know, I don't think you realize how old-fashioned you've become—the village poet with the guitar—hating the System—man, that's *over.*

WALTER: What the hell, am I in some kind of originality contest or something?! I'm not trying to live up to some Public Relations image of myself! I don't care how unfashionable something is if it *feels* right to *me!*

BOLTON *(pleasantly):* Well, if you're so big with the instinctive approach, why don't you wait to see what my help *feels* like before you reject it? You can't *feel* in advance, you know.

DORIS: I think he's got you, Walter.
BOLTON: Why don't you give it a try?
WALTER: Because the idea of *trying* it *feels* terrible.

Walter agrees to try, and it is a little victory for Bolton. Doris starts to tell her father that the baby is coming, but Bolton is intent on pressing his advantage. Gently, he argues for a hospital. He calls on their instinct for protecting the young. He is tolerant of their views but points out that parents often must sacrifice everything, even their convictions, for their children.

Equally gently, Doris tells her father that they refuse to make sacrifices for their child because they do not want it to feel guilty later when it will learn of the debt of sacrifice and know it cannot make amends.

Bolton warns them that sheer love for their child will change all their notions—they'll get theirs in their turn. This is an expression of parental love that brings tears to Doris' eyes. She tells her father, tenderly, that she is going to have the baby—right now. All Bolton's self-possession vanishes.

BOLTON *(starting to panic):* Come on! We've got to get her to a hospital! *(He starts out, stops.)* Wait! I'll call first!
     He moves toward the phone, but Walter blocks his way. He stops.
Now listen! I've had enough of this nonsense!
DORIS: *Daddy!*
     The sound of her voice turns him around.
You promised you wouldn't spoil this! You promised me!
BOLTON *(without thinking):* Yes, but I didn't mean it!
DORIS: You didn't mean it?!
BOLTON: Well, I . . .
DORIS: But you promised me! I've always believed you, you're my father! What else didn't you mean?
BOLTON: If he won't protect you, I have to! Any way I can!
DORIS: Daddy, don't force me to choose between you and Walter!
BOLTON *(after a long pause):* How am I supposed to boil this water?

Doris hugs her father, while Walter goes to make the bedroom ready. Doris has another contraction. Bolton gets an idea; he pretends that they will need cigars, lots of cigars. He phones a "wholesaler," Stan Herman, but Stan (the doctor) is not at his office. The nurse at the other end of the phone conversation is obviously confused by all this camouflaging talk. Something she tells Bolton makes him grab his coat and run out to find his "cigars."

WALTER: Boy, that's a PR man for you, the first thing he thinks of is handing out cigars!
DORIS *(bewildered and suddenly rather afraid):* I *wish* he hadn't run off and left us like this . . .
     Walter touches her reassuringly, and drawing strength from him, she says:
We didn't need any help nine months ago, why should we need it now?
     They embrace. The curtain falls.

ACT III

At curtain rise, Walter is stringing clotheslines across the room upstage. Doris is lying on the sofa, having changed into a white terrycloth robe. She is breathing in a special way she has studied, and it is working fine. The contractions are coming one a minute. Walter is nervous, at concert pitch.

The doorbell rings—it is not Bolton ("He looked to me like a man who had chickened out and was headed for the nearest bar," Walter comments), but Ken Powell. Ken introduces himself, and Walter and Doris cannot help being impressed when they hear he is fiction editor of *Cutlass Magazine* and interested in Walter's work. They're very hip at *Cutlass*.

Walter gives Ken his manuscript and goes to make Ken a drink. Ken compliments Walter on his pictures and describes *Cutlass* as "a magazine for intellectuals who like girls." He turns to one of Walter's poems.

KEN *(opening to a poem at random):* Well, let's see . . . "Pitfalls of Youth." Good subject! Most of our readers are young-thinking men, and they look to us for guidance. We have a deep moral responsibility to be up-to-the-minute. *(Reads.)* "Pitfalls of Youth" . . .

If in your youth, you struggle free,
And even once live naturally,
Then later, when you fail to make it,
You won't be cool enough to fake it.
After a pause.

Your work has a fine old Ogden Nash quality, but, uh, there's a certain pessimistic note here that our readers would find discouraging. I mean, they like something more inspiring like, say, "If you can't make it, fake it!" See? Upbeat! *(Snapping his fingers.)* This is nice, but it needs a little work, it's not inspiring enough.

Bolton dashes into the apartment, out of breath with frustration (obviously he hasn't been able to fetch Dr. Herman). He is over-cordial to Ken and name-drops the center ad spread in *Cutlass,* which sets Ken to reading again.

Bolton explains to Walter that the "cigars" will be over later—the "wholesaler" is delayed by an emergency.

Bolton and Ken discuss Walter's poems. Bolton suggests that *Cutlass* run a biography of Walter with all the trimmings including color pictures (an idea which seems to captivate Walter and Doris), but Ken is having none of it. Ken explains: ". . . as an editor, I am a bridge—an intellectual bridge, if you will—between writer and reader. I have to help the author get his neurosis synchronized with the audience's neurosis so that this magic acceptance thing will happen to his neurotic retail products. . . ."

Winn comes in (Bolton had hoped it was Stan) and under cover of his entrance Doris slips into the bedroom.

Ken continues to explain that Walter's work will have to be changed quite a lot before publication—particularly his writing about doctors. Ken reminds his listeners that most people are fond of their doctors. Ken appalls Bolton and Walter as he outlines what he would consider a good *Cutlass* story: a story about a pediatrician and a nymphomaniac whose child catches them in the act and then kills himself ("Now *there's* a story for you! A tough, gusty yarn. . . .").

Winn likes the story—or says he does—and much as Bolton loathes it he permits himself to suggest that Walter could write it for *Cutlass*. Walter refuses coldly and follows Doris into the bedroom.

Ken is starving hungry, and so Bolton sends Winn to take him out to dinner. Bolton pretends to Winn that everything is under control (he is no longer willing to let Winn know the true state of affairs, that the baby's arrival is imminent), and he is relieved to see Ken and Winn depart.

> . . . *Walter sticks his head out of the bedroom door, looks to see if they have gone, and quickly crossing to the stove, takes a pair of rubber surgical gloves out of a package and drops them in a pot of water, which he puts on to boil. He is wearing a makeshift surgical gown fashioned from a sheet.*

BOLTON: What's happening? How's she doing?

WALTER: She'll be all right—now *that's* over!

BOLTON: Did they throw her off?

WALTER: What threw her was your sneaky attempt to make me compromise myself! You almost sucked me in there. Boy, you have to watch yourself every minute!

BOLTON (*crossing to pour himself a drink*): Okay, okay, I'll admit he was *impossible*. You were right to reject him. But that doesn't mean you should always reject *everything*.

WALTER: Listen, don't do me any more favors!

BOLTON: But it's not that *simple!*

> *Walter turns angrily away.*

Wait! Wait! Let me finish! Please! . . . Sometimes, sometimes you have to, uh . . . not compromise! Not compromise! You have to, uh, use *jujitsu* on the System. You have to fall back, see, and utilizing the weight of the System against itself, you, uh, *flip* the System, and uh . . .

> *He trails off, feeling absurd under Walter's glare. He picks up the bottle to pour himself a drink.*

WALTER: Are you going to help us, or are you just going to get drunk?

BOLTON (*startled, he freezes, then slowly sets the bottle down without pouring and says shakily*): What do you want me to do?

Walter wants him to help hang bedsheets on the clotheslines, to be used for sterile wrappings after Bolton sprays them with disinfectant. There is no time to lose. If they have fallen behind schedule, Bolton suggests, why not outsmart the System by using a hospital? Walter can blame Bolton for getting the birth off to a bad start and causing the change in plans.

WALTER: She's going to be all right! You just spray these sheets and keep an eye on that water, and stay off my back! I'm going to do this *my* way, because this is *my* child, and *my* wife, and *my* house! Remember that! *(He starts back toward the bedroom.)*

BOLTON: Don't worry, I know what it means to have a wife and child . . . I just wish you did.

Walter whirls around, glaring.

You're still thinking like a single man . . .

Walter turns angrily back toward the door.

. . . and if you keep it up, you may *be* one again.

WALTER *(freezes, his hand on the knob; he looks back at Bolton and says in a strained voice):* She's going to be all right! *(He exits into the bedroom, his face tense with anxiety.)*

Bolton begins to spray the sheets. Winn returns, pretending he forgot his hat. Bolton requests Winn to level, and Winn admits he noticed Doris was in labor. He got rid of Ken and came back to help because his "personal desire to help and his duty to the agency coincide."

Winn suggests the police, or Dr. Herman. Bolton rejects the first and explains that Dr. Herman is busy delivering the child of a drummer named Hey-Hey Hallahan (a nervous father who drummed on all the furniture and drove Bolton crazy). Dr. Herman will come as soon as he can.

While Bolton sprays (and he can hardly bear the heavy responsibility of getting the sheets perfectly clean), Winn takes the possibility of an "obstetrical accident" into matter-of-fact consideration. There would be police to be dealt with, and night court reporters. . . .

BOLTON: Yes, well, all right, but let's hope that isn't necessary, for God's sake! *(He sprays madly.)*

WINN: Uh, sir, in the event that some sort of statement is necessary, I wonder if you've thought of anything.

BOLTON: What do you mean?

WINN: Well, you know, something euphemistic I could use in the event that something happens to Doris or the baby. I've already taken a crack at it myself—all the copy people are off on Sunday—but the only thing I've been able to come up with so far is: *(reading from a notebook.)* uh, "the pregnancy resulted in a negative nativity."

BOLTON *(regards Winn for a beat):* "Negative nativity" . . . small "n", I assume?

WINN: Yes, sir. We wouldn't want to get into that whole religious thing . . .

BOLTON: Well, that's very nice, Winn. Dignified, yet obscure.

WINN: Thank you, sir. I have sat at the feet of the Master.

Bolton grimaces.

Winn is causing Bolton to see himself as he really is; what scares Bolton most is, maybe if he had his life to live all over again he would find that this is the way he really wanted to be.

There is a crisis with the rubber gloves—the water has boiled away, and Bolton is afraid that this is the beginning of disaster that will be blamed on him. But the gloves are all right, he caught them in time.

Walter comes out of the bedroom—he is worried, but his worry turns to anger when he sees Winn there and learns that Winn knows all about the birth. Bolton chills Walter with a reminder that they may need a lawyer before the night is over. Walter goes back into the bedroom.

Winn helps Bolton hang sheets. Winn has noticed that Bolton hasn't told Walter about Dr. Herman; Bolton wants to insinuate Dr. Herman into Walter's life so that Walter can get to like him before he learns he's a doctor.

Bolton suddenly gets the idea of calling an ambulance to have it wait downstairs. Walter catches him doing this and stops him; Walter will have no part of an ambulance. He orders Winn out of the apartment. Obviously worried, Walter grabs the book on obstetrics and runs back into the bedroom protesting "It's going to be all right!"

Bolton tries to relax, but can't. Sneakily he calls the ambulance again on a phone whose loud dial clicks nearly betray him. In an undertone, he orders the ambulance.

>*Without thinking, he slams down the phone in triumph, and then freezes, with his hands still on it. Walter bursts out of the bedroom.*

WALTER *(furious):* You called it, didn't you?

BOLTON *(getting angry himself):* I called it for myself, not for you! I'm going to the hospital in it! I need an emergency operation on my ulcer!

WALTER: You're lying!

BOLTON: By the time it gets here, I won't be.

WALTER *(wildly):* Get out! Get out of here! You *cheat!*

DORIS' VOICE: Walter!

>*Walter forgets about Bolton at the sound of her voice, whirls and dashes back into the room.*

Winn is happy that the ambulance is on the way, but Bolton feels that somehow the ambulance spoils it a little for Doris and Walter. He hopes the baby will be born before the ambulance arrives. He listens at the bedroom door and worries about the peculiar sound of Doris's breathing.

Stan comes in, reeling; to Bolton's intense relief, he is only *playing* drunk, as a form of disguise in case Walter is there. Hey-Hey Hallahan's wife had a nice healthy boy, so now Stan can turn his attention to Doris. The trouble is, Bolton hasn't yet prepared them for Stan's taking part in the delivery.

Stan listens at the bedroom door with his stethoscope and tells Bolton that Doris is riding out the contractions very well. Bolton asks Stan to stay, and Stan sits, waiting.

>*Bolton more or less from force of habit resumes spraying the sheets. He stops when he becomes aware of Stan staring curiously at him.*

BOLTON *(self-consciously):* I'm uh, spraying a, uh, disinfectant on these sheets.

STAN: Oh, very good idea.
BOLTON *(pleased):* Really?!
STAN: Yes, it gives you something to do.
BOLTON: It kills the germs! . . . Doesn't it?
STAN: Yeah, I guess so.
BOLTON: You *guess* so?
STAN: Well, let's say it definitely makes them very nervous.
BOLTON *(angrily; resumes spraying):* Well, I'm going to do it anyway! . . . It gives me something to do.

Winn is concerned about Walter's hostility to outsiders and wants Stan to have a plausible explanation for his presence. Winn suggests that Stan use his war record to impress Walter, and of course Stan ridicules the suggestion.

Stan stethoscopes the door again, amused by the thought that maybe Walter is listening with another stethoscope on *his* side of the door.

> *Stan, still chortling to himself, crosses to the door and listens. He moves his stethoscope along the wall, over near the coats, and down about the height of a bed. The expression on his face becomes solemn. Apparently he hears something of significance. He catches Bolton watching him, and, quickly smiling, he renews the image of Walter's stethoscope following his around the wall with some quick funny pantomime, which doesn't quite conceal his concern. He listens some more, and then, casually crossing to the stove, he takes some instruments out of the paper bag, and from his pockets, and slips them into a pot of boiling water.*

STAN: Jim, this is some of the finest boiling water I've ever seen.

But Bolton senses something is wrong. He prods Stan until Stan tells him there's nothing much to worry about, it's just a breech delivery, a little awkward.

BOLTON: How can you tell from here?
STAN: Something he said. He's just starting to realize that he's in trouble.
> *Listens again with the stethoscope in his ears so that he can't hear Bolton's desperate whispers.*
BOLTON: Then why don't you go in there for God's sake! Go in there!
STAN *(turns, shakes his head in admiration):* He's quite a guy.
> *Notices Bolton's frantic gestures and removes the stethoscope from his ears.*
What?
BOLTON: What are you waiting for? Go in there!
STAN: Jim, he's under a terrific strain, I can't just suddenly walk in there on him; there's no telling how he might react. Is he a big guy?
BOLTON: Yes . . .
> *Stan shakes his head and resumes listening.*
Oh, God, it's all my fault! I should have prepared him for this! Suppose he

doesn't feel protective enough . . . Suppose he doesn't have the right stuff in him after all . . .

> *Suddenly Stan hurries away from the door. It bursts open and Walter dashes out, headed for the stove. He stops at the sight of Stan with the stethoscope around his neck.*

BOLTON *(realizing it's now or never, blurts out):* This is my old friend, Stan, he's an obstetrician! . . .

> *Walter stares, hung in space. Bolton snatches up the book of verse and says in desperation:*

He—He digs your work!!

WALTER *(stares at Stan for a long beat, then says shakily):* I could use some help.

STAN: I'll be right with you, Walt. Go tell her not to push.

Stan fetches his instruments from the stove and goes into the bedroom. Winn congratulates Bolton on the way he handled the matter, the way he used the word "dig" at the right time.

In front of Bolton (and thus nailing down the fact that the agency has been spying on Bolton), Winn calls the agency vice president and reports that the crisis is over. In response to a question, Winn tells his boss that Bolton has "hardly touched" the bottle of Scotch. As Winn hangs up, Bolton is furious that the agency should question his drinking habits.

Cool as ever, Winn makes Bolton a present of this swindle-sheet bottle of Scotch—and suggests that they both deduct it.

BOLTON *(automatically):* Oh, fine. It all adds up, you know.

WINN: Right! Well, I guess that wraps it . . . *(He starts to leave.)*

BOLTON: There's one minor correction you might want to make in your report to the vice president: the key word wasn't "dig," it was "work."

WINN: Oh, really! Well, I'll have to remember that. Thank you. Goodnight. *(Polite, pleasant and smiling to the end, he exits.)*

> *Bolton closes the door, gives his head a shake as if to clear it, and then runs to the bedroom door. He listens, but apparently hears nothing significant. He crosses to the table, pours some Scotch into his glass and downs it. Then, still absorbed with thoughts of Doris, he absently takes his expense-account book out of his shirt pocket, and is going to make a notation on the Scotch, but since he still has Walter's book of verse under his arm, it is difficult to write. As he starts to put the verse down, he freezes for a moment, one book in each hand. Then, in a sudden wave of revulsion, he savagely crumples the expense-account book and hurls it from him. Sitting, he opens Walter's book and after a moment begins to sing softly to himself.*

BOLTON: . . . I put my IBM card in that old pianola and it played out my whole life song . . .

> *Walter bursts out of the bedroom. Bolton snaps the book shut. Walter is too upset to notice.*

What's the matter! What happened!

WALTER *(almost in tears):* He gave her a shot! She's going to miss it!

BOLTON: Miss what?!

WALTER: Seeing the birth! Gee, she wanted to so much.

BOLTON: But is she going to be all right?!

WALTER: He said she would. She's resting now.

    Pause.

He wants two of your sheets.

BOLTON *(thrilled, leaps into action):* Oh! Well! Let's see now . . .

    He can't figure out how to get them down without contaminating them. He panics.

I can't get them down!

WALTER: I'll help you. Just touch the corners. We'll fold them.

BOLTON: Careful now!

    They each take a corner and fold toward each other. They find themselves face-to-face.

WALTER *(after a beat):* Thanks, for everything.

BOLTON: That's all right.

WALTER: I'll hang this one over here for a minute. *(He accidentally steps on Bolton's crumpled expense book.)* Oh, I . . . ! Did you throw this away?

BOLTON *(rather embarrassed):* Uh, yeah . . .

WALTER: Oh. *(He smiles at Bolton.)*

BOLTON: Thanks, for everything.

WALTER: That's all right.

    They start to get the other sheet down. Suddenly there is the cry of a newborn baby! Walter is stunned.

That's the baby. *I missed it too!*

BOLTON: Oh . . . Well, maybe some day you and Doris can . . .

WALTER *(interrupting excitedly):* That's right! You know, I never thought of that! *(He whirls around and goes running into the bedroom, shouting.)* Hey, Doris! Let's have another baby!

    Turning front, Bolton lifts his hands helplessly, as the curtain falls.

THE ROYAL HUNT OF THE SUN

A Play in Two Acts

BY PETER SHAFFER

Cast and credits appear on page 382

PETER SHAFFER was born in England, at Liverpool, in 1926. He attended St. Paul's School in London and spent three years at Trinity College, Cambridge. In 1951, at the age of 25, he came to the United States where for three years he worked in the Acquisitions Department of the New York Public Library while pursuing his writing career. His The Salt Land, The Prodigal Father *and* Balcony of Terror *appeared on British television. In 1958 his play* Five Finger Exercise *was a success in London, and on December 2, 1959 it was presented at the Music Box and was named a Best Play of that season.*

A pair of Shaffer one-acters, The Private Ear *and* The Public Eye, *were produced October 9, 1963 at the Morosco after a London production that ran eighteen months. Shaffer's* The Royal Hunt of the Sun *was the first work by a contemporary playwright to be done by England's National Theater under the directorship of Laurence Olivier. Shaffer's* Black Comedy *was produced on the London stage this season and his* The Public Eye *is soon to be seen in a movie version starring Julie Andrews and directed by Mike Nichols.*

Time: June 1529-August 1533

Place: Two early scenes in Spain and Panama; then the Up-per Province of the Inca Empire, now South Ecuador and Northwestern Peru. Act II takes place in the town of Cajamarca.

ACT I—THE HUNT

SYNOPSIS: The bare stage is dominated by a wooden back wall on which hangs a huge metal medallion with four black crucifixes pointed like swords. The medallion is twelve feet in diameter, and its circumference is ringed with twelve hinged petal-like shapes.

> *When closed, these interlock to form a great medallion on which is incised the emblem of the Conquistadors; when opened, they form the rays of a giant golden sun, emblem of the Incas. Each petal has an inlay of gold magnetized to it: when these inlays are pulled out the great black frame remaining symbolizes the dese-cration of Peru . . . Old Martin, grizzled, in his middle fifties, ap-pears. He wears the black costume of a Spanish hidalgo in the mid-sixteenth century.*

OLD MARTIN: Save you all. My name is Martin. I'm a soldier of Spain and that's it. Most of my life I've spent fighting for land, treasure and the cross. I'm worth millions. Soon I'll be dead and they'll bury me out here in Peru, the land I helped ruin as a boy. This story is about ruin. Ruin and gold. More gold than any of you will ever see even if you work in a counting house. I'm going to tell you how one hundred and sixty-seven men conquered an empire of twenty-four million. . . .

As Old Martin imagines how it was to be a boy and dream of heroism and conquest, Young Martin enters, duelling the air with a stick. He is Martin as a boy of fifteen, about 40 years before. Young Martin's entrance is closely followed by that of Francisco Pizarro.

> *He is a man in late middle age: tough, commanding, harsh, wasted, secret. The gestures are blunt and often violent; the expression in-tense and energetic, capable of fury and cruelty, but also of sud-den melancholy and sardonic humor. At the moment he appears more neatly than he is ever to do again: hair and beard are trimmed, and his clothes quite grand, as if he is trying to make a fine impression.*

Pizarro is recruiting in his birthplace, Trujillo, for his third expedition—the King has given him sole right of discovery in Peru and named him Viceroy of anything he can conquer with an army to be raised at his own expense.

Accompanying Pizarro are his second-in-command, Hernando de Soto *(His whole air breathes an unquestioning loyalty. . . . He is an admirable soldier and a staunch friend)* and the Dominican Fray Vincente de Valverde *(A peasant priest whose zeal is not greatly tempered by intelligence, nor sweetened by any anxiety to please).* Pizarro's audience of villagers includes Salinas, a blacksmith; Rodas, a tailor; Vasca, Domingo and the Chavez brothers; and Diego, whom Pizarro names Master of Horse. Rodas the tailor refuses Pizarro's offer of employment. Then Pizarro turns to Young Martin (at first Old Martin speaks his words but then exits as Young Martin begins to speak for himself). Young Martin is filled with the ideals of chivalry and wants to sign on as a page.

PIZARRO: Why do you want to come?

YOUNG MARTIN: It's going to be glorious, sir.

PIZARRO: Look you, if you served me you'd be Page to an old slogger: no titles, no traditions. I learnt my trade as a mercenary, going with who best paid me. It's a closed book to me, all that chivalry. But then, not reading or writing, all books are closed to me. If I took you you'd have to be my reader and writer, both.

YOUNG MARTIN: I'd be honored my Lord. Oh, please my Lord!

PIZARRO: General will do. Let's see your respect. Greet me.

The boy bows.

Now to the Church. That's Brother Valverde, our Chaplain.

VALVERDE: The blessing of God on you, my son. And on all who come with us to alter the heathen.

PIZARRO: Now to our Second-in-Command, Cavalier de Soto. I'm sure you all know the Cavalier well by reputation: a great soldier. He has fought under Cordoba! No expedition he seconds can fail.

He takes a roll of cloth, woven with the design of a llama, from De Soto.

Now look at this! Indian stuff! Ten years ago standing with the great Balboa, I saw a chieftain draw this beast on the leaf of an aloe. And he said to me: Where this roams is unaccountable wealth!

RODAS: Oh, yes, uncountable! Ask Sanchez the farrier about that. He listened to talk like that from him five years ago.

DIEGO: Who cares about him?

RODAS: Unaccountable bloody wealth? It rained six months and his skin rotted on him. They lost twenty-seven out of fifty.

PIZARRO: And so we may again. What do you think I'm offering? A walk in the country? Jellies and wine in a basket, your hand round your girl? No, I'm promising you swamps. A forest like the beard of the world. Sitting half-buried in earth to escape the mouths of insects. You may live for weeks on palm tree buds and soup made out of leather straps. And at night you will sleep in thick wet darkness with snakes hung over your heads like bell ropes —and black men in that blackness: men that eat each other. And why should you endure all this? Because I believe that beyond this terrible place is a

DAVID CARRADINE (AS ATAHUALLPA) AND CHRISTOPHER PLUMMER
(AS PIZARRO) IN "THE ROYAL HUNT OF THE SUN"

kingdom, where gold is as common as wood is here! I took only two steps in
and found cups and pans made out of it solid.

Pizarro claps his hands and Felipillo enters. He is an Ecuador Indian wearing golden ornaments. While the villagers examine the trinkets and agree that
they are gold, Valverde stresses the spiritual goal of the expedition, to bring
God to such heathens as this. The villagers, even Rodas, sign on and follow
Diego offstage. Pizarro takes on Young Martin as Page, and the lad goes off
with Valverde.

Left alone with de Soto, Pizarro confesses that it isn't gold that is beckon-
ing him to another expedition into the jungle.

PIZARRO: . . . At my age things become what they really are. Gold turns
into metal.

DE SOTO: Then why? You could stay here now and be hero for a province.
What's left to endure so much for—especially with your infirmity? You've
earned the right to comfort. Your country would gladly grant it to you for
the rest of your life.

PIZARRO: My country, where is that?

DE SOTO: Spain, sir.

PIZARRO: Spain and I have been strangers since I was a boy. The only
spot I know in it is here—this filthy village. This is Spain to me. Is this where
you wish me comfort? For twenty-two years I drove pigs down this street

because my father couldn't own to my mother. Twenty-two years without one single day of hope. When I turned soldier and dragged my arquebus along the roads of Italy, I was so famished I was beyond eating. I got nothing and I gave nothing, and though I groaned for that once I'm glad with it now. Because I owe nothing . . . Once the world could have had me for a petty farm, two rocky fields and a Senor to my name. It said "No." Ten years on it could have had me for double—small estate, fifty oranges and a Sir to them. It said "No." Twenty years more and it could still have had me cheap: Balboa's trusty lieutenant, marched with him into the Pacific and claimed it for Spain: State pension and dinner once a week with the local Mayor. But the world said "No." Said "No" and said "No." Well, now it's going to know me. If I live this next year I'm going to get me a name that won't ever be forgotten. A name to be sung here for centuries in your ballads, out there under the cork trees where I sat as a boy with bandages for shoes. I amuse you.

DE SOTO: Surely you see you don't.

PIZARRO: Oh yes, I amuse you Cavalier de Soto. The old pigherd lumbering after fame. You inherited your honor—I had to root for mine like the pigs. It's amusing.

Pizarro kneels as the lights grow whiter and colder. There is organ music, and Valverde enters bearing a large wooden Christ and accompanied by his assistant Fray Marcos de Nizza, a serene and intellectually mature priest. The Villagers enter dressed in white cloaks and carrying banners; among them is the Venetian captain Pedro de Candia (wearing a pearl in one ear and walking with a lazy stealth that at once suggests danger). Old Martin comes in to explain that they are all consecrating their weapons in the Cathedral Church at Panama. They number 187 men, twenty-seven of whom are mounted.

Estete enters—stiff, imperious, dressed in the black of the Spanish court. He is Royal Veedor and Overseer in the name of the King, Carlos V. He infuriates Pizarro by insinuating that he, Estete, has the supreme authority in non-military matters, matters which might infringe upon the King's majesty. Pizarro shouts his defiance by naming de Soto absolute Second-in-Command, responsible only to the supreme authority of Pizarro (whose partner, Almagro, is to stay behind and organize reinforcements to follow in three months). Then Pizarro collapses in pain from an old knife-thrust. De Soto marches the expedition out, leaving Pizarro to follow in the care of Young Martin.

Pizarro warns the boy against romanticizing about the army. Soldiers are for killing, period. Army tradition is "nothing but years of Us against Them. Christ-men against Pagan-men. Men against men." There is nothing noble about the pain and the dying. Young Martin will learn this in the forest, Pizarro warns as he limps off.

> The boy is left alone. The stage darkens and the huge medallion high on the back wall begins to glow. Great cries of "Inca!" are heard. The boy bolts offstage. Exotic music mixes with the chanting. Slowly the medallion opens outwards to form a huge golden sun with twelve great rays. In the center stands Atahuallpa, sov-

ereign Inca of Peru, masked, crowned, and dressed in gold. When he speaks, his voice, like the voices of all the Incas, is strangely formalized. Enter below the Inca court: Villac Umu, the High Priest, Challcuchima, Manco and others, all masked, and robed in terracotta. They prostrate themselves.

MANCO: Atahuallpa! God!

ATAHUALLPA: God hears.

MANCO: Manco your Chasqui speaks. I bring truth from many runners what has been seen in the Farthest Province. White men sitting on huge sheep. The sheep are red! Everywhere their leader shouts aloud "Here is God!"

ATAHUALLPA: The White God!

VILLAC UMU: Beware, beware Inca!

ATAHUALLPA: All-powerful spirit who left this place before my ancestors ruled you. The White God returns!

CHALLCUCHIMA: You do not know this.

ATAHUALLPA: He has been long waited for. If he comes, it is with blessing. Then my people will see I did well to take the Crown.

The omens are bad, but Atahuallpa believes that the White God is coming to bless him and his rule. The court retires but Atahuallpa remains motionless in his sunflower through the scenes which follow.

The light becomes mottled; in the province of Tumbes a band of Conquistadors led by de Candia chases a group of Indians and captures their Chief, upon which they become passive. With Felipillo as interpreter, the Spaniards demand gold. The Chief tells them there is no gold, it was all taken by Atahuallpa for his war. Pizarro wants to know more about Atahuallpa.

PIZARRO: . . . Who did he fight?

CHIEF: His brother Huascar. His father the great Inca Huayana grew two sons. One by a wife, one by a not-wife. At his death he cut the Kingdom in two for them. But Atahuallpa wanted all. So he made war, and killed his brother. Now he is lord of earth and sky.

PIZARRO: And he's the bastard?

All the Indians cry out.

Answer! He's the bastard?

CHIEF: He is Son of the Sun. He needs no wedded mother. He is God.

INDIANS (*chanting*): Sapa Inca! Inca Capac!

PIZARRO: God?

CHIEF: God!

PIZARRO: God on earth?

VALVERDE: Christ defend us!

DE SOTO: Do you believe this?

CHIEF: It is true. The sun is God. Atahuallpa is his child sent to shine on us for a few years of life. Then he will return to his father's palace and live forever.

PIZARRO: God on earth!

Villaverde is scandalized. At sword's point he forces the Indians to chant "Jesus Christ Inca" as they are herded offstage. Atahuallpa in his sunflower remarks "He surely is a god. He teaches my people to praise him."

De Soto declares, as he exits, that the Inca God has a shock coming. Pizarro agrees, adding that "we've got a God worth a thousand of yours. A gentle God with gentle priests, and a couple of big cannon to blow you out of the sky!"

As Pizarro exits, Atahuallpa's henchmen come onstage with another warning. His people are weeping and groaning as the Spaniards advance. But Atahuallpa orders Challcuchima: go tell Pizarro to rendezvous at Cajamarca, behind the great mountains. If Pizarro is a god, he will keep the appointment, if a man, he will die on the journey, which is arduous.

The lights fade; it is night in the forest. Vasca and Domingo, on duty, hear wild bird cries and complain of rusting armor and absence of gold.

De Candia enters with Estete and sends the two soldiers off with a warning about talking while on duty. De Candia examines his arquebus, "Strozzi's most perfect model. She can stop a horse at five hundred paces."

Pizarro and Young Martin enter. Watching them, Estete and de Candia agree that Pizarro is mad and dangerous.

Pizarro is lecturing Young Martin on the law of life in the forest: rip and tear, no chivalry about it. But Young Martin clings to his high hopes, to his ideals, and to his hero-worship of Pizarro, even though Pizarro warns Martin that he would rip him too, along with the rest of the well-ordered, respectable world. "Little Lord of Hope," Pizarro tells the boy, "I'm harsh with you. You own everything I've lost. I despise the keeping, and I loathe the losing. Where can a man live, between two hates?"

Pizarro approaches de Candia and Estete and exchanges polite animosities. Pizarro's plan is to press forward, and he challenges Estete to write to the King criticizing his leadership.

After they depart their separate ways, the light brightens to morning and Old Martin comes on to describe the next stage of the expedition.

OLD MARTIN: We were in the forest for six weeks, but at last we escaped and found on the other side our first witness of a great empire. There was a road fifteen feet wide, bordered with mimosa and blue glories, with walls on both sides the height of a man. We rode it for days, six horses abreast: and all the way, far up the hillsides, were huge fields of corn laid out in terraces, and a net of water in a thousand canals. (Exit.)

Atahuallpa is apprised of the Spaniards' progress; the sight of a llama apparently delights them, for some reason, the Chief is told.

A large group of Spaniards watches a large group of Indians singing a toilsong, miming sowing and reaping. Felipillo interprets the Headman's description of Inca life.

HEADMAN: Here all work together in families: fifty, a hundred, a thousand. I am head of a thousand families. I give out to all food. I give out to all clothes. I give out to all confessing.

DE NIZZA: Confessing?

HEADMAN: I have priest power . . . I confess my people of all crimes against the laws of the sun.

DE NIZZA: What laws are these?

HEADMAN: It is the seventh month. That is why they must pick corn.

ATAHUALLPA *(intoning):* In the eighth month you will plough. In the ninth, sow maize. In the tenth, mend your roofs.

HEADMAN: Each age also has its tasks.

ATAHUALLPA: Nine years to twelve, protect harvests. Twelve to eighteen, care for herds. Eighteen to twenty-five, warriors for me—Atahuallpa Inca!

FELIPILLO: They are stupid; always do what they are told.

DE SOTO: This is because they are poor?

FELIPILLO: Not poor. Not rich. All same.

ATAHUALLPA: At twenty-five all will marry. All will receive one tupu of land.

HEADMAN: What may be covered by one hundred pounds of maize.

ATAHUALLPA: They will never move from there. At birth of a son one more tupu will be given. At birth of a daughter, half a tupu. At fifty all people will leave work forever and be fed in honor till they die.

DE SOTA: I have settled several lands. This is the first I've entered which shames our Spain.

ESTETE: Shames?

PIZARRO: Oh, it's not difficult to shame Spain. Here shames every country which teaches we are born greedy for possessions. Clearly we're made greedy when we're assured it's natural. But there's a picture for a Spanish eye! There's nothing to covet, so covetousness dies at birth.

There are very few nobles, the Headman tells Pizarro, but many messengers so that the King always has his eye on things.

Challcuchima enters with Manco bringing greetings from the Son of the Sun-God to the Spaniards (who offer blessings from their Son of God). Challcuchima delivers the Inca's message: Pizarro is ordered to visit him at Cajamarca behind the great mountains. Pizarro boasts he will make this difficult one-month climbing journey in two weeks and sends the ambassadors off to tell Atahuallpa so.

Estete advises Pizarro to wait for the reinforcements, but Pizarro ignores the advice. He orders Estete to stay behind with a garrison of twenty men. Then Pizarro calls his soldiers to assembly; he tells them they can remain and be killed by Atahuallpa's mighty forces; they can retreat and be killed, or they can go on toward the gold and maybe they will still be killed. Rodas decides to stay, but the others follow Pizarro as he moves them out, ordering them to behave like the gods the Incas think they are and to "follow the pig-boy to his glory!"

Young Martin, ordered to stay by Pizarro but insistent upon going, beats the drum for the Spaniard slow-march as masked Indians move on to the upper level. The approach of 167 Spaniards—marching in step and looking neither to the right nor to the left—is reported to Atahuallpa and convinces him more than ever that this is a god and his priests sent to do Atahuallpa homage. Villac Umu urges Atahuallpa to kill the Spaniards, but the Inca refuses.

The Spaniards are bathed in cold blue light and fall down on the stage at their first glimpse of the towering Andes. Pizarro will need the horses for his meeting with Atahuallpa, and Diego promises him the horses will make the journey safely. Pizarro hurls his defiance at the mountains, and at the Inca. As he does this, Atahuallpa beckons to him three times and then withdraws backward from his position in the sun and disappears into the blackness.

The Spaniards press on in "The Mime of the Great Ascent," simulating a stumbling, tortuous, dangerous, painful climb, *"performed to an eerie, cold music made from the thin whine of huge saws."* Old Martin comes on to describe this agonizing progress.

OLD MARTIN: Have you ever climbed a mountain in full armor? That's what we did, him going first the whole way up a tiny path into the clouds, with drops sheer on both sides into nothing. For hours we crept forward like blind men, the sweat freezing on our faces, lugging skittery leaking horses, and pricked all the time for the ambush that would tip us into death. Each turn of the path it grew colder. The friendly trees of the forest dropped away, and there were only pines. Then they went too, and there were just scrubby little bushes standing up in ice. All round us the rocks began to whine with cold. And always above us, or below us, those filthy condor birds, hanging on the air with great tasseled wings.

> *It grows darker. The music grows colder yet. The men freeze and hang their heads for a long moment, before resuming their desperate climb.*

Then night. We lay down twos and threes together on the path, and hugged like lovers for warmth in that burning cold. And most cried. We got up with cold iron for bones and went on. Four days like that; groaning, not speaking; the breath a blade in our lungs. Four days, slowly, like flies on a wall; limping flies, dying flies, up an endless wall of rock. A tiny army lost in the creases of the moon.

INDIANS *(off, in echo):* Stand!

> *The Spaniards whirl round. Villac Umu and his attendants appear, clothed entirely in white fur. The High Priest wears a snow-white llama head on top of his own.*

VILLAC UMU: You see Villac Umu. Chief Priest of the Sun. Why do you come?

PIZARRO: To see the Great Inca.

VILLAC UMU: Why will you see him?

PIZARRO: To give him blessing.

VILLAC UMU: Why will you bless him?

PIZARRO: He is a God. I am a God.

VALVERDE *(sotto voce):* General!

Villac Umu delivers the Inca's orders: the Spaniards are to go to the town of Cajamarca, below, to rest, and tomorrow the Inca will join them. Valverde doesn't approve of Pizarro's masquerading as a god, but Pizarro tells him, "To conquer for Christ, one can surely usurp his name for a night, Father."

The Spaniards descend and fan out "onto a huge plain of eucalyptus trees," where they settle into the eerie, empty town. There are 10,000 Indians on the hillsides, and Valverde suspects a death trap.

Pizarro plans with de Soto, de Candia, de Nizza and Diego: they must ring the square with their 167 men and ambush the Great Inca. Once a knife is placed at the Inca's throat, his subjects will surrender: "Grab the King, grab the Kingdom!" Pizarro plans the deployment of his forces and gives the watchword for the ambush: "San Jago." Others pray. If they get out alive, Pizarro promises Young Martin, he will give the lad anything he asks; and all that Young Martin wants is a sword.

In the night, Pizarro exchanges confidences with de Soto. Pizarro has been cheated by time, robbed of hope. He once lay on a rock with a girl by the sea—but time passed and so did that moment, and he never married or had a son because no woman he wanted would marry a bastard. "Try and halt a moment in our lives and it becomes maggoty at once. . . . You can't escape maggots unless you go with Time, and if you go, they wriggle in you anyway." Pizarro once tried to capture beauty in women by means of lust, but finally time robbed him even of that.

PIZARRO: . . . I've been cheated from the moment I was born because there's death in everything.

DE SOTO: Except in God.

A pause.

PIZARRO: When I was young, I used to sit on the slope outside the village and watch the sun go down, and I used to think: if only I could find the place where it sinks to rest for the night, I'd find the source of life, like the beginning of a river. I used to wonder what it could be like. Perhaps an island, a strange place of white sand, where the people never died. Never grew old, or felt pain, and never died.

DE SOTO: Sweet fancy.

PIZARRO: It's what your mind runs to when it lacks instruction. If I had a son, I'd kill him if he didn't read his book . . . Where does the sun rest at night?

DE SOTO: Nowhere. It's a heavenly body set by God to move round the earth in perpetual motion.

PIZARRO: Do you know this?

DE SOTO: All Europe knows it.

PIZARRO: What if they were wrong? If it settled here each evening, somewhere in those great mountains, like a God laid down to sleep? To a savage mind it must make a fine God. I myself can't fix anything nearer to a thought of worship than standing at dawn and watching it fill the world. Like the coming of something eternal, against going flesh. What a fantastic wonder that anyone on earth should dare to say. "That's my father. My father: the sun!" It's silly—but tremendous. . . .

The thought of Atahuallpa fascinates Pizarro; he doesn't hate Atahuallpa, he feels as though all his life had been lived toward this one dawn of November 16, 1532.

Priests and soldiers are chanting. All take their appointed places for Atahuallpa's coming and for the ambush; and for an hour . . . five hours . . . ten hours nothing stirs. Then, towards evening, with the sun red as though someone had stabbed it, "squirting blood all over the sky," the Spaniards see movement among the Indians on the hills as thousands sweep the path clean for the approaching Inca. The thousands are armed with axes and spears (the Spaniards report as they watch the Indians' approach) but they throw their weapons down as they prepare to meet the white gods.

Strange music grows louder and louder signifying Atahuallpa's approach. The priests remain in the square, but seven gunners are deployed onto the roofs and the rest of the soldiers take cover.

> *The music crashes over the stage as the Indian procession enters in an astonishing explosion of color. The King's attendants—many of them playing musical instruments: reed pipes, cymbals and giant marraccas—are as gay as parrots. They wear costumes of orange and yellow, and fantastic headdresses of gold and feathers, with eyes embossed on them in staring black enamel. By contrast, Atahuallpa Inca presents a picture of utter simplicity. He is dressed from head to foot in white: across his eyes is a mask of jade mosaic, and round his head a circlet of plain gold. Silence falls. The King glares about him.*

ATAHUALLPA (*haughtily*): Where is the God?

VALVERDE (*through Felipillo*): I am a priest of God.

ATAHUALLPA: I do not want the priest. I want the God. Where is he? He sent me greeting.

VALVERDE: That was our General. Our God cannot be seen.

ATAHUALLPA: *I* may see him.

Valverde and de Nizza explain that Christ was killed by men and ascended into heaven, leaving the Pope as his Regent on earth. This Pope has commanded the Spaniards' King to bring all men to true belief, to make them vassals of Christ.

ATAHUALLPA: I am the vassal of no man. I am the greatest Prince on earth. Your King is great. He has sent you far across the water. So he is my brother. But your Pope is mad. He gives away countries that are not his. His faith also is mad.

VALVERDE: Beware!

ATAHUALLPA: Ware you! You kill my people; you make them slaves. By what power?

VALVERDE: By this. (*He offers a Bible.*) The Word of God.

> *Atahuallpa holds it to his ear. He listens intently. He shakes it.*

ATAHUALLPA: No word. (*He smells the book, and then licks it. Finally he throws it down impatiently.*) God is angry with your insults.

VALVERDE: Blasphemy!

ATAHUALLPA: God is angry.

VALVERDE: Francisco Pizarro, do you stay your hand when Christ is insulted? Let this pagan feel the power of your arm. I absolve you all! San Jago!

> *Pizarro appears above with drawn sword, and in a great voice sings out his battle-cry.*

PIZARRO: SAN JAGO Y CIERRA ESPAÑA!

> *Instantly from all sides the soldiers rush in echoing the great cry.*

SOLDIERS: SAN JAGO!

> *There is a tense pause. The Indians look at this ring of armed men in terror. A violent drumming begins, and there ensues "The Mime of the Great Massacre." To a savage music, wave upon wave of Indians are slaughtered and rise again to protect their lord who stands bewildered in their midst. It is all in vain. Relentlessly the Spanish soldiers hew their way through the ranks of feathered attendants towards their quarry. They surround him. Salinas snatches the crown off his head and tosses it up to Pizarro, who catches it and to a great shout crowns himself. All the Indians cry out in horror. The drum hammers on relentlessly while Atahuallpa is led off at sword-point by the whole band of Spaniards. At the same time, dragged from the middle of the sun by howling Indians, a vast bloodstained cloth bellies out over the stage. All rush off; their screams fill the theater. The lights fade out slowly out on the rippling cloth of blood. Curtain.*

ACT II—THE KILL

The stage is in darkness, and an Inca lament is heard. As the lights come up the bloodstained cloth is still spread out.

> *In the sun chamber Atahuallpa stands in chains, his back to the audience, his white robe dirty with blood. Although he is unmasked, we cannot yet see his face, only a tail of black hair hanging down his neck. Old Martin appears. From opposite, Young Martin comes in, stumbling with shock. He collapses on his knees.*

OLD MARTIN: Look at the warrior where he struts. Glory on his sword. Salvation in his new spurs. One of the knights at last. The very perfect knight Sir Martin, tender in virtue, bodyguard of Christ. Jesus, we are all eased out of kids' dreams; but who can be ripped out of them and live loving after? Three thousand Indians we killed in that square. The only Spaniard to be wounded was the General, scratched by a sword while protecting his Royal prisoner. That night, as I knelt vomiting into a canal, the empire of the Incas stopped. The spring of the clock was snapped. For a thousand miles men sat down not knowing what to do.

> *Enter De Soto.*

DE SOTO: Well, boy, what is it? They weren't armed, is that it? If they had been we could be dead now.

YOUNG MARTIN: Honorably dead! Not alive and shamed.

DE SOTO: And Christ would be dead here too, scarcely born . . .

It is their duty to stay alive and bring Christ to these pagans, de Soto tells the boy, who still fails to understand.

Pizarro rebukes Young Martin for forgetting his manners. Then he approaches Atahuallpa.

PIZARRO: My lord, I am Francisco Pizarro, General of Spain. It is an honor to speak with you. *(Pause.)* You are very tall, my lord. In my country are no such tall men. *(Pause.)* My lord, won't you speak?

> *Atahuallpa turns. For the first time we see his face, carved in a mould of serene arrogance. His whole bearing displays the most entire dignity and natural grace. When he moves or speaks, it is always with the consciousness of his divine origin, his sacred function and his absolute power.*

ATAHUALLPA *(to Felipillo):* Tell him I am Atahuallpa Capac, Son of the Sun, Sun of the Moon, Lord of the Four Quarters. Why does he not kneel?

FELIPILLO: The Inca says he wishes he had killed you when you first came.

PIZARRO: Why didn't he?

ATAHUALLPA: He lied to me. He is not a God. I came for blessing. He sharpened his knives on the shoulders of my servants. I have no word for *him* whose word is evil.

FELIPILLO: He says he wants to make slaves of your best warriors, then kill all the others. Especially you he would kill because you are old; no use as slave.

Felipillo is lying, playing a devious game of his own in order to steal one of Atahuallpa's wives, named Oello, whom Felipillo has admired. But Young Martin detects Felipillo's fraud because he knows a few words of the language including the word "slave," which Atahuallpa did not use. Felipillo is dismissed by Pizarro and from now on Young Martin is interpreter.

Later, to pass the time, Young Martin teaches 33-year-old Atahuallpa a Spanish card game in which the cards represent Churchmen, Nobles, Merchants (with their gold) and Poor—in this way Atahuallpa learns that there are poor in Spain, and that the Conquistadors are after his gold. He faces Pizarro with this knowledge at their next meeting.

ATAHUALLPA: You want gold. That is why you came here.

PIZARRO: My lord—

ATAHUALLPA: You can't hide from me.

> *Showing him the card of the Poor.*

You want gold. I know. Speak.

PIZARRO: You have gold?

ATAHUALLPA: It is the sweat of the sun. It belongs to me.

PIZARRO: Is there much?

ATAHUALLPA: Make me free. I would fill this room.

PIZARRO: Fill?

DE SOTO: It's not possible.

ATAHUALLPA: I am Atahuallpa and I say it.

PIZARRO: How long?

ATAHUALLPA: Two showings of my Mother Moon. But it will not be done.

PIZARRO: Why not?

ATAHUALLPA: You must swear to free me and you have no swear to give.

PIZARRO: You wrong me, my lord.

ATAHUALLPA: No, it is in your face, no swear.

PIZARRO: I never broke word with you. I never promised you safety. If once I did, you would have it.

De Soto warns Pizarro: do not promise what it would not be politic to perform. But Pizarro will have the gold. "He's offering more than any conqueror has ever seen. Alexander, Tamberlaine, or who you please. I mean to have it." Besides. . . .

PIZARRO: . . . He has some meaning for me, this Man-God. An immortal man in whom all his people live completely. He has an answer for time.

DE SOTO: If it was true.

PIZARRO: Yes, if . . .

DE SOTO: General, be careful. I don't understand you in full but I know this: what you do now can never be undone.

But Pizarro swears to set Atahuallpa free in exchange for the roomful of gold, and Atahuallpa swears to keep the peace and not to try to escape. The room is 22 feet long, 17 feet wide and nine feet high; the gold can be in whatever shape it is collected, so Atahuallpa gets the benefit of any interstices of air between trinkets. He calls on all the cities of his empire to send him gold for ransom.

The Inca's attendants dress him in fresh clothing and bring him food. Oello serves him with her own hands and prepares to burn what the Inca does not eat, when Felipillo flings her to the ground and and challenges Atahuallpa and his court to do anything about it. Young Martin, Valverde and de Nizza enter and they chase Felipillo off. Atahuallpa sends his attendants away and enters into a discussion with the priests.

Villac Umu explains that the Sun sends a succession of Gods to look after the Incas, reassimilating each God in the Sun's own time. Valverde wants to know what would happen if one of these man-Gods was killed in battle; Villac Umu replies that the Sun would revive him the next day. But so far this has never happened. All the Incas have departed in the Sun's own good time.

Atahuallpa scoffs at the Christians for what seems to him the cannibalistic symbolism of their Mass.

De Nizza attempts to explain Christ's motives: Christ wanted to share death with man; to share the prison of sin which is each man's life, his dependence on physical needs and a need for companionship. Atahuallpa boasts that he needs no one; he is the Sun. When de Nizza tells him the sun is only a ball of fire, Atahuallpa rises, furious and almost strikes him.

De Nizza continues: the weakness of the Inca life is that there is no choice and therefore no love in it. Marriage, the piece of land—all is ordered by law. To have love there must be freedom of choice. "Love is the only door from the prison of ourselves," de Nizza tells the Inca, and in his view God shares this prison of pain and lust with each man.

"The First Gold Procession" takes place: Indian porters carrying trinkets and utensils parade across the stage, guarded by Spanish soldiers. Then the objects are hung in the middle of the sun. But Pizarro complains to Atahuallpa that a month has gone by and the room is only a quarter full; and there are rumors of revolt. The Inca suggests that Pizarro check for himself that the capital, Cuzco, is entirely quiet. Pizarro sends de Soto with thirty men to check.

Valverde sees Atahuallpa as an embodiment of Satan. De Nizza feels that the true evil of the Inca empire is its levelling; its elimination of hunger, of inequality, of hope and therefore of love. He will not rest until he converts Atahuallpa; but Atahuallpa only declares once more his belief in the overpowering physical and therefore spiritual presence of the father-Sun.

After both the priests have gone, Atahuallpa denounces them as fools.

ATAHUALLPA: You do not believe them.
PIZARRO: You dare not say that to me. . . .
ATAHUALLPA: You do not believe them. Their God is not in your face.
    Pizarro retreats from Atahuallpa, who begins to sing in a strange voice:
You must not rob, O little finch.
The harvest maize, O little finch.
The trap is set, O little finch.
To seize you quick, O little finch.

Ask that black bird, O little finch.
Nailed on a branch, O little finch.
Where is her heart, O little finch.
Where are her plumes, O little finch.

She is cut up, O little finch.
For stealing grain, O little finch.
See, see the fate, O little finch.
Of robber birds, O little finch.

This is a harvest song. For you.
PIZARRO: For me?
ATAHUALLPA: Yes.
PIZARRO: Robber birds.
ATAHUALLPA: Yes.
PIZARRO: You're a robber bird yourself.

ATAHUALLPA: Explain this.

PIZARRO: You killed your brother to get the throne.

ATAHUALLPA: He was a fool. His body was a man. His head was a child.

PIZARRO: But he was the rightful king.

ATAHUALLPA: I was the rightful God. My Sky Father shouted "Rise up! In you lives your Earth Father, Huayana the Warrior. Your brother is fit only to tend herds but you were born to tend my people." So I killed him, and the land smiled.

PIZARRO: That was my work long ago. Tending herds.

ATAHUALLPA: It was not your work. You are a warrior, it is in your face.

PIZARRO: You see much in my face.

ATAHUALLPA: I see my father.

PIZARRO: You do me honor, lad.

ATAHUALLPA: Speak true. If in your home your brother was King, but fit only for herds, would you take his crown?

PIZARRO: If I could.

ATAHUALLPA: And then you would kill him.

PIZARRO: No.

ATAHUALLPA: If you could not keep it for fear of his friends, unless he was dead, you would kill him.

PIZARRO: Let me give you another case. If I come to a country and seize the King's crown but for fear of his friends cannot keep it unless I kill him, what do I do?

ATAHUALLPA: So.

PIZARRO: So.

> *Atahuallpa moves away, offended.*

Oh, it is only a game we play. Tell me—did you hate your brother?

ATAHUALLPA: No. He was ugly like a llama, like his mother. My mother was beautiful.

PIZARRO: I did not know my mother. She was not my father's wife. She left me at the church door for anyone to find. There's talk in the village still, how I was suckled by a sow.

ATAHUALLPA: You are not then . . . ?

PIZARRO: Legitimate? No, my lord, no more than you.

ATAHUALLPA: So.

PIZARRO: So.

> *A pause.*

ATAHUALLPA: To be born so is a sign for a great man.

PIZARRO (*smiling*): I think so too.

> *Atahuallpa removes one of his golden earrings and hangs it on Pizarro's ear.*

And what is that?

ATAHUALLPA: The sign of a nobleman. Only the most important men may wear them. The most near to me.

YOUNG MARTIN: Very becoming, sir. Look.

> *He hands him a dagger. The General looks at himself in the blade.*

PIZARRO: I have never seemed so distinguished to myself. I thank you.

Atahuallpa then dances, lithely, a very difficult ritual mime of a warrior killing foes. Then he invites Pizarro to follow suit. Pizarro must accept the challenge but performs it clumsily, finally slips and laughs at his own awkwardness.

PIZARRO *(to Atahuallpa):* You make me laugh! *(In sudden wonder.) You make me laugh!*
> *Atahuallpa consults his young interpreter, who tries to explain. The Inca nods gravely. Tentatively Pizarro extends his hand to him. Atahuallpa takes it and rises. Quietly they go off together.*

"The Second Gold Procession" and "The Rape of the Sun" take place in an atmosphere of rising greed. Spanish soldiers guarding the Indian porters are grabbing at trinkets and becoming unruly. The treasure room, now half full, is guarded by Diego and the Chavez brothers.

> *They begin to explore the sun itself, leaning out of the chamber and prodding at the petals with their halberds. Suddenly Diego gives a cry of triumph, drives his halberd into a slot in one of the rays, and pulls out the gold inlay. The sun gives a deep groan, like the sound of a great animal being wounded. With greedy yelps, all the soldiers below rush at the sun and start pulling it to bits; they tear out the gold inlays and fling them on the ground, while terrible groans fill the air. In a moment only the great gold frame remains; a broken, blackened sun.*

De Soto returns from Cuzco to tell of a terrible silence throughout the kingdom; men standing in the fields, waiting. He describes the wondrous gold objects he has seen, and as he does so Indians place these same objects in the treasure-chamber: gold maize planted in gold soil; apple trees of gold; gold birds, gold butterflies and twenty life-sized golden llamas grazing in a field.

With the addition of these objects, the treasure room is full. The soldiers talk of the share-out, of what they will buy with their loot: a farm, a house of prostitution. Vasca wants to keep a round gold sun he risked his life to pluck from the very top of a temple, but he is reminded that all gold is community property until it is officially parceled out. The soldiers want to run to the treasure-house and divide the loot immediately, but de Soto brings them under control.

Pizarro and Atahuallpa enter, fencing furiously, a game which the younger, agile Inca wins by knocking the sword from Pizarro's hand. They pour some maize wine in friendship, as de Soto reminds Pizarro that the treasure room is full and that to keep the men quiet it would be well to share the gold out at once. Pizarro agrees, and he dictates to Martin: "The Inca Atahuallpa has today discharged his obligation to General Pizarro. He is therefore a free man."

Atahuallpa kneels and thanks the sun, then rises as Pizarro assures de Soto the Inca will give his word not to harm any Spaniard. Meanwhile, Atahuallpa is fascinated by Young Martin's writing. To test its efficacy, he has Martin write the word for "ransom" on his nail, then shows it to de Soto and is amazed that de Soto knows that this sign says "ransom." Atahuallpa tries this magic out on Pizarro, who is discussing a plan to melt down the precious golden objects. Pizarro must reveal that he cannot read, he never learned. Atahuallpa declares that they will learn together, like brothers—but not tomorrow. Tomorrow he will go.

PIZARRO: . . . What will you do then?

ATAHUALLPA: I will not hurt you.

PIZARRO: Or my army?

ATAHUALLPA: That I do not swear.

PIZARRO: You must.

ATAHUALLPA: You do not say this till now.

PIZARRO: Well, now I say it. Atahuallpa, you must swear to me that you will not hurt a man in my army if I let you go.

ATAHUALLPA: I will not swear this.

PIZARRO: For my sake.

ATAHUALLPA: Three thousand of my servants they killed in the square. Three thousand, without arms. I will avenge them.

PIZARRO: There is a way of mercy, Atahuallpa.

ATAHUALLPA: It is not my way. It is not your way.

Pizarro insists he can't let Atahuallpa go without assurance that he won't attack the Spanish soldiers; Atahuallpa, angered, threatens to kill them all and make drums of their bodies. Pizarro adds to his dictated statement that for the time being, for the good of the country, Atahuallpa must stay on as a "guest" of the army.

Pizarro sends de Soto off to melt down the gold despite the beauty of some of the objects. Young Martin reproaches Pizarro for betraying Atahuallpa. Pizarro resorts to exerting his authority over Young Martin, commanding the lad's obedience and thereby losing his devotion. Young Martin exits, as Old Martin comments that he will never give such devotion to anyone again.

Pizarro is taken by one of his seizures, to Atahuallpa's astonishment. Atahuallpa kneels beside Pizarro. . . .

> . . . Uncertain what to do, he extends his hands, first to the wound, and then to Pizarro's head, which he holds with a kind of remote tenderness. The lights go down all around them.

PIZARRO: Leave it now. There's no cure or more easing for it. Death's entered the house you see. It's half down already, like an old barn. What can you know about that? Youth's in you like a spring of blood, to spurt, for ever. Your skin is singing: "I will never get old." But you will. Time is stalking you, as I did. That gold flesh will cold and blacken. Your eyes will curdle, those wet living eyes . . . They'll make a mummy of your body—I know the custom—and wrap you in robes of vicuna wool, and carry you through all your Empire down to Cuzco. And then they'll fold you in two and sit you on a chair in darkness . . . Atahuallpa, I'm going to die! And the thought of that dark has for years rotted everything for me, all simple joy in life. All through old age, which is so much longer and more terrible than anything in youth, I've watched the circles of nature with hatred. The leaves pop out, the leaves fall. Every year it's piglet time, calving time, time for children in a gush of blood and water. Women dote on this. A birth, any birth, fills them with love. They clap with love, and my soul shrugs. Round and round is all I see: an endless sky of birds, flying and ripping and nursing their young to fly and rip and nurse their young—*for what?* Listen, boy. That prison the Priest calls Sin Original, I know as Time. And seen in time everything is trivial. Pain. Good. God is trivial in that seeing. Trapped in this cage we cry out "There's a gaoler; there must be. At the last, last, last of lasts he will let us out. He will! He will!" . . . But, oh my boy, no one will come for all our crying.

> *Pause.*

I'm going to kill you, Atahuallpa. What does it matter? Words kept, words broken, it all means nothing. Nothing. You go to sleep earlier than me, that's all. Do you see? Look at your eyes, like coals from the sun, glowing forever in the deep of your skull. Like my dream . . . Sing me your little song. *(Singing.)* O little finch . . .

> *Atahuallpa intones a few lines of the song.*

Nothing. Nothing . . . *(In sudden anguish, almost hatred.)* O, lad, what am I going to do with you?

The gold has been melted down and the richest booty in history is shared out: 57,220 gold pieces for Pizarro; 17,640 for de Soto; 2,200 for the Church and a fifth of everything for the Crown (Estete has joined them in time to receive it. And he has seen nothing of the reinforcements); 971,000 to be divided among the others, except for cowardly Rodas, who gets nothing.

De Candia reminds Pizarro that they are maintaining their authority by hanging Indians for all offenses, and he wants to know when they are to hang the Inca. Pizarro, disturbed, tears Atahuallpa's gold ring from his ear and hurls it on the ground. He stalks off. Estete and de Candia plan to relieve the Spanish Crown of the embarrassment of Atahuallpa if Pizarro doesn't do it.

Now that they are in possession of their spoils, the soldiers gamble and carouse, watched intently by the Indians, who are awaiting their chance, making bird-noises. Pizarro is pacing up and down in mental anguish, trying to reach a decision. Salinas and Rodas fight over the gold. De Soto intervenes to stop the fight and he sends all the soldiers to their quarters.

De Soto councils Pizarro to keep his word and let Atahuallpa go, but Pizarro fears that if he does so the Indians will wipe them all out, their story will be forgotten and years later someone else will "discover" Peru. Pizarro's word is law, and he can take it back even from Atahuallpa if he wishes.

But when the other course—to kill the Inca—is urged on him by Estete in the name of the King, Pizarro denounces the King and cites the promise he gave to Atahuallpa. Valverde argues that no Christian promise to a pagan is valid. Pizarro vilifies him and turns to de Nizza for advice: "If Christ was here now, do you think he would kill my Inca?" De Nizza's advice is true to his belief: Peru is a choiceless Empire of vegetables, loveless and Godless and must be stamped out along with its leader for the great spiritual good of everyone. The advice is: kill.

Diego rushes onstage, having just killed a man in a quarrel without meaning to.

DIEGO: May I speak free, sir?

PIZARRO: What? I've got to kill him, is that it?

DIEGO: What other way is there? The men are out of their wits. They feel death all round them.

PIZARRO: So it is and let them face it. I promised them gold, not life. Well, they've got gold. The cripples have gold crutches. The coughers spit gold snot. The bargain's over.

DIEGO: No, sir, not with me. To me you're the greatest General in the world. And we're the greatest company.

PIZARRO: Pizarro's boys, is that it?

DIEGO: Yes, sir. Pizarro's boys.

PIZARRO: Ah, the old band. The dear old regiment. Fool! Look, you were born a man. Not a Blue man or a Green man but A MAN. You are able to feel a thousand separate loves unordered by fear or solitude. Are you going to trade them all in for Gang-love? Flag-love? Carlos-the-Fifth-love? Jesus-the-Christ-love? All that has been tied on you; it is only this that makes you bay for death.

VALVERDE: I'll give you death. When I get back to Spain, a commission will hale you to the stake for what you have said today.

PIZARRO: If I let the Inca go, Father, you'll never get back to Spain.

ESTETE: You madman: see here, you put him underground by sunset or I'll take the knife to him myself.

PIZARRO: ATAHUALLPA!

Atahuallpa enters with Young Martin.

They ache for your death. They want to write psalms to their God in your blood. By they'll all die before you—that I promise.

> *He binds Atahuallpa's arm to his own with a long cord of rope last used to tie some gold.*

There. No, no, some here. Now no one will kill you unless they kill me first.

Pizarro pulls Young Martin's sword from its scabbard and prepares to defend himself against Estete, Diego and de Candia. But Atahuallpa pulls him back and asks the attackers for a few moments with Pizarro. All but Young Martin exit.

Atahuallpa reassures Pizarro that nothing can happen to an Inca unless God wills it.

ATAHUALLPA: Only my father can take me from here. And he would not accept me killed by men like you. Men with no word. You may be King in this land but never God. I am God of the Four Quarters and if you kill me tonight I will rise at dawn when my Father first touches my body with light.

PIZARRO: You believe this?

ATAHUALLPA: All my people know it—it is why they have let me stay with you.

PIZARRO: They knew you could not be harmed. . . .

ATAHUALLPA: So.

PIZARRO: Was this the meaning? The meaning of my dream? You were choosing me?

YOUNG MARTIN: My lord, it's just a boast. Beyond any kind of reason.

PIZARRO: Is it?

YOUNG MARTIN: How can a man die, then get up and walk away?

PIZARRO: Let's hear your creed, boy. "I believe in Jesus Christ, the Son of God, that He suffered under Pontius Pilate, was crucified, dead and buried" . . . and what?

YOUNG MARTIN: Sir?

PIZARRO: What?

YOUNG MARTIN: "He descended into Hell, and on the third day He rose again from the dead . . ."

PIZARRO: You don't believe it!

YOUNG MARTIN: I do! On my soul! I believe with perfect faith!

PIZARRO: But Christ's to be the only one, is that it? What if it's possible, here in a land beyond all maps and scholars, guarded by mountains up to the sky, that there were true Gods on earth, creators of true peace? Think of it! Gods, free of time.

YOUNG MARTIN: It's impossible, my lord.

PIZARRO: It's the only way to give life meaning! To blast out of time and live forever, *us,* in our own persons. This is the law: die in despair or be a God yourself! . . . Look at him: always so calm as if the teeth of life never bit him . . . or the teeth of death. What if it was really true, Martin? That I've gone God-hunting and caught one. A being who can renew his life over and over?

Pizarro works himself into a hysteria; he wants to worship the sun, he has the sun on a string. He runs around and around Atahuallpa at the end of the rope tying them together until finally he falls to the ground, exhausted.

Quietly the Inca pulls in the rope. Then at last he speaks.

ATAHUALLPA: Pizarro. You will die soon and you do not believe in your God. That is why you tremble and keep no word. Believe in me. I will give you a word and fill you with joy. For you I will do a great thing. I will swallow death and spit it out of me.

Pause. This whole scene stays very still.

PIZARRO *(whispering):* You cannot.

ATAHUALLPA: Yes, if my father wills it.

PIZARRO: How if he does not?

ATAHUALLPA: He will. His people still need me. Believe.

PIZARRO: Impossible.

ATAHUALLPA: Believe.

PIZARRO: How? . . . How? . . .

Atahuallpa (Old Martin explains) puts Pizarro through a pagan ritual of confession. Then the Inca cuts himself loose from Pizarro and gives himself up to the soldiers, who set up a pole in the sun and haul Atahuallpa up onto it, as Pizarro tells him: "Fly up, my bird, and come to me again."

Atahuallpa is tried and convicted of killing his brother and usurping the throne; sentence, death by fire. To avoid burning, so that he may have a body for the sun to revive, he makes a deal with Valverde and embraces the Christian faith and is baptized Juan de Atahuallpa on August 29, 1533. In exchange for this baptism he earns the right to be strangled instead of burned.

> *The Inca suddenly raises his head, tears off his clothes and intones in a great voice:*

ATAHUALLPA: INTI! INTI! INTI!

VALVERDE: What does he say?

PIZARRO: The Sun. The Sun. The Sun.

VALVERDE: *Kill him!*

> *Soldiers haul Atahuallpa to his feet and hold him to the stake. Rodas slips a string over his head and while all the Spaniards recite the Latin Creed below, and great howls of "Inca!" come from the darkness, the Sovereign King of Peru is garrotted. His screams and struggles subside; his body falls slack. His executioners hand the corpse down to the soldiers below, who carry it to the center of the stage and drop it at Pizarro's feet. Then all leave save the old man, who stands as if turned to stone. A drum beats. Slowly, in semi-darkness, the stage fills with all the Indians, robed in black and terracotta, wearing the great golden funeral masks of ancient Peru. Grouped round the prone body, they intone a strange Chant of Resurrection, punctuated by hollow beats on the drums and by long, long silences in which they turn their immense triangular eyes inquiringly up to the sky. Finally, after three great cries appear to summon it, the sun rises. Its rays fall on the body. Atahuallpa does not move. The masked men watch in amazement—disbelief—finally, despair. Slowly, with hanging, dejected heads, they shuffle away. Pizarro is left alone with the dead King. He contemplates him. A silence. Then suddenly he slaps it viciously, and the body rolls over on its back.*

PIZARRO: Cheat! You've cheated me! Cheat . . .

> *For a moment his old body is racked with sobs; then, surprised, he feels tears on his cheek. He examines them. The sunlight brightens on his head.*

What's this? What is it? In all your life you never made one of these, I know, and I not till this minute. Look.

> *He kneels to show the dead Inca.*

Ah, no. You have no eyes for me now, Atahuallpa: they are dusty balls of amber I can tap on. You have no peace for me, Atahuallpa: the birds still scream in your forest. You have no joy for me, Atahuallpa, my boy: the only joy is in death. I lived between two hates: I die between two darks: blind eyes and a blind sky. And yet you saw once. The sky sees nothing, but you saw. Is there comfort there? The sky knows no feeling, but we know them, that's sure. Martin's hope, and de Soto's honor, and your trust—your trust which hunted me: we alone make these. That's some marvel, yes, some marvel. To sit in a great cold silence, and sing out sweet with just our own warm breath: that's some marvel, surely. To make water in a sand world: surely, surely . . . God's just a name on your nail; and naming begins cries and cruelties. But to live without hope of after, and make whatever God there is, oh, that's some immortal business surely . . . I'm tired. Where are you? You're so cold. I'd warm you if I could. But there's no warming now, not ever now. I'm colding too. There's a snow of death falling all round us. You can almost see it. It's over, lad, I'm coming after you. There's nothing but peace to come. We'll be put into the same earth, father and son in our own land. And that sun will roam uncaught over his empty pasture.

OLD MARTIN: So fell Peru. We gave her greed, hunger and the Cross: three gifts for the civilized life. The family groups that sang on the terraces are gone. In their place slaves shuffle underground and they don't sing there. Peru is a silent country, frozen in avarice. So fell Spain, gorged with gold; distended; now dying.

PIZARRO (singing):
    Where is her heart, O little finch . . .

OLD MARTIN: And so fell you, General, my master, whom men called the Son of His Own Deeds. He was killed later in a quarrel with his partner, who brought up the reinforcements. But to speak truth, he sat down that morning and never really got up again.

PIZARRO (singing):
    Where are her plumes, O little finch . . .

OLD MARTIN: I'm the only one left now of that company: landowner— slaveowner—and forty years from any time of hope. It put out a good blossom, but it was shaken off rough. After that I reckon the fruit always comes sour, and doesn't sweeten up much with age.

PIZARRO (singing):
    She is cut up, O little finch.
    For stealing grain, O little finch . . .

OLD MARTIN: General you did for me, and now I've done for you. And there's no joy in that. Or in anything now. But then there's no joy in the world could match for me what I had when I first went with you across the water to find the gold country. And no pain like losing it. Save you all.

    He goes out. Pizarro lies beside the body of Atahuallpa and quietly
    sings to it.

PIZARRO (singing):
    See, see the fate, O little finch,
    Of robber birds, O little finch.
        The sun glares at the audience. Curtain.

HOGAN'S GOAT

A Play in Two Acts

BY WILLIAM ALFRED

Cast and credits appear on page 425

Unlike the first-generation 1890 Irish-American characters of his Hogan's
Goat, *WILLIAM ALFRED was Brooklyn-born (on August 16, 1922), Brook-
lyn-bred (the son of a bricklayer) and Brooklyn-educated. His last year at
Brooklyn College was interrupted by army service from 1941 to 1945 in
World War II, ending in New Guinea and Manila. Alfred returned to Brook-
lyn College to get his BA degree. Then he went to Harvard for his MA and
PhD, and he has been teaching at Harvard since 1954, as a Professor of En-
glish since 1963.*

Hogan's Goat *(the only off-Broadway play to make the Best Plays list in
1965-66) is William Alfred's first professional production. His published
works include a new translation of* Beowulf *and another verse play,* Agamemnon, *which is to be produced in 1966 in Paris, starring Ingrid Bergman. Alfred's theatrical work-in-progress is a comedy about long Irish engagements
called* The Curse of an Aching Heart; *and he intends writing a play about
Agnes Hogan and the events preceding those of* Hogan's Goat.

Time: April 1890

Place: The City of Brooklyn

ACT I

Scene 1: The parlor of Matthew Stanton's flat

SYNOPSIS: It is Thursday, April 28, 1890, 10 p.m. A two-level set represents a house on Fifth Street in Brooklyn which the Stantons share with the Haggerty family. Downstairs is the kitchen of the Haggertys' apartment (blacked out at curtain rise). A narrow, steep staircase at right leads to the Stantons' parlor on the upper floor.

> *Enter Matthew Stanton, carrying a bottle of champagne. He is a handsome, auburn-haired man in his late thirties, dressed carefully in a four-buttoned suit of good serge, and a soft black hat. . . .*

Matthew Stanton bounds up the stairs, hides the bottle of champagne behind the sofa in a room whose furniture is tufted and fringed and whose windows are draped in the manner of the period. Stanton, who is Leader of the Sixth Ward of Brooklyn, calls out for his wife Kathleen.

> *Enter Kathleen Stanton, closing the door behind her. She is tall and slim and dressed in a black broadcloth suit which brings out the redness of her hair and the whiteness of her skin.*

KATHLEEN:

I wish you wouldn't take those stairs so fast;
They're wicked: You could catch your foot and fall—
I had a bit of a headache and lay down.
Why, Mattie darling, what's the matter with you?
You're gray as wasp's nests.

STANTON:

I'm to be the mayor!
No more that plug who runs the Court Café
And owes his ear to every deadbeat sport
With a favor in mind and ten cents for a ball,
But mayor of Brooklyn, and you the mayor's lady.
They caught Ned Quinn with his red fist in the till,
The Party of Reform, I mean, and we
"Are going to beat their game with restitution
And self-reform." Say something, can't you, Kate!

KATHLEEN (*sits down heavily and puts her hand to her temple*):
Oh, Mattie, Mattie.

STANTON:

Jesus! Are you crying?

I've what I wanted since I landed here
Twelve years ago, and she breaks into tears.
KATHLEEN: It's that I'm—
STANTON: What? You're what?
KATHLEEN: Afraid.

She is afraid, and she believes that he is, too. They have a quarrel which ends in an embrace.

Kathleen asks Stanton to seek a dispensation from Father Coyne, so that they can be secretly re-married by their Church.

STANTON: Now?
KATHLEEN:
     Yes, Matt, now. Before it is too late.
     We aren't married.
STANTON:
          What was that in London,
     The drunkard's pledge I took?
KATHLEEN:
          We're Catholics, Matt.
     Since when can Catholics make a valid marriage
     In a city hall? You have to tell the priest—
STANTON:
     Shall I tell him now? Do you take me for a fool
     To throw away the mayor's chair for that?
KATHLEEN:
     I slink to Sunday mass like a pavement nymph.
     It's three years now since I made my Easter Duty,
     Three years of telling Father Coyne that we
     Receive at Easter Mass in the Cathedral,
     Mortal Sin on Mortal Sin, Matt. If I died,
     I'd go to Hell—

Stanton doesn't believe God would punish Kathleen for a mere technicality; Kathleen sees their City-Hall marriage as no mere technicality, but "three years' fornication." She lights a cigarette, and Matt calls smoking a "whore's habit."

Stanton will arrange for a church marriage some day, but in the meantime, he fears that he will lose the mayorality if their temporary arrangement is discovered by the voters. Kathleen warns him to consider, not his ambition, but his soul, and Stanton blurts out his own Godfearing but anti-dogmatic creed: men will be men, and "God sets no traps."

STANTON: . . . What if they should make a scandal of us?
KATHLEEN: Could we be worse off than we are?
STANTON: Kathleen!
KATHLEEN: Could we be worse off than we are, I said?

STANTON:

> Could we! We could. You don't know poverty.
> You don't know what it is to do without,
> Not fine clothes only, or a handsome house,
> But men's respect. I do. I have been poor.
> "Mattie, will you run down to the corner,
> And buy me some cigars" or "Mattie, get
> This gentleman a cab." Nine years, I served
> Ned Quinn and Agnes Hogan, day by day,
> Buying my freedom like a Roman slave.
> Will you ask me to put liberty at stake
> To ease your scrupulous conscience? If you do,
> You're not the woman that I took you for
> When I married you. Have you no courage, Kate?

Yes, she has courage; the courage to endure her homesickness for Dublin, where women's smoking is accepted and the talk was of books and such. Here the talk is not intellectual, but the gossip of those who have been cooks and maids; "servants' talk." She is lonely.

STANTON:

> Are you the only exile of us all?
> You slept your crossing through in a rosewood berth
> With the swells a hundred feet below your portholes,
> And ate off China on a linen cloth,
> With the air around you fresh as the first of May.
> I slept six deep in a bunk short as a coffin
> Between a poisoned pup of a seasick boy
> And a slaughtered pig of a snorer from Kildare,
> Who wrestled elephants the wild nights through,
> And sweated sour milk. I wolfed my meals,
> Green water, and salt beef, and wooden biscuits,
> On my hunkers like an ape, in a four-foot aisle
> As choked as the one door of a burning school.
> I crossed in mid-December: seven weeks
> Of driving rain that kept the hatches battened
> In a hold so low of beam a man my height
> Could never lift his head. And I couldn't wash.
> Water was low; the place was like an icehouse;
> And girls were thick as field mice in a haystack
> In the bunk across. I would have died of shame,
> When I stood in the landing shed of this "promised land,"
> As naked as the day I first saw light,
> Defiled with my own waste like a dying cat,
> And a lousy red beard on me like a tinker's,
> While a bitch of a doctor, with his nails too long,
> Dared tell me: "In Amurrica, we bathe!"

I'd have died with shame, had I sailed here to die.
I swallowed pride and rage, and made a vow
The time would come when I could spit both out
In the face of the likes of him. I made a vow
I'd fight my way to power if it killed me,
Not only for myself, but for our kind,
For the men behind me, laughing out of fear,
At their own shame as well as mine, for the women,
Behind the board partition, frightened dumb
With worry they'd be sent back home to starve
Because they'd dirty feet. I was born again.
It came to me as brutal as the cold
That makes us flinch the day the midwife takes
Our wet heels in her fist, and punches breath
Into our dangling carcasses: Get power!
Without it, there can be do decency,
No virtue and no grace. I have kept my vow.
The mayor's chair is mine but for the running.
Will you have me lose it for your convent scruples?
        Pause.
KATHLEEN: You never told me that about your landing.

He has won Kate's sympathy, and now he asks for her patience. On Sunday next, on the steamer ride to Seagate for Mayor Quinn's birthday clambake the candidacy is to be announced (after Stanton settles his differences with Quinn so that there will be unity within the Party). Stanton promises he'll see the priest about re-marriage as soon as he wins the election. They open the champagne for a toast to the future.

Scene 2: The back room of Stanton's saloon, The Court Café

At 11 o'clock that night, three people are gathered in the back room of Stanton's saloon. Double glass-paned doors upstage lead to the bar. At left is a Ladies' Entrance from the street. The furniture includes tables, chairs, an upright piano with a dead fern sitting on it. There are a few paper decorations, as though there had recently been a celebration. The three seated at one of the tables with whiskeys in front of them are:

> . . . *John "Black Jack" Haggerty, in his late sixties, wearing his Sunday clothes, his hair parted in the middle and swagged over his eyebrows in dove's wings, his handlebar mustache repeating the design. Both hair and mustache are dyed an improbable black. To Haggerty's left, Petey Boyle, a young tough in his twenties, his heavy hair parted in the middle and combed oilily back, the teeth marks of the comb still in it. His rachitic frame is wiry as a weed; and he is dressed in a Salvation Army suit that droops in the seat, balloons at the knees and elbows. Next to Boyle, but facing the*

> *audience, Bessie Legg, a blonde girl in her late twenties or early thirties, her hair in a pompadour under a Floradora hat that looks like an ostrich nest, a long feather boa on, together with many strands of glass beads, and rings on every finger but her thumbs, all cheap. Her doll's face is a bit crumpled, but there is no petulance in it, merely jocose self-indulgence.*

They are discussing Stanton's candidacy; "Black Jack" Haggerty is Assistant Leader of the Ward and head of the Matthew Stanton Association. Stanton has a couple of personal problems in his past, but Haggerty thinks things will work out. Quinn is to be told by Boss Murphy and persuaded to go along with Stanton and the Party, sometime during the four days before his planned birthday celebration down in Seagate.

Maria Haggerty comes in by the Ladies' Entrance.

> *She is a tall, raw-boned woman in her late sixties, with loose-stranded, iron-gray hair pulled back around a center part in a tight bun. She wears a rusty black toque, and a long black woolen coat with a frayed hem, and is carrying a large handbag, which she sets down on the floor as she settles wearily into the chair to stage right of Haggerty, her husband.*

Haggerty urges them all, including his wife, to put away their doubts and celebrate Stanton's candidacy.

MARIA:
 I'm sure I'm glad for Matt's sake. He's worked hard,
 And he's been good, giving us the flat and all.
 But in a way, you know, Ned Quinn is right:
 Matt's hard on people, harder than he should be.
 He's a lot to answer for before he dies.
BESSIE: You mean Ag Hogan?
MARIA: Yes, I do.
BESSIE:
       Poor girl.
 When I was there this morning, she looked awful.
MARIA:
 She'll never live to comb out a gray head.
 I've just come now from giving her her tea,
 In that coffin of a furnished room in Smith Street.
 I looked at the cheesecloth curtains hung on strings;
 And I thought of all those velvet-muffled windows,
 Those carpets red as blood and deep as snow,
 Those tables glistening underneath the lamps
 Like rosy gold, in her big house in Seagate.
 And I said to myself, if it weren't for Agnes Hogan,
 Matt would be a grocery clerk at Nolan's,

And not the owner of The Court Café.
And candidate for mayor; and there she lies,
Flat on her back with two beanbags of buckshot
On her shriveled breasts, to chain her to the mattress,
As if she could move, her eyes in a black stare
At the white paint peeling off that iron bedstead,
Like scabs of a rash; and he never once comes near her,
For fear, I suppose, they'd call him Hogan's Goat,
And his missis might find out about their high jinks.
And yet if Matt were any kind of man,
Wouldn't he go and take her in his arms,
And say, "You hurt me bad three years ago;
But I hurt you as bad. Forgive and forget."
Maybe it's because the girl's my niece,
But I think I'd feel the same if she were not.

Haggerty provokes Bessie with a remark about one of *her* indiscretions. At the height of their quarrel, Matt Stanton comes in from the bar with a crowd of well-wishers singing "He'll make a jolly good mayor!" The candidacy is supposed to be a secret until Quinn is told, but friends call on Stanton to make a speech.

STANTON:
        . . . When I returned from England
Three years ago with my new wife, I thought
My chances to get back into the Party
Were gone for good. Yet in those three short years
You stuck by me so fast, the Party made me
Leader of the Ward in which the mayor
I had a falling-out with lives; and now
You're bent on giving me his place.
Ned Quinn—

Petey Boyle jumps onto a table and leads a song whose burden is that Ned Quinn is a swindler, "Says the Shan Van Vocht." Father Coyne enters, unnoticed, wearing his biretta and an old black overcoat over his cassock.

Father Coyne reproaches them for mocking Ned Quinn: hate the sin but love the sinner. Evil can arise sometimes from good, Father Coyne warns Stanton; punish the evil, but do not over-react and drive out the good too. Take Quinn's office away, but don't condemn him.

Stanton disagrees. Corruption must be disowned along with those who create it. . . .

STANTON:
        . . . Before they can infect us with the pox
We came across the ocean to avoid,
Liberty gone blind, the death of honor!—

Would you have the big men of this city say
That they were right in keeping us cheap labor,
Because we are not fit for nobler service,
We dirty what we touch? Say that they will,
And with full right, unless we dare cut free
From these enfeebling politics of pity,
And rule the city right. Ned Quinn must go—

The crowd cheers Stanton, but Father Coyne warns him: judge not. Stanton promises he'll make no move against Quinn unless Quinn moves first.

The others leave, as Father Coyne asks to see Stanton alone. Father Coyne urges Stanton to go see Agnes Hogan, who's dying. But Stanton doesn't want to re-stimulate old gossip that his wife might hear. And, Stanton remembers, it was Quinn who was most to blame for Ag's downfall from a combination of tuberculosis and whiskey and other excesses. Josie Finn had exposed the whole scandal.

STANTON: . . . I was the goat for fair.
FATHER COYNE:
    Ag was fully clothed.
    And so was Quinn.
STANTON:
    You didn't see them, Father.
    They were leg in leg when Josie brought me in.
    Asleep, I grant you, but his ham of a hand
    Was tangled in the fullness of her hair—

Still, Father Coyne urges Stanton: don't let Agnes die unreconciled. Someone is bound to tell Kathleen Stanton about Agnes, anyhow, during the political campaign. But Stanton can't bring himself to admit to his wife he "serviced" Ag Hogan for three years. He was faithful to Ag during those years, he assures Father Coyne, but she played him false with Quinn.

Father Coyne is not swallowing this. Stanton never married Ag, Father Coyne declares, because he wanted her for fun only, he was afraid she'd spoil his chances for mayor, he was afraid he'd be called "Hogan's Goat" forever, he was glad when he found Quinn with her, it gave him an excuse to break away. Stanton is a good man at heart, Father Coyne pleads, a good man who should not permit himself to do wrong.

FATHER COYNE:
    . . . Hogan's goat or not,
    Pocket your pride, and tell your wife about her.
    Go talk with Ag, and let her die in peace,
    Or else you'll be her goat in the Bible sense,
    With all her sins on your head, and the world a desert. . . .

Still, Stanton is reluctant to upset Katie with this old story. Father Coyne argues to the contrary. Telling Katie may help to ease the stiffness that lies between them.

STANTON:
Who dares to say that something stands between us?
That's a pack of lies!
FATHER COYNE: Is it? Tell Katie, Matt—

Boyle bursts in with the news that Ag is dying. Stanton agrees to accompany Father Coyne to her deathbed, and they leave.

Scene 3: The all-night Printer's Church in the Newspaper Row of Brooklyn on lower Fulton Street.

At midnight that same night, Stanton is kneeling on a prie-dieu, confessing to Father Maloney; confessing a wrong against Agnes Hogan.

STANTON:
I lived with her three years before I married.
They pulled the sheet over her face an hour ago.
The hem of it gave. It was gray as a buried rag.
She wouldn't have the priest. She lay there sweating,
And they around her with their lighted candles.
She glowered and said, "If such love was a sin,
I'd rather not make peace with God at all."
They pressed her hard. She shook and shook her head.
She kept on shaking it until she died—
Absolve her through me!

But Father Maloney has no power to absolve Agnes by proxy; he can only absolve Stanton. Stanton explains further to the priest: a long time ago he found Agnes Hogan in bed with another man and left her screaming at him. This night, as she lay dying, she welcomed him back with joyous open arms.

Still Father Maloney can give Stanton no comfort. Agnes Hogan died "in the Devil's arms", unrepentant and unshriven. And Father Maloney's judgment of Stanton will be no less severe because Stanton has come furtively to confession in a strange parish, with a strange priest.

Stanton, furious, rejects forgiveness by the likes of Father Maloney, whom he accuses of dragging men down. Yes, down to earth, to become humble, Father Maloney agrees, and he warns angry Stanton to be careful or he will receive no absolution himself.

STANTON:
. . . Who can absolve us but ourselves!
I am what I am. What I have done, I'd cause for.
It was seeing what life did to her unmanned me;

It was looking in her eyes as they guttered out
That drove me here like a scared kid from the bogs
Who takes the clouds that bruise the light for demons.
But thanks to the words from the open grave of your mouth
I see that fear for the wind in fog that it is
And it is killed for good. I'm my own man now.
I can say that for the first time in my life.
I'm free of her; and I'm free of you and yours.
Come what come may to me, from this day forward,
I'll not fall to my knees for man or God.
    Stanton rises and quickly strides out. Father Maloney rises.
FATHER MALONEY: Will you dare to turn your back on the living God!

Scene 4: The back room of Fogarty's Saloon

"Palsy" Murphy, Boss of Brooklyn and head of the Edward Quinn Association, is seated at a table holding a sheaf of papers. . . .

> . . . *He is a florid, rather stout man in his late fifties, with black hair* en brosse, *graying at the temples. Mayor Edward Quinn stands facing Murphy like a statue of a lawyer in a park. He is a tall, husky, big-boned man in his seventies, bald, but with hair growing out of his ears. He is dressed in rumpled morning clothes.*

With interruptions and outbursts from Quinn, Murphy is reading aloud a speech delivered by Stanton at a "non-political" gathering at Father Coyne's church (Quinn: "I roofed his sieve of a church and glazed it too. . . . There's not a priest you can trust!") to raise money to pay Agnes Hogan's debts. The Party of Reform ("A Lutheran lawyer with a flytrap mouth!") is in possession of some affidavits ("Got by collusion and by audits forged!") that the treasury is missing $15,000 ("They couldn't even get that business right, it's twenty thousand, Palsy, if it's a cent!") and they will expose this shortage unless Quinn withdraws his candidacy in the next election ("See, that's Matt's game. He's out to get my job . . . as sneaky as a rat in a hotel kitchen!").

Quinn recalls how he gave 25-year-old Stanton his break (at Ag Hogan's urging) after Stanton had lost a job with a grocer. Quinn put Stanton on with Judge Muldooney. Ag loved Stanton ever after and welcomed him on her deathbed, from which Agnes barred Quinn.

Murphy observes that Mrs. Stanton knows only that Agnes helped her husband, not about the love affair.

Quinn reminds Murphy that if he goes to jail Murphy goes too—no more "hundred-dollar suits and fancy feeds with tarts in Rector's." Quinn accuses his fellow party members of wanting to tear him down and pretend to be respectable now that they have "reached the shore."

Murphy counters by reading more of Matt's speech. Stanton had recommended that they put up the money to keep Quinn out of jail and cover his peculation. Stanton agreed to pledge $3,000. But Quinn rejects help and sympathy from "a greenhorn that I picked up in a barroom to run my sweetheart's errands."

QUINN:

  . . . He took Ag from me first; that's how he started.
He ran her roadhouse for her. "He was handsome!
He'd skin like milk, and eyes like stars in winter!"
And he was young and shrewd! She taught him manners:
What clothes to wear, what cutlery to begin with,
What twaddle he must speak when introduced
To the state bigwigs down from Albany.
He told her that he loved her. She ditched me.
I'm twenty years her senior. Then that day,
That famous Labor Day three years ago,
We'd a drink or two, you know, for old times' sake,
And we passed out, and that bitch Josie Finn
Found out about us, and brought Matt in on us,
Our arms around each other like two children.
And he spat on poor Ag's carpet, called her a whore,
Me a degenerate. Three years ago,
The very year he married this Kathleen,
The Lord knows who, James, from the Christ knows where,
In some cosy hocus-pocus there in London,
To show Ag he could do without her. He never spoke
To Ag at all until he found her done for,
Dying lung by lung. He'd never speak to me at all
If I were not in trouble.
Don't you see the triumph of it, Palsy Murphy!
He takes his vengeance in a show of mercy.
He weeps as he destroys! He's a crocodile—

Now it's time for Murphy to get down to brass tacks and Party policy. The Party agrees with Stanton; the Party will restore the missing money, on condition that Quinn resign his office.

Quinn is furious; he will *not* resign. He'll fight—he'll make restitution himself, and he'll see them all in the soup together before he'll let Matt Stanton take his job.

MURPHY: The Party will disown you!
QUINN:

      Let them try!
I'll grease the palm of every squarehead deadbeat
From Greenwood Cemetery to the Narrows
Who'll stagger to the polls for three months' rent,
I'll buy the blackface vote off all the fences
Down Fulton Street from Hudson Avenue.
I'll vote from every plot in Holy Cross

With an Irish headstone on it. I'll win this fight—
MURPHY: I'll telegraph to Albany. I warn you!
QUINN: Damn Albany! Get out of here! Get out!

Murphy leaves, and Quinn calls in Bill, his hanger-on, a wiry drunk, about seventy. He sends Bill on an errand to get Agnes Hogan a big wreath with a gold-lettered message "For Agnes Mary Hogan, gone but not forgotten." *That should help to get gossip started.* . . .

Scene 5: The Haggertys' kitchen beneath the Stantons' parlor

At 8 o'clock that evening, the wake for Agnes Hogan is taking place in the Haggertys' flat in Stanton's house. The kitchen furniture is cheap and well-worn. Behind the kitchen table is the cooking stove placed in the chimney whose mantle is a clutter of odds and ends. At right of the stove, under a brown velour portiere, is the entrance to the rest of the flat, from which the sounds of the wake can be heard. The door at right to the hall and the Stantons' stairway is held ajar by Quinn's flower piece leaning against it.

> *Seated to stage left of the table is Josie Finn, a tall, rather handsome woman in her late thirties, with her black hair in a loose bun. Opposite her sits Ann Mulcahy, a small, plump woman with a face like a withered apple, red hair gone white, and fine searching eyes.*

They are waiting for the tea kettle to boil, and talking. They agree that Stanton should have luck for letting the wake be held here. Petey Boyle comes in and assumes Josie has come here to gloat at Ag's death, hurls an obscenity at her and departs. Josie is another one whom Ag wouldn't allow near her deathbed.

Josie vows to guard her tongue and her temper from now on and almost gets angry at Ann, just as Father Coyne enters. Father Coyne wants to know why for three years Josie has been going to other churches instead of to his parish, where she belongs. Gentle Ann prevents Father Coyne from pursuing this subject, and he departs.

Ann is worried for fear that Stanton and Quinn will confront each other at this wake, and she goes to see what she can do to prevent it. While Josie is brewing the tea, Quinn comes into the kitchen.

Quinn wants to know why Agnes is wearing a wedding ring, and Josie tells him: it was her mother's, Agnes requested that she be buried wearing it. Josie confesses to Quinn her shame that she betrayed Agnes, broke her heart three years ago by helping to create that drunken misunderstanding.

JOSIE:
    I'll never interfere that way again.
    If it were not for me, they'd have been married,
    And there'd have been no sin. Has Ag gone to Hell?
    Do you think that, Ned? For that would be my fault.

Have I destroyed her life forever, Ned,
In this world and the next?
        Pause.
QUINN:
        You're talking blather.
Ach, God's more merciful than Father Coyne,
Be sure of that, or we'd have been roasted black,
The whole damned lot of us, long since.
        Pause.
Come on.
Wouldn't you like to make it up to Ag, Jo?
Do something for her dead? That's all I'm asking.
Shouldn't Matt pay for what he did to her?
All that you'd need to say's a single sentence,
When the Lady Duchess Kathleen Kakiak
Descends in visitation: "Mrs. Stanton,
Sure, God will bless you for your charity."
"My charity?" she'll ask. You'll say, "You know,
Ag having lived with Matt three years and all."
That's all you'd have to say.

Josie knows it is not revenge for Agnes that Quinn really wants, but City Hall. She urges Quinn to give up his "murderous pride." Quinn declares that he *must* fight. Albany has threatened to destroy him, so he had to send a letter, yielding—but it's only a tactic, he means to fight on and win.

Josie wishes she had cast out pride and begged Agnes for forgiveness. Quinn accuses Josie of still loving Matt Stanton, and she doesn't deny it. Quinn tells her that Stanton is a traitor to her, making derogatory remarks about her behind her back. Quinn cites a ridiculing toast Stanton made concerning Josie, at a party. Quinn warns her: Stanton has been false to him, to Ag and to Kathleen, he'll be false to Josie too.

QUINN: . . . And when Stanton plays you false, don't whine to me.
        *Enter Kathleen, Stanton and Murphy, Murphy is carrying a case
        of liquor, which he sets on the chair nearest him, his eyes fixed on
        Quinn and Stanton confronting each other.*
STANTON:
        I will not play her false, nor will I you . . .
I got your letter; and I thank you for it.
I'm sorry that my winning means your loss.
        Pause. Quinn glares at Stanton, then takes a step towards the door.
MURPHY: Wait, Ned!
STANTON:
        I swear, I'll see you through this trouble.
I want to be your friend again. Shake hands.
Come on, man. And what better place than here.
I'm sure Ag would have wanted it. Come on—

QUINN:

   Good, God! The goat can talk. When Ag was living, though,
   You rarely met the livestock in the house!
      Stanton hurls himself at Quinn, and takes him by the throat. Kath-
      leen screams. Josie and Murphy rush to get between them.
STANTON: I'll kill him!

While Murphy is holding Stanton, Quinn carefully looks at Stanton and then spits in his face. He departs, while Josie hands Stanton a rag to wipe his face. Stanton turns on Josie with a remark that hurts her feelings. Kathleen protests, but the more she protests the more callous Stanton becomes.

KATHLEEN: Matt, beg her pardon.
STANTON:

   For what? For what? Don't waste your sympathy
   On that one. And stay clear of her as can be:
   She has a wicked tongue. Watch out for her—
KATHLEEN: The woman heard you!—
STANTON:

   Devil a bit I care!
   Will you come into the parlor!
KATHLEEN: Matt, she's crying.
      Stanton strides over towards Josie, awkward with remorse.
STANTON: Josie—
JOSIE: Never mind. I heard you, Matt.
STANTON:

   The devil
   Take you then, for your big ears!
JOSIE: The devil take me, Matt.

All exit but Josie, who picks up the rag. Maria Haggerty comes in; she wants Josie to make it up with Stanton, who can be forgiven for becoming over-wrought by Ag's death and other problems. Contemptuously, Josie calls him "Hogan's Goat," her "fancy boy." Josie agrees to make it up with Stanton—maybe—if he makes the first move.

Kathleen comes in to talk with Josie as Maria leaves to get Stanton.

KATHLEEN:

   . . . Mrs. Finn, please. Matthew meant no harm . . .
   He has a dreadful temper. You know that.
   And he's like a scalded cat since yesterday
   When he got the news that Agnes Hogan died.
      Pause.
   He told me just how much she'd meant to him
   When he was starting out on his career.
   You know that better, maybe, than myself—

JOSIE:

    He told you that, did he! Did he tell you how
    He lived with her three years in a state of sin
    In a love nest of a roadhouse down in Seagate?
    And the devil take the talk! Did he tell you, too,
    She drank herself consumptive for his sake
    Because he threw her over three years since,
    When he'd got all he wanted from her, missis,
    And married you—

> *Kathleen gasps and runs out the door. Josie looks straight ahead into the air before her face, brings both hands to her forehead with a slap, and sits swaying in her chair. Curtain.*

ACT II

Scene 1: The parlor of Matthew Stanton's flat

At 11 o'clock that evening, there is the sound of a scuffle and then the lights come up, revealing Stanton on the sofa dabbing blood from a cut on his forehead and Kathleen holding the silver hand mirror with which she has just struck him. Fury has ebbed from Kathleen, and she stands limp; under the influence of drink, but with her mind still working.

Kathleen has been drinking in Stanton's own saloon with blowsy Bessie Legg. How could she do this to Stanton on the night that he has won, with Quinn's resignation in hand? Because she feels that they are not really married—no more than Matt and Ag were.

Now Stanton knows that Kathleen *knows*. A flare-up between them ends in an embrace.

STANTON: I married you because I love you, Kate.
KATHLEEN:

    Then why was I the one soul in this city
    Who didn't know of you and Agnes? Why?
STANTON: I didn't want to hurt you.
KATHLEEN:

        Well, you have—
    How do I know you won't abandon me
    If I don't get you what you want from life?
STANTON: Don't say such things.
KATHLEEN:

    No wonder they seemed strange,
    Your what-d'ya-callem's, your constituents:
    They none of them could look me in the face
    For fear they might let on. Didn't Bessie Legg
    Tell me she thought the only reason Agnes Hogan
    Went to bed with Quinn was to prove to herself

That there was someone loved her, when she saw
Your feelings for her dying like wet coal,
And realized she'd lost you? How do I know
The same thing will not happen to myself;
And people won't be saying a year from now,
Kate went the same way as the poor dead whore?
STANTON: Kate. Don't call her that.
KATHLEEN: Why not? Don't they?
STANTON:
They don't. And don't you call her out of name.
You never knew her. And the talk you've heard
Has been about her as she was in public,
Stripping the heavy diamonds off her fingers
To keep the party going one more hour.
I knew what lay behind it. It was mine:
Her will to fullness. She contained a man
As the wind does, the first giddy days of spring,
When your coat blows open, and your blood beats hard,
As clear as ice, and warm as a chimney wall.
'Twas she first gave me heart to dare be free.
All threats turned promise when she talked to you.
With her on your arm, you saw your life before you
Like breast-high wheat in the soft dazzle of August.
She had a way of cupping her long hands
Around my bulldog's mug, as if I were
Some fancy fruit she'd bought beyond her means,
And laughing with delight. She put nothing on
She did not feel, and felt with flesh and soul.
I don't believe she knew what shame might be.
You could not resist her. *I* could not. I tried.
I was twenty-five years old when I first met her.
I'd never . . .
KATHLEEN: What?
STANTON: I was what you'd call a virgin . . .
KATHLEEN: The saints preserve us!
STANTON:
        Yes, it's funny now;
It wasn't funny then.
        Pause.
It was she wooed me.
It seemed—Lord knows, I don't—unnatural.
She was ten years my senior. But, oh, Kate,
To look at her downstairs, you'd never know
What once she was! Her hair was bronze and silver
Like pear trees in full bloom, her eyes were opal,
Her skin was like new milk, and her blue veins
Trembled in the shimmer of her full straight neck

Like threads of violets fallen from her hair
And filliped by the breeze . . .

Agnes bought Stanton presents; she asked him to help run her gaming
rooms. When he caught her with Quinn, he broke with her. He had realized
the first time he heard himself called "Hogan's Goat" that if he continued
the relationship it was goodbye to all his ambitions. And, at the last, Agnes
was treating him like a chattel.

Once when Agnes and Stanton had a fight, Stanton went to Newark (he
won't tell Kathleen what happened there). Agnes followed him. They made
up their quarrel in some mysterious way, and then came back. Kathleen thinks
that maybe Stanton still loves Agnes, but no; part of him died when he caught
her with Quinn, only to be reborn when Stanton met Kathleen in London.
He had to marry Kathleen quickly, for fear of losing her. Stanton didn't tell
Kathleen about Agnes, partly because . . .

STANTON:
          . . . I was ashamed
That I had let her woo me like a girl,
And I could not resist her or say no
For three long years. It was that slavery
I was ashamed of most—
KATHLEEN:
          That slavery,
My dear, is love—
STANTON: What is it you just said?
KATHLEEN: I'm terrible drunk.
STANTON:
          Sure, don't I know that!
And if you weren't, Kate, you'd be a widow.
You'd have brained me good and proper with that mirror,
If your eye had not been blurred—

Stanton summons Kathleen to bed as she rambles on: Stanton didn't come
looking for her in the saloon; he waited for her to come crawling home to
him. Kathleen is afraid of Agnes Hogan's continuing influence.

KATHLEEN:
          . . . Those things you said about you and Ag Hogan,
About resenting how you felt for her,
They go for me—Oh, Matt, we're like twin children:
The pride is in our blood—I'd like to kill you,
Or die myself. Do you understand me, Matt!
Don't let me. I am sick with shame. I love you—
          Stanton kisses her on the mouth, lifts her to her feet, and helps her
          towards the bedroom.
STANTON: You're crying drunk—

KATHLEEN:
> In vino veritas.
> There's truth in drink.

STANTON:
> God! Now she's quoting Latin,
> And me so ignorant that all I know
> Is that I'm cold and want my wife beside me
> Before I can feel warm again or rest.
> Ag's dead, Kate, dead.
> But, Katie, we're alive.
> Come with me out of the cold. Ag's gone for good.

Scene 2: The back room of Stanton's saloon, The Court Café

At midnight the same night, there is a "Stanton for Mayor" sign hung in the back room of Stanton's saloon. Bessie Legg is seated, staring at an empty glass. Bill (Quinn's hanger-on) peeks in the door of the Ladies' Entrance to see who's there, and then Bill and Quinn enter.

Bessie fears that Quinn's presence in Stanton's saloon will start a riot. Quinn gives her money to go into the bar and buy drinks and arrange to have the back room to herself for a while. Bessie obeys, pretending that she has an amorous customer and wants absolute privacy. Quinn posts Bill outside the Ladies' Entrance as a lookout.

Quinn wants a favor from Bessie.

QUINN:
> I hear you've been spelling out May Haggerty
> Looking after Ag this past year, Bessie.
> I wonder did Ag still have a cowhide trunk?

BESSIE: A yellow leather trunk? She did.

QUINN: Where is it?

BESSIE:
> It's around the corner in her room in Smith Street,
> The Haggertys didn't have time to cart it home.

QUINN:
> There's something in it that I'd like to have,
> For a keepsake, don't you know. Have you the key?

BESSIE: The key to Ag's room? Yeah.

QUINN: Good. Give it here.

What is it Quinn wants? An onyx brooch that was his mother's; it would be in a tin box in Agnes' trunk, together with some old papers. Bessie's instinct is to run to Matt Stanton with the key, but Quinn threatens to have her in jail for soliciting if she doesn't give it to him. She throws it at him and he passes it out the door to Bill, who is heard departing on his errand.

Bessie is Quinn's prisoner till Bill gets back. She throws her drink in Quinn's face; she is disgusted with herself for ratting.

Bill runs in with Agnes Hogan's tin box, then goes back on watch. Quinn kicks it open. In it are a number of mementos, including a bundle of scorched letters addressed to Matthew Stanton in Newark (where Stanton went the time he left Agnes). There is also a vilifying letter to Matt which Agnes never sent.

Quinn gave this box to Agnes himself and he knows its secrets, including a false bottom. In the false bottom he finds a paper, charred (Agnes Hogan obviously meant to burn it but didn't). Quinn puts this paper in his pocket, replaces the rest of the box's contents.

QUINN:
>   . . . I'm through now. We can part. Don't worry, child.
>   I'm putting these things in the box, and Bill will return it
>   And lock the trunk and room behind him. But mark me.
>   You're not to say a thing of this to Stanton.
>   He's a worse suspicious nature than your own;
>   And we've got to come, you know, to a meeting of minds
>   At the Clambake on my birthday Sunday, Bessie,
>   Stanton and I. It would only throw him off
>   If he heard I had been going through Ag's things.
>   We wouldn't want that, Bessie; would we, child,
>   Any more than you'd want that stretch in jail.
>   I hope you take my meaning—I must leave you, Bessie.
>> *Quinn rises with the box under his arm, and moves towards the Ladies' Entrance.*

BESSIE: I hope you rot in Hell!

QUINN:
>   You must love me, child,
>   That you should want my company forever.

Quinn leaves. Bessie weeps as she pockets some money Quinn has left her.

Scene 3: The stern of a Coney Island steamer bound for Seagate

It is twilight on Sunday evening, May 1, 1890. Above the upper deck of the steamer's stern are hung large portraits of Stanton and Quinn, with bunting and a shield reading "For the Public Good." On the lower deck at right are a table with carpet-seated folding chairs and—set off with its back to the table—a carpet-seated armchair.

Haggerty (in a green and gold sash reading "The Matthew Stanton Association"), Boyle and Ann Mulcahy are seated at the table as Maria Haggerty enters with a loaded tea tray. She proceeds to pour and serve.

Kathleen is sleeping off a touch of seasickness in her husband's stateroom. Quinn has made a sentimental speech to his friends and voters. Quinn and Stanton haven't made up, but Haggerty is convinced they will do so for the good of all.

They exit to the front of the boat to see the lights of Coney Island, as Quinn enters with Bill and with Father Coyne. Father Coyne is trying to arrange a peace parley, and he goes off to find Stanton.

QUINN:

> Look at that now, Billy.
> Brooklyn, how are you! For the public good!
> A whore for a mayor and a spoiled nun for his lady!
> We mustn't let that happen, must we now?—
> Play lose me, Billy. Here's the lot of them.

> > *Exit Bill, stage right. Enter Father Coyne, followed by Murphy and Stanton. Stanton walks forward, keeping his eyes straight ahead. Quinn rakes all three of them with his eyes, then averts his gaze from Stanton.*

QUINN *(to Murphy):*

> If it isn't the Lord Beaconsfield of Brooklyn
> With the ten thumbs of his fine Italian hands
> Done up in ice-cream gloves.

> > *He turns suddenly to Stanton.*

> How are you since?—

STANTON:

> I'll speak no word until he begs my pardon.
> I told you, Father. Has he grown so old and silly
> He thinks men can do harm without amends!

FATHER COYNE:

> Do you want him to get down on his knees to you!
> He's lost enough already. Leave him his pride.

MURPHY:

> The food in the mouth of the voters is at stake,
> It's bread and lard for lunch for thousands, thousands,
> If this election's lost; and it will be lost
> Unless you join your hands and pull together.

QUINN:

> For all that's passed between us, I'll shake his hand,
> If he will mine.

MURPHY: Come on now, Matt. Come on.

QUINN:

> When he gets as old as I am, he'll understand
> It was death I spat at that night at the wake,
> And wish he'd come to terms with an old man's rage.

> > *Pause. Stanton suddenly grabs Quinn's hand. Quinn gives him a clumsy bear hug, his face appearing over Stanton's shoulder.*

STANTON:

> Go on now, Ned. You're not that old. You've years.
> There's years of use in you.

QUINN: Matt boy.

Murphy rejoices at their reconciliation. Quinn puts it to Matt that the landing should be a thundering, band-playing ceremony with the massed members of both their associations. Stanton agrees; maybe a taste of glory will lift Kathleen's spirits.

They all exit about their business just before Kathleen enters, alone, dressed in travelling black. She moves the armchair into the shadow, where the Haggertys, Ann Mulcahy, Boyle and Bessie do not notice her when they come in with still another pot of tea.

In Kathleen's hearing, they remember a clambake Agnes Hogan gave, with "wagonloads of beer," and with Agnes dancing a jig on up-ended beer kegs; it was the night Matt Stanton caught Agnes with Quinn. The Haggertys begin a jig to a ribald song sung by Boyle, when Stanton enters. He sees his wife Kathleen (whom the others haven't yet noticed in her armchair) and reproaches them for taking such liberties in a lady's presence.

The four exit, and Kathleen is embarrassed at the scene—but Stanton tells her she has a position to maintain now, he has won the candidacy for mayor, and Quinn wants to meet her.

Still, Kathleen can't throw off a sense of foreboding. Stanton smells brandy on her breath and extracts her firm promise not to drink any more.

Stanton leaves to find Quinn, and Bessie enters. Bessie, in whose flat Kathleen had passed out the night she got drunk, remembers better days when she and her husband, Jack Legg, had a flat of their own. Tearfully, she recalls that Legg left her God knows why, for God knows where. She hopes he is dead.

Boyle comes in, and before making her exit with him, Bessie tells Kathleen that nothing can harm her, because she is a lady.

Maria Haggerty enters and persuades Kathleen to take half a glass of brandy, in spite of her promise. Sentimentally, almost mystically, Kathleen summons up memories of a village ceremony dedicated to the Virgin, back home in Ireland; she weeps at the spotless purity of the festival and its adored object. As Maria warns Kathleen that her mood is the result of dead spirits "whining in her blood," Quinn enters. Kathleen sends Maria to get some perfume from her cabin. She wants to talk to Quinn alone.

Quinn warns Kathleen: trust no one, not even Matt Stanton. Kathleen calls this "slander" and Quinn, angry, throws it in Kathleen's face that she herself is living in sin, she wasn't married in a Catholic church, and he has his knowledge straight from England.

KATHLEEN:
    You rejoice when people go wrong, don't you, Mayor!
QUINN:
    We've no time now to talk morality.
    We'll wait for Stanton, then go get Father Coyne
    And the rest, and walk down to my stateroom
    And arrange what we will say. I've bought off those accountants,
    Paid back that little sum from the funds I borrowed,
    And the books are doctored. All that now remains is

> To find a way to break the joyous news
> That I will run again. I think Matt should do it!

KATHLEEN:

> If you're a man who'd ruin two reputations
> To gain your ends, what have you done with your life?

QUINN:

> What I have done with my life is my affair!
> Do you think I'll let that bastard have my office?
> I loved the woman that he took from me,
> And I let her go with him, but I kept my office.
> And I heard them here in Seagate making sport
> Of all I'd done for them, but I kept mum,
> And I kept my office. And I watched the poor bitch die
> While he grew high and mighty, but I kept my office.
> Keep my office I will to the day I die,
> And God help those who try to take it.

Kathleen begs Quinn to refrain from making a scandal of her London marriage. Quinn rejects her plea. Kathleen then warns him that the Party will defend her marriage with Stanton; after all, they are married legally, if not in the Catholic Church. Not so, says Quinn—and Kathleen calls him a lying devil.

Quinn pulls from his pocket the scorched piece of paper he found in the false bottom of Agnes Hogan's tin box and throws it into Kathleen's lap.

QUINN:

> I'm a lying devil, am I! Look at that!
> Look at it, why don't you. Are you blind!
> How can you be his wife when he married Ag
> In the Sacred Heart in Newark in '86!
>> *Repeated sound of ship's bell. People are gathering, preparing to get off. Sound of winches, lowering gangplank. Kathleen sits as if shot, the paper in her hands.*

DECKHAND: Seagate! Seagate! Everybody off.

KATHLEEN: All gone. All gone.

>> *Kathleen rises suddenly, the paper in her hand, swaying with shock, as if drunk. The disembarking passengers look curiously at her.*

> God damn the day I met him.
> God damn this mouth that spoke him fair, these eyes
> That flooded my blood with his face. God damn this flesh
> That kindled in his arms, and this heart that told me,
> Say yes, say yes, to everything he asked.
> It would have been better had I not been born.
>> *Quinn grabs the paper out of Kathleen's hand and puts it back into his pocket fast.*

QUINN:

> For God's sake, missis. Don't take on this way.

We have to keep this quiet. There's people watching.

Quinn runs to the table and fetches the half-finished glass of brandy. Kathleen, still swaying, her arms at her side, automatically accepts the glass from him and, as if by reflex, presses it to her breast. She does not see the people who are staring at her. Enter Stanton with Murphy and Father Coyne, a group of voters around him.

STANTON:

It isn't in the courts reform must work
But in each striving heart . . .

Stanton sees the people staring at Kathleen and Quinn. He breaks away from those around him and hurries over to her. He speaks in a steely whisper.

Look at you. Look at you, for the love of Jesus.
In front of all these people. You're owl-eyed drunk,
With the bands about to fife us off the boat!
I'll get Maria to help you sober up.
Quinn and I will walk ashore together.
You are not fit for decent men to be seen with!

Kathleen smashes the glass to the floor. She speaks in a ringing voice.

KATHLEEN:

Did you think that—
Did you think that when you lied to me in London,
And I let you marry me in the City Hall,
Because you said you couldn't wait for the banns,
You wanted me so much! Did you think that
When you had me in the bed in sacrilege
Above the corpse of your true-wedded wife,
Ag Hogan!

Hostile reaction from the crowd. The sound of the bands suddenly blares out.

Scene 4: The parlor of Matthew Stanton's flat and the Haggertys' kitchen beneath it.

Very late that same night, Kathleen is moving in and out of the bedroom in the Stantons' flat upstairs, packing one of two big trunks visible in the parlor. Downstairs, the Haggertys, Father Coyne, Boyle, Bessie and Murphy enter with all their picnic paraphernalia.

Maria complains that she will leave this house of Stanton's and find somewhere else to live, even if she becomes a pauper. Haggerty invites his friends to come into the parlor for a warming fire and glass of whiskey. All follow him under the portiere off into the next room.

Stanton comes into the hall, goes upstairs and sees Kathleen packing. It's all over for him as far as the mayoralty is concerned. They have given the nomination back to Quinn. Everyone has betrayed Stanton, even his own wife.

KATHLEEN:

It ill becomes you, man, to talk betrayals.

Can you tell me whom you've known you've not betrayed!—

You killed Ag Hogan. But you won't kill me!

STANTON: I had the right to leave her. She played me false—

KATHLEEN:

Had you the right to marry me? The right

To cut me off from all that I hold holy?

STANTON:

Would "all that you hold holy," our precious Church,

Have granted me a divorce from Agnes Hogan,

An adulteress!—

KATHLEEN:

What kind of man are you!

That woman died without the Sacraments

Because in her last fever she was afraid

If she confessed her sins she might betray you.

She died cut off from God to spare you harm.

And you have the worst word in your mouth for her.

Do you know why? Because you're no good, man.

You waited for your chance to throw her over.

You saw that with her you'd be nothing. Nothing.

You had to be the mayor of this city

And she was in the way. You married me

To make yourself respectable again.

That's the only reason.

STANTON:

I loved . . . I loved you, Kate.

Kathleen, I've nothing left.

I need you.

KATHLEEN:

Yes. To patch your kick-down fences.

But I have my pride too!—

STANTON:

Go then, God damn you!

Do you think I'll kneel on the floor and beg your help!

I never begged for help from man or God,

And I won't now. You'll not drive me to my knees!

KATHLEEN:

To sit and tell me you have nothing left!

No more do I! You've taken it out of me

By demanding more than anyone can give.

That's what evil is,

The starvation of a heart with nothing in it

To make the world around it nothing too.

You never begged from man or God! You took!

You've taken all your life without return!

You never gave yourself to a single soul
For all your noble talk. —Even in bed
You stole me blind!—
STANTON:
      Get out of here! Get out!
You're not a woman. You're a would-be nun!
You were from the beginning.
KATHLEEN: God help you, Matt.

Kathleen finishes packing and puts on her hat. She tells Matt she has left behind everything he gave her, including the jewelry and furs. She goes to the head of the stairs, and Stanton sees that this is final, she is leaving him here alone.

      Stanton rushes out the door and grabs Kathleen.
STANTON: You'll not leave me! I'll see to that!
      Blackout. Kathleen screams and hits the bottom of the stairs.

The group downstairs hears the noise. When they get a kerosine lamp lit and gather in the hall they see Kathleen lying in a crumpled heap at the foot of the stairs—her head at an odd broken-neck angle—and Stanton standing halfway down, nearly fainting.

They gather around Kathleen, whose first thought is to protect her husband.

KATHLEEN:
      Ah, Jack. And May. And is that the Father there?
      Amn't I a shame and a disgrace
      To get so legless drunk I fall downstairs
      Like an unwatched child—

They send for a doctor. Stanton cradles her in his arms, begs her forgiveness. But Kathleen hushes him—whatever happened is their secret, no need for him to assume any public blame.

KATHLEEN:
      . . . Do you know what stopped my breath up on the landing?
      I love you still. I thought of us on the boat from England.
      There's few have been as happy as we were—
      Is that the Father there? I want the Father.

As Kathleen makes her confession to Father Coyne, Boyle comes in with a policeman and a doctor.

Stanton pulls Kathleen away from Father Coyne and kisses her as she dies murmuring "the boat from England," and with Stanton promising her they will go home to Ireland to live. But, as the doctor confirms, Stanton is making these tender promises to a corpse.

Father Coyne tries to finish his absolution, but Stanton holds his dead wife tighter and defends her reputation, defiantly, by denying that Kathleen was drunk and confessing, "I flung her down the stairs to keep her here."

Stanton turns the body of his wife over to Father Coyne and rises, ready to accompany the policeman to the precinct house.

STANTON:

Maria, lay my wife out on the bed
With some degree of decency, and spill
That bottle of the Worth perfume she loved
Over that bedspread that she was so proud of,
And sit with her until the coroner comes . . .
I will not have her stink, or lie alone—
With great difficulty, Stanton brings himself to turn and look at his wife and the priest.
With all her sins on my head, and the world a desert.
Stanton throws his arms out in a begging embrace and falls on his knees. Enter Murphy and Quinn, unnoticed by Stanton.
Maisie, Jack. And Petey. Bessie, Father,
Help me, for the love of Jesus help me.
Dear God in Heaven, help me and forgive me.
The Haggertys rush to him and grasp his hands. Haggerty raises him, and relinquishes him to Father Coyne.

MURPHY: God have mercy on her. Our election's lost.
Stanton wheels around. His eyes meet with Quinn's.

QUINN:

I never meant to do this to you, Matt.
I didn't know. I never meant to do it.
I only meant to look out for my good.
I'm nobody. I'm no one, if I'm not the mayor.
I'm nothing, Matt. I'm nobody. I'm nothing—
Stanton rakes Quinn's face with a blind man's stare. Exit Stanton.

FATHER COYNE:

Why are you standing around like imbeciles!
Carry her up the stairs, and lay her out
As Mattie asked you to.
Haggerty and Boyle lift Kathleen, and start up the stairs with her. Maria follows, her mouth in the crook of her elbow, shaking with tears. Quinn and Murphy, Bessie and Father Coyne look on from below.
Well you may cry!
Cry for us all while you're at it. Cry for us all!
Curtain.

MAN OF LA MANCHA

A Musical in One Act

BOOK BY DALE WASSERMAN

MUSIC BY MITCH LEIGH

LYRICS BY JOE DARION

Cast and credits appear on page 386

DALE WASSERMAN (book) was born in Rhinelander, Wisconsin, in 1917. He was destined to live a modern version of a real Huckleberry Finn childhood. His father's occupation—building and operating movie theaters in Minnesota, Wisconsin and Iowa—brought him early into contact with show business. But he was also orphaned early, at age 11, and struck out on his own footloose adventure. Every so often, in this town or that, some well-meaning person would collar the little drifter and place him in school, but like Huck he soon escaped from any environment that threatened to hold him. Finally, at Belmont High School in Los Angeles, he stayed long enough to complete the three-year course in one and a half years, in special examinations for those with special ability.

At 19 Wasserman entered show business, with plenty of time to pursue several careers. For more than seven years he managed Katherine Dunham's dance troupe. He directed operas and he directed plays. He won awards for lighting design. Ten years ago, in 1956, he wrote his first script, Elisha and the Long Knives, *which was cited as the best TV play of its season. This was the first of forty-seven (at this writing) Wasserman scripts, all of which without exception have been produced or are in production for stage, screen and television.*

Wasserman's TV credits include The Fog, The Power and the Glory *(which starred Laurence Olivier),* The Lincoln Murder Case, The Stranger *and* I, Don Quixote, *which has become* Man of La Mancha. *For the movies he wrote* The Vikings, Mister Buddwing *and the first of many scripts for the Elizabeth Taylor-Richard Burton* Cleopatra. *His first stage work was* Livin' the Life, *a musical version of the Tom Sawyer-Huck Finn story, produced off Broadway in 1957. He was last represented on Broadway by his adaptation of Ken Kesey's novel* One Flew Over the Cuckoo's Nest *(1963). At present, Wasserman has his own film company in partnership with Delbert Mann and Douglas Laurence.*

MITCH LEIGH *(music) was born in New York City on January 31, 1928. He attended New York schools and studied with Paul Hindemith at the Yale School of Music in New Haven. Back in New York, he organized and founded Music Makers, Inc., a commercial production house which has won every major radio and TV award for its work. Mr. Leigh composes in a wide range from jazz to opera. He was previously represented on Broadway by incidental music for the plays* Too True to Be Good *(1963) and* Never Live Over a Pretzel Factory *(1964).* Man of La Mancha *is his first score for a Broadway musical.*

JOE DARION *(lyrics) is a native New Yorker. He was educated in New York Schools and at City College, Class of 1930. He served in the Navy in World War II. His popular songs have sold more than ten million records, and among them are "Ricochet," "Changing Partners," "The Ho-Ho Song" and "Midnight Train." He has written an opera,* Archy and Mehitabel, *which he then adapted into his only previous Broadway musical,* Shinbone Alley *(1957), for which he wrote both lyrics and book (the latter in collaboration with Mel Brooks). This season, in addition to* Man of La Mancha, *his work includes the oratorio* Galileo, *written for television in collaboration with Ezra Laderman.*

INTRODUCTION BY THE PLAYWRIGHT

I was in Madrid that summer, writing a movie that had nothing to do with Madrid, when my eye caught an item in the newspapers which stated that my purpose in Spain was research for a stage version of *Don Quixote*. That was chuckling-matter, for like most people who know *Don Quixote* I had not even read it. The time and place seemed appropriate for repair of that omission, however, so I set forth on the two-volume journey and arrived at its end with two firm conclusions. The first was that this archetypal work could not and should not be adapted for the stage. The second had to do not with the novel but with its author.

I was aware, of course, that *Don Quixote* had been attempted for the theater hundreds of times. Having seen a dozen of these attempts—ballet, motion picture, play and opera—I was aware too that the attempts invariably fell short. The reason was plain: trying to capture this work in dramatic form was much like attempting to force the sea into a bucket; ambitious but impractical. But what continued to haunt my thoughts was not the novel but the shadowy figure behind it.

Miguel de Cervantes y Saavedra . . . who was he? What manner of man could pour into a magnum opus so incredible a wealth of wit and wisdom, could range so widely over the spectrum of human behavior that nearly all living literature is still in his debt? With interest that was to become very nearly obsessive I set out in search of Cervantes.

I learned that his life was scarcely less mysterious than that of his contemporary, William Shakespeare. A few documents attest to his existence . . . a baptismal certificate of October 9, 1547; a record of army service, disablement, enslavery for five years in Algiers; embroilments with the law which netted him at least three prison terms; an excommunication by the church; a failed marriage, an illegitimate daughter . . . but the list of misfortunes begins to overwhelm.

Misfortune, in fact, was the pattern of his life. He was dealt blow after blow by the blind malice of fate. Failure and disaster, this is the record—until, in his 50s, shamefully poor, infirm of body and with dimming eyesight, he undertook the writing of a book which he hoped might bring him ease in his remaining years.

Here I discovered the design for the play I wanted to write: not an adaptation of *Don Quixote* but a tribute to the spirit of his creator. I wanted to interweave and merge their identities—for what I had learned was that in all essential ways Miguel de Cervantes *was* Don Quixote. The upsets of existence never dimmed the brightness of his vision, never soured his compassion nor his humor, never stripped him of his faith.

The motif of the attempt I found in a quotation from another brilliant Miguel, Unamuno, who said: "Only he who attempts the absurd is capable of achieving the impossible." In that Quixotic spirit the play was written, a deliberate denial of the prevailing spirit of our own time which might be expressed as aesthetic masochism and which finds its theatrical mood in black comedy and the deification of despair.

But those are subjective reasons. Most simply, *Man of La Mancha* is my way of paying tribute to the indomitable soul of Miguel de Cervantes, the man who was Don Quixote.

DALE WASSERMAN

Time: The end of the 16th century

Place: Spain. A prison in the city of Seville and various places in the imagination of Miguel de Cervantes

SYNOPSIS:The action is continuous, without intermission, on an abstract platform which at first serves as a prison common room, then as any environment for the adventurous fancies of Miguel de Cervantes.

As a prison area, the stage is reached by a stairway lowered from above like a drawbridge. A trap in the floor leads to a still lower dungeon. There are crannies for prisoners to huddle in, an open well at left and a fire covered by a grill at right.

> *The primary effect to be achieved is that of improvisation; it must seem as though all scenic, prop and costume items are adapted from materials already on stage, augmented by effects from Cervantes' theatrical trunk. This scheme is fundamental to the play.*
>
> *Only in the inner play—as devised by Cervantes—is there musical style and form. The prison scenes framing the inner play are not "musicalized" in the sense that there is no singing or dancing in these except as may be motivated realistically. The performance is played without intermission.*

Later on, when the scene changes, the prisoners will slip into the various roles of Cervantes' tale. Now they are seen in their roles as prisoners, eating, gambling, one strumming a guitar, one dancing.

A strange chant with handclaps, drums and clanking chains is heard. It is the Theme of the Inquisition.

The stairway is lowered and down it steps Miguel de Cervantes with his Manservant, guarded by the Captain of the Inquisition and two soldiers. Cervantes is lean and spare as though from a lifetime of penury, with the strong, clearly-defined features of the dreamer and the manners of a gentleman. His rotund Manservant is carrying a large, shabby straw trunk.

The Captain tells the prisoner Cervantes that this is a place for waiting; some wait a lifetime here, and the least fortunate wait for their turn at the Inquisition, as Cervantes is doomed to do. The Captain departs with his soldiers up the stairway which is then drawn up after him. Cervantes examines this jail and his fellow-prisoners.

CERVANTES *(sensing potential danger—turning on all his charm):* Good morning gentlemen . . . ladies. I regret being thrust upon you in this manner, and hope you will not find my company objectionable. In any case I trust I shall not be among you long. The Inquisition—

> *With a yell, the prisoners attack. Cervantes and the Manservant are seized, tripped up, pinned to the floor. The prisoners are busy rifling their pockets as The Governor, a big man of obvious authority, who has been asleep in the corner, awakens and yells.*

IRVING JACOBSON (AS SANCHO), RICHARD KILEY (AS DON QUIXOTE)
AND JOAN DIENER (AS ALDONZA) IN "MAN OF LA MANCHA"

THE GOVERNOR: Enough! Noise, trouble fights . . . kill each other if you must but for God's sake, do it quietly! *(To Cervantes.)* Who are you? Eh? Speak up!

CERVANTES *(gasping, as his throat is freed):* Cervantes. Don Miguel de Cervantes.

THE GOVERNOR: A gentleman!

CERVANTES: It has never saved me from going to bed hungry.

The Governor informs Cervantes that like all newcomers he must be tried by his fellow-prisoners (defendants are generally found guilty and fined all their possessions). Cervantes is a poet—a poet of the theater, a playwright and actor. The inmates rummage in his trunk, finding his property sword and other parts of costumes. The Governor finds a heavy bundle, a manuscript, which he prepares to throw into the fire. Cervantes begs him not to destroy the manuscript, and The Governor pauses, granting Cervantes the right to defend himself before judgment is pronounced.

CERVANTES: . . . You see, I had been employed by the government as a tax-collector. . . .

THE GOVERNOR: Poet, actor, *tax-collector?*

CERVANTES: A temporary thing to keep us from starvation.

THE GOVERNOR: How does a tax-collector get in trouble with the Inquisition?

CERVANTES: I made an assessment against the monastery of La Merced. When they refused to pay, I issued a lien on the property.

THE GOVERNOR: You did *what?*

MANSERVANT: He foreclosed on a church.

THE GOVERNOR *(to the Manservant):* But why are *you* here?

MANSERVANT: Someone had to tack the notice on the church door. *(Dolefully he indicates himself.)*

THE GOVERNOR: These two have empty rooms in their heads!

CERVANTES: The law says treat everyone equally. We only obeyed the law!

The Duke, a cynically clever prisoner, steps forward. He is later described by Cervantes as "A man who carries his own self-importance as though afraid of breaking it." In The Duke's character there is no room for emotion or imagination, and he charges Cervantes with being "an idealist, a bad poet and an honest man."

CERVANTES: It is true I am guilty of these charges. An idealist? I have never had the courage to believe in nothing. A bad poet? That comes a bit more painfully . . . still . . .

THE GOVERNOR *(impatiently):* Let's hear your defense!

CERVANTES *(an idea seems to strike him):* Your Excellency, if you've no objection I should like to present it in the manner I know best . . . in the form of a charade—

THE GOVERNOR: Charade?

CERVANTES: An entertainment, if you will—

THE DUKE: Entertainment!

CERVANTES: At worst it may beguile your time. *(To the other prisoners.)* And if any of *you* should care to enter in . . .

THE DUKE: Governor! I should like to protest!

THE GOVERNOR: No, no, let's hear him out!

CERVANTES: Then . . . may I set the stage?

> The Governor waves assent. The prisoners shift position to become audience as Cervantes gestures to his Manservant, who scurries, like a well-trained stage manager, to assist as required. Music begins, softly, under, as Cervantes, seated center, begins a make-up transformation through the following speech.

I shall impersonate a man . . . come, enter into my imagination and see him! His name . . . Alonso Quijana . . . a country squire, no longer young. Bony, hollow-faced . . . eyes that burn with the fire of inner vision. Being retired, he has much time for books. He studies them from morn to night, and often through the night as well. And all he reads oppresses him . . . fills him with indignation at man's murderous ways toward man. He broods . . . and broods . . . and broods—and finally from so much brooding his brains dry up. He lays down the melancholy burden of sanity and conceives the strangest project ever imagined . . . to become a knight-errant and sally forth into the world to right all wrongs. No longer shall he be plain Alonso Quijana . . . but a dauntless knight known as—Don Quixote de La Mancha!!!

The transformation of Cervantes into Don Quixote is now complete. The Manservant, who will become Sancho Panza, assists further by dressing him, providing him with props, during the beginning of the song.

DON QUIXOTE *(Singing, a little tongue in cheek, an actor aware that he's performing)*:

Hear me now, oh thou bleak and unbearable world!
Thou art base and debauched as can be;
And a knight with his banners all bravely unfurled
Now hurls down his gauntlet to thee!

I am I, Don Quixote,
The Lord of La Mancha,
My destiny calls and I go;
And the wild winds of fortune will carry me onward,
Oh whithersoever they blow.

Whithersoever they blow,
Onward to glory I go!

He turns away from the prisoners to build two "horses"—from wooden frames and masks he's presumably brought with him. As he does, his servant, now attired as Sancho Panza, takes over.

SANCHO *(sings)*:

I'm Sancho! Yes, I'm Sancho!
I'll follow my master till the end.
I'll tell all the world proudly
I'm his squire! I'm his friend!

They finish building their "horses"—the frames are now worn by dancers— and then "ride" away, singing their songs in counterpoint as the prisoners fade from sight. They are on the high road of adventure. The "horses" dance a lively flamenco as they go.

DON QUIXOTE: Well, Sancho—how dost thou like adventuring?

SANCHO: Oh, marvelous, Your Grace. But it's peculiar—to me this great highway to glory looks exactly like the road to El Toboso where you can buy chickens cheap.

DON QUIXOTE: Like beauty, my friend, 'tis all in the eyes of the beholder. Only wait and thou shalt see amazing sights.

SANCHO: What kind?

DON QUIXOTE: Why, knights and nations, warlocks, wizards . . . a cavalcade of vast, unending armies!

SANCHO: They sound dangerous!
The horses listen too. They react throughout—after all they under-
stand.

DON QUIXOTE: They *are* dangerous. But one there'll be who leads them
. . . and he will be the most dangerous of all!

SANCHO: Well, who is he? Who?

DON QUIXOTE: The Great Enchanter. Beware him, Sancho . . . for his
thoughts are cold and his spirit shriveled. He has eyes like little machines,
and where he walks the earth is blighted. But one day we shall meet face to
face . . . and on that day—! *(He shakes his lance ferociously.)*

Suddenly, Don Quixote sees in the distance what he takes to be a giant, an
ogre by name Matagoger.

DON QUIXOTE: . . . You can tell him by the four great arms awhirling on
his back!

SANCHO: It's a windmill.

DON QUIXOTE *(shouting):* Ho! Feckless giant standing there! Avast! Avaunt!
On guard! Beware! *(He charges off.)*

SANCHO: No, no, Your Grace, I swear by my wife's little black moustache,
that's not a giant, it's only a—
Offstage a crash; the horses run for cover. To musical accompani-
ment the combat begins as the projected shadows of a windmill's
sails cross the stage. As Sancho watches, horrified, Quixote's hel-
met comes flying back onstage, then the butt of his lance, splayed
and splintered. The final crash; and Quixote crawls back into view,
his sword a corkscrew. A doleful picture, he comes rolling down-
stage as Sancho hurries to plump himself down and stop him.

SANCHO: Didn't I tell you? Didn't I say, "Your Grace, that's a windmill?"

DON QUIXOTE *(hollowly):* The work of my enemy.

SANCHO: The Enchanter?

DON QUIXOTE: At the last moment, he transformed that ogre into a windmill.

Don Quixote believes he's at the Enchanter's mercy because he's never
been properly dubbed a knight. Only a lord of a castle can perform this ceremony—and sure enough, there in the distance is a castle, banners "flaunting"
in the wind. Sancho sees it as an inn which may be full of dangerous rowdies,
but Don Quixote pushes on straight for the "castle's" drawbridge.

The scene fades back to the prison, where inmates are setting up the main
room of a lowly country inn. Cervantes concedes to his audience that this
may indeed be an inn and Don Quixote could still see it as a castle. To each
his own vision.

As the prison fades out once more and becomes the main room of the inn,
a noisy gang of Muleteers is being served a great pot of stew. The serving
girl is Aldonza, and the woman prisoner who plays her always keeps to her-

self during the prison scenes like a woman apart, a very special creature. Here at the inn, Aldonza is fierce, shapely and extremely durable, though shopworn. The Muleteers' flirting with her takes the form of grabbing and pushing.

PEDRO: My *mules* are not as stubborn. *(He snaps his whip at her.)*

ALDONZA: Fine! Make love to your mules!

> *The Muleteers laugh, then sing, moving toward her in various amorous attitudes, reaching for her again.*

MULETEERS *(sing):*

I come for love,
I come for love,
I come to Aldonza for love!

ALDONZA *(pushes them away and sings):*

One pair of arms is like another,
I don't know why or who's to blame,
I'll go with you or with your brother,
It's all the same, it's all the same!

This I have learned: that when the light's out,
No man will burn with special flame,
You'll prove to me, before the night's out,
You're all the same, you're all the same!

So do not talk to me of love,
I'm not a fool with starry eyes,
Just put your money in my hand,
And you will get what money buys!

Aldonza continues singing and fending off the Muleteers. Pedro shakes a bag full of coins at her, then tosses the bag on the floor. She spits at the money but lifts her skirt in Pedro's face. Now Pedro offers her the money pleadingly as she ends her contemptuous song.

The Innkeeper (who is also The Governor) enters with his wife Maria and Fermina, a serving girl, to straighten up the mess left by the activity in the preceding number. Suddenly their ears are assailed by the sound of a bugle atrociously blown. The Innkeeper expects that it is the pig butcher, but it turns out to be Sancho and Don Quixote, who has tied the limb of a tree to the butt of his shattered lance.

DON QUIXOTE *(haughtily):* Is the lord of the castle at hand?

> *No reply from the flabbergasted innkeeper.*

I say, is the Castellano here?

INNKEEPER *(with an effort):* I am in charge of this place.

DON QUIXOTE *(coldly):* We waited, sire, for a dwarf to mount the battlements and announce us, but none appeared.

INNKEEPER: The . . . dwarfs are all busy.

The Innkeeper is willing to play along. As he tells his wife, "Madmen are the children of God." He offers the travelers food, shelter and stable.

In the grand manner, Don Quixote places his knightly self at the service of the Innkeeper and his guests. When Aldonza enters to set the table he is stricken by her presence. As he looks at her, he is a man staring directly at the sun. He addresses her "Sweet lady . . . fair virgin" and implores her to speak her name.

ALDONZA *(a loud growl):* Aldonza!

DON QUIXOTE *(approaching her):* The name of a kitchen-scullion . . . or mayhap my lady's serving-maid?

ALDONZA: I told you my name! Now get out of the way.

DON QUIXOTE *(smiling, still keeping his eyes averted):* Did my lady think to put me to a test? Ah, sweet sovereign of my captive heart, I shall not fail thee, for I *know. (Turning toward her, sings.)*

I have dreamed thee too long,
Never seen thee or touched thee, but known thee with all of my heart,
Half a prayer, half a song,
Thou hast always been with me, though we have been always apart.

Dulcinea . . . Dulcinea . . .
I see heaven when I see thee, Dulcinea,
And thy name is like a prayer an angel whispers . . .
Dulcinea . . . Dulcinea!
    She moves away from him. He follows.
If I reach out to thee,
Do not tremble and shrink from the touch of my hand on thy hair,
Let my fingers but see
Thou are warm and alive, and no phantom to fade in the air.

Dulcinea . . . Dulcinea . . .
I have sought thee, sung thee, dreamed thee, Dulcinea!
Now I've found thee, and the world shall know thy glory.
Dulcinea . . . Dulcinea!

The Innkeeper leads Don Quixote away to show him his rooms, and the Muleteers parody the song. Aldonza belabors her tormentors, driven wild by their teasing. As she does so, the scene fades back to the prison.

The Duke objects to Cervantes' defense, and to its very form, but The Governor allows Cervantes to continue. The womenfolk of Alonso Quijana, alias Don Quixote, are embarrassed by his eccentric behavior (Cervantes tells his prison audience).

The scene fades to a church confessional. Quixote-Quijana's niece, Antonia, and his Housekeeper are telling a Padre their family troubles. Antonia is afraid her uncle's madness will scare off her husband-to-be. But even so (Antonia says), she has only her uncle's best interests at heart; she's not thinking of herself, she is only thinking of him.

ANTONIA *(holier-than-thou, into the screen, to the Padre who is listening.* Sings):

> I'm only thinking of him,
> I'm only thinking of him,
> Whatever I may do or say,
> I'm only thinking of him!
> In my body, it's well known,
> There is not one selfish bone—
> I'm only thinking and worrying about him!
>> *More confidential, then more passionate.*
> I've been told he's chasing dragons and I fear it may be true.
> If my groom should hear about it, heaven knows what he will do!
> Oh, I dearly love my uncle but for what he's done to me
> I would like to take and lock him up and throw away the key!
>> *She's realized what she's said.*
> But if I do . . .
> But if I do . . .
> There is one thing I swear will still be true . . .

ANTONIA	*(In counterpoint.)*	PADRE
I'm only thinking of him;		I know, I know my dear;
I'm only thinking of him;		Of course you are, my dear;
I'm only thinking and worrying about him.		I understand.

The Housekeeper joins their hypocritical chant: her master is lonely, but if he reaches out in her direction she'll defend her honor. Ironically, the Padre says he believes the two ladies' motives to be pure.

Cervantes intrudes into the action to introduce Antonia's fiance, Doctor Sanson Carrasco (played by The Duke). Dr. Carrasco is a Bachelor of Science, a graduate of Salamanca, bursting with self-importance. Cervantes places him at a corner of the stage, then places Antonia, the Housekeeper and the Padre at the other corners. Their position is eccentric but their conversation is realistic and rapid-fire.

Dr. Carrasco will accept no polite euphemism for Don Quixote's condition. He is a doctor, and he knows that his uncle-to-be is insane. Suffering as he is from delusions, he is certainly ridiculous and maybe even dangerous. It will be most embarrassing to have a lunatic in the family.

Antonia brings up the subject of her uncle's property. She had hoped that it would pass, eventually, to her betrothed. The Padre echoes her concern about the property; then, more cleverly, he changes his tune and stresses the challenge to their ingenuity in finding Don Quixote and persuading him to come home. Drawn by the challenge (or the potential loot), Dr. Carrasco decides to go after Don Quixote. But (as all of them sing once more) they are only thinking of *him*.

Cervantes draws his audience back to the inn's kitchen, where pots are steaming and Aldonza is ladling. Sancho enters with a "missive" from Don Quixote. Neither Aldonza nor Sancho can read, but Sancho has learned the words of the missive by heart. He sings the words of the letter while Aldonza eats supper.

SANCHO: "Most lovely sovereign and highborn lady—"

ALDONZA: Ho.

SANCHO: "The heart of this, thy vassal knight, faints for thy favor."

ALDONZA: Ha. *(She wipes her mouth with the back of her hand, then wipes her hand on her skirt.)*

SANCHO: "Oh, fairest of the fair, purest of the pure, Incomparable Dulcinea—"

ALDONZA: *That* again. My name is Aldonza!

SANCHO *(patiently):* My master calls you Dulcinea.

ALDONZA *(glowering):* Why?

SANCHO: I don't know, but I can tell you from experience that knights have their own language for everything, and it's better not to ask questions because it only gets you into trouble.

Aldonza shrugs, then gestures for him to continue.

"I beg thee grant that I may kiss the nethermost hem of thy garment—"

ALDONZA: Kiss my *which?*

SANCHO: If you keep interrupting, the whole thing will be gone out of my head!

ALDONZA: Well, what does he *want?*

SANCHO: I'm getting to it! "—And send to me a token of thy fair esteem that I may carry as my standard into battle."

ALDONZA: What kind of a token?

SANCHO: He says generally it's a silken scarf.

Aldonza, angry at what she cannot understand, flings him the filthy rag with which she wiped her bowl. But she is intrigued nevertheless, and she asks Sancho to explain why he follows Don Quixote.

SANCHO *(he is at a loss for a reason; finally, giving up, he sings, simply):*
I like him.
I really like him.
Tear out my fingernails one by one, I like him!

I don't have
A very good reason.
Since I've been with him cuckoonuts have been in season—

But there's nothing I can do,
Chop me up for onion stew,
Still I'll yell to the sky,
Though I can't tell you why,
That I like him!

What does *Sancho* get out of it? Nothing. But, as he sings again with great dignity—he likes him. Sancho exits, leaving Aldonza troubled, unsure, as the scene changes to the stable. She sings of her confusion at the enigma of Don Quixote—what does he want of her with his manners and his missive? The "horses" bed down for the night, the lights dim and then come up on the prison.

Cervantes is showing the prisoners playing Muleteers how to create the illusion of an innyard. And he is teaching one of them, Anselmo, a song.

ANSELMO *(sings):*
    Little bird, little bird,
    In the cinnamon tree,
    Little bird, little bird,
    Do you sing for me?
    Do you bring me word
    Of one I know?
    Little bird, little bird, I love her so,
    Little bird, little bird, I have to know,
    Little bird, little bird.

The scene changes to the innyard, where the Muleteers sing the song to Aldonza as she makes her way to the well. Pedro snatches the missive. She tries to retrieve it but Pedro holds her and she bites him. Anselmo reads from it.

ANSELMO *(haltingly, mispronouncing words):* "Most lovely sovereign and high-born lady—!" It's from her knight. A love letter!

ALDONZA *(still held):* It's a stupid joke.

TENORIO: Then why so hot about it?

PEDRO: Has he touched your heart?

ALDONZA *(breaking away and snatching back the letter):* Nobody touches my heart.

ANSELMO: All those fine words—!

ALDONZA *(she picks up her buckets of water and starts off):* Fine words. He's a man, isn't he? All right, he wants what every other man wants.
    Pedro stops her, holds her with a question.

PEDRO: Aldonza?

ALDONZA: Later . . . when I'm finished in the kitchen.

While the Muleteers sing "Little Bird" once more in an insinuating tone, the Padre and Dr. Carrasco enter and ask the serving girl Fermina to tell Don Quixote of their arrival.

Don Quixote enters and to their surprise he greets them warmly, as friends.

PADRE *(in deep relief):* Ah, Senor Quijana—

DON QUIXOTE *(reproving but kind):* I should prefer that you address me properly. I am Don Quixote, knight-errant of La Mancha.
The Padre quails, sinks to a seat.
DR. CARRASCO: Senor Quijana—
DON QUIXOTE *(another gentle correction):* Don Quixote.
DR. CARRASCO: There are no giants. No kings under enchantment. No chivalry. No knights. There have been no knights for three hundred years.
DON QUIXOTE *(to the Padre, pityingly):* So learned—yet so misinformed.
DR. CARRASCO *(losing his temper):* These are *facts.*
DON QUIXOTE: Facts are the enemy of truth.

Sancho enters and proffers Aldonza's rag. Don Quixote accepts it as "gossamer," extolling his lady Dulcinea. "To each his Dulcinea," the Padre observes sadly. At this moment there is an interruption: a Barber is heard singing as he approaches.

> BARBER *(singing offstage):*
> Oh, I am a little barber
> And I go my merry way,
> With my razor and my leeches
> I can always earn my pay.
>
> Though your chin be smooth as satin,
> You will need me soon I know,
> For the Lord protects his barbers,
> And he makes the stubble grow.

The Barber enters carrying all the paraphernalia of his trade, including a brass shaving basin on his head. Don Quixote intercepts him. At sword's point he demands that the Barber hand over the Golden Helmet. Even Sancho protests, along with the Barber, that it is a shaving basin, but Don Quixote recognizes it as the Golden Helmet of Mambrino. With his foot on the prostrate Barber, he handles the basin with great reverence.

> DON QUIXOTE *(sings):*
> Thou Golden Helmet of Mambrino,
> With so illustrious a past,
> Too long has thou been lost to glory,
> Th'art rediscovered now at last!
>
> Golden Helmet of Mambrino,
> There can be no
> Hat like thee!
> Thee and I, now,
> Ere I die, now,
> Will make golden
> History!

The Barber looks to the Muleteers for support, but they are amused by Don Quixote's antics. Don Quixote removes his own helmet, goes over to the Padre and indicates he'd like the Padre to crown him with the new "helmet."

Dr. Carrasco indicates that the Padre should do it. He wants to see how far Don Quixote will go in eccentric behavior.

Don Quixote insists that Dulcinea's favor be attached before he is crowned. As the Barber watches in disbelief, Sancho attaches the rag and the Padre completes the ceremony of coronation, much to the Muleteers' amusement.

Since everyone else seems to take Don Quixote seriously, the Barber succumbs to the mood of the moment and joins in a final hymn to the Golden Helmet. Only the Padre and Dr. Carrasco remain unimpressed. One of the Muleteers is actually awestruck, as all exit, leaving Don Quixote alone with his prize.

The Innkeeper enters and Don Quixote confesses to him that he has never been dubbed a knight. He asks the Innkeeper, as lord of this castle, to perform this service for him. The Innkeeper agrees. Don Quixote will keep vigil in the courtyard under the stars; then at sunrise he'll be dubbed knight.

> *The lights change and pick up the Padre and Dr. Carrasco en route back home.*

PADRE: There is either the wisest madman or the maddest wise man in the world.

DR. CARRASCO: He is mad.

PADRE: Well . . . in any case we have failed.

DR. CARRASCO *(tightly):* Not necessarily. We know the sickness. Now to find the cure. *(He exits.)*

PADRE *(stopping and reflecting for a moment):* The cure. May it be not worse than the disease. *(Sings.)*

To each his Dulcinea,
That he alone can name . . .
To each a secret hiding place
Where he can find the haunting face
To light his secret flame. . . .

As the Padre sings, Don Quixote is seen preparing for his vigil and Aldonza for her date with Pedro.

PADRE *(sings):*

There is no Dulcinea,
She's made of flame and air,
And yet how lovely life would seem
If every man could weave a dream
To keep him from despair.

To each his Dulcinea
Though she's naught but flame and air!

After finishing his song, the Padre follows Dr. Carrasco. Aldonza disappears from sight. Don Quixote is pacing the innyard alone at night, lance in hand.

DON QUIXOTE: Now I must consider how sages of the future will describe this historic night. *(He strikes a pose . . . then continues his march.)* Long after the sun had retired to his couch, darkening the gates and balconies of La Mancha, Don Quixote, with measured tread and lofty expression, held vigil in the courtyard of a mighty castle! *(He changes tone.)* Oh, maker of empty boasts. On this, of all nights, to give way to vanity. Nay, Don Quixote —take a deep breath of life and consider how it should be lived. *(He kneels.)* Call nothing thy own except thy soul.
    Pause.
Love not what thou art, but only what thou may become.
    Pause.
Do not pursue pleasure, for thou may have the misfortune to overtake it.
    Pause.
Look always forward; in last year's nest there are no birds this year.
    *Aldonza has entered the courtyard en route to her rendezvous with
    Pedro. She stops, watching Don Quixote and listening.*
Be just to all men. Be courteous to all women.
    Pause.
Live in the vision of that one for whom great deeds are done . . . she that is called Dulcinea.
    ALDONZA: Why do you call me that?
    DON QUIXOTE: My lady!

Aldonza bids him rise from his knees and questions him to probe the mystery of his adoration of her. Woman, he tells her, is "the radiance that lights man's way . . . glory!" This leaves her as puzzled as before.

    ALDONZA: What do you want of me?
    DON QUIXOTE: Nothing.
    ALDONZA: Liar!
    DON QUIXOTE: I deserved the rebuke. I ask of my lady . . .
    ALDONZA: *Now* we get to it.
    DON QUIXOTE: . . . that I may be allowed to serve her. That I may hold her in my heart. That I may dedicate each victory and call upon her in defeat. And if at last I give my life I give it in the sacred name of Dulcinea.

Still, Aldonza does not understand. To her, "The world's a dung heap and we are the maggots that crawl on it." Don Quixote insists that the quest is all-important; whether he wins or loses does not matter.

    ALDONZA: . . . What does that mean—quest?
    DON QUIXOTE: It is the mission of each true knight . . . his duty—nay, his privilege. *(Sings.)*

To dream the impossible dream,
To fight the unbeatable foe,
To bear with unbearable sorrow,
To run where the brave dare not go.

To right the unrightable wrong,
To love, pure and chaste, from afar,
To try, when your arms are too weary,
To reach the unreachable star!

That, sings Don Quixote, is his quest—and one man's striving can make the world a better place.

ALDONZA *(quite still after the song . . . then):* Once—just once—would you look at me as I really am?

DON QUIXOTE *(looking directly at her):* I see beauty. Purity. I see the woman each man holds secret in his heart. Dulcinea.

Aldonza backs away into the arms of Pedro, who has approached stealthily. Don Quixote pushes Pedro with his lance, knocks him over, prods him in the buttocks. Pedro cries to the Muleteers for help. Don Quixote shouts defiance to them all, and a broadly comic, choreographed melee ensues.

Don Quixote catches Juan's whip with his lance and teeters him off the edge of the stage.

Pedro grabs the whip, but Aldonza knocks the wind out of him with the flat of Don Quixote's sword. Pedro falls into the well.

Jose and Anselmo attack Don Quixote with a rake and a pot, and Don Quixote times his dodging so that his two attackers merely injure each other. The pot becomes stuck over Don Quixote's head, but Sancho arrives and helps to get it off him.

Aldonza flails about with the lance, while the Muleteer Jose is poked by Sancho with the rake and then gets stuck sitting in the now-empty pot. Jose is bludgeoned and thrown into the well.

Anselmo and the Muleteers drive at Don Quixote with a ladder, which entraps the knight. They take away his lance but are attacked by Sancho and Aldonza.

Don Quixote, caught in the ladder, revolves it. The last two Muleteers, hanging onto the ladder's ends, are thrown off by centrifugal force. The fight is over. "Victory!" gasps the knight; "Victory!" echoes his squire, and "Victory!" cries his lady Dulcinea, brandishing his sword.

The Innkeeper enters and is appalled by signs of the struggle. Don Quixote's wounds are bound up as the Muleteers limp off the field of battle.

The Innkeeper tells Don Quixote, most respectfully, that this is a peaceful inn, and the fire-eating knight must leave the premises as soon as convenient. Don Quixote reminds him of his promise to dub him knight. Don Quixote has kept vigil and proven himself in battle and is now ready for the honor of knighthood.

The Innkeeper takes Don Quixote's bent sword and swiftly dubs him knight. But this is not quite satisfactory.

DON QUIXOTE: Your Lordship . . .

INNKEEPER: Something else?

DON QUIXOTE: It is customary to grant the new knight an added name. If Your Lordship could devise such a name for me . . . ?

INNKEEPER: Hmmm. *(He reflects a moment, then circles Don Quixote; is suddenly inspired. Sings.)*
> Hail, Knight of the Woeful Countenance,
> Knight of the Woeful Countenance!
> Wherever you go
> People will know
> Of the glorious deeds of the Knight of the Woe-
> Ful Countenance!
>
> Oh valorous knight, go and fight for the right,
> And battle all villains that be.
> But oh, when you do, what will happen to you
> Thank God I won't be there to see!

The Innkeeper indicates that Aldonza and Sancho join him in the ceremony.

INNKEEPER, ALDONZA and SANCHO *(sing):*
> Hail, Knight of the Woeful Countenance,
> Knight of the Woeful Countenance!
> Wherever you go
> People will know
> Of the glorious deeds of the Knight of the Woe-
> Ful Count—te—nance!

Don Quixote is delighted with his new name. He moves immediately to perform his next duty: minister to his enemies and bind up their wounds. Aldonza picks up the bandages and goes to carry out this duty for him, an act which confirms his adoration of her.

In the inn's large room, the Muleteers are taking stock of their injuries. Aldonza moves to help Juan. He grabs her and rolls her over, and the rape of Aldonza by the Muleteers takes place in choreography.

Aldonza is bound and gagged; her skirt is pulled off.

> *Tenorio forces her to dance with him and finally pushes her down onto the table. As he bends over her, Fermina enters, screams and Pedro pulls Tenorio off. Anselmo strikes Fermina, who watches fascinated as Aldonza is raised in the air; Anselmo sings a vicious parody of "Little Bird." Aldonza is struck by Pedro's whip, beaten further by two of the other Muleteers and finally falls unconscious as Pedro is about to strike again. Realizing her state, he gestures to the others to stop and to carry Aldonza off. Fermina, who has*

*been sadistically fascinated, picks up Aldonza's skirt and watches
the Muleteers, the brutalized Aldonza slung over Juan's back, exit.
As Fermina looks off, the lights pick up Don Quixote and Sancho
at the other edge of the stage.*

DON QUIXOTE: Ah, Sancho, how I do envy my enemies.

SANCHO: Envy?

DON QUIXOTE: To think they know the healing touch of my lady Dulcinea.
Let this be proof to thee, Sancho. Nobility triumphs. Virtue always prevails.
Now in the moment of victory, do I confirm my knighthood and my oath.
For all my life this I do swear—*(Sings.)*

To dream the impossible dream,
To fight the unbeatable foe,
To bear with unbearable sorrow,
To run where the brave dare not go . . .

The lights make the transition back to prison, as the Theme of the Inquisition makes itself heard. All the prisoners are tense and fearful, Cervantes
included. The stairway descends.

CERVANTES: Are they coming for me?

THE DUKE: Very possibly. Are you afraid, Cervantes? *(Mockingly.)* Where's
your courage? Is that in your imagination, too?

Cervantes is obviously terrified. The Duke pursues inexorably.
No escape, Cervantes. This is *happening.* Not to your brave man of La Mancha, but to *you.* Quick, Cervantes—call upon him. Let him shield you. Let
him save you, if he can, from *that!*

*On the stairway the Men of the Inquisition have appeared. They
are robed, hooded, frightening in aspect. Cervantes is paralyzed
with fear, only his eyes moving, following them as they descend
into the vault. . . .*

They approach the trembling Cervantes—then move past him to a trap in
the floor. They drag up another poor sufferer from the dungeon below and
haul him up the stairs, which recede together with the Inquisition Theme. It
was not Cervantes' turn—this time.

Cervantes is offered wine and urged to continue his "defense." For the moment, he is too shaken to return to La Mancha.

THE DUKE: . . . Why are you poets so fascinated with madmen?

CERVANTES: I suppose . . . we have much in common.

THE DUKE: You both turn your backs on life.

CERVANTES *(pulling himself together):* We both select from life what pleases
us.

THE DUKE: A man must come to terms with life as it is!

CERVANTES: My friend, I have lived almost fifty years, and I have seen
life as it is. Pain, misery, hunger . . . cruelty beyond belief. I have heard the
singing from taverns and the moans from bundles of filth on the streets. I

have been a soldier and seen my comrades fall in battle . . . or die more slowly under the lash in Africa. I have held them in my arms at the final moment. These were men who saw life as it is, yet they died despairing. No glory, no gallant last words . . . only their eyes filled with confusion, whimpering the question: "Why?" I do not think they asked why they were dying, but why they had lived.

> *He rises, and through the following speech moves into the character of Don Quixote as musical underscore and change of setting begin.*

When life itself seems lunatic, who knows where madness lies? Too much sanity may be madness. To seek treasure where there is only trash. Perhaps to be practical is madness. And maddest of all, to see life as it is and not as it should be.

The "I am I, Don Quixote" theme comes up. Prisoners disappear and horses make their entrance, as the lights change the setting.

DON QUIXOTE *(sings):*
    I am I, Don Quixote,
    The Lord of La Mancha,
    Destroyer of evil am I,
    I will march to the sound of the trumpets of glory,
    Forever to conquer or die!
        He laughs.

Aldonza has gone off with the Muleteers—no doubt for some noble reason, Don Quixote insists to Sancho. They come upon a Moorish Gypsy encampment. Sancho fears that these are thieves and murderers, but his master prefers to give them the benefit of the doubt.

The Gypsies examine the horses, then push forward a Gypsy lass who attempts to seduce Don Quixote. He takes her for the daughter of a noble African lord. She and her colleagues lead the knight into a dance which cannot be performed in armor. Don Quixote takes his off, and it is piled onto the horses.

DON QUIXOTE: Sweet maiden, what wilt thou?
SANCHO: I think I know what she wilt!
        The Girl seizes one of Don Quixote's hands, presses it to her right breast.
DON QUIXOTE *(to Sancho, trying to explain):* She wishes me to feel the beating of her heart. And such is her innocence she does not even know where it is.
        The Girl seizes Don Quixote's other hand and presses it to her other breast.
SANCHO: Or even how many she has!

Don Quixote interprets a Moorish wail as a tale of their noble African's lord's capture. Their master is being held for ransom, which these good retainers are trying to raise. Don Quixote gives money to the Girl, while her friends rob him of his purse. Don Quixote makes Sancho drop a coin, too, and they all join in a dance which gives the Gypsies an opportunity to sneak away one by one.

After Don Quixote and Sancho fall exhausted from dancing, they see that they are alone and have been robbed of every possession.

The scene changes to the inn, where the Innkeeper opens his door to the destitute Don Quixote over his wife's protests. He cannot deny sanctuary to a knight dubbed by his own hand.

Don Quixote intends to go after the Gypsies because he cannot allow evil to flourish. But Aldonza enters, her clothes torn, her flesh bruised.

DON QUIXOTE: . . . Dulcinea—

ALDONZA (backing away from him): Enough of that! Get yourself to a madhouse. Rave about nobility where no one can hear.

DON QUIXOTE: My lady—

ALDONZA: I am not your lady! I am not any kind of a lady! (Trying to make him understand. Sings.)

> I was spawned in a ditch by a mother who left me there
> Naked and cold and too hungry to cry;
> I never blamed her, I'm sure she left hoping
> That I'd have the good sense to die!
>
> Then, of course, there's my father—I'm told that young ladies
> Can point to their fathers with maidenly pride;
> Mine was some regiment here for an hour,
> I can't even tell you which side!
>
> So of course I became, as befitted my delicate birth,
> The most casual bride of the murdering scum of the earth!

Yet she is still Dulcinea, Don Quixote protests. She exhorts him in song to look at her, look at the slut she is. And she hates Don Quixote for making her glimpse a better life.

ALDONZA (sings):

> Can't you see what your gentle insanities do to me?
> Rob me of anger and give me despair!
> Blows and abuse I can take and give back again,
> Tenderness I cannot bear!
>
> So please torture me now with your "Sweet Dulcineas" no more!
> I am no one! I'm nothing! I'm only Aldonza the whore!

DON QUIXOTE: Now and forever thou art my lady Dulcinea!

After a scream of despair, Aldonza collapses. At this moment a warlike fanfare of trumpets is heard.

The gate opens and in comes—incredibly—a Knight, a towering, larger-than-life-sized figure helmeted and visored, wearing plumes on his casque and glittering highlights on his armor.

The huge knight challenges Don Quixote as a charlatan and a pretender. Don Quixote recognizes this Knight as his arch-enemy the Enchanter and throws down his gauntlet, the gage of battle. If Don Quixote is beaten, declares the stranger Knight, he must forfeit his freedom. If the stranger is beaten, Don Quixote will require that he kneel and beg mercy of the lady Dulcinea. The stranger looks upon Aldonza and declares her "an alley cat!"

DON QUIXOTE (drawing his sword in fury): Monster! Defend thyself!

KNIGHT OF THE MIRRORS (stepping back): Hold! Thou asked my name, Don Quixote. Now I shall tell it. I am called—the Knight of the Mirrors!

> As he says this, the Knight takes a shield from one of his attendants and swings it forward. Its surface is a mirror which blinds and bewilders Don Quixote. In a choreographed pattern, Don Quixote attempts to fight with the Knight, but the reflection of the mirror keeps blinding him and he turns away. The Knight taps the ground with his sword to indicate where he is, and each time Quixote lurches at the place he's heard the sound, the Knight moves swiftly away. Finally, Quixote is forced to turn into his own reflection in the mirror. He turns away from it, but wherever he moves on stage, one of the attendants, bearing a similar mirror, brings him up short. Don Quixote reels from one to the other.

KNIGHT OF THE MIRRORS: Look, Don Quixote! Look in the mirror of reality and behold things as they truly are. Look! What dost thou see, Don Quixote? A gallant knight? Naught but an aging fool!

> Don Quixote recoils from his own image, only to be brought up against another.

Look! Dost thou see him? A madman dressed for a masquerade!

> Attempting escape, Don Quixote finds himself facing another mirror.

Look, Don Quixote! See him as he truly is! See the clown!

> Don Quixote reels away, only to find the mirrors converging as the Knight and his attendants close down upon him.

Drown, Don Quixote. Drown—drown in the mirror. Go deep—deep—the masquerade is ended!

> Quixote falls to his knees.

Confess! Thy lady is a trollop, and thy dream the nightmare of a disordered mind!

DON QUIXOTE (in dazed desperation): I am Don Quixote, knight errant of La Mancha . . . and my lady is the Lady Dulcinea. I am Don Quixote, knight errant . . . and my lady . . . my lady . . . (Finally beaten, he sinks to the floor, weeping.)

KNIGHT OF THE MIRRORS (removing the casque from his head): It is done!

Of course the Knight of the Mirrors is Dr. Carrasco, with his "cure" for Don Quixote's "illness." Aldonza is seized with pity for the fallen knight.

The scene changes swiftly to the prison, where the Captain of the Inquisition warns Cervantes he is soon to be summoned. The story is finished as far as Cervantes is concerned, but his fellow-prisoners don't like his ending. If they will allow him a little more time, Cervantes pleads, maybe he will improvise . . .

The scene changes to Alonso Quijana's bedroom, where Don Quixote lies in a deep coma. Dr. Carrasco and the Padre can do nothing more; Antonia and the Housekeeper must resign themselves to the inevitable, which is soon to occur. Dr. Carrasco feels somewhat guilty and cannot elicit the reassurance from the Padre he would like to have. Sancho enters.

SANCHO (to the Padre): Your Reverence, could I talk to him?
PADRE: I'm afraid he won't hear you.
SANCHO (moving toward the bed): Well, then I won't say much.
DR. CARRASCO: And no mention of knight-errantry!
SANCHO: Of course not. Does one speak of the rope in the house of the hanged? Oh—excuse me, Your Grace.
ANTONIA (bitterly): Your Grace.
SANCHO: Just a few words . . . to lighten his heart. (Sings.)
  A little gossip . . . a little chat . . .
  A little idle talk . . . of this and that . . .
  I'll tell him all the troubles I have had
  And since he doesn't hear, at least he won't feel bad.

Sancho sings and chatters of how he came home and his wife seemed to have lost the knack of beating him. His confidences to his unconscious master finally take this form:

SANCHO (sings):
  Oh, I haven't fought a windmill in a fortnight
  And the humble joys get duller every day.
  Why, when I'm asleep a dragon with his fiery tongue a-waggin'
  Whispers, "Sancho, won't you please come out and play?"

Dr. Carrasco chastises Sancho for raising the taboo subject of chivalry. Don Quixote comes out of his coma and recognizes his friend Sancho as "a fat little bag stuffed with proverbs." Antonia speaks words of comfort to her uncle, and Dr. Carrasco asks him to say his name. He does: Alonso Quijana.

Don Quixote senses that he is dying and decides to make a will. Vaguely he remembers a strange dream he had during his illness . . . but he returns to the question of the will and dictates to the Padre his wish to leave everything to Antonia, except for a few small bequests.

There is a loud interruption, a knocking, and Aldonza forces her way into the sickroom. Dr. Carrasco tries to throw her out, but Don Quixote (although he doesn't recognize her) insists on courtesy in his house. Aldonza calls him "My Lord" and "Don Quixote"; still he does not remember her.

Again, Dr. Carrasco tries to send her from the room, but she pleads with Don Quixote to call her by that other name; to bring back the dream.

ALDONZA (sings):
    . . . Dulcinea . . . Dulcinea . . .
    Won't you please bring back the dream of Dulcinea . . .
    Won't you bring me back the bright and shining glory
    Of Dulcinea . . . Dulcinea . . .
DR. CARRASCO: I'm afraid I must insist—
DON QUIXOTE: Let be!
        Carrasco lets her go.
Then perhaps . . . it was not a dream . . .
    ALDONZA (kneeling beside Don Quixote): You spoke of a dream. And about the quest!
    DON QUIXOTE (his mind stirring): Quest?
    ALDONZA: How you must fight and it doesn't matter whether you win or lose if only you follow the quest!
    DON QUIXOTE: The words. Tell me the words!
    ALDONZA (speaking to the music of "The Quest"): "To dream the impossible dream . . ." But they're your own words! "To fight the unbeatable foe . . ." Don't you remember? "To bear with unbearable sorrow . . ." You must remember! "To run where the brave dare not go—"
    DON QUIXOTE (remembering, speaks, then finally sings):
        To right the unrightable wrong . . .
    ALDONZA (a whisper): Yes . . .
    DON QUIXOTE:
        To love, pure and chaste, from afar . . .
    ALDONZA: Yes . . .
    DON QUIXOTE:
        To try, when your arms are too weary,
        To reach the unreachable star!
    ALDONZA: Thank you, my lord!
    DON QUIXOTE: But this is not seemly, my lady. On thy knees? To me?
    ALDONZA (in protest as he tries to rise): My lord, you are not well!
    DON QUIXOTE (growing in power): Not well? What is sickness to the body of a knight-errant? What matter wounds? For each time he falls he shall rise again—and woe to the wicked! (A lusty bellow.) Sancho!
    SANCHO (moving forward): Here, Your Grace.
    DON QUIXOTE: My armor! My sword!
    SANCHO (delightedly): More misadventures!
    DON QUIXOTE: Adventures, old friend. (Struggling up out of bed, singing.)
        Oh the trumpets of glory now call me to ride,
        Yes, the trumpets are calling to me,
            Reaching out to Aldonza and Sancho.
        And wherever I ride, ever staunch at my side,

My squire and my lady shall be.
>   *They help him out of bed.*
I am I, Don Quixote . . .
DON QUIXOTE, ALDONZA and SANCHO *(sing):*
>   . . . the Lord of La Mancha,
Our destiny calls and we go!
>   *Don Quixote moves a couple of steps, Aldonza and Sancho assisting him.*
And the wild winds of fortune shall carry us onward
Oh, whithersover . . .
>   *Don Quixote falters.*
ALDONZA *(a cry of apprehension):* My lord—!
SANCHO: Master—!
DON QUIXOTE *(reassuring them, sings on):*
Whithersoever they blow,
Onward to glo—ah!
>   *A cry from deep within his chest. Then a whisper.*
. . . I . . . go . . .
>   *He crumples to the floor. Sancho and Aldonza lower him gently.*

Dr. Carrasco examines him; Don Quixote is dead. The Padre chants in Latin.

ALDONZA: Don Quixote is not dead. Believe Sancho, believe.
SANCHO *(in confused hope):* Aldonza?
ALDONZA: My name is Dulcinea.

As the lights fade and change the scene back to prison, the Captain of the Inquisition is standing at the head of the stairway, summoning Cervantes to "submit his person to purification."

CERVANTES *(with wry bravado as he removes his Don Quixote beard and moustache):* How popular a defendant I am. Summoned by one court before I've quite finished with another. Well? How says the Jury?
THE GOVERNOR *(musingly, weighing the package now held in his hands):* I think I know what this contains. The history of your mad knight?
>   *Cervantes nods assent. The Governor hands him the package.*
Plead as well there as you did here and you may not burn.
CERVANTES: I've no intention of burning. *(To his Manservant.)* Shall we go, old friend?
>   *He sees that his Manservant is rigid with fear; moves to him and puts a reassuring arm about his shoulder.*
Courage.
>   *He leads him toward the stairs.*
THE GOVERNOR: Cervantes.
>   *Cervantes pauses.*
I think Don Quixote is brother to Don Miguel.

CERVANTES: God help us—we are both men of La Mancha.

The hooded Inquisitors appear with the guards to take the two prisoners away. As Cervantes and Sancho bravely mount the stairs the prisoner who played Aldonza, standing apart from the other prisoners, begins to sing "The Quest." The others join in as their eyes follow Cervantes.

PRISONERS *(sing):*
> . . . To reach the unreachable star,
> Though you know it's impossibly high,
> To live with your heart striving upward
> To a far, unattainable sky!
>> *By now the song has swelled in full chorus, overwhelming the In-*
>> *quisition chant. The lights fade and the play ends.*

INADMISSIBLE EVIDENCE

A Play in Two Acts

BY JOHN OSBORNE

Cast and credits appear on page 389

JOHN OSBORNE was born in London on December 12, 1929. His father, a commercial artist, died when Osborne was still a child, and the boy was brought up by his mother, who worked as a barmaid. He attended Belmont College in Devon and then began an acting career at 19. A year later he wrote his first play, which was produced in 1949. His first script staged in a London production was Look Back in Anger *(1956, at the Royal Court Theater). It became a major example of England's controversial "angry young man" attitude and was produced on Broadway in 1957.*

Other Osborne plays produced in New York were The Entertainer *(London, 1957; Broadway, 1958),* Epitaph for George Dillon *(London, 1958; Broadway, 1958) and* Luther *(London, 1960; Broadway, 1963). All were named Best Plays of their respective seasons, and both* Look Back in Anger *and* Luther *won New York Drama Critics Circle Awards.*

Other Osborne plays produced in London were The World of Paul Slickey *(1959),* Plays for England *(The Blood of the Bambergs and Under Plain Cover, 1962),* Inadmissible Evidence *(1964) and* A Patriot for Me *(1965). His script for the movie* Tom Jones *won the 1963 Academy Award.*

Inadmissible Evidence *is a composition made from a middle-aged man's cries of pain as he is buried in the ruins of his own life. In the following synopsis, the first act has been more than usually condensed to leave space for a detailed account of his final spasms, including all of his exhortation to his daughter in Act II.*

Time: The Present

Place: A solicitor's office in East London

ACT I

SYNOPSIS: The setting is described as *"The location where a dream takes place."* It is a solicitor's office with desk at right, with a clutter of dusty law-books and other paraphernalia, with the suggestion upstage of an outer office for clerks and a telephone girl. In this dream, however, a courtroom is super-imposed on the office. The prisoner in the dock is Bill Maitland facing one of Her Majesty's judges sitting high up on a bench above the setting, under a Royal Coat of Arms. Bill Maitland is middle-aged, dressed in the uniform of respectability including dark suit and striped tie.

The Clerk of the Court is reading the indictment.

CLERK: William Henry Maitland, you are accused of having unlawfully and wickedly published and made known, and caused to be procured and made known, a wicked, bawdy and scandalous object. Intending—

BILL: Object?

JUDGE: Proceed, proceed.

CLERK: Object. Intending to vitiate and corrupt the morals of the liege subjects of our Lady the Queen, to debauch and poison the minds of divers of the liege subjects of our Lady and to raise and create in them lustful de-sires, and to bring the liege subjects into a state of wickedness, lewdness and debauchery. How do you plead? Guilty or Not Guilty?

BILL: Not guilty.

Pause.

CLERK: Place your right hand on the book and repeat after me: I swear by Almighty God—

BILL: I swear . . . My lord, I wish to affirm.

JUDGE: Very well.

CLERK: Do you swear and affirm?

BILL: I swear and affirm . . . *(Pause. Then a hoarse rattle. Clearing his throat at intervals.)* I hearby swear and affirm. Affirm. On my . . . Honor? By my belief. My belief in . . . in . . . the technological revolution, the press-ing, growing, pressing, urgent need for more and more scientists, and more scientists, for more and more schools and universities and universities and schools, the theme of change, realistic decisions based on a highly developed and professional study of society by people who really know their subject, the overdue need for us to adapt ourselves to different conditions, the theme and challenge of such rapid change, change, rapid change. . . .

Bill continues talking in a kind of verbal shortland.

BILL: . . . above all the facts, inescapable. Anna, my wife, Hudson, I mean my managing clerk, Hudson, Joy, the telephonist, the enrichment of our standard of living. I've lost my prescription, Jane, my father's too old to be here, thank God, the National Research, Research Development Council, the Taylor Report, the Nayler Report, failure report, and a projected budget of five hundred thousand million, millions for this purpose, the practical dangers of pre-marital in the commanding heights of our declining objects. . . .

The defendant wishes to conduct his own case, the Clerk tells the Judge. Bill will begin his defense (the prosecution should begin and the defendant have the last word; but this trial is as irregular as a dream) if he could only find his pills to relieve his headache—"like a gimlet, up behind the eyeballs."

Bill has always expected that he would be brought to account like this, and so of course he is ready.

BILL: . . . I wish I could open my eyes. My eyelids. They're like oysters. However, this is my concern and not yours. I'll think of something. *(He presses his eyeballs.)* My name is William Henry Maitland. I am thirty-nine years old, practising solicitor and commissioner for oaths at 34, Fleet Chambers E.C.3. I have worked in service of the law—if you can call being a solicitor, working in the service of the law—for nearly twenty-five years. In fact I started work in this very office, this court, since I was at least fifteen. . . . That—*(Points to Judge's seat.)*—is my old boss's chair. You see, I took his position over from him. My managing clerk, old Hudson, he was working for the old man even then. Not that he was much older than me. He just always seemed older. Anyway, he works for me now. I don't even know why I took up the law. I don't think there was any reason at all much. I can't think of any now, and I couldn't think of any then. Perhaps I did think I might land up on the bench even. Or with learned counsel. Mr. Jones. No, but I never seriously thought of myself being brilliant enough to sit in that company, with those men, among any of them with their fresh complexions from their playing fields and all that, with their ringing, effortless voice production and their quiet chambers, and tailors and mess bills and Oxford Colleges and going to the opera God knows where and the 400, whatever I used to think that was. I can't remember at the time. I have always been tolerably bright.

JUDGE: Always been?

BILL: Bright. *Only* tolerably bright, my lord. But, to start with, and potentially and finally, that is to say, irredeemably mediocre. . . .

In order to become even a "small market place solicitor" Bill studied exceptionally hard. He imagines he sees his ex-wife and his father in the courtroom . . . then he gets back onto the track of self-analysis. He was always a quick study but doesn't retain much, so that he "must be getting less and less good" at his job. He has a flair for snap decisions but is basically an indecisive person.

BILL: . . . I am almost forty years old, and I know I have never made a decision which I didn't either regret, or suspect was just plain commonplace or shifty or scamped and indulgent or mildly stupid or undistinguished. As you must see. As for why I am here, I have to confess this: I have to confess that: that I have depended almost entirely on other people's efforts. Anything else would have been impossible for me, and I always knew in my own heart that only that it was that kept me alive and functioning at all, let alone making decisions or being quick minded and all that nonsense about me . . . That I have never really been able to tell the difference between a friend and an enemy, and I have always made what seemed to me at the time to make the most exhausting efforts to find out. The difference. But it has never been clear to me, and there it is, the distinction, and as I have got older, and as I have worked my way up—up—to my present position. I find it even more, quite impossible. And out of the question. And then, then I have always been afraid of being found out.

Found out? Yes, he has always had the foreboding that some day he would be brought to judgment and committed to all the indignities of prison, like any other guilty defendant.

He feels unwell; he would like to leave the box. He has tried to make friends with women and to love them, and he has failed in both efforts. ". . . I can't escape it, I can't forget it. And I can't begin again. You see?"

As he moans, the dream courtroom fades to the "reality" of lawyer's office. The Judge and the Clerk take off their wigs and robes and become Hudson, the managing clerk and Jones, another clerk, in Bill's office. They move into the office area, ready to take up their daily tasks.

> *During this, Bill remains still. The actor has to indicate the painful struggle into consciousness, without, at the same time, making the physical metaphor too explicit: the difficulty of breathing, the violent inner effort to throw off the burden, the fishy, palpitating struggle of the heart being landed into wakefulness. The gasping will takes over. The dream, the prison of embryonic helplessness for the moment, recedes, but not altogether. The focus fades on Bill, who emerges slowly out of it. Presently, he makes his way out of it, into the outer office, then through into the office itself.*

The office day begins as usual; Bill has cut himself shaving and is suffering from a hangover. He greets his secretary, Shirley, with "Hello, sexy" when she brings him the mail.

BILL: What—no make-up this morning?

SHIRLEY: You *do* remember Mrs. Garnsey's coming at 9:30?

BILL: Of course, I forgot you girls don't really wear make-up nowadays, do you? All leaking eyeshadow and red noses. Go and put on some lipstick, dear. What's the matter? Isn't he giving it to you?

SHIRLEY: Finished?

BILL: Don't tell me you're getting too much. I don't believe it.

SHIRLEY: Oh, knock it off.

BILL: Well, something's made you bad tempered this morning, and I don't believe that languid pipe cleaner of an accountant you're engaged to has got *that* much lead in his pencil.

SHIRLEY: Do you ever think of anything else?

BILL: Not so much. Probably less than you do though.

SHIRLEY: Me?

BILL: I just talk about it at great boring length mostly to boring, bad-tempered and silly girls. Without make-up.

SHIRLEY: You know what you can do! And quick.

Hudson and Jones tell Bill that Shirley is quitting at the end of the week. Bill goes out of his way to make a hostile remark to Jones (who seems accustomed to this rough treatment from his boss). Then Bill launches into a diatribe against Shirley's "droopy young bookkeeper" boy friend, blaming his type for creating and enjoying all the banalities of modern living (such as placing mascots in the rear windows of autos). Following this, Bill has some scorn left over to hurl at Jones, who endures stoically these unwarranted gibes from his employer. Jones is, in Bill's words, "a tent peg. Made in England. To be knocked into the ground."

Bill asks Shirley to fetch him a glass of water, but she objects. Hudson warns Bill not to underestimate Jones. Then in comes the blonde and shapely telephone girl, Joy, who is agreeably willing to fetch a glass of water and the file on Mrs. Garnsey.

Bill confides to Hudson that he feels strange this morning; things are going against him; empty taxis would not stop for him. He is sure that computers will take over the work of lawyers and put them all out of business. The papers are full of Britain's problems, but what about *his* problems.

Hudson tries to joke him out of his melancholy. Joy comes in with the water and the Garnsey file. Hudson wants to talk business, but Bill is preoccupied with thoughts of Joy's love-making potential. Bill takes some of his pills, then receives the message that his wife, Anna, has been trying to get in touch with him.

BILL: ... If Anna rings will you speak to her, say I'm with Mrs. Garnsey? *Hudson nods.*
It's only about next weekend.

HUDSON: I thought you were going to Blackpool. On a business trip.

BILL: Yes, with Liz. We'd planned it before Christmas. We haven't really had a long weekend together since last summer when Anna took the kids with her down to North Devon.

HUDSON: So what's happening?

BILL: I don't know. Anna's fixed some crazy do for the entire weekend for the girl's birthday.

HUDSON: How old is she?

BILL: I don't know. Seventeen. Eighteen. Anyway, too old and too sophisticated and too unhampered by anything in particular to need my presence at her birthday for two whole days.

HUDSON: Does your wife know about Blackpool?

BILL: Cancel it, she says. Business doesn't mean all that to *you*. Give your daughter a good time.

HUDSON: She knows you were going with Liz?

BILL: Why else should she arrange this daft junket? She doesn't like the kids' chums any more than I do. It'll be all jazz and noise and black leather and sour teenage squalor and necking, and oh—

HUDSON: You've always been pretty fond of necking and—

BILL: Squalor! I may have helped to knock it together often enough but I haven't enjoyed it, and I haven't ever been made to feel sharp or with it or representative of any damned thing. I was never, at any time, like that bunch of kids my daughter runs around with, so don't compare me to them.

HUDSON: Sorry.

BILL: And as for necking, I never went in for it, never would, and pray God I am never so old, servile or fumbling that I ever have to wriggle through that dingy assault course. Do you like it, do you want it, those are the only questions I have ever thought worth while going into. You think I'm not telling the truth? Well, it's as near the truth as I can find at this moment; for one thing I have never had very strong fingers which is why I had to give up learning the piano.

Bill doesn't seem to attract his rightful share of tenderness, either from his wife Anna or from his mistres Liz. Sex doesn't offer him a satisfactory escape, nor does his work.

Bill should visit the Scrubs today to check on a client charged with indecent assault, but he doesn't want to; neither does he want to take on Mrs. Garnsey's divorce problems because "I dread those clients, clients like Mrs. Garnsey. I've got all the lumber I can carry."

They discuss another case, and it seems that Bill is trying to put all of the day's chores, all of his own normal and rightful duties, onto Hudson and Jones.

Bill asks Joy to get his wife on the phone. Meanwhile Liz calls, but Bill can't speak with her just yet. While Joy is ringing Mrs. Maitland, Bill tells Hudson about his son; about how little communication there is between them, and how the boy actually *wanted* to go away to school. He asks Hudson's advice about whether he should leave his wife. Hudson replies it doesn't make any difference to Bill whether he leaves her or not.

Bill picks up the phone to talk to his wife. His conversation with her is a kind of rejection, partially unintentional, on all levels. He can't tell her what time he's coming home, he can't meet her for lunch, he doesn't think he can go on the weekend she is planning for their daughter Jane. The conversation leaves him drained.

Hudson has to leave the office on business, and it seems to Bill a form of desertion. Then Shirley comes in to give notice. She is leaving Friday and glad to go. She is two months' pregnant and engaged to be married. Bill wants her to stay and even offers her a raise. He is almost gentle with her, but she is unremittingly hostile.

BILL: . . . You're accusing me. But I haven't touched you. Not for three months. At least.

SHIRLEY: Thanks so much.

BILL: Oh, for God's sake throw off that half baked, cheap, show-girl act and listen to me.

SHIRLEY: Why? What have you ever done for me?

BILL: Nothing. I suppose. But I do know we had some affection for one another, beneath all the arguing and banter and waste of breath. I know I liked you. And when we were in bed together you dropped all your pretenses and deceits, after a while anyway. Perhaps I did even. I don't think I let you think it was an enduring love affair—in the sense of well of endless, wheedling obligations and summonses and things. But, if you think back on it, detail by detail, I don't think you can say it was fraudulent. Can you?

SHIRLEY: No.

BILL: You can't *disown* it. If you do that, you are helping, you are conspiring to kill me.

Shirley remembers each incident of love-making, she does not disown their affair. But on second thought she will not wait till Friday, she is leaving right now.

Joy announces Mrs. Garnsey. Bill asks her to wait, asks to speak to his mistress Liz. Panicky, Bill stops Hudson before he can leave the office and offers him a partnership in the firm. But Hudson is wary. Frankly, he has received offers from other firms and wants to think things over. Hudson departs . . . so does Shirley . . . and at first Joy can't get Liz on the line; finally she does.

BILL (on phone): Liz? My darling, I've been trying to get hold of you . . . Are you all right? . . . Well, no . . . Everything's . . . I said everything's . . . What? Oh, I couldn't get a taxi for a start, well, not a start . . . Well, you know, if I keep my head upright and don't move it about too much, and talk fairly slowly . . . Look, try and bear with me a minute . . . What was what like? Oh, last night . . . Well, yes there was an Anna situation . . . oh, before we went out and afterwards . . . Yes, that was bad enough, but the whole thing was very strange . . . It's difficult to explain . . . No, I can't quite . . . I'm sorry. I just don't seem to retain very much of anything, of anything that happened . . . I just felt everyone was cutting me . . . cutting me . . . I know, I should care! I like them as much as they like me . . . I don't know whether they're more afraid than I am . . . I think they really *want* to be liked . . . in that sort of way . . . I don't exactly do my best do I. No, well then . . . No, Anna quite enjoyed herself while she was there . . . Oh, the usual shower . . . They all seem to adore her . . . I know, but more than ever . . . it's only all right when I'm with her . . . Yes . . . But it seemed at my expense this time, it seemed to be out of me . . . as if they were disowning me . . . it's wonderful to hear your voice . . . Well, I don't know yet . . . sometime this evening . . . Look, please don't *you* press me . . . Yes. It'll be all right . . . I may not sound like it, but it will be . . . you don't think I want to go to her silly birthday junket, do you? . . . Do you think I don't know that. Of course it's Anna . . . Well, I'll probably talk to the kid myself . . . Look, love, I've got to go . . . Can I ring you back? I've got this client and she's been waiting about . . . Let me ring you . . . You *will* be in, won't you? . . . Yes, but you will *be* there . . . Promise? Don't go out till I ring you back . . . I need to talk to you . . . It'll be all right. Don't worry. *(To Joy.)* I'll see Mrs. Garnsey now.

Though Bill is extremely polite to Mrs. Garnsey, she is somewhat put off by having to see Bill. She is used to dealing with Hudson and has told him everything already; how she is getting a divorce on the grounds of her husband's adultery with three other women. Bill's duty is to tell her what the law is so that she can make up her mind how she wants to proceed. But Bill ventures onto dangerous ground, asking her how she feels about her marriage. She and her husband continually disappoint each other, and she is sorry for him.

MRS. GARNSEY: . . . what kills me is that he is being hurt so much.
BILL: How do you mean?
MRS. G: By everyone. He comes home to me, and I know that nothing really works for him. Not at the office, not his friends, not even his girls. I wish they would. God knows, he tries hard enough. I wish I could help him. But I can't, and everyone, everyone, wherever, we go together, whether it's a night out, or an evening at our club, or an outing with the children, everyone's, I know, everyone's drawing away from him. And the more people have been good and kind and thoughtful to me, the worse it's been for him. I know. And now. Now: *I'm* doing the same thing. The children hardly notice him. And now it's *me*. I can't bear to see him rejected and laughed at and scorned behind his back and ignored—
    All this last is scarcely audible.
And now it's *me*. I've got to leave him.
    Nothing more meaningful comes from her. Bill gets up to comfort her but is paralysed.

Mrs. Garnsey is near collapse and so is Bill, shaken by her description of her husband's plight, which so resembles his own. Joy leads Mrs. Garnsey away and then returns. She tries, as ordered, to get Bill's mistress (Liz Eaves) on the phone, but there is no answer.

BILL: Joy.
JOY: Yes?
BILL: Will you stay on a bit tonight?
JOY: Is it important?
BILL: Yes.

JOY: If you like.
BILL: Thank you.
Joy turns to go.
JOY: What shall I do about Mrs. Eaves?
BILL: Keep trying her.
JOY: Will you speak to her?
BILL: No. But. Say I'll be round this evening.
JOY: What time?
BILL: Tell her: to expect me when she sees me.
Curtain.

ACT II

It is early morning. Bill has been sleeping on the sofa. He struggles to wake up (as he did after the "trial" scene in Act I), and finally the ringing telephone helps him to rouse himself. He answers it, but the line is dead.

He begins his morning ritual by swallowing a pill with soda water. This gags him. As he prepares to take two more pills, he dials Liz's number.

> *This telephone conversation and the ones that follow it and some of the duologues should progressively resemble the feeling of dream and unreality of Bill's giving "evidence" at the beginning of Act I. Some of the time it should all seem actually taking place at the particular moment, naturally, casual, lucid, unclouded. At others the grip of the dream grows tighter; for example, in the call that follows now, the presence of the person on the other end should be made very real indeed, but, sometimes it should trail off into a feeling of doubt as to whether there is anyone to speak to at all.*

Liz answers, and Bill blurts out his condition: he has a terrible headache, he slept at the office, he should have phoned her to tell her he wasn't coming instead of just standing her up. Liz is obviously needling him about Joy. He takes the other two pills, then has to leave the phone and disappear into the lavatory to vomit them.

When he returns to the phone, Bill assures Liz that he loves her. He tells her what happened the night before. At 7:30 his wife Anna turned up at the office and dragged him off to dinner with a couple whose hobbies are Sociology and Sex.

BILL: . . . All tables and diagrams and unreadable . . . Yes. All it adds up to in the end is either do it or don't. We do . . . You've got it. Every time she drops one he's in there in the room with a surgical mask on and popping away with his camera . . . Yes . . . being encouraging . . . Well, it's pretty discouraging to look at them together . . . Oh sure, *rotten* dinner . . . Oh, wooden bowls, yes, sort of *Sunday Times* Supplement Primitive . . . *very* badly cooked . . . Hullo . . . Hullo . . . Are you there? . . . Oh . . . I keep thinking you're not there . . . Well, you weren't saying anything and I suddenly . . . Hullo . . . Hullo . . . Oh, hell's bloody bells. . . .

Bill fears the possibility of being cut off from Liz, but she is still on the wire and listening. Bill continues unburdening himself. Last night Bill decided to tell his wife Anna the truth: that he wants to go away for the weekend with Liz. Tough luck for the birthday weekend planned for his daughter Jane. (The information that Bill told his wife the truth seems to disturb Liz at the other end of the conversation.) After this confession about the weekend, they went out to dinner. Bill got drunk, there was a row. Bill dropped Anna at home and came to sleep at the office.

Bill hadn't wanted to break in on Liz at that late hour . . . He will try to call on her some time this morning, but in the meantime he earnestly hopes she will stay home in case he needs to telephone her again.

> *He puts the phone down. Picks it up again several times to see if it is alive. Gets out a razor, brush and mirror and looks at them dully. Dials phone again. More than ever the ambiguity of reality is marked, of whether the phone is dead, of whether the person at the other end exits. He trails back and forth between lucidity and near off-handedness and fumbling and fear and addressing himself. . . . The telephone is stalked, abused, taken for granted, feared. Most of all the fear of being cut off, of no sound from either end.*

It is his wife Anna whom Bill has dialed this time. He tells her he slept at the office, recriminates about the dinner party.

BILL: . . . well, it wasn't exactly a load of old fun was it? . . . Well, *you* were a success, but then you always are . . . I didn't mean it unkindly, you deserve to be. It's just that the more they despise me the more admirable and courageous and decent spirited you become . . . sometimes I think you're my only grip left, if you let me go, I'll disappear, I'll be made to disappear, nothing will work, I'll be like something in a capsule in space, weightless, unable to touch anything or do anything, like a groping baby in a removed, putrefying womb . . . No, I'll not leave you . . . I've told you. I'll not leave you . . . *you* are leaving me. . . .

But Jane's birthday weekend is out. Bill confesses to Anna his need for Liz, Anna can think of him what she will. As for his daughter, Bill knows that he "bores the jeans off her." He wants to speak to her, however, and Anna puts Jane on the phone.

Bill makes a few pleasantries to Jane and then asks her to come to the office to see him. He invites her to lunch. She can't make it, but she'll drop in at the office for a few minutes.

With his wife back on the phone, Bill tries to tell her of his confusion, his feeling that it is all too much for him, and Hudson and Jones are less and less help to him. Bill and Anna love each other, but "It just doesn't do much good, does it?"

As Bill hangs up the receiver, someone enters the outer office. Bill hopes it is Joy, but it turns out to be Hudson, shortly followed by Jones. Bill admits to Hudson that he failed with Mrs. Garnsey, then asks Hudson about the offer of a partnership. Hudson is still thinking it over.

Joy arrives, and Bill gives her conflicting orders: call Mrs. Eaves, call Mrs. Garnsey. Joy makes Bill understand that Shirley, his secretary has really left him and is not coming back. Bill talks on the phone briefly to Liz Eaves, for reassurance; then he absorbs from Joy the information that Mrs. Garnsey has changed her mind and isn't returning for further consultation.

He and Joy discuss the previous evening, which they spent together until Anna came to pick Bill up at 7:30. Bill is "Sorry," but Joy sees no need for that, as they both enjoyed themselves.

JOY: I have one flaw in my character. Well, not just one, but one that crops up all the time. You see I want to have sex constantly, I mean I'm always wanting it, I always have.

BILL: Joy; for a woman to make that admission is no shame, believe you me.

JOY: Ah, but everyone tells you differently. Right? You lose a man's respect, you lose your own sense of respect and all that old load of rubbish. Right?

BILL: Right.

JOY: So. So I've always felt guilty. There it is, daft, but I am. So I have to get them to say "I love you." And then, then I say "I love you."

BILL: And then?

JOY: And then. Then: I feel better. *(Pause.)* You see.

BILL: I'm sorry.

JOY: Don't be. You don't love me. And I don't love you. But it's all right. Isn't it?

She kisses him lightly.

You're a funny old thing. You're scared aren't you?

BILL: Yes.

JOY: Well, Joy won't leave you. Not yet a while. What do you want doing?

BILL: I don't know. Just cope, will you?

JOY: Sure.

It's all Bill can do to keep his agenda straight in his mind—the cases, his daughter, Mrs. Garnsey. Jones comes in, and the usual banter makes Jones wonder if he's done something wrong. No, Bill admits, he's tried to catch Jones in error but Jones is "pretty solid." Would Jones accept an offer from another firm? He might. Take over Hudson's position? He might. He's not committing himself.

Jones brings up an indecent assault case that is pending. Bill will talk to the client, Maples; maybe they can get him off by "leaning" on the evidence a little. Bill admits that someone will probably blow the whistle on him some day at the Law Society, and he wonders who it will be. . . .

Jones reminds Bill that the firm has lost Mrs. Garnsey's business. Bill knows he scared her off and hopes to get her back with a letter. He tells Jones: "I'm the wrong man for these things. You and Hudson should do them. *You're* the right people. You can handle them—I can't."

A client, Mrs. Tonks, comes in to go over her divorce petition with Bill (she is played by the same actress as Mrs. Garnsey). Mrs. Tonks reads aloud the petition which describes the sexual excesses and eccentricities of her husband. Bill refers to her husband's deposition which answers these charges, so that, in a dreamlike way, it seems almost as though Bill himself is being accused.

BILL: There were difficulties between us. Such that my wife failed to reach satisfaction.

MRS. TONKS: That. On frequent occasions at the said addresses whilst he was having intercourse with the petitioner he did . . .

BILL: My wife visited the Marriage Guidance Council on at least three occasions who told her they believed the difficulty was due to my wife's reluctance . . .

MRS. T: Notwithstanding the fact that he knew the petitioner found this conduct revolting and upsetting.

BILL: We've none of us been reluctant much have we? Well, there were girls like Maureen, and even with you there were difficulties but not revolting or upsetting. At least, not much, I don't think so. You weren't reluctant, you should be happy, you didn't cling onto it like it was the crown jewels. You were generous, loving, bright, you should have been able to cope. *I* should have been able to cope.

MRS. T: He told petitioner he liked to hear the noise made by . . .

BILL: To have another child. Another child. In spite of the advice given to her by the Counsel she refused to use this.

MRS. T: That. It was his desire to have sexual intercourse with a woman in this street to whom he referred . . .

BILL: Because she said it was nasty. Nasty and messy.

MRS. T: He constantly referred to as "that great big beautiful blonde bat."

BILL: I wonder if it was real or dyed. Not that it matters.

MRS. T: On at least eleven occasions during the marriage he attempted to commit . . .

BILL: I deny that I persisted.

MRS. T: And did in fact.

BILL: There is no truth at all in this.

MRS. T: Upon the person of the petitioner, compelling the petitioner with force to submit.

BILL: I respected my wife's feelings at all times and especially . . .

MRS. T: To these malpractises. That. In March 1961 when the petitioner was seven months pregnant with the child Laura, the respondent violently chastised the child Edward with a heavy brush of a type . . .

BILL: No truth at all in these allegations. . . .

Joy interrupts to say that another client is waiting. Bill passes Mrs. Tonks on to Jones, at the same time begging her to believe that she is not being "passed on."

The new client, Mrs. Anderson, enters Bill's office (she is played by the same actress as Mrs. Garnsey and Mrs. Tonks). It is another divorce case, caused by husband's neglect rather than excess. Once again, the client's complaints send Bill into a world of his own where he is answering his own charges against himself for being a poor husband. He imagines his own funeral, with Anna in black and an assembly-line cremation. He imagines what it might be like if Anna died: he might have a cup of coffee at Lyons (smiling at the waitress), buy a new suit, enjoy a very slow dinner topped off by a cigar and liqueur, then a show and to bed with a good book. . . .

There is nothing Bill can do for Mrs. Anderson, not even listen to her petition. Joy leads her out of the office. He asks Joy to connect him with a colleague named Winters, whose managing clerk pretends that Winters is not available. In desperation he phones Liz Eaves and pours out to her, on the telephone, his suspicion that his former colleague is brushing him off or even conspiring against him. Again, he asks Liz to stay home in case he needs to telephone her.

Joy ushers in the indecent assault client, Maples. He is played by the same actor who plays Jones.

> *Jones-Maples has some of Jones's unattractiveness but with other elements. In place of his puny arrogance and closed mind, there is a quick-witted, improvising nature, not without courage. His flashes of fear are like bursts of creative energy, in contrast to Jones's whining fixity and confidence.*

BILL: Mr. Maples. Sorry about all this waiting about for you. I'm afraid it's . . . do sit down. No calls, Joy. Right?

JOY: What about Mr. Winters?

BILL: Oh. Yes. Him.

JOY: And.

BILL: I don't know do I? Use your judgment. Well, try me if you're not sure. But I must see to Mr. Maples, I must see he's looked after. We *must* get on with it.

> *Slight pause as he falters into another distraction. They watch him. He wrenches himself out and dismisses her.*

All right.

> *Joy goes out.*

Now, at last. So sorry. You've (*He looks for Maples' file. Flips through papers.*) You've, yes, you've been seeing—Mr. Jones.

> *Maples nods.*

Yes, there's a fairly longish statement. And, of course, a copy of your statement to the police. And these other things . . . It doesn't make a very clear . . . at the moment, does it? Shall we start more or less . . .

> *Joy buzzes.*

JOY: (*off*): Your daughter's here.

BILL: Ask her to wait.

JOY: Only thing is she says she's not got very long. Shall I—

BILL: Who has? Tell her to wait. Give her a cup of tea and discuss your teenage interest together.

JOY: I'm no teenager, thank you!

BILL: No one would know it. And look—don't let her go. She's got to stay and see me. After I'm through with Mr. Maples. Tell her that. *(Switches off.)* Fresh start was right. Yes, let me say to you—

> *He is thrown by the image of his daughter waiting outside. She is just visible to the audience.*

As your lawyer you have no, no obligations to me. Whatsoever. However, if you wish me to act in your interests, you should regard me like the, the Queen, with the right to, to be consulted, to encourage and to warn I don't even ask for the truth. You may not be capable of it, it's difficult to retain for most of us, some of us at least, and when you're in a spot of trouble, as well, you are, let's be quite honest about it, and you feel you are gradually being deserted and isolated, it becomes elusive, more than ever, one can grasp so little, trust nothing, it's inhuman to be expected to be capable of giving a decent account of oneself . . . Could you just shift your chair a little nearer to the desk. There, then I can see you properly. I hate to have my clients half way across the room, having to talk to themselves. Instead of to me. Shall we see if we can't find anything that's been left out. *(Pause.)* Who *are* you?

> *When Maples replies, his delivery adopts roughly the same style as in the Mrs. Garnsey-Anderson-Tonks dialogue.*

MAPLES: How can I describe myself to you? I do seem to be very ordinary, don't I?

BILL: I don't know. I wish I could see you more clearly. This statement . . .

MAPLES: Isn't true.

BILL: Well, I knew that before you came in.

> *Presently he gives his evidence, like Bill himself. Mostly at speed, more polemic than reflection.*

MAPLES: All right them. My name is John Montague, after my uncle Monty, Maples. I am married, I am quite young though I don't feel as if being young ever happened to me. I've always been married or in the army or living with my parents. I have one child, aged six, a little girl, Daphne, Susan, my wife's choice not mine. My wife's name is Hilda. That was about the only name she didn't need to be talked out of as she hated it too. I met Hilda when I was still doing my National Service, which was a bit of a difficult time for me. But it isn't very interesting to tell anyone because I don't have any proper characteristics at all, save one, and there's not even any interest in that, any more than there is in being five feet seven or prone to hay fever. Physically I'm lazy, on the whole, that is, but it doesn't stop me being restless. I can't stop at home but most of the time I'm scared to death of putting my nose outside the front door. But sometimes I do. I'm there somehow, on the, because of some row with Hilda, or some excuse or I get back late from one of the shops, and in twenty-five minutes I'm in the West End. I used to like to play tennis, which I'm rather good at—And badminton, that too, I played that at school. Hilda doesn't like anything like that, and I haven't bothered. But I used to be rather good and full of energy and I could beat quite a lot of the others. There were always a few, though, and we used to have wonderful, great long duels when we should have been doing our homework. And it might even end up in a bit of a fight. A couple of times I even burst into tears when I was playing against someone called Shipley, his name was. He thought I was a bit mad, but it was all right. We were old friends. Nothing else. We talked about girls constantly, all the time.

Bill tries to take some of this in. Maples sees the effort and slows down the concentration for a few moments.

Maples is in the drapery business. He had met his wife Hilda while still in the army, and her father owned a run-down ribbon-and-button shop. Maples has built up the business until now there are two new shops in addition to the old one.

MAPLES: I'll have to tell you about Denis.

BILL: Denis who? Oh, all right, tell me later.

MAPLES: Well, a year ago I nearly left Hilda. I fell in love. I still think it was the first time. But I couldn't bear the thought that I couldn't get over it, that it was bigger than me, however ordinary I might be. I never liked girls except my sister but she wasn't always easy to talk to. She could be suspicious and sort of unwelcoming. We all talked about girls all the time and we'd play games like seeing how we could look up their skirts when they were playing games or going upstairs on the bus.

BILL: I'll bet Shipley was good at that.

MAPLES: Yes. He was.

BILL: So was I, I'm afraid.

MAPLES: The only thing that excited me was playing tennis, and especially the badminton with him. I'd sweat for hours, before, during and afterwards, and I couldn't get my homework done in time for bed which scared me because I was terrified of getting into trouble. . . .

Maples was also scared into marrying Hilda because he had gotten her pregnant; his mother had always told him this was the rottenest thing a man can do. Maples liked his father better than his mother. He never liked girls, but he never liked effeminate men, either. He always lets the other person make the first advances.

Maples' wife knows about the indecent assault charge, because one of the detectives came around to his house. Maples doesn't want to change; he wants to remain as he is, but he wants to stay out of trouble with the law.

MAPLES: . . . I'd even given up Denis four months ago, I hadn't spoken to him even for four months and this happened. On the way back from the new Hounslow shop. Hilda's mother tries to call it a boutique, but I think I've talked her out of that now. I used to have to get drunk first, like I did when I forced myself into bed with Hilda and got married for it. But I haven't had to do that for a long time. Do you think I should plead guilty?

BILL: Not yet.

MAPLES: What's the advantage?

BILL: Of pleading guilty? It has the advantage of certainty, that's all.

MAPLES: That sounds very attractive at the moment.

BILL: Well, I can't even guarantee that yet.

Joy buzzes.

JOY: I'm sorry, but your daughter wants to know how much longer, because she can come back.

BILL: Tell her she's got to wait. I don't care. She's got to wait. Now tell her. *(Switches off.)* Can I offer you anything?

MAPLES *(shakes his head):* Sometimes I would think I was unique, of course. You know, years ago. I hoped I was. But I'm not. I'm ordinary. But I wish I wasn't. I didn't have a clue. Nothing happened until after I was married, after Daphne was born. For some reason I got on the wrong train, but it was the right direction more or less and I just stayed on it, standing up, all those bodies pressed together and suddenly I felt two, maybe three, fingers touch me, very lightly. Every time the train stopped more people got out and there was more room. I was scared to look up from my paper and there wasn't any longer any excuse to be so close to anyone. A great draught of air came in from the platform and I felt cold, and it was Gunnersbury Station which is not too far from me, so I looked up and got out. I didn't dare look back but I heard the footsteps behind me. That was the first time and I'd had a few drinks first and I was very cold, at the back of some row of shops called something Parade, by the Midland Bank. About half past seven at night. That's about all I remember of it. When I got in, my dinner was all overcooked and simmering on a plate over the gas stove with the gravy gone hard round the edge of the plate, which is a bit like the way Hilda does things, spills them or upsets them or does them too much and she wasn't feeling well and couldn't get the baby to sleep. I went out into the garden, put my fingers down my throat and then buried it all with a trowel. If I wasn't married I'd have done it all the time, one to another, I suppose, but I don't think so. That's never been what I wanted. Oh, not that I haven't behaved . . . They're right to get me, people like me. There was a young fellow, a sales manager at a store in Kingston. Do you know what I did? He was married. Nice girl. Rather attractive, not long married. Well, I set my sights and one night the three of us went out, got drunk, and while, all the time, while his wife was in the front—

BILL: Driving?—

MAPLES: Driving—

BILL: Actually in the back?

MAPLES: And she never knew. We were so damned sharp, she never knew from beginning to end. Still doesn't know. Like Hilda, she never knew about Denis, about giving him up. I gave him up, you see. He wanted me to leave Hilda and take on a new life altogether. He begged me. He threatened to phone up or write to me. But he hasn't. He kept his promise. I longed to break the whole thing, and I think I would have done this particular night.

BILL: Do you still want to give him up?

MAPLES: No.

BILL: Do you think he's given you up?

Pause.

MAPLES: Yes. Probably. What's going to happen to me?

BILL: I don't know enough yet. I need to know more than that. I should think Sir Watkin Glover Q.C. is sure to apply the full rigor of the law and send the both of us down. What about the police?

MAPLES: I've only had one brush with the police before. Late one night by Turnham Green. He flashed his torch on us. He let the other one go, but he took my name and address and made me meet him the next night. Only about three times. I know you think I haven't tried. I can't make any more effort, any more, I want to plead guilty.

BILL: Well, you can't, now go on!

MAPLES: He asked me for a light, this policeman.

BILL: In plain clothes?

MAPLES: Naturally.

BILL: Look, try to help me, will you. Where?

MAPLES: Piccadilly Tube Station.

BILL: You're crazy.

MAPLES: I know. But I knew it was going to happen. Sounds camp, but then the truth so often is. He was quite young, younger than I am, with lots of fair, wavy hair, like mine used to be, when I just went in the army, before I met Hilda, before it started to go; he looked up. In the usual way. His eyes were pale and his cheekbones looked sharp and frail as if you could have smashed them with a knock from your finger, but when he walked away, you could see how really strong he must be. He walked straight into the cottage at number one entrance, you know, by the Regent Palace. And that was it. There was another one in there and they both of them grabbed me. Savile Row Station. Oh, quite gently. And no surprise to any of us. Denis and I had often talked about it happening. They seemed nice enough at first. I began to feel better and relaxed, as if I was being loved openly and attended on, and then, then the pressure turned on. What I ought to do. What the magistrate would say. What they knew. The one who had asked for the light had seen me with Denis. He said they knew all about him. About both of us. I had to keep him out of it. I knew nothing could be worse. So I, I signed this statement. And there it is, In front of you. So. Are you all right?

BILL (just audible): Yes.

MAPLES: You haven't taken anything down. Was it . . .

BILL: Don't worry. We'll go through it all again with Hudson.

MAPLES: No. I don't think so.

Bill is losing Maples as a client because Maples realizes there isn't anything Bill can do for him except put him off onto someone else like Hudson. Maples departs and Bill's daughter Jane comes into the office. The lights fade and then they fade up again.

Fade up on Jane and Bill together. Bill's speech must be started at the full flood. When he fails it is with his longing. His daughter is cool, distressed, scared.

BILL: They're all pretending to ignore me. No they're not pretending, they are! And that'll be the going of you except that it's happened already. Of course it has, ages ago. Look at me. Why you can't have looked at me and seen anything, what, not for years, not since you were a little tiny girl and I used to take you out and hold your hand in the street. I always used to think then that when you're the age you are now, I'd take you out to restaurants for dinner, big restaurants like I used to think posh restaurants were like, with marble columns and glass and orchestras. Like Lyons used to be before you knew it. And I thought we'd behave like a rather grand married couple, a bit casual but with lots and lots of signals for one another. And waves of waiters would pass in front of us and admire us and envy us and we'd dance together. *(Holds her to him.)* Very slowly.

    Pause.

And when we got back to our table, and when it was all over, we'd lean forward and look at each other with such, such oh, pleasure—we'd hardly be able to eat our dinner. *(Releases her.)* So that when we got up, after a bit too much champagne, we'd have to hang on to each other very tightly indeed. And then: go home . . . I always wish I'd been brought up in the country you know. Won't be possible much longer. There isn't any place for me, not like you. In the law, in the country, or, indeed, in any place in this city. My old father lives in the country, as you know, but he doesn't want to see me these days. Can't say I blame him. When I went to see him the other day— whenever it was, do you know, I tried to remind him of all sorts of things we'd done together, but he simply wouldn't, he wouldn't remember. And then the old devil got mad and told me I was imagining it. I had to go in the end. He was tired and he wanted me to go. When I bent down and kissed him, he didn't look up . . . Your other grandparents can hardly bring themselves to acknowledge me. The old woman crossed to the other side of the street once when I was pushing you in the pram so as to avoid speaking to me. Which surprised me. With you, I mean. They have you over there and your mother goes, I know, and they still give you generous presents Christmas and birthday, but do you know when they write to your mother, they never even mention me by name, love to Bill, how's Bill, nothing, not for ten years, and they only did it in the early years after you were born because they thought they had to if they were going to be able to see you! And then they discovered that they didn't even have to mime that genteel little courtesy. How much do you think your safety depends on the goodwill of others? Well? Tell me. Or your safety? How safe do you think you are? How? Safe?

    She turns away increasingly frightened.

Do you want to get rid of me. Do *you?* Um? Because I want to get rid of you.

    She moves to the door. He is toweringly cool for awhile.

Just a moment, Jane. You can't go yet. Till I tell you. About this famous weekend.

    She shrugs impatiently.

Oh, I know it's none of your fault. But you should know I shan't be with you, or, at least, your mother then, just because I shall be with Liz—a subject that bores you, I know, as much as it's beginning to her, if you see—I'll be with her for three whole days or something, if she'll have me, I don't know

that she will, but I'll be with her instead of you on your seventeenth—is it
seventeen?—anyway, birthday and the reason for that is because I know:
that when I see you, I cause you little else but distaste or distress, or, at the
least, your own vintage, swinging, indifference. But nothing, certainly not
your swinging distaste can match what I feel for you.
    Small pause as he changes tack.
Or any of those who are more and more like you. Oh, I read about you, I
see you in the streets. I hear what you say, the sounds you make, the few
jokes you make, the wounds you inflict without even longing to hurt, there is
no lather or fear in you, all cool, dreamy, young, cool and not a proper blem-
ish, forthright, unimpressed, contemptuous of ambition but good and pushy all
the same. You've no shame of what you are, and, very little, well, not much
doubt as to what you'll become. And quite right, at least so I used to think.
They're young, I said, and for the first time they're being allowed to roll about
in it and have clothes and money and music and sex, and you can take or
leave any of it. No one before has been able to do such things with such
charm, such ease, such frozen innocence as all of you seem to have, to me.
Only you, and girls like you, naturally, could get on that poor old erotic cart-
horse, the well known plastic mac and manage to make it look pretty. Pretty,
mark you! Chic. Lively. You've stopped its lumbering, indecent, slobbering
ancient longing and banged it into the middle of the Daily Express—where
they're only allowed to say the word "rape" if a black African's involved.
Or perhaps a nun. *You* don't even, not moved, to wear make-up any longer.
Your hair looks like a Yorkshire terrier's come in from out of the monsoon.
And, yet, somehow, perversely, you are more beautiful and certainly more
dashing than any of the girls I used to know and lust after from morning to
night, with their sweety, tacky lipsticks and silk stockings on coupons and
permanent waves and thick hipped heavy skirts. I don't know what you have
to do with me at all, and soon you won't, you'll go out of that door and I'll
not see you again. I am quite sure of *that* by this time if nothing else. You
hardly drink except for some wine and pintfuls of murky coffee. You'll go
anywhere and more or less seem to do anything, you've already permanent
sunless, bleached stains beneath your breasts and two, likewise, crescents, on
your buttocks. You'll read any menu without bothering, order what you want,
and, what's more, get it. Then maybe leave it. You'll hitch hike and make
your young noises from one end of Europe to the other without a thought of
having the correct currency or the necessary language. And you're right. And
you dance with each other, in such a way, I would never have been able to
master. *(He gazes longingly across.)* But, and this is the but, I still don't
think what you're doing will ever, even, even, even approach the fibbing,
mumping, pinched little worm of energy eating away in this me, of mine, I
mean. That is: which is that of being slowly munched and then diminished
altogether. That worm, thank heaven, is not in your little cherry rose. You
are unselfconscious, which I am not. You are without guilt, which I am not.
Quite rightly. Of course, you are stuffed full of paltry relief for emergent countries, and marches and boycotts and rallies, you, you kink your innocent way
along tirelessly to all that poetry and endless jazz and folk worship *and* look-

ing gay and touching and stylish all at the same time. But there isn't much loving in any of your kindnesses, Jane, not much kindness, not even cruelty, really, in any of you, not much craving for the harm of others, perhaps just a very easy, controlled sharp, I mean "sharp" pleasure in discomfiture. You're flip and offhand and if you are the unfeeling things you appear to be, no one can really accuse you of being cruel in the proper sense. If you should ever, and I hope you shan't, my dear, I truly do for I've leapt at the very idea of you, before you were ever born, let alone the sight and smell of you; if you should one day start to shrink slowly into an unremarkable, gummy little hole into a world outside the care or consciousness of anyone, you'll have no rattlings of shame or death, there'll be no little sweating, eruptions of blood, no fevers or clots or flesh splitting anywhere or haemorrhage. You'll have done everything well and sensibly and stylishly. You'll know it wasn't worth any candle that ever burned. You will have to be blown out, snuffed, decently, and not be watched spluttering and spilling and hardening. You know what God is supposed to have said, well in Sunday School, anyway? God said, He said: Be fruitful and multiply and replenish the earth. And *subdue* it. It seems to me Jane, little Jane, you don't look little any longer, you are on your way at last, all, to doing all four of them. For the first time. Go on now.

    She waits. They elude each other. She goes out. Fade. Fade up on
    Bill.

Joy enters wearing her overcoat. She reviews the situation: Hudson has decided to quit and take a job with another firm. He has gone home, and so has Jones, who says that the Law Society is "on to" Bill's practices. Joy is going home now, too. Maybe she'll be back the next day; maybe she won't. "You know what," she tells him, "I think they're all right. I don't like you either."

Liz comes in and delivers a few sarcasms about the departed Joy. Liz really loves Bill, but he constantly puts their relationship under great strain. "Frankness" as practised by Bill is a destructive form of criticism.

Bill's wife Anna phones. Bill can't be bothered to lie, tells her he's with Liz and will call her back. He unburdens himself to Liz, who is truly worried about him.

    BILL: . . . I can't grasp anything. I used to be good at my job because I had what they called an instinct and a quick brain. Quick! I can't get through the Law reports. I leave everything to Hudson and now he's gone, and I wouldn't leave a camel's breakfast to Jones even if he *were* still here.

    LIZ: Bill. What are we going to do?

    BILL: Go away. I suppose.

Liz reminds him that he gets no escape, no release from travel. She senses the inevitable.

    LIZ: I was thinking: perhaps you'd rather I didn't come away for the weekend.

Silence. He faces her.

I just thought you seemed . . . as if . . . you might . . . want to be alone.

Pause.

BILL: I was only waiting, from the moment you came in, for you to say that.

LIZ: I'm sorry to be so predictable. One often is, you know, when someone knows you well and loves you.

BILL: As I do. As I certainly do.

LIZ: I was trying my hardest to be honest. It's a failing—

BILL: Well, why don't you take something for it.

LIZ: I don't care what you are or what you do—

BILL: Or who I am.

LIZ: I need you.

BILL: Not that word, please.

LIZ: You pretend to be ill and ignorant just so you can escape reproach. You beggar and belittle yourself just to get out of the game.

BILL: Whenever I do it, I enjoy, I think you do know, being some, some sort of, sort of good and comfort and pleasure to you because I love you. I don't love you for the sake of that pleasure. I can get it anywhere.

She touches his shoulder and kisses the back of his head. He won't look up.

LIZ: You can always ring me.

BILL: But you won't be there.

She can't reply.

You do know that I love you?

LIZ: Yes.

BILL: And I shall never forget your face or anything about you. It won't be possible. I think I'm quite certain, not that it matters, I loved you more than anyone.

LIZ: More than Jane?

BILL: Yes.

LIZ: Goodbye.

She goes out. Bill takes a pill with a glass of water. He dials a number on the telephone.

BILL: Anna? Anna, what time is it? I can't see very clearly . . . Do you think I should come home . . . I don't think there's much point, do you? . . . Please don't cry, love . . . I, I think it must be better if you don't see me . . . don't see me . . . yes . . . don't. Please don't don't . . . I'll have to put the receiver down . . . I think I'll stay here . . . Well the Law Society or someone will, sometime . . . I think I'll just stay here . . . Goodbye.

He replaces the receiver and sits back waiting. Curtain.

"IT'S A BIRD   IT'S A PLANE   IT'S SUPERMAN"

A Musical Comedy in Two Acts

BOOK BY DAVID NEWMAN
and ROBERT BENTON

MUSIC BY CHARLES STROUSE

LYRICS BY LEE ADAMS

Based on the comic strip, Superman

Cast and credits appear on page 405

DAVID NEWMAN and ROBERT BENTON (book) met on the staff of Esquire, *where Newman was an editor and Benton an art director, and where they soon began to collaborate on various literary projects. Newman was born in New York, in 1937, and grew up in the suburbs, in Mount Vernon. He went to the University of Michigan, where he won the Avery Hopwood drama contest. Benton was born, raised and educated in Texas: born in Dallas in 1932, raised in Waxahachie, and went to college at University of Texas. Since their meeting at the magazine, their output has included a political satire entitled* Extremism; *an original screen play; a monthly column in* Mademoiselle *called "Man Talk," and numerous free-lance assignments for various magazines.*

Benton has collaborated with another writer on The In and Out Book *and* The Worry Book. *He is married, with one child; Newman is married, with two children. They continue at* Esquire *as contributing editors. Their book for the musical* Superman *is the Broadway writing debut of both.*

CHARLES STROUSE (music) and LEE ADAMS (lyrics) have written three scores together before Superman—*those of* Bye Bye Birdie *(1960),* All American *(1962) and* Golden Boy *(1964). Strouse is a native New Yorker, born in 1928. He has composed since the age of 12, and he studied at the Eastern School of Music and in private lessons from Aaron Copeland and Nadia Boulanger. Adams was born in 1924 in Mansfield, Ohio and attended Columbia University Graduate School of Journalism. He did not get into writing lyrics until after a period of working on newspapers, magazine, TV and radio.*

Strouse and Adams began writing for the theater at Green Mansions, a resort in the Adirondacks where they had to come up with a new show every Saturday night. They have worked together for 17 years, during which time they have published more than 300 songs. In addition to their Broadway musicals, their work has included 15 revues, a television special and songs for two movies. Each is married, with one child.

The musical Superman *brought the Man of Steel from his natural habitat in the paneled pages of drawings to the scene-by-scene, number-by-number environment of the musical stage. Our method of synopsizing* Superman *in the pages following the Introduction by the authors of its book differs from that used for the other nine Best Plays. In the case of* Superman *we represent the stage story mostly in pictures, so that you can see him in action as you are accustomed to do in his printed adventures.*

The photographs and drawings represent the succession of scenes as produced and directed by Harold Prince on March 29, 1966 at the Alvin Theater, with the dances and musical numbers staged by Ernest Flatt, in the scenery designed by Robert Randolph and the costumes designed by Florence Klotz. Our special thanks go to Mr. Prince and his press staff headed by Mary Bryant and Robert Pasolli for help in obtaining the excellent photos by Friedman-Abeles and Van Williams. Special thanks, too, to Mort Weisinger, Executive Editor, Superman, *through whose courtesy this synopsis of the musical includes several drawings which were not part of the show, but which picture the real Superman in action.*

INTRODUCTION BY THE PLAYWRIGHTS

"It's a Bird   It's a Plane   It's SUPERMAN" deals with the problems of a schizoid Kryptonian (and by extension, *all* schizoid Kryptonians) and his relationships with ten-time Nobel Prize losers, jealous gossip columnists and Chinese acrobats. Its universal qualities are, therefore, immediate and unshakable. In addition, the great modern dilemma of Alienation is thoroughly explored in the tragic character of Lois Lane, girl reporter, who is unable to pierce the emotional defense ("the Freudian mask") of Superman's blocked psyche. The latter is fully explored by the existential (in that it arises from an *acte gratuit*) probing of Dr. Abner Sedgwick, a 20th century Gilles de Raie.

Nor does this deeply despairing theatrical event ignore the concept of Loss of Communication, in that Clark Kent can't tell people that there is a red "S" underneath his white shirt. Loss of Identity, here expressed by the symbolic act of leaving one's street clothes in a phone booth, is equally explored. To be sure, *Superman* has elements of the Theater of Cruelty: witness the scene in which the Chinese acrobats hit the hero with shovels, blackjacks and gongs. Lastly, the play contains aspects of Theater of the Absurd (note the lyrics: "Pow! Bam! Zonk!") and many of the characteristics of the "happening," i.e., the ever-present possibility that the wire will break and send the actor flying around the stage crashing downward.

In short, *Superman* is a testament to the harrowing perplexities of 20th century Man, especially one who walks around in a red cape and blue tights; and we are exhausted from writing it. Perhaps you noticed.

DAVID NEWMAN and ROBERT BENTON

Time: The present
Place: In and around Metropolis

ACT I

Scene 1: A muscled figure in blue and red cape swoops from the sky, picks up the getaway car of a gang of bank robbers and flings it into the air. It's not a bird . . . it's not a plane . . . it's Superman. Having stopped the bank robbers, Superman then races up a side street to a phone booth where he can put on his Clark Kent disguise, singing:

Ev'ry man
Has a job to do,
And my job is doing good!

Ev'ry night,
When the job is through,
I fold my tights, proud to know
I've done all I could!

It's a satisfying feeling
When you hang up your cape,
To know that you've averted
Murder, larceny and rape. . . .

Ev'ry man
Has his job to do,
And my job is doing good!
I'll never stop doing good!

Oh, It's hard to keep on wearing
The old Clark Kent smile,
But I know I have to do it
'Cause my work is so worthwhile! . . .

So here you go,
Bravery gone . . .
Meek and mild . . .
Glasses on . . .
Superman,
Now you're Clark Kent.

(And now he is, *left.*)

Max Mencken (*left,* Jack Cassidy), columnist on the Metropolis *Daily Planet* sneers at Superman, wonders "Who needs him?"

"I need him!" cries Lois Lane (*below center,* Patricia Morand, arms upraised), a reporter on the *Daily Planet.* "They need me!" cues Superman and "We need him!" the citizens echo in song.

CITIZENS:
In a world of evil and doubt,
We need him!
We need him! . . . .
Trouble looms and somehow he knows
We need him!
We need him! . . . .

WOMAN:
He saved my baby from a fire!
MAN:
He caught the thug who was mugging Uncle Meyer!
CITIZENS:
Yes, when a bad situation grows dire,
We need him!—himmm. . . .

Scene 2: At the *Daily Planet,* meek Clark Kent (Bob Holiday) covers lowly Shipping News while Lois, a city room star, covers the Superman story. Superman often saves Lois's life (Clark reminds her), flies her around free, gives her exclusives. But, Lois expresses her doubts in song—"Oh how I wish I weren't in love with Superman!/A wasted life, that's all I've got with Superman!/To hope that it could ever be,/It's just a schoolgirl's fantasy,/Oh, is there no one else for me but Superman?". . . .

Enter Dr. Abner Sedgwick (*below,* Michael O'Sullivan). He needs Superman's help urgently. There's a dangerous buildup in his nuclear reactor (notice Clark Kent eavesdropping). Suddenly Clark Kent departs. . . .

Scene 2A: Clark Kent whips off his glasses, his hat, his Clark Kent disguise.

Scene 3: He soars to the rescue, to the nuclear reactor room of Metropolis Institute of Technology (MIT), where he alights . . . . as . . . . SUPERMAN! →

While Superman and Dr. Sedgwick (in a lead suit) enter the nuclear reactor to repair it, Lois and Dr. Sedgwick's assistant Jim Morgan (*below,* Don Chastain) squeeze behind a shield and sing of who matters and who doesn't:

VAN WILLIAMS

JIM:
. . . . One big boom,
    And it'll all be over,
    Or perhaps the smog will finish
    Our short dull history!
    We don't matter at all. . . .
    So here we are
    An earnest girl reporter,
    And you think you're something
      special
    In this vast eternity!
    Baby, you and I,
    We're just about as special
    As a walnut or a fly!
    We don't matter at all!
    We don't matter at all!
    We don't really matter at all.
  LOIS:
. . . . Wrong approach!
    To me I'm much more special
    Than a walnut or a roach
    Oh, we matter, we do
    What's the matter with you?
    People really matter—they do!

The reactor is fixed; Metropolis is saved; the others have gone; and Dr. Sedgwick, in his tattered lead suit, is seething. Sedgwick wants revenge on the human race because he's never won the Nobel Prize. He had hoped that radiation would destroy the world's symbol of goodness, Superman.

SEDGWICK:

In nineteen forty-nine
I thought I had it made,
My work in light diffusion
Put my colleagues in the shade!
But then my hopes were shattered
By some Hindu in Ceylon!
They gave the prize in physics
To Sir Chandra V. Raman!
Revenge!
Revenge!
I'll have it on them all!
No single slight will I forget,
I'll show no mercy, you can bet!
They'll all get theirs the day I get
Revenge! ! . . . .

. . . . Ah! But the thing that really
    drove me to a fury:
They gave the prize to Harold
    Urey!
The shocking thing about the
    matter is:
My heavy hydrogen was heavier
    than *his!* . . .
Revenge!
Revenge!
That's all I live for now!
I'll make 'em wince and cringe
    and cry!
I'll spit in their collective eye!
I'll have one thing before I die—!
Revenge! ! ! !

Scene 4: At the *Daily Planet,* Max brushes off devoted Sydney (*above left,* Linda Lavin) who has brought him the makings of a gadget to trap Superman into giving away his identity.

Then Max makes a pass at Lois, who wants no part of him. Max sings:

.... You're the woman for the man
    who has ev'rything!
    Let me show you how to live!
    Girls who get are girls who give!
    You're the woman for the man
    Who has ev'rything!
    I'm a man who has ev'rything
    Ev'rything but you. . . .

    At ev'ry opening night I'm there!
    Headwaiters know me ev'rywhere!
    Of course it's freebies all the way,
    A check for me? They wouldn't
      dare!
    A chick is seen with me today,
    Tomorrow Zanuck starts to call!
    So relax, kid,
    This is Max, kid!
    Don't give me a stall! . . . .

Max in his turn is brushed off by Lois. Meanwhile, Sydney's only remaining possibility is shy, awkward Clark Kent. Sydney leaps into Clark's arms (*below*) to sing to him of possibilities:

Haircut, simply terrible,
Necktie—the worst!
Bearing, just unbearable,
What to tackle first?
Still you've got possibilities,
Though you're horribly square,
I see possibilities,
Underneath, there's something there!

You won't be shy
When I get through
Come on and roar
You tiger, you!

Somewhere way down deep in you
There's life, no doubt!
It's just been asleep in you,
Let me bring it out!
You've got possibilities,
Maybe even a lot!
Red-hot possibilities,
Why be shy and ill at ease?
I see possibilities
You don't even know you've got!

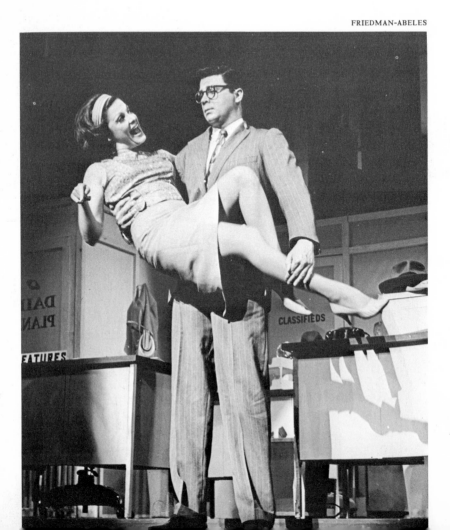

PHOTOS BY FRIEDMAN-ABELES

Scene 5: Dr. Sedgwick phones to tell Lois he will name the new Physics building Superman Hall. Lois invites him to the *Daily Planet* to see a movie of Superman's life as background for his dedication speech.

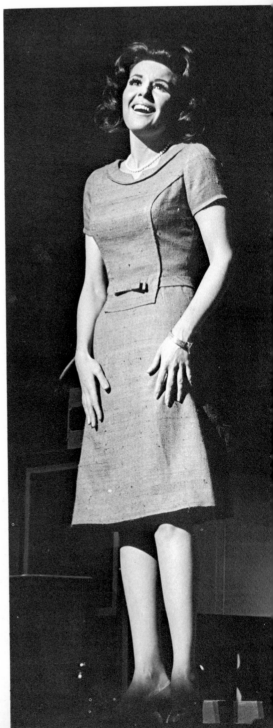

Scene 6: At the *Daily Planet* screening room, Dr. Sedgwick's assistant Jim arrives early and kisses Lois. Now, at last, she knows "What I've Always Wanted":

Well, well, look at me
The girl who wanted the unattainable
    man,
But now suddenly
Life has handed me a totally different
    plan.
One kiss and something in me melts.
And what I've always wanted—
Turns out to be,
Something else. . . .

What I've always wanted,
What I've always wanted,
Just to be a wife, that corny life
Is what I've always wanted. . . .

Dr. Sedgwick arrives at the screening room. The movie starts. It tells how a scientist on the planet Krypton became convinced his planet was going to explode—so he made one final effort to save his baby son. (Over. . . .)

BARELY IN TIME BEFORE THE FATAL HOUR, **JOR-EL** FINISHED ANOTHER ROCKET--WITH HIS BABY SON AS THE PASSENGER THIS TIME...

I AIMED THE ROCKET TOWARD A LIVING PLANET I DISCOVERED IN MY TELESCOPE! OUR SON WILL LIVE A NEW LIFE ON... **EARTH!**

GOODBYE, MY BABY! GOOD LUCK...

BEHIND THE SPEEDING ROCKET, MIGHTY KRYPTON EXPLODED INTO GREEN, RADIOACTIVE FRAGMENTS, LATER TO BE KNOWN AS **KRYPTONITE!** *

*ONE FLOCK OF GREEN KRYPTONITE METEORITES LATER PASSED THROUGH A RADIOACTIVE COSMIC CLOUD TO BECOME **RED KRYPTONITE!** — EDITOR

TIME PASSED--AS THE TINY ROCKET NEARED ITS DESTINATION--**EARTH!**

UPON LANDING, THE ROCKET'S IMPACT TOSSED **KAL-EL** OUT VIOLENTLY...BUT **UNHARMED!**...FOR, AS IT LATER PROVED, ALL PEOPLE AND THINGS FROM KRYPTON BECAME **INVULNERABLE** ON EARTH!

KRASH!

THUD!

. . . . and so the baby from Krypton arrived on Earth and grew up into Superman. The movie recapitulates some of his good deeds: catching criminals, playing checkers with old folks, entertaining children. At the end of the film, Superman makes a little speech to the audience.

SUPERMAN: Kids, being Superman is a full-time job. But there's a lot you can do to help. First, be good and listen to your parents and teachers. Believe me, they're on your side. Second, be healthy, in mind and body. You know, it's not easy combating all the criminals and evil-doers in a city this size. No matter how hard I work, there will always be men who want to take the "easy way" out. But if I know that the youth of Metropolis is behind me one hundred per cent, and if I can feel confident that tomorrow's citizens will be decent, upright men and women, my job will be that much simpler.

The film ends, and Lois leaves Dr. Sedgwick alone to think. Sedgwick tells himself that Superman needs his admirers as much as they need *him*. Sedgwick will hatch "Plan B" against Superman. Once again he sings "Revenge."

Scene 7: The Flying Lings are enemies of Superman because while he's around nobody will pay to see the Lings fly in their acrobatic act. They will help Dr. Sedgwick against Superman. They plan to rendezvous at City Hall Tower.

Scene 8: At the *Daily Planet,* Max Mencken has narrowed his Superman suspects to five. He brings them to the newspaper and pretends there is a bomb going off so that whoever is Superman will have to give himself away. But Clark Kent manages to save the situation, surreptitiously, thus protecting his disguise.

Scene 9: Atop City Hall Tower, Dr. Sedgwick meets the Lings and gives them several sticks of dynamite (invented by Alfred P. Nobel). Sedgwick instructs the Lings to blow up City Hall Tower.

FRIEDMAN-ABELES

Scene 10: On the MIT campus, Superman flies in for the ceremonies naming new Superman Hall. Dr. Sedgwick is on the platform. There are photographers present to take Superman's picture, and crowds to cheer him, and the girls of Kappa Kappa Kappa (*next page, top*) to sing and dance "It's Super Nice."

GIRLS:

> It's super nice
> To be with you
> We only hope
> You feel it too
> So glad you're here
> All red and blue
> A super nice nice
> Per-person like you! . . . .

> It's a bird it's a plane it's a—
> It's a bird it's a plane it's a—
> There goes Superman! A-look
> Look up in the sky,
> There goes Su-baby my oh my
> (Scream) . . . .
> Yeah yeah yeah!

To show his gratitude, Superman lifts the crowded platform (*below*). But what's that in the background? City Hall Tower dynamited, falling, and Superman is trapped, powerless to help! Dr. Sedgwick smiles gleefully. All look at Superman accusingly, as the curtain falls on Act I.

ACT II

Scene 1: Newspaper headlines shout Superman's disgrace, **WHERE WAS SUPERMAN?** Max is happy. His mock-farewell is sung with irony:

So long, big guy,
It's tough to say goodbye.
So long, big guy,
Here's mud in your X-ray eye!

Farewell, old pal,
You know we'll all miss you,
You had your day,
So what is there left to say?

Sure, you were doing swell,
Too bad you fell, big fella!

You might as well
Turn in those tights, big guy,
Take your last bow,
And look who's the big guy now! . . . .

Go on and cry,
I understand, big guy,
You're through, and how,
And me, I'm the big guy—

So long, ta ta, and adios!
Chin-chin, shalom and toodle—oo!
Arrivederci, daddy-o!—now!

Scene 2: In Clark Kent's apartment, a haggard Superman is bearing his humiliation alone, as best he can. Lois arrives and is surprised to find Superman at Clark Kent's. Superman expresses his hurt bewilderment in song:

Why can't the strongest man in the world
Be the happiest man in the world?

Why does the strongest man in the world
Have the heaviest heart in the world!

Why must I, the Man of Steel,
Feel as helpless as a man of straw!

They used to hold me in such awe!

Now the cheers
Have turned to jeers!

Why must the strongest man in the world
Be the bluest man—tell me why?

Don't they know the strongest man
Can cry? . . . .

Lois can relieve Superman's mind on one point: she won't be an emotional burden to him any more. She loves Jim Morgan. Having "reassured" Superman, she leaves so abruptly that she doesn't hear Superman call out after her: ". . . Lois, I love you!"

VAN WILLIAMS

Scene 3: All week long "the skies have been empty," as Max (*above,* with Sydney) writes in his column. Max suggests that Sydney write a book about him called "My Years With Max." Sydney replies in song:

Ooh, do you love you!
Ooh, do you love you!

I've seen nothing to match
Such pure conceit
You're so sold on yourself
It's sort of sweet. . . .

You're what you enjoy
Boy! It's boy meets boy!

You've found your Mister Right,
It's you-know-who!
Ooh, do you love you!

While Sydney is singing, the Lings hit Max on the head and carry him off in a laundry basket.

Scene 4: Max is taken to Dr. Sedgwick's laboratory. Dr. Sedgwick's computer, the Brainiac 7, indicates that Max may be Superman. Max laughs, suggests Sedgwick might as well have said Clark Kent. Sedgwick has never programmed Clark Kent. He does so, and the computer declares Kent *is* Superman. Max and Sedgwick pledge themselves to each other as a team to destroy Superman, in exuberant song and dance (*at right*). . . . →

MAX:
>You've got what I need, baby!
>You've got it, and how!
>You've got what I need, baby!
>Together we can scale the heights,
>And I mean right now!
>
>You've got what it takes, sweetie!
>All the way from A to Z!
>You've got what I need, baby,
>And from now on baby,
>>you've got me!

VAN WILLIAMS

VAN WILLIAMS

FRIEDMAN-ABELES

BOTH:
>Here comes the new team, mister!
>We'll be great, just wait and see!
>You've got what I need, baby,
>And from now on, baby—
>Don't mean maybe—
>From now on, baby, you've got me!

Scene 5: Meanwhile, in a number staged in comic-strip panels, Lois is still thinking of Superman when she should be thinking only of Jim. Sydney meets Clark Kent and kisses him (*below right*). Max's comment is part of a song:

MAX:

She doesn't know who's kissing her—
it's Superman!

LINGS:

Why are we always out of a job—
it's Superman!

ALL:

Who is the man you can't ignore?
It's Superman!
From Budapest to Baltimore—
it's Superman!
His figure whirling round my brain!
A creature science can't explain!
It's not a bird, it's not a plane—
it's Superman!

JIM:

I find a girl, and she's hung up on Superman!

SEDGWICK:

Who will we soon have in our net—

LINGS:

—it's Superman! . . . .

ENSEMBLE:

Why's the sky so empty?
Superman, where is he?
How could he desert us?
Superman, how could you?
Who is the man you can't forget—
it's Superman!

Scene 6: Max leads Clark Kent and Sydney into Sedgwick's trap in an abandoned power station. Max sends Sydney away. The Lings bring in Lois, unconscious and strapped to a chair which they connect to a 6,000-volt generator, so that Superman can't make a move without endangering her life. The Lings drag Max off.

Sedgwick tells Clark he knows he's Superman, and he attacks the Man of Steel psychologically. Is he *really* doing good? If so, why doesn't he prevent crime instead of just catching crooks after the fact? Why does he wear an ostentatious cape? (Slowly, Superman peels off his Clark Kent disguise.) Why, in fact, call himself *Super*man? It is because, rejected from his native planet, he needs the adulation of millions.

> *Superman, shaken, falling apart, drops in a chair.*

SUPERMAN: But they do love me—

SEDGWICK: Oh do they? Yes, they love the performer, the stunt man who flies in the sky—(*As if he had just thought of it.*) Flying? You know, of course, that flying is a well-known dream symbol of frustration, but let that pass. (*Patronizingly.*) I know you really *can* fly. Of course Clark Kent can't fly. But then he doesn't need to. He has a job, a home, friends. Remember, the world created Superman, but *you* have created Clark Kent. Why have you found it necessary to lead this double life? Could it be because you are unable to accept responsibilities?

SUPERMAN: Dr. Sedgwick, I . . . can't . . . think anymore—

SEDGWICK (*heading for home, driving hard*): Superman, this is *truth*. A child who is rejected thinks in his childish way that he has done something wrong. A creature, who walks among men, disguised as one of them, and yet rejects the idea of living as one of them?? Such a man is consumed by *guilt!* Such a man will perform so-called good deeds in the hope of alleviating that guilt!

SUPERMAN: Have I no right to my job?

SEDGWICK (*relentlessly, ruthlessly, hammering him down*): Who gave you that right? Who set you up as the judge? Who told you that men couldn't deal with their own lives? *Who told you that we needed a Superman?*

> *Superman slowly puts his head in his hand, beaten. Totally self-absorbed and broken.*

I did it! I did it!

Jim rushes in looking for Lois, and the Lings knock him on the head and he falls a foot away from where Superman sits brooding. But Superman pays no attention. His inertia is as complete as his defeat.

Scene 7: That night, Lois is still strapped to the generator and Max is a prisoner too, guarded by the Lings. Lois sings her confidence that "I'm not finished yet!/Superman won't let me die!" Sedgwick comes in followed by humble, obedient Superman. The Flying Lings reveal themselves as representatives of Red China. They pin a peace medal on Sedgwick, who is almost crazed by his victory. They will all escape to Red China in a helicopter, taking Superman with them.

Lois shouts to Superman that this is *wrong*. Jim protests, and they shoot him. This brings Superman out of his fog. "I'll never stop doing good!" he cries and attacks the Lings—POW! BAM! ZONK!

PHOTOS BY VAN WILLIAMS

SUPERMAN:

    You boys—pow!
    Are good! Bam!
    I like a crook who really tries!
    Come on! Pow!
    Let's go! Bonk!
    You'll learn a trick or two! . . . .

    Good night!
    Sweet dreams!
    So solly to mess up your plan!
    But now you know—
    Splat!
    Pow!
    You can't fool around
    Wham!
    Zow!
    With Superman!

LINGS:

Ooof!
Arghhh!
Grunt!
Gasp!
Uggggh!
Ow!
Choke!
Aieeeee . . .!
Thud!
Sob!
Arghhh!
Oof!
Groan!
Choke!

Having disposed of the Lings, Superman hears Lois cry, "Help! Help, Superman!" and flies to her rescue. Sedgwick tries to escape as the Chinese helicopter lowers a rope ladder—but Sedgwick falls to his death in a cloud of electric sparks.

Lois goes to Jim's aid—he is wounded, but he will live. And now at last, Lois knows—it is really Superman she loves.

Max tries to tell Sydney that Clark Kent is Superman, but she doesn't believe him; like all others to whom Max would tell this, Sydney thinks he's crazy. She makes Max walk over and apologize to Superman for all the trouble he caused.

A policeman rushes in with the news that a missile is headed in the direction of Metropolis. "A missile!" exclaims Superman, "This is a job for Superman! Up, up. . . ."

FRIEDMAN-ABELES

. . . . and awayyy!"

THE END

CACTUS FLOWER

A Comedy in Two Acts

BY ABE BURROWS

Based on a play by Pierre Barillet and Jean-Pierre Gredy

Cast and credits appear on page 390

ABE BURROWS belongs to the majority (52 per cent) of established Broadway playwrights who were born in New York City. December 18, 1910 was the date. His father was in the wallpaper and paint business. His education—at College of the City of New York and the New York University School of Finance—aimed him straight at Wall Street, but he struck it only a glancing blow. He began writing for radio and soon reached a peak as head writer for one of the masters of radio comedy, Ed Gardner and his Duffy's Tavern.

Burrows *made his Broadway debut as co-author of the book of* Guys and Dolls *(1950, a Best Play and a Critics best) under the direction of a master of stage comedy, George S. Kaufman. His major Broadway musical credits since that date are as follows:* Can-Can *(1953, author of the book and director);* Silk Stockings *(1955, co-author of the book);* Happy Hunting *(1956, director);* Say, Darling *(1958, co-author of the book and director);* First Impressions *(1959, director);* How to Succeed in Business Without Really Trying *(1961, a Best Play and a Critics and Pulitzer Prize winner; co-author of the book and director), and* What Makes Sammy Run? *(1964, director). It is known that he contributed "uncredited revisions" to the book of* Make a Wish *(1951), but the full extent of his uncredited work on friends' shows is unknowable, even by Burrows himself.*

The adaptation of Cactus Flower *is Burrows' first work for the record on a non-musical script. He also directed this comedy, and he directed* Reclining Figure *(1954) and* The Golden Fleecing *(1959). Burrows' writings for media other than the stage have included the screen play for* The Solid Gold Cadillac *and the recent TV series* O.K. Crackerby.

PIERRE BARILLET and JEAN-PIERRE GREDY wrote a comedy called Le Don D'Adele *for the French theater ten years ago. It ran for three years and was followed by their equally successful* Ami, Ami. *During the decade the French stage has enjoyed many other works of this leading comedy-writing team, including adaptations of the American plays* Sunday in New York *and* Goodbye, Charlie. *Their* Fleur de Cactus, *from which* Cactus Flower *was translated literally in title but considerably Americanized in content, was a hit in Paris last season.*

Time: The present

Place: Uptown and downtown Manhattan

ACT I

Scene 1: Toni's apartment in Greenwich Village

SYNOPSIS: It is 4 a.m. in Toni's one-room apartment, which is compactly furnished with bed, stove, a few living room pieces. The entrance door is upstage center and a door to the bathroom leads off right. Next to it is a large window, outside of which the fire escape can be seen. There is just barely enough light to see that Toni is at home.

> *She is lying on the bed, face down, unconscious, her head hanging off the front of the bed. She's a beautiful girl, wearing an attractive short nightgown. A small radio on the shelf at window is on and rock 'n' roll music is playing. We hear someone pounding at the door.*

It is Igor, from across the hall—and he smells gas. When no one answers his knock, he goes to the fire escape, smashes a window pane, opens the window and enters.

> *He's a good looking young fellow, very athletic and quick in his movements. He is dressed in T-shirt and chino pants.*

Swiftly, Igor sizes up the situation and does what is to be done: turn off the gas, open all windows, give artificial respiration and mouth-to-mouth resuscitation. As he does so, Toni kisses him.

> *He very sensibly holds still for a long kiss. Then he pulls back.*

TONI *(in a very sleepy voice, her arms still around his neck):* Julian. Julian . . .

IGOR: Hey, I'm not Julian . . . Wake up, wake up.

TONI *(same sleepy voice):* Julian, kiss me.

IGOR *(looking around):* Sorry, Julian, whoever you are.
    They kiss again.

TONI *(pulling away):* Who are you—what are you doing?

IGOR: Mouth-to-mouth resuscitation.

TONI: You were kissing me.

IGOR *(releasing her):* It sort of got away.

TONI: Wait a minute, where am I? I was trying to . . .

IGOR: Look, I live next door and I smelled gas.

TONI: Gas? I'm alive! I fizzled it! I fizzled it! Oh boy, I really fizzled it! *(She falls back into her former position.)*

Toni blames Igor for interfering and saving her life. Igor tries to joke her out of her depression. He is an unproduced playwright (full name, Igor Sullivan). She is Antoinette Simmons and she works in an LP record shop. There she chanced to meet Julian—handsome, successful Dr. Julian Winston, a dentist.

IGOR: . . . You just found out that Dr. Julian Winston, D.D.S., Park Avenue, has a wife and three children.

TONI: I *didn't* just find it out. Julian told me he was married the first time we met. That's one of the things that attracted me to him. Made me love him more.

IGOR: You go for married men, huh?

TONI: I like honesty. All my life people have lied to me and I can't stand it. Julian had the decency to warn me right away that he had a wife and a family. I was in love with him and I accepted it.

IGOR: So what's the problem?

TONI: I couldn't accept it. At first I thought it was all going to be a carefree, gay fling. Whoopee. Then came all those times when he couldn't see me. Night after night I'd be ready and waiting, then, bang! there'd be a phone call or a note.

Julian cancelled their date last night (says Toni, putting on Julian's robe) and it depressed her particularly because it was the first anniversary of their meeting. She had been cooking him her special chicken cacciatore which boiled over while she was unconscious, stopping up the burners and probably saving her life.

Igor, it seems, is living on an allowance from his father. Though he's not a snappy dresser like Julian, he is not entirely the struggling, poor young writer.

Toni tries to go to sleep, and Igor leaves. Then Toni suddenly remembers that she mailed a letter to Julian telling him she intended to kill herself. She pounds on the wall and Igor comes back into the room.

TONI: . . . now that I fizzled it, he's got to be told before he reads my letter. Igor, you must call him for me.

IGOR: Why don't you call him yourself?

TONI: First of all, I'll be sleeping. Second of all, I'm through with him and I won't give him the satisfaction of hearing me cry. *(Lying down on the bed.)* Besides, he's liable to call the cops or something.

Obligingly, Igor agrees to call Julian the next morning and tell him Toni is alive.

Scene 2: Dr. Julian Winston's office

In the center of Dr. Winston's reception room is the desk of his secretary-assistant (on it, in addition to the telephone and other office necessities, is a small cactus plant). At right are chairs for the patients and upstage center is the door to the doctor's operating room, behind which we can see the glare of fluorescent lighting. At right is the door to the waiting room, upstage left the door to a supply closet. Among other prominent features of this office are a stereo-hi-fi set (playing at curtain rise) and several modern paintings.

Stephanie Dickinson, the dentist's assistant, enters from the operating room.

> *Stephanie is the completely efficient nurse. She's dressed in a white uniform, low-heeled shoes, very little makeup. She walks to the desk and picks up mail, looks through it quickly. Phone rings. She goes left to the stereo, turns down the sound. The music keeps playing, but at a much lower level. She crosses back to the phone and picks it up and answers it. When Stephanie speaks, her voice is soft, soothing, yet impersonal. Her voice, plus the soft music, creates an effect that is supposed to be very soothing for the patients.*

The phone call is from a patient who needs an emergency appointment with the popular Dr. Winston. Stephanie graciously grants this patient some time a week from Thursday.

Riffling through the mail, Stephanie finds Toni's letter marked "Personal and confidential." She doesn't open it. Igor's phone call comes through, but Stephanie can't disturb the doctor, who is working on a patient. Igor must call back later.

Mrs. Dixon Durant, a society matron, comes in, late for her appointment, which has been given to someone else.

MRS. DURANT: Please hurry the doctor. I must be through in half an hour. Charles will be waiting.

STEPHANIE: Charles?

MRS. DURANT: Mr. Charles. The hairdresser. Today he's taking care of me personally. I can't keep him waiting.

STEPHANIE: Really, Mrs. Durant, your teeth are more important than your hair.

MRS. DURANT *(looking at her for a moment):* You really think that, don't you? How sad.

> *She goes into waiting room. Stephanie is thrown by this for a moment, reaches up and touches her hair. . . .*

Dr. Julian Winston comes in from his operating room, having finished with the patient (who is Harvey Greenfield, a very good friend of his). Julian is a young man, good-looking, self-possessed, giving off an aura of both charm and capability: in short, he is perfectly equipped to be a successful Park Avenue dentist.

Stephanie reminds Julian that his friend Harvey Greenfield never pays his bill, but Julian can't bring himself to demand payment.

Harvey comes in from the operating room. He comments on the richness of the office apointments and exchanges veiled sarcasms with Stephanie on the subject of bill paying. Stephanie goes to make the operating room ready for Mrs. Durant.

HARVEY: That dame makes me feel like I'm back with the Seabees.

JULIAN: She is very efficient.

HARVEY *(tone of disgust):* Come on. I always figured you'd have a nurse who was a . . . *nurse.* You're Julian Winston. Bachelor, connoisseur . . .

JULIAN *(cutting in):* Harvey, Miss Dickinson is my assistant for the very reasons you complain about. *(Pushing chair into desk.)* She's like a wife, a good wife . . . devoted, efficient, takes care of everything for me . . . during the day! And at night she goes home, to *her* home. And I, with no cares, no problems, go to my girl. My life is arranged the way I like it.

Harvey notices that Julian used the singular "girl." Julian confesses he has had one girl, only one, for a year now. Just last night, he tried playing the field as he once did—he made a date with a spectacular Swedish blonde airline stewardess. . . .

Julian's story is interrupted by the entrance of Mrs. Durant. Julian immediately turns on the charm, which is part of the treatment. Stephanie ushers Mrs. Durant into the operating room.

Julian continues to Harvey: he could do nothing with the stewardess, Toni's image intervened. Harvey warns Julian that this could lead to marriage, but Julian denies and rejects this idea. It would ruin his cozy set-up, which he enjoys so much—one girl for the office, one after office hours.

Besides, Julian says, Toni Simmons thinks he's already married.

HARVEY: Julian. You pulled that old stunt on her?

JULIAN: I've never done it before, but this time I had to. When I first set eyes on Toni I knew this was the one. She could make me do anything.

HARVEY: It's scary.

JULIAN: She could change this whole pleasant life of mine. So . . . I told her I had a wife and three children.

HARVEY: The three children is a nice touch.

JULIAN: And I told it to her right away. Five minutes after we met—so that everything between us would be open and above board.

HARVEY: Very good. Very good. It's such a big dirty rotten lie that it has class.

Harvey, too, has a girl he is worrying about; a girl who looks like Botticelli's Springtime, only she has this trouble with her teeth. . . . Julian knows he is being hustled, but he agrees to take her on as a patient. He goes to the operating room to work on Mrs. Durant.

HARVEY: *(approaching Stephanie carefully)* Excuse me, Sergeant, uh, Miss Dickinson, Dr. Winston said I was to make an appointment for a lady friend of mine.

STEPHANIE *(trying to get rid of him quickly):* How about two weeks from Wednesday at seven a.m.

HARVEY: You're kidding. I'm asleep at seven a.m.

STEPHANIE: I thought the appointment was for a lady.

HARVEY: That's right. We're both asleep at seven a.m. *(He chuckles, then quickly.)* I'm sorry. I hope I'm not shocking you. *(Leans on desk.)*

STEPHANIE: No, but it must be a terrible shock for her. . . .

In their badinage, it is revealed that Harvey is by profession a television actor (his specialty is soap commercials) and Stephanie has never seen him on TV. Harvey makes the appointment for Botticelli's Springtime and leaves.

Julian comes in to inquire about the next patient, leaving Mrs. Durant in the chair with her mouth open. Stephanie demonstrates her efficiency: she has made him sandwiches for lunch and sent a plant to his sister for her birthday. She hands Julian the letter marked "Personal and confidential," which, of course, is Toni's suicide letter. Julian reads it, grabs his coat and prepares to run off to try to save Toni.

STEPHANIE: Doctor, I know that letter came from a woman. Really, if your girl friends start coming before your patients . . .

JULIAN *(opens door, turns back to her):* Miss Dickinson, shut up!

STEPHANIE *(shocked):* Doctor, you've never said that to me before.

JULIAN: Remind me to say it more often. *(He goes.)*

Stephanie, flustered, answers the phone; it is Igor's call to tell Julian that Toni is safe—too late. Mrs. Durant comes in from the operating room, her mouth still open and packed, but making complaining noises. Stephanie tells *her* to shut up.

Scene 3: Toni's apartment in Greenwich Village

When Julian bursts in, Toni is sitting at the table, with Coke and potato chips and a magazine.

Julian thinks the whole suicide was a fake, nothing really happened. Toni tells him she is through, she can't continue like this any longer. Igor brings Toni some fruit, and Julian reacts coldly to his presence.

But when Igor asks Toni how she feels and mentions the gas, Julian realizes Toni really *did* try suicide. As Igor leaves, Julian is sitting there reproaching himself.

JULIAN: I'm a bastard. The biggest bastard in the whole world.

TONI: Julian, please, you're starting to make it sound like bragging.

She rises and stands directly behind him.

It wasn't really your fault. I knew what I was getting into. You've always told me the truth.

JULIAN: I should have kept my mouth shut.

TONI: You couldn't, Julian. You're a decent guy. And that's why I've loved you. And now I'm returning you to your wife and children, and I hope you will be very happy.

Making motion as though hitting him in back of head.

JULIAN: No, Toni, no! It's going to be all right with us. I'm going to make up for everything.

TONI *(crosses to bed):* Oh, I know how it will be. We'll go to Easthampton for a weekend . . . we'll be happy. *(Sits on bed.)* Then I'll get another one of your cancellations and I'll feel worse than before.

JULIAN *(rises):* No, Toni, no weekends. I'm talking about a whole lifetime. Toni, I'm going to marry you.

TONI: What do you mean, "marry"?

JULIAN: You know, "Do you? I do. Do I? You do" . . . marry. Right away.

TONI: What about your wife?

JULIAN: My wife? I'll divorce her.

TONI: What about your children?

JULIAN: I'll divorce them too.

TONI: Julian, this isn't funny.

JULIAN: I'm very serious. I should've thought of this long ago. Oh, baby, when I think you were ready to die because of me. *(Crosses, sits by her on the bed.)*

TONI: Then you really do love me, Julian?

JULIAN *(tenderly):* Are you just now finding it out?

They embrace.

Julian has no trouble getting used to the idea of marriage with Toni; but Toni cannot get second thoughts about Julian's supposed "wife" and "children" out of her head. Julian assures Toni that he and his wife are little better than strangers.

Julian has invented his wife, and it is a simple matter for him to tell Toni that this imaginary wife really *wants* an imaginary divorce. This satisfies Toni —almost. She doesn't want to spend the rest of her days hiding from this wife, she wants to meet her face-to-face. As they embrace, Julian will promise Toni anything, and foolishly he promises to introduce her to his wife.

Scene 4: Dr. Julian Winston's office

That same afternoon, about 5 o'clock, Stephanie rises from her desk to open the door to Senor Arturo Sanchez, a dapper South American. Senor Sanchez is overjoyed to discover that his dentist appointment must be cancelled and is perfectly agreeable to waiting until next year for another one.

Senor Sanchez has an eye for the ladies, and he can see in Stephanie what is concealed from most others.

SANCHEZ: That uniform doesn't fool me. We Latins have a great eye for hidden beauty. You see, for centuries our women were all covered up . . . mantillas, long dresses, veils . . . so in self-defense Latin men had to develop an instinct for guessing what was underneath. You are a woman worth knowing.

STEPHANIE *(takes another pencil. After a look):* What about next Thursday?

SANCHEZ *(crossing toward her):* Wonderful! Where shall we meet?

STEPHANIE: This is you and Dr. Winston!

SANCHEZ *(crossing to her):* Oh. But I'd like for us to have dinner one of these evenings . . . a small dinner . . . candlelight, guitars . . .

STEPHANIE *(with a twinkle):* Will you bring along your wife?

SANCHEZ *(dead serious):* My wife? You wouldn't like her. Nobody likes her. Now let's make it next Thursday after my appointment.

STEPHANIE *(a bit more sharply):* Senor Sanchez, I can't. You're a married man.

SANCHEZ *(crossing away right):* I don't understand. If I'm married, that's *my* problem. What has that got to do with you? I would not be prejudiced if *you* were married.

Stephanie's answer remains "no." Julian enters just as Senor Sanchez moves to depart—but Senor Sanchez runs out on his dentist appointment anyway.

Stephanie has smoothed over the situation in Julian's absence, even placating Mrs. Durant.

The phone rings—it is Toni. Julian hangs up immediately after reassuring her that he will arrange for her to meet his "wife."

Julian asks Stephanie to stay, telling her he wants to get to know her better—they never have a chance to talk. Under Julian's urging, Stephanie tries to describe herself and her life.

Stephanie thinks for a moment, then begins to talk in the manner of a person discussing something she's never discussed before. Or even thought about. The words will come out fairly slowly and carefully as she goes through her life, item by item.

STEPHANIE: I live in Jackson Heights . . .

JULIAN: Alone.

STEPHANIE: Yes. I mean, no. I live with my mother. We have three rooms, actually three and a half . . . there's a dining alcove. It's a very big dining alcove so you could really call it four rooms. That's where we keep the television. We like to watch the news when we're eating. I like Walter Cronkite. My mother likes Huntley and Brinkley better. So we don't often watch Walter Cronkite.

> *There is a long silence. Julian has been studying her carefully, during this long recital. Now, when the silence happens, he helps her a bit.*

JULIAN: And what do you do after Huntley-Cronkite . . . after dinner?

STEPHANIE: I go for a walk with Frieda, my cocker spaniel.

JULIAN: Frieda? That's a hell of a name for a cocker spaniel.

STEPHANIE: Frieda loves it. And some evenings I visit my sister. She and my brother-in-law and I like to play Scrabble.

She has two nephews, and she likes Marcello Mastroianni. On her vacation, she and her mother and Frieda go to Cape Cod in an MG.

The point is, there are no men in Stephanie's life. But she is not inexperienced. She was very much in love, once, but the guy was married.

Julian hints that he is in great trouble, and Stephanie offers to help him, no matter what it is.

> JULIAN: You could do me a great service, Miss Dickinson, I'm greatly in need . . . of a wife.
>> *As he says the word "wife," Stephanie's chair slides from under her and she falls forward on the desk. This is a quick fall. She catches herself with her arms and recovers quickly.*
>
> STEPHANIE: A wife! Doctor, I . . .
>> *She is tremendously flustered. She straightens her desk, puts on her glasses.*
>
> JULIAN *(suddenly realizing what she thinks):* Oh, please understand something . . . *(Crossing to her.)*
>
> STEPHANIE *(still flustered):* I . . . this is something I never expected. Wife!
>
> JULIAN *(going on):* I need a wife temporarily . . . fifteen or twenty minutes.

Julian explains the Toni situation: he is going to marry her, but first Toni wants to meet his "wife" and Stephanie could play the part. Stephanie urges Julian to solve his problem by telling Toni the truth, but the scene ends with Julian still wheedling: if Stephanie would just go around to the LP record shop where Toni works and have a talk with her. . . .

Scene 5: The LP record shop in the Village

In the afternoon, a few days later, Toni is putting records on a shelf. Music is playing at the back of the shop and there is one customer, a listener not a buyer.

> *Stephanie enters from the street door stage right. Actually, it's her first change of clothes in the play. She's wearing a very attractive suit and very smart hat and shoes. She carries gloves and a good looking purse. As she comes in, she spots Toni and looks her over.*

Stephanie orders a record and asks that it be sent to "Mrs. . . . Julian . . . Winston."

Toni realizes that this is no coincidence, and Stephanie admits she came here on purpose, because her "husband" Julian asked her to. Playing the role Julian assigned to her, Stephanie assures Toni she wants a divorce.

Toni, in turn, assures Stephanie that she loves Julian. Stephanie tries to get away, but Toni brings up the subject of the three children—who will tell them? Stephanie hadn't known about the "children," but after her initial surprise she manages to sail through the subject safely.

The subject of Julian's nurse, Miss Dickinson, crops up.

TONI: One of those sterling old maids. Probably madly in love with the boss.

STEPHANIE: Did Julian tell you that?

TONI: No. But the way he described her . . .

STEPHANIE: How *did* he describe her?

TONI: He didn't really describe her. But once when he was working late, I felt a sudden pang of jealousy about Miss Dickinson, and I told Julian about it and he laughed and laughed . . .

Toni laughs. Stephanie responds by laughing rather painfully.

Toni insists that Stephanie tell her the truth about her feelings for Julian. The situation, and the influence of the music of Albioni's adagio in the background, cause Stephanie to daydream that perhaps she *is* Julian's wife, as she describes all his little foibles and habits like a woman who is leaving her husband not without some pain after all the intimacies of ten years of marriage.

Toni is wholly convinced (and so is Stephanie, almost). Stephanie buys the record which set the mood for the strange marriage reverie.

TONI: Mrs. Winston, I want to say . . . well, I can't let you go without telling you that I think you're a gracious, charming, very attractive woman.

STEPHANIE *(tastes the compliment for a second, then, in the manner of every queen and great lady of history):* Thank you, my dear.

She sweeps through the door. Toni watches her go.

Scene 6: Toni's apartment in Greenwich Village

In early evening of the same day, Julian enters, carrying roses, but Toni isn't there. As he fixes the flowers in a coffee pot, Igor comes in wearing only a towel around his waist. He is looking for his razor (Toni likes Igor's better than Julian's electric).

Julian reacts sullenly to Igor's presence, naked, in his fiancee's room. Igor in his turn resents Julian stringing Toni along. Julian insists he really *is* going to marry Toni.

Toni comes in, and Igor leaves them alone. Toni tells Julian of his "wife's" visit to the LP shop.

Just as Julian begins to feel that things are now settled and his lie about a wife and family has run its course safely, Toni goes on about this "fine woman" who really loves Julian underneath it all. Toni feels sorry for Stephanie, she feels kinship for her, as though she were an older sister—particularly after having seen her across the street with two of the "children" (Julian figures Stephanie must have brought her two nephews on this errand to the LP shop). Toni questions Julian about these children's ages, and of course Julian gets caught in his own net of lies.

TONI *(persisting teasingly):* Your older boy. That's Peter, isn't it?

JULIAN: Yes, that's Peter all right. Well, uh . . . let's see, uh . . . how old would he be now? *(Looks at his watch.)*

TONI: You told me he was eight.

JULIAN: Well, if I told you he's eight, he's eight.

TONI: Why do men fib about their children's age? Julian, I saw that boy. He looks eleven or twelve.

JULIAN: Well, I guess I'm caught. Peter is eleven or twelve.

TONI: That's very interesting, considering you're married only ten years.
        Julian is stuck.
Come on, Julian, the truth.

JULIAN: All right. The truth is that Peter was a premature baby. Born before we were married.

TONI: I'm glad. It confirms everything.

JULIAN: How's *that?*

TONI: Don't you see? Here's a woman who gave herself to you before you were married. This was not a marriage of convenience, it was love.

JULIAN: Oh, for God's sake!

TONI: And she still loves you.

Julian has to think of something, fast, or Toni's sentimental fondness for the idea of his "wife" will upset their marriage plans. Julian tells Toni that his "wife" *wants* a divorce, she has a lover. At first this makes Toni feel better. Then she gets that look in her eye . . . if this lover is going to marry Stephanie and be a father to Julian's children, hadn't they better arrange to meet him to see what he's like?

Julian refuses, and Toni threatens to call his wife herself, to arrange a meeting. So Julian must agree to arrange for them to meet his "wife" Stephanie's "lover." He pounds on the wall in frustration, not knowing that this is the customary signal to Igor, who enters, still wrapped in his towel, to see if there is anything wrong.

Scene 7: Dr. Julian Winston's office

The next day, Stephanie is saying "No" as the scene begins. She will *not* play the part of the wife again. Julian has just finished with Mrs. Durant—he hurt her a little and she suggests it was because Julian is overtired from too much night life.

After Mrs. Durant leaves, Julian accuses Stephanie of having played the role of wife too well. For one thing, she should never have brought those children along.

If she can't take her nephews along on her day off, Stephanie retorts, then she's handing in her two weeks' notice.

Julian switches tactics and argues with Stephanie that further help is part of her *professional* duty.

JULIAN: Yes. My problems with Toni are beginning to affect my work. You know what happened in there just now? I *hurt Mrs. Durant*. She felt pain! It's the first time I have ever hurt a patient.

STEPHANIE *(smugly):* I've predicted your disintegration.

JULIAN *(crossing to her):* Miss Dickinson, you played my wife once and I know you enjoyed yourself. The truth, Miss Dickinson. You did enjoy it.

STEPHANIE: It wasn't too bad.

JULIAN: Now here's your chance to play it again. You don't want to give up that role without one more performance. Why, it's . . . it's . . . like an actress doing a great Joan of Arc and then playing it for only one night.

> Stephanie covers her face with her hands, seems to be sobbing. Her shoulders shake.

What's the matter? Did I upset you? *(Leans over her.)*

STEPHANIE *(taking her hands away and revealing the fact that she has been laughing. She speaks in a tired, amused voice that conveys the feeling that she has given up fighting):* I'm sorry, no. I was just thinking that between the two roles, Joan of Arc has the happy ending.

Weakly, Stephanie agrees to play wife one more time, but it is up to Julian to find someone to play the part of her lover. Stephanie suggests Senor Sanchez. Julian, his eyebrows raised somewhat, vetoes this suggestion.

The doorbell rings—it's Harvey Greenfield, who had phoned earlier to say that his filling dropped out, he needed emergency attention. Over Stephanie's loud protests, Julian designates Harvey to play the part of the lover. Julian will do anything for Harvey, include fix his girl's teeth free, and so of course Harvey will not mind doing a little favor for Julian. . . .

Scene 8: A small night spot

A few evenings later the plan is put into action. A rendezvous is set up in a small, dimly-lit night club. Harvey is sitting by himself on a banquette at right. A waiter serves him a drink.

> Stephanie's silhouette appears, stage left. For this scene Stephanie's clothes go up another notch. She is wearing a chic dinner dress. Her hair is done smartly and there is further progress in the emergence of Stephanie as a looker.

Stephanie and Harvey exchange mild hostilities in the semi-darkness and wait to play their parts. There is no one else in the place because it is only midnight, and this is a late night spot.

Toni and Julian enter and choose a banquette at left. Much against their inclinations, Stephanie and Harvey assume flirtatious attitudes. Toni spots them, excitedly calls Julian's attention to his "wife" and her "lover." Toni is embarrassed, but she can't help watching them, as they perform for Toni's benefit.

Stephanie drags Harvey onto the dance floor to make it look good, and Toni goes to the dance floor with Julian, to get a closer view. They bump into each other. After awkward introductions, all four sit down at Harvey's banquette.

The conversation opens with Julian's comment that his "wife" Stephanie has turned into "quite a swinger."

STEPHANIE *(to Toni):* You see, Toni, Dr. Winston never realized that I couldn't go out much because of our children. They were too young.

TONI *(sympathetically):* Of course. *(Turning quickly to Harvey.)* By the way, Mr. Greenfield . . .

HARVEY: Yes?

TONI: How do you like children?

HARVEY: Grilled, medium rare. *(He laughs at his own joke.)*

JULIAN: Ha ha. That's very funny, Mr. Greenfield, but, actually, it's the kind of joke made by a man hiding a profound emotional feeling.
        Harvey just stares at him.
Deep down I know you love children.

HARVEY: Huh?

STEPHANIE: Deep down.

HARVEY *(getting it):* Oh, deep down, yes. Especially yours. I'm nuts about them.

Harvey overdoes his make-believe affection for Stephanie, who fights him off earnestly. As Harvey pours a round of drinks, "Botticelli's Springtime"— a big, handsome brunette—enters and goes to the center of the dance floor. Finally she spots Harvey.

BOTTICELLI'S SPRINGTIME: Oh, there you are, Harvey. Sorry I'm late, honey. Hello, everybody.
        They all stare at her in dead silence. Harvey's reaction is an interesting one. He also stares in dead, shocked silence.
STEPHANIE *(finally):* Won't you join us?

HARVEY *(leaping up):* No, she doesn't want to! We have to talk . . . uh . . . business.
        He crosses to her.
BOTTICELLI'S SPRINGTIME: What is this? Did we have a date tonight or didn't we?

HARVEY: Come, we'll talk at the bar. *(Turning back to the group.)* Please excuse us, folks, this is important. She's the daughter of one of my sponsors. Silly debutante. I'll be right back.

BOTTICELLI'S SPRINGTIME: What are you trying to pull? We had a . . .

HARVEY *(cutting in quietly):* Quiet or you'll be stuck with your old teeth.

While Harvey escorts Springtime to the bar, Stephanie goes to powder her nose like any woman jilted. Toni has decided that Harvey is a two-timing bum, not good enough for Stephanie, and Julian must snatch her from his grasp.

Julian stages a mock fight with Harvey, grabbing his lapels and pulling him to the dance floor, accusing Harvey of mistreating Stephanie, calling him names, offering to punch him, pretending to force Harvey to leave the night club.

Toni, impressed, thought Julian was "beautiful" in anger.

JULIAN *(modestly):* It was nothing.

TONI: I liked it.

JULIAN *(he snuggles with her a minute and his voice turns sexy, as it usually does when they snuggle):* Let's go home, Toni. What do you say? Let's go home where we can be alone.

TONI *(purring):* I feel that way myself, but . . . *(Suddenly pulls herself away.)* Stop it. Here's your wife.

Stephanie approaches to tell them she's called a taxi and is going home. Toni will not hear of her going home alone, insists that Julian escort her. Julian suggests that they all three leave together and drop Stephanie off first. No—Toni insists that Julian take Stephanie home, by himself. Limply, Julian agrees. Stephanie moves away to allow Toni and Julian to say goodnight.

JULIAN: What the hell am I going to do with her?

TONI: You're going to be "very nice."

JULIAN *(startled):* Now wait a minute . . .

TONI: "Very nice." To please me.
    Stephanie has been putting on her gloves. She's still waiting. Julian crosses to Stephanie.

JULIAN *(grimly):* All right, let's go.

STEPHANIE *(a small needle):* It's been such a long time, dear, since we've gone home together.

JULIAN *(through clenched teeth):* A very long time. Come on. *(He walks out left.)*

STEPHANIE: Good night, Toni.

TONI: Good night, Stephanie.

STEPHANIE: You've been very thoughtful.
    Julian reappears in entrance.

JULIAN: For God's sake, will you come on!

STEPHANIE *(as though she's afraid):* Oh, I'd better hurry. God knows what he'll do! *(She goes.)*
    Cocktail piano music swells. Curtain.

ACT II

Scene 1: Dr. Julian Winston's office

Early the next morning, Stephanie is cheerfully watering her cactus plant. She turns on the music. Julian enters looking grim, but Stephanie greets him happily with a comment about the beautiful day.

JULIAN *(studying her grimly):* What the hell are you so happy about?

STEPHANIE *(very casually):* Doctor, is there anything wrong with my being happy?

JULIAN *(turns off the stereo):* Yes. I don't like it.

STEPHANIE *(crossing to desk):* Now, Doctor, you've been complaining that I'm too grim and efficient. You compared me with my cactus plant. Well, Doctor, every once in a while this prickly little thing puts forth a lovely flower that some people think . . .

JULIAN *(interrupting sharply):* Cut it out! I know why you're happy. You're happy because last night was a complete and utter disaster.

Julian didn't sleep well because he hates sleeping alone; he is snappish and quarrelsome. He couldn't return to Toni last night, because Toni had asked him to stay with Stephanie and comfort her.

STEPHANIE: But you didn't comfort me.

JULIAN: You're damn right I didn't.

STEPHANIE *(rises, crosses to him):* Look, I'm in this so deep now I just want to get our stories straight as far as Toni's concerned. Did we . . . did we spend the night together?

JULIAN: No.

STEPHANIE: Good. I only asked because, with your imagination, I never know what you'll have me doing next.

JULIAN: You'll be glad to know you didn't do *that.*

STEPHANIE: But what about Toni? When she hears that we *didn't,* she's liable to insist that we *do* and ask to come over and watch.

Julian figures it's about time he told Toni the truth. Unfairly, Julian blames Stephanie for butting into his affairs; for being too harsh to Harvey. She hates Harvey and, Julian observes, maybe she hates all men.

JULIAN: I'm not speaking as a layman, you know. At dental school we had a whole year of psychiatry.

STEPHANIE: I'd still only trust you with my teeth and gums.

JULIAN *(going right on):* Miss Dickinson, as a trained observer, I detect in you a strong ambivalence about men.

STEPHANIE *(another shout):* I don't give a damn about men.

JULIAN: Again you're loud . . . and a bit coarse.

STEPHANIE *(a whisper):* I don't give a hoot about men.

JULIAN: But you don't hate them.

STEPHANIE *(a shout):* No! *(Catches herself and whispers.)* No.

JULIAN: You know, I think I believe you.

Pompously, Julian puts his little psychiatric learning to use, accusing Stephanie of deliberately defeminizing herself, giving the impression that she hates men because, in truth, she *fears* them. This comment makes Stephanie weep that she is "a nurse, not a geisha girl."

Mrs. Durant comes in and catches Stephanie weeping. And for a moment the doctor cannot even remember Mrs. Durant's name.

MRS. DURANT: You know, Doctor, I don't think you're up to being a bachelor. Too tough. You see, you're always surrounded by women. Women patients and . . . *(Looks at Stephanie, then dismisses her.)* Well, anyway, lots of women. And you know that chic white coat gives you a lot of razzmatazz. It must put you under quite a strain. Makes you very nervous.

JULIAN: I—I—I'm not nervous.

MRS. DURANT: Better pay attention to me, Doctor. I know what I'm talking about. I have a great nose for sexual tension. *(She goes into operating room.)*

Julian has decided maybe it's high time he married Toni—then he can forget her. He tries to apologize to Stephanie, but his apology turns into another accusation of hiding her light under a bushel.

Scene 2: The LP record shop in the Village

Toni is up on the ladder as Julian enters carrying a big box. It is a present for her. She descends the ladder and opens the box—a mink stole! Toni assumes it is a peace offering because Julian, as directed, would have been "very nice" to his wife the night before.

In another sense the stole really *is* a peace offering; Julian intends to tell Toni the whole truth about not being married, and the stole is sugar coating for this pill. Julian tries to unburden himself but is interrupted by a customer. After Toni gets rid of the customer she turns to Julian and urges him to continue, tell her all, she "can forgive everything except a lie." That finishes Julian's effort to come clean.

Toni tries to guess what is bothering Julian. She guesses that Stephanie is a nymphomaniac, and Julian lets her think that this is true. This cuts into Toni's admiration of Stephanie somewhat, although Toni still intends to send her some records she thought Stephanie might like.

Julian parts with Toni fondly, and leaves. Igor comes into the shop. Igor is depressed, guesses he is in love (we can guess who he loves, but Toni can't). Toni invites him to join herself and Julian for dinner that night, to cheer him up. She puts on the stole and parades for Igor.

TONI *(crossing to center):* Poor Julian. He thought this would please me.

IGOR: It pleased *him*. That kind of character gets his kicks by draping his women in mink.

TONI: That's very unkind, Igor. Boy, when I think of all the women who would give their souls for this.

She rolls stole up in a ball, stuffs it back into the box.

And here am I, not really wanting it. *(Sudden thought.)* Hey! Igor!

IGOR: What?

TONI: Here's my chance to do a good deed. I was going to send his wife these records.

He looks at her.

I'll send her the mink.

IGOR: Oh, boy.

TONI: What's wrong? She'll love it.

IGOR *(tenderly):* Toni, you're the most ridiculous, wonderful kook I ever knew. But Mrs. Winston would never accept a mink stole from you.

TONI *(ignoring him):* Where's that card?

She looks on counter, picks up card, shows it to Igor.

IGOR *(reading):* "As ever, Julian."

She takes card, puts it in the box, closes box.

IGOR & TONI: Aahhhh!

TONI: Now we're all even. I stole her husband, I give her a stole.

They both laugh.

Scene 3: Dr. Julian Winston's Office

Later that afternoon, Julian gives Stephanie some work to send to the lab.

STEPHANIE: Oh, by the way, there was a call from your home a while ago. Seems there was a package there addressed to me. Or, rather, to Mrs. Winston.

JULIAN: Oh?

STEPHANIE: Your maid was puzzled so I just told her to send it along to the office.

JULIAN: Oh, I know what that is. It's for you.

STEPHANIE: But what . . . ?

JULIAN: You'll understand when you get it. Now quickly, please, the lab. *(He goes.)*

Stephanie admits Senor Sanchez, who for once is *early* for his dentist appointment. It is because he wants to see Stephanie; he invites her to the April in Paris Ball. Stephanie declines, she has no clothes . . . but Senor Sanchez will buy her anything, he has twenty million in a Swiss bank. Still Stephanie declines.

Julian comes in and interrupts; he can take Senor Sanchez now. Both men disappear into the operating room, as Julian asks Stephanie for Senor Sanchez's X-rays.

The messenger arrives with the box and Stephanie opens it. She is staggered and dazed by the mink stole and the card: "As ever, Julian." She hands

Julian Harvey's X-rays by mistake, and when Julian comes in to get the right ones he sees that Stephanie is about to faint.

JULIAN: What's wrong, Miss Dickinson?

STEPHANIE: Nothing, nothing. I felt a little dizzy.

JULIAN: Do you want to go home?

STEPHANIE: No, Doctor, no, I'm fine. It's just that it came and . . . oh, it's too much.

> *This section is staged so that Julian doesn't see the mink until we want him to.*

JULIAN: What the hell are you talking about? *(Puts Harvey's X-rays on desk.)*

STEPHANIE: The gift. It's overwhelming . . . unbelievable . . .

JULIAN: Holy smoke, it's not that great a thing. Just a few . . .

STEPHANIE *(raving on):* And your card. How sweet.

JULIAN *(reads):* "As ever, Julian." Well I must say I did spend considerable time trying to pick out the sort of thing you like. After all, you've put up with a lot from me lately.

STEPHANIE: I'll never be able to thank you enough.

JULIAN: I'm glad to have given you so much pleasure. I know you love beautiful music. *(He goes into operating room.)*

STEPHANIE: Music! What a lovely way of describing this.

> *She takes the stole from box, puts it on and twirls around. . . .*

Stephanie's first instinct is to call her mother, but Julian comes back before she can complete the call. Julian does a double-take as he sees the stole and now it's *his* turn to stagger and feel a little dizzy. Senor Sanchez fears that they are reacting to his X-rays. With a sickly laugh, Julian pushes Senor Sanchez back into the operating room. Stephanie phones her mother to tell her she is going to buy an expensive dress, because she is going to the April in Paris Ball.

Scene 4: A small night spot

Later that night, it looks as though Igor is getting over his depression. He is dancing with Toni while Julian mopes on the banquette.

While Igor goes to fetch some cigarettes, Julian reproaches Toni for giving away his expensive present, with his card in it.

Igor and Toni go to the dance floor again, just as Harvey and Botticelli's Springtime arrive. Harvey thinks Julian really meant all those insults the night before; Julian assures him no, he'll explain later.

As Toni and Igor come back to the table, Senor Sanchez comes in with Stephanie, who is wearing the mink stole over "a sensational evening gown." They order champagne as Senor Sanchez compliments her on her gown: "absolute poetry."

Seeing Stephanie with Senor Sanchez confirms Toni's belief that Stephanie likes to wander from man to man. Igor likes Stephanie's looks, and he and Toni accuse each other of liking older people.

Stephanie spots Julian, and they wave at each other. Stephanie flirts with Senor Sanchez for Julian's benefit.

Harvey tries to explain all the cross-relationships to Botticelli's Springtime, who is appropriately shocked by it all.

Senor Sanchez and Stephanie get up to dance, and Julian resents their leaving the mink stole unguarded. Somewhat roughly, Julian invites Toni to dance. They bump into the other couple. Toni starts doing a swinging new step to the rock 'n' roll music; Stephanie imitates her. Soon Julian and Senor Sanchez are on the sidelines, and Igor joins the two women in the rock 'n' roll dance.

Stephanie, in her dancing euphoria, even hurls a cheery greeting at Harvey. In full dance, Toni introduces Igor to Stephanie, and the three do the Swim, the Backstroke and a dance they make up called the Dentist.

> *They do this for a moment. Toni starts dancing right and heads for the center dance platform. Toni sees Julian sitting alone and hurries to him. Stephanie, who is left with Igor, crosses to the right of him, turns around, grabs his necktie and follows Toni, pulling Igor along. When they arrive on the center platform, the rock 'n' roll music is coming to a finish. Stephanie starts for table, pulling Igor by his tie. The music segues into a slow, dreamy ballad. Senor Sanchez rises as though to go. He picks up stole. Stephanie is stopped by Igor and they both start dancing to the ballad. Senor Sanchez folds stole, replaces it on chair and sits. Toni's back is to them, but Julian is watching intently.*

Stephanie and Igor dispose of the problem of the difference in their ages and dance on affectionately. Their obvious merriment begins to annoy Julian and Toni.

JULIAN: I must say, that Igor of yours is a pretty vulgar dancer.

TONI: What do you mean, Igor? She's the one that's plastering herself against him. That's no lady, that's a barracuda. And when I think of all I've done for her.

Igor kisses Stephanie on the neck.

JULIAN: I don't know what's come over her. Hey, did you see that? He just kissed her on the neck.

Senor Sanchez rises.

TONI: I have a feeling that perhaps we're in the way. Oh boy, Julian, everything you said about Stephanie sure was true.

JULIAN *(stunned with surprise):* Yes it was, wasn't it??? Look at them now! Toni, if someone doesn't stop that man, he's going to make love right in the middle of the floor.

TONI *(hiding her irritation with nonchalance):* I don't care to watch any more. Let's get out of here.

They rise; the music switches back to rock 'n' roll, and once again Igor and Stephanie go into a wild dance. Stephanie grabs the stole and swings it, making it part of the dance. Senor Sanchez rises—even he is showing signs of jealousy. Toni stalks out in anger; Julian, on his way to following her, grabs the stole from Stephanie, folds it and hands it to Senor Sanchez. Then he leaves too. Stephanie and Igor remain behind as part of the happy, growing pandemonium.

Scene 5: Dr. Julian Winston's office

As the curtain rises, a spotlight is directed at the cactus plant on Stephanie's desk. It has grown a large, lovely flower.

Then the lights come on, and it is the next morning. Julian comes in, impatiently, from the operating room. Then Stephanie tiptoes in through the waiting room door, obviously late (two patients have come and gone), and still in her evening clothes. Julian tries to play it cool but finally cannot resist shouting "Where the hell have you been?"

First, Stephanie recalls, they drank tequila and gin with crowds of late-late revelers until the night club closed; then they went to a jam session where Stephanie took a puff of pot just to be a sport; but best of all was sunrise on the beach at Coney Island.

Julian fears that he has created a monster; but no, Stephanie assures him, this was her true self, letting herself go and having fun.

And, Julian learns, it was Igor and not Senor Sanchez she was having fun with throughout her "night of debauchery." Julian accuses her of robbing the cradle; she throws Toni right back at him.

Julian had called Stephanie repressed; well, now she let herself go, and he sounds almost as though he were jealous. It was hard for Stephanie to go out with Senor Sanchez and cut loose, but now she's glad she did it.

JULIAN: Well, it certainly freed your neck for Igor.

STEPHANIE (sharply): Never mind Igor. He was fine, warm, sincere, and he thought I was beautiful . . . he even said sexy!

JULIAN (tolerantly): Well, with those dim lights . . . and with my mink . . .

STEPHANIE (cutting in): Charming. Sure, the soft lights helped. But there was something else. There was a spark . . . electricity . . . I could feel it, and it was my electricity.

JULIAN: Oh, well, if you brought along your own battery . . .

STEPHANIE (she means this): Don't joke about this, Doctor. If you do, I'll kick you.

JULIAN: Now, Miss Dickinson, I was just trying to . . .

STEPHANIE (through clenched teeth as she grabs the lapels of his suit): Drop it, Doctor. I warn you, drop it.

 Gives him a small shove.

JULIAN (he's decided he's gone too far): Oh, let's not be angry, Stephanie.

You spent a gay, wild evening and it went to your head. I'm sure there's no harm done. After all, it was just a little flirtation. Right?
She stands there, steaming.

Julian can't resist asking her if she went to bed with Igor. He insists on "a husband's right" to know. Infuriated, she demands a divorce. She has put up with too much—lipstick on handkerchiefs, pictures of girls in bikinis, wild weekends in Easthampton. . . .

JULIAN: How did you know about my wild weekends in Easthampton? *(Crosses to left, turns back.)* You spied on me! You had me followed! All right, you want war. You can have it. I'll tell the whole world about you. Your drunkenness! Your marijuana parties! Your orgies on the beach! *You* want a divorce. It's *I* who wants a divorce.
STEPHANIE: Well, you can have it. I'm through as your wife and through as your personal slave.
As she says this, she crosses above desk, wraps the mink around his neck.
Give that to your child concubine. *(She starts for the door right.)*
JULIAN: Stephanie, I warn you, if you go out that door don't ever try to come back.
STEPHANIE *(at door, turns back):* Come back? Do you think I'm a masochist? *(Switches to great dignity.)* Don't worry, Dr. Winston, you'll never, never see me again. *(She opens the door, starts through it, stops and turns.)* And that goes for the children too. *(She goes.)*

Scene 6: Toni's apartment in Greenwich Village

That evening, Toni is asking Igor the same question Julian asked Stephanie. At first Igor is not telling; but finally he is trapped into admitting that they did *not* go to bed together. But Igor found Stephanie fun to talk to, and very appealing.
Stephanie arrives to talk to Toni. She greets Igor warmly but sends him out of the apartment.
Toni is still fuming about the previous evening with Igor, but Stephanie wants to talk about Julian. She means to tell Toni the truth, at last.

TONI: . . . Are you keeping him or not? Do I take him or can't you spare him? I have to know.
STEPHANIE: There's something else you have to know first. *(Puts hand on her shoulder.)* Sit down, dearie. You won't have so far to fall.
Toni sits on bed. Stephanie paces a moment.
TONI *(a little frightened):* What can it be?
STEPHANIE *(crossing left):* I have no patience with people who shilly-shally about these things. I'm going to come straight to the point. Julian and I . . .
She stops, turns, looks at Toni.

Oh, God, this isn't as easy as I thought.

TONI (*sudden thought*): I know what it is. You're pregnant.

STEPHANIE: I don't think so. Where did you ever get a crazy thought like that?

TONI: Crazy? Not for the swinging Mrs. Winston.

STEPHANIE: I'm not Mrs. Winston. I'm *Miss* Dickinson.

At first Toni doesn't believe Stephanie is "that old maid." But gradually she comprehends that Julian is not married and that she has been swindled by a pack of lies. Stephanie reminds her that Julian wants to marry her, after all. Stephanie's motive in coming here has been to untangle the snarl of lies and make things neat for Julian, who really loves Toni.

STEPHANIE: . . . Now look, Toni, one of these days Julian will come to you and tell you the truth on his own. When he does, try to help him, accept him. Well, try to. (*Crosses to door.*)

TONI: A man who lies cannot love.

STEPHANIE: That sounds like something out of a fortune cookie. (*She goes.*)
Toni picks up picture of Julian from headboard.

TONI (*to photo*): Dirty married bachelor!

Toni summons Igor into her room and kisses him again and again. He senses she is doing it to wipe out Julian—and then there is a knock on the door. Obviously, it is Julian. Igor goes to hide in the bathroom.

Julian has come for help, understanding—and confession. He has something to tell Toni. It is this: his wife Stephanie no longer wants a divorce. She refuses to go through with it and Julian cannot afford the scandal of a messy contested divorce (while Julian is telling her this lie, Toni, furious, is making Karate chops at him behind his back).

So, Julian concludes, he and Toni must go on as before, snatching happiness whenever they can. Toni agrees—they will go on as before, with Julian sharing her with Igor.

Julian refuses to believe that there is anything serious between Toni and Igor. Toni insists that Igor is hiding in the bathroom right now.

JULIAN: All right, cut it out, Toni. You know damned well that if I thought for one moment that beatnik was in there, I'd be out of here like a shot.
The bathroom door opens quickly and Igor appears. He's wearing nothing but a towel around his waist. Julian stares at him. Igor stares back.

IGOR: Hi, there.
Julian gives Toni a long look, then turns and heads for the door. He opens it.

TONI (*follows him*): Julian, don't feel too bad about this. You'll get over the . . .

JULIAN (*cutting her off with dignity as he turns back*): I'll be fine, Toni. You broke up my home. You took me away from my wife. You alienated me

from my children. But, thank God, I still have one thing left—my integrity.
He goes, leaving the door open. Toni closes the door with an attitude of finality. Toni and Igor look at each other. Toni gives Igor a salute. He returns it.

Igor goes back to the bathroom to change back into his clothes. Toni asks him to stay for dinner—she'll cook him some chicken cacciatore. Igor comes out of the bathroom to smile and nod as he agrees.

Scene 7: Dr. Julian Winston's office

At 10 o'clock the next morning, the phone is ringing and the doorbell chiming. Stephanie disposes of the patient on the phone and then opens the door. It is Julian, hung over, expecting that there would be no one there because Stephanie had quit. But Stephanie feels it is her duty to keep things under control until Julian finds a replacement.

Julian admits that he and Toni are through. Stephanie confesses that she had visited Toni and told her the truth. This doesn't upset Julian as much as it should. Julian admits that the real reason he told Toni one more lie was to get out of marrying her; the idea of marrying her was a mistake to begin with, and when he caught her with Igor it was the last straw.

But that's not why he went out and got drunk.

JULIAN: When I walked out of there I was angry. Absolutely furious! Homicidal!
STEPHANIE *(sits in desk chair):* So that's why you . . .
JULIAN: Stop interrupting! I was sure as hell sore at Toni. And then all at once . . . it was like magic . . . my anger disappeared, and all I felt was a delicious feeling of relief. Blessed, joyous relief. I never loved Toni and she never loved me. Now I was out of it. I said to myself, "Julian, thank God that's over. Now you can go home to your wife." I scampered down the stairs singing to myself, and then . . . bam! I remembered. I had no wife! When I got home there would be nobody. And when I got to the office, you wouldn't be there either.
STEPHANIE *(excited, rises):* So you went out and got drunk.
JULIAN: Stinking!
STEPHANIE *(crossing to him):* That's marvelous, marvelous!
In her happiness, she puts her arms around him, then quickly takes them away.
That's very nice, Doctor.

Julian moves to kiss Stephanie, who has no objections. He kisses her.

JULIAN: I feel as though you've always been my wife. We don't even need to bother getting married.
STEPHANIE: Well, just as a matter of form.
Phone rings.

JULIAN: Hey! I'm going to need a new nurse.

STEPHANIE: After all the trouble I went to, I'm not going to give another old maid a crack at you. *(Picks up phone.)*

JULIAN *(crosses to closet)*: After all the trouble *you* . . . *(Goes into closet to change into white coat.)*

STEPHANIE *(on phone)*: Hello, Dr. Winston's office. Well, the doctor's busy. May I take a message?

Listens a moment as Julian re-enters, crosses to right of desk.

I see. One moment, please.

Turns to Julian, who is buttoning on his white coat.

It's a young lady. She's a stewardess with Swedish Airlines. She says she's free this evening.

JULIAN *(slightly rueful)*: Tell her I've been grounded.

STEPHANIE *(back to phone)*: Hello, I'm sorry, Miss, but Dr. Winston doesn't do that sort of work any more.

She hangs up, turns on stereo, which plays the "Hallelujah Chorus", crosses to him and they kiss. Curtain.

THE PERSECUTION
AND ASSASSINATION
OF MARAT
AS PERFORMED
BY THE INMATES OF THE
ASYLUM OF CHARENTON
UNDER THE DIRECTION OF
THE MARQUIS DE SADE

A Play in Two Acts

BY PETER WEISS

English version by Geoffrey Skelton

Verse adaptation by Adrian Mitchell

Cast and credits appear on page 393

PETER WEISS was born in Nowawes, near Berlin, in 1916. He left Germany in 1934, shortly after the Nazis appeared on the scene. Since 1939 he has been living in Stockholm, Sweden, where he works as a writer, painter and movie director. He is now a Swedish citizen but continues to write in German. Among his works are translations of two Strindberg plays, various experimental films which have been shown internationally, a novel entitled Leave-taking *and a new play about the Auschwitz trials at Frankfurt,* The Investigation, *which opened in October, 1965, at various theaters in both East and West Germany.*

269

Weiss's play with the long title usually abbreviated as Marat/Sade *was of course written in German and had its premiere in April, 1964, at the Schiller Theater in West Berlin. The production in English presented on Broadway was the one mounted by the Royal Shakespeare Company at the Aldwych Theater in London, under the direction of Peter Brook. Weiss designed his own set for the Berlin version, and his wife, Gunilla Palmstierna-Weiss, designed the costumes for both productions.*

Mr. Brook's staging of Marat/Sade *differed considerably from the staging described in the published version. In the following synopsis it is Mr. Brook's direction that is used insofar as possible.*

INTRODUCTION BY THE PLAYWRIGHT *

Even before his confinement in the stronghold of Vincennes and the Paris Bastille Sade had produced plays in his residence La Coste. During the thirteen years of his imprisonment, between the ages of 33 and 46, he wrote seventeen plays in addition to his large prose works.

From 1801 until his death in 1814 Sade was interned in the asylum of Charenton, where over a period of years he had the chance of producing plays among the patients and appearing as an actor himself.

In exclusive Paris circles it was considered a rare pleasure to attend Sade's theatrical performances in the "hiding place for the moral rejects of civilised society." It is of course probable that these amateur performances consisted in the main of declamatory pieces in the prevailing style: the bulk of Sade's dramatic work does not reach up to the boldness and consistency of his prose.

Sade's encounter with Marat, which is the subject of this play, is entirely imaginary, based only on the single fact that it was Sade who spoke the memorial address at Marat's funeral. Even in this speech his real attitude towards Marat is questionable, since he made the speech primarily to save his own skin; at that time his position was in danger, his name on the list of those marked out for the guillotine.

What interests me in bringing together Sade and Marat is the conflict between an individualism carried to extreme lengths and the idea of a political and social upheaval. Even Sade knew the Revolution to be necessary; his works are one single attack on a corrupt ruling class. He flinched however from the violent methods of the progressives and, like the modern advocate of a third approach, fell between two stools.

His claim that he had suffered at the hands of the old regime cannot be taken as evidence of heroism, since his imprisonment was due to charges of sexual extravagance and not to political acts. These excesses, in monstrous written form, were once again to cause his downfall under the new regime.

Sade's plays represent his last attempt to communicate with his fellow beings, but with advancing age he relapsed entirely into solitariness. A doctor

---

* These comments are excerpts from an historical note by Mr. Weiss appended to Atheneum's published version of *Marat/Sade* and designated by him to introduce his play here.

at Charenton wrote, "I frequently encountered him as he walked alone, with heavy dragging steps, very negligently dressed, through the corridors near his home. I never saw him speak with anybody. . . ."

If the idea of bringing Sade into contact with Marat in his final hour is my own invention, the picture of Marat at this time accords with fact. The psychosomatic skin disease from which he suffered in the last years of his life—a legacy of privation in the cellars in which he hid—forced him to spend many hours in the bath in order to soothe his itching. And here he was on Saturday, July 13, 1793, when Charlotte Corday came three times to his door before she gained entry and stabbed him.

Marat's words in the play correspond in content and often almost exactly in expression with the writings he left behind. What is said about the various phases of his life is also authentic. He left home at the age of 16, studied medicine, lived for some years in England, was renowned as a physician, misunderstood as a scientist, won social honors. Subsequently, however, after subjecting society to the shafts of his criticism, he placed himself entirely in the service of the Revolution and, on account of his violent and uncompromising character, was made the scapegoat for many acts of cruelty.

Scarcely any other personality of the French Revolution has been depicted in so revolting and bloodthirsty a light by the bourgeois historians of the 19th century as Marat. This is not really surprising, since his ideas lead in a direct line to Marxism, though they also come perilously near to the idea of dictatorship, even when he himself protested, "Dictator: the word must be abolished. I hate anything to do with masters and slaves."

Beside Marat in the play I have placed the former priest Jacques Roux, who surpassed Marat in his rabble-rousing and passionate pacifism. I have ignored the fact that Marat in the last days of his life turned away from Roux and, perhaps in an attack of persecution mania, disowned him.

I have also taken liberties in the portrayal of Duperret, the Girondist deputy. Here he is shown as the conservative patriot, one of many thousands of similar sort. He is also pressed into service as Charlotte Corday's lover, a role held in reality by M. Tournelis.

Charlotte Corday had in fact let nobody into her secret. Schooled by convent life in the art of ecstatic withdrawal, she went her way alone and, with thoughts of Joan of Arc and the Biblical Judith in mind, made a saint out of herself.

PETER WEISS

Time: July 13, 1808

Place: The asylum at Charenton in France

ACT I

SYNOPSIS: The stage area is the bath hall of the asylum of Charenton with benches, massage tables, etc. The baths themselves are depressions in the stage flooring covered over by duckboards. The center of the stage is a circle of these baths, and downstage in the apron there are three more. The duckboards are arranged on edge as a kind of screen masking Marat's bath at left center. De Sade's chair will be placed at right center, and downstage left are benches for spectators. The theater auditorium itself is, in a way, part of the setting, and the audience is a group of "guests" who have been invited to watch the inmates perform.

Five musician-inmates have taken their positions in the front boxes on either side. As the action begins. . . .

1: Assembly

. . . is taking place. The inmates of Charenton are gathering in the bath hall to present a play to the asylum director and a selected audience. The play is a form of therapy. The inmates are attended by Male Nurses (who look like butchers with batons in their aprons) and athletic-looking Sisters.

Some of the patients are almost normal in appearance and behavior, like the Marquis de Sade. . . .

> . . . *Sixty-eight years old, extremely corpulent, gray hair, smooth complexion. He moves heavily, breathes at times with difficulty, as if asthmatic. His clothing is of good quality, but worn. He is wearing white breeches with bows, a wide-sleeved white shirt with ornamental front and lace cuffs and white buckled shoes.*

Most of the patients, however, are eccentric to the point of revulsion in both looks and behavior. They shuffle, crab-fashion; they drool; they make erotic and neurotic gestures. They are mindless, shameless, human gargoyles. . . .

> . . . *According to need they appear either in their white hospital uniforms or in primitive costumes with strong color contrasts. Any not required in the play devote themselves to physical exercises. Their presence must set the atmosphere behind the acting area. They make habitual movements, turn in circles, hop, mutter to themselves, wail, scream and so on.*

De Sade is preparing the area for his actors and his play. As he gives a sign, the elegant Coulmier, director of this asylum, and his glittering wife and daughters enter in a procession down the aisle of the auditorium. Coulmier carries a walking stick and has a penchant for Napoleonic attitudes.

The actors, patients who will take the leading roles in de Sade's play, enter. The men and women come in from opposite sides.

> *Jean-Paul Marat is in his fiftieth year, suffering from a skin disease. He is draped in a white cloth and has a white bandage round his temples.*

Among the principals is the patient playing Simonne, Marat's mistress. She is attentive to him in odd, graceless movements and changes his head bandage whenever possible. The patient playing Charlotte Corday is led to a bench by two Sisters.

> *She is aged twenty-four. Her clothing consists of a thin white blouse of Empire cut. The blouse does not conceal the bosom, but she wears a flimsy white cloth over it. Her long auburn hair hangs down on the right side of her neck. She wears pink leather boots with high heels, and when she is "on stage" a ribboned hat is tied to her. She is attended throughout by two Sisters, who support her, comb her hair and arrange her clothes. She moves like a somnambulist.*

Others move into position. There is Duperret, a Girondist Deputy played by an erotomaniac patient who flings himself at Charlotte Corday whenever he can sneak near her. He is dressed in a short waistcoat and smooth, tight trousers somewhat revealingly stained in front.

There is Jacques Roux, a former priest, a radical socialist, played by an inmate whose sleeves are tied together over his hands so that he is limited to straitjacket movements. There are Four Singers, a woman and three men, in caps of the Revolution.

There is the Herald with bells on his cap and a beribboned staff in his hand, dressed in harlequin smock over hospital shirt. The actors take their positions as the asylum Director, Coulmier, reaches the acting area.

> *The Patients in the background stand tensely. One of them adopts an eccentric pose, another comes slowly forward with outstretched arms. Fanfare.*

2: Prologue

COULMIER:
> As Director of the Clinic of Charenton
> I would like to welcome you to this salon
> To one of our residents a vote
> of thanks is due Monsieur de Sade who wrote
> and has produced this play for your delectation

and for our patients' rehabilitation
We ask your kindly indulgence for
a cast never on stage before
coming to Charenton But each inmate
I can assure you will try to pull his weight
We're modern enlightened and we don't agree
with locking up patients We prefer therapy
through education and especially art
so that our hospital may play its part
faithfully following according to our lights
the Declaration of Human Rights
I agree with our author Monsieur de Sade
that his play set in our modern bath house won't be marred
by all these instruments for mental and physical hygene
Quite on the contrary they set the scene
For in Monsieur de Sade's play he has tried
to show how Jean-Paul Marat died
and how he waited in his bath before
Charlotte Corday came knocking at the door.

3: Preparation

Coulmier and his family take their seats downstage left. The duckboards
are taken down and placed flat, as covers. This action reveals the patient playing Marat seated in his portable bathtub, head swathed in a cloth.

4: Presentation

HERALD (knocking three times with his staff, as the music stops):
Already seated in his place
here is Marat observe his face
    Points his staff at Marat.
Fifty years old and not yet dead
he wears a bandage around his head
    Points staff at bandage.
His flesh burns it is yellow as cheese
    Points at his neck.
because disfigured by a skin disease
And only water cooling every limb
    Points to bath.
prevents his fever from consuming him
    Marat takes his pen and begins to write.
To act this important role we chose
a lucky paranoiac one of those
who've made unprecedented strides since we
introduced them to hydrotherapy. . . .

The Herald introduces Simonne to the audience, and then Charlotte Corday. Corday is from a landed Caen family, and she is "phenomenally pulchritudinous." She is played by a sufferer from sleeping sickness and melancholia.

The Herald introduces Duperret, a Girondist "on Marat's black list" (and the erotomaniac playing him tries to paw Charlotte Corday but is pulled back). The Herald introduces Jacques Roux, Marat's ally, who works his straitjacketed arms and utters the one word "Liberty," at which Coulmier raises a warning forefinger.

HERALD:
   . . . Now meet this gentleman from high society
     Points at de Sade who turns his back on the public in a bored way.
   who under the lurid star of notoriety
   came to live with us just five years ago
   It's to his genius that we owe this show
   The former Marquis Monsieur de Sade
   whose books were banned his essays barred
   while he's been persecuted and reviled
   thrown into jail and for some years exiled
   The introduction's over now the play
   of Jean-Paul Marat can get under way
   Tonight the date
   is the thirteenth of July eighteen-o-eight
   And on this night our cast intend
   showing how fifteen years ago night without end
   fell on that man that invalid
     Points at Marat.
   And you are going to see him bleed
     Points at Marat's breast.
   and see this woman after careful thought
     Points at Corday.
   take up the dagger and cut him short
   Homage to Marat

The principals move out of the way so that the Four Singers—Kokol, Polpoch, Cucurucu and the woman Rossignol—can move near to Marat.

5: Homage to Marat

The Four Singers and their chorus of Patients recall that four years after the Revolution Marat was still writing, still struggling for liberty against the generals and the ruling class. Marat is crowned with a wreath, lifted from the bath and carried around the room.

FOUR SINGERS *(sing):*
   Four years he fought and he fought unafraid
   sniffing down traitors by traitors betrayed

Marat in the courtroom Marat underground
sometimes the otter and sometimes the hound

Fighting all the gentry and fighting every priest
businessman the bourgeois the military beast
Marat always ready to stifle every scheme
of the sons of the arse-licking dying regime

We've got new generals our leaders are new
They sit and they argue and all that they do
is sell their own colleagues and ride on their backs
and jail them and break them or give them all the axe

Screaming in language no man understands
of rights that we grabbed with our own bleeding hands
when we wiped out the bosses and stormed through the wall
of the prison they told us would outlast us all

CHORUS and FOUR SINGERS *(sing):*
    Marat we're poor and the poor stay poor
    Marat don't make us wait any more
    We want our rights and we don't care how
    We want our revolution NOW.

Marat is placed back in the bath, with some ceremony. Simonne pulls off
the wreath, throws it to one side, arranges the bandages.

> *De Sade sits unmoving, looking across the stage with a mocking*
> *expression on his face.*

HERALD:
    The Revolution came and went
    and unrest was replaced by discontent

6: *Stifled Unrest*

Playing hungry and protesting Revolution rabble, the Patients cry "Freedom" as though they were referring to their own case. They become so ardent
(and tactless) in their cries for freedom that Coulmier interrupts.

COULMIER *(knocking with his stick on the railing):* Monsieur de Sade *(De
Sade takes no notice.)*
    It appears I must act as the voice of reason
    What's going to happen when right at the start of the play
    the patients are so disturbed
    Please keep your production under control
    Times have changed times are different
    and these days we should take a subtler view of old grievances

The Male Nurses control the patients.

7: Corday Is Introduced

As though it were a ritual, the Sisters lead Charlotte Corday forward. "She stands outside his door ready and poised to kill," the Herald declares; the act will take place, it is inevitable.

CORDAY *(sleepily and hesitantly):*
    Poor Marat in your bathtub
    your body soaked saturated with poison
        Waking up.
    Poison spurting from your hiding place
    poisoning the people
    arousing them to looting and murder
    Marat
    I have come
    I
    Charlotte Corday from Caen
    where a huge army of liberation is massing
    and Marat I come as the first of them Marat

She sings her disillusionment with Marat. Once they both followed the same ideal of freedom. But Marat's way led over "mountains of dead." To Charlotte Corday, on the contrary, the *Fraternité* of revolution meant brotherly love; a less violent solution. Now, she sings, "I go to murder you Marat and free all mankind."

De Sade waves a large wooden knife, tantalizing Corday. She follows it, manages to get ahold of it and kneels, holding it.

8: I Am the Revolution

Marat is writing his July 14 exhortation. The itching is almost unbearable, but Simonne warns him not to scratch; his bath water is turning red.

MARAT:
    And what's a bath full of blood
    compared to the bloodbaths still to come
    Once we thought a few hundred corpses would be enough
    then we saw thousands were still too few
    and today we can't even count all the dead
    Everywhere you look
    everywhere
        Marat raises himself up in the bath. The Four Singers stretched
        out on the floor play cards, taking no notice of Marat.
    There they are
    Behind the walls

Up on the rooftops
Down in the cellars
Hypocrites
They wear the people's cap on their heads
but their underwear's embroidered with crowns
and if so much as a shop gets looted
they squeal
Beggars villains gutter rats
Simonne Simonne
my head's on fire
I can't breathe
There is a rioting mob inside me
Simonne
I am the Revolution
Corday is led into position by the Sisters.

9: Corday's First Visit

Charlotte Corday tries to see Marat, pretending she wishes to report on the rebellious situation in Caen. Simonne will not let her in. Corday indicates that's she's eager to thrust in the knife, but de Sade explains to her: not yet, she must come to Marat's door three times. Corday withdraws.

10: Song and Mime of Corday's Arrival in Paris

As an accompaniment to the song, Patients come forward as mimes. They walk singly around the arena. With simple disguises they present types in the street. One is an "Incroyable," another a "Merveilleuse" or a banner-bearer, a salesman and cutler, an acrobat or flower seller, and there are also some prostitutes. Corday circles the arena in the opposite direction. She represents the country girl who has come to town for the first time.

FOUR SINGERS *(sing):*
Charlotte Corday came to our town
heard the people talking saw the banners wave
Weariness had almost dragged her down
weariness had dragged her down

Charlotte Corday had to be brave
she could never stay at comfortable hotels
Had to find a man with knives to sell
had to find a man with knives. . . .

In the song, Charlotte Corday finds her knife and pays forty sous for it. She strolls in Paris and hears "the singing Guillotine." She watches a cart pass by with its load of condemned. She is shocked by the bloody horror of the Paris street scene.

11: Death's Triumph

Marat justifies the bloody revenge of the people.

MARAT:
> . . . it's too late
> to start crying over spilt blood
> What is the blood of these aristocrats
> compared with the blood the people shed for you
> Many of them had their throats slit by your gangs
> Many of them died more slowly in your workshops

The Patients are aroused by Marat's harangue. Coulmier rises to protest that they are becoming overexcited and showing to bad advantage before the invited audience. De Sade ignores this protest.

The Herald calmly advises everyone that these barbarous practices are shown as history. They could not be repeated in the present, more civilized era.

Nobles are lined up for the guillotine, and Corday resolves to imitate their self-possession "when it's all over."

SADE:
> Look at them Marat
> these men who once owned everything
> See how they turn their defeat into victory
> Now that their pleasures have been taken away
> the guillotine saves them from endless boredom
> Gaily they offer their heads as if for coronation
> Is not that the pinnacle of perversion

The execution proceeds. As the nobles are executed, a bucket of red blood is poured down a nearby drain. Then the King is executed and the blood emptied from the bucket is blue.

The body of the King is thrown into the downstage center bath. As pieces of it are flung out, the Patients are excited into pandemonium. They are quieted by the attendants. Corday is led to her bench, while the Patients go down into the baths and cover themselves over with the duckboards.

12: Conversation Concerning Life and Death

Marat and de Sade discuss death across the empty arena. Death is of no importance, de Sade insists, and Nature would not care if the whole human race were destroyed.

SADE:
> I hate Nature
> this passionless spectator this unbreakable iceberg-face

that can bear everything
this goads us to greater and greater acts
    Breathing heavily.
Haven't we always beaten down those weaker than ourselves
Haven't we torn at their throats
with continuous villainy and lust
Haven't we experimented in our laboratories
before applying the final solution

De Sade recalls the gruesome execution of Damiens for the attempted murder of Louis XV; how they scorched Damiens with molten lead and boiling oil, burned off his hands and then tore him limb from limb.

SADE:
    . . . there's no passion in our post-revolutionary murders
    Now they are all official
    We condemn to death without emotion
    and there's no singular personal death to be had
    only an anonymous cheapened death
    which we could dole out to entire nations
    on a mathematical basis
    until the time comes
    for all life
    to be extinguished

Marat accuses de Sade of lack of compassion. De Sade characterizes compassion as a form of aristocratic contempt, like a gift to a beggar.

SADE:
    . . . No Marat
    no small emotions please
    Your feelings were never petty
    For you just as for me
    only the most extreme actions matter
MARAT:
    If I am extreme I am not extreme in the same way as you
    Against Nature's silence I use action
    In the vast indifference I invent a meaning
    I don't watch unmoved I intervene
    and say that this and this are wrong
    and I work to alter them and improve them
    The important thing
    is to pull yourself up by your own hair
    to turn yourself inside out
    and see the whole world with fresh eyes

13: Marat's Liturgy

The Herald announces the liturgy; music and bells are heard as the Patients come out of the baths to listen to Marat tell them how once the kings were their "dear fathers." The priests "settled down among their treasures and ate and drank with princes" and told the masses that injustice and suffering were the will of God. Paradise was to be the reward. As Marat speaks, Patients and Singers perform a cynical mime of churchly doings.

Again, Director Coulmier rises to protest; the church and the clergy have been restored to favor under the Emperor. Why, this very asylum is partly dependent on the church's good will.

And once again the Herald must remind his listeners that the play's tactless utterances about the church belong to the rebellious past, not the God-fearing present.

14: A Regrettable Intervention

A Patient, a former abbot, comes forward and delivers a Satanic parody of the Lord's Prayer. He is then suppressed. Again, the Herald apologizes and the Patients settle down on their benches.

15: Continuation of the Conversation Between Marat and de Sade

De Sade muses that "What we do is just a shadow of what we want to do," and "I do not know if I am hangman or victim." He is horrified by the very horrors he is able to imagine, and yet as he thinks of them he is able to feel them. He believes himself to be unpredictably capable of any act, like a little tailor of his acquaintance who beat a man to death and tore out his heart.

A Patient speaks, partly to Coulmier.

PATIENT:
    A mad animal
    Man's a mad animal
    I'm a thousand years old and in my time
    I've helped commit a million murders
    The earth is spread
    The earth is spread thick
    with squashed human guts
    We few survivors
    We few survivors
    walk over a quaking bog of corpses
    always under our feet
    every step we take
    rotted bones ashes matted hair
    under our feet
    broken teeth skulls split open
    A mad animal
    I'm a mad animal

And the peak of horror hasn't yet been reached, the Patient declares as he's led away by de Sade. Because of this interruption, Marat falters over his lines but soon regains his place.

De Sade tells Marat his dreams there, in that womblike bathtub, no longer apply to the realities of life outside. And, de Sade adds, external revolution is unimportant compared to the world of imagination.

Wrong, Marat declares. The pen isn't really mightier than the sword. Ideas can't really break down walls.

MARAT:
    We're all so clogged with dead ideas
    passed from generation to generation
    that even the best of us
    don't know the way out
    We invented the Revolution
    but we don't know how to run it
    Look everyone wants to keep something from the past
    a souvenir of the old regime
        This man decides to keep a painting
        This one keeps his mistress
        This man keeps his horse
        He *(Pointing.)* keeps his garden
        He *(Pointing.)* keeps his estate
        He keeps his country house
        He keeps his factories
        This man couldn't part with his shipyards
        This one kept his army
        and that one keeps his king
    And so we stand here
    and write into the declaration of the rights of man
    the holy right of property
    And now we find where that leads
    Every man's equally free to fight
    fraternally and with equal arms of course
    Every man his own millionaire
    Man against man group against group
    in happy mutual robbery
        The Patients stand up slowly, some step forward. The Four Singers
        take up their positions.
    And ahead of them the great springtime of mankind
    the budding of trade and the blossoming of industry
    and one enormous financial upsurge
    We stand here more oppressed than when we begun
        Points across the auditorium.
    and they think that the revolution's been won

16: The People's Reaction

The mob protests its poverty and powerlessness, in song. They want their revolution NOW. While Duperret and the Sisters try to rouse Charlotte Corday for the next scene, the Herald exhorts his hearers:

HERALD:
   . . . Work for and trust the powerful few
   what's best for them is best for you
   Ladies and gentlemen we'd like to see
   people and government in harmony
   a harmony which I should say
   we've very nearly reached today

17: First Conversation Between Corday and Duperret

Young Charlotte Corday has left her Caen convent to seek out the noble and very well-reputed Girondist Monsieur Duperret. The patient playing Corday is in a dreamlike state and (ironically) the erotomaniac playing Duperret paws her and makes advances to her as they discuss politics.

Corday believes Marat wants anarchy so he can rule. Duperret bids her return to the shelter of the nuns and scoffs at Marat.

DUPERRET:
   You talk about Marat but who's this Marat
   A street salesman a funfair barker
   a layabout from Corsica sorry I mean Sardinia
   Marat the name sounds Jewish to me
   perhaps derived from the waters of Marah in the Bible
   But who listens to him
   Only the mob down in the streets
   Up here Marat can be no danger to us

Duperret tries to get at Corday, but she pulls away from him and the Sisters rescue her. In doing so, Duperret falls into the downstage center bath. He continues trying to get at her and thus misses several cues while discussing the political situation. He tells Corday (prompted by the Herald) that the English, the Spaniards, the Prussians, the Austrians will soon overrun France and set things right. He will stay with her (instead of going on a mission to Caen, as she had ordered) until "with Marat's mob interred" France regains true freedom.

Duperret is chained to the proscenium arch right to prevent his getting at Corday, who is led back to her bench.

18: De Sade Turns His Back on All the Nations

De Sade derides patriotism as lunacy, and again asylum Director Coulmier gives warning that they are treading on dangerous ground. De Sade believes in no causes, only in himself. Angrily Marat defends his belief in the Revolution—which, he says, has been betrayed because the bourgeosie have won it and the people have lost.

The Four Singers sing a ribald song about "Those fat monkeys covered in banknotes."

19: First Rabble-Rousing of Jacques Roux

The straitjacketed figure of Jacques Roux springs onto a bench and calls the rabble to arms.

ROUX:
> . . . Up there they despise you
> because you never had the cash
> to learn to read and write
> You're good enough for the dirty work of the Revolution
> but they screw their noses up at you
> because your sweat stinks
> You have to sit way down there
> so they won't have to see you
> And down there
> in ignorance and stink
> you're allowed to do your bit
> towards bringing in the golden age
> in which you'll all do the same old dirty work. . . .

Stand up, Roux urges the people; stand up and let the poets who sing of life see how numerous are the suffering rabble.

COULMIER *(springing up):*
> Do we have to listen to this sort of thing
> We're citizens of a new enlightened age
> We're all revolutionaries nowadays
> but this is plain treachery we can't allow it.

The Herald explains that this is the notorious Roux, an ex-priest who stepped down from pulpit to soap box. He is Marat's "chief apostle."

Roux cries out for reforms, including the conversion of the churches into schools, which makes Coulmier wince again. Roux demands an end to war between supposedly glorious armies which are, after all, merely frightened men.

COULMIER *(shouting over him):*
> This is outright defeatism
> At this very moment our soldiers are laying down their lives
> for the freedom of the world and for our freedom
> *Turning violently to Sade.*
> This scene was cut

But de Sade ignores Coulmier and congratulates Roux, who is overpowered and strapped to a bench. He cries out for Marat to "Come out and lead the people."

20: Monsieur de Sade Is Whipped

Today they love Marat, tomorrow they will scorn him, declares de Sade as he moves downstage center, slowly unbuttoning his shirt. He will tell them what he thinks of the Revolution.

SADE:

> . . . When I lay in the Bastille
> my ideas were already formed
> I sweated them out
> under the blows of my own whip
> out of hatred for myself
> and the limitations of my mind
> In prison I created in my mind
> monstrous representatives of a dying class
> who could only exercise their power
> in spectacularly staged orgies
> I recorded the mechanics of their atrocities
> in the minutest detail
> and brought out everything wicked and brutal
> that lay inside me
> In a criminal society
> I dug the criminal out of myself
> so I could understand him and so understand
> the times we live in
> My imaginary giants committed
> desecrations and tortures
> I committed them myself
> and like them allowed myself to be bound and beaten
> And even now I should like to take
> this beauty here
>> *Pointing to Corday, who is brought forward.*
> who stands there so expectantly
> and let her beat me
> while I talk to you about the Revolution

De Sade discards his shirt and kneels with Corday standing behind him. At various times she will "whip" him by swinging her body and slowly drawing her long hair across de Sade's naked back—and each time it is as though he had been struck by a whip.

At first, de Sade declares, he thought the Revolution would be an orgiastic release of revenge. He soon realized, though, that he himself wasn't capable of sending even the guilty to punishment.

SADE:

    . . . I saw I wasn't capable of murder
            Whiplash. Sade groans asthmatically.
    although murder
    was the final proof of my existence
    and now
            Whiplash. He gasps and groans.
    the very thought of it
    horrifies me
    In September when I saw
    the official sacking of the Carmelite Convent
    I had to bend over in the courtyard
    and vomit
            Corday stops, herself breathing heavily.
    as I saw my own prophecies coming true
    and women running by
    holding in their dripping hands
    the severed genitals of men

Corday continues her "whipping" as de Sade recalls how so many people went to the scaffold that revenge became merely a mechanical process, unfeeling, dull. At last de Sade crumples under the "punishment" of the whip. Corday is pulled back by the Sisters. De Sade begins to get up, very slowly, while prophesying where the Revolution is heading.

SADE:

    To the withering of the individual man
    and a slow merging into uniformity
    to the death of choice
    to self denial
    to deadly weakness
    in a state
    which has no contact with individuals
    but which is impregnable
    So I turn away
    I am one of those who has to be defeated
    and from this defeat I want to seize
    all I can get with my own strength
    I step out of my place
    and watch what happens
    without joining in
    observing
    noting down my observations
    and all around me
    stillness
            Pauses, breathing heavily.
    And when I vanish

I want all trace of my existence
to be wiped out
> *He takes his shirt and returns to his chair, slowly dressing.*

21: Poor Old Marat

Marat complains of his crawling flesh, and of the darkness; he cannot find his pen and paper to write his call to the people. Simonne finds it for him. The Singers take up their song.

FOUR SINGERS *(sing):*
> . . . Poor old Marat in you we trust
> You work till your eyes turn as red as rust
> but while you write they're on your track
> The boots mount the staircase the door's flung back
> > *Together with Chorus.*
> Marat we're poor and the poor stay poor
> Marat don't make us wait any more
> We want our rights and we don't care how
> We want our revolution NOW
> > *Music finale, Singers withdraw.*

22: Second Conversation Between Corday and Duperret

The Herald explains that this is to be a scene of pure love and purely spiritual contact.

Duperret and Corday speak and sing of the ideal society which will exist some day; a society in which each individual will be free and happy. They agree that this Utopia will come true.

Duperret slips his chain and dives at Corday. The Sisters protect her. Duperret crawls after her but Marat puts his hand on Duperret's shoulders and stops him; then pushes him away.

23: These Lies They Tell

MARAT:
> These lies they tell about the ideal state
> The rich will never give away their property
> of their own free will
> And if by force of circumstances
> they have to give up just a little
> here and there
> they do it only because they know
> they'll soon win it back again. . . .

Marat warns "the people" they will have to use force, they mustn't be fooled by the appearance of prosperity and equality. This drives Coulmier to protest to de Sade, who doesn't respond.

De Sade moves downstage as Duperret is put back into chains.

MARAT:
    . . . Watch out
    for as soon as it pleases them
    they'll send you out
    to protect their gold
    in wars
    whose weapons rapidly developed
    by servile scientists
    will become more and more deadly
    until they can with a flick of the finger
    tear a million of you to pieces

To Coulmier's satisfaction, de Sade interrupts Marat and derides his principles of justice and equality.

24: Song and Mime of the Glorification of the Beneficiary

> *The Four Singers perform a mime, in which they illustrate the cash value of all the things de Sade names.*

SADE:
    One always bakes the most delicate cakes
    Two is the really superb masseur
    Three sets your hair with exceptional flair
    Four's brandy goes to the Emperor
    Five knows each trick of advanced rhetoric
    Six bred a beautiful brand-new rose
    Seven can cook every dish in the book
    And eight cuts you flawlessly elegant clothes
    Do you think those eight would be happy
    if each of them could climb so high
    and no higher
    before banging their heads on equality. . . .

No, says de Sade, even the idealists are falling out and would like to leap at each other's throats. Marat argues that this is normal, the weaker fellow-travelers are always purged, and rebuilding can't take place until the old building has been torn down. Meanwhile, Marat warns, the counter-revolutionaries plot and plan.

The Four Singers promenade and wonder, in song, what the people are waiting for now that the king is gone and the Revolution is accomplished.

25: Corday's Second Visit

Charlotte Corday is led forward to pantomime knocking on Marat's door. She delivers a letter to Simonne and asks to see Marat, pleading for his aid. Simonne refuses to admit her.

MARAT: Who was that at the door Simonne
    Simonne hesitates in confusion between Corday and Marat.
HERALD *(prompting):* A girl from Caen with a letter a petitioner
    Corday is sunk into herself. She moves off.
SIMONNE *(confused and angry):*
    I won't let anyone in
    They only bring us trouble
    All these people with their convulsions and complaints
    As if you had nothing better to do
    than be their lawyer and doctor and confessor
        She tears the letter up.

In his chair and surrounded by the Four Singers, de Sade describes the Revolution and its motives: a poet is looking for poetry, an angler for fish. Each person follows the Revolution because he believes it will bring him his heart's desire—which, of course, it does not.

The song of the Four Singers deplores Marat's condition and fears that he is losing his grip.

FOUR SINGERS *(sing):*
    . . . Marat Marat can you explain
    how once in the daylight your thought seemed plain
    Has your affliction left you dumb
    Your thoughts lie in shadows now night has come

26: The Faces of Marat

Marat in his bath is moved downstage center. He is feverish, and his troubled dreams come to life onstage in a dumb show of characters entering though a mist of steam; characters representing Science, the Church, the Newly Rich; characters from his past life including his mother and father, all grotesquely costumed.

SCHOOLMASTER *(sings in a falsetto voice):*
    Even as a child
    this Marat
    made groups of his friends
    rush screaming at each other
    they fought with wooden swords
    but real blood flowed
        Cries are heard in the background.

and they took prisoners
and bound and tortured them
and nobody knew why

Then it is Marat's mother's turn to recall that for days at a time he wouldn't eat, and they whipped him for it.

MOTHER *(laughs shrilly):*
   . . . locked him up in the cellar of course
but nothing helped
There was no getting at him
Oh
     She starts laughing again.
FATHER *(springing forward, in a hurried voice):*
When I bit him he bit back
his own father
Threw himself down when I wanted to hang him up
and when I spat at him he lay there stiff as a poker
cold as ice
     Starts to laugh harshly.
MARAT:
Yes I see you
hated father hated mother.

Marat hears the two figures laugh "like executioners." He is so feverish that Simonne tries to make him stop writing, but he feels he must compose his call to the nation.

Then the feverish dreams begin again; the Schoolmaster recalls how the youth boasted of his erudition. Marat calls for his old manuscripts, a novel and a book about slavery, but Simonne won't bring them. Dream-figures recite Marat's biography.

MILITARY REPRESENTATIVE:
One book published under the name of a count
The other under the name of a prince
Just look at him
this charlatan
greedy for titles and court distinctions
who turned on those he once flattered
only because they did not recognize him
A SCIENTIST:
What did he do in England this shady Marat
Wasn't he a dandy in the highest society
who had to run away
because he was caught red-handed embezzling and stealing . . .

Then Marat was appointed physician to the Count d'Artois, the Scientist continues. During this time he consorted with aristocrats—and with their ladies.

A NEWLY-RICH:
>And when at last they let him drop
>back to his kind the simple poor
>and when he spoke and couldn't stop
>each word from branding him a boor
>and when they found he was a quack
>with watered drugs and pills of chalk
>and when they threw him on his back
>He raised his battered head to squawk
>   Property is Robbery
>   *Cries in the background.*
>Down with all Tyrants
>   *The cry is taken up in the background.*

A dream-Voltaire enters. He mentions a small book of Marat's entitled "Man," as Marat gets out of his tub and lowers himself into the downstage center bath (momentarily the paranoiac patient playing Marat is forgetting himself as an actor and seeking the security of his therapeutic bath). In his book, Marat had advanced the theory that the soul exists in the brain and sends messages to the body by means of nerves. Voltaire ridicules the whole idea; it is beneath even his laughter.

The scientist Lavoisier appears and ridicules another theory of Marat's, advanced to the Academy, that fire is not an element, but combustion of air, and heat is made of rays in a universe in which "electrified magnetic particles whizz about and rub against each other."

>*The figures mime the attitude of judges about to give a verdict.*
>VOLTAIRE: So this frustrated Newton's eyes
>PRIEST: turned to the streets He thought it best
>SCHOOLMASTER: To join the revolutionaries
>NEWLY RICH: and beat his dilettante breast
>PRIEST: crying out The oppressed must rise
>LAVOISIER: He meant of course I am oppressed

Mother and father and dream figures depart. Duperret slips his chain again and makes for Corday but is stopped. Roux springs to Marat's defense, crying woe to him who would try to advance mankind.

ROUX:
>. . . You wanted enlightenment and warmth
>and so you studied light and heat
>You wondered how forces can be controlled
>so you studied electricity

You wanted to know what man is for
so you asked yourself What is this soul
this dump for hollow ideals and mangled morals
You decided that the soul is in the brain
and that it can learn to think
For to you the soul is a practical thing
a tool for ruling and mastering life
And you came one day to the Revolution
because you saw the most important vision
That our circumstances must be changed fundamentally
and without these changes
everything we try to do must fail

Softly, the Patients sing a reprise of "Revolution NOW" as they retreat upstage. Marat crawls out of the downstage center bath and, naked, crawls upstage to his tub and gets into it.

The Herald interrupts the play to announce an intermission, a "drinking
thinking time." Marat will be there in his bath when the audience returns, the
Herald assures them.

Coulmier and his wife and daughters exit into the wings and the asbestos
curtain comes down.

ACT II

27: The National Assembly

The asbestos curtain has risen before the intermission is over, revealing
the Patients waiting to begin the play again, improvising. Coulmier has returned to the stage and is chatting with de Sade, and Coulmier's wife and
daughters have regained their seats. To signal the beginning of the action, the
Herald knocks with his stick and the house lights dim.

The Four Singers enter, as Jacobites. Marat (who has been draped in a
towel) stands up in his tub to address the Assembly, the majority of which
jeers him and shouts for Robespierre and Danton.

MARAT:
Fellow citizens
members of the National Assembly
our country is in danger
From every corner of Europe armies invade us
led by profiteers
who want to strangle us
and already quarrel over the spoils
And what are we doing
    Apathetic noises.
Our minister of war
whose integrity you never doubted

> has sold the corn meant for our armies
> for his own profit to foreign powers
> and now it feeds the troops
> who are invading us.
>> *Cries and whistles.*

The few cheer for Marat and the many jeer as he continues his speech. The chief of the revolutionary army, Dumouriez, is a traitor (Marat says), and most generals favor the emigres. The finance minister is lining his pockets and the leading banker is encouraging British espionage (Here Coulmier interrupts with the admonition that this same banker is now in favor with Napoleon).

There is civil war, Marat continues, and famine. Labor is being exploited. And Marat wishes that there were room in the Assembly for thousands to come and hear what is under discussion.

DUPERRET:
> What is he trying to do
> He's trying to rouse the people again
> Look who sits on the public benches
> Knitting-women concierges and washerwomen
> with no one to employ them any more
> And who has he got on his side
> Pickpockets layabouts parasites
> who loiter in the boulevards
>> *Indignation among the onlookers.*
> and hang around the cafes

Marat tells the members of the Assembly they don't understand the people, they are too far removed from them. Even Danton and Robespierre "sit at high-class tables making cultural conversation."

MARAT:
> And you still long to ape them
> those powdered chimpanzees
> Necker Lafayette Talleyrand
COULMIER *(interrupting)*:
> That's enough
> *(These are my friends and the friends of France)
> If you use any more of these (slanderous)
> passages we agreed to cut
> I will stop your play
MARAT *(breaking in)*:
> and all the rest of them
> What we need now is a true deputy of the people. . . .

* Words in parentheses were added to the text in the Peter Brook production.

. . . an incorruptible to rule them, declares Marat. The word "dictator" is hurled at him, but he disowns it.

Duperret calls for thought instead of agitation. He is knocked down, as Roux rushes forward to echo Marat's call to action. The crowd becomes disorderly, calling out for and against Marat.

KOKOL & POLPOCH *(dancing, singing):*
> Hit at the rich until they crash
> Throw down their god and divide their cash

CUCURUCU & ROSSIGNOL *(dancing, singing):*
> We wouldn't mind a tasty meal
> of pate de foie and filleted eel

CHORUS: Marat Marat Marat Marat Marat
> *De Sade raises his hands. They all freeze. Roll of drums and beginning of music.*

28: Poor Marat in Your Bathtub Seat

Marat, in his bath, is exhausted. Sisters and Nurses push the Patients back while the Four Singers deliver a song.

FOUR SINGERS *(accompanied, singing):*
> Poor Marat in your bathtub seat
> your life on this planet is near complete
> closer and closer to you death creeps
> though there on her bench Charlotte Corday sleeps

This is the eve, the Four Singers warn Marat. They sit on a bench upstage. The Patients know this is supposed to be a quiet scene; they sssh each other and are still.

Marat calls for Simonne, but it is de Sade who answers him and urges him to give up.

SADE:
> . . . Long ago I abandoned my masterpiece
> a roll of paper thirty yards long
> which I filled completely with minute handwriting
> in my dungeon years ago
> It vanished when the Bastille fell
> it vanished as everything written
> everything thought and planned
> will disappear

But Marat refuses to heed de Sade's defeatism.

MARAT *(raising himself up):*
> I had time for nothing but work

Day and night were not enough for me
When I investigated a wrong it grew branches
and every branch grew twigs
Wherever I turned
I found corruption

Marat describes his feverish, all-consuming process of writing his book about slavery which was suppressed. After each of his pamphlets, too, "they came with cannons." Marat fears the knock on the door may happen again; he is anxious to finish his July 14 call to the people of France.

De Sade points to the Four Singers, playing "Lost revolutionaries," helpless, aimless creatures, lost in drink. De Sade wonders where Marat could possibly lead them; and does Marat now favor authority where he once denounced it? In the background the Patients are doing tricks at their guardians' command: standing on one foot or walking in a circle.

Marat is confused. The Four Singers come forward for their song.

THE FOUR SINGERS *(singing and dancing):*
Poor old Marat you lie prostrate
while others are gambling with France's fate
Your words have turned into a flood
which covers all France with her people's blood

29: *Preparations for the Third Visit*

The Herald, Duperret and other Patients are urging Charlotte Corday to wake up and carry out her role. The Herald hands her a knife. She rises and hides it in her dress during the following speech.

CORDAY *(her eyes still closed, speaking softly, nervously):*
Now I know what it is like
when the head is cut off the body
Oh this moment
hands tied behind the back
feet bound together
neck bared
hair cut off
knees on the boards
the head already laid
in the metal slot
looking down into the dripping basket
The sound of the blade rising
and from its slanting edge
the blood still drops
and then the downward slide
to split us in two
    Pause.

they say
that the head
held high in the executioner's hand
still lives
that the eyes still see
that the tongue still writhes
and down below the arms and legs still shudder

Duperret urges Corday to throw the knife away and go home to Caen. But Corday recalls Judith, who saved her city by slaying Holofernes with a single blow. She becomes hysterical and is quieted by the Sisters.

Now Paris must be saved from its orgy of blood, so ferocious now that little children are playing with toy guillotines, executing dolls filled with red ink. Marat's death will end the blood orgy, Corday believes.

30: Corday's Third and Last Visit

One last time Duperret urges Corday to desist, but she will not. She waves him out of her way and he drops to the floor.

Marat resolves that he has been right all the time and will state his convictions once more in his July 14 call. De Sade approaches him and asks him to see Corday as a virgin carrying a knife "to intensify the love-play."

Corday moves closer, as Marat asks Simonne who was knocking. De Sade again advises Marat to see Corday as a country maiden who has enjoyed erotic dreams of life out in the great world.

SADE (to musical accompaniment):
    And then she was tired of her isolation
    and stirred up by the new age
    and gathered up in the great tide
    and wanted to be part of the Revolution
    And what's the point of a revolution
    without general copulation
CHORUS:
    And what's the point of a revolution
    without general
    copulation copulation copulation
        Continues as a round.
SADE:
    Marat
    as I sat there in the Bastille
    for thirteen long years
    I learned
    that this is a world of bodies
    each body pulsing with a terrible power
    each body alone and racked with its own unrest
    In that loneliness

marooned in a stone sea
I heard lips whispering continually
and felt all the time
in the palms of my hands and in my skin
touching and stroking
Shut behind thirteen bolted doors.
my feet fettered
I dreamed only
of the orifices of the body
put there
so one may hook and twine oneself in them

The inner self (Sade continues, as the Patients listen intently), is so deep and secure a dungeon that those who fight revolutions for external freedom are fighting mutinies within a prison.

The Patients mime copulation to music. The Attendants move Marat downstage as de Sade returns to his chair.

"Who's at the door?" Marat asks Simonne, who replies, "The girl from Caen." Marat asks Simonne to let her in.

Reluctantly, Simonne moves back as Corday approaches Marat, her hand on the hidden knife.

Marat urges Corday to come closer so he can see her better, and hear more clearly the names she is reciting of those who are gathering against him in Caen (he can know their names, since he is soon to die). As Corday comes closer still, Marat rises in his bath and cries out one more time that he wishes to make his July 14 call to the people of France.

Corday stands immediately behind Marat and places her left hand close to his chest as he sits, pen still in hand. She pulls the knife from its hiding place and raises it in her right hand, poised to strike. Simonne screams.

All on stage freeze in their tracks. Marat sits quietly, leaning forward.

31: Interruptus

HERALD:

Now it's a part of Sade's dramatic plan
to interrupt the climax so this man
Marat can hear and gasp with his last breath
at how the world will go after his death
With a musical history we'll bring him up to date
From seventeen-ninety-three to eighteen-eight

The Four Singers sing of events to come as the Herald unfolds banners showing the dates of these events. Charlotte Corday takes the opportunity to lie down on the floor behind the bench.

The song tells of the beheading of Marat's enemies, including Corday and Duperret. It tells of "Fifteen glorious years;" of Bonaparte's conquest of

Egypt and all Europe except England, which is to fall soon (despite the set-back at Trafalgar).

FOUR SINGERS *(sing):*
    . . . Now the Prussians retreat *(Banner 1806.)*
    Russia faces defeat *(Banner 1807.)*
    All the world
    bends its knee
    to Napoleon
    and his family
    Fight on land and on sea *(Banner 1808.)*
    All men want to be free
    If they don't
    never mind
    we'll abolish all mankind

    Fifteen glorious years
    Fifteen glorious years
    years of peace
    years of war
    each year greater
    than the one before
    Marat
    we're marching on
    behind Napoleon

32: The Murder

Corday gets up. Simonne screams again as Corday lowers the knife and kills Marat, with de Sade standing behind her watching her movements closely.

The Patients cry out and Corday faints. Marat comes to rest in the pose of the famous David painting, holding pen and paper.

Polpoch brings in a bucket of blood and pours it down the drain. This time the blood is white.

And this is the end of de Sade's play.

33: Epilogue

The play is over, and the Herald is asking de Sade: who won? But the author refuses to elucidate.

SADE:
    (Husband and wife most certainly will quarrel
    He'll say it's filthy she'll insist it's moral
    Well, you may create all your varying theses
    and keep them on your mantlepieces)

Marat, putting forth his own opinion eagerly, says the important thing is to "see the whole world with fresh eyes."

Coulmier steps forward to speak a polite word or two to the audience as they leave the imaginary, bloody past and return to the civilized, sure-to-be-victorious present.

The orchestral music in the background begins to define itself as a march. The Patients are sensitive to this, and nervous. The Four Singers put words to the music, words about the new era:

FOUR SINGERS (sing):
. . . We can say what we like without favor or fear
and what we can't say we can breathe in your ear
And though we're locked up we're no longer enslaved
and the honor of France is eternally saved
the useless debate the political brawl
are over there's one man to speak for us all
For he helps us in sickness and destitution
he's the leader who ended the Revolution
and everyone knows why we're cheering for
Napoleon our mighty Emperor

Coulmier is chatting with de Sade and several members of the cast. But the music is swelling, insistent, and the Patients grouped upstage are restless. They form a line and begin to advance as a column, four steps forward, three steps back.

Coulmier motions the Patients back, but they come on despite all restraints.

The Herald loses control of himself and becomes violent. Coulmier's family panics, and de Sade incites Duperret to run after Coulmier's daughter. Coulmier shows a cowardly streak as he urges his wife to save their daughter from Duperret. She is finally saved by a Nurse and a Sister.

ALL (in confused and rhythmic shouts in time to the marching):
Charenton Charenton
Napoleon Napoleon
Nation Nation
Revolution Revolution
Copulation Copulation
    The shouting grows. The column reaches the front. The struggle
    between Nurses and Herald develops and catches the attention of
    the others. Suddenly the whole stage is fighting. De Sade watches
    with a faint smile, almost indulgent.

The Patients who played leading roles have moved to one side, out of the riot, as though they had spent all emotion on the play. Nurses shake their batons as Roux springs forward in front of the marchers, his arms still strait-jacketed.

ROUX:

    When will you learn to see
    When will you learn to take sides

    He tries to force them back but is drawn in and vanishes from
    sight in the still advancing ranks. The Patients are fully at the
    mercy of their mad marchlike dance. Many of them hop and spin
    in ecstasy. Coulmier incites the Nurses to extreme violence.

Some Patients are struck down, but the majority overcome the few Nurses and Sisters. Coulmier and family flee. The Four Singers, now completely out of hand, escape from the stage and run out into the auditorium and up into the balcony.

De Sade stands downstage laughing at the turmoil.

At the very height of the activity, the stage manager walks onstage and blows a whistle. All action stops; then the actors stand and applaud the audience.

When the audience starts to applaud the actors, the actors change to a slow hand-clap which stops this applause. Then the actors walk off the stage. The house lights come up. The play is over.

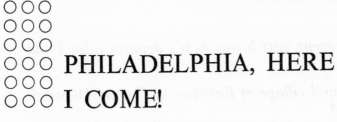

PHILADELPHIA, HERE I COME!

A Play in Three Episodes

BY BRIAN FRIEL

Cast and credits appear on page 398

BRIAN FRIEL was born in Northern Ireland at Derry City and, at 36, with a wife and two children, he still lives there. Until 1960 he was a school teacher; since that date he has devoted himself to writing. His short stories have appeared in The New Yorker *and have been collected in a volume entitled* The Saucer of Larks *and in a forthcoming one called* The Gold In the Sea. *Mr. Friel had three plays produced in Belfast and Dublin before this present work; they were* This Doubtful Paradise, The Blind Mice *and* The Enemy Within.

Philadelphia, Here I Come! was produced in Dublin in September, 1964. It was performed there and on Broadway in the soft, familiar accents of Southern Ireland, but it is clearly a Northern Ireland play. Its characters are not the loquacious, shamrock-hued types of most Irish stage literature; they are taciturn, Scottish-Irish Northerners (though no special point is made of this in the play, one way or the other).

Mr. Friel has a new play, The Loves of Cass McGuire, *whose world premiere is planned for 1966-67, either in New York or Dublin.*

Time: The present, just before Gar's departure for Philadelphia

Place: The small village of Ballybeg in County Donegal, Ireland

EPISODE I

SYNOPSIS: In the living quarters of County Councillor S.B. O'Donnell and his son Gar, behind the Ballybeg general store which they own and operate, the dining-living area called the "kitchen" occupies (at left) more than half the visible area of the ground floor. The large table is set for tea. Behind it is a breakfront for storing dishes. At left is a large clock. The door to the "scullery" is at left. The main exit to the store and beyond is upstage center. At right a door leads into Gar's bedroom—a small room with a window in the wall at right. In this room can be seen a bed, a dresser, a crockery jug and bowl for washing and, very prominently, a record player.

> *. . . Madge, the housekeeper, enters from the scullery with a tray in her hands and finishes setting the table. She is a woman in her sixties. She walks as if her feet were precious.*

Madge calls Gar for his tea. In from the shop door comes a young man, excited with the anticipation of leaving on a journey to Philadelphia in America, the next day. He is Gar—Public Gar, as differentiated from Private Gar, whom we will meet in a few moments.

> *The two Gars, Public Gar and Private Gar, are two views of the one man. Public Gar is the Gar that people see, talk to, talk about. Private Gar is the unseen man, the man within, the conscience, the alter ego, the secret thoughts, the id. Private Gar, the spirit, is invisible to everybody, always. (Ed. note: by "people" and "everybody" is meant all the characters in the play. Both Gars, Public and Private, played by two different actors, are audible and visible to the audience at all times.) Nobody except Public Gar hears Private Gar talk. But even Public Gar, although he talks to Private Gar occasionally, never sees him and never looks at him. One cannot look at one's alter ego.*

Gar—whose full name is Gareth Mary O'Donnell—grabs Madge and waltzes her around as she protests.

MADGE: Please, Gar . . .
PUBLIC GAR *(tickling her):* Will you miss me, I said?
MADGE: I will—I will—I will—I——

PUBLIC: That's better. Now tell me: What time is it?

MADGE: Agh, Gar——

PUBLIC: What time is it?

MADGE *(looking at clock):* Ten past seven.

PUBLIC: And what time do I knock off at?

MADGE: At seven.

PUBLIC: Which means that on my last day with him he got ten minutes overtime out of my hide.

> *He releases Madge.*

Instead of saying to me *(Grandly.)* "Gar, my son, since you are leaving me forever, you may have the entire day free," what does he do? Lines up five packs of flour and says *(In flat dreary tones.)* "Make them up into two-pound pokes.

MADGE: He's losing a treasure, indeed!

PUBLIC: So d'you know what I said to him? I just drew myself up and looked him straight in the eye and said to him: "Two-pound pokes it will be" —just like that.

MADGE: That flattened him.

> *She goes off to the scullery. He stands at the door and talks in to her.*

PUBLIC: And that wasn't it all. At six o'clock he remembered about the bloody pollock, and him in the middle of the Angelus *(Stands in imitation of the father; head bowed, hands on chest. In flat tones—)* "Behold-the-hand-maiden-of-the-Lord-Gut-and-salt-them-fish." So by God I lashed so much salt on those bloody fish that any poor bugger that eats them will die of thirst. But when the corpses are strewn all over Ballybeg, where will I be? In the little old U.S.A.! Yip-eeeeee! *(He swings away from the scullery door and does a few exuberant steps as he sings:)* "Philadelphia, here I come, rightah backah where Ah started from—"

> *He goes into his bedroom, flings himself down on his bed, rests his head on his hands, and looks at the ceiling. Sings alternate lines of "Philadelphia"—first half—with Private Gar, who is offstage.*

PUBLIC GAR: It's all over.

PRIVATE GAR *(offstage, in an echo-chamber voice):* And it's all about to begin. It's all over.

PUBLIC GAR: And all about to begin.

PRIVATE GAR *(now onstage):* Just think, Gar.

PUBLIC: Think . . .

PRIVATE: Think . . . Up in that big bugger of a jet, with its snout pointing straight for the States, and its tail belching smoke over Ireland; and you sitting up at the front *(Public acts this.)* with your competent fingers poised over the controls; and then away down below in the Atlantic you see a bloody bugger of an Irish boat out fishing for bloody pollock and—

> *Public nose-dives, engines screaming, machine-guns stuttering.*

Public and Private finish their fantasy of flying a plane and sinking a fishing boat. Then Public takes off his shop coat, rolls it up and throws it on the floor, and there is a fantasy of making a soccer goal, to the cheers of the crowd.

Then there is a fantasy of Gar defending himself before a judge for leaving Ireland to go to "a profane, irreligious, pagan country of gross materialism."

Madge comes in with an old suitcase, a rope to tie it up with and a bundle of Gar's clothes. She cannot see or hear Private Gar, of course. She speaks to Public Gar about his father, S.B. O'Donnell.

MADGE: . . . He's said nothing since, I suppose?

PUBLIC: Not a word.

PRIVATE: The bugger.

MADGE: But he hasn't paid you your week's wages?

PUBLIC: Three pounds, fifteen shillings—that'll carry me far.

MADGE: He'll have something to say then, you'll see. And maybe he'll slip you a couple of extra pounds.

PUBLIC: Whether he says goodby to me or not, or whether he slips me a few miserable quid or not, it's a matter of total indifference to me, Madge.

MADGE: Ay, so. Your tea's on the table—but that's a matter of total indifference to me.

PUBLIC: Give me time to wash, will you?

MADGE: And another thing: just because he doesn't say much doesn't mean that he hasn't feelings like the rest of us.

PUBLIC: Say much. He's said nothing!

MADGE: He said nothing either when your mother died. It must have been near daybreak when he got to sleep last night. I could hear his bed creaking.

PUBLIC: Well to hell with him—

MADGE (leaving): Don't come into your tea smelling like a lobster pot.

PUBLIC: If he wants to speak to me he knows where to find me! But I'm damned if I'm going to speak to him first!

Madge goes off to the scullery. Public calls after her.
And you can tell him I said that if you like!

PRIVATE: What the hell do you care about him. Screwballs! Skin-flint! Skittery Face! You're free of him and his stinking bloody shop. And tomorrow morning, boy, when that little ole plane gets up into the skies, you'll stick your head out the window *(Public acts this.)* and spit down on the lot of them!

> *S.B. O'Donnell appears at the shop door. He is in his late sixties. Wears a hat, a good dark suit, collar and tie, black apron. S.B. O'Donnell is a responsible, respectable citizen.*

S.B.: Gar!

Public reacts instinctively. Private keeps calm.

PRIVATE: Let the bugger call.

S.B. *(louder):* Gar!

> *Instinct is stronger than reason: Public rushes to his door and opens it. But as soon as he opens it and looks out at his father he assumes in speech and gesture a surly, taciturn gruffness. He always behaves in this way when he is in his father's company.*

PUBLIC: Aye?

S.B.: How many coils of barbed-wire came in on the mail-van this evening?

PUBLIC: Two or was it three?

S.B.: That's what I'm asking you. It was you that carried them into the yard.

PUBLIC: There were two—no, no, no three—yes, three—or maybe it was . . . was it two?

S.B.: Agh!

> *S.B. retires to the shop. Public and Private come back into the bedroom.*

Private tries to remember how many rolls of barbed wire there were, but he cannot; after tomorrow he won't care, anyhow.

Private assumes the fantasy role of Patrick Palinakis, head of a big American hotel chain, to whom Public is explaining his qualifications for a job. Public is 25, with one year at University College, Dublin (he quit because he realized the academic life was not for him). His father is in a business of many products. . . . Then Public breaks off the fantasy by rolling on the bed and reciting his own special verbal talisman, a charm to ward off all kind of spells: "It is now sixteen or seventeen years since I saw the Queen of France, then the Dauphiness, at Versailles."

Public puts the first movement of Mendelssohn's violin concerto on the record player; they fantasize an important concert; after which Public examines the battered suitcase. He finds it empty, except for a newspaper dated January 1, 1937—the day of his parents' wedding. The suitcase hasn't been opened since their honeymoon.

PRIVATE: She was small, Madge says, and wild, and young, Madge says, from a place called Bailtefree beyond the mountains; and her eyes were bright, and her hair was loose, and she carried her shoes under her arm until she came to the edge of the village, Madge says, and then she put them on . . .

PUBLIC: Eternal rest grant unto her, O Lord, and let perpetual light shine . . .

She was 19, and S.B. was 40, and maybe she cried herself to sleep many a night, and maybe it was good (Private thinks out loud) that she died three days after Gar was born. Private wrenches himself out of this mood: "It is now sixteen or seventeen years since I saw the Queen of France, etc."

Public changes the Mendelssohn for lively Ceilidhe Band music. He dances around, nodding to imaginary people on the dance floor. Private reminds Public that this tune was Katie Doogan's tune; he loved her once, does he love her still?

Public switches off the record player, flips out his wallet with its picture of Katie Doogan and sits contemplating it. Private curses Kate and her whole family, but Public blames himself for what happened that night, 10 months ago. While Private is describing what an ass Gar made of himself, Public goes off right. He soon returns at left, strolling with his sweetheart Kate; it is that night, 10 months before.

Gar and Katie Doogan are very much in love; their marriage plans are set; engaged at Christmas and married at Easter, but Gar can hardly wait. They plan to have fourteen children, seven boys and seven girls, the latter "gentle and frail and silly" like their mother.

But Kate fears that Gar's 3 pounds, 15 shillings a week isn't enough to live on. Public swears he'll ask for a raise, and he tells Kate his secret: he buys eggs from the farms and sells them to the Hotel at a profit, with S.B. none the wiser.

> *They kiss. Suddenly Kate breaks off. Her voice is urgent.*

KATE: We'll go now rightaway, and tell them.

PUBLIC: Who?

KATE: Mammy and Daddy. They're at home tonight.

> *She catches his arm and pulls him towards the left.*

Come on. Quickly. Now, Gar, now.

PUBLIC *(adjusting his tie):* God, Kathy, I'm in no—look at the shoes—the trousers—

KATE: What matter. It must be now, Gar, now!

PUBLIC: What—what—what'll I say?

KATE: That you want their permission to marry me next week.

PUBLIC: God, they'll wipe the bloody floor with me!

KATE: Gar!

> *She kisses him passionately. . . .*

Manfully, Public Gar tackles Senator Doogan—but before he can put the question, Doogan sends Kate into the house to greet a certain Francis King who is visiting; Francis King, whose father studied medicine while Senator Doogan was studying law, who will be a doctor and probably will get the good dispensary job. All the Doogans hope Francis King will marry Kate.

As Doogan crushes all Public Gar's hopes with this story, Private Gar is ridiculing the poor lover.

PRIVATE: . . . And all the time she must have known—the aul bitch!— And you promised to give her breakfast in bed every morning! And you told her about the egg money!

DOOGAN: . . . your father, Gareth?

PRIVATE: He's talking to you, thick-skull.

PUBLIC: What—what—what's that?

DOOGAN: Your father—how is he?

PUBLIC: Oh he—he—he's grand, thanks.

PRIVATE: Get out! Get out!

PUBLIC: Look, Mr. Doogan, if you'll excuse me, I think I'd better move on—

DOOGAN: Aren't you waiting for supper? The others will be along in a moment for—

PUBLIC: No, I must run. I've got to make up half-a-hundredweight of sugar bags.

PRIVATE: Brilliant!

PUBLIC: Say goodby to—

DOOGAN: Certainly—certainly. Oh, Gareth—
> *Public pauses. Doogan speaks awkwardly, with sincerity.*

Kate is our only child, Gareth, and her happiness is all that is important to us—

PRIVATE: *(sings):*
> Give the woman in the bed more porter—

DOOGAN: What I'm trying to say is that any decision she makes will be her own.

PRIVATE *(sings):*
> Give the man beside her water,
> Give the woman in the bed more porter—

DOOGAN: Just in case you should think that her mother or I were . . . in case you might have the idea . . .

PUBLIC *(rapidly):* Good night, Mr. Doogan. *(Rushes off.)*

DOOGAN: Goodby . . . Gareth.
> *Doogan stands lighting his pipe. Kate enters down right of Doogan and sees that Gar is no longer there.*

KATE: Where's Gar?

DOOGAN: He didn't seem anxious to stay.

KATE: But didn't he—did he—?

DOOGAN: No, he didn't.

The memory figures fade, as Public puts away the photo and washes up. Private is goading Public about Kate's marriage (which has now taken place) and Majorca honeymoon with up-and-coming Dr. King. Well, Private admits, maybe there are other fish in the sea, and maybe the Senator would have been pretty hard to take—harder even than S.B.

Private mimics S.B. drily giving his reasons for hardly ever travelling (it causes him to suffer from constipation).

Private and Public fantasize a street-corner pickup until Madge enters and scolds Gar: his tea is getting cold. They go into the dining room, and before Madge goes into her scullery she tells them her joyous news—her sister has just had another girl.

PUBLIC: How many's that you have now?

MADGE: Four grandnieces and three grandnephews. *(Pause.)* And they're going to call this one Madge—at least so she *says.*

PUBLIC: I'll send it a—a—a—an elephant out of my first wages! An elephant for wee Madge!

MADGE: I had a feeling it would be a wee girl this time. Maybe I'll take a run over on Sunday and square the place up for her. She could do with some help, with seven of them.

PUBLIC: You're a brick, Madge.

MADGE: Aye, so. *(As she goes to the scullery.)* Wee Madge, maybe . . .
> *Public sits at the table. Private leans against the wall beside him.*

PRIVATE: And now what are you sad about? Just because she lives for those Mulhern children, and gives them whatever few half-pence she has? Madge,

Madge, I think I love you more than any of them. Give me a piece of your courage, Madge.

> *S.B. enters from the shop and goes through his nightly routine. He hangs up the shop keys. He looks at his pocket watch and checks its time with the clock on the wall. He takes off his apron, folds it carefully, and leaves it on the back of his chair. Then he sits down to eat.*

S.B. performs these actions ponderously, and Private mocks him in a chattery monologue, calling him Screwballs. He ridicules the predictability of S.B.'s conversation by uttering the phrases before S.B. says them: "Another day over" and "I suppose we can't complain."

S.B. discusses rats: he didn't find as many about this year. He removes his false teeth—now his informality is complete, as also is Private's attitude of contempt.

> *As the following speech goes on all trace of humor fades from Private's voice. He becomes more and more intense and it is with an effort that he keeps his voice under control.*

PRIVATE: Screwballs, we've eaten together like this for the past twenty-odd years, and never once in all that time have you made as much as one unpredictable remark. Now, even though you refuse to acknowledge the fact, Screwballs, I'm leaving you forever. I'm going to Philadelphia to work in an hotel. And you know why I'm going, Screwballs, don't you. Because I'm twenty-five, and you treat me as if I were five—I can't order even a dozen loaves without getting your permission. Because you pay me less than you pay Madge. But worse, far worse than that, Screwballs, because—*we embarrass one another.* If one of us were to say, "You're looking tired" or "That's a bad cough you have," the other would fall over backways with embarrassment. So tonight do you know what I want you to do? I want you to make one unpredictable remark, and even though I'll still be on that plane tomorrow morning, I'll have doubts: maybe I should have stuck it out; maybe the old codger did have feelings; maybe I have maligned the old bastard. So now, Screwballs, say . . . *(Thinks.)* . . . "Once upon a time a rainbow ended in our garden" . . . say, "I like to walk across the White Strand when there's a misty rain falling" . . . say "Gar, son—" say, "Gar, you bugger you, why don't you stick it out here with me for it's not such a bad aul bugger of a place." Go on. Say it! Say it! Say it!

S.B.: True enough . . .

PUBLIC *(almost inaudibly):* Aye?

S.B.: I didn't find as many about the year.

Instinctively, Public cries aloud for Madge, then pretends he wants more bread. Madge, grumbling, remarking about the silence between father and son, goes to fetch it.

S.B. gives Public his week's pay ("It's all there—you needn't count it." "I didn't say I was going to count it, did I?"). Public knows it is no more, or less, than usual. Then Public offers his father more tea, and is refused; then silence as Private picks up his mockery where he left off. Madge comes in and out, again remarking on the silence that lies like a wall between any hope of father-son communication.

Private parodies a son asking his father's advice about emotional problems. Gar and his friends may all be sex maniacs. Why? Because they are unmarried; continuously boastful about their adventures with the fair sex; and, to a man, all virgins.

Master Boyle enters from the scullery.

> *He is around sixty, white-haired, handsome, defiant. He is shab-bily dressed; his eyes, head, hands, arms are constantly moving— he sits for a moment and rises again—he puts his hands in his pock-ets and takes them out again—his eyes roam around the room but see nothing. S.B. is barely courteous to him.*

S.B. excuses himself and goes into the store to get away from this tired old wreck of a schoolmaster with his mind on the bottle. Boyle confesses to Gar that he has had another run-in with the Canon, who doesn't fire him only be-cause the organization is behind Boyle. Boyle boasts that he has been offered a big teaching job in Boston.

Boyle elicits from Gar that Gar is leaving on the mail van the next morning at 7:15 o'clock; he is going to stay in Philadelphia with his mother's sister, his Aunt Lizzy Gallagher. Boyle knew Gar's mother, Maire, and might have been Gar's father if things had turned out differently. Boyle has brought Gar a book of Boyle's own poems as a going-away present along with the advice: "Don't look over your shoulder. Be one hundred per cent American." At the same time, Boyle, who is headed for the pub, needs a bit of a loan, and Gar willingly gives him a pound from his wages.

The gift from his old schoolmaster—the kind of a gesture he misses from his own father—has touched Gar deeply, and he is moved as they shake hands in parting. Emotion is Gar's enemy on this eve of his journey, and yet he longs to feel it.

BOYLE: . . . I'll—I'll miss you, Gar.
PRIVATE: For God's sake get a grip on yourself.
PUBLIC: Thanks for the book and for—
        Boyle embraces Public briefly.
PRIVATE: Stop it! Stop it! Stop it!
        Boyle breaks away and goes quickly off through the scullery. He bumps into Madge who is entering.
MADGE: Lord, the speed of him! His tongue out for a drink!
PRIVATE: Quick! Into your room!
MADGE: God knows I don't blame the Canon for wanting rid of that—
        Public rushes to the bedroom. Private follows.
Well! The manners about this place!
        She gathers up the tea things. Public stands inside the bedroom

door, his hands up to his face. Private stands at his elbow, speaking urgently into his ear.

PRIVATE: Remember—you're going! At seven-fifteen. You're still going! He's nothing but a drunken aul schoolmaster—a conceited, arrogant wash-out!

PUBLIC: O God, the Creator and Redeemer of all the faithful—

PRIVATE: Get a grip on yourself! Don't be a damned sentimental fool! *(Sings:)*

   Philadelphia, here I come—

PUBLIC: Maire and Una and Rose and Agnes and Lizzy and Maire—

PRIVATE: Yessir, you're going to cut a bit of a dash in them thar States! Great big sexy dames and night clubs and high living and films and dances and—

PUBLIC: Kathy, my own darling Kathy—

PRIVATE *(sings):*

   Where bowers of flowers bloom in the spring

PUBLIC: I don't—I can't.

PRIVATE *(sings):*

   Each morning at dawning, everything is bright and gay

   A sun-kissed miss says

   Don't be late

Sing up, man!

PUBLIC: I—I—I—

PRIVATE *(sings):*

   That's why I can hardly wait.

PUBLIC *(sings limply):*

   Philadelphia, here I come.

PRIVATE: That's it, laddybuck!

TOGETHER *(sing):*

   Philadelphia, here I come.

      Curtain.

EPISODE II

A short time later, Public is lying on the bed and Private is slumped in a chair. Private goads Public, prodding him to prevent the onset of homesickness in contemplation of the Philadelphia journey. Private breaks Public's train of sentimental thought with "It is now sixteen or seventeen years since I last saw the Queen, etc."

They fantasize an American political career for Gar; chairman of the Senate Foreign Aid Committee, investigating Doogan. They hear their beloved "aul fluke-feet" Madge moving around the dining area.

PUBLIC *(calls softly):* Madge.

   Private drops into the armchair. Public stands listening until the sound has died away.

PRIVATE *(wearily):* Off again! You know what you're doing, don't you, laddybuck? Collecting memories and images and impressions that are going to make you bloody miserable; and in a way that's what you want, isn't it?

PUBLIC: Bugger!

Public and Private go over the checklist of the trip—passport, vaccination certificate. Public re-reads his letter from Uncle Con and Aunt Lizzy, who will meet him at the airport. Gar will have the spare room in their apartment —TV, air conditioning, his own bathroom with shower. He starts work on the 23rd at the Emperor Hotel, owned by Mr. Patrick Palinakis, who is half-Greek and half-Irish.

And, P.S., there is no hurry about paying back the passage money.

As Public finishes reading the letter, Private reminds him of the visit Aunt Lizzy and Uncle Con and their friend Ben Burton paid to Ireland the previous September 8 (Public can't prevent it flashing into his mind that September 8 was also Kathleen Doogan's wedding day). Gar was so curious about his mother's sister, Aunt Lizzy, that he could hardly keep his eyes off her. Gar's memory of this visit is acted out in flashback.

> *Three people have moved into the kitchen: Con Sweeney, Lizzy Sweeney and Ben Burton. All three are in the 55 to 60 age region. Burton is American, the Sweeneys Irish-American. . . . The three guests have glasses in their hands. None of them is drunk, but Lizzy is more than usually garrulous. She is a small energetic woman, heavily made-up, impulsive. Con, her husband, is a quiet, patient man. Burton, their friend, sits smiling at his glass most of the time. As she talks, Lizzy . . . has the habit of putting her arm around, or catching the elbow of, the person she is addressing. This constant physical touching is new and disquieting to Public.*

Lizzy is walking around telling a story to the seated men and to Public (and Private) standing at the door of the bedroom. She is describing Gar's mother's wedding day; but she digresses into a warm appreciation of Ben Burton's friendship (she kisses him on top of his head). When the Sweeneys went out to American in 1937 (or 1938), Ben befriended them, gave them an apartment until Con found a job. But Gar wants to hear about his mother.

PUBLIC: You were telling us about that morning.

LIZZY: What's he talking about?

PUBLIC: The day my father and mother got married.

LIZZY: That day! Wasn't that something? With the wind howling and the rain slashing about! And Mother, poor Mother, may God be good to her, she thought that just because Maire got this guy with a big store we should all of got guys with big stores. And poor Maire—we were so alike in every way, Maire and me. But he was good to her. I'll say that for S.B. O'Donnell—real good to her. Where the hell is he anyhow? Why will S.B. O'Donnell, my brother-in-law, not meet me?

CON: He told you—he's away at a wedding.

LIZZY: What wedding?

CON: Some local girl and some Dublin doc.

LIZZY: What local girl? You think I'm a stranger here or something?

CON *(to Public):* What local girl?

PUBLIC: Senator Doogan's daughter.

PRIVATE: Kathy.

LIZZY: Never heard of him. Some Johnny-hop-up. When did they start having Senators about this place for Gawd's sake?

BEN *(to Public):* You have a senate in Dublin, just like our Senate, don't you?

LIZZY: Don't you start telling me nothing about my own country, Ben. You got your own problems to look after. Just you leave me to manage this place, okay?

BEN: Sorry, Elise.

LIZZY: Ben!
      She kisses the top of his head.

Madge comes in and out disapprovingly. Lizzy and Con both urge Gar to come to America to get a job. But Gar wants Lizzy to continue talking about his mother's wedding day.

PUBLIC: You were about to tell us about what Agnes whispered to you.

LIZZY *(crying):* Poor Aggie—dead. Maire—dead. Rose, Una, Lizzy—dead —all gone—all dead and gone . . .

CON: Honey, you're Lizzy.

LIZZY: So what?

CON: Honey, you're not dead.

LIZZY *(regarding Con cautiously):* You gone senile all of a sudden? *(Confidentially, to Ben.)* Give him no more to drink. *(To Con.)* For Gawds sakes who says I'm dead?

BEN: You're very much alive, Elise.
      She goes to him and gives him another kiss.

Lizzy transfers her slightly maudlin feelings for Ben to America itself ("Gawd's own country") where they have acquired color TV and $15,000 in Federal bonds, and a deep freeze, and a back yard, and Christmas—and Lizzy weeps again, this time because she and Con have no child of their own to share all this bounty. Gar is the only child of the five sisters, and Lizzy is tearfully prepared to offer him all they have, as well as all the love they have in them.

Ben goes to get the car. Lizzy is making a scene, she knows, but that's the way it has always been with the Gallagher girls, either laughing or crying, not like "the O'Donnells—you know—kinda cold."

Impulsively, Public Gar agrees to go to America (Private warns him: No!). Lizzy is overjoyed; this is what she came to Ireland for, this is why she is "half-shot-up." She throws her arms around Public and calls him "my son." Blackout.

When the lights come up, Public and Private are in the bedroom and the memory figures have gone. Private is needling Public with criticism of Aunt Lizzy—her grammar, her vulgarity, her lack of self-control. Public agreed to go to Philadelphia only because he had been softened up by the fact that it was Kathy's wedding day, plus his aunt's reference to "cold O'Donnells." Now the time for the trip has come, and Public begins to panic: "It is not sixteen or seventeen years since I saw . . ." but even this charm fails to work. Instinctively, he cries for Madge and then has to think up an excuse about his coat when Madge comes to see what's wanted.

As Public and Private leave to say goodby to "the boys" at the pub, Madge throws it in Gar's face that the boys did not come here to see *him*. Public, exiting, asks Madge to call him at 6:30 next morning.

S.B. enters and sits down to read his paper. Madge's emotions are being stirred by Gar's departure, and she takes it out on a surprised S.B. She reproaches him for sitting there in front of her without his teeth.

s.b. *(puzzled):* Eh?

madge: I mean it. It—it—it—it just drives me mad, the sight of you! *(The tears begin to come.)* And I have that much work to do: the stairs have to be washed down, and the store's to be swept, and your room has to be done out—and—and—I'm telling you I'll be that busy for the next couple of weeks that I won't have time to lift my head!

> She dashes off. S.B. stares after her, then out at the audience. Then, very slowly, he looks down at the paper again—it has been upside down—and turns it right side up. But he can't read. He looks across at Gar's bedroom, sighs, rises, and exits very slowly to the shop.

A moment or two later Public and Private Gar enter boisterously with "the boys"—Ned, Tom and Joe. They are joking and pulling bottles of stout from their pockets, opening them and filling glasses.

> . . . But their bluster is not altogether convincing. There is something false about it. Tranquility is their enemy; they fight it valiantly. At the beginning of this scene Gar is flattered that the boys have come to him. When they consistently refuse to acknowledge his leaving—or perhaps because he is already spiritually gone from them—his good humor deserts him. He becomes apart from the others. Ned is the leader of the group. Tom is his feed-man, subserviently watching for every cue. Joe, the youngest of the trio, and not yet fully committed to the boys' way of life, is torn between fealty to Ned and Tom and a spontaneous and simple loneliness over Gar's departure. Nothing would suit him better than a grand loud send-off party. But he cannot manage this, and his loyalty is divided. He is patently gauche, innocent, obvious.

They talk of playing football; they joke at Madge, who looks in on them sourly. Gar boasts to Madge that he met them on their way to call on *him*.

When Gar mentions that he'll be thinking of them when he's far away, Ned quickly shifts the conversation over to their favorite topic—women.

They have noticed two English blondes staying at the hotel, and a "big red thing"—one of the McFadden girls.

NED: Annie? Is Annie home?

JOE: Aye, she is. So I heard the mammy saying.

NED: Bloody great! That's me fixed up for the next two weeks! Were any of youse ever on that job?

JOE: No, I wasn't, Ned.

TOM: For God's sake, she wouldn't spit on you!

NED: Game as they're going, big Annie. But you need the constitution of a horse. I had her for the fortnight she was home last year and she damned near killed me.

PUBLIC: Big Annie from up beyond the quarry?

JOE: You know, Gar—the one with the squint.

NED (with dignity): Annie McFadden has no squint.

PUBLIC: Away and take a running race to yourself, Ned.

NED (with quiet threat): What do you mean?

PUBLIC: You were never out with big Annie McFadden in your puff, man.

NED: Are you calling me a liar?

PRIVATE (wearily): What's the point.

TOM (quickly): Oh, by God, Ned was there, Gar, manys and manys the time. Weren't you, Ned?

PUBLIC: Have it your own way.

JOE (nervously): And maybe she got the squint straightened out since I saw her last. All the women get the squints straightened out nowadays. Dammit, you could walk from here to Cork nowadays and you wouldn't see a woman with a—

NED: I just don't like fellas getting snottery with me, that's all.

In the short silence that follows, Private comments that there never used to be this tension with the boys, there used to be a lot of laughing. Tom jokes Ned out of his mood by reminding him about two girls from Greenock and a fat one from Dublin—lucky Ned, who preens himself as Tom reminds them all of Ned's power over women. But there is another silence.

Public begins to talk about Philadelphia, but again Ned quickly changes the subject, recalling a night at the caves with two Dublin skivvies from the Lodge. Ned tells how he and the boys went swimming, naked, except for little Jimmy Crerand, who stayed in the cave with the two women. The women took Jimmy's trousers off and chased after him until he ran home.

NED (to Public Gar): You missed that night.

TOM (mimicking Jimmy): "Save me, boys, save me!"

NED: I don't think we went to bed that night at all.

TOM: You may be sure we didn't.

NED: Powerful.

Another silence descends. After a few seconds Private speaks.

PRIVATE: We were all there that night, Ned. And the girls' names were Gladys and Susan. And they sat on the rocks dangling their feet in the water. And we sat in the cave, peeping out at them. And then Jimmy Crerand suggested that we go in for a swim; and we all ran to the far end of the shore; and we splashed about like schoolboys. Then we came back to the cave, and wrestled with one another. And then out of sheer boredom, Tom, you suggested that we take the trousers off Crerand—just to prove how manly we all were. But when Ned started towards Jimmy—five foot nothing, remember?—wee Jimmy squared up and defied not only the brave Ned but the whole lot of us. So we straggled back home, one behind the other, and left the girls dangling their feet in the water. And that was that night.

Public breaks the silence with more talk of the coming football game, but Ned has his mind on women. He bets that he can make it with one of the English girls at the Hotel—he is for a "dirty big booze-up" and then the women. Gar begs off because he must get up early. Joe hangs back, too, but Tom is ready to follow Ned, who declares that his blood is up.

Ned makes for the exit, apparently without any goodbys for Gar or any notice that Gar is leaving. But Ned pauses by the door.

> *. . . Ned begins taking off the broad leather belt with the huge brass buckle that supports his trousers.*

NED *(shyly, awkwardly):* By the way, Gar, since I'll not see you again before you go—

TOM: Hi! What are you at? At least wait till you're sure of the women!

NED *(impatiently to Tom):* Agh, shut up! *(To Public.)* If any of them Yankee scuts try to beat you up some dark night, you can . . .

> *Now he is very confused and flings the belt across the room to Public.*

. . . you know . . . there's a bloody big buckle on it . . . manys a get I scutched with it.

TOM: Safe enough, lads: he has braces on as well!

NED: I meant to buy you something good, but the aul fella didn't sell the calf to the jobbers last Friday . . . and he could have, the stupid bastard, such a bloody stupid bastard of an aul fella!

PUBLIC *(moved):* Thanks, Ned . . . thanks . . .

JOE: Damnit, I have nothing for you, Gar.

TOM *(quickly):* Are we for the sandbanks or are we not?

NED: You'll make out all right over there . . . have a . . .

TOM: I know that look in his eyes!

> *Ned wheels rapidly on Tom, gives him more than a playful punch.*

NED *(savagely):* Christ, if there's one get I hate, it's you! *(He goes off quickly.)*

Tom hesitates, then runs after Ned. Public urges Joe to go too, but Joe hasn't yet learned how to make himself believe his own fantasies, and he knows the pursuit of women is all make-believe: "Sure you know yourself they'll hang about the gable of the hotel and chat and do nothing." But Public encourages Joe to join the game of pretend, so that Joe begins to think his blood is up too. He prepares to leave.

JOE: Good luck, Gar. And tell Madge that the next time she asks us up for tea we'd bloody well better get it.
PUBLIC: She *asked* you?
JOE: That's why I was joking her about us keeping our word. As if we wanted tea, for God's sake! But I'd better catch up with the stirk before they do damage . . . So long, aul cock! *(He runs off.)*
PUBLIC: Madge . . . Oh God . . .

Private counsels Public: he would be like his friends, he would have to amuse himself with these immature pretenses at romantic adventure, were it not for Aunt Lizzy and Philadelphia. Now Public can remember the laughter without having to remember how really bleak and empty the so-called good times were. Experience will be refined by memory into "gold, precious gold."

There is a knock on the door; it is Gar's ex-sweetheart Kate, come to say goodbye. Public is constrained in his conversation, but Kate is very much at ease. She agrees with Gar that he will make a lot of money in America and come home with a million dollars, "driving a Cadillac and smoking cigars and taking movie-films."

This image, together with Kate's small-talk questions about his father, begins to release in Gar his pent-up emotion, his distress at leaving all that he loves. His feelings pour out of him in the form of aggressive vituperation at Ballybeg and all its inhabitants: his father, his friends, Master Boyle, everyone. Kate protests, "It isn't as bad as that—", but Gar insists it's a quagmire and everyone in it is crazy. He wouldn't stay another minute if you gave him the whole place. He is "free as the bloody wind."

KATE: All I meant was—
PUBLIC: Answerable to nobody! All this bloody yap about father and son and all this sentimental rubbish about "homeland" and "birthplace"—yap! Bloody yap! Impermanence—anonymity—that's what I'm looking for; a vast restless place that doesn't give a damn about the past. To hell with Ballybeg, that's what I say!

Politely, Kate takes her leave ("Goodby, Gar") and Gar can do no better than usher her out with friendly cliches like "name the first one after me."

> She is gone. Public returns and immediately buries his face in his hands.
PRIVATE: Kate . . . sweet Katie Doogan . . . my darling Kathy Doogan . . .
> Public uncovers his face and with trembling fingers lights a cigarette and takes a drink. As he does, Private continues very softly.
Oh my God, steady man, steady—it is now sixteen or seventeen years since I

saw the Queen of France, then the Dauphiness, at Versailles, and surely never lighted on this orb—Oh God, Oh my God, those thoughts are sinful *(Sings.)* as beautiful Kitty one morning was tripping with a pitcher of milk—
>*Public attempts to whistle his song, "Philadelphia Here I Come."*
>*He whistles the first phrase and the notes die away. Private keeps*
>*on talking while Public attempts to whistle.*

We'll go now, right away, and tell them—Mammy and Daddy—they're at home tonight—now, Gar, now—it must be now—remember, it's up to you entirely up to you—gut and salt them fish—and they're going to call this one Madge, at least so she *says*—
>*Public makes another attempt to whistle.*

—a little something to remind you of your old teacher—don't keep looking back over your shoulder, be one hundred per cent American—a packet of cigarettes and a pot of jam—seven boys and seven girls—and our daughters'll all be gentle and frail and silly like you—and I'll never wait till Christmas— I'll burst, I'll bloody well burst—goodby, Gar, it isn't as bad as that—goodby, Gar, it isn't as bad as that—goodby, Gar, it isn't as bad as that—

PUBLIC *(in whispered shout):* Screwballs, say something! Say something, father!
>*Quick curtain.*

EPISODE III

Part 1

A short time later, Madge, S.B. and Public are kneeling saying the rosary. But Gar doesn't have his mind on the prayers, and so Private is talking about Philadelphia, the time differential—then Gar's mind goes back to the rosary, and Private speaks its words in unison with Public.

Gar doesn't concentrate on the prayer for long. Soon Private is again rambling on, envisioning his interesting future as a bachelor type—a *romantic* bachelor type—who, at 43, may just possibly fall in love with a 19-year-old Russian princess.

Then Private concentrates on his father; does S.B. ever dream of the past, of "the young, gay girl from beyond the mountains who sometimes cried herself to sleep?"

PRIVATE *(softly, nervously, with growing excitement):* God—maybe— Screwballs—behind those dead eyes and that flat face are there memories of precious moments in the past? My God, have I been unfair to you? Is it possible that you have hoarded in the back of that mind of yours—do you remember—it was an afternoon in May—oh, fifteen years ago—I don't remember every detail but some things are as vivid as can be: the boat was blue and the paint was peeling and there was an empty cigarette packet floating in the water at the bottom between two trout and the left rowlock kept slipping and you had given me your hat and had put your jacket round my shoulders because there had been a shower of rain. And you had the rod in your left hand—I can see the cork nibbled away from the butt of the rod—and maybe we had been chatting—I don't remember—it doesn't matter—but between us at that moment there was this great happiness, this great joy—you must have felt it too—it was so much richer than a content—it was a great, great happiness, and active, bubbling joy—although nothing was being said—just the two of us fishing on a lake on a showery day—and young as I was I felt, I knew, that this was precious, and your hat was soft on the top of my ears—I can feel it—and I shrank down into your coat—and then, then for no reason at all except that you were happy too, you began to sing. *(Sings:)*

All round my hat I'll wear a green colored ribbono,
All round my hat for a twelve month and a day.
And if anybody asks me the reason why I wear it,
It's all because my true love is far, far away.

The rosary is over, but Public and Private do not notice until Madge and S.B. have risen to their feet. Tartly, Madge interrupts Gar's reverie. Embarrassed at being caught day-dreaming, Public and Private rise while Madge goes to get supper.

PRIVATE: Go on! Ask him! He must remember!

S.B.: The days are shortening already. Before we know we'll be burning light before closing time.

PRIVATE: Go on! Go on!

PUBLIC *(in the churlish, off-hand tone he uses to S.B.):* What ever happened to that aul boat on Lough na Cloc Cor.

S.B.: What's that?

PRIVATE: Again!

PUBLIC: That aul boat that used to be up on Lough na Cloc Cor—an aul blue thing—d'you remember it?

S.B.: A boat? Eh? *(Voices off.)* The Canon!

PRIVATE: Bugger the Canon!
     The Canon enters; a lean, white man with alert eyes and a thin mouth.

The Canon is joking with Madge as he enters. Madge has told him he waits to call "till the rosary's over and the kettle's on," and this tickles him. The Canon asks after the O'Donnell family, and S.B. pretends that all is as usual; this is a night like any other night. They begin their game of checkers.

The Canon alludes to Gar's imminent departure, but S.B. directs his attention back to the game. Private mocks their conventional small talk about the weather, and about the stakes in this contest: S.B. wants to raise them but the Canon makes it the usual, a half-penny a game.

Madge brings tea and biscuits. Public urges Madge to run over to her sister's and see the new baby, Public will do the washing-up. Before Madge leaves, Public tries to find out whether his mother went with Master Boyle before she went with S.B. Madge will tell him nothing, except that his mother married the better man.

Public takes his tea into his room and leaves the door open. But evidently Gar is still thinking about the two locked in checkers combat, because Private stands at the table between S.B. and the Canon, mocking them, while Public, in the bedroom, mimes all of Private's actions.

Private ridicules their concentration and their silence. He jokes at the human enigma of S.B.; no one can understand him except, possibly, the Canon —and here, in spite of himself, Private's tone changes from raillery almost to serious pleading. He wishes the all-understanding Canon would explain his father to him, would translate S.B. into some language that Gar could understand.

Private tries to sing a couple of bright, ribald songs, but somehow his song becomes "Auld Lang Syne." In the bedroom, Public puts the second movement of Mendelssohn's violin concerto onto the record-player.

> *The record begins. Private runs to the table and thrusts his face between the players.*

PRIVATE: Listen! Listen! Listen! D'you hear it? D'you know what the music says? *(To S.B.)* It says that once upon a time a boy and his father sat in a blue boat on a lake on an afternoon in May, and on that afternoon a great beauty happened, a beauty that has haunted the boy ever since, because he wonders now did it really take place or did he imagine it. There are only the two of us, he says; each of us is all the other has; and why can we not even look at each other? Have pity on us, he says; have goddam pity on every goddam bloody man jack of us.

> *He comes away from the table and walks limply back to the bedroom. When he gets to the bedroom door he turns, surveys the men.*

To hell with all strong silent men!

> *He goes into the bedroom, drops into the chair, and sits motionless. Public sinks back on to the bed again.*

The Canon notices a "noise." S.B. explains that it is one of Gar's records.

S.B.: All he asks is to sit in there and play them records all day.
CANON: It makes him happy.
S.B.: Terrible man for the records.
CANON: Just so, now. It'll be getting near his time, he tells me.
S.B.: Tomorrow morning.
CANON: Tomorrow morning.
S.B.: Aye, tomorrow morning. Powerful the way time passes, too.
CANON: You wait, says she, till the rosary's over and the kettle's on.
S.B.: A sharp one. Madge.
CANON: Ah-hah. There's hope for you yet.
S.B.: I don't know is there.
CANON: No. You're not too late yet.
S.B.: Maybe . . . maybe . . .
CANON: No, I wouldn't say die yet—not yet I wouldn't.
> *Slow curtain.*

Part 2

In the small hours of the morning, Gar's things are packed and lying in the dimly-lit "kitchen" just outside his bedroom door. Public is lying on the bed, Private sitting in the chair in the darkened bedroom.

S.B. enters from the scullery, carrying a cup of tea, shoeless, coatless, but with his hat on. He sits and looks at Gar's door and Gar's luggage. His cough wakes Gar up—Private alertly, Public sleepily.

Private reminds Public that with only four hours to go he is doing and seeing everything for the last time. Public shuts him up. He goes to get some aspirin, followed by Private, and discovers his father sitting at the dining table.

S.B. and Public admit that neither can sleep. Private tells Public: now's his chance to talk to his father. Public goes to get a cup of tea, returns, and reaches out for contact with S.B. in conversation about the routine matters of the shop, the dangling ends of business: a new tire for the van, an order of fence posts, the pliers, plug tobacco, new methods of heating and cooking, anything to keep the talk going. Private warns, "It's the silence that's the enemy." It's Gar who first refers to his departure.

PUBLIC: Better get these pills and then try to get a couple of hours sleep.

S.B.: You're getting the mail van to Strabane?

PUBLIC *(gives him a quick, watchful look):* At a quarter past seven.

S.B. *(awkwardly):* I was listening to the weather forecast there . . . moderate westerly winds and occasional showers, it said.

PUBLIC: Aye?

S.B.: I was thinking it—it—it—it would be a fair enough day for going up in thon plane.

PUBLIC: It should be, then.

S.B.: Showers—just like the Canon said . . . And I was meaning to tell you that you should sit at the back . . .

PRIVATE: It is now sixteen or seventeen years—the longest way round's the shortest way home—

S.B.: So *he* was saying, too . . . you know there—if there was an accident or anything—it's the front gets it hardest—

PUBLIC: I suppose that's true enough.

S.B.: So *he* was saying . . . not that I would know—just that he was saying it there . . .

PRIVATE *(urgently, rapidly):* Now! Now! He might remember—he might. But if he does, my God laddo—what if he does?

PUBLIC *(with pretended carelessness):* D'you know what kept coming into my mind the day?

S.B.: Eh?

PUBLIC: The fishing we used to do on Lough na Cloc Cor.

S.B. *(confused, on guard):* Oh, aye, Lough na Cloc Cor—aye—aye—

PUBLIC: We had a throw on it every Sunday during the season.

S.B.: That's not the day nor yesterday.

PUBLIC *(more quickly):* There used to be a blue boat on it—d'you remember it?

S.B.: Many's the fish we took off that same lake.

PUBLIC: D'you remember the blue boat?

S.B.: A blue one, eh?

PUBLIC: I don't know who owned it. But it was blue. And the paint was peeling.

S.B. *(remembering):* I mind a brown one the doctor brought from somewhere up in the—

PUBLIC *(quickly):* It doesn't matter who owned it. It doesn't even matter that it was blue. But d'you remember one afternoon in May—we were up there—the two of us—and it must have rained because you put your jacket round my shoulders and gave me your hat—

S.B.: Aye?

PUBLIC: —and it wasn't that we were talking or anything—but suddenly —suddenly you sang "All Round My Hat I'll Wear a Green Colored Ribbono"—

S.B.: Me?

PUBLIC: —for no reason at all except that we—that you were happy. D'you remember? D'you remember?

There is a pause while S.B. tries to recall.

S.B.: No . . . no, then, I don't . . .

Private claps his hands in nervous mockery.

PRIVATE *(quickly):* There! There! There!

S.B.: "All Round My Hat"? No, I don't think I ever knew that one. It wasn't "The Flower of Sweet Strabane," was it? That was my song.

PUBLIC: It could have been. It doesn't matter.

PRIVATE: So now you know: it never happened! Ha-ha-ha-ha-ha.

S.B.: "All Round My Hat"?—that was never one of mine. What does it go like?

PUBLIC: I couldn't tell you. I don't know it either.

PRIVATE: Ha-ha-ha-ha-ha-ha-ha-ha.

S.B.: And you say the boat was blue?

PUBLIC: It doesn't matter. Forget it.

S.B. *(justly, reasonably):* There was a brown one belonging to the doctor, and before that there was a wee flat-bottom—but it was green—or was it white? I'll tell you, you wouldn't be thinking of a punt—it could have been blue—one that the curate had down at the pier last summer—

Private's mocking laughter increases. Public rushes quickly into the shop. Private, still mocking, follows.

—a fine sturdy wee punt it was, too, and it could well have been the . . .

He sees that he is alone and tails off. Slowly he gets to his feet and goes toward the scullery door. He meets Madge entering. She is dressed in outside clothes. She is very weary.

Madge is just back from her sister's. The baby is fine—and they're going to call it Brigid (says Madge, swallowing her immense disappointment).

S.B. wants to talk, and he tells Madge he can manage the business all right without Gar; he doesn't have as many customers as he once did, he'll manage. He remembers the old days; he has *his* "blue boat" memories, too.

s.b: D'you mind the trouble we had keeping him at school just after he turned ten. D'you mind nothing would do him but he'd get behind the counter. And he had this wee sailor suit on him this morning—

MADGE: A sailor suit? He never had a sailor suit.

s.b.: Oh, he had, Madge. Oh, Madge, he had. I can see him, with his shoulders back, and the wee head up straight, and the mouth, aw, man, as set, and says he this morning, I can hear him saying it, says he, "I'm not going to school. I'm going into my daddy's business"—you know—all important—and, d'you mind, you tried to coax him to go to school, and not a move you could get out of him, and him as manly looking, and this wee sailor suit as smart looking on him, and—and—and at the heel of the hunt I had to go with him myself, the two of us, hand in hand, as happy as larks—we were that happy, Madge—and him dancing and chatting beside me—mind? You couldn't get a word in edge-ways with all the chatting he used to go through . . . Maybe, Madge, maybe it's because I could have been his grandfather, eh?

MADGE: I don't know.

s.b.: I was too old for her, Madge, eh?

MADGE: I don't know. They're a new race—a new world.

s.b. *(leaving):* In the wee sailor suit—all the chatting he used to go through . . . I don't know either . . .

Madge contemplates the suitcase; Gar will be mighty homesick for awhile, she believes. She tries saying "Brigid Mulhern" and then "Madge Mulhern" for the sound of the names: "Madge Mulhern—I don't know—it's too aul'-fashioned or something."

Madge fetches two pound notes from her dresser, money she'd been saving to have her feet attended to, and puts it in Gar's coat pocket for "a cup of tea on the plane." She muses that when S.B. was Gar's age "he was the very same as him: leppin' and eejitin' about and actin' the clown; as like as two peas." When Gar gets to be the same age that S.B. is now, Madge decides, "he'll turn out just the same. And although I won't be here to see it, you'll find he's learned nothing in-between times."

Public and Private come in from the shop. Madge lets Gar think that the baby is to be named Madge, as hoped.

PUBLIC: Did you tell her she's getting an elephant out of my first wages?

MADGE: Aye, so. The jars are up?

PUBLIC: They are.

MADGE: And the dishes washed?

PUBLIC: All done.

MADGE: I'll give you a call at half-six, then.

PUBLIC: Madge—Madge, you'd let me know if—if he got sick or anything?

MADGE: Who else would there be?

PUBLIC: Just in case . . . not that it's likely—he'll outlive the whole of us . . .

MADGE: Good night.

PUBLIC: Sleep well, Madge.

MADGE: Sleep well yourself.

Public and Private watch Madge shuffle off.

PRIVATE: Watch her carefully, every movement, every gesture, every little peculiarity: keep the camera whirring; for this is a film you'll run over and over again—Madge Going to Bed On My Last Night At Home . . . Madge . . .

Public and Private go into the bedroom.

God, boy, why do you have to leave. Why? Why?

PUBLIC: I don't know. I—I—I don't know.

Quick curtain.

THE LION IN WINTER

A Play in Two Acts

BY JAMES GOLDMAN

Cast and credits appear on page 400

JAMES GOLDMAN was born in Chicago in 1927. His father was a business man. He attended the University of Chicago as an undergraduate and Columbia as a graduate student until his studies there were interrupted by the Korean War. Following two years' military service, he began working toward his goal of becoming a playwright. He made it to Broadway in 1961 with the comedy Blood, Sweat and Stanley Poole *and in 1962 with the book for* A Family Affair, *both of these written in collaboration with his brother William. A play written on his own,* They Might Be Giants, *was staged in London in 1961 by Joan Littlewood.*

Mr. Goldman now lives in New York City with his wife Marie and his daughter Julia. The Lion in Winter *is his Broadway debut with a script written alone, without a collaborator.*

INTRODUCTION BY THE PLAYWRIGHT *

Comedy, as far as I'm concerned, is just as limited, particular and circumscribed a form as tragedy. They are, to oversimplify it, polar opposites. *Blithe Spirit* is no more a comedy, in this sense, than *The Petrified Forest* is a tragedy. Laughter, fundamentally, has little more to do with comedy than tears have to do with tragedy. One gets a good cry from *The Browning Version,* not from *King Lear.* Just as something larger and more terrible than tears comes out of tragedy, so something larger and more penetrating than a good laugh is the product and the aim of comedy.

* These comments appeared in an article by Mr. Goldman in the Sunday *Herald Tribune's New York* section and were chosen by him to introduce his play here.

The Lion in Winter is concerned with things that ordinarily are somber: hatred, vengeance, lost love, greed, the threat of death, to name a few. What must be realized, I think, is that the subject matter of comedy and tragedy is the same. All passions are equally available to each. It is only when the passions get specific and particular that we get one form or the other. There's not way to make a comedy of *Hamlet:* but there is a comic play in overwhelming hatred coupled with the inability to act. A man as driven as he is immobilized is stuff for comedy.

Ultimately, what seems to separate the two forms is the author's basic view of life. Those authors having one will tend to see existence as a comic or tragic enterprise. I tend to see it comic and the basic source of comedy for me —this year, at any rate—is this: that man, by nature, has a fundamental need to organize a world that won't be put in order.

We have a deep need to make sense of life. We've absolutely got to organize and classify. The world, however, won't be ordered. This is not to say that nature is chaotic. Rather, it is infinitely reorganizable. We see or feel or think new things and all life changes. Newton comes along or Freud or Keppler or Spinoza and the world is not the same. If, which I doubt, the day should come when there is nothing to discover, when at last we get things right, then comedy will stop.

Concretely, what this means is that we are forever trying to act logically on insufficient data. We tend never to know what we're really doing, what we truly want or how to get it but we spend our lives behaving as if we did. And this, it seems to me, is what comedy arises from.

This kind of comedy, left unadorned, tends to be heavily ironic, somewhat grim and not much fun. The elements of what we ordinarily understand as comedy—wit, humor, style, verve, bright coloring—are much to be desired. A comedy ought to be both fun and funny. There are no jokes in *The Lion in Winter,* but comic things go on and comic things get said. The fabric of the play was cut for laughter.

The Lion in Winter is only apparently historical. While founded on the facts we have, these facts reveal only the outcome of relationships—such things as who kills whom and when. The content of those relationships, the people and their passions, while congruent with the facts, are fictions. More important, though, are the content and the style of the piece which are—or, heaven knows, were meant to be—entirely contemporary.

The play, then, is an odd one. It is comedy but not the kind we're used to seeing. It wants to be amusing and upsetting both. It wants—because the people in it are—to be funny and a little terrifying. And above all, it wants to be a vision of a world with tears but without tragedy, with passion, pain and funny things all caught in bright clear comic light.

JAMES GOLDMAN

Time: Christmas, 1183

Place: Henry II's Castle at Chinon in France

ACT I

Scene 1

SYNOPSIS: The palace of Henry II, King of England, at Chinon is represented by a single setting of stone arches and pillars which can represent any part of the edifice. Changes of place are accomplished with banners, tapestries, Christmas decorations, etc., but there is very little furniture to hinder the movement to and fro of the royal characters. These personages are consistent with the few historical facts available but the projection of their personalities and emotions in detail is fictional. And:

> *The play, finally, contains anachronisms in speech, thought, habit, custom and so on. Those the author is aware of—the way, for instance, Christmas is celebrated—are deliberate and not intended to outrage the historical aspects of the script.*

At curtain rise the set represents the bedroom of Alais (pronounced Alice) Capet, dressed for a formal occasion and removing a crown from her head. She is 23, beautiful, in love with Henry Plantagenet, King of England, who is standing near the doorway.

> *Henry Plantagenet has just turned 50, an age at which, in his time, men were either old or dead. Not Henry. Though arthritis comes occasionally and new battle wounds don't heal the way the old ones did, he still is very nearly all he ever was. He is enjoying that final rush of physical and mental vigor that comes to some men not before the end but just before the start of the decline. He wears, as always, plain, dull, unimpressive clothes.*

Henry comments that "It's going to be a jungle of a day; if I start growling now I'll never last." He is trying to solve the problem of royal succession among his three sons—Richard, Geoffrey and John—and reunion with his wife. All are his potential enemies.

ALAIS: How great a matter am I?

HENRY: Alais, in my time I've known contessas, milkmaids, courtesans and novices, whores, gypsies, jades and little boys but nowhere in God's Western world have I found anyone to love but you.

ALAIS: And Rosamund.

HENRY: She's dead.

ALAIS: And Eleanor.

HENRY: The new Medusa? My good wife?

ALAIS: How is your Queen?

HENRY: Decaying, I suppose.

ALAIS: You haven't seen her?

HENRY: No, nor smelled nor touched nor tasted. Don't be jealous of the gorgon; she is not among the things I love. How many husbands do you know who dungeon up their wives? I haven't kept the great bitch in the keep for ten years out of passionate attachment. (*Extending his hand.*) Come. I've heard she's aging badly; let's go look.

ALAIS: Would it be troublesome if I betrayed you?

HENRY: We've no secrets, Eleanor and I. How can you possibly betray me?

ALAIS: I could give away your plans.

HENRY: You don't know what they are.

ALAIS: I know you want to disinherit Richard.

HENRY: So does Eleanor. She knows young Henry's dead. The young king died in summer and I haven't named an heir. She knows I want John on the throne and I know she wants Richard. We are very frank about it.

ALAIS: Henry, I can't be your mistress if I'm married to your son.

HENRY: Why can't you? Johnny wouldn't mind.

But Alais dislikes young John—he's pimply and unattractive. All Alais wants is Henry—but their relationship is under fire. Alais is the elder sister of Philip, King of France. Henry accepted Alais as a prospective bride for one of his sons when Alais was only seven years old, in order to acquire her dowry (a little province named the Vexin). Henry has come to love Alais himself and has made her his mistress, but her brother Philip wants either to see Alais truly married to a prince of England, or the dowry back. The latter alternative is out of the question, the Vexin is "vital" to Henry.

HENRY: It's been my luck to fall in love with landed women. When I married Eleanor, I thought: "You lucky man. The richest woman in the world. She owns the Aquitaine, the greatest province on the Continent—and beautiful as well." She was, you know.

ALAIS: And you adored her.

HENRY: Memory fails. There may have been an era when I did.

Gently arranging a wisp of her hair.

Let's have one strand askew; nothing in life has any business being perfect.

With her crown or without it, Alais must carry out Henry's plans, even though she pleads with him not to force her into marriage. Henry explains that it is necessary to secure the succession. John loves his father (Henry is convinced), so John is to be King and marry Alais.

Alais argues that none of Henry's conniving sons loves him. But Henry explains that it is natural for a prince to plot and snap his way toward the throne; he expects this of his sons. He "can hear the thinking through the walls."

Alais warns him she is going to fight to keep him; she is no longer the pliant, obedient adolescent. Henry avows that he doesn't intend to give her up, but he will "make an heir of John, a petty prince of Richard." Together Henry and Alais prepare to join their royal family gathering.

Dim and blackout.

Scene 2:

Now the setting represents the Reception Hall. It has acquired a refectory table, banners and a pile of holly boughs in a corner upstage.

Onstage at curtain rise are the three Plantagenet princes, Henry II's sons (his eldest son, Henry, having died the previous summer).

Richard Coeur de Lion, at 26, looks both like his father and his legend. He is taller than Henry, thick and powerful but at the same time graceful, handsome, impressive and exquisitely dressed. He has been a famous soldier since his middle teens and is thoroughly at home with power and politics.
Geoffrey, Count of Brittany, is 25, tall, thin, darkly attractive, quick of speech and movement; the best brain of a brainy family. John, at 16, does indeed have pimples. Shorter than his brothers and pudgy without being fat, he has a round open face and a sweet smile.

The princes are hanging up holly boughs and discussing their family and the succession to the throne. "I'm father's favorite; that's what counts," says John, and Richard warns: "I'm a constant soldier and sometime poet and I will be King." Geoffrey says nothing.

Eleanor enters.

Eleanor of Aquitaine is 61 and looks nothing like it. She is a truly handsome woman of great temperament, authority and presence. She has been a Queen of international importance for 46 years and you know it. Finally, she is that most unusual thing: a genuinely feminine woman thoroughly capable of holding her own in a man's world.

GEOFFREY *(delighted):* Mother.

ELEANOR: Geoffrey—oh but I do have handsome children. John—you're so clean and neat. Henry takes good care of you. And Richard. Don't look sullen, dear; it makes your eyes go small and piggy and your chin look weak. Where's Henry?

RICHARD: Upstairs with the family whore.

ELEANOR: That is a mean and tawdry way to talk about your fiancee.

JOHN: My fiancee.

ELEANOR: Whosever fiancee, I brought her up and she is dear to me and gentle. Have we seen the French King yet?

GEOFFREY: Not yet.

ELEANOR: Let's hope he's grown up like his father—simon pure and simon simple. Good, good Louis; if I'd managed sons for him instead of all those little girls, I'd still be stuck with being Queen of France and we should not have known each other. Such, my angels, is the role of sex in history. How's your father?

JOHN: Do you care?

ELEANOR: More deeply, lamb, than you can possibly imagine. Is my hair in place? I've given up the looking glass; quicksilver has no sense of tact.

RICHARD: He still plans to make John King.

ELEANOR: Of course he does. My, what a greedy little trinity you are: king, king, king. Two of you must learn to live with disappointment.

Henry enters with Alais on his arm.

HENRY: Ah—but which two?

ELEANOR: Let's deny them all and live forever.

HENRY: Tusk to tusk through all eternity. How was your crossing? Did the Channel part for you?

ELEANOR: It went flat when I told it to; I didn't think to ask for more. How dear of you to let me out of jail.

HENRY: It's only for the holidays.

ELEANOR: Like school. You keep me young. Here's gentle Alais.

Alais wants to curtsey, but Eleanor embraces her like one of her own— Eleanor was Alais's foster-mother from the age of 7. Henry has sent for the 17-year-old French King, Philip. He orders his sons to back him up in nego- tiations with Philip, and Eleanor warns that Philip is "quite impressive" for his age, as Philip enters.

> *Philip Capet is indeed gorgeous. He is tall, well-proportioned and handsome without being at all pretty. His manner is open, direct and simple and he smiles easily. He has been King of France for three years and has learned a great deal.*

Philip bows to Eleanor, then tells Henry: either Alais marries Richard or he takes the Vexin back immediately. Henry explains that he must leave be- hind him when he dies three contented sons, or there will be civil war. Richard already has the Aquitaine, he would be too powerful with Alais too, which would also give him Philip for an ally.

Nevertheless Philip will hold Henry to the original terms agreed on with his father King Louis. Henry refuses, calling Philip "boy."

PHILIP: I'm a king; I'm no man's boy.

HENRY: A king? Because you put your ass on purple cushions?

PHILIP: Sir. *(He turns on his heel, starts to go.)*

HENRY: Philip, you haven't got the feel of this at all. Use all your voices: when I bellow, bellow back.

PHILIP *(white with anger):* I'll mark that down.

Henry advises him also to mark that as kings they have their nations' peace in their hands and must treat it with civilized care. Coldly, Philip lets Henry

know he has his *own* advisers. As Philip leaves, Henry admits "You're better
at this than I thought you'd be," grinning at him. Philip, grinning back, exits
on the line "I wasn't sure you'd noticed."

Now, to his family assembled, Henry declares that he is no King Lear. The
nation he built will be passed on intact. Richard openly avows his intention
to fight to win Alais, Aquitaine and the crown for himself, then he departs,
characterizing his rival John as a "walking pustule."

John is petulantly offended but is told by Henry: go and eat. John obeys.
Geoffrey tells his parents he's to be King John's Chancellor.

GEOFFREY: It's not as nice as being King.

HENRY: We've made you Duke of Brittany. Is that so little?

GEOFFREY: No one thinks of crowns and mentions Geoff. Why is that? I
make out three prizes here—a throne, a princess and the Aquitaine. Three
prizes and three sons; but no one ever says, "Here, Geoff, here Geoff boy,
here's a bone for you."

HENRY: I should have thought that being Chancellor was a satisfying bone.

GEOFFREY: It isn't power that I feel deprived of; it's the mention that I
miss. There's no affection for me here. You wouldn't think I'd want that,
would you? *(Exit.)*

Eleanor decides she doesn't like any of their children except her foster-child
Alais. Eleanor remembers Rosamund Clifford, whom Henry brought from
Wales; Rosamund has been dead 7 years, 2 months and 18 days (Eleanor
made the numbers up to annoy Henry). But the memory also hurts Alais, who
suspects that Henry will leave her too some day. Alais declares herself too
easy a victim for Eleanor's sport, and leaves.

HENRY: She is lovely, isn't she?

ELEANOR: Yes, very.

HENRY: If I'd chosen, who could I have picked to love to gall you more?

ELEANOR: There's no one. *(Moving to the holly boughs.)* Come on; let's
finish Christmassing the place.

Henry admits that Eleanor doesn't look so bad for her age, and Eleanor im-
modestly agrees. For someone who has borne six girls and five boys and been
married to Henry 31 years, she is in good condition.

Henry admits that he misses Eleanor at times. He even admits that his attachment for Alais is "an old man's last attachment; nothing more."

HENRY: . . . How hard do you find living in your castle?

ELEANOR: It was difficult in the beginning but that's past. I find I've seen
the world enough. I have my maids and menials in my courtyard and I hold
my little court. It suits me now.

HENRY: I'll never let you loose. You led too many civil wars against me.

ELEANOR: And I damn near won the last one. Still, as long as I get trotted out for Christmas Courts and state occasions now and then—for I do like to see you—it's enough. Do you still need the Vexin, Henry?

HENRY: Need you ask?

His policy requires that he quarter troops there, 20 miles from Paris. Eleanor moves the first piece in the chess game between them: she threatens Henry that if Alais doesn't marry Richard, she'll see he loses the Vexin. Richard is to be King, not John. Eleanor doesn't really care . . . except that Henry cares so much, it is her instinct to thwart him.

Yes, Henry cares. During Philip's minority, without France as a constant threat, he has learned the pleasures of peace, of concerning his kingly self with cattle instead of armies. He wants the peace to continue and last.

HENRY: If you oppose me, I will strike you any way I can.

ELEANOR: Of course you will.

HENRY (taking her arm as before): We have a hundred barons we should look the loving couple for.

     They stand regally, side by side.

ELEANOR (smiling a terrible smile at him): Can you read love in that?

HENRY (nodding, smiling back): And permanent affection.

ELEANOR (as they start, grand and stately, for the wings): Henry?

HENRY: Madam?

ELEANOR: Did you ever love me?

HENRY: No.

ELEANOR: Good. That will make this pleasanter.

     Dim and blackout.

Scene 3

A short time later, in Eleanor's chamber, Eleanor is seated at a table wrapping Christmas presents. Richard enters; he has been summoned for what Eleanor hopes will be "a reunion." Eleanor says he looks well; she has followed his career as a great warrior; she loves him. But Richard doesn't believe her. He suspects that what she really loves is Aquitaine, which Richard holds at present. He tells his mother she is "so deceitful you can't ask for water when you're thirsty."

John and Geoffrey come in, closely followed by Henry and Alais. Brusquely, Henry tells them: the crown and Alais are to go to Richard. Richard is to be King.

JOHN: What about me? I'm your favorite, I'm the one you love.

HENRY: John, I can't help myself. Stand next to Richard. See how you compare. Could you keep anything I gave you? Could you beat him on the field?

JOHN: You could.

HENRY: But John, I won't be there.

JOHN: Let's fight him now.

HENRY: How can I? There's no way to win. I'm losing too, John. All my dreams for you are lost.

Power is the only fact, says Henry, so let's face it—Richard is the ablest and would simply seize the crown if Henry didn't give it to him. Richard is still sullen and suspects this gift of the crown and Alais. Henry informs them he's getting the one thing he wants most, an intact England.

Henry leaves them to discuss his decision. Alais follows him after declaring that among all this royalty "I'm the only pawn. I haven't got a thing to lose: that makes me dangerous."

John wonders: why is this happening to him, why is brother Richard his enemy? Why was his mother never close to him? When John was a child, Richard was "everything a little brother dreams of," says John in a rare moment of sincerity that moves Eleanor to try, for once, to mother him. But of course John wrenches away from her embrace, commenting "I'm the family nothing. Geoffrey's smart and Richard's brave and I'm not anything."

John orders Geoffrey to follow him out, but pragmatic Geoffrey sloughs John off; John is now a fallen candidate for power. John departs alone. Geoffrey offers Eleanor his services as Chancellor.

ELEANOR: It's a bitter thing your mummy has to say.

GEOFFREY: She doesn't trust me.

ELEANOR: You must know Henry isn't through with John. He'll keep the Vexin 'til the moon goes blue from cold and as for Richard's wedding day, we'll see the second coming first; the needlework alone can last for years.

GEOFFREY: I know. You know I know. I know you know I know, we know that Henry knows and Henry knows we know it. We're a knowledgeable family. Do you want my services or don't you?

ELEANOR: Why are you dropping John?

GEOFFREY: Because you're going to win.

They spar with one another. It's difficult to tell whether the devious Geoffrey is playing a double or triple game. Geoffrey has a gift for hating, Eleanor tells him, as Geoffrey declares his only hoped-for reward is the fun of watching Eleanor and Henry tearing each other to pieces.

Eleanor asks Geoffrey to be Richard's Chancellor. Since Geoffrey refuses with the word "rot" as he departs, Eleanor decides this must mean that Geoffrey will agree to help if they need him. "Scenes," she declares. "I can't touch my sons except in scenes."

Eleanor's next "scene" is to be with Richard, alone. He hands her a glass of wine, as she tells him she wants to see him King. But Richard knows the only thing she really wants is "Father's vitals on a bed of lettuce." For this, she would betray them all to Philip, or the Franks, or the Holy Romans.

RICHARD: You are Medea to the teeth but this is one son you won't use for vengeance on your husband.

ELEANOR: I could bend you. I could wear you like a bracelet—but I'd sooner die.

RICHARD: You're old enough to die, in any case.

ELEANOR: How my captivity has changed you. Henry meant to hurt me and he's hacked you up instead. More wine.

He takes the glass, goes and pours. Eleanor gazes at the hand that held the glass.

Men coveted this talon once. Henry was eighteen when we met and I was Queen of France. He came down from the North to Paris with a mind like Aristotle's and a form like mortal sin. We shattered the Commandments on the spot. I spent three months annuling Louis—and in spring, in May not far from here, we married. Young Count Henry and his Countess. But in three years time, I was his Queen and he was King of England. Done at twenty-one. Five years your junior, General.

RICHARD: I can count.

ELEANOR: No doubt the picture of your parents being fond does not hang in your gallery—but we were fond. There was no Thomas Becket then, or Rosamund. No rivals—only me. And then young Henry came and you and all the other blossoms in my garden. Yes, if I'd been sterile, darling, I'd be happier today.

RICHARD: Is that designed to hurt me?

ELEANOR: What a waste. I've fought with Henry over who comes next, whose dawn is it and which son gets the sunset and we'll never live to see it. Look at you. I loved you more than Henry and it's cost me everything.

RICHARD: What do you want?

ELEANOR: I want us back the way we were.

RICHARD: That's not it.

ELEANOR: All right, then. I want the Aquitaine.

She will see to it that Richard really acquires the throne and Alais—if Richard will promise her the Aquitaine. And she will make a will leaving everything to Richard.

Richard's reaction is the same as Geoffrey's: "rot." Wills can be burned or otherwise destroyed. Eleanor tries to arouse some filial emotion in Richard, but to no avail; he regards his mother as inhuman, dead and deadly.

ELEANOR: This won't burn. I'll scratch a will on this.

Baring her forearm, a small knife suddenly in her other hand.

To Richard, everything. *(She draws the blade across the flesh.)*

RICHARD: Mother!

ELEANOR: Remember how I taught you numbers and the lute and poetry.

RICHARD *(softly, as they hold each other)*: Mother.

ELEANOR: See? You do remember. I taught you dancing, too, and languages and all the music that I knew and how to love what's beautiful. The sun was warmer then and we were every day together.

Dim and blackout.

Scene 4

Immediately following, in the Reception Hall (which has now acquired a Christmas tree), John is drinking from a bottle. Geoffrey hurries in and begins a council of war with John, as though nothing had happened between them. But John is still smarting under Geoffrey's betrayal. Geoffrey explains: this was only to fool the others, and it has worked. John is Geoffrey's only way to power.

Geoffrey proposes a deal with Philip for a war to finish Richard off. "We're extra princes now," Geoffrey tells John. "You know where extra princes go." John wants to think this over.

Philip enters, early for an audience with Henry. Philip has been eavesdropping and wants John's answer: yes or no to war against Richard? Philip tells Geoffrey, "If John wants a war he's got one." John hasn't quite agreed, when Phillip and Geoffrey go off to hatch more plots—just as Henry enters with Alais.

John, petulant, cancels a birthday hunting trip with his father. John accuses Henry of not loving him, of giving everything to Richard, and then he goes off to find Philip.

HENRY: What in hell was that about?

ALAIS: He heard you disinherit him upstairs and wondered if you meant it.

HENRY: If I meant it? When I've fathered him and mothered him and babied him? He's all I've got. How often does he have to hear it? Every supper? Should we start the soup with who we love and who we don't?

ALAIS: I heard you promise me to Richard.

HENRY: You don't think I meant it?

It was part of his policy; he must somehow arrange to get the Aquitaine for John. Eleanor is opposing him, "wooing" Richard just to torture Henry (Henry has been eavesdropping on the scene between Eleanor and Richard).

Eleanor comes in laden with Christmas packages and sets them under the tree. Henry tells Alais he loves her in order "to keep her spirits up," and Alais exits.

Henry and Eleanor bargain together—Henry's aim is to leave a political structure behind him that will last. He wants Alais and the throne for Richard and Aquitaine for John. They digress when Eleanor mentions Rosamund.

HENRY: What's your count? Let's have a tally of the bedspreads you've spread out on.

ELEANOR: Thomas Becket's.

HENRY: That's a lie.

ELEANOR: I know it. Jealousy looks silly on us, Henry.

Henry has the documents for her to sign away the Aquitaine to John. What persuasion will he use? Torture? Bribes? Seduction? ("Save your aching arches. That road is closed.")

No, Henry has a richer prize than that to offer Eleanor: her freedom.

ELEANOR: You're good.

HENRY: I thought it might appeal to you. You always fancied travelling.

ELEANOR: Yes, I did. I even made poor Louis take me on Crusade. How's that for blasphemy? I dressed my maids as Amazons and rode bare breasted halfway to Damascus. Louis had a seizure and I damn near died of windburn but the troops were dazzled. Henry, I'm against the wall.

HENRY: Because I've put you there, don't think I like to see it.

Freedom is the one thing Eleanor craves; she'll sign away the Aquitaine in exchange for it, on one condition: that Alais's wedding take place immediately. Henry admits that he loves Alais, and this will hurt him (which is exactly what Eleanor wants). In another stab, Eleanor brings up old gossip about an affair between her and Henry's father, Geoffrey. Henry counterstabs with "Rosamund, I loved you."

But Henry will keep his part of the bargain—he shouts for a priest to perform the marriage, as Philip, John and Geoffrey come on from one side and Richard and Alais from the other. John, understanding that the marriage is to take place immediately, calls his mother "a bag of bile" and protests to his father.

Eleanor sends Geoffrey to get a bishop. Alais believes this situation is merely more of Henry's plotting, but Henry warns her that love or not, they are through, she is no Helen to fight wars over. As a sort of marriage procession forms around her, Alais appeals to her brother Philip, then to Henry.

ALAIS: . . . It makes no sense. Why give me up? What do you get? What are you gaining?

HENRY: Why, the Aquitaine, of course.

RICHARD (stopping dead): What's that?

HENRY: Your mother gets her freedom and I get the Aquitaine. (To Eleanor.) That is the proposition, isn't it? You did agree.

RICHARD (to Eleanor): Of course she did. I knew, I knew it. It was all pretense. You used me. God, and I believed you. I believed it all.

ELEANOR: I meant it all.

RICHARD: No wedding. There will be no wedding.

Henry demands that Richard go through with it; he has promised Philip, and all. But Richard defies him: "Damn the wedding and to hell with your position."

Philip calls Richard a dunce for not seeing that Henry is only feigning anger and doesn't really want the wedding at all. Henry turns his wrath on Philip, vowing that Alais will never marry while Henry is alive, or give back the Vexin either. Philip stands up to him, and then exits.

RICHARD: Listen to the lion. Flash a yellow tooth and frighten me.

HENRY: Don't spoil it, Richard—Take it like a good sport.

RICHARD: How's your bad leg?

HENRY: Better, thank you.

RICHARD: And your back and all the rest of it. You're getting old. One day you'll have me once too often.

HENRY: When? I'm fifty now. My God, boy, I'm the oldest man I know. I've got a decade on the Pope. What's it to be? The broadsword when I'm eighty-five?

RICHARD: I'm not a second son. Not now. Your Henry's in the vault, you know.

HENRY: I know; I've seen him there.

RICHARD: I'll have the crown.

HENRY: You'll have what Daddy gives you.

RICHARD: I am next in line.

HENRY: To nothing.

RICHARD: Then we'll have the broadswords now.

HENRY: This minute?

RICHARD: On the battlefield.

Richard has 2,000 men at Poitiers—but Henry has Richard and will hold him prisoner (Richard can have the run of the castle) until Richard agrees that John is to be King. Richard threatens to escape, and exits. John is happy again, and Geoffrey is happy—they exit. But Eleanor is not happy.

ELEANOR: I came close, didn't I? *(To Alais.)* I almost had my freedom and I almost had you for my son. I should have liked it, being free. *(To Henry.)* You played it nicely. You were good.

HENRY: I really was. I fooled you, didn't I? God, but I do love being King.

ELEANOR: Well, Henry, liege and lord, what happens now?

HENRY: I've no idea. I know I'm winning and I know I'll win but what the next move is—*(Looking at her closely.)* You're not scared?

ELEANOR: No.

Alais resents Henry's playing with her feelings like this. He tells her it's not possible for him to give her up.

Eleanor asks Henry if she may watch him and Alais kiss. She imagines it every night, and she wants to see how accurate her vision is.

HENRY *(turning to Alais, opening his arms):* Forget the dragon in the doorway: come. *(Holding her.)* Believe I love you, for I do. Believe I'm yours forever, for I am. Believe in my contentment and the joy you give me and believe—

> Breaking, turning to Eleanor.

You want more?

> Their eyes burn at each other. Then, turning slowly back to Alais.

I'm an old man in an empty place. Be with me.

> They kiss. Eleanor stands in the doorway, watching. Dim and blackout.

Scene 5

In Eleanor's chamber, shortly afterwards, Eleanor is alone and thinking out loud. She has lost this round, but four seasons will pass and next Christmas she will win. She picks up her crown and tells it that they are locked in for another year.

Geoffrey comes in to report: Richard is storming around the castle, with John in pursuit, calling him names.

Eleanor holds out the crown to Geoffrey, mockingly, and Geoffrey is hurt. He can remember back to this third birthday, and he can remember nothing but indifference from his parents. Why? Eleanor doesn't know. Perhaps she was indifferent to everything then, as (she tells Geoffrey) she used to hear Abelard speak without really listening to what he said, or caring. She'd listen now. But at the moment, she's sick of all her children and their cleverness.

John comes in to gloat; Richard to announce "The bastard's boxed us up." Richard is aching to get to Poitiers and war with Henry, but Eleanor explains to him that they've lost this round; Richard will be king, but not this year; go to bed and forget it.

Richard thinks out loud that John might die and puts his hand to his dagger. Eleanor expects such behaviour ("We all have knives. It is eleven eighty-three and we're barbarians.") but she wishes it were not so. Mass war, she tells them, is the result of individual hatreds, and if they could just love each other a little they might achieve the beginning of something like peace.

Geoffrey wonders: "While we hugged each other, what would Philip do?" John, startled, remembers that he has made an agreement with Philip for a war; now that Richard has fallen from favor and war is unnecessary, John must call it off before his father finds out. John rushes off. Eleanor sends Geoffrey after him to keep him away from Philip until Eleanor says they can meet. Then Eleanor sends Richard to find Philip, with orders to promise him anything—the Vexin, Brittany, anything—to spring Richard loose from the castle. Then, with Richard free and John out of favor, Eleanor will plan the next move. . . .

ELEANOR: I haven't lost. It isn't over. Oh, I've got the old man this time. The damn fool thinks he loves John, he believes it. That's where the knife goes in. Knives, knives . . . it was a fine thought, wasn't it. Oh, Henry, we have done a big thing badly. *(Looking for her mirror.)* Where's that mirror? I am Eleanor and I can look at anything. *(Gazing into the mirror.)* My, what a lovely girl. How could her king have left her?
  Dim and blackout.

Scene 6

In Philip's chambers, immediately following, Philip is making ready for bed (a canopied bed with curtains; the room also holds a tapestry, a chair and a table with decanter and glasses).

Geoffrey is the first to appear, and he comes right to the point with an offer to Philip.

GEOFFREY: All of England's land in France, from Normandy down to the Spanish border, once I'm King.

PHILIP: All that. What could I do that's worth all that?

GEOFFREY: By morning, I can be the chosen son. The crown can come to me. But once it does, once Henry's favor falls my way, the war begins.

PHILIP: We have so many wars. Which one is this?

GEOFFREY: The one that Richard, John and Eleanor will make. I'll have to fight to keep what Henry, in his rage, is going to give me.

Philip pretends that he might accept the offer. Geoffrey tells him he's on his way to Henry to tell him John is a traitor . . . and John bursts from behind the screen where he had been hiding. John is angry enough to want to kill Geoffrey, who is as cool and unperturbed. John has spoiled it all, says Geoffrey. Geoffrey wasn't *really* going to betray John to their father—but Philip would have.

Richard is heard approaching. Confused John—who no longer can tell who are his friends—and inscrutable Geoffrey hide behind the screen.

Richard unburdens himself to Philip; he must have soldiers to fight his father. Philip has not seen his boyhood friend Richard for two years, during which he's studied to be king; and Philip wants to know why did Richard never write to him? And why should he make Richard King and have doughty Richard to fight instead of "the cretin or the fiend?"

Richard wouldn't fight Philip, he argues—and besides, he offers him the Vexin and all of Geoffrey's Brittany in exchange for his assistance.

PHILIP: And in return, what do you want from me?

RICHARD: Two thousand soldiers.

PHILIP: And what else?

RICHARD: Five hundred knights on horse.

PHILIP: And what else?

RICHARD: Arms and siege equipment.

PHILIP: And what else?

RICHARD: I never wrote because I thought you'd never answer.
  Philip says nothing.
You got married.

PHILIP: Does that make a difference?

RICHARD: Doesn't it?

PHILIP: I've spent two years on every street in hell.

RICHARD: That's odd: I didn't see you there.
  Philip takes Richard's hand. They start moving to the bed.
You haven't said you love me.

PHILIP: When the times comes.

HENRY (*offstage calling*): Philip.

Richard hides in the bed, and Henry enters. He wants to reach a settlement with Philip. He knows his children will offer Philip whole provinces to fight Henry, who offers Philip peace.

Philip taunts Henry; he doesn't need Henry's friendship, or to fight Henry. He doesn't have to. Time is on his side; Henry is getting older each day, and therefore weaker. If Henry attacked him, Philip wouldn't even have to resist. He could yield province by province waiting for Henry to die.

Henry guesses that Philip will make an alliance with Richard—and then withdraw his forces before the fight starts. "Why fight Henry when his sons will do it for you?"

Henry bids Philip good night, and this really surprises Philip; he feels that negotiation and discussion should continue. But Henry declares he is satisfied, he was won this round.

PHILIP: . . . You haven't won a damn thing.

HENRY: I've found out the way your mind works and the kind of man you are. I know your plans and expectations. You have burbled every bit of strategy you've got. I know exactly what you will do and exactly what you won't. And I've told you exactly nothing. To these aged eyes, boy, that's what winning looks like. *Dormez bien.*

PHILIP: One time, when I was very small, I watched some soldiers take their dinner pig and truss it up and put the thing, alive and kicking, on the fire. That's the sound I'm going to hear from you.

HENRY: And I thought you lacked passion.

PHILIP: You—you made my father nothing. You were always better. You bullied him, you bellied with his wife, you beat him down in every war, you twisted every treaty, you played mock-the-monk and then you made him love you for it. I was there: his last words went to you.

HENRY: He was a loving man and you learned nothing of it.

PHILIP: I learned how much fathers live in sons. A king like you has policy prepared on everything. What's the official line on sodomy? How stands the Crown on boys who do with boys?

HENRY: Richard finds his way into so many legends. Let's hear yours and see how it compares.

PHILIP: He found me first when I was fifteen. We were hunting. It was nearly dark. I lost my way. My horse fell. I was thrown. I woke to Richard touching me. He asked me if I loved him—Philip, do you love me?—and I told him yes.

HENRY: I've heard much better.

PHILIP: You know why I told him yes? So one day I could tell you all about it. You cannot imagine what that yes cost. Or perhaps you can. Imagine snuggling to a chancred whore and, bending back your lips in something like a smile, saying, "Yes I love you and I find you beautiful." I don't know how I did it.

RICHARD (*charging from the bed*): No—it wasn't like that.

Richard believes that Philip loved him, and challenges him to pick up his sword and fight. But Philip declines, and Richard turns on his father. Henry always loved his eldest son Henry best and never paid Richard any attention. Richard never cared about the crown, he only wanted his father to love him.

Henry refuses to take the blame for Richard's emotional weakness. Besides, Richard always belonged to his mother, Eleanor. Henry thanks God that he has another son, John. Geoffrey leaps from hiding to tell Henry that he alone is a fit candidate to become King. Devious Geoffrey explains: Richard and John are both traitors. Richard offered Geoffrey the Chancellorship if he would advise John to commit treason. And John has done so.

Henry doesn't believe it, so Geoffrey pulls aside the tapestry to reveal John in hiding.

JOHN *(to Geoffrey, from the heart):* You turd.

HENRY: Well, John?

JOHN: It isn't what you think.

HENRY: What do I think?

JOHN: What Geoffrey said. I wouldn't plot against you, ever.

HENRY: I know; you're a good boy.

JOHN: Can I go now, please? It's late. I ought to be in bed.

HENRY: You fool.

JOHN: Me? What have I done now?

HENRY: Couldn't you wait? Couldn't you trust me? It was all yours. Couldn't you believe that?

JOHN: Will you listen to the grief.

HENRY: What do you think I built this kingdom for?

JOHN: Me? Daddy did it all for me? When can I have it, Daddy? Not until we bury you?

HENRY: You're just like them. And after all I've given you.

JOHN: I got it; I know what you gave.

HENRY: I loved you.

JOHN: You're a cold and bloody bastard, you are, and you don't love anything.

GEOFFREY: I'm it, I'm all that's left. Here, Father; here I am.

HENRY: My life, when it is written, will read better than it lived. Henry Fitz-Empress, first Plantagenet, a King at twenty-one, the ablest soldier of an able time. He led men well, he cared for justice when he could and ruled for thirty years, a state as great as Charlemagne's. He married, out of love, a woman out of legend. Not in Alexandria or Rome or Camelot has there been such a Queen. She bore him many children—but no sons. King Henry had no sons. He had three whiskered things but he disowned them. You're not mine. We're not connected. I deny you. None of you will get my crown. I leave you nothing and I wish you plague. May all your children breach and die. *(Moving unsteadily toward the door.)* My boys are gone. I've lost my boys. *(Stopping, glaring up.)* You dare to damn me, do you? Well, I damn you back. God damn you. All my boys are gone. I've lost my boys. Oh Jesus, all my boys.

   Blackout and curtain.

ACT II

Scene 1

Alais is preparing spiced wine at a brazier in Henry's chamber, a short time later. Somewhat earlier, Henry had wandered in and out, in a melancholy mood. Alais is ignorant of the events that took place in Philip's bedroom; but Eleanor, who comes in, is not.

Alais wonders whether Eleanor ever loved Henry. The two women talk of Rosamund. Eleanor resented Henry's giving Rosamund her seat at the head of the table, but she didn't hate Rosamund enough to poison her, as rumors have it.

ALAIS: Green becomes you. You must always wear it.

ELEANOR: Are you dressing me in envy?

ALAIS: I've tried feeling pity for you but it keeps on turning into something else.

ELEANOR: Why pity?

ALAIS: You love Henry but you love his kingdom too. You look at him and you see cities; acreage, coastline, taxes. All I see is Henry. Leave him to me, can't you?

ELEANOR: But I left him years ago.

ALAIS: You are untouchable. And I thought I could move you. Were you always like this? Years ago, when I was young and worshipped you, is this what you were like?

ELEANOR: Most likely. Child, I'm finished and I've come to give him anything he asks for.

ALAIS: Do you know what I should like for Christmas? I should like to see you suffer.

But Alais throws herself into Eleanor's arms with a cry of *"Maman,"* and Eleanor comforts her with a Christmas song. Henry comes in and sends Alais away so he can talk to Eleanor.

Both Henry and Eleanor pretend to be limp and beaten, like fighters trying to draw a careless punch. Eleanor pretends that she is willing to exchange even the Aquitaine for a little peace; she will sign away anything, if only she will be left alone locked up in England.

But Henry has decided he doesn't want her signature any more, he doesn't care any longer about John or Richard. He wants only one thing—a new wife. The Pope owes him a favor, he'll grant an annulment so that he can marry Alais. Why? He wants a son.

Eleanor is truly astonished. He has enough bastard sons to "populate a country town," not to speak of the three princes. Henry vilifies dead Henry ("vain, deceitful, weak and cowardly"), Geoffrey ("wheels and gears"), John, the traitor, and Richard . . .

HENRY: . . . How could you send him off to deal with Philip?

ELEANOR: I was tired. I was busy. They were friends.

HENRY: Eleanor, he was the best. The strongest, bravest, handsomest and from the cradle on you cradled him. I never had a chance.

ELEANOR: You never wanted one.

HENRY: How do you know? You took him. Separation from your husband you could bear. But not your boy.

ELEANOR: Whatever I have done, you made me do.

HENRY: You threw me out of bed for Richard.

ELEANOR: Not until you threw me out for Rosamund.

HENRY: It's not that simple. I won't have it be that simple.

ELEANOR: I adored you.

HENRY: Never.

ELEANOR: I still do.

HENRY: Of all the lies, that one is the most terrible.

ELEANOR: I know. That's why I saved it up for now.

And suddenly they are in each other's arms.

Oh Henry, we have mangled everything we've touched.

HENRY: Deny us what you will, we have done that. And all for Rosamund.

ELEANOR: No, you were right: it is too simple. Life, if it's like anything at all, is like an avalanche. To blame the little ball of snow that starts it all, to say it is the cause is just as true as it is meaningless.

HENRY: Do you remember when we met?

ELEANOR: Down to the hour and the color of your stockings.

HENRY: I could hardly see you for the sunlight.

ELEANOR: It was raining but no matter.

HENRY: There was very little talk as I recall it.

ELEANOR: Very little.

HENRY: I had never seen such beauty—and I walked right up and touched it. God, where did I find the gall to do that?

ELEANOR: In my eyes.

HENRY: I loved you.

ELEANOR: No annulment.

HENRY: What?

ELEANOR: There will be no annulment.

HENRY: Will there not.

ELEANOR: No; I'm afraid you'll have to do without.

HENRY: Well—it was just a whim.

ELEANOR: I'm so relieved. I didn't want to lose you.

HENRY: Out of curiosity, as intellectual to intellectual, how in the name of bleeding Jesus can you lose me? Do you ever see me? Am I ever with you? Ever near you? Am I ever anywhere but somewhere else?

ELEANOR: I'm not concerned about your geographical location.

HENRY: Do we write? Do I send messages? Do dinghies bearing gifts float up the Thames to you? Are you remembered?

ELEANOR: You are.

HENRY: You're no part of me. We do not touch at any point. How can you lose me?

ELEANOR: Can't you feel the chains.

HENRY: You know enough to know I can't be stopped.

ELEANOR: But I don't have to stop you; I have only to delay you. Every enemy you have has friends in Rome. We'll cost you time.

HENRY: What is this? I'm not moldering; my paint's not peeling off. I'm good for years.

ELEANOR: How many years? Suppose I hold you back for one; I can—it's possible. Suppose your first son dies; ours did—it's possible. Suppose you're daughtered next; we were—that, too, is possible. How old is Daddy then? What kind of spindly, ricket-ridden, milky, semi-witted, wizened, dim-eyed, gammy-handed, limpy line of things will you beget?

HENRY: It's sweet of you to care.

ELEANOR: And when you die, which is regrettable but necessary, what will happen to frail Alais and her puny prince? You can't think Richard's going to wait for your grotesque to grow?

HENRY: You wouldn't let him do a thing like that?

ELEANOR: Let him? I'd push him through the nursery door.

HENRY: You're not that cruel.

ELEANOR: Don't fret. We'll wait until you're dead to do it.

HENRY: Eleanor, what do you want?

ELEANOR: Just what you want: a king for a son. You can make more. I can't. You think I want to disappear? One son is all I've got and you can blot him out and call me cruel. For these ten years you've lived with everything I've lost and loved another woman through it all. And I'm cruel. I could peel you like a pear and God Himself would call it justice. Nothing I could do to you is wanton; nothing is too much.

So Henry threatens to go to Rome at once, and Eleanor counter-threatens him with war: Richard, Geoffrey, John, Eleanor of Aquitaine and Philip allied against him. At last they have a common cause—new sons.

Eleanor believes she has "got him." Still Henry threatens to hold them all locked up there at Chinon while he goes to Rome.

Eleanor offers him anything to give up this plan for an annulment. He refuses. Then she attacks him with her ultimate weapon (her certain knowledge of whether or not she had an affair with his father Geoffrey) at his weakest point (his uncertainty about whether or not this affair took place). She fires at Henry again and again: "I never touched you without thinking Geoffrey, Geoffrey" and "I've put more horns on you than Louis ever wore." This battering finally wears down his defenses.

ELEANOR: I loved your father's body. He was beautiful.

HENRY: It never happened.

ELEANOR: I can see his body now. Shall I describe it?

HENRY: Eleanor, I hope you die.

ELEANOR: His arms were rough, with scars here—

HENRY: Stop it!

ELEANOR: I can feel his arms. I feel them.

HENRY: AAH!

ELEANOR: What's that? Have I hurt you?

HENRY: Oh, my God, I'm going to be sick.

ELEANOR *(hurling it after him as he exits):* We did it. You were in the next room when he did it!

    Henry is gone.

Well, what family doesn't have its ups and downs?

    At the brazier, spreading her hands over it.

It's cold. I can't feel anything. *(Huddling close to the coals.)* Not anything at all. *(Hugging herself, arms around tight.)* We couldn't go back, could we, Henry.

    Dim and blackout.

Scene 2

In Alais's chamber early the next morning, Alais is asleep in a chair. Henry marches in briskly and wakes her up. They are packed, the train of attendants and supplies is ready, they are off to Rome for an annulment. They will be married by the Pope himself.

But Alais fears that Eleanor will find a way to stop them, even though Henry is "launching her for Salisbury," down the River Vienne, back to prison, by lunchtime. The boys are locked up deep in the wine cellar. Henry invites Alais to marry him, have five children and they'll call the first one Louis, in honor of France.

Alais construes the situation: the boys must be kept down "forever," or when Henry dies they will break out and kill Alais's children. That is her ultimatum. Kill them, or find himself "another widow."

HENRY *(so weary):* Incredible, but I have children who would murder children. Every time I've read *Medea,* I've thought: "Absurd. Fish eat their young, and foxes: but not us." And yet she did it. I imagine she was mad; don't you? Yes, mad she must have been. *(He rises.)*

ALAIS: Henry—are you going down?

HENRY: Down? Yes.

ALAIS: To let them out or keep them in?

HENRY: Could you say, to a child of yours, "You've seen the sunlight for the last time?"

ALAIS: Can you do it, Henry?

HENRY: Well, I'd be a master bastard if I did.

ALAIS: I must know. Can you?

HENRY: I shall have to, shan't I? *(He turns, starts for the door.)*

    Dim and blackout.

Scene 3

Immediately following, John is tapping a barrel and Richard holding two cups, in the wine-cellar dungeon. Barrelheads line the wall. There are candles and a table but no chairs.

GEOFFREY: Don't you know what's going to happen?

JOHN: No, and you don't either. You and your big cerebellum. *(Doing Geoffrey.)* "I'm what's left. Here, Daddy; here I am." And here you are.

RICHARD: But not for long.

GEOFFREY: You think we're getting out?

RICHARD: No; deeper in. The fortress at Vaudreuil has dungeons down two hundred feet. That's where I'd keep us.

GEOFFREY: And if I were Father, I'm not sure I'd keep the three of us at all. You don't take prisoners, do you, Dick. And with good reason. Dungeon doors can swing both ways but caskets have no hinges.

JOHN: I know you. You only want to frighten me.

GEOFFREY: John, the condition of your trousers, be they wet or dry, could not concern me less. I think I'm apt to die today and I am sweating, John. I'm sweating cold.

John is sure they'll be rescued, and Richard is determined not to beg his father. The dungeon door opens—but it is only Eleanor, carrying a covered breakfast tray as a gift for her boys before she sails down the river. She drops the tray onto the table with a great clank, and when she takes the cloth away the princes see that the tray is heaped with daggers and short swords.

The imputation is obvious. Eleanor tells them there is only one guard outside. Richard begins to organize his brothers, tells them "when you run, run hard." But Geoffrey has other ideas. If they stay, and Henry comes to the dungeon, it will be three knives against one.

John balks at murder and Eleanor recoils from Geoffrey and his suggestion. Geoffrey dares Eleanor to swear that murder wasn't on her mind when she brought the daggers. And, Geoffrey warns, she is in stalemate, because "warn him, it's the end of us: warn him not and it's the end of him."

Eleanor pretends to call the guard, but cannot. Richard decides that Geoffrey is right; they should stay. Bitterly, Richard denounces his mother for her feigned squeamishness: "You stand there looking like a saint in pain when you brought us the knives to do your work."

Eleanor calls Richard an "unnatural animal," and Richard tells her that he learned to fight Henry by watching her. She tried to kill Henry often enough, even with crossbowmen ("That was in the field."). Certainly she showed Richard that she wanted Henry dead; she tried to kill him. Why? "I wanted Henry back . . . I wanted Henry."

Watching Eleanor, Geoffrey begins to suspect that she will warn Henry. This, Eleanor declares, puts Geoffrey in stalemate, too. "You don't dare let me stay here and you don't dare let me go."

John jumps to get the cover back on the tray, as Henry enters, carrying an armful of large candlesticks. He fills them with candles and Alais, following with a taper, lights them.

Henry wonders aloud whether he can let them go, and Richard warns him: he'll never stop fighting Henry. What has he to fight with? Eleanor reveals the knives on the tray.

HENRY: . . . You're killers, aren't you? I am. I can do it. *(To Geoffrey.)* Take a knife. *(To Richard.)* Come on. What is it? Come for me.

RICHARD: I can't.

HENRY: You're Richard, aren't you?

RICHARD: But you're Henry.

HENRY: Please—we can't stop and we can't go back. There's nothing else.

JOHN: Daddy? Take me back. Please. Can't we try again?

HENRY: Again?

JOHN: We always have before.

HENRY: Oh yes—We always have.

JOHN *(running toward him, arms outstretched):* Oh, Daddy—
> *He comes skidding to a stop as Henry draws his sword, holds it dead still, leveled at John's vitals.*

ELEANOR: Go on. Execute them. You're the King. You've judged. You've sentenced. You know how.

HENRY: By God, I will. Come Monday and they'll hang you with the washing. There'll be princes swinging from the Christmas trees.

ELEANOR: Why wait? They are assassins, aren't they? This was treason, wasn't it? You gave them life—you take it.

HENRY: Who's to say it's monstrous? I'm the King. I call it just. *(To his sons.)* Therefore, I, Henry, by the Grace of God King of the English, Lord of Scotland, Ireland and Wales, Count of Anjou, Brittany, Poitou and Normandy, Maine, Gascony and Aquitaine do sentence you to death. Done this Christmas Day in Chinon in God's year eleven eighty-three.
> *He takes his sword and with the flat of it makes a great swipe at Richard's shoulder. It makes a stinging slap-crack of a sound. Richard staggers very slightly but beyond that neither moves nor registers a thing. A whimper is heard in the ensuing silence. It comes from Henry. Then, soft and thoughtful—*

Surely that's not what I intended. Children . . . children are . . . they're all we have.
> *Spent, shattered, unable to look at anyone or anything, he waves them from the room.*

Go on. I'm done, I'm done. I'm finished with you. Never come again.
> *John, Geoffrey and Richard exit.*

Alais senses that in some way Eleanor has contrived this, contrived to save her sons, knowing that they will kill Henry "the next time or the next." Eleanor always wins—except the one prize she really wants.

Henry embraces Alais to annoy Eleanor, then sends her away to wait for him. Henry feels that his life's work has been wasted because of Eleanor, she has brought him to this nothing, this dark cellar.

ELEANOR: Lost your life's work, have you? Provinces are nothing: land is dirt. I've lost you. I can't ever have you back again. You haven't suffered. I could take defeats like yours and laugh. I've done it. If you're broken, it's because you're brittle. You are all I've ever loved. Christ, you don't know what nothing is. I want to die.

Wait long enough and it will happen, Henry suggests. Eleanor smiles.

HENRY: We're in the cellar and you're going back to prison and my life is wasted and we've lost each other and you're smiling.
ELEANOR: It's the way I register despair. There's everything in life but hope.
HENRY: We have each other and for all I know that's what hope is.
ELEANOR: We're jungle creatures, Henry, and the dark is all around us. See them? In the corners, you can see the eyes.
HENRY: And they can see ours. I'm a match for anything. Aren't you?
ELEANOR: I should have been a great fool not to love you.
HENRY: Come along; I'll see you to your ship.
ELEANOR: So soon?
HENRY: There's always Easter Court.
ELEANOR: You'll let me out for Easter?
HENRY *(nodding):* Come the resurrection, you can strike me down again.
ELEANOR: Perhaps I'll do it next time.
HENRY: And perhaps you won't.
ELEANOR *(taking his arm, moving to go):* It must be late and I don't want to miss the tide.
HENRY *(as they go):* You know, I hope we never die.
ELEANOR: I hope so, too.
HENRY: You think there's any chance of it?
ELEANOR *(as they exit):* Oh, Henry.
HENRY: What about Methuselah?
ELEANOR: You think he lived?
　　　Curtain.

OUTSTANDING PERFORMANCES
1965-66

On this page: Richard Kiley as Don Quixote
In *Man of La Mancha*

Above, in victory with Irving
Jacobson as Sancho; *right,* in
defeat by the Knight of the
Mirrors (Jon Cypher)

Rosemary Harris
as Eleanor in
The Lion in Winter

Nicol Williamson as Bill
Maitland in *Inadmissible
Evidence* (FAR RIGHT)

Barbara Harris as Daisy
Gamble in *On a Clear
Day You Can See
Forever* (FAR LEFT)

Ian Richardson as
Marat in *Marat/Sade*

Mairin D. O'Sullivan as
Madge in *Philadelphia,
Here I Come!*

David Carradine as
Atahuallpa in *The Royal
Hunt of the Sun*
(FAR RIGHT)

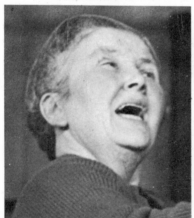

Zoe Caldwell as Polly in
The Gnadiges Fraulein,
part of *Slapstick Tragedy*
(FAR LEFT)

Paul Ford as Bascom
Barlow in *3 Bags Full*

Lauren Bacall as
Stephanie in
Cactus Flower

Michael O'Sullivan as
Dr. Abner Sedgwick in
Superman (FAR RIGHT)

Robert Preston as Henry
II in *The Lion in Winter*
(FAR LEFT)

Angela Lansbury as
Mame Dennis in *Mame*

Gwen Verdon as Charity
in *Sweet Charity*

Alan King as Doctor
Jack Kingsley in
The Impossible Years
(FAR RIGHT)

Henry Fonda as
Jim Bolton in
Generation (FAR LEFT)

Eamon Kelly as
S. B. O'Donnell in
*Philadelphia, Here
I Come!*

Lauren Bacall and Brenda Vaccaro (*left*) in a night club scene from *Cactus Flower*. Half-hidden behind them are Barry Nelson (*left*) and Arny Freeman

Above, Howard Bay's sketch for the thrust-stage setting of *Man of La Mancha. Below,* his sketches for two of that show's costumes by himself and Patton Campbell: Sancho (*left*) and the Knight of the Mirrors (*right*)

Above, Nicol Williamson, Lois Daine (his daughter) and Valerie French (his mistress) in John Osborne's *Inadmissible Evidence* from London

Below, Donal Donnelly *(front)* as Private Gar and Patrick Bedford as Public Gar, two halves of one character, in *Philadelphia, Here I Come!* from Dublin

The Persecution and Assassination of Marat as Performed by the Inmates of the Asylum of Charenton (*above*, played by members of The Royal Shakespeare Company) *Under the Direction of the Marquis de Sade* (*above*, played by Patrick Magee)—an importation from London more succinctly known as *Marat/Sade*. *Below*, sketches by Gunilla Palmstierna-Weiss for costumes in *Marat/Sade*, which was written by her husband, Peter Weiss.

Conquistadors encounter Incas in Peter Shaffer's *The Royal Hunt of the Sun.*
Pizarro (*second from right*) was played by Christopher Plummer; the Inca
chieftain Atahuallpa (*in background,* in his sun-like recess) by David Carradine

Two generations (Henry Fonda, father-in-law, Richard Jordan, son-in-law)
cooperate in folding sheets in William Goodhart's *Generation*

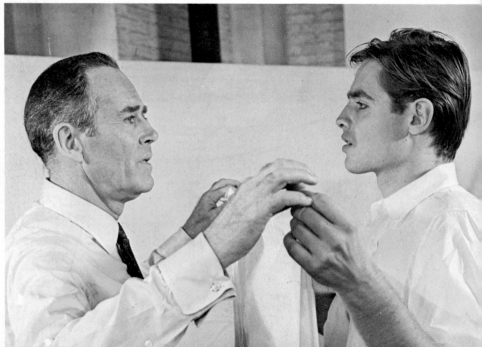

PORTRAITS OF THE SEASON

Above, Shepperd Strud-wick (*top*) and Jason Robards in *The Devils*

Above, Louis Gossett and Menasha Skulnik as *The Zulu and the Zayda*.

PHOTOS BY FRIEDMAN-ABELES

Above, Ruth Gordon and Ernest Truex in *A Very Rich Woman*

Left, Sarah Badel and Charles D. Gray in *The Right Honourable Gentleman*

MUSICALS

Angela Lansbury as Mame, with the ensemble, in the Jerry Herman number "Mame," from the musical *Mame* with book by Jerome Lawrence and Robert E. Lee. *Below* are two of Robert Mackintosh's *Mame* costume sketches— *at left,* for Mame herself and *at right* for Mame's best friend Vera Charles (played by Beatrice Arthur)

Above, the singing, dancing, instrument-playing cast of the South African revue *Wait a Minim!*; *below,* the *Sweet Charity* dancers doing Bob Fosse's "Rich Man's Frug"

FRIEDMAN-ABELES

Julie Harris dances for an assortment of spectators in *Skyscraper*

SAM SIEGEL

Above, Harry Secombe as Pickwick in *Pickwick*

Left, John Cullum and Barbara Harris in *On a Clear Day You Can See Forever*

A pair of thrillers: *Hostile Witness* (*left*) with Melville Cooper as the judge and Ray Milland as the defendant; *Wait Until Dark* (*below*) with Lee Remick as a blind girl victimized by villain Robert Duvall

The APA Repertory Company (*below*) was just one big happy family (including, seated on floor, Rosemary Harris and Clayton Corzatte) in their Broadway hit revival of *You Can't Take It With You*

In the royal parade in *The Lion in Winter* were Geoffrey (Dennis Cooney), John (Bruce Scott), Philip, King of France (Christopher Walken), Henry II (Robert Preston), Eleanor of Aquitaine (Rosemary Harris), Richard (James Rado) and Alais (Suzanne Grossmann). Their palace setting, Chinon, was designed by Will Steven Armstrong; so were their 12th century costumes (*left to right, below,* are Armstrong's sketches for Eleanor, Alais and Henry)

Janet Ward, Alan King and Jane Elliot played mother, father and daughter in *The Impossible Years*

Will Steven Armstrong designed a Madison Avenue town house in the art nouveau style for Jerome Chodorov's *3 Bags Full*. *Above* is Armstrong's sketch, carried out *at right* in a scene with Paul Ford, John Richards and Rufus Smith

"The Dadda" has a fainting spell in Joe Orton's *Entertaining Mr. Sloane* (with Lee Montague, George Turner, Sheila Hancock, Dudley Sutton)

VISITORS

Bavarian State Theater's *Die Ratten* (Max Mairich and Gerd Brüdern)

Harpagon (Michael Aumont) bends over a victim in The Comédie Français' *L'Avare*

Vivien Leigh and John Gielgud in *Ivanov*

MARTHA HOLMES

Faye Dunaway as Kathleen Stanton and Tom Ahearne as Mayor Quinn in William Alfred's verse drama *Hogan's Goat*

The Mad Show folk: MacIntyre Dixon, Marcia Rodd, Jo Anne Worley, Paul Sand, Dick Libertini

BERT ANDREWS

BROADWAY

Right, Gloria Foster as Medea in *Medea*

ADGER COWANS

Left, Judith Granite, Philip Baker Hall and Joe Servello in *The World of Gunter Grass*

Left, John Colicos (as Musgrave), Jeanne Hepple and Charlotte Jones in John Arden's *Serjeant Musgrave's Dance*

FRIEDMAN-ABELES

Avra Petrides (*standing*), John Karlen, Carolan Daniels, Jess Osuna in
Monopoly

Above, Jeremy Geidt in *The Trigon; left,*
Frank Langella and Carrie Nye in *The
White Devil*

LINCOLN CENTER REPERTORY

Above, a Jo Mielziner sketch for Repertory Theater of Lincoln Center's *Danton's Death. At left,* a scene from the production

PHOTOS BY PETER DANESS

Right, Lincoln Center's *The Caucasian Chalk Circle* (Beatrice Manley, Ronald Weyand, Ronnie Misa, Robert Symonds, Elizabeth Huddle)

THEATER AROUND THE UNITED STATES

IVOR PROTHEROE

Los Angeles Theater Group's production of *The Deputy* (*above,* with Ronald Long, Ian Wolfe, Philip Bourneuf, Alan Napier, Robert Brown), went on an extended tour. *Below,* Long Wharf Theater's (in New Haven, Conn.) production of *The Crucible* (foreground, Sally Noble)

New plays—*above,* Richard Halverson and Philip Kerr in Milton Geiger's *Carved in Snow* (about Edwin Booth), Cleveland Play House; *right,* Jon Voight and Dorothea Hammond in Loring Mandel's *Project Immortality,* Arena Stage, Washington; *below,* Rosemary Harris and Sydney Walker in Archibald MacLeish's *Herakles,* APA Repertory at University of Michigan

GEORGE DE VINCENT

Charles Gaines and Lester Rawlins in *A Man for All Seasons,* Buffalo Studio Theater

SHERWIN GREENBERG, MC GRANAHAN & MAY

WALT BURTON

Above, Mary Sinclair and Dennis Longwell in *Ghosts,* Cincinnati Playhouse in the Park; *left,* Jane McLeod, Edward Moore and Charles Kimbrough in Genet's *The Balcony,* Hartford, Conn., Stage Company

A GRAPHIC GLANCE

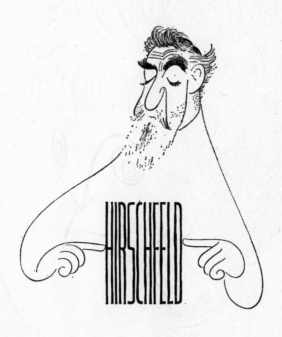

ZOHRA LAMPERT, SAM LEVENE AND ESTELLE WINWOOD IN
"NATHAN WEINSTEIN, MYSTIC, CONNECTICUT"

JULIE HARRIS AND CHARLES NELSON REILLY IN "SKYSCRAPER"

ROLAND CULVER, EDWARD ATIENZA, VIVIEN LEIGH, JOHN GIELGUD, JENNIFER HILARY,

ETHEL GRIFFIES, JOHN MERIVALE AND PAULA LAURENCE IN THE REVIVAL OF "IVANOV"

LOUIS GOSSETT AND MENASHA SKULNIK IN "THE ZULU AND THE ZAYDA"

ZOE CALDWELL, KATE REID AND MARGARET LEIGHTON IN
"SLAPSTICK TRAGEDY"

BEATRICE ARTHUR, ANGELA LANSBURY

AND JANE CONNELL IN "MAME"

MICHAEL KERMOYAN, IRRA PETINA, CONSTANCE TOWERS AND LILLIAN GISH
IN "ANYA"

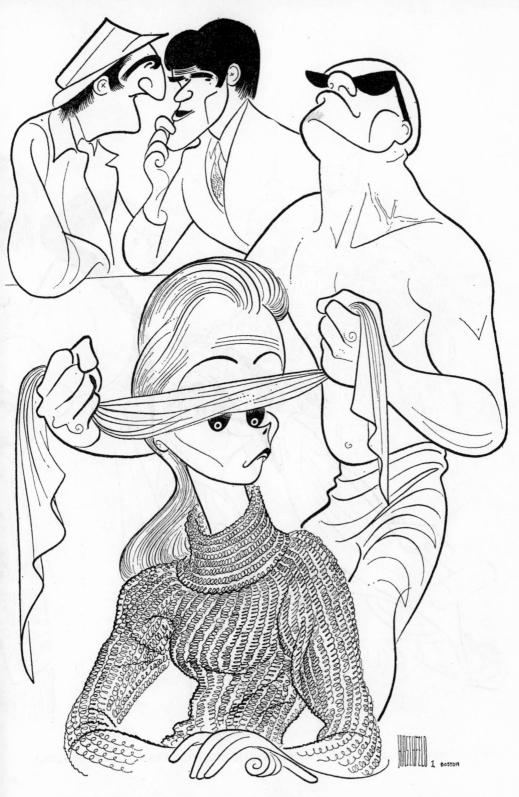

VAL BISOGLIO, MITCHELL RYAN, ROBERT DUVALL AND LEE REMICK
IN "WAIT UNTIL DARK"

EDWARD WINTER, ROBERT SYMONDS, ELIZABETH HUDDLE, GLENN MAZEN, BEATRICE

MANLEY, PAUL MANN AND BROCK PETERS IN "THE CAUCASIAN CHALK CIRCLE"

HELEN GALLAGHER, GWEN VERDON AND THELMA OLIVER IN "SWEET CHARITY"

PLAYS PRODUCED
IN THE
UNITED STATES

PLAYS PRODUCED ON BROADWAY

Figures in parentheses following title indicate number of performances. Plays marked with an asterisk (*) were still running on May 31, 1966, and their number of performances is figured from opening night through that date, not including previews or extra non-profit benefit performances.

HOLDOVERS FROM PREVIOUS SEASONS

Plays which were running on June 1, 1965 are listed below. More detailed information about them is to be found in previous Best Plays volumes of appropriate years. Important cast changes are recorded in a section of this volume.

* **Barefoot in the Park** (1,084). By Neil Simon. Opened October 23, 1963.

* **Hello, Dolly!** (989). Musical suggested by Thornton Wilder's *The Matchmaker;* book by Michael Stewart; music and lyrics by Jerry Herman. Opened January 16, 1964.

* **Any Wednesday** (951). By Muriel Resnik. Opened February 18, 1964.

What Makes Sammy Run? (540). Musical based on the novel by Budd Schulberg; book by Budd and Stuart Schulberg; music and lyrics by Ervin Drake. Opened February 27, 1964. (Closed June 12, 1965)

* **Funny Girl** (885). Musical with book by Isobel Lennart; music by Jule Styne; lyrics by Bob Merrill. Opened March 26, 1964.

The Subject Was Roses (832). By Frank D. Gilroy. Opened May 25, 1964. (Closed May 21, 1966)

* **Fiddler on the Roof** (702). Musical based on Sholom Aleichem's stories; book by Joseph Stein; music by Jerry Bock; lyrics by Sheldon Harnick. Opened September 22, 1964.

Golden Boy (568). Musical based on the play by Clifford Odets; book by Clifford Odets and William Gibson; music by Charles Strouse; lyrics by Lee Adams. Opened October 20, 1964. (Closed March 5, 1966)

* **Luv** (647). By Murray Schisgal. Opened November 11, 1964.

The Owl and the Pussycat (427). By Bill Manhoff. Opened November 18, 1964. (Closed November 27, 1965)

Bajour (232). Musical based on *New Yorker* stories by Joseph Mitchell; book by Ernest Kinoy; music and lyrics by Walter Marks. Opened November 23, 1964. (Closed June 12, 1965)

I Had a Ball (199). Musical with book by Jerome Chodorov; music and lyrics by Jack Lawrence and Stan Freeman. Opened December 15, 1964. (Closed June 12, 1965)

Baker Street (311). Musical based on stories by Sir Arthur Conan Doyle; book by Jerome Coopersmith; music and lyrics by Marian Grudeff and Raymond Jessel. Opened February 16, 1965. (Closed November 14, 1965)

Catch Me If You Can (103). By Jack Weinstock and Willie Gilbert. Opened March 9, 1965. (Closed June 5, 1965)

* **The Odd Couple** (510). By Neil Simon. Opened March 10, 1965.

This Was Burlesque (124). Revue based on Ann Corio's recollection of burlesque. Opened March 16, 1965. (Closed June 6, 1965)

Do I Hear a Waltz? (220). Musical with book by Arthur Laurents based on his play *The Time of the Cuckoo;* music by Richard Rodgers; lyrics by Stephen Sondheim. Opened March 18, 1965. (Closed September 25, 1965)

The Amen Corner (84). By James Baldwin. Opened April 15, 1965. (Closed June 26, 1965)

* **Half a Sixpence** (458). Musical based on H.G. Wells' *Kipps;* book by Beverley Cross; music and lyrics by David Heneker. Opened April 25, 1965.

The Glass Menagerie (175). Revival of the play by Tennessee Williams. Opened May 4, 1965. (Closed October 2, 1965)

Flora, the Red Menace (87). Musical based on Lester Atwell's novel *Love Is Just Around the Corner;* book by George Abbott and Robert Russell; music by John Kander; lyrics by Fred Ebb. Opened May 11, 1965. (Closed July 24, 1965)

The Roar of the Greasepaint—The Smell of the Crowd (231). Musical with book, music and lyrics by Leslie Bricusse and Anthony Newley. Opened May 16, 1965. (Closed December 4, 1965)

PLAYS PRODUCED JUNE 1, 1965—May 31, 1966

New York City Center Light Opera Company. Four musical revivals. **South Pacific** (15) based on James M. Michener's *Tales of the South Pacific;* book by Oscar Hammerstein II and Joshua Logan; music by Richard Rodgers; lyrics by Oscar Hammerstein II. Opened June 2, 1965. (Closed June 13, 1965). **The Music Man** (15) based on a story by Meredith Willson and Franklin Lacey; book, music and lyrics by Meredith Willson. Opened June 16, 1965. (Closed June 27, 1965). Plus *Guys and Dolls* and *Kiss Me Kate* (see 1964-65 *Best Plays* volume). Produced by the New York City Center Light Opera Company, Jean Dalrymple, director, at New York City Center.

SOUTH PACIFIC

Ngana	Dana Shimizu	Abner	Victor Duntiere
Jerome	Keenan Shimizu	Stewpot	Tom Pedi
Henry	Sab Shimono	Luther Billis	Alan North
Ensign Nellie Forbush	Betsy Palmer	Professor	Mickey Karm
Emile de Becque	Ray Middleton	Lt. Joseph Cable,	
Bloody Mary	Honey Sanders	U.S.M.C.	Richard Armbruster
Bloody Mary's Assistant	Maureen Tionco	Capt. George Brackett, U.S.N.	Murvyn Vye

Cmdr. William Harbison,
  U.S.N. ....Sam Kirkham
Yeoman Herbert Quale ....Walter P. Brown
Marine Sgt.
  Kenneth Johnson .....William C. Wendt
Seaman Richard West ....Ken Ayers
Seabee Morton Wise ....Scott Blanchard
Seaman Tom O'Brien ....Mel Gordan
Radio Operator
  Bob McCaffrey ....Gregg Nickerson
Staff Sgt. Thomas Hassinger ....Philip Lucas
Lt. Genevieve Marshall ....Carol Joplin
Ensign Dinah Murphy ....Terri Baker
Ensign Janet MacGregor ..Nancy McGeorge

Ensign Cora MacRae ....Renee Gorsey
Ensign Bessie Noonan ....Patricia O'Riordan
Ensign Connie Walewska ......Marlene Kay
Ensign Pamela Whitmore ..Dorothy Hanning
Ensign Sue Yaeger ....Jody Lane
Ensign Teya Ryan ....Mary E. Small
Ensign Lisa Minelli ....Maria Hero
Seaman James Hayes ....Philip Rash
Marine Cpl. Hamilton Steeves .Michael Quinn
Seaman John Clark ....Don Yule
Liat ....Eleanor A. Calbes
Lt. Buzz Adams ....Stan Page
Shore Patrol Officer ....Joe Bellomo

Standby: Miss Sanders—Doris Galiber. Understudies: Mr. North—Mickey Karm; Mr. Armbruster—Stan Page; Mr. Vye—Phil Lucas; Mr. Kirkham—Scott Blanchard; Mr. Pedi—Mike Quinn; Mr. Page—Joe Bellomo; Mr. Karm—Phil Rash; Miss Calbes—Maureen Tionco.

Directed by James Hammerstein; musical director, Anton Coppola; dance director, Albert Popwell; scenery, Jo Mielziner; costumes, Stanley Simmons; lighting, Peggy Clark; production stage manager, Herman Shapiro; stage managers, Chris Ryan, Beau Tilden; press, Tom Trenkle.

Time: World War II. Place: two islands in the South Pacific.

South Pacific was first produced April 7, 1949, by Richard Rodgers, Oscar Hammerstein II, Leland Hayward and Joshua Logan at the Majestic Theater for 1,925 performances. It was revived at the City Center May 4, 1955, for 15 performances; April 24, 1957, for 23 performances, and April 26, 1961, for 23 performances.

THE MUSIC MAN

Travelling Salesmen ......Russell Goodwin,
  John Herbert, Jack Davison, Ronald
  Stratton, Howard Kahl, Joseph Carow,
  Ronn Forella
Charlie Cowell ....Alan Dexter
Conductor ....Van Stevens
Harold Hill ....Bert Parks
Mayor Shinn ....Milo Boulton
The Buffalo Bills
  Ewart Dunlop ....Al Shea
  Oliver Hix ....Wayne Ward
  Jacey Squires ....Vern Reed
  Olin Britt ....Dale Jones
Marcellus Washburn ....Art Wallace

Tommy Djilas ....William Glassman
Marian Paroo ....Gaylea Byrne
Mrs. Paroo ....Sibyl Bowan
Amaryllis ....Garda Hermany
Winthrop Paroo ....Dennis Scott
Eulalie Mackecknie Shinn ....Doro Merande
Zaneeta Shinn ....Sandy Duncan
Gracie Shinn ....Roma Hermany
Alma Hix ....Adnia Rice
Maud Dunlop ....Jeanne Schlegel
Ethel Toffelmier ....Amelia Varney
Mrs. Squires ....Paula Trueman
Constable Locke ....Van Stevens

River City Townspeople and Kids: Robin Adair, Rita Agnese, Barbara Beck, Carol B. Bostick, Bonnie Gene Card, Joanna Crosson, Suzanne Crumpler, Joan Lindsay, Sandra Ray, Alice Mary Riley, Joy Serio, Betty Chretien, Peggy Cooper, Laurie Franks, Jodell Ann Kenting, Ora McBride, Addi Negri, Jeannette Seibert, Peggy Wathen, Lynn Wendell, Joseph Carow, Ronn Forella, Carlos Macri, David Moffat, Eric Paynter, Michael Scotlin, Ronald Stratton, George Tregre, Gary Wales, Arthur Whitfield, Austin Colyer, Jack Davison, Russell Goodwin, John Herbert, Howard Kahl, Ben Laney, Ripple Lewis, Dan Resin, Van Stevens.

Understudies: Miss Byrne—Laurie Franks; Mr. Boulton—Russell Goodwin; Miss Bowan—Adnia Rice; Mr. Wallace—Ripple Lewis; Mr. Glassman—Arthur Whitfield; Miss Duncan—Bonnie Gene Card; Mr. Scott—Michael Maitland; Miss Rice—Betty Chretien; Miss Varney—Addi Negri; Garda Hermany—Roma Hermany; Mr. Reed—Ben Laney; Mr. Shea—Austin Colyer; Mr. Ward—Dan Resin; Mr. Jones—Russell Goodwin; Misses Schlegel and Trueman—Lynn Wendell.

Directed by Gus Schirmer Jr.; musical director, Liza Redfield; choreography, Vernon Lusby (based on the original by Onna White); scenery and lighting, Howard Bay; costumes, Raoul Pène du Bois; vocal arrangements, Herbert Greene; orchestrations, Don Walker; dance arrangements, Lawrence Rosenthal; production stage manager, Chester O'Brien; stage managers, Bert Wood, Maxine Taylor; press, Tom Trenkle.

Time: 1912. Place: River City, Iowa.

The Music Man was first produced by Kermit Bloomgarden with Herbert Greene (in association with Frank Productions, Inc.) at the Majestic Theater, December 19, 1957, for 1,375 performances.

Music Theater of Lincoln Center. Two musical revivals. **Kismet** (48). Book by Charles Lederer and Luther Davis, based on the play by Edward Knoblock; music and lyrics by Robert Wright and George Forrest, based on themes by Alexander Borodin. Opened June 22, 1965. (Closed July 31, 1965). **Carousel** (48). Based on Ferenc Molnar's *Liliom;* book and lyrics by Oscar Hammerstein II; music by Richard Rodgers. Opened August 10, 1965. (Closed September 18, 1965). Both musicals produced by the Music Theater of Lincoln Center, Richard Rodgers, president and producing director, at the New York State Theater at Lincoln Center for the Performing Arts.

KISMET

Imam ....Rudy Vejar	Chief Policeman ....Alfred Toigo
Muezzins ......Grant Spradling, Paul Veglia,	Second Policeman ....Allen Peck
Vincent Henry, Martin Jewell	The Wazir of Police ....Henry Calvin
Mullah ....Julius Fields	Wazir's Guards ....Nick Littlefield,
First Beggar ....Earle MacVeigh	Jerry Meyers
Second Beggar ....Robert Lamont	Lalume ....Anne Jeffreys
Third Beggar ....Andre St. Jean	Attendants ......Henry Baker, James Wamen
Dervishes ....Buddy Bryan, Eddie James	The Princesses of Ababu ....Reiko Sato,
Omar ....Don Beddoe	Diana Banks, Nancy Roth
A Public Poet,	The Caliph ....Richard Banke
later called Hajj ....Alfred Drake	Slave Girls ....Michele Evans, Carol Hallock,
Marsinah, his daughter ....Lee Venora	Eleanore Kingsley, Ingeborg Kjeldsen
A Merchant ....Neil McNelis	A Servant ....Paul Veglia
Hassan-Ben ....Frank Coleman	Princess Zubbediya of Damascus ..Sally Neal
Jawan ....Truman Gaige	Ayah to Zubbediya ....Anita Alpert
The Bangle Man ....Rudy Vejar	Princess Samaris of Bangalore .Beatrice Kraft
Street Dancer ....Sally Neal	Prosecutor ....Earle MacVeigh
Akbar ....Buddy Bryan	The Widow Yussef ....Anita Alpert
Assiz ....Eddie James	

Singers: Bonnie Glasgow, Bobbi Lange, Joyce McDonald, Lucille Perret, Susan Sanders, Wanda Saxon, Bonnie Ellen Spark, Henry Baker, Frank Coleman, Vincent Henry, Martin Jewell, Richard Khan, Nick Littlefield, Neil McNelis, Bob Neukum, Allen Peck, Grant Spradling, Paul Veglia.

Dancers: Joanne DiVito, Marti Hespen, Shai Holsaert, Indra-nila, Bette Scott, Susan Sigrist, Jenny Workman, Julius Fields, Andre St. Jean.

Understudies: Mr. Drake—Earle MacVeigh; Miss Jeffreys—Ingeborg Kjeldsen; Miss Venora—Joyce McDonald; Mr. Calvin—Alfred Toigo; Mr. Banke—Rudy Vejar; Mr. Beddoe—Truman Gaige; Mr. Gaige—Robert Lamont; Mr. Toigo—Allen Peck; Miss Alpert—Susan Sanders; Mr. Peck—Nick Littlefield; Mr. MacVeigh—Richard Khan; Mr. Lamont—Andre St. Jean; Mr. Coleman—Neil McNelis; Misses Sato, Banks, Roth—Joanne DiVito; Messrs. Bryan, James—Julius Fields; Miss Neal—Jenny Workman; Miss Kraft—Bette Scott; Misses Evans, Hallock, Kingsley, Kjeldsen—Bobbi Lange; Miss Alpert—Bonnie Ellen Spark.

Directed by Edward Greenberg; choreography and musical staging, Jack Cole; musical director, Franz Allers; scenery, Lemuel Ayers; costumes, Frank Thompson; lighting, Peter Hunt; orchestrations and choral arrangement, Arthur Kay; production stage manager, Bill Ross; stage manager, Ben Strobach; press, Richard Maney.

Time and Place: one day in Baghdad.

Kismet was first produced on Broadway by Charles Lederer at the Ziegfeld Theater (with Alfred Drake in the role of Hajj), December 3, 1953, for 583 performances.

CAROUSEL

Carrie Pipperidge ....Susan Watson	Jigger Craigin ....Jerry Orbach
Julie Jordan ....Eileen Christy	Hannah ....Jenny Workman
Mrs. Mullin ....Benay Venuta	Boatswain ....Birl Jonns
Billy Bigelow ....John Raitt	Arminy ....Dixie Carter
Policeman ....Thomas Barry	Captain ....John Dorrin
Mr. Bascombe ....Ralston Hill	Heavenly Friend
Nettie Fowler ....Katherine Hilgenberg	(Brother Joshua) ....Gwyllum Evans
Enoch Snow ....Reid Shelton	Starkeeper ....Edward Everett Horton

ANNE JEFFREYS, ALFRED DRAKE AND LEE VENORA IN THE REVIVAL

OF "KISMET"

Louise	Linda Howe	Enoch Snow Jr.	Alan Johnson
Carnival Boy	Birl Jonns	Principal	John Dorrin

Singers: Lynn Carroll, Ronn Carroll, Dixie Carter, Cathy Corkill, Gene Davis, Audrey Dearden, John Dorrin, Dorothy Emmerson, Cleo Fry, Ben Laney, Terry Marone, Laried Montgomery, Bob Neukum, Lucille Perret, Joseph Pichette, Philip Rash, Sean Walsh, Peggy Wathen.

Dancers: Bonnie Gene Card, Dennis Cole, Richard Cousins, Victor Duntiere, Lois Etelman, Frank Hoopman, Anita Jones, Linda Keeler, Lucia Lambert, Arnott Mader, Richard Oliver, Carol Perea, J. Hunter Ross, Terry Ryland, Eva Marie Sage, Melissa Stoneburn, Kathy Wilson, Toodie Wittmer.

Standby: Mr. Raitt—Jerry Orbach. Understudies: Miss Christy—Dorothy Emmerson; Miss Watson—Dixie Carter; Mr. Shelton—Philip Rash; Miss Hilgenberg—Cleo Fry; Mr. Orbach—Thomas Barry; Mr. Horton—Gwyllum Evans; Mr. Evans—Ralston Hill; Mr. Hill—John Dorrin; Mr. Barry—Ronn Carroll.

Directed by Edward Greenberg; choreography, Agnes de Mille; musical director, Franz Allers; scenery, Paul C. McGuire; costumes, Stanley Simmons; lighting, Peter Hunt; orchestrations, Don Walker; choreography restaged by Gemze de Lappe; production stage manager, Bill Ross; stage manager, George Quick; press, Richard Maney.

Time: 1873-1888. Place: the New England Coast in Maine.

Carousel was first produced on Broadway by the Theater Guild at the Majestic Theater (with John Raitt in the role of Billy Bigelow), April 19, 1945, for 890 performances. It was revived by the Theater Guild at the City Center, January 25, 1949, for 48 performances, and by the New York City Center Light Opera Company at the City Center, June 2, 1954, for 79 performances and September 11, 1957, for 24 performances.

Oliver! (64). Return engagement of the musical based on Charles Dickens' *Oliver Twist;* book, music and lyrics by Lionel Bart. Produced by David Merrick and Donald Albery at the Martin Beck Theater. Opened August 2, 1965. (Closed September 25, 1965)

Oliver Twist ....Victor Stiles	At the Thieves' Kitchen:
At the Workhouse:	Fagin ....Robin Ramsay
Mr. Bumble, the Beadle .....Alan Crofoot	The Artful Dodger ....Joey Baio
Mrs. Corney, the Matron ...Dawna Shove	Nancy ....Maura K. Wedge
Old Sally, a pauper ....Sherill Price	Bet ....Donnie Smiley
At the Undertaker's:	Bill Sikes ....Danny Sewell
Mr. Sowerberry,	At the Brownlow's:
the Undertaker ....John Miranda	Mr. Brownlow ....Bram Nossen
Mrs. Sowerberry, his wife ....Sherill Price	Dr. Grimwig ....Fred Miller
Charlotte, their daughter ...Lynda Sturner	Mrs. Bedwin ....Dodi Protero
Noah Claypole,	
their apprentice ....Billy Brandon	

Workhouse Boys and Fagin's Gang: Tommy Battreall, Paul Dwyer, Anthony Endon, Eugene Endon, Lee Koenig, Greg Lange, Bart Larsen, Christopher Month, Jackie Perkuhn, Sonny Rocco, Ricky Rosenthal, Brett Smiley.

Londoners: Walter Blocher, Ted Bloecher, Reese Burns, Dominic Chianese, Sally Cooke, Marise Counsell, Georgia Dell, Walter Hook, Lesley Hunt, Michael McCormick, Richard Miller, Moose Peting, Terry Robinson, Virginia Sandifur, Gretchen Van Aken, Richard Wulf.

Understudies: Mr. Ramsay—Richard Miller; Miss Wedge—Gretchen Van Aken; Mr. Crofoot—Fred Miller; Miss Shove—Georgia Dell; Mr. Nossen—Walter Hook; Mr. Miller—John Kimbro; Mr. Sewell—Richard Wulf; Miss Price—Marise Counsell; Mr. Miranda—Dominic Chianese; Mr. Stiles—Mr. Smiley; Misses Sturner and Smiley—Lesley Hunt; Mr. Brandon—Michael McCormick; Miss Protero—Georgia Dell.

Directed by Peter Coe; scenery and costumes, Sean Kenny; orchestrations, Eric Rogers; musical director, Robert McNamee; lighting, John Wyckham; technical supervisor, Ian Albery; production stage manager, Ben D. Kranz; stage manager, Geoffrey Johnson; press, Lee Solters, Harvey B. Sabinson, Jay Russell.

Oliver is a foreign play previously produced in England. It was first produced on Broadway by David Merrick and Donald Albery at the Imperial Theater, January 6, 1963, for 774 performances.

Mrs. Dally (53). By William Hanley. Produced by Martin Gabel at the John Golden Theater. Opened September 22, 1965. (Closed November 6, 1965)

Evalyn ....Arlene Francis	Sam ....Ralph Meeker
Frankie ....Robert Forster	

Understudy: Messrs. Forster and Meeker—Jim Oyster.

Directed by Joseph Anthony; scenery and lighting, David Hays; costumes, Ann Roth; production stage manager, Paul A. Foley; press, Harvey B. Sabinson, Lee Solters, Bob Ullman.

Time: the present. Place: an apartment in New York City. Part 1: Mrs. Dally Has A Lover (an afternoon in January). Part 2: Today Is Independence Day (a morning in July).

Middle-aged Mrs. Dally reaches out for love and reassurance, but she is disappointed both by her lover, who is immature, and her husband Sam, who is preoccupied with his own shortcomings and guilt feelings in the death of their son. Part 1 is an extensive re-working of Mr. Hanley's one-act play *Mrs. Dally Has a Lover,* presented off Broadway Oct. 1, 1962 for 48 performances.

New York City Opera fall and spring repertory included revivals of works which originated on Broadway: **The Saint of Bleecker Street** (2) words and music by Gian Carlo Menotti, opened September 29, 1965; **Street Scene** (6) with music by Kurt Weill, book by Elmer Rice based on his play, lyrics by Lanston Hughes, opened February 24, 1966; **The Consul** (3) words and music by Gian Carlo Menotti, opened March 17, 1966. (Repertory closed March 27, 1966). Produced by New York City Opera, *The Saint of Bleecker Street* at New York City Center and *Street Scene* and *The Consul* at the New York State Theater of Lincoln Center.

PERFORMER	"THE SAINT OF BLEECKER STREET"	"STREET SCENE"	"THE CONSUL"
Florence Anglin		Shirley Kaplan	
Richard Armbruster		Steve Sankey	
Joan August		1st Nursemaid	
Ludmilla Azova			Anna Gomez
Donna Babbs		Grace Davis	
Herbert Beattie			Police Agent
William Beck	Salvatore		
Jack Bittner		George Jones	Assan
Tom Brooke		Charlie Hildebrand	
Gene Bullard			The Magician
Don Carlo		Dr. Wilson	
Elizabeth Carron		Anna Maurrant	Foreign Woman
Nico Castel		Abraham Kaplan	
William Chapman		Frank Maurrant	
Catherine Christensen		Rose Maurrant	
L. D. Clements		Daniel Buchanan	
Paul Corder		Fred Cullen	
Kay Creed		Mrs. Hildebrand	
Anita Darian	Maria Corona		
Jack DeLon		Lippo Fiorentino	
Philip Erikson			1st Plainclothesman
Beverly Evans			The Secretary
Elisabeth Farmer			Vera Boronel
Harriet Greene		Salvation Army Girl	
Muriel Greenspon	Assunta	Olga Olsen	
Don Henderson	Bartender		
Betsy Hepburn		Jennie Hildebrand	
Lila Herbert		3rd Graduate	
George S. Irving		Carl Olsen	
Mary Jennings	Carmela		
Jodell Kenting	Young Woman	2d Nursemaid	
Ruth Kobart		Emma Jones	
Richard Krause	1st Guest		
William Ledbetter	2d Guest		
Sondra Lee		Mae Jones	
William Lewis		Sam Kaplan	
Dolores Mari		Greta Fiorentino	
Barney Martin		Vincent Jones	
Mabel Mercer			Voice on Record
Julia Migenes	Annina		
Sherrill Milnes			John Sorel
Janet Morris		2d Graduate	
Leslie Morris		Joan	
Wendy Morris	Concettina	Violin Girl	
Robert Mosley		Henry Davis	
Patricia Neway			Magda Sorel
Mark Novak		Joe	
Bruce Papa		Willie Maurrant	
Richard Park			2d Plainclothesman
Alan Peterson		Dick McGann	
Anne Pretzat		Salvation Army Girl	

	"THE SAINT OF		
PERFORMER	BLEECKER STREET"	"STREET SCENE"	"THE CONSUL"
Seth Riggs		Harry Easter	
Evelyn Sachs			The Mother
Anthony Safina	Young Man		
David Smith		Officer Murphy	Mr. Kofner
Malcolm Smith	Don Marco		
Jeanne Tanzy		Mary Hildebrand	
Harry Theyard	Michele		
Debbie Thomas		Myrtle	
Clyde Ventura	Dumb Son		
Alyce Elizabeth Webb		Mrs. Davis	
Beverly Wolff	Desideria		
Don Yule		City Marshall	

THE SAINT OF BLEECKER STREET production supervised by Gian Carlo Menotti; scenery and costumes, Robert Randolph; stage director, Francis Rizzo; conductor, Vincent La-Selva.

Time: the present. Place: New York City. *The Saint of Bleecker Street* was presented at the Broadway Theater, December 27, 1954, for 92 performances.

STREET SCENE directed by Herbert Machiz; scenery and costumes, Paul Sylbert; choreography, Richard Tone; conductor, Charles Wilson.

Time: the present, in June. Place: New York City. *Street Scene* as a play was first presented January 10, 1929, for 601 performances. Its musical version was presented at the Adelphi Theater, January 9, 1947, for 148 performances.

THE CONSUL directed by Gian Carlo Menotti; scenery, Horace Armistead; conductor, Vincent LaSelva; assistant to Mr. Menotti, Francis Rizzo.

Time: the present. Place: somewhere in Europe. *The Consul* was presented at the Ethel Barrymore Theater, March 15, 1950 for 269 performances.

For all three productions: executive stage manager, Hans Sondheimer; stage managers, Dan Butt, Bill Field; press, Nat & Irvin Dorfman.

A Very Rich Woman (28). By Ruth Gordon; based on a play by Philippe Hériat. Produced by Garson Kanin at the Belasco Theater. Opened September 30, 1965. (Closed October 23, 1965)

Mrs. Lord	Ruth Gordon	Linus Bailey III	Peter Turgeon
Mrs. Minot	Madge Kennedy	Alex Rovenesco	Jack Ryland
Johnny	Larry Oliver	Dalphne Bailey	Heidi Murray
Mae	Ethel Griffies	Oliver Sears	Ernest Truex
Dennis	Jon Richards	Pearl	Katharine Houghton
Edith Shaw	Joan Wetmore	Miss Moran	Diana Muldaur
Ursula Bailey	Carrie Nye	The Supervisor	Stefan Schnabel
Patrick	Raymond Walburn		

Standby: Miss Gordon—Sylvia Field. Understudies: Others in cast—Dick Van Patten, Jon Richards, Larry Oliver, Eileen Letchworth, Katharine Houghton.

Directed by Garson Kanin; scenery, Oliver Smith; costumes, Audré; lighting, John Harvey; associate producer, Al Goldin; associate director, David Pardoll; stage manager, Dick Van Patten; press, Nat Dorfman, Irvin Dorfman.

Time: the present. Place: in and around Boston, Mass.

Comedy about a very rich and resourceful Boston widow who fights off the efforts of her two heartless daughters to acquire her wealth by having her declared incompetent.

Pickwick (55). Musical based on Charles Dickens' *Pickwick Papers;* book by Wolf Mankowitz; music by Cyril Ornadel; lyrics by Leslie Bricusse. Produced by David Merrick in association with Bernard Delfont at the Forty-sixth Street Theater. Opened October 4, 1965. (Closed November 20, 1965)

Hot Toddy Seller ....Jim Connor	Mr. Jingle ....Anton Rodgers
Cold Drinks Seller ....Edmond Varrato	Major Domo ....Jim Connor
Bird Seller ....Roger LePage	Dr. Slammer ....Peter Costanza
Hot Potato Man ....Gerrit de Beer	1st Officer ....Richard Neilson
Turnkey ....Allan Lokos	2nd Officer ....Haydon Smith
Roker ....Peter Costanza	Landlord ....Edmond Varrato
Pickwick ....Harry Secombe	Mrs. Leo Hunter ....Elizabeth Parrish
Augustus Snodgrass ....Julian Orchard	Mr. Leo Hunter ....Gerrit de Beer
Tracy Tupman ....John Call	Dodson ....Michael Darbyshire
Nathaniel Winkle ....Oscar Quitak	Fogg ....Tony Sympson
Sam Weller ....Roy Castle	Wicks ....Haydon Smith
Mr. Wardle ....Michael Logan	Jackson ....Keith Perry
Rachel ....Helena Carroll	Usher ....Taylor Reed
Isabella ....Nancy Haywood	Bailiff ....Stanley Simmonds
Emily ....Sybil Scotford	Sgt. Buzfuz ....Peter Bull
Fat Boy ....Joe Richards	Judge ....Richard Neilson
Mrs. Bardell ....Charlotte Rae	Sgt. Snubbins ....Allan Lokos
Bardell, Jr. ....Brian Chapin	Jury Foreman ....Roger LePage
Mary ....Nancy Barrett	

Passers-by, Oslers, Debtors, Maids, Drinkers and Pot Boys: Jill Alexander, Michael Amber, Bill Black, William Coppola, Ann Davies, Selma Marcus, Ann Tell, Bill Nuss, Edmond Varrato, Larry Whiteley, Gerrit de Beer, Clyde Laurents, Keith Perry, Taylor Reed, Bruce Becker, Susan Cartt, Jo Freilich, Mary Keller, Don Lawrence, Ginia Mason, Lani Michaels, Ross Miles, Nancy Stevens, Don Strong, Haydon Smith, Roger LePage. Children: Michael Easton, Richard Easton, Tracy Evans, Leslie Ann Mapes, Bonnie Turner.

Understudies: Mr. Secombe—Taylor Reed; Mr. Castle—Roger LePage; Mr. Orchard—Keith Perry; Mr. Quitak—Larry Whiteley; Mr. Call—Taylor Reed; Miss Rae—Ann Tell; Mr. Logan —William Coppola; Mr. Darbyshire—Keith Perry; Miss Barrett—Mary Keller; Mr. Sympson— Gerrit de Beer; Mr. Bull—Peter Costanza; Mr. Rodgers—Richard Neilson; Miss Carroll— Elizabeth Parrish; Miss Scotford—Ann Davies; Miss Haywood—Jill Alexander; Miss Parrish— Selma Marcus; Master Chapin—Michael Easton; Mr. Neilson—Clyde Laurents; Mr. Costanza— Stanley Simmonds.

Directed by Peter Coe; choreography, Gillian Lynne; musical direction and vocal arrangements, Ian Fraser; scenery, Sean Kenny; costumes, Roger Furse and Peter Rice; lighting, Jules Fisher; orchestrations, Eric Rogers; production stage manager, William Dodds; stage manager, Peter Stern; press, Harvey B. Sabinson, Lee Solters, Lila King.

Time: 1827. Place: in and around London and Rochester. Act I, Scene 1: The Pickwickians. Scene 2: Introduces Mr. Pickwick to a new and not uninteresting scene in the great drama of life. Scene 3: The first day's adventures. Scene 4: Strongly illustrative of the position, that the course of true love is not a railway. Scene 5: Descriptive of a very important proceeding on the part of Mr. Pickwick; no less an epoch in his life, then in his history. Scene 6: Too full of adventure to be briefly described. Act II, Scene 1: Some account of Eatanswill; the state of parties therein; and of the election of a member to serve in Parliament for that ancient, loyal and patriotic borough. Scene 2: How the Pickwickians, when Mr. Pickwick stepped out of the frying pan, walked gently and comfortably into the fire. Scene 3: Showing how Dodson and Fogg were men of business; and how an affecting interview took place between Mr. Weller and his employer. Scene 4: Is wholly devoted to a full and faithful report of the memorable trial of Bardell against Pickwick. Scene 5: What befell Mr. Pickwick when he got into the Fleet; what prisoners he saw there; and how he passed the night. Scene 6: In which the Pickwick Club is finally dissolved and everything concluded to the satisfaction of everybody.

The adventures and romances of the Pickwick Club members set to music and presented in a format "designed for the introduction of diverting characters and incidents attempting no ingenuity of plot" (Dickens' own words in his *Pickwick Papers* preface). A foreign play previously produced in London.

ACT I

"I Like the Company of Men" ....Pickwick, Snodgrass, Tupman, Winkle	
"That's What I'd Like for Christmas" ....Pickwick, The Company	
"The Pickwickians" ....Pickwick, Snodgrass, Tupman, Winkle	
"A Bit of a Character" ....Jingle, Snodgrass, Winkle, Tupman	
"There's Something About You" ....Jingle, Rachel, The Company	

"A Gentleman's Gentleman" ....Sam, Mary
"You Never Met a Feller Like Me" ....Pickwick, Sam Weller
"I'll Never Be Lonely Again" ....Pickwick, Mrs. Bardell

ACT II

"Fizkin and Pickwick" ....The Company
"Very" ....Jingle, Pickwick, Wardle
"If I Ruled the World" ....Pickwick, The Company
"I'll Never Be Lonely Again" (Reprise) ....The Pickwickians
"Talk" ....Sam, The Company
"That's the Law" ....Pickwick, Dodson, Fogg, The Company
"Damages" ....Pickwick, Mrs. Bardell
"If I Ruled the World" (Reprise) ....Pickwick, The Company

* **Generation** (269). By William Goodhart. Produced by Frederick Brisson at the Morosco Theater. Opened October 6, 1965.

Walter Owen	Richard Jordan	Stan Herman	A. Larry Haines
Jim Bolton	Henry Fonda	Winston Garand	Don Fellows
Doris Owen	Holly Turner	Ken Powell	Sandy Baron

Understudies: Miss Turner—Lynn Morris; Messrs. Haines and Baron—Joseph Bernard.

Directed by Gene Saks; incidental music, Jerry Bock; lyrics, William Goodhart; scenery and lighting, George Jenkins; costumes, Albert Wolsky; associate producer, Victor Samrock; production manager, Fred Hebert; production stage manager, Wayne Carson; Stage manager, Joseph Bernard; press, Sol Jacobson, Lewis Harmon, Mary Ward.

Time: the present. Place: the studio-loft-apartment of Walter Owen in Lower Manhattan. Act I: Late Saturday afternoon. Act II: Sunday afternoon. Act III: That evening.

Comedy about the gulf of understanding between the generations, as a successful middle-aged advertising executive visits his newlywed daughter (who is about to have a baby without the help of a doctor, with only her adamant young husband in attendance) in her pad in Manhattan's Bohemia.

Michael Arquette replaced Sandy Baron 10/25/65-11/9/65. Peter Lombard replaced Richard Jordan and Paul Collins replaced Sandy Baron 5/16/66.

A Best Play; see page 121

Minor Miracle (4). By Al Morgan. Produced by Zev Bufman and Howard Erskine at Henry Miller's Theater. Opened October 7, 1965. (Closed October 9, 1965)

Mrs. Doody	Pert Kelton	Bishop William O'Leary	Dennis King
Father Maurice Britt	Lee Tracy	Mrs. Fuller	Zamah Cunningham
Herman Wekstein	Robert H. Harris	Reporters	Douglas McLean, Kate Tomlinson, Maurice Brenner, Roger Johnson Jr., Gina MacClay Joel Fredrick, Robert Horen
Mrs. Prosser	Julie Bovasso		
Rickie Prosser	Glenn Scimonelli		
Father Kincaid	Conard Fowkes		

Understudies: Messrs. Tracy and King—Douglas McLean; Misses Kelton, Bovasso and Cunningham—Kate Tomlinson; Mr. Harris—Maurice Brenner; Mr. Fowkes—Roger Johnson Jr.; Mr. Scimonelli—Eugene Pressman.

Directed by Howard Erskine; scenery, Robert Randolph; costumes, Theoni V. Aldredge; lighting, Tharon Musser; production stage manager, Howard Whitfield; stage manager, Roger Johnson Jr.; press, Lee Solters, Harvey D. Sabinson, Bob Ullman.

Time: the present. Place: New York City. Act I, Scene 1: The parlor of the Parish House of St. Martin's Catholic Church in the Yorkville section of Manhattan—Saturday morning, 10 a.m. Scene 2: The same—6 p.m. that evening. Act II: The parlor of the Parish House—Sunday afternoon, 2 p.m. Act III, Scene 1: The parlor of the Parish House, Monday evening, 6:30 p.m. Scene 2: The same—9:30 that night.

A neighborhood lad claims to have seen a vision of the Virgin, which creates a stir in the parish of an elderly, horse-playing priest.

Drat! The Cat! (8). Musical with book and lyrics by Ira Levin; music by Milton Schafer. Produced by Jerry Adler and Norman Rosemont at the Martin Beck Theater. Opened October 10, 1965. (Closed October 16, 1965)

The Mayor ....Alfred Spindelman
Pincer,
    Superintendant of Police ..Charles Durning
Mallet, Chief of Detectives ....Gene Varrone
Roger "Bulldog" Purefoy,
    Former Chief of Detectives ....David Gold
Kate Purefoy, His Wife ....Lu Leonard
The Doctor ....Leo Bloom
Emma, a Patrolwoman ....Sandy Ellen
Bob Purefoy, the Purefoys' Son,
    a Patrolman ....Elliott Gould
The Van Guilder's Butler ...Harry Naughton
Matilda Van Guilder,
    a Socialite ....Jane Connell

Lucius Van Guilder, Her Husband,
    a Millionaire ....Jack Fletcher
Alice Van Guilder,
    Their Daughter ....Lesley Ann Warren
The Maid ....Jacque Dean
The Minister ....Al Lanti
The Mayor's Wife ....Marian Haraldson
Julietta Onderdonck, a Dowager
    from Boston ....Mariana Doro
The Judge ....David Gold
The Prosecutor ....Leo Bloom

Patrolmen: Leo Bloom, Ralph Farnworth, Ian Garry, David Gold, Barney Johnston, Al Lanti, William Lutz, George Marcy, Larry Moss, Harry Naughton, Ronald Paré, James Powers, Dan Siretta, Bill Starr.

Others in the Ensemble: Jeri Barto, Nancy Lynch, Carmen Morales, Mary Zahn, Lillian Bozinoff, Beth Howland, Meg Walter, Margery Gray.

Directed by Joe Layton; choreography, Joe Layton; scenery and lighting, David Hays; costumes, Fred Voelpel; musical direction and vocal arrangements, Herbert Grossman; orchestrations, Hershy Kay and Clare Grundman; dance music, Genevieve Pitot; choreographic associate, James Moore; production stage manager, George Thorn; stage manager, Tom Porter; press, Mike Merrick Co., Barry Kobrin, Ruth Cage.

Time: the latter part of the 19th Century, spring. Place: New York City and environs.

A "musical spoof" of cops-and-robbers melodrama, in a tale of a larcenous heiress and a bumbling policeman.

ACT I

Scene 1: Various places in New York City
    "Drat! The Cat!" ....Citizens, Patrolmen, the Mayor, Pincer, Mallet
Scene 2: A bedroom in the Purefoys' flat
    "My Son, Uphold the Law" ....Roger, Patrolmen
Scene 3: Lucius Van Guilder's study and counting room
    "Holmes and Watson" ....Alice, Bob
    "She Touched Me" ....Bob
Scene 4: Alice Van Guilder's boudoir and a secret chamber
    "Wild and Reckless" ....Alice
Scene 5: The Purefoys' kitchen
    "She's Roses" ....Bob, Kate
Scene 6: Pier Fourteen
    Ballet: "Ignoble Theft of the Idol's Eyes" ....Cat, Patrolmen, Attendants of the Idol
Scene 7: Van Guilder's study and the garden
    "Dancing with Alice" ....Bob, Alice, Mr. & Mrs. Van Guilder, Guests
    "Drat! The Cat! (Reprise) ....Mr. & Mrs. Van Guilder, Guests
Scene 8: The Van Guilders' cellar
    "Purefoy's Lament" ....Bob

ACT II

Scene 1: Police Headquarters
    "A Pox Upon the Traitor's Brow" ....Pincer, Mallet, Emma, Patrolmen
Scene 2: The cellar
    "Deep in Your Heart" ....Bob

Scene 3: Van Guilder's study
"Let's Go" ....Alice and Bob
"It's Your Fault" ....Mr. & Mrs. Van Guilder
Scene 4: The woods north of the city
"Wild and Reckless" (Reprise) ....Bob
Scene 5: Various places in the city
Ballet: "The Upside-Down Thief" ....Bob, Citizens, Patrolmen, Kate
Scene 6: The woods and the city
"Today Is a Day for a Band to Play" ....Pincer, Mallet, Emma, Patrolmen, Citizens
"She Touched Me" (Reprise) ....Bob and Alice
Scene 7: Van Guilder's study
"I Like Him" ....Alice
Scene 8: A courtroom
"Justice Triumphant" ....Entire Company
"Today Is a Day for a Band to Play" (Reprise) ....Entire Company

Entertaining Mr. Sloane (13). By Joe Orton. Produced by Slade Brown, Tanya Chasman and E.A. Gilbert in association with Michael Codron and Donald Albery at the Lyceum Theater. Opened October 12, 1965. (Closed October 23, 1965)

Kath	Sheila Hancock	The Dadda	George Turner
Sloane	Dudley Sutton	Ed	Lee Montague

Understudies: Miss Hancock—Michaele Myers; Mr. Sutton—Geoff Garland; Messrs. Turner and Montague—Harry Bergman.
Directed by Alan Schneider; scenery and costumes, William Ritman; production stage managers, Mark Wright, Duane Camp; press, Dorothy Ross, Richard O'Brien.
Time: the present. Place: a house in London. Act I: The sitting room, evening. Act II: Some months later, morning. Act III: Immediately following.
Members of a family living on the edge of a junkyard are human junk: a selfish father, his faded and sex-starved daughter, his homosexual son. Each in his own way uses a young murderer who becomes their lodger. A foreign play previously produced in London (May 6, 1964).

* **The Impossible Years** (262). By Bob Fisher and Arthur Marx. Produced by David Black and Walter A. Hyman at The Playhouse. Opened October 13, 1965.

Doctor Jack Kingsley	Alan King	Wally	Kenneth Carr
Linda Kingsley	Jane Elliot	Dennis	Jeff Siggins
Abbey Kingsley	Neva Small	Andy	Scott Glenn
Alice Kingsley	Janet Ward	Bartholomew Smuts	Michael Hadge
Ricky Fleisher	Terrence Logan	Doctor Harold Fleisher	Michael Vale
Richard Merrick	Bert Convy	Arnold Brecher	Jack Hollander
Miss Hammer	Sudie Bond	Irwin Kniberg	Kenneth Kealey
Francine	Donna Baccala		

Understudies: Messrs. King, Vale, Hollander—Jack Sorian; Misses Ward, Bond—Eulalie Noble; Misses Elliot, Baccala—Pamela Murphy; Mr. Convy—Robert Jundelin; Messrs. Logan, Siggins, Glenn—Kenneth Carr; Mr. Hadge—Jeff Siggins; Miss Small—Jan Rhodes.
Directed by Arthur Storch; scenery, William Pitkin; costumes, Ann Roth; lighting, Martin Aronstein; production stage manager, James Gelb; stage manager, Doreen Richards; press, Frank Goodman, Martin Shwartz.
Time: the present. Place: the den and living room of the Kingsley home in Old Westbury, L.I. Act I, Scene 1: A late afternoon in spring. Scene 2: Saturday morning, about 10 o'clock. Scene 3: A month later, about noon. Scene 4: Two weeks later, mid-morning. Act II, Scene 1: The following evening. Scene 2: The next morning. Scene 3: The same day, mid-afternoon.
Comedy in which a famous psychiatrist is writing a book about bringing up teen-agers but is continually being stumped by his own teen-aged daughter and her friends.
Alan King was replaced by Ed McMahon and Jane Elliot was replaced by Pamela Murphy 1/17/66 through 1/22/66.

The World of Charles Aznavour (29). Solo program of songs, many of them in the French language, composed and sung by Charles Aznavour. Produced by Norman Twain and Sid Bernstein in association with Henry Goldgran at the Ambassador Theater. Opened October 14, 1965. (Closed November 6, 1965)

Scenery and lighting, Ralph Alswang; music director, Henry Byrs; stage manager, Martin Gold; press, Max Eisen, Jeannie Gibson Merrick.

A foreign show previously produced in Paris.

Part I: "Le Temps," "Avec," "For Me Formidable," "Je Te Rechaufferais," "Who," "J'ai Perdu La Tete," "Never Again," "Parceque," "Isabelle," "The Boss Is Dead," "Reste," "Two Guitars," "Que C'est Triste Venice," "You've Let Yourself Go." Part II: "I Dig You That Way," "C'est Fini," "The Time Is Now," "Quand Tu Viens Chez Moi," "L'amour C'est Comme Un Jour," "I'm Wrong," "Et Pourtant," "Les Comediens," "Love At Last You Have Found Me," "Paris Is At Her Best in May," "La Boheme," "You've Got To Learn," "La Mamma."

* **On A Clear Day You Can See Forever** (260). Musical with book and lyrics by Alan Jay Lerner; music by Burton Lane. Produced by Alan Jay Lerner in association with Rogo Productions at the Mark Hellinger Theater. Opened October 17, 1965.

Dr. Mark Bruckner ....John Cullum	Warren Smith ....William Daniels
Mrs. Hatch ....Evelyn Page	Prudence Cumming .....Barbara Remington
Student ....Gerald M. Teijelo Jr.	Edward Moncrief ....Clifford David
Daisy Gamble ....Barbara Harris	Flora ....Carol Flemming
Muriel Bunson ....Barbara Monte	Dr. Paul Bruckner ....Gerry Mathews
James Preston ....William Reilly	Dr. Conrad Bruckner ....Michael Lewis
Samuel Welles ....Gordon Dilworth	Evans Bolagard ....Hamilton Camp
Mrs. Welles ....Blanche Collins	Themistocles Kriakos ....Titos Vandis
Sir Hubert Insdale ....Byron Webster	T.A.A. Official ....David Thomas
Dolly Wainwhistle .....Hanne Marie Reiner	and
Blackamoor ....Bernard Johnson	Melinda ....Barbara Harris
Millard Cross ....Gerald M. Teijelo Jr.	

Singing Ensemble: Rudy Challenger, Paul Eichel, Eddie Erickson, Stokely Gray, Bennett Hill, Art Matthews, Dan Resin, Ken Richards, Rita Golden, Joy Holly, Zona Kennedy, Pat Lysinger, Caroline Parks, Nancy Reeves, Jeannette Seibert, Dixie Stewart.

Dancing Ensemble: Sterling Clark, Luigi Gasparinetti, Bernard Johnson, Louis Kosman, Kazimir Kokich, Marco Pogacar, Ronald B. Stratton, Gerald M. Teijelo Jr., William Reilly, Rita Agnese, Carol Flemming, Marion Fels, Leslie Franzos, Bettye Jenkins, Charlene Mehl, Barbara Monte, Hanne Marie Reiner, Barbara Remington.

Standbys: Mr. Cullum, Mr. David—Hal Linden; Miss Harris, Rita Gardner. Understudies: Mr. Vandis—Gordon Dilworth; Mr. Daniels—Dan Resin; Mr. Lewis—Art Matthews; Miss Allen—Pat Lysinger; Messrs. Webster and Dilworth—Michael Lewis; Mr. Thomas—Ken Richards; Mr. Camp—David Thomas; Miss Collins—Jeanette Siebert.

Directed by Robert Lewis; dances and musical numbers staged by Herbert Ross; scenery, Oliver Smith; costumes, Freddy Wittop; lighting, Feder; orchestrations, Robert Russell Bennett; music continuity and vocals, Trude Rittman; dance music, Betty Walberg; musical director, Theodore Saidenberg; Miss Harris' modern clothes, Donald Brooks; production supervisor, Stone Widney; production stage manager, Ross Bowman; stage managers, Pat Chandler, Edward Preston; press, Mike Merrick Co., Barry Kobrin.

Time: the present. Place: New York City. Act I, Scene 1: A lecture room at the Bruckner Clinic, late afternoon, spring. Scene 2: The solarium of the Clinic, several days later. Scene 3: Dr. Mark Bruckner's office, immediately following. Scene 4: The rooftop of Daisy's apartment, later that night. Scene 5: Dr. Mark Bruckner's office, the following afternoon. Scene 6: Dr. Mark Bruckner's office, early evening, a week later. Act II, Scene 1: The solarium of the Clinic, a week later. Scene 2: Dr. Mark Bruckner's office, immediately following. Scene 3: The rooftop of Daisy's apartment, late that night. Scene 4: Dr. Mark Bruckner's office, afternoon, one week later. Scene 5: The Municipal Airport, later that day.

A handsome psychiatrist is first clinically, then romantically fascinated by a seemingly feather-headed young woman, who is so acutely clairvoyant that under hypnosis she can recall all the details of her previous 18th century incarnation, including a love affair.

ACT I

"Hurry! It's Lovely Up Here" ....Barbara Harris
"Ring Out the Bells" ....Gordon Dilworth, Blanche Collins, Byron Webster, Servants
"Tosy and Cosh" ....Miss Harris
"On A Clear Day You Can See Forever" ....John Cullum
"On the S.S. Bernard Cohn" ....Miss Harris, Barbara Monte, William Reilly,
                                                                Gerald M. Teijelo, Jr.
"At the Hellrakers' " ....Dance Ensemble
"Don't Tamper With My Sister" ....Clifford David, Webster, Ensemble
"She Wasn't You" ....David
"Melinda" ....Cullum

ACT II

"When I'm Being Born Again" ....Titos Vandis
"What Did I Have That I Don't Have" ....Miss Harris
"Wait 'Til We're Sixty-Five" ....William Daniels, Miss Harris
"Come Back To Me" ....Cullum
"On a Clear Day" (Reprise) ....Cullum

The Right Honourable Gentleman (118). By Michael Dyne. Produced by Peter Cookson, Amy Lynn and Walter Schwimmer at the Billy Rose Theater. Opened October 19, 1965. (Closed January 29, 1966)

Mr. Bodley ....Ed Zimmermann	Mrs. Donald Crawford (Nia) ...Sarah Badel
Sir Charles Dilke ....Charles D. Gray	Mr. Donald Crawford ...Henderson Forsythe
Brookes (a servant) ....Frederick Young	Sir James Russell ....Staats Cotsworth
Mrs. Ashton Dilke (Maye, Dilke's	Mrs. Sarah Gray ....Eve Collyer
sister-in-law) ....Frances Sternhagen	Mrs. Rossiter (Lila) ....Coral Browne
Mrs. Emilia Pattison,	Mrs. Garland (Helen) ....Marie Wallace
later Lady Dilke ....M'el Dowd	Mrs. Pelham ....Louise Larabee
Mr. Joseph Chamberlain ....William Roerick	Captain Forster ....Francis Bethencourt

Understudies: Mr. Gray—Francis Bethencourt; Miss Browne—Eve Collyer; Misses Badel, Sternhagen and Wallace—Nancy Reardon; Misses Dowd, Collyer, Larabee and Mr. Young— Sylvia O'Brien; Mr. Roerick—Henderson Forsythe; Messrs. Zimmermann, Forsythe, Cotsworth and Bethencourt—Frederick Young.

Directed by Frith Banbury; scenery and costumes, Loudon Sainthill; lighting, Lloyd Burlingame; costume supervisor, Ray Diffen; production stage manager, John Maxtone-Graham; stage manager, William H. Batchelder; press, Sol Jacobson, Lewis Harmon, Mary Ward.

Time: 1885. Place: London. Act I, Scene 1: Sir Charles Dilke's study at 76 Sloane Street, a May morning. Scene 2: Mrs. Rossiter's sitting room at 52 Prince's Gate, night, early June. Scene 3: Sir Charles Dilke's study, afternoon, late June. Scene 4: The Rossiter house, early evening, July. Act II, Scene 1: Sir Charles Dilke's study, morning, early September. Scene 2: Mrs. Rossiter's sitting room, early evening, two weeks later. Scene 3: Sir Charles Dilke's study, early evening, a week later.

The play is based on a real public scandal (and uses the real names) in which an accusation of adultery ruined the career of a distinguished Parliamentarian colleague of Gladstone's in Victorian England. A foreign play previously produced in London (opened May 28, 1964 and ran for 17 months).

* **Repertory Theater of Lincoln Center for the Performing Arts.** Repertory of four plays. **Danton's Death** (46). By Georg Buechner; new English version by Herbert Blau. Opened October 21, 1965. (Closed November 27, 1965). **The Country Wife** (54). A revival of the play by William Wycherley. Opened December 9, 1965. (Closed January 23, 1966). **The Condemned of Altona** (46). American premiere of the play by Jean-Paul Sartre; adapted by Justin O'Brien. Opened February 3, 1966. (Closed March 13, 1966). * **The Caucasian Chalk Circle** (77). New York premiere of the play by Bertold Brecht; English version by Eric Bentley. Opened March 24, 1966. All four plays produced by the Repertory Theater of Lincoln Center, under the direction of Herbert Blau and Jules Irving, at the Vivian Beaumont Theater.

PERFORMER	"DANTON'S DEATH"	"THE COUNTRY WIFE"	"THE CONDEMNED OF ALTONA"	"THE CAUCASIAN CHALK CIRCLE"
Ruth Attaway	Woman			Maro
Frank Bayer	Young Man With Balloon	Matou		Young Peasant; stableboy
Stanley Beck	Executioner			Drunken Peasant
Alan Bergmann	George Danton			
Roscoe Lee Browne	St. Just			
John Carpenter				Cook; Merchant; Doctor; Farmer
Edward Cicciarelli	Young Gentleman; Soldier			Messenger
Leonardo Cimino				Surab; Architect No. 1; Farmer
Oliver Clark				Bizergan Kazbeki; Sosso
Carolyn Coates		Miss Alithea	Johanna	Asja; Merchant
Mariclare Costello	Robespierre's Servant			
George Coulouris			The Father	
John Devlin				Tzereteli
James Dukas	Dumas		The S.S.	Mikadze; Blockhead
Elaine Eldridge				Very Old Woman
Gail Fisher	Lucille, Camille's Wife			
Ray Fry	Morel	Sir Jasper Fidget		Delegate; Architect No. 2; Merchant; Monk; Invalid
Robert Gerringer	Simon			
Michael Granger	Hérault-Séchelles	A Quack		Lavrenti
James Greene	Husband; Citizen			
Edith Gresham	Citizen	Old Lady Squeamish		Peasant Woman; Kitchen Maid
William Haddock				Peasant Man; Groom; Very Old Man
Robert Haswell	General Dillon	Mr. Pinchwife	Heinrich	Major Domo; Farmer
Marcie Hubert	Marion	Lucy		Girl Tractorist; Suliko
Elizabeth Huddle	Woman; Eugénie	Mrs. Margery Pinchwife		Surab's Wife; Grusha
James Earl Jones	Philippeau			
Stacy Keach	Cutler; Turnkey	Mr. Horner		Groom; Musician
Lincoln Kilpatrick	Beggar; Citizen			Irakli
Marketa Kimbrell				Agriculturist; Soloist
Judith Lowry				Peasant Woman
Beatrice Manley	Lady; Wife	Mrs. Squeamish		Governor's Wife
Paul Mann	Collot d'Herbois			Fat Prince
Glenn Mazen	Fouquier			The Governor; Jussup
Carlo Mazzone-Clementi	Puppeteer			
Ronnie Misa				Michael

PERFORMER	"DANTON'S DEATH"	"THE COUNTRY WIFE"	"THE CONDEMNED OF ALTONA"	"THE CAUCASIAN CHALK CIRCLE"
Earl Montgomery				Loladze; Grand Duke; Blackmailer; Shuboladze
Claudette Nevins	Julie, Danton's Wife			
Brock Peters				Storyteller
Robert Phalen	Laflotte			Wounded Soldier
Priscilla Pointer	Lady	My Lady Fidget	Leni	Kitchen Maid; Aniko
Judith Propper				Masha
Doris Rich				Cook
Tom Rosqui	Citizen Barère		Frantz	Limping Man
Diane Shalet	Rosalie			
Robert Stattel	Camille Desmoulins	Mr. Harcourt		Servant; Messenger
David J. Stewart	Lacroix			
David Sullivan	Young Man; Gentleman		Klages	Servant; Musician; Invalid's Servant
Robert Symonds	Robespierre	Mr. Sparkish		Judge; Azdak
Boris Tumarin				Aleko; Oboladze; Old Peasant
Murvyn Vye				Corporal; Innkeeper
Shirley Jac Wagner	Simon's Wife	Mrs. Dainty Fidget		Makinä; Kitchen Maid; Grusha's Mother-in-law; Granny Grusinia
Jack Waltzer	Citizen			
Ronald Weyand	Legendre; Executioner			Peasant Husband; Policeman
Kate Wilkinson	Woman; Madame			
Edward Winter	Deputy From Lyons; Soldier; Jailer	Mr. Dorilant	Werner	Simon Shashava
Erica Yohn	Woman; Adelaide			Nina; Peasant Woman; Ludovica
Louis Zorich	Billaud		Assistant S.S.	

Children in *Danton's Death:* Eileen Dolphin, Matthew Pryor, Paul Dwyer; alternates, Barry Symonds, Victoria Symonds.

Understudies for *Danton's Death:* Mr. Bergmann, Tom Rosqui; Mr. Granger—Glenn Mazen; Mr. Jones—David Sullivan; Mr. Stattel—Robert Phalen; Mr. Browne—Lincoln Kilpatrick; Messrs. Symonds, Weyand—Stacy Keach; Messrs. Zorich, Mazen, Rosqui—James Greene; Mr. Mann—Robert Haswell; Mr. Stewart—Ray Fry; Mr. Phalen—Edward Cicciarelli; Mr. Haswell—Ronald Weyand; Mr. Gerringer—James Dukas; Misses Nevins, Fisher—Mariclare Costello; Misses Hubert, Huddle—Priscilla Pointer; Misses Shalet, Yohn—Elizabeth Huddle; others—Frank Bayer, Stanley Beck, Howard Fischer, Edith Gresham, Shirley Jac Wagner, Jack Waltzer, Timothy Ward.

Merchants, Thieves, Pimps and Bawds in *The Country Wife:* Ruth Attaway, Stanley Beck, Edward Cicciarelli, Mariclare Costello, Jeff David, James Dukas, Paul Dwyer, Elaine Eldridge, Amy Irving, Lincoln Kilpatrick, Richard Levy, Glenn Mazen, Carlo Mazzone-Clementi, Robert Phalen, Tom Rosqui, David Sullivan, Barry Symonds, Victoria Symonds, Jack Waltzer, Craig Ward, Angela Wood, Erica Yohn, Louis Zorich. Alternates for Children, David Speyer, Lara Speyer. Understudies: Mariclare Costello, James Dukas, Elaine Eldridge, Glenn Mazen, Robert Phalen, David Sullivan, Jack Waltzer, Angela Wood, Erica Yohn.

Understudies for *The Condemned of Altona:* Miss Coates—Beatrice Manley; Mr. Winter—Robert Stattel; Miss Pointer—Erica Yohn; Mr. Coulouris—Robert Haswell; Mr. Rosqui—Stacy Keach; Messrs. Dukas, Haswell—Louis Zorich; Mr. Sullivan—Robert Phalen.

In *The Caucasian Chalk Circle*—Ironshirts: Stanley Beck, Edward Cicciarelli, Jeff David, Michael Granger, Robert Phalen. Beggars: Elaine Eldridge, Richard Levy, Carlo Mazzone-Clementi, Priscilla Pointer, Judith Propper, Tom Rosqui, Shirley Jac Wagner, Ronald Weyand. Villagers: Ruth Attaway, John Carpenter, Carolyn Coates, Elaine Eldridge, Edith Gresham, Marcie Hubert, Carlo Mazzone-Clementi, Robert Phalen, Priscilla Pointer, Judith Propper, Ronald Weyand, Erica Yohn. Children: Steven Chall, Buster Davis (alternates, Scooter Jolley, Barry Symonds. Chorus: Elizabeth Cole, Barbara Smith Conrad, Elizabeth S. Corrigan, Mary Delson. Musicians: mandolin-balalaika, Jacob Glick; percussion, Richard Fitz; accordion, Martha Gerhart; guitar, Elizabeth S. Corrigan.

Understudies for *The Caucasian Chalk Circle:* Mr. Peters—John Carpenter; Miss Manley— Carolyn Coates; Mr. Devlin—Tom Rosqui; Mr. Mann-Earl Montgomery; Mr. Winter—Robert Phalen; Mr. Vye—Ronald Weyand; Miss Huddle—Marcie Hubert; Mr. Mazen—David Sullivan; Mr. Symonds—Ray Fry; Mr. Weyand—Tom Rosqui; Messrs. Montgomery, Tumarin— Glenn Mazen; others—Frank Bayer, Stanley Beck, Edward Cicciarelli, Leonardo Cimino, Oliver Clark, John Devlin, James Dukas, Elaine Eldridge, Robert Haswell, Stacy Keach, Beatrice Manley, Judith Propper, Robert Stattel, Robert Symonds, Edward Winter.

DANTON'S DEATH directed by Herbert Blau; scenery and lighting, Jo Mielziner; costumes, James Hart Stearns; costumes supervised by John Boyt; electronic music and songs, Morton Subotnick; production stage managers, Frederic de Wilde, James Kershaw; stage manager, Howard Fischer; press, Barry Hyams, Susan Bloch.

Time: March 24 to April 5, 1794. Place: Paris.

The historical conflict between humanistic Danton and ferociously idealistic Robespierre is resolved by the guillotine in a pageant of the French Revolution. *Danton's Death* is a 19th-century German play. It was previously produced on Broadway, in another version, by Orson Welles and John Houseman at the Mercury Theater, November 2, 1938, for 21 performances.

THE COUNTRY WIFE directed by Robert Symonds; scenery and costumes, James Hart Stearns; associate designer, James F. Göhl; costumes supervised by Deidre Cartier; lighting, Jean Rosenthal; music and songs, Stanley Silverman; production stage manager, James Kershaw; stage manager, Howard Fischer; press, Barry Hyams, Susan Bloch.

Time: the latter half of the 17th century. Place: London.

The Country Wife was first produced at the Drury Lane Theater, London, in 1675. Recent notable stagings took place in London in 1924 (Phoenix Society) and in 1936 (Old Vic, with Ruth Gordon, in a production which also played New York that winter). It was produced in New York by the Playwrights Company in 1957 (with Julie Harris and Laurence Harvey) and in San Francisco by the Messrs. Blau and Irving in their Actor's Workshop during the 1964-65 season.

THE CONDEMNED OF ALTONA directed by Herbert Blau; scenery, Robin Wagner; costumes, Deidre Cartier; lighting, Martin Aronstein; sound, Charles Gross; production stage manager, James Kershaw; press, Barry Hyams, Susan Bloch.

Time: 1959. Place: the Gerlach house in Altona, Germany. ACT I: The Council Room, Sunday afternoon. Act II, Scene 1: Frantz's room, Monday afternoon. Scene 2: The Council Room, Saturday, late afternoon. Act III, Scene 1: Frantz's room, same day, early evening. Scene 2: The Council Room, an hour later.

Members of a non-Nazi German industrial family suffer various forms of self-punishment for varying degrees of guilt in playing along with the Nazis. Guiltiest of all is the oldest son who killed two prisoners while serving as an officer on the Russian front. He has prisoned himself in his room for 13 years in order to pretend to himself that Germany is still wrecked and on her knees in expiation of her national sins. A foreign play previously produced in Paris and London and in a screen version starring Maximilian Schell, Sophia Loren and Frederic March.

THE CAUCASIAN CHALK CIRCLE directed by Jules Irving; scenery, costumes and masks, James Hart Stearns; lighting, Richard Nelson; music and songs, Morton Subotnick; associate designer, James F. Gohl; music director, Stanley Silverman; production stage manager, James Kershaw; stage managers, Russell McGrath, Timothy Ward; press, Barry Hyams, Susan Bloch.

Time: for the Prologue, summer, 1945; for the play, 1200 A.D. Place: a war-ravaged Caucasian village and the same area in ancient times. Act I, Scene 1: The Prologue. Scene 2: The Noble Child. Act II, Scene 1: The Flight to the Northern Mountains. Scene 2: The Northern Mountains. Act III, Scene 1: The Story of the Judge. Scene 2: The Caucasian Chalk Circle.

The Caucasian Chalk Circle is a foreign play written by Brecht in Germany in 1945. But its world premiere took place in the United States, in a college production of an English version in 1948. Its first professional production was at the Hedgerow Theater in 1948. This is its first professional production in New York.

* **The Royal Hunt of the Sun** (247). By Peter Shaffer. Produced by Theater Guild Productions, Theodore Mann, Gerard Oestreicher in association with Hope Abelson at the ANTA Theater. Opened October 26, 1965.

The Spaniards:
Martin Ruiz ....George Rose
Martin Ruiz as a boy ....Paul Collins
Franciso Pizarro, Commander of the
    Expedition ....Christopher Plummer
Hernardo de Soto,
    Second-in-Command .....John Vernon
Fray Vincente de Valverde, Dominican,
    Chaplain to the Expedition .Ben Hammer
Diego de Trujillo, Master of
    the Horse ....Michael Lamont
Salinas, blacksmith ....Nelson Phillips
Rodas, tailor ....Jake Dengel
Soldiers
    Vasca ....Tony Capodilupo
    Domingo ....George Sampson
    Juan Chavez ....Clyde Burton
    Pedro Chavez ....John Church
Felipillo, an Indian boy employed as
    interpreter to Pizarro ..Gregory Rozakis

Fray Marcos de Nizza,
    Franciscan Friar ....Michael Levin
Pedro de Candia, Commander
    of Artillery ....Cal Bellini
Miguel Estete,
    Royal Overseer ....Thayer David
The Incas:
Atahuallpa, Sovereign Inca
    of Peru ....David Carradine
Villac Umu, High Priest
    of Peru ....Mylo Quam
Challcuchima, an Inca
    General ....Clayton Corbin
Manco, a Messenger ....Marc Maskin
Chieftain ....Robert Berdeen
Headman ....Judd Jones
Oello, a wife of Atahuallpa ...Sandy Leeds
Inti Coussi, step-sister of
    Atahuallpa ....Julie Sheppard

Peruvian Indians: Barry Burns, Paul Charles, Kurt Christian, Edilio Ferraro, Roy Lozano, Hector Mercado, Ken Novarro, B.J. Desimone, Don Silber.

Musicians: Herbert Harris, Norman Grossman, Charles Birch, Steve Silverman.

Understudies: Mr. Rose—Thayer David; Master Collins—Paul Charles; Messrs. Hammer, Sampson, Levin—John Church; Mr. Lamont—B.J. De Simone; Messrs. Phillips, Dengel, Capodilupo—George Sampson; Mr. Church—Kurt Christien; Mr. Rozakis—Robert Berdeen; Mr. Bellini—George Sampson; Mr. David—Tony Capodilupo; Mr. Carradine—Clayton Corbin; Messrs. Quam, Corbin—Don Silber; Mr. Maskin—Barry Burns; Mr. Berdeen—Roy Lozano; Mr. Jones—Mark Maskin.

Directed by John Dexter; scenery and costumes, Michael Annals; lighting, Martin Aronstein; mime, Madame Claude Chagrin; music and sound effects, Marc Wilkinson; musical director, Herbert Harris; associate producer, Don Herbert; an ANTA presentation by arrangement with David Susskind and Daniel Melnick; production stage manager, Randall Brooks; New York production supervised by George Jenkins and Ben Edwards; stage manager, Maxine S. Taylor; press, Merle Debuskey, Violet Welles, Larry Belling.

Time: June 1529 to August 1533. Place: apart from two early scenes in Spain and Panama, the play is set in the Upper Province of the Inca Empire: what is now South Ecuador and Northwestern Peru. The whole of Act II takes place in the town of Cajamarca. Act I: The Hunt. Act II: The Kill.

Pizarro, at the time of the conquest of Peru, has seen so much evil violence that he yearns to believe in a power greater than death; he sacrifices the Inca man-God Atahuallpa as an experiment, in hope that Atahuallpa will be able to rise from the dead. A foreign play previously produced in London.

Robert Burr replaced John Vernon 1/4/66. Robert Burr replaced Christopher Plummer and Don Silber replaced Robert Burr 3/29/66. Clayton Corbin replaced David Carradine, Judd Jones replaced Clayton Corbin, Paul Charles replaced Paul Collins and John Church replaced Michael Levin 5/10/66.

A Best Play; see page 146

Postmark Zero (8). By Robert Nemiroff, based on the book of *Last Letters from Stalingrad* translated by Frank Schneider and Charles Gullans, and other factual material. Produced by Burton C. D'Lugoff, Robert Nemiroff and Franklin Fried in association with Triangle Productions at the Brooks Atkinson Theater. Opened November 1, 1965. (Closed November 6, 1965)

Cast: Hardy Kruger, John Heffernan, Viveca Lindfors, Edward Grover, Curt Lowens, Alvin Epstein, John Karlen, Clotilde Joano.

Standby: Misses Lindfors, Joano—Jane Cronin.
Directed by Peter Kass; scenery, costumes, lighting, Jack Blackman; production associates, Howard Bennett, Joel Dein; production stage manager, Norman Rothstein; stage manager, Bud Coffey; press, Robert W. Larkin.
Time: summer, 1942, to January 31, 1943. Place: Germany and Russia.
Terror, hatred, suffering expressed in a dramatization of the letters of nameless German soldiers in the Battle of Stalingrad, and in some home-front incidents.

Mating Dance (1) By Eleanor Harris Howard and Helen McAvity. Produced by Elliot Martin at the Eugene O'Neill Theater. Opened and closed at the evening performance, November 3, 1965.

Kelly Lewis	Marian Hailey	Senator Lucia Barrett	Marian Winters
Jeff	Rick Lenz	Lyn Hoyt	Esther Jane Coryell
Mrs. Grindell	Ruth Newton	Ramesh Ramru	Don Calfa
Oscar Davenport	J.D. Cannon	Junior	Robert H. Wiensko
Deedee Dinehart	Judith Barcroft	Roger MacDougall	Richard Mulligan
Bruce Barrett	Van Johnson	Officer Lynch	Paul Sorvino

Understudies: Mr. Johnson—Robert H. Wiensko; Miss Winters, Miss Coryell—Ruth Newton; Miss Hailey—Judith Barcroft; Mr. Mulligan—Rick Lenz; Mr. Wiensko—Don Calfa.
Directed by Ronny Graham; scenery, Eldon Elder; costumes, Florence Klotz; lighting, John Harvey; title song, Albert A. Beach, Lawrence Grossman; production stage manager, Wally Peterson; press, Mary Bryant, Fred Weterick, Robert Pasolli.
Time: the present. Act I, Scene 1: Kelly's apartment, Saturday, late. Scene 2: Several days later, evening. Act II, Scene 1: Three weeks later, evening. Scene 2: One hour later. Scene 3: The following morning.
Comedy about a TV personality married to a lady Senator but dallying with someone else; and scandal must be avoided until after the campaign is over.

Xmas in Las Vegas (4). By Jack Richardson. Produced by Fred Coe and David Karr at the Ethel Barrymore Theater. Opened November 4, 1965. (Closed November 6, 1965)

Edward T. Wellspot	Tom Ewell	Michel Wellspot	Heywood Hale Broun
Lionel Wellspot	Joe Ponazecki	Mrs. Edna Simon	Mabel Albertson
Emily Wellspot	Judy Frank	Willy	MacIntyre Dixon
Eleanor Wellspot	Shannon Bolin	Spiros Olympus	Robert H. Harris

Standbys: Messrs. Ewell, Harris, Broun—John Cecil Holm; Misses Bolin, Albertson—Sylvia Davis; Messrs. Ponazecki, Dixon—Ronald Boston; Miss Frank—Anne Baker.
Directed by Fred Coe; scenery and lighting, Robert Randolph; costumes, Ruth Morley; production stage manager, Porter Van Zandt; stage manager, Ellen Wittman; press, Karl Bernstein.
Time: the present, two days before Christmas. Place: Las Vegas, Nevada. Act I, Scene 1: A gambling casino. Scene 2: The Wellspot hotel suite. Scene 3: The office of Spiros Olympus. Scene 4: The Wellspot hotel suite. Act II, Scene 1: A gambling room at the casino. Scene 2: The Wellspot hotel suite. Scene 3: The gambling room. Scene 4: The Wellspot hotel suite.
A compulsive gambler is in Las Vegas for his annual visit to try to make his fortune at blackjack; meanwhile his family indulges in neurotic sexual yearnings and exploits.

The Zulu and the Zayda (179). By Howard Da Silva and Felix Leon; music and lyrics by Harold Rome; based on a story by Dan Jacobson. Produced by Theodore Mann and Dore Schary at the Cort Theater. Opened November 10, 1965. (Closed April 16, 1966)

Johannes	Ossie Davis	Arthur Grossman	Philip Vandervort
Koofer	James Higgins	David Grossman	John Pleshette
Harry Grossman	Joe Silver	Eric	John Randolph Jones
Helen Grossman	Sarah Cunningham	Zayda	Menasha Skulnik

Tommy Layton	Norman Barrs	William	Ed Hall
Paulus	Louis Gossett	Mr. Lamene	Charles Moore
Woman with Baby Carriage	Sandra Kent	Mrs. Lamene	Ella Thompson
Policeman	David Mogck	Groenwald	Robert Hewitt
Peter	Peter DeAnda	Dyckboom	Max Jacobs
John	Yaphet Kotto	Mourner	Sholom Ludvinsky
Joan	Christine Spencer	Nurse	Sandra Kent

Understudies: Sandra Kent, Charles Moore, Ella Thompson.

Directed by Dore Schary; scenery and lighting, William and Jean Eckart; costumes, Frank Thompson; musical supervision and orchestrations, Meyer Kupferman; conductor, Michael Spivakowsky; production stage managers, Jeb Schary and Harry Young; press, Merle Debuskey, Violet Welles, Reuben Rabinovitch, Lawrence Belling.

Time: the present. Place: Johannesburg, Republic of South Africa.

Comedy about a frisky Jewish granddad (zayda) whose family hires a Zulu as a companion for him. Their friendship bridges the gulf between age and youth, white and black, Europe and Africa, but it is troubled by the strong local prejudices. This is a straight play in which the characters sometimes pause to sing a song.

ACT I

"Tkambuza" .... Ossie Davis
"Crocodile Wife" .... Davis
"Good To Be Alive" .... Menasha Skulnik, Louis Gossett
"The Water Wears Down The Stone" .... Davis
"Rivers of Tears" .... Skulnik
"Like The Breeze Blows" .... Peter DeAnda, Christine Spencer, Ensemble
"Oisgetzaychnet" .... Skulnik, Ensemble

ACT II

"Some Things" .... Ensemble
"Zulu Love Song" .... Gossett
"L'Chayim" .... Skulnik
"Cold, Cold Room" .... Davis
"Good To Be Alive" (Reprise) .... Skulnik, Gossett

* **Skyscraper** (227). Musical based on Elmer Rice's *Dream Girl;* with book by Peter Stone; music by James Van Heusen; lyrics by Sammy Kahn. Produced by Feuer and Martin at the Lunt-Fontanne Theater. Opened November 13, 1965.

Georgina	Julie Harris	Woman Customer	Georgia Creighton
Mrs. Allerton	Nancy Cushman	Auctioneer	Burt Bier
Mr. Allerton	Donald Burr	Harry The Waiter	John Anania
Charlotte	Lesley Stewart	Cab Driver	Ken Ayers
Mayor	Burt Bier	Jazz Musician	Walter P. Brown
Doctor	Richard Korthaze	Photographer	Christian Gray
Herbert Bushman	Dick O'Neill	Appearing in the film sequence:	
Stanley	Rex Everhart	Paola	Pola Chapelle
Timothy Bushman	Peter L. Marshall	Francesco	Paul Sorvino
Roger Summerhill	Charles Nelson Reilly		

Singers: John Anania, Ken Ayers, Burt Bier, Walter P. Brown, Christian Gray, Randy Phillips, Casper Roos, Eleanor Bergquist, Georgia Creighton, Ceil Delli, Maryann Kerrick.

Dancers: Ray Chabeau, Gene Gavin, Curtis Hood, Gene Kelton, Ray Kirchner, Richard Korthaze, Darrell Notara, Bill Starr, Kent Thomas, Barbara Beck, Trudy Carson, Marilyn Charles, Suzanne France, Ellen Graff, Lauren Jones, Renata Powers.

Standby: Miss Harris—Lesley Stewart. Understudies: Mr. Reilly—Christian Gray; Mr. Marshall—Randy Phillips; Miss Cushman—Georgia Creighton; Mr. O'Neill—Burt Bier; Mr. Burr—Casper Roos; Mr. Everhart—John Anania; Miss Stewart—Maryann Kerrick.

Directed by Cy Feuer; dances and musical numbers staged by Michael Kidd; scenery and lighting, Robert Randolph; costumes, Theoni V. Aldredge; musical director, John Lesko; orchestrations, Fred Werner; dance music arranged by Marvin Laird; production stage manager, Phil Friedman; stage manager, Jack Leigh; press, Merle Debuskey, Violet Welles, Lawrence Belling.

Time: yesterday. Place: in and around a large skyscraper and a small brownstone in New York City.

Our heroine is given to daydreaming herself into romantic entanglements with all the men she meets. In the meantime, she is in a real entanglement, as the skyscraper-builders next door try to persuade her by fair means and foul to sell them her little brownstone dwelling and antique shop.

ACT I

"Occasional Flight of Fancy" ....Julie Harris, Officials
"Run For Your Life" ....Peter L. Marshall, Dick O'Neill
"Local 403" ....Rex Everhart, Construction Workers, Girls
"Opposites" ....Miss Harris, Marshall
"Run For Your Life" (Reprise) ....Marshall
"Just the Crust" ....Charles Nelson Reilly, Dick O'Neill
"Everybody Has A Right To Be Wrong" ....Miss Harris, Marshall
"Everybody Has A Right To Be Wrong" (Reprise) ....Miss Harris
"Wrong!" ....Miss Harris, Nancy Cushman, Lesley Stewart, Customers
"The Auction" ....Customers
"Occasional Flight of Fancy" (Reprise) ....Miss Harris

ACT II

"The Gaiety" ....Customers
"More Than One Way" ....Marshall, Construction Workers
"Haute Couture" ....Everhart, Models, Construction Workers
"Don't Worry" ....Reilly, O'Neill
"Don't Worry" (Reprise) ....Miss Harris, Reilly
"I'll Only Miss Her When I Think of Her" ....Marshall
"Spare That Building" ....Miss Harris, Marshall, Reilly, Company

The Devils (63). By John Whiting; based on *The Devils of Loudun* by Aldous Huxley. Produced by Alexander H. Cohen at the Broadway Theater. Opened November 16, 1965. (Closed January 8, 1966)

Mannoury, a surgeon ....Bernard Kates
Adam, a chemist ....Mark Gordon
Jean D'Armagnac, the Governor
  of Loudun ....Hugh Franklin
Guillame De Cerisay, the Chief
  Magistrate ....John Baragrey
Louis Trincant, the Public
  Prosecutor ....John Milligan
Phillipe Trincant, his daughter ...Lynda Day
A Sewerman ....James Coco
Urbain Grandier, the Vicar of St.
  Peter's Church ....Jason Robards
Ninon, a widow ....Barbara Colby
De La Rochepozay, the Bishop
  of Poitiers ....Shepperd Strudwick
Father Rangier ....Michael Lombard

Father Barre ....Albert Dekker
Sister Jeanne Of The Angels, the Prioress
  of St. Ursula's Convent ....Anne Bancroft
Richelieu ....Tom Klunis
Louis XIII, King of France ...Richard Lynch
De Laubardemont, the King's Special
  Commissioner to Loudun ....John Coliços
Sister Claire ....Karen Ludwig
Sister Louise ....Erin Martin
Sister Gabrielle ....Anna Shaler
Father Mignon ....Patrick Hines
Clerk ....John Milligan
Prince Henri De Conde ......Louis Turenne
Bontemps, a jailer ....Alan Mixon
Father Ambrose ....Edgar Stehli
Old Man ....Eugene R. Wood

Townspeople, People from the Country, Capuchins, Carmelites, Jesuits, Soldiers: Harry Clark, Linda Geisler, Judy Granite, Patricia Hammack, George Morse, Martha Neag, Frank Rowley, Lucretia Simmons, Holland Taylor, Joseph Aulisi, Richard Botham, Eric Bruno, Susan Carr, Diane Deckard, Jonathan Fox, Ron Frederics, Mary McKenzie Gordon, Adrienne Hazzard, Betsy Langman, Terry Lomax, Robert Nadder, P.L. Pfeiffer, Julie Prince, Robbie Reed, Malcolm Taylor.

Standby for Miss Bancroft—Jenny Egan. Understudies: Messrs. Baragrey, Strudwick, Klunis, Mixon—Roy Shuman; Messrs. Gordon, Lombard, Milligan, Wood—George Morse; Miss Colby —Anna Shaler; Messrs. Milligan, Stehli—Eugene R. Wood; Miss Day—Erin Martin; Messrs. Kates, Coco, Robards—Alan Mixon; Messrs. Franklin, Colicos, Turenne—Tom Klunis; Mr. Dekker—Michael Lombard; Mr. Lynch—Frank Rowley; Miss Ludwig—Lucretia Simmons; Miss Martin—Holland Taylor; Miss Shaler—Linda Geisler; Mr. Hines—John Milligan.

Directed by Michael Cacoyannis; scenery, Rouben Ter-Arutunian; costumes, Motley; lighting, Jules Fisher; production associate, Hildy Parks; production stage manager, Jean Barrere; stage manager, Jake Hamilton; press, James D. Proctor, Max Gendel, Louise Weiner.

Time: 1623-1634. Place: France, in and near the town of Loudun, and briefly in Paris.

The play is based on true events in which a roue priest is falsely accused by a hysterical nun of possessing her with diabolical, erotic visions; the priest discovers some of the truth about his own soul and its hidden strength in the course of his subsequent torture and execution. A foreign play previously produced in London (1961).

Zoe Caldwell replaced Anne Bancroft at most performances during Miss Bancroft's illness the final two weeks of the play's run.

Marcel Marceau (24). Programs of pantomimes by Marcel Marceau. Produced by New York City Center Drama Company, Jean Dalrymple, director, in association with Ronald A. Wilford Associates, Inc., at the New York City Center. Opened November 17, 1965. (Closed December 12, 1965)

Marcel Marceau performed in programs selected from the following repertory: Part I—The Kite, The Man and His Boat, The Magician, The Bureaucrats, The Cage, Circus Performer, The Seven Deadly Sins, Walking, Walking Against the Wind, The Staircase, The Sculptor, The Public Garden, The Mask Maker, Youth, Maturity, Old Age and Death; Part II—BIP goes to an Audition, BIP as a Matador, BIP dreams he is Don Juan, BIP as a Soldier, BIP goes Traveling, BIP in the Subway, BIP as a Baby Sitter, BIP at a Society Party, BIP as a Lion Tamer, BIP takes an Ocean Voyage, BIP hunts Butterflies, BIP plays David and Goliath, BIP the Street Musician, BIP looks for a job on New Year's Eve. Presentation of cards by Pierre Verry.

Production stage manager, Tennent McDaniel; stage manager, Louis Thomas; press, Herbert Breslin.

Marcel Marceau last appeared on Broadway at the New York City Center January 1, 1963, for 32 performances.

* Man of La Mancha (216). Musical with book by Dale Wasserman; music by Mitch Leigh; lyrics by Joe Darion; suggested by the life and works of Miguel de Cervantes y Saavedra. Produced by Albert W. Selden and Hal James at ANTA Washington Square Theater. Opened November 22, 1965.

Don Quixote (Cervantes) .....Richard Kiley	The Housekeeper ....Eleanore Knapp
Sancho ....Irving Jacobson	Jose, a Muleteer ....Eddie Roll
Aldonza ....Joan Diener	Juan, a Muleteer ....John Aristedes
The Innkeeper ....Ray Middleton	Paco, a Muleteer ....Antony De Vecchi
The Padre ....Robert Rounseville	Tenorio, a Muleteer ......Fernando Grahal
Dr. Carrasco ....Jon Cypher	Maria, The Innkeeper's
Antonia ....Mimi Turque	Wife ....Marceline Decker
The Barber ....Gino Conforti	Fermina, a Slavey ....Gerrianne Raphael
Pedro, Head Muleteer ....Shev Rodgers	Captain of the Inquisition ....Renato Gibelli
Anselmo, a Muleteer ....Harry Theyard	Guitarist ....David Serva

Directed by Albert Marre; choreography, Jack Cole; scenery and lighting, Howard Bay; costumes, Howard Bay and Patton Campbell; musical direction and dance arrangements, Neil Warner; musical arrangements, Music Makers, Inc.; production stage manager, Marnel Sumner; stage manager, Michael Turque; press, Arthur Cantor, Artie Solomon.

Time: the end of the 16th century. Place: a dungeon in Seville and various places in the imagination of Miguel de Cervantes. The action is played without intermission.

Thrown into the Inquisition's prison, Cervantes tells his fellow-inmates the story of Don Quixote's idealistic exploits. As Cervantes concludes his hymn to the human imagination, he finds in himself a Don Quixote kind of bravery with which to face the Inquisitors.

José Ferrer replaced Richard Kiley for two weeks beginning 5/28/66.

A Best Play; see page 195

"Man of La Mancha" ....Richard Kiley, Irving Jacobson, Horses
"It's All the Same" ....Joan Diener, Muleteers
"Dulcinea" ....Kiley
"I'm Only Thinking of Him" ....Robert Rounseville, Mimi Turque, Eleanore Knapp,
                                                                        Jon Cypher
"I Really Like Him" ....Jacobson
"What Does He Want of Me" ....Miss Diener
"Little Bird, Little Bird" ....Harry Theyard, Muleteers
"Barber's Song" ....Gino Conforti
"Golden Helmet" ....Kiley, Jacobson, Conforti, Muleteers
"To Each His Dulcinea" (To Every Man His Dream) ....Rounseville
"The Quest" (The Impossible Dream) ....Kiley
"The Combat" ....Kiley, Miss Diener, Jacobson, Muleteers
"Knight of the Woeful Countenance" ....Ray Middleton, Miss Diener, Jacobson
"The Abduction" ....Miss Diener, Muleteers
"Moorish Dance" ....Ensemble
"Aldonza" ....Miss Diener
"The Knight of the Mirrors" ....Ensemble
"A Little Gossip" ....Jacobson
"Dulcinea" (Reprise) ....Miss Diener
"Man of La Mancha" (Reprise) ....Kiley
"The Psalm" ....Rounseville
"The Quest" (Reprise) ....Entire Company

* **You Can't Take It With You** (217). Revival by Association of Producing Artists Repertory Company of the comedy by Moss Hart and George S. Kaufman. Produced by the Phoenix Theater (A Project of Theater Incorporated), T. Edward Hambleton, managing director, at the Lyceum Theater. Opened November 23, 1965.

Penelope Sycamore	Dee Victor	Henderson	James Greene
Essie	Jennifer Harmon	Tony Kirby	Clayton Corzatte
Rheba	Paulette Waters	Boris Kolenkhov	Keene Curtis
Paul Sycamore	Sydney Walker	Gay Wellington	Patricia Connolly
Mr. De Pinna	Joseph Bird	Mr. Kirby	Richard Woods
Ed	Gordon Gould	Mrs. Kirby	Betty Miller
Donald	Nat Simmons	Three Men	Chuck Daniel, Robert Moss,
Martin Vanderhof	Donald Moffat		George Pentecost
Alice	Rosemary Harris	Olga	Claribel Baird

Understudies: Misses Victor, Miller—Cavada Humphrey; Misses Harmon, Baird—Patricia Conolly; Misses Waters, Conolly—Mira Waters; Messrs. Walker, Bird—James Greene; Messrs. Gould, Corzatte, Greene—George Pentecost; Messrs. Simmons, Greene—Chuck Daniel; Mr. Moffat—Joseph Bird; Mr. Woods—Gordon Gould; Messrs. Daniel, Moss, Pentecost—Sean Gillespie; Miss Harris—Jennifer Harmon.

Directed by Ellis Rabb; scenery and lighting, James Tilton; New York supervision, Norris Houghton; costumes, Nancy Potts; production stage manager, Robert Moss; stage managers, Bruce A. Hoover, Sean Gillespie; press, Ben Kornzweig, Reginald Denenholz, Anne Woll.

Time: 1936. Place: the home of Martin Vanderhof in New York. Act I: A Wednesday evening (during this act the curtain is lowered to denote the passing of several hours). Act II: A week later. Act III: The next day.

You Can't Take It With You was first produced on Broadway by Sam H. Harris at the Booth Theater, December 14, 1936, for 837 performances. Its 1965 production was first mounted as a part of the Association of Producing Artists-Phoenix repertory season in residence at Ann Arbor under the auspices of the University of Michigan Professional Theater Program.

Kathleen Widdoes replaced Rosemary Harris 1/10/66. Late in the season many of the roles were re-cast two or three times with various mmbers of the repertory company.

Anya (16). Musical with book by George Abbott and Guy Bolton, based on the play *Anastasia* by Marcelle Maurette and Guy Bolton; music and lyrics by Robert Wright and George Forrest, based on themes of S. Rachmaninoff. Produced by

Fred R. Fehlhaber at the Ziegfeld Theater. Opened November 29, 1965. (Closed December 11, 1965)

Anya	Constance Towers	Olga	Laurie Franks
Nurse	Patricia Hoffman	Masha	Rita Metzger
Bounine	Michael Kermoyan	Sleigh Driver	Lawrence Boyll
Josef	Boris Aplon	Anouchka	Elizabeth Howell
Count Drivinitz	Lawrence Brooks	Tinka	Barbara Alexander
Count Dorn	Adair McGowan	Mother	Maggie Task
Sergei	Jack Dabdoub	Father	Michael Quinn
Yegor	Walter Hook	Dowager Empress	Lillian Gish
Katrina	Irra Petina	Prince Paul	John Michael King
Petrovin	Ed Steffe	Countess Drivinitz	Elizabeth Howell
Balalaika Player	Konstantin Pio-Ulsky	First Policeman	Lawrence Boyll
Genia, the Countess		Second Policeman	Bernard Frank
Hohenstadt	Karen Shepard	Police Sergeant	Howard Kahl
Chernov	George S. Irving	Baroness Livenbaum	Margaret Mullen

Dancers: Barbara Alexander, Ciya Challis, Patricia Drylie, Juliette Durand, Kip Andrews, Steven Boockvor, Randy Doney, Joseph Nelson.

Singers: Laurie Franks, Patricia Hoffman, Rita Metzger, Mia Powers, Lourette Raymon, Diane Tarleton, Maggie Task, Darrel Askey, Lawrence Boyll, Les Freed, Horace Guittard, Walter Hook, Howard Kahl, Adair McGowan, Richard Nieves, J. Vernon Oaks, Robert Sharp, John Taliaferro, Bernard Frank.

Understudies: Miss Towers—Karen Shepard; Mr. Kermoyan—Lawrence Brooks; Miss Gish—Margaret Mullen; Miss Petina—Maggie Task; Mr. Irving—Jack Dabdoub; Mr. King—Horace Guittard; Miss Shepard—Lourette Raymon; Miss Mullen—Elizabeth Howell; Miss Alexander—Ciya Challis; Mr. Aplon—Bernard Frank; Mr. Steffe—Jack Dabdoub.

Directed by George Abbott; choreography and musical numbers, Hanya Holm; scenery, Robert Randolph; costumes, Patricia Zipprodt; lighting, Richard Casler; musical direction, Harold Hastings; orchestrations, Don Walker; production stage manager, John Allen; stage manager, Frank Gero; press, Mary Bryant, Robert Pasolli.

Time: 1925. Place: Berlin.

The book of *Anya*, like the play on which it is based, is about the Czar's daughter Anastasia who, according to legend, may have alone escaped the mass slaughter of her royal family during the Russian Revolution.

ACT I

Choral Prelude
"Anya"
Scene 1: The Sanatorium
"A Song From Somewhere" ....Anya
Scene 2: The Cafe Czarina
"Vodka, Vodka!" ....Katrina, Josef, Emigrés
"So Proud" ....Bounine, Chernov, Petrovin, Josef
"Homeward" ....Katrina, Emigrés
Scene 3: The Chateau
"Snowflakes and Sweethearts" ("The Snowbird Song") ....Tinka, Anya, Father, Mother, Peasants
"On That Day" ....Chernov, Petrovin, Josef, Katrina
Scene 4: The Library
"Anya" ....Bounine
"Six Palaces" ....Anya, Bounine, Chernov, Petrovin
Livadia, on the Black Sea
Young Prince Paul—Randy Doney
Young Anya—Barbara Alexander
The Palace of Peterhof
The Winter Palace
Dowager Empress—Lillian Gish
Scene 5: The Courtyard
"Hand in Hand" ....Anya, Prince Paul
"This Is My Kind of Love" ....Anya, Bounine

Scene 6: The Library
Scene 7: The Chateau
"On That Day" (Reprise) ....Prince, Paul, Investors

ACT II

Scene 1: The Chateau
"That Prelude!" ....Bounine, Katrina, Petrovin, Josef, Chernov, Sergei,
Yegor, Masha, Olga, Policemen
Scene 2: The Empress' Drawing Room in Copenhagen
"A Quiet Land" ....Anya
Scene 3: The Courtyard
"Here Tonight, Tomorrow Where?" ....Chernov, Petrovin, Josef
"Leben Sie Wohl" ....Katrina, Policemen
"If This Is Goodbye" ....Anya, Bounine
Scene 4: The Library
"Little Hands" ....The Empress, Anya
Scene 5: The Chateau
"All Hail The Empress" ....Emigrés
Choral Finale

Inadmissible Evidence (166). By John Osborne. The English Stage Company Production, produced by David Merrick Arts Foundation at the Belasco Theater. Opened November 30, 1965. (Closed April 23, 1966)

Bill Maitland		Shirley	Jeanne Hepple
(Evenings)	Nicol Williamson	Joy	Lois Daine
(Matinees)	James Patterson	Mrs. Garnsey	Madeleine Sherwood
Hudson	Peter Sallis	Jane Maitland	Jill Townsend
Jones	Ted van Griethuysen	Liz	Valerie French

Understudies: Messrs. Sallis, van Griethuysen—Mitchell Erickson; Misses Sherwood, French—Barbara Lester; Misses Hepple, Daine, Townsend—Susan Tabor.
Directed by Anthony Page; scenery and costumes, Jocelyn Herbert; lighting and design supervision, Lloyd Burlingame; associate producer, Samuel Liff; production stage manager, Ben Kranz; stage manager, Mitchell Erickson; press, Max Eisen, Carl Samrock.
Time: the present. Place: a solicitor's office in East London.
The climb from his lower-class background has been too steep for this middle-aged lawyer; he is exhausted and falling apart. His business is disintegrating, his love affairs are unsatisfying, his family is alienated from him, he cannot stop protesting and everything he says worsens his predicament. A foreign play previously produced in London.
Susan Tabor replaced Lois Daine 1/18/66.
A Best Play; see page 221

The Playroom (33). By Mary Drayton. Produced by Kermit Bloomgarden and Trude Heller in association with Max Youngstein and David Karr at the Brooks Atkinson Theater. Opened December 5, 1965. (Closed January 1, 1966)

Christopher	Peter Kastner	Charlot	Alan Howard
Judy	Karen Black	Ellen	Christopher Norris
Louise	Augusta Dabney	Lt. McAfee	P. Jay Sidney
David	Tom Helmore	Detective Sullivan	Stan Watt
Eric	Richard Thomas	Patrolman Young	Jon DeHart
Paulie	Bonnie Bedelia		

Understudies: Mr. Helmore—Stan Watt; Messrs. Sidney, Watt—Don Doherty; Miss Black—Bonnie Bedelia; Misses Bedelia, Norris—Barbara Myers; Messrs. Kastner, Thomas, Howard—Don Scardino.
Directed by Joseph Anthony; scenery and lighting, Jo Mielziner; costumes, Theoni V. Aldredge; production supervisor, Bill Ross; production stage manager, Don Doherty; press, James D. Proctor, Louise Weiner.

Time: the present. Place: an apartment building called "The Montana" in New York City.
A teen-ager who adores her father so resents her stepmother that she kidnaps her young
stepsister and holds her for ransom, aided by four teen-aged friends so extremely neurotic and
dissolute that they decide to murder their little victim in order to avoid getting caught.

Me and Thee (1). By Charles Horine. Produced by Delancey Productions at the
John Golden Theater. Opened and closed at the evening performance, December
7, 1965.

Alice Carter	Barbara Britton	Dr. Grant Reeves	Charles Braswell
Paul Carter	Durward Kirby	Lela	Carolan Daniels
Roger Carter	Randy Kirby		

Understudies: Messrs. Durward Kirby, Braswell—Earl Rowe; Misses Daniels, Britton—Lynn
Bernay; Mr. Randy Kirby—David Eliscu.
Directed by Perry Bruskin; scenery and costumes, Charles Evans; fashion co-ordination, A.
Christina Giannini; lighting, V.C. Fuqua; music and theme song "Me and Thee" by George
Fischoff, lyrics by Charles Horine and Hank Miles; production stage manager, Ben Janney;
stage manager, David Eliscu; press, David Lipsky.
Time: the present. Place: the living room of the Carters' New York City apartment. Act I,
Scene 1: Late afternoon on a rainy day in December. Scene 2: The following evening. Act II,
Scene 1: Late afternoon on Christmas Eve, a week later. Scene 2: Early evening on New
Year's Eve. Scene 3: Early the following morning.
Comedy about a couple who are urged to stop conforming and let themselves go; they at-
tempt it, with dire results.

* Cactus Flower (199). By Abe Burrows; based on a play by Pierre Barillet and
Jean Pierre Gredy. Produced by David Merrick at the Royale Theater. Opened
December 8, 1965.

Toni	Brenda Vaccaro	Senor Sanchez	Arny Freeman
Igor	Burt Brinckerhoff	Customer	Will Gregory
Stephanie	Lauren Bacall	Waiter	Michael Fairman
Mrs. Durant	Eileen Letchworth	Botticelli's Springtime	Marjorie Battles
Julian	Barry Nelson	Music Lover	Michael Fairman
Harvey	Robert Moore		

Standby: Miss Bacall—Eileen Letchworth. Understudies: Mr. Nelson—Will Gregory; Miss
Vaccaro—Marjorie Battles; Messrs. Brinckerhoff and Moore—Michael Fairman.
Directed by Abe Burrows; scenery, Oliver Smith; costumes, Theoni V. Aldredge; lighting,
Martin Aronstein; associate producer, Samuel Liff; production stage manager, Charles Durand;
stage manager, May Muth; press, Harvey B. Sabinson, Lee Solters, Bob Ullman.
Time: the present. Place: 15 scenes scattered around uptown and downtown Manhattan.
Comedy about a bachelor-dentist who weaves a tangled web of romantic deceit with the
help of his angular, efficient nurse; finally she catches him in this same web.
A Best Play; see page 245

The Yearling (3). Musical based on the novel by Marjorie Kinnan Rawlings; book
by Herbert Martin and Lore Noto; music by Michael Leonard; lyrics by Herbert
Martin. Produced by Lore Noto at the Alvin Theater. Opened December 10, 1965.
(Closed December 11, 1965)

Jody Baxter	Steve Sanders	Millwheel Forrester	Tom Fleetwood
Ezra (Penny) Baxter	David Wayne	Lem Forrester	Robert Goss
Ora Baxter	Dolores Wilson	Mrs. Hutto	Carmen Mathews
Fodder-Wing	Peter Falzone	Oliver Hutto	David Hartman
Ma Forrester	Fay Sappington	Eulalie	Janet Campano
Buck Forrester	Allan Louw	Twink	Carmen Alvarez
Arch Forrester	Rodd Barry	Doc Wilson	Gordon B. Clarke
Pack Forrester	Roy Barry	Preacher	Frank Bouley
Gabby Forrester	Bob LaCrosse	Captain	David Sabin

Townspeople: Loyce Baker, Lynette Bennett, Lois Grandi, Bobbi Lange, Ruth Lawrence, Barbara Miller, Bella Shalom, Myrna Strom, Mimi Wallace, Trudy Wallace, Vito Durante, Anthony Endon, Harrison Fisher, Scott Hunter, Martin Ross, Herbert Sanders, Ted Sprague.

Understudies: Miss Wilson—Lizabeth Pritchett; Messrs. Louw, Rodd Barry, Roy Barry, La-Crosse, Fleetwood, Goss, Hartman, Clarke—David Sabin; Master Sanders, Master Falzone—Bryant Fraser; Miss Alvarez—Mimi Wallace; Miss Campano—Lois Grandi; Messrs. Barry, La-Crosse—Vito Durante; Miss Sappington—Barbara Miller.

Directed by Lloyd Richards; choreography, Ralph Beaumont; scenery and costumes, Ed Wittstein; lighting, Jules Fisher; musical direction and vocal arrangements, Julian Stein; orchestrations, Larry Wilcox; dance music, David Baker; associate producer, Michael Balistreri; production stage manager, Mortimer Halpern; stage manager, Edward Julien; press, Harvey B. Sabinson, Lee Solters, David Powers.

Time: just after the Civil War. Place: Northern Florida.

A lonely boy softens his hard country life with affection for a fawn. Loss of this pet brings him at last to maturity.

ACT I

Scene 1: The Baxter Clearing
"Let Him Kick Up His Heels" ....Penny, Ora
Scene 2: The Forrester Clearing
"Boy Talk" ....Jody, Fodder-Wing
"Bear Hunt" ....Penny, Jody, Forresters
"Some Day I'm Gonna Fly" ....Jody, Fodder-Wing, Forresters
Scene 3: The Woods
"Lonely Clearing" ....Penny
Scene 4: The Hutto House
"Everything In The World I Love" ....Jody, Mrs. Hutto
Scene 5: The Town of Volusia
"I'm All Smiles" ....Twink
"I'm All Smiles" (Reprise) ....Oliver
Scene 6: The Glen
Scene 7: The Woods
Scene 8: The Forrester Clearing
Scene 9: The Baxter Cabin
"The Kind Of Man A Woman Needs" ....Ora
"What A Happy Day" ....Ora, Jody, Doc, Buck, Millwheel
"What A Happy Day" (Reprise) ....Jody, Doc, Buck, Millwheel

ACT II

Scene 1: The Baxter Cabin, the week before Christmas
"Ain't He A Joy?" ....Penny, Jody
"Why Did I Choose You?" ....Penny, Ora
"One Promise" ....Ora
Scene 2: Volusia
"One Promise" (Reprise) ....Ora, Townspeople
"Bear Hunt" (Reprise) ....Entire Company
Scene 3: Wharf
"Everything In The World I Love" (Reprise) ....Penny, Jody, Mrs. Hutto, Oliver,
                                                      Twink, Townspeople
Scene 4: The Baxter Cabin
"What A Happy Day" (Reprise) ....Jody
Scene 5: The Baxter Cabin
"Nothing More" ....Penny, Jody
Scene 6:The Runaway
Scene 7: The Baxter Clearing
"Everything Beautiful" ....Ora

La Grosse Valise (7). Musical with book by Robert Dhery; music and orchestrations by Gerard Calvi; lyrics by Harold Rome. Produced by Joe Kipness and Arthur Lesser at the Fifty-fourth Street Theater. Opened December 14, 1965. (Closed December 18, 1965)

Traveler to Bordeaux ....Jacques Ebner
Antoine, a customs inspector....Michel Modo
Spanish Tourists ....Marcello Gamboa,
                                Diane Coupe
Pepito, a customs inspector ....Guy Grosso
Jean-Loup Roussel, assistant chief
  of customs ....Ronald Fraser
La Fouillette, an airport police
  officer ....Tony Doonan
La Nana ....France Arnell
Photographers ....Max Vialle, Bernard
                                Gauthron
Nicolas ....Brigitte Valadin
Svatsou, the clown
  (M. Cheri) ....Victor Spinetti
Vlaminsky ....Guy Bertil

Raoul ....Barry L. Martin
Chief of customs ....John Maxim
The Little Porter ....Bert Michaels
DeWalleyne ....Sybil Bartrop
Baby's Maid ....Maureen Byrnes
Chief d'Etat, a diplomatic
  official ....Max Vialle
Old Lady ....Rita Charisse
Andre ....Jean-Michel Mole
Baby ....Joyce Jillson
Mireille ....Mireille Chazal
Pedralini, Head Scout ....John Maxim
1st Scout ....George Tregre
Bald Man ....Bernard Gauthron
Berthozeau ....Tony Doonan

Others: Diana Baffa, Maureen Byrnes, Ronn Forella, Pat Gosling, Carolyn Kirsch, Alex McKay, Donna Sanders, Mary Zahn.

Directed by Robert Dhery; choreography, Colette Brosset; associate choreographer, Tom Panko; scenery and costumes, Jacques Dupont, supervised by Frederick Fox; lighting, John Gleason; musical director, Lehman Engel; assistant conductor, Karen L. Gustafson; associate producer, Arthur Cantor; stage manager, Bob Burland; press, Arthur Cantor, Arthur Solomon.

Time: the present. Place: Customs, Orly Airport, Paris, France.

A clown attempts to get his enormous piece of luggage through customs. When opened, it spills out a show full of zany sketches and song and dance numbers. A foreign play previously produced in Paris.

ACT I

"La Grosse Valise" ....Roussel, M. Cheri, Nicolas, Company
"A Big One" ....Roussel, Antoine, Pepito, M. Cheri, Nicolas, Company
"C'est Defendu" ....Roussel, La Nana, Pepito, Antoine
"Hamburg Waltz" ....Principals, Dancing Girls and Boys
"Happy Song" ....Roussel, Pepito, Antoine, Chief of Customs
"For You" ....Baby
"Sandwich for Two" ....M. Cheri, Nicolas
"La Java" ....La Nana, Chief of Customs, Baby, Dancing Girls and Boys
"Xanadu" ....La Nana, M. Cheri, Roussel

ACT II

"Slippy Sloppy Shoes" ....M. Cheri, Roussel, Dancing Girls and Boys
"Spanish Dance" ....Roussel, Mireille
"For You" (Reprise) ....Roussel, Baby
"Delilah Done Me Wrong" ....M. Cheri, La Nana, the Slaves
"Hawaii" ....La Nana, Baby, Dancing Girls

Oklahoma! (24). Revival of the musical based on *Green Grow the Lilacs* by Lynn Riggs; book and lyrics by Oscar Hammerstein II; music by Richard Rodgers. Produced by the New York City Center Light Opera Company, Jean Dalrymple, director, by arrangement with Rodgers & Hammerstein, at the New York City Center. Opened December 15, 1965. (Closed January 2, 1966)

Aunt Eller ....Ruth Kobart
Curly ....John Davidson
Laurey ....Susan Watson
Will Parker ....Richard France
Jud Fry ....Daniel P. Hannafin

Ado Annie Carnes ....Karen Morrow
Ali Hakim ....Jules Munshin
Gertie Cummings ....Loi Leabo
Andrew Carnes ....Sammy Smith
Cord Elam ....Herbert Surface

Dancers: Cathy Conklin, Joanna Crosson, Carolyn Dyer, Carol Estey, Sharon Herr, Loi Leabo, Jane Levin, Marie Patrice, Betty Ann Rapine, Rande Rayburn, Julie Theobald, Toodie Wittmer, Don Angelo, Dean Crane, Gerry Dalton, Jeremy Ives, Brynnar Mehl, Phillip Rice, Bud Spencer, Fabian Suart.

Singers: Vicki Belmonte, Maria Bradley, Judie Elkins, Jeanne Frey, Marie Hero, Joyce Olson, Susan Sidney, Maggie Worth, Kenny Adams, Brown Bradley, Roger Alan Brown, Joseph Corby, Peter Clark, Lance Des Jardins, Konstantin Moskalenko, Stephen John Rydell, Herbert Surface, Victor Helou.

Understudies: Mr. Davidson—Joseph Corby; Miss Watson—Laurie Franks; Messrs. Munshin, Smith—Victor Helou; Miss Morrow—Maria Hero; Mr. France—Kenny Adams; Miss Kobart—Maggie Worth; Mr. Hannafin—Roger Alan Brown; Miss Leabo—Carolyn Dyer; Mr. Albright—Dean Crane; Miss Watson—Sharon Herr. Swing girl, Carolyn Dyer. Dance captain, Loi Leabo.

Directed by John Fearnley; original dances by Agnes de Mille restaged by Gemze de Lappe; scenery, Lemuel Ayers; costumes, Stanley Simmons; lighting, Peggy Clark; musical director, Pembroke Davenport; assistant conductor, Abba Bogin; production stage managers, Herman Shapiro, Chet O'Brien; press, Jean Dalrymple, Homer Poupart.

Time: just after the turn of the century. Place: Indian territory (now Oklahoma).

Oklahoma! was first produced by the Theater Guild, March 31, 1943, for 2,212 performances. It was last revived on Broadway by the New York City Center Light Opera Company in spring, 1963, for 30 performances in two engagements of 15 performances each.

The Persecution and Assassination of Marat as Performed by the Inmates of the Asylum of Charenton Under the Direction of the Marquis de Sade (144). By Peter Weiss; English version by Geoffrey Skelton; verse adaptation by Adrian Mitchell. Produced by David Merrick Arts Foundation by arrangement with the Governors of the Royal Shakespeare Theater, Stratford Upon-Avon, presenting the Royal Shakespeare Company at the Martin Beck Theater. Opened December 27, 1965. (Closed April 30, 1966)

M. Coulmier	Clifford Rose	Marquis de Sade	Patrick Magee
Mme. Coulmier	Brenda Kempner	Duperret	John Steiner
Mlle. Coulmier	Ruth Baker	Abbot	Mark Jones
Herald	Michael Williams	A mad animal	Morgan Sheppard
Cucurucu	Freddie Jones	Schoolmaster	James Mellor
Kokol	Hugh Sullivan	The Military Representative	Ian Hogg
Polpoch	Jonathan Burn	Mother	Mark Jones
Rossignol	Jeanette Landis	Father	Henry Woolf
Jacques Roux	Robert Lloyd	A newly-rich lady	John Hussey
Charlotte Corday	Glenda Jackson	Voltaire	John Harwood
Jean-Paul Marat	Ian Richardson	Lavoisier	Leon Lissek
Simonne Evrard	Susan Williamson		

Others: Patients—Mary Allen, Michael Farnsworth, Maroussia Frank, Tamara Fuerst, Guy Gordon, Sheila Grant, Michael Percival, Lyn Pinkney, Carol Raymont; Nuns—Heather Canning, Jennifer Tudor; Guards—Timothy Hardy, Stanford Trowell.

Musicians: Patrick Gowers (music director, harmonium, tuba), Richard Callinan (percussion), Michael Gould (trumpet), Nicholas Moes (guitar, harmonium), Rainer Schuelein (flute, piccolo, alto flute).

Understudies: Mr. Richardson—Robert Lloyd; Mr. Magee—Morgan Sheppard; Miss Jackson—Sheila Grant; Mr. Williams—John Steiner; Mr. Rose—John Hussey; Mr. Steiner—Mark Jones; Miss Williamson—Maroussia Frank.

Directed by Peter Brook; scenery and properties, Sally Jacobs; costumes, Gunilla Palmstierna-Weiss; choreographer, Malcolm Goddard; lighting and design supervision, Lloyd Burlingame; music, Richard Peaslee; assistant to the director, Ian Richardson; stage manager, Christine Staley; press, Harvey B. Sabinson, Lee Solters, David Powers.

Time: the Napoleonic Era. Place: the insane asylum at Charenton in France.

Charenton asylum inmates, gibbering mad folk, act out a play about Marat's assassination, under de Sade's direction, as a form of occupational therapy. The play itself is a conflict of revolutionary zeal (embodied by Marat) with inward-seeking existentialism (embodied by de Sade). A foreign play previously produced in West Berlin and London.

A Best Play; see page 269

UTBU (7). By James Kirkwood. Produced by Lyn Austin at the Helen Hayes Theater. Opened January 4, 1966. (Closed January 8, 1966)

Connie Tufford	Margaret Hamilton	J. Francis Amber	Tony Randall
Anastasia Amber	Cathryn Damon	Eugene Boyer	Tom Aldredge
William Uggims	Alan Webb	Valerie Rogers	Constance Ford
Madge Kempton	Doris Rich	Miss——Rogers	Susan Priolo
Shirley Amber	Thelma Ritter	Jimmy Newton	Clyde Williams

Understudies: Messrs. Randall, Webb—Tom Aldredge; Misses Ritter, Hamilton, Rich—Mary Farrell; Misses Damon, Ford—Laurinda Barrett; Mr. Aldredge—Charles Gray; Miss Priolo—Trudy Bordoff; Mr. Williams—Valdo Williams.

Directed by Nancy Walker; scenery and lighting, David Hays; costumes, Theoni V. Aldredge; associate producer, Bruce W. Stark; production stage manager, Frederic de Wilde; stage manager, Charles Gray; press, Samuel Lurie, Stanley F. Kaminsky.

Time: the present. Place: the Manhattan apartment of J. Francis Amber overlooking the East River. Act I: A morning in early fall. Act II, Scene 1: The afternoon of the same day. Scene 2: The next afternoon.

Comedy about the systematic bumping-off of undesirable persons by a group whose name (as per the initials in the play's title) stands for Unhealthy To Be Unpleasant.

Malcolm (7). By Edward Albee; based on the novel by James Purdy. Produced by Theater 1966 (Richard Barr and Clinton Wilder) at the Sam S. Shubert Theater. Opened January 11, 1966. (Closed January 15, 1966)

Malcolm	Matthew Cowles	Jocko	Robert Viharo
Cox	Henderson Forsythe	Melba	Jennifer West
Laureen	Estelle Parsons	A man	William Callan
Kermit	John Heffernan	Heliodoro	Victor Arnold
A young man	Victor Arnold	A park attendant, Miles, a policeman,	
Madame Girard	Ruth White	a doctor	Henderson Forsythe
Girard Girard	Wyman Pendleton	A street walker,	
Eloisa Brace	Alice Drummond	Madame Rosita	Estelle Parsons
Jerome Brace	Donald Hotton	Various people	Vicki Blankenship, Joseph
Gus	Alan Yorke		Cali, William Callan, Robert Viharo

Standby: Misses White, Drummond—Doris Roberts.

Understudies: Mr. Cowles—Douglas Anderson; Misses Parsons, West—Vicki Blankenship; Messrs. Heffernan, Pendleton—William Callan; Mr. Hotton—Victor Arnold; Messrs. Yorke, Arnold—Robert Viharo.

Directed by Alan Schneider; scenery, William Ritman; costumes, Willa Kim; lighting, Tharon Musser; music, William Flanagan; song "Hot in the Rocker" music by William Flanagan, lyrics by Edward Albee; production stage manager, Mark Wright; stage manager, Arthur Pepine; press, Howard Atlee, David Roggensack.

Time: the present. Place: anywhere. The play is divided into two acts.

A lad of fifteen, a symbol of innocence, is ordered to go out into the world, where each person he meets is corrupt and adds to his experience but diminishes him until finally he is destroyed.

The Wayward Stork (5). By Harry Tugend. Produced by Garrick Productions and Martin Lee at the Forty-sixth Street Theater. Opened January 19, 1966. (Closed January 22, 1966)

Robert Stevens	Bob Cummings	Mrs. Galbraith	Molly Ardrey
Mrs. Julia Stevens	Lois Nettleton	Nurse	Linn Mason
Mrs. Maggie Stevens	Arlene Golonka	Dr. Justin Kempp	Bernie West
Mrs. Peters	Arlene Walker	Dr. Stanley Carter	Gary Pillar
Mrs. Hoyt	Rosalind Cash	Roy Bailey	Art Lund

Understudies: Mr. Cummings—Bernie West; Misses Nettleton, Golonka, Mason, Walker, Cash—Molly Ardrey; Mr. West—Art Lund; Messrs. Lund, Pillar—Chet Leaming.

Directed by Dan Levin; scenery, Will Steven Armstrong; costumes, Ann Roth; lighting, Peter Hunt; production stage manager, Kenneth Mays; stage manager, Chet Leaming; press, Nat and Irvin Dorfman.

Time: the present. Place: Los Angeles, Calif. Act I, Scene 1: The Stevens' home, West Los Angeles, early September afternoon. Scene 2: Dr. Justin Kempp's offices, University Medical Center, Los Angeles. Scene 3: The Stevens' home, 10 a.m., two weeks later. Scene 4: The same, that night at 9 o'clock. Act II, Scene 1: The Stevens' home, the next morning. Scene 2: The same, evening, three weeks later. Scene 3: Dr. Kempp's offices, the following morning.

Comedy about a sterile husband who connives to have his wife artificially inseminated—but by mistake his widowed sister-in-law receives this treatment.

* **Sweet Charity** (139). Musical based on the screenplay *Nights of Cabiria* by Federico Fellini, Tullio Pinelli and Ennio Flaiano; book by Neil Simon; music by Cy Coleman; lyrics by Dorothy Fields. Produced by Fryer, Carr and Harris at the Palace Theater. Opened January 29, 1966.

Charity ....Gwen Verdon	Carmen ....Carmen Morales
Dark Glasses; Mike ....Michael Davis	Nickie ....Helen Gallagher
Bystander; Waiter ....John Stratton	Doorman ....I. W. Klein
Married Couple ...Bud Vest, Elaine Cancilla	Ursula ....Sharon Ritchie
Woman With Hat; Receptionist;	Vittorio Vidal ....James Luisi
Good Fairy ....Ruth Buzzi	Manfred ....Bud Vest
Ice Cream Vendor ....Gene Foote	Old Maid ....Elaine Cancilla
Football Player ....John Sharpe	Oscar ....John McMartin
Ballplayers ....Harold Pierson, Eddie Gasper	Daddy Johann Sebastian
Career Girl; Rosie ....Barbara Sharma	Brubeck ....Arnold Soboloff
Young Spanish Man ....Lee Roy Reams	Brother Harold;
1st Cop; Herman ....John Wheeler	Policeman ....Harold Pierson
2nd Cop; Barney ....David Gold	Brother Eddie ....Eddie Gasper
Helene ....Thelma Oliver	

The singers and dancers of Times Square: I. W. Klein, Mary Louise, Alice Evans, Betsy Dickerson, Kathryn Doby, Suzanne Charny, Elaine Cancilla, Carmen Morales, Christine Stewart, Charlene Ryan, David Gold, Gene Foote, Harold Pierson, Bud Vest, Lee Roy Reams, John Sharpe, Eddie Gasper, Michael Davis, Patrick Heim.

Understudies: Miss Verdon—Helen Gallagher; Mr. McMartin—John Stratton; Mr. Luisi—Michael Davis; Miss Gallagher—Elaine Cancilla; Miss Oliver—Barbara Sharma; Miss Ritchie—Charlene Ryan; Miss Sharma—Suzanne Charney.

Directed, conceived and choreographed by Bob Fosse; scenery and lighting, Robert Randolph; costumes, Irene Sharaff; musical direction and dance music arrangements, Fred Werner; orchestrations, Ralph Burns; production manager, Robert Linden; associate producer, John Bowab; stage managers, Paul Phillips, Michael Sinclair, Nick Malekos; press, Betty Lee Hunt, Fred Weterick.

Time: the present. Place: New York City.

A warm-hearted dance hall hostess goes from man to man, looking for the right one. She is always the loser, even at last when she thinks she is finally winning.

Marie Wallace replaced Sharon Ritchie 2/14/66.

ACT I

Prologue: Charity's Wish
Scene 1: The Park
"You Should See Yourself" ....Gwen Verdon, Michael Davis
"The Rescue" ....Passers-By
Scene 2: Hostess Room
Scene 3: Fan-Dango Ballroom
"Big Spender" ....Helen Gallagher, Thelma Oliver, Fan-Dango Girls
"Charity's Soliloquy" ....Miss Verdon
Scene 4: New York Street
Scene 5: Pompeii Club
"Rich Man's Frug" ....Barbara Sharma, Eddie Gasper, John Sharpe, The Patrons
Scene 6: Vittorio Vidal's Apartment
"If My Friends Could See Me Now" ....Miss Verdon
"Too Many Tomorrows" ....James Luisi
Scene 7: Hostess Room

"There's Gotta Be Something Better Than This" ....Misses Verdon, Gallagher, Oliver
Scene 8: YMHA—92d Street "Y"
"I'm The Bravest Individual" ....Miss Verdon, John McMartin

ACT II

Scene 1: YMHA—92d Street "Y"
Scene 2: Rhythm of Life Church
"Rhythm of Life" ....Arnold Soboloff, Harold Pierson, Gasper, Worshippers
Scene 3: Going Cross-town
Scene 4: Charity's Apartment
"Baby Dream Your Dream" ....Misses Gallagher, Oliver
Scene 5: Coney Island
"Sweet Charity" ....McMartin
Scene 6: Fan-Dango Ballroom
"Where Am I Going" ....Miss Verdon
Scene 7: Times Square
Scene 8: Barney's Chile Hacienda
Scene 9
"I'm a Brass Band" ....Miss Verdon and her Brass Band
Scene 10: Fan-Dango Ballroom
"I Love To Cry At Weddings" ....John Wheeler, Davis, Miss Gallagher,
Miss Oliver, Girls, Patrons
Scene 11: The Park

The Great Indoors (7). By Irene Kamp. Produced by George W. George and Frank Granat at the Eugene O'Neill Theater. Opened February 1, 1966. (Closed February 5, 1966)

Hattie Gaines	.............Rosetta LeNoire	Willy Kane	.................Logan Ramsey
Oriane Brice	...............Geraldine Page	Bonnie Doon	................Dolph Sweet
Arnolt Zend	..................Curt Jurgens	Kurt Schonforn	............Hans Gudegast
Hector Case	........Clarence Williams III	Francis X. Daugherty	.......House Jameson
Billie Mae McCune	........Margaret Ladd	Lila Sparrow	...............Joan Wetmore

Understudies: Misses Page, Wetmore—Eunice Anderson; Mr. Jurgens—House Jameson; Mr. Williams—Gene Boland; Miss Ladd—Carol Guilford; Messrs. Ramsey, Sweet, Jameson—Wallace Englehardt; Mr. Gudegast—Reinhard Jahn.
Directed by George Schaefer; scenery, Peter Larkin; costumes, Noel Taylor; lighting, Tharon Musser; "Cold" music by Jacques Urbont, lyrics by Irene Kamp; production stage manager, Robert Downing; stage manager, Nelle Nugent; press, Harvey B. Sabinson, Lee Solters, Lila King.
Time: late summer, 1964. Place: the Belvedere—a summerhouse on a former plantation in the Delta region of the American South. Act I: A Friday morning. Act II: Saturday evening. Act III: Early Sunday evening.
Drama of racial and religious tensions set in the Deep South, where a former German munitions-maker (who also happens to be a Jew) confronts his two offspring: a Negro whose mother was a former house servant and a German whose mother was a dancer tortured by the Nazis.

* **Wait Until Dark** (136). By Frederick Knott. Produced by Fred Coe at the Ethel Barrymore Theater. Opened February 2, 1966.

Mike Talman	................Mitchell Ryan	Sam Hendrix	..............James Congdon
Sgt. Carlino	.................Val Bisoglio	Gloria	......................Julie Herrod
Harry Roat Jr.	.............Robert Duvall	Policemen	.....William Jordan, Richard Kuss
Susy Hendrix	.................Lee Remick		

Standby: Miss Remick—Dixie Marquis. Understudies: Mr. Duvall—James Tolkan; Messrs. Ryan, Congdon—William Jordan; Mr. Bisoglio—Richard Kuss; Miss Herrod—Susan Dunfee.
Directed by Arthur Penn; scenery and lighting, George Jenkins; costumes, Ruth Morley; stage manager, Ellen Wittman; press, Karl Bernstein, Michael Bruno.

Time: the present, Place: a basement apartment in Greenwich Village. Act I, Scene 1: Friday evening. Scene 2: Saturday afternoon. Act II, Scene 1: Twenty minutes later. Scene 2: About an hour later. Act III, Scene 1: Immediately afterwards. Scene 2: A few minutes later. Scene 3: A minute later.

A blind woman is menaced by a gang of criminals who are trying to recover, by guile or by force, a heroin-stuffed doll they suppose is concealed in her apartment.

James Tolkan replaced Robert Duval in mid-May.

The Comédie Française. Repertory of four plays in the French language. **L'Avare** (8). Revival of the comedy by Molière (Jean-Baptiste Poquelin). Opened February 8, 1966. (Closed February 27, 1966). **Le Cid** (5). Revival of the tragedy by Pierre Corneille. Opened February 11, 1966. (Closed February 13, 1966). **La Reine Morte** (4). By Henri de Montherlant. Opened February 15, 1966. (Closed February 24, 1966). **Un Fil à la Patte** (8). Revival of the comedy by Georges Feydeau. Opened February 17, 1966. (Closed February 22, 1966) Produced by S. Hurok under the auspices of the New York City Center of Music and Drama, by arrangement with the French government, at the New York City Center.

PERFORMER	L'AVARE	LE CID	UN FIL A LA PATTE	LA REINE MORTE
Marthe Alycia			La Baronne	
Jean-Claude Arnaud	Maitre Jacques		Firmin	Don Eduardo
			Le Concierge	Capt. Bathala
Michel Aumont	Harpagon		Bouzin	
Geneviève Casile	Elise	L'Infante	Nini	Inès de Castro
Jacques Charon			Bois-d'Enghein	
François Chaumette	Anselme	Don Gomez		Egas Coelho
Paul-Emile Deiber		Don Diègue	Le Général	Le Roi Ferrante
Lise Delamare	Frosine	Léonor	Marceline	
Jacques Destoop	Brindavoine	Don Rodrigue	Un Monsieur	Lt. Martins
Michel Duchaussoy	Mâitre Simon	Don Arias	Chenneviette	Alvar Gonçalvès
Maurice Escande		Le Roi		
Christine Fersen		Chimène	Une dame	L'Infante
Alain Feydeau	La Merluche		Fontanet	
Max Fournel	Le Commissaire	Don Alonse	Emile	Le Grand Amiral
				Don Manuel
				Ocayo
Catherine Hubeau	Mariane		Viviane	
Jean-Louis Jemma	Cléante	Don Sanche	Lantery	Don Christoval
Francoise Kanel	Dame Claude	Dona Elvire	Miss Betting	
Michel Martin	Un pâtissier	Le page	Le fleuriste	Dino del Moro
Alain Pralon	La Flèche		Jean	Un Serviteur
Catherine Samie			Lucette	
Jacques Toja	Valère		Antonio	Prince don Pedro

L'AVARE directed by Jacques Mauclair; scenery and costumes, Jacques Noël; music, Georges Delerue.

Time: the 17th century. Place: Paris.

L'Avare was first performed September 9, 1668 at the Palais-Royal, with Molière himself in the role of Harpagon. From 1680 to 1960, The Comédie Française performed it 1,989 times.

LE CID directed by Paul-Emile Deiber; scenery and costumes, André Delfau; music, Marcel Landowski.

Time: the 11th century, under the reign of Don Fernand. Place: Seville, Spain.

Le Cid was first performed at the Marais in Paris in 1636. From 1680 to 1952, The Comédie Française performed it 1,220 times.

LA REINE MORTE directed by Pierre Franck; scenery and costumes, Pierre Simonini.

Time: the Middle Ages. Place: Portugal. Act I, Scene 1: In the Royal Palace. Scene 2: In Inès de Castro's house. Act II, Scene 1: The King's study. Scene 2: The entrance to Santarem Castle. Act III: A room in the Royal Palace.

La Reine Morte concerns a Portuguese king whose son defies his wishes and marries as he chooses. The king has his son's wife killed but dies of emotion from this act, whereupon the prince enthrones his dead bride. The play was written in 1942 for The Comédie Française and has been performed in France and in many other countries. This production is its American premiere.

UN FIL A LA PATTE directed by Jacques Charon; scenery and costumes, André Levasseur. Time: the *Belle Epoque*. Place: Paris.

Un Fil à la Patte was first performed January 9, 1894, at the Palais-Royal. Its 200th Comédie Française performance took place on November 11, 1964.

Administrator-general of The Comédie Française, Maurice Escande; director-general, Roger Hoff; simultaneous English translations, Helen Gillespie, Edward Greer; stage managers, Max de Guy, Irving Sudrow; press, Martin Feinstein, Michael Sweeley.

Philadelphia, Here I Come! (119). By Brian Friel. Produced by David Merrick Arts Foundation, by arrangement with Oscar Lewenstein and Michael White, at the Helen Hayes Theater. Opened February 16, 1966.

Madge .... Mairin D. O'Sullivan	Master Boyle .... Joseph Boland
Gareth O'Donnell	Lizzy Sweeney .... Mavis Villiers
In Public .... Patrick Bedford	Con Sweeney .... Joseph Warren
In Private .... Donal Donnelly	Ben Burton .... John Cecil Holm
S.B. O'Donnell,	Ned .... Thomas Connolly
County Councillor .... Eamon Kelly	Tom .... Dermot McNamara
Kate Doogan .... Lanna Saunders	Joe .... Eamon Morrissey
Senator Doogan .... William Griffis	Canon Mick O'Byrne .... Donald Marye

Understudies: Mr. Donnelly—Dermot McNamara; Messrs. Bedford, Connolly, McNamara, Morrissey—David Haviland; Mr. Kelly—Joseph Boland; Messrs. Boland, Marye—John Cecil Holm; Messrs. Warren, Holm, Griffis—Joseph Hill; Misses Villiers, O'Sullivan—Grace Carney; Miss Saunders—Lesley Hunt.

Directed by Hilton Edwards; scenery and costumes, Lloyd Burlingame; associate producer, Samuel Liff; production stage manager, Mitchell Erickson; stage manager, Joseph Hill; press, Harvey B. Sabinson, Lee Solters, Jay Russell.

Time: the present, the night before Gar's departure for Philadelphia. Place: the living quarters behind the general store of County Councillor S.B. O'Donnell in Ballybeg, Ireland. The play is divided into three acts.

An Irish youth preparing to come live in America is swept by emotion as he severs his ties with friends and neighbors (his innermost feelings are expressed by a second character representing his private self). In particular, he tries (and fails) to evoke some small sign of affection from his father, with whom he is unable to communicate. A foreign play previously produced in Dublin.

A Best Play; see page 301

* Hostile Witness (118). By Jack Roffey. Produced by Jay Julien and Andre Goulston by arrangement with Peter Saunders at The Music Box. Opened February 17, 1966.

Charles Milburn .... Norman Barrs	Mr. Naylor .... Anthony Kemble Cooper
Percy .... Harvey Jason	Clerk of the Court .... Walter Thomson
Sheila Larkin .... Angela Thornton	Policeman .... Arthur Marlowe
Simon Crawford .... Ray Milland	Superintendent Eley .... Gerald Peters
Sir Peter Crossman .... Michael Allinson	Dr. Wimborne .... Peter Pagan
Hamish Gillespie .... Edgar Daniels	Mr. Justice Osborne .... Melville Cooper
Major Hugh Maitland .... Geoffrey Lumsden	Prison Officer .... John Clark
Court Usher .... Stafford Dickens	Lady Gregory .... Margot Stevenson

Spectators and Court Personnel: Katherine Hynes, Dorothy James, Robert Murch, Alex Reed, Tom McDermott, Jim Oyster.

Understudies: Messrs. Barrs, Peters—Alex Reed; Messrs. Allinson, Kemble Cooper—Tom McDermott; Mr. Lumsden—Peter Pagan; Miss Thornton—Dorothy James; Mr. Daniels— Walter Thomson; Mr. Melville Cooper—Stafford Dickens; Messrs. Dickens, Thomson—Arthur Marlowe; Messrs. Pagan, Clark, Marlowe—Jim Oyster; Miss Stevenson—Katherine Hynes; Mr. Jason—John Clark.

Directed by Reginald Denham; scenery and lighting, Ralph Alswang; associate producer,

Anthony Parella; production stage manager, Paul A. Foley; stage manager, Arthur Marlowe; press, Harvey B. Sabinson, Lee Solters, Leo Stern.

Time: the present. Place: London. Act I, Scene 1: The chambers of Simon Crawford, Q.C., early evening of a day in April. Scene 2: Court No. 1, Central Criminal Court, Old Bailey, an afternoon some weeks later. Act II, Scene 1: A consultation cell, Old Bailey, a few minutes later. Scene 2: Same as Act I, Scene 2, the following morning.

A successful Q.C. is accused of murdering a judge. His friends rally round him as he is brought to trial, but only by clever deductions followed by clever courtroom tactics is he saved and the real murderer exposed. A foreign play previously produced in London.

Slapstick Tragedy (7). A program of two one-act plays *(The Mutilated* and *The Gnadiges Fraulein)* by Tennessee Williams. Produced by Charles Bowden and Lester Persky in association with Sidney Lanier at the Longacre Theater. Opened February 22, 1966. (Closed February 26, 1966)

THE MUTILATED

Celeste	Kate Reid	Cop	Jordan Charney
Henry	Ralph Waite	Bernie	Tom Aldredge
Trinket	Margaret Leighton	Woman at Bar	Adelle Rasey
Slim	James Olson	Pious Queen	Dan Bly
Bruno	Ralph Waite	Tiger	Henry Oliver
Maxie	David Sabin	Shore Police	Hank Brunjes
Bird Girl	Renee Orin		

Singers: Hank Brunjes, Jordan Charney, Alan Crofoot, Larry Ellis, Ronn Hansen, Henry Oliver, Renee Orin, Art Ostrin, Adelle Rasey, David Sabin.

THE GNADIGES FRAULEIN

Polly	Zoe Caldwell	The Gnadiges Fraulein	Margaret Leighton
Molly	Kate Reid	Cocaloony	Art Ostrin
Permanent Transient	Dan Bly	Indian Joe	James Olson

Standbys: Miss Leighton—Adelle Rasey; Misses Reid, Caldwell—Renee Orin. Understudies: Mr. Olson—Hank Brunjes; Mr. Waite—Jordan Charney; Mr. Aldredge—Dan Bly.

Directed by Alan Schneider; scenery, Ming Cho Lee; costumes, Noel Taylor; music, Lee Hoiby; lighting, Martin Aronstein; produced in association with Frenman Productions, Inc.; production stage manager, Mark Wright; stage managers, Patrick Horrigan, Elizabeth Roberts; press, David Rothenberg.

THE MUTILATED Time: the 1930s. Place: the Old French Quarter in New Orleans. Two floozies in a run-down hotel room—one who has had a breast removed and one who has been battered emotionally—console each other in a quarrelsome friendship and also find a degree of comfort in their faith in the Virgin Mary. THE GNADIGES FRAULEIN Time: the present. Place: Cocaloony Key. Drifters living in a bunkhouse on a Florida key include a gossip columnist, a mad ex-vaudevillian and a has-been singer whose eyes are pecked out by birds.

Nathan Weinstein, Mystic, Connecticut (3). By David Rayfiel. Produced by Philip Rose, Herschel Bernardi and Jeanne Otto at the Brooks Atkinson Theater. Opened February 25, 1966. (Closed February 26, 1966)

Rachel Weinstein	Zohra Lampert	Man Patient	Michael Beckett
Arnold Rose	Anthony Holland	Mrs. Snow	Estelle Winwood
Nathan Weinstein	Sam Levene	Harry Wang	Robert Barend
Dr. Lance Augenblick	Gerry Matthews	Deborah Wang	Doris Belack
Goldfish Girl	Alixandria Walsh	Lem Fowler	John Wardwell
Lady Visitor	Sylvia Davis	Chief Kim Bong Choy	Saeed Jaffrey
Hospital Attendant	David Miller		

Standby: Miss Winwood—Sylvia Davis. Understudies: Mr. Levene—Robert Barend; Misses Lampert, Belack—Anna Shaler; Mr. Barend—Norman Shelly; Messrs. Jaffrey, Wardwell—David Miller; Messrs. Holland, Matthews—Michael Beckett.

Directed by Peter Kass; scenery and lighting, Ben Edwards; costumes, Jane Greenwood; music composed and arranged by Joseph Garvey; production stage manager, Leonard Auerbach; stage manager, Norman Shelly; press, Merle Debuskey, Violet Welles, Mae S. Hong, Larry Belling.

Time: the present. Place: New York City and Mystic, Conn. Act I, Scene 1: "Incident at a Retirement Party." Scene 2: "Hospital Life." Scene 3: "A Plan Is Born." Scene 4: "Visiting Hours—Part One." Scene 5: "Visiting Hours—Part Two." Scene 6: "Start of the Pilgrimage." Act II: "A Father's Desperate Scheme." Act III, Scene 1: "the united . . . states." Scene 2: "The New King."

Comedy about a retired Jewish Post Office employee trying to find out the cause of his daughter's neurosis.

First One Asleep, Whistle (1). By Oliver Hailey. Produced by Edgar and Bruce Lansbury at the Belasco Theater. Opened and closed at the evening performance, February 26, 1966.

Elaine	Salome Jens	David	Frank Converse
Susan	Marya Zimmet	Esther	Louise Shaffer

Alternate: Elissa Leeds had been scheduled to play the role of Susan at matinee performances. Standbys: Miss Jens—Nina Wilcox; Mr. Converse—Sam Waterston.

Directed by John Berry; scenery and lighting, Lloyd Burlingame; costumes, Theoni V. Aldredge; production stage manager, Gigi Cascio; press, Max Eisen, Robert Larkin, Jeannie Gibson Merrick.

Time: the present. Place: Elaine's apartment in New York City. Act I, Scene 1: Late evening. Scene 2: 8 a.m., a few days later. Scene 3: A month later, 4 a.m. Scene 4: Another month later, 11 p.m. Act II, Scene 1: Another month later, midafternoon. Scene 2: Late that night.

Emotional tangle involving a neurotic young mother in an ill-fated romance with an immature lover.

Where's Daddy? (22). By William Inge. Produced by Michael Wager (by arrangement with Robert Whitehead) at the Billy Rose Theater. Opened March 2, 1966. (Closed March 19, 1966)

Teena	Barbara Dana	Helen	Barbara Ann Teer
Tom	Beau Bridges	Razz	Robert Hooks
Mrs. Bigelow	Betty Field	Pinky	Hiram Sherman

Standbys: Miss Field—Dortha Duckworth; Mr. Bridges—John Crowther. Understudies: Mr. Sherman—Howard Fischer; Mr. Hooks—Booker T. Bradshaw Jr.; Miss Dana—Katharine Houghton; Miss Teer—Abigail Rosen.

Directed by Harold Clurman; scenery and lighting, Ben Edwards; clothes, Jane Greenwood; production stage manager, Frederic de Wilde; stage manager, Howard Fischer; press, Samuel Lurie, Stanley F. Kaminsky.

Time: the present. Place: a hall and one-room apartment in Midtown Manhattan. Act I: A late afternoon in early summer. Act II: The next morning.

Comedy about a young husband so fearful of parenthood that he persuades his wife (much to the chagrin of family and friends) that they should give the baby up for adoption and break up their marriage. But after the child is born they can't go through with these plans.

The Lion in Winter (92). By James Goldman. Produced by Eugene V. Wolsk, Walter A. Hyman and Alan King with Emanuel Azenberg at the Ambassador Theater. Opened March 3, 1966. (Closed May 21, 1966)

Henry II, King of England	Robert Preston	Richard, the oldest son, sometimes called the Lionheart	James Rado
Alais, a French princess	Suzanne Grossmann		
John, the youngest son	Bruce Scott	Eleanor, Henry's wife	Rosemary Harris
Geoffrey, the middle son	Dennis Cooney	Philip, King of France	Christopher Walken

Standbys: Miss Harris—Ludi Claire; Mr. Preston—Bruce Glover. Understudies: Messrs. Cooney, Scott, Walken—Ty McConnell; Miss Grossmann—Leslie Vega; Mr. Rado—Bruce Glover.

Directed by Noel Willman; scenery and costumes, Will Steven Armstrong; lighting, Tharon

Musser; incidental music, Thomas Wagner; production manager, Jose Vega; stage manager, Roger Johnson Jr.; press, Frank Goodman, Martin Schwartz, Ruth Cage.

Time: Christmas, 1183. Place: Henry's castle at Chinon, France. Act I, Scene 1: Alais' chamber, early afternoon. Scene 2: Reception hall, immediately following. Scene 3: Eleanor's chamber, a short time later. Scene 4: Reception hall, immediately following. Scene 5: Eleanor's chamber, not long afterward. Scene 6: Philip's chamber, immediately following. Act II, Scene 1: Henry's chamber, some time later. Scene 2: Alais' chamber, early the next morning. Scene 3: The wine cellar, immediately following.

An imaginary gathering of a real, historical royal family at which Henry II of England means to decide upon an heir among his three sons; he favors the youngest, John. He has released his captive wife, the celebrated Eleanor of Aquitaine, to join the gathering, and she favors her eldest son Richard. This situation prompts a fierce love-hate struggle between Henry and Eleanor.

A Best Play; see page 324

3 Bags Full (33). By Jerome Chodorov; based on a play by Claude Magnier. Produced by Leonard S. Field at Henry Miller's Theater. Opened March 6, 1966. (Closed April 2, 1966)

Jenkins	Jon Richards	Jeanette	Leigh Taylor-Young
Kathleen	Sharon Gans	Boris	Dick Sabol
Bascom Barlow	Paul Ford	Mr. Cottingham	Rufus Smith
Richard Foyle	Joe Ponazecki	Charlotte	Iris Whitney
Angela	April Shawhan	Preston Cottingham	Philip Cusack
Genevieve	Nancy Marchand		

Standby: Mr. Ford—Gordon B. Clarke. Understudies: Misses Marchand, Whitney—Parker McCormick; Mr. Ponazecki—Philip Cusack; Messrs. Sabol, Smith, Richards, Cusack—John Hallow.

Directed by Gower Champion; scenery and lighting, Will Steven Armstrong; costumes, Freddy Wittop; production stage manager, John Drew Devereaux; stage manager, John Hallow; press, Abner D. Klipstein.

Time: summer in the early 1900s. Place: a private residence on Madison Avenue, New York City. Act I: One evening. Act II: A few moments later.

Comedy about a wealthy sporting goods tycoon trying not quite successfully to keep track of three young romances, several surprises of parenthood and three similar-appearing carpetbags: one full of diamonds, one full of cash and one full of ladies' undergarments.

* **Wait a Minim!** (98). Leon Gluckman's musical revue. Produced by Frank Productions Inc. at the John Golden Theater. Opened March 7, 1966.

Andrew Tracey	Michel Martel	Dana Valery
Paul Tracey	Nigel Pegram	Sarah Atkinson
Kendrew Lascelles	April Olrich	

Musical accompaniments: Andrew Tracey—guitar, guitar-lute, bamboo pipe, Portuguese guitar, mandolin, treble and soprano recorder, Rhodesian mbira, Chopi timbila, Lozi drums, tuba, bagpipes, Indian tabla drums, clarinet, Trinidadian steel drum, sousaphone, Indian gong; Paul Tracey—guitar, H.M. Bull Fiddle, flute, Chopi timbila, Lozi drums, piccolo, melodica, squeezebox, bagpipes, kalimba, tuba, sousaphone, Indian gong; Nigel Pegram—guitar, H.M. Bull Fiddle, double respiratory linguaphone, Lozi drums, bagpipes, Japanese koto zither, trombone, Chopi timbila, penny whistle, Indian tanpura drone; Kendrew Lascelles—trumpet: other percussion instruments—The Company.

Devised and directed by Leon Gluckman; musical arrangements and direction, Andrew Tracey; scenery and lighting, Frank Rembach and Leon Gluckman; scenery executed by Frank Rembach; costumes, Heather MacDonald-Rouse; choreography, Frank Staff and Kendrew Lascelles; lighting and design supervision, Klaus Holm; costume supervision, Patton Campbell; stage manager, Frank Rembach; press, Reuben Rabinovitch.

Revue features many folk songs—African, European and Asian—played on a great variety of instruments, with occasional dances and comedy pantomimes satirizing political and social eccentricities, particularly the South African policy of *apartheid*. A foreign play previously produced in South Africa, Rhodesia and London.

PART I

THIS IS THE LAND
  "Ndinosara Nani?" (Karanga folk song, Southern Rhodesia) ....Andrew, Michel, Nigel,
                                                                      Dana, Paul
  "Hoe Ry Die Boere" (Afrikaans folk song) ....Nigel, Paul, Andrew
  "This Is Worth Fighting For" ....Sarah
  "Subuhi Sana" (Swahili) ....Andrew
  "Jikel' Emaweni" (Xhosa fighting song, Transkei) ....Dana
DINGERE DINGALE
  "Ajade Papa" (Tamil lullaby) ....Michel
  "Dingere Dingale" (Tamil song) ....The Company
  Tuba Man ....Kendrew
OVER THE HILLS
  "I Know Where I'm Going" (Irish folk song) ....Paul, Sarah, Andrew
  "Over The Hills" ....April, Andrew
  "I Gave My Love a Cherry" (English folk song) ....Paul, Dana, Michel, Nigel, Andrew
  "Black-White Calypso" ....Nigel (Song by Jeremy Taylor)
DIE MEISTERTRINKER
  "Deutches Weinlied" ....The Company
  "Gretl's Cow" ....April
  "Eine kleine bombardonmusik" ....Nigel, Paul, Andrew, Kendrew
  "Watschplattlanz" ....The Company
  "Butter Milk Hill" (Irish-American) ....Dana
  "Aria" ....Paul
OUT OF FOCUS ....The Company
  Snap Happy ....April, Kendrew
  "Hoshoryu" (Japanese folk song) ....Michel, Sarah
  The Gentle Art ....Kendrew, Michel, Paul
  "Dirty Old Town" ....Andrew, Paul, Nigel, Dana (Song by Ewan MacColl)
  "Last Summer" ....Andrew, Paul, Nigel, Kendrew
VIVE LA DIFFERENCE
  "Lalirette" ....Paul, Andrew, Michel, Nigel
  "Le roi a fait battre tambour" ....Michel, Nigel, Paul, Andrew
  Tour de France ....Kendrew, April, Andrew, Paul, Michel
  "A Piece of Ground" ....Nigel (Song by Jeremy Taylor)
  "Ayama" ....Andrew, Paul, Michel
NORTH OF THE 'POPO
  Professor Piercing ....Paul
  The Chairman ....Nigel
  "Mgeniso waMgodo waShambini" (Chopi timbila) ....Andrew, Paul, Nigel
  "Kupura Kupika" (Pounding Song, Nyasaland) ....Sarah, Dana, April
  "The Izicatulo Gumboot Dance" ....The Company

PART II

TUNES OF GLORY
  "The Wee Cooper o'Fife" (Doric Diddling) ....Paul, Andrew, Nigel
  "Red, Red Rose" (Burns) ....Paul
  "Hammer Song" ....Andrew, Nigel, Michel, Paul (Song by Seeger-Hays)
  "London Talking Blues" ....Nigel (Song by Jeremy Taylor)
  "The Love Life of a Gondolier" ....Kendrew, Michel, April
  "Foyo" (Haitian patios lullaby) ....Paul, Andrew, Nigel
  "Cool" ....Dana, Paul, Nigel, Andrew (Song by Andrew and Paul Tracey)
  On Guard ....Kendrew, April
SIR OSWALD SODDE
  Opening Knight ....The Company
  "Sir Oswald Sodde" (Words and music by Jeffrey Smith) ....Andrew, Sarah, Nigel,
                                                                    Paul, Michel
  "Table Bay" (Cape Malay) ....Dana (Arranged and adapted by Stanley Glasser and
                                                                    Adolf Wood)
THIS IS SOUTH AFRICA
  "Chuzi Mama Gwabi Gwabi" (Marabi dance song) ....Dana, Michel
  "Celeste Aida" ....Michel

"Cingoma Chakabaruka" (Tumbuka or Henga, Nyasaland) ....The Company
"Skalo-Zwi" (Music by Stanley Glasser, words by Gwigwi Mrwebe, Pedi Pipe Dance
   specially arranged by Andrew Tracey) ....Dana and The Company
"Samandoza-we!" (Ndau, Southern Rhodesia) ....The Company
"Amasalela" (Baca fighting song, Transkei) ....The Company

Happily Never After (4). By J.A. Ross. Produced by George W. George and Frank Granat at the Eugene O'Neill Theater. Opened March 10, 1966. (Closed March 12, 1966)

Harry Mills	..........Gerald S. O'Loughlin	Peter Kingsley	..............Ken Kercheval
Joan Mills	.................Barbara Barrie	Sarah Mills	..................Karen Black
Mary Kingsley	.............Rochelle Oliver		

Standby: Miss Barrie—Nancy Franklin. Understudies: Mr. O'Loughlin—Robert Baines; Misses Oliver, Black—Nancy Tribush; Mr. Kercheval—Don Travanty.

Directed by Joseph Anthony; scenery, Peter Larkin; lighting, Jean Rosenthal; costumes, Theoni V. Aldredge; production stage manager, William Dodds; stage manager, Robert Baines; press, Harvey B. Sabinson, Lee Solters, David Powers.

Time: the present. Place: a beach house on the North Shore of Long Island. Act I: Saturday, 1 a.m., a weekend in June. Act II, Scene 1: Saturday morning, 6 a.m. Scene 2: Early afternoon, the same day. Act III: 9 o'clock in the evening.

Comedy about a couple's weekend on Long Island, interrupted by family problems and friends' marital difficulties.

Bunraku (16). Puppet theater of Japan presented in the Japanese language. Produced by Paul Szilard in association with the New York City Center of Music and Drama, Inc., under the distinguished patronage of leaders of the Japanese diplomatic corps and their wives, at the New York City Center. Opened March 15, 1966. (Closed March 27, 1966)

Singers, reciters: Tsubamedayu Toyotake, Tsudaiyu Takemoto, Harukodayu Takemoto, Mojidayu Takemoto, Oritayu Takemoto. Samisen players: Matsunosuke Nozawa, Yashichi Takezawa, Katsutaro Nozawa, Danroku Takesawa, Katsuhei Nozawa. Drummer: Tatsuhachiro Mochizuki. Puppet manipulators: Monjuro Kiritake, Eiza Yoshida, Kamematsu Kiritake, Tamao Yoshida, Kanjuro Kiritake, Seitjuro Toyomatsu, Minosuke Yoshida, Bunjaku Yoshida, Tamasho Yoshida, Bunsho Yoshida, Monya Kiritake, Monju Kiritake, Tamako Yoshida, Icho Kiritake.

Director of advisory board, Hiroshi Kawazoe; general manager, Masahiko Imai; scenery, Kazuo Sugimoto; lighting and set supervision, Ronald Bates; simultaneous translation, Kazu Obayashi; stage managers, Eisuke Kamada, Ronald Bates; press, Shirley E. Herz.

Bunraku dates from the 18th century. Its repertory in this engagement included *The General's Daughter* (1764), by Fuemi Wakatake; *Fishing for Wives,* adapted from a Noh comedy; *The Greengrocer's Daughter* (1773), by Sensuke Suga, Wackichi Matsuda and Fuemi Wakatake; *The Revenge of the Forty-Seven Ronin* (1748), by Izumo Takeda with Shoraku Miyoshi and Senryu Namiki, and *The Tale of the Morning Glory* (1832), by Kagashi Yamada.

Pousse-Café (3). Musical with book by Jerome Weidman; music by Duke Ellington; lyrics by Marshall Barer and Fred Tobias. Produced by Guy de la Passardiere at the Forty-sixth Street Theater. Opened March 18, 1966. (Closed March 19, 1966)

Ellis	......................Ellis Larkins	Solange	..........................Lilo
Havana	...................Travis Hudson	Sailor	........................Dom Angelo
Duchess	.................Madge Cameron	Policeman	...................Hal Norman
Monty	.......................Al Nesor	Paul	........................Don Crabtree
Harry	....................Tommy Karaty	Maurice	...................Charles Durning
Sourball	....................Robert Rovin	Artie	.......................Coley Worth
Bill	..........................Ben Bryant	Louise	...................Marlena Lustik
Arthur Owen Jr.	................Jeff Siggins	Dean Stewart	.............Charles Durning
John Harmon	.............Gary Krawford	Danny	.....................Richard Tone
Professor George Ritter	.....Theodore Bikel		

Ensemble: Dom Angelo, Kay Cole, Joel Conrad, Mervin Crook, Elaine Giftos, Altovise Gore, Peter Hamparian, Jo Ann Lehmann, Marlena Lustik, Iva March, Simon McQueen, Rita O'Connor, Martin Ross, Barbara Saatan, Scotty Salmon.

Standby: Mr. Bikel—Peter Johl. Understudies: Lilo—Simon McQueen; Miss Hudson—Madge Cameron; Mr. Tone—Dom Angelo; Mr. Krawford—Tommy Karaty; Messrs. Rovin, Bryant, Nesor—Marty Ross; Mr. Karaty—Joel Conrad; Mr. Siggins—Scotty Salmon; Mr. Worth—Charles Durning; Messrs. Durning, Crabtree—Hal Norman; Miss Cameron—Fran Stevens.

Directed by José Quintero; scenery, Will Steven Armstrong; lighting. V.C. Fuqua; costumes, Patricia Zipprodt and Albert Wolsky; musical direction, Sherman Frank; production consultant, Charles Conaway; orchestrations, Larry Wilcox; music numbers and dances staged by Marvin Gordon; choreography, Valerie Bettis; associate producer, Monty Shaff; production stage manager, Henri Caubisens; stage manager, Herman Magidson; press, Bill Doll, Midori Tsuji, Bob Ganshaw, Dick Spittel.

Time: the early 1920s. Place: New Orleans. Act I, Scene 1 (following Prologue): Schoolroom. Scene 2: Cafe and bar. Scene 3: Solange's dressing room. Scene 4: Cafe and bar. Scene 5: Dormitory. Scene 6: Solange's dressing room; Scene 7: Same, the next morning. Scene 8: Professor's quarters. Scene 9: Professor's quarters and Solange's dressing room. Scene 10: Cafe and bar. Act II, Scene 1: Cafe and bar. Scene 2: Solange's dressing room. Scene 3: Cafe and bar. Scene 4: Professor's quarters. Scene 5: Cafe and bar. Scene 6: Solange's dressing room. Scene 7: Schoolroom.

Pousse-Café is based on the 1930 movie *The Blue Angel,* a German film which starred Marlene Dietrich in the story of a professor's infatuation with a cabaret entertainer.

ACT I

"The Spider and the Fly" ....Travis Hudson, Dance Ensemble
"Rules and Regulations" ....Theodore Bikel, Gary Krawford, Robert Rovin,
Ben Bryant, Jeff Siggins, Tommy Karaty
"Follow Me Up The Stairs" ....Lilo
"Goodbye Charlie" ....Miss Hudson, Ensemble
"C'est Comme Ca" ....Lilo
"Thank you, Ma'am" ....Bikel, Lilo
"The Eleventh Commandment" ....Al Nesor, Rovin, Siggins, Karaty
"Someone To Care For" ....Bikel
"The Wedding" ....Ensemble

ACT II

"Entre Acte" ....Orchestra
"Let's" (Rehearsal Scene) ....Richard Tone, Marlena Lustik, Dance Ensemble
"The Good Old Days" ....Lilo, Don Crabtree, Nesor, Coley Worth, Charles Durning
"Easy to Take" ....Tone, Lilo
"C'est Comme Ca" (Reprise) ....Bikel
"C'est Comme Ca" (Reprise) ....Lilo
"Let's" ....Lilo, Male Dancers
"Old World Charm" ....Bikel
"The Spider and the Fly" (Reprise) ....Miss Hudson

*Mark Twain Tonight! (71). One-man performance by Hal Holbrook as Mark Twain in writings and speeches by Mark Twain. Produced by Emanuel Azenberg, Eugene V. Wolsk and Leonard Soloway in association with John Lotas at the Longacre Theater. Opened March 23, 1966.

Mr. Holbrook's program was selected from the material by Mark Twain: "On My Return to the Pulpit;" "Slow Train, Long Dog" from *Following the Equator;* "Smoke Rings;" "Poet Story," "Stealing a Clerical Hat," "Compliments," "How to be Seventy" and "Mary Ann" from *Speeches;* "Hunting the Water Closet" and "His Grandfather's Old Ram" from *Mark Twain's Notebook;* "A Genuine Mexican Plug," "Missionaries" and "Reporting in San Francisco" from *Roughing It;* "Bone Treatment" from *Christian Science;* "The Lord Will Provide," "Susy's Prayer," "Boyhood on the Farm," "My Trained Presbyterian Conscience" and "Praying for Gingerbread" from *Autobiography;* "The Opera" from *A Tramp Abroad;* "That Grand Old Asylum" from *The Gilded Age;* "The Italian Guide" and "I Took Along the Window Sash" from *Innocents Abroad:* "Encounter With An Interviewer" from *Sketches;* "Decay in the Art of Lying" from *Essays* and other sources; "Huck and Jim," "Lost in the Fog" and "Shooting of Boggs" from *Huckleberry Finn;* "Our Country Right or Wrong," "The Damned Human Race," "Noah and the Ark," "Is Man An Angel" and "Heaven or Hell?" from *Letters From The Earth;* "Evolution" and "Man, That Poor Thing" from Biography; "The Christian Bible"; "O Kind Missionary Come Home" from *Essays;* "The Virgin Mary" from *Ladies Home Journal;* "A Ghost Story" and "My Ancestor Satan" from *Short Stories;* "Get Rich Quick Disease"; "Sunrise on the River" from *Life on the Mississippi* and "Adam and Eve" from *Extracts From Adam's Diary.*

Production supervisor, Jerry Adler; press, Harvey B. Sabinson, David Powers.

The first New York presentation of Mr. Holbrook's *Mark Twain Tonight!* took place off Broadway in 1959. This is its first Broadway presentation.

The Best Laid Plans (3). By Gwen Davis. Produced by Hillard Elkins in association with Donald J. Mitchell at the Brooks Atkinson Theater. Opened March 25, 1966. (Closed March 26, 1966)

Alicia Hopper	Marian Hailey	Dr. Ralph Brodie	Kenneth Mars
Jason Beckman	Edward Woodward	Evelyn Hopper	Polly Rowles
Lorna	Cynthia Harris		

Standbys: Messrs. Woodward, Mars—Lawrence Keith; Misses Hailey, Harris—Rue McClanahan; Miss Rowles—Ethel Britton.

Directed by Arthur Storch; scenery, Oliver Smith; costumes, Florence Klotz; lighting, Peggy Clark; associate producer, George Platt; production supervisor, Michael Thoma; production stage manager, Vincent Lynne; press, Lee Solters, Harvey B. Sabinson, Harry Nigro.

Time: the present. Act I, Scene 1: The apartments of Alicia Hopper and Jason Beckman, morning. Scene 2: Dr. Ralph Brodie's office, 11 a.m. that morning. Scene 3: Both apartments, about noon. Act II, Scene 1: The apartment of Jason and Alicia, three weeks later, late afternoon. Scene 2: Dr. Brodie's office, immediately afterwards. Scene 3: The apartment, later that evening. Act III, Scene 1: Alicia's apartment, the following Monday morning. Scene 2: Dr. Brodie's office, the same morning. Scene 3: Alicia's apartment, about noon.

Comedy about a business woman who shares the same psychoanalyst with a well-known playwright. She poses as a beatnik in order to attract his attention.

*"It's a Bird It's a Plane It's SUPERMAN" (75). Musical with book by David Newman and Robert Benton, based on the comic strip "Superman"; music by Charles Strouse; lyrics by Lee Adams. Produced by Harold Prince in association with Ruth Mitchell at the Alvin Theater. Opened March 29, 1966.

Superman and Clark Kent	Bob Holiday	Citizens of Metropolis	
Max Mencken	Jack Cassidy	Byron, the Bank Guard	Eugene Edwards
Lois Lane	Patricia Marand	Harvey,	
Perry White	Eric Mason	the Tour Guide	Bob Scherkenbach
Sydney	Linda Lavin	Bonnie, the Moll	April Nevins
Dr. Abner Sedgwick	Michael O'Sullivan	Sue-Ellen, the Teenager	Tina Faye
Jim Morgan	Don Chastain	Marnie, the Model	Judy Newman
Father Ling	Jerry Fujikawa	Gordon, the Student	Bick Goss
Dong Ling	Bill Starr	Annette, the Secretary	Michelle Barry
Tai Ling	Murphy James	Wanda, the Waitress	Gay Edmond
Fan Po Ling	Juleste Salve	Rosalie, the High	
Ming Foo Ling	Michael Gentry	School Girl	Marilyne Mason
Joe Ling	Joseph Gentry	Leslie, the Shopper	Jayme Mylroie
The Suspects		Cathy, the Child	Lori Browne
1.	Les Freed	Barbie, the Receptionist	Mara Landi
2.	Dick Miller	Al, the Bank Robber	George Bunt
3.	Dal Richards	Milton, the Hood	Dallas Edmunds
4.	John Grigas	Kevin, the College Boy	Roy Smith
5.	John Smolko	William, the	
		Exchange Student	Haruki Fujimoto

Understudies: Mr. Cassidy—Dick Miller; Mr. O'Sullivan—Dal Richards; Mr. Holiday—John Smolko; Miss Marand—Marilyne Mason; Mr. Chastain—Eric Mason; Miss Lavin—Jayme Mylroie; The Flying Lings—Haruki Fujimoto; Mr. Fujikawa—Juleste Salve.

Directed by Harold Prince; dances and musical numbers staged by Ernest Flatt; scenery and lighting, Robert Randolph; costumes, Florence Klotz; musical direction, Harold Hastings; orchestrations, Eddie Sauter; dance arrangements, Betty Walberg; filmed sequences produced by MPO Pictures, Inc.; stage manager, Ben Strobach; press, Mary Bryant, Robert Pasolli.

Time: the present. Place: in and around the city of Metropolis, U.S.A.

A dastardly professor, boiling with envy because he's never won a Nobel Prize, wants to gain notoriety; so he plots with one of Clark Kent's fellow reporters on *The Daily Planet* to unmask and overcome Superman. The professor does find a chink in the invulnerability of Superman (he needs to be loved) but is foiled before he can bring his nefarious scheme to its climax.

A Best Play; see page 242

ACT I

Scene 1: Outside the Chase-Metropolis Bank
"Doing Good" ....Bob Holiday
"We Need Him" ....Jack Cassidy, Patricia Marand, Holiday, Company
Scene 2: The offices of *The Daily Planet*
"It's Superman" ....Miss Marand
Scene 3: A telephone booth
Scene 4: The nuclear reactor at Metropolis Institute of Technology
"We Don't Matter At All" ....Don Chastain, Miss Marand
"Revenge" ....Michael O'Sullivan
Scene 5: The offices of *The Daily Planet*
"The Woman For The Man" ....Cassidy
"You've Got Possibilities" ....Linda Lavin
Scene 6: Dr. Sedgwick's study
Scene 7: The screening room
"What I've Always Wanted" ....Miss Marand
"Revenge" (Reprise) ....O'Sullivan
Scene 8: Dr. Sedgwick's home
"Everything's Easy When You Know How" ....The Flying Lings
Scene 9: The offices of *The Daily Planet*
Scene 10: Atop City Hall Tower
Scene 11: The M.I.T. dedication grounds
"It's Super Nice" ....The Company

ACT II

Scene 1: The front page, one week later
"So Long, Big Guy" ....Cassidy
Scene 2: Clark Kent's apartment
"The Strongest Man in the World" ....Holiday
Scene 3: A street in Metropolis
"Ooh, Do You Love You!" ....Miss Lavin
Scene 4: Dr. Sedgwick's laboratory
"You've Got What I Need" ....Cassidy, O'Sullivan
Scene 5: Meanwhile
"It's Superman" (Reprise) ....The Company
Scene 6: An abandoned power station outside Metropolis
Scene 7: The power station, next morning
"I'm Not Finished Yet" ....Miss Marand
"Pow! Bam! Zonk!" ....Holiday, the Flying Lings

Bavarian State Theater. Two programs of revivals in the German language. **Die Mitschuldigen** (*The Accomplices*) by Johann Wolfgang von Goethe with **Woyzeck** (8) by Georg Büchner. Opened April 5, 1966. (Closed April 10, 1966) **Die Ratten** (*The Rats*) (8) by Gerhart Hauptmann. Opened April 12, 1966. (Closed April 17, 1966) Produced by Gert von Gontard and Felix G. Gerstman in cooperation with Deutsches Theater, Inc., under the patronage of the German Federal Republic and the Bavarian Government, at New York City Center.

PERFORMER	"DIE MITSCHULDIGEN"	"WOYZECK"	"DIE RATTEN"
Jürgen Arndt		Karl	Doctor Kegel
Martin Benrath	Alcest		Bruno Mechelke
Carin Braun		Margret	Walburga
Gerd Brüdern			John
Erwin Faber		Old Man	
Peter Fricke		Andres	Erich Spitta
Darel Glaser		Monkey	
Gustl Halenke			Selma Knobbe
Karl Hanft		Innkeeper	
Harry Hertzsch		1st Man	Policeman Schierke
Jörg Holm			Käferstein
Hannes Kaetner		2d Man	
Walter Kohutek		A Jew	Nathaniel Jettel
Elfriede Kuzmany			Mrs. Knobbe
Max Mairich	Innkeeper	Captain	Quaquaro
Friedrich Maurer		Barker	Pastor Spitta
Herbert Mensching	Söller	1st Apprentice	
A. Moosholzer		Marie's Child	
Elisabeth Orth	Sophie	Marie	Alice Rütterbusch
Christine Ostermayer			Pauline Piperkarcka
Ilse Ritter		A Girl	
Horst Sachtleben	Waiter	2d Apprentice	
Edmund Saussen		Sergeant	
Karl Maria Schley			Harro Hassenreuter
Helmut Schmid		Drum-Major	
Edith Schultze- Westrum		Grandmother	Mrs. Hassenreuter
Klaus Schwarzkopf		Doctor	
Heinrich Schweiger		Woyzeck	
Sigfrit Steiner		Policeman	
Annemarie Wernicke		Käthe	Mrs. Kielbacke
Maria Wimmer			Mrs. John

Soldiers, students, citizens in *Woyzeck:* Patricia Aldrich, Lee Callahan, Lynne Garmston, Zola Long, Nikki Nardone, Erna Rossmann, Patricia Sinnott, Ludmilla Tchor, Chris Yule, Robert Coldiron, James G. Demas, Lee H. Doyle, Cornelius T. Frizell, Werner T. Graber, John Keeler, Fred H. Kolouch, Alec Murphy, Mell Reynolds, Walter Rivera, Frederick S. Roffman, Ivan Smith, Carl W. Stewart. Children: Silvia Lemberger, Robert Puleo, Lisa Puleo.

DIE MITSCHULDIGEN and WOYZECK directed by Hans Lietzau; music, *(Woyzeck)* Peter Zwetkoff, *(Die Mitschuldigen)* Mark Lothar; choreography, Heino Hallhuber; assistant to director, Ursula Heilmann.

Die Mitschuldigen is a tale of thievery and the cuckolding of the thief, told in three scenes. *Woyzeck,* in 24 scenes, is the drama of a peasant's murder of his unfaithful sweetheart.

DIE RATTEN directed by Helmut Henrichs; assistant to director, Ursula Laerum.

Die Ratten time: about 1910. Place: Berlin. Act I: Attic of a former barracks, now an apartment house. Act II: Mrs. John's apartment in the same house. Act III: Same as Act I. Acts IV and V: Same as Act II. The lives of human vermin are examined in a manner that is almost farcical, except that they are working real evil.

For both programs, Helmut Henrichs, general manager; scenery and costumes, Jürgen Rose; technical director, Dieter Ganzemüller; lighting, Frithjof Elbertshagen; simultaneous translation, Iris Merlis, Lisa Smart; press, Jean Dalrymple.

*New York City Center Light Opera Company. Spring season of four Frank Loesser musical revivals. **How to Succeed in Business Without Really Trying** (23) book by Abe Burrows, Jack Weinstock and Willie Gilbert; music and lyrics by Frank Loesser. Opened April 20, 1966. (Closed May 8, 1966). **The Most Happy Fella** (15) book, music and lyrics by Frank Loesser; based on Sidney Howard's play *They Knew What They Wanted.* Opened May 11, 1966. (Closed May 22, 1966). ***Where's Charley?** (8) book by George Abbott; based on Brandon Thomas'

Charley's Aunt; music and lyrics by Frank Loesser. Opened May 25, 1966; was scheduled to close June 5, 1966 and to be followed by *Guys and Dolls* June 8, 1966. Produced by New York City Center Light Opera Company, Jean Dalrymple, director, at New York City Center.

HOW TO SUCCEED

Finch	Leo Gochman	Miss Jones	Justine Johnston
Gatch	Lang des Jardins	Mr. Twimble	Lou Cutell
Jenkins	Austin Colyer	Hedy	Betty Linton
Peterson	Reese Burns	Scrubwomen	Natasha Grishin,
Tackaberry	Henry Lawrence		Renee Gorsey
J.B. Biggley	Billy De Wolfe	Miss Krumholtz	Del Green
Rosemary	Sheila Sullivan	Ovington	Richard Marr
Bratt	Art Barnett	Policeman	Paul Adams
Smitty	Pat McEnnis	Womper	Lou Cutell
Frump	Lee Goodman		

Singers: Paul Adams, Reese Burns, Austin Colyer, Lang des Jardins, Walter E. Hook, Mickey Karm, Henry Lawrence, Richard Marr, Marie Bradley, Jane Coleman, Jacque Dean, Renee Gorsey, Del Green, Maria Hero, Judy McMurdo.

Dancers: Doria Avila, Richard Denny, Garold Gardner, Jerry Kent, Stan Mazin, Leo J. Muller, Terry Nicholson, Roger Allan Raby, Nephele Buecher, Patricia Cope, Mickey Gunnersen, Natasha Grishin, Rosie Holotik, Beth Howland, Joan Lindsay, Sharron Miller.

Understudies: Mr. Gochman—Mickey Karm; Mr. De Wolfe—Art Barnett; Miss Sullivan—Maria Hero; Mr. Goodman—Paul Adams; Mr. Barnett—Richard Marr; Miss Linton—Judy McMurdo.

Directed by Gus Schirmer; scenery, Robert Randolph; costumes, Stanley Simmons; lighting, Peggy Clark; musical direction, Anton Coppola; production stage managers, Herman Shapiro, Herman Magidson; stage manager, Michael Foley; press, Homer Poupart, John Clugstone.

How to Succeed in Business Without Really Trying opened October 14, 1964 and closed March 6, 1965, after becoming Broadway's fifth longest-running musical at 1,417 performances. It won the New York Drama Critics Circle Award and the Pulitzer Prize for its 1961-62 season. This is its first revival.

THE MOST HAPPY FELLA

The Cashier	Lee Cass	Joe	Art Lund
Cleo	Karen Morrow	Giuseppe	Montes de Oca
Rosabella	Barbara Meister	Pasquale	Will Roy
The Waitresses	Joanna Crosson, Rita	Ciccio	Edward Becker
	O'Connor, Joy Serio, Susan Sigrist	The Doctor	Carl Nicholas
The Postman	Lee Cass	The Priest	Dick Ensslen
Tony	Norman Atkins	Tessie	Karen Grant
Marie	Fran Stevens	Gussie	Jody La Rocco
Max	Joe McGrath	Sissy	Marci Phillips
Herman	Jack De Lon	Neighbor Ladies	Joyce Olson, Rosemary
Clem	James Hobson		McNamara, Rita Metzger
Jake	Robert E. Maxwell Jr.	Brakeman	Dale Westerman
Al	John A. Boni	Bus Driver	Doug Hunt

All the Neighbors and All the Neighbors' Neighbors: Lillian Bozinoff, Susan Cogan, Jeanne Frey, Marlene Kay, Evelyn Kingsley, Rosemary McNamara, Rita Metzger, Barbara Miller, LaVergne Monette, Joyce Olson, Patti Winston, Gene Albano, John A. Boni, Marvin Goodis, James Hobson, Doug Hunt, Philip Lucas, Stuart Mann, Robert E. Maxwell Jr., Joe McGrath, George T. McWhorter, Dale Westerman, Wilson Robey, Diane Arnold, Linda Bonem, Connie Burnett, Kay Cole, Joanna Crosson, Judith Dunford, Ina Kurland, Rita O'Connor, Joy Serio, Susan Sigrist, Myrna Strom, Dom Angelo, Frank Coppola, Vito Durante, Jerry Fries, Bob La Crosse, Teak Lewis, Carlos Macri, Donald Mark, Victor Pieran, Dom Salinaro, Marc Scott.

Standby: Mr. Atkins—Dick Ensslen. Understudies: Miss Meister—Jeanne Frey; Mr. Lund—John A. Boni; Miss Stevens—Rita Metzger; Mr. De Lon—Wilson Robey; Miss Morrow—Rosemary McNamara; Mr. Nichols—Dale Westerman; Mr. Cass—Dick Ensslen; Mr. de Oca—Joe McGrath; Mr. Roy—Marvin Goodis; Mr. Becker—Stuart Mann; Mr. Hobson—Phil Lucas; Mr. Maxwell—Doug Hunt; Mr. Boni—George McWhorter.

BETTY LINTON AND BILLY DE WOLFE IN THE REVIVAL OF "HOW TO SUCCEED
IN BUSINESS WITHOUT REALLY TRYING"

Directed by Ralph Beaumont; choreography, Ralph Beaumont; scenery, Jo Mielziner; costumes, Frank Thompson; lighting, Peggy Clark; musical direction, Abba Bogin; production stage manager, Chet O'Brien; stage managers, Phil King, Sean Cunningham.

The Most Happy Fella was first presented on Broadway May 3, 1956, for 676 performances. It was last revived by the New York City Center in 1959.

WHERE'S CHARLEY?

Brassett	Tom Bate	Mr. Spettigue	Mort Marshall
Professor Fortesque	Donald Barton	Donna Lusia D'Alvadorez	Eleanor Steber
Jack Chesney	David Smith	Photographer	Stan Mazin
Charley Wykeham	Darryl Hickman	Patricia	Maria Hero
Kitty Verdun	Karen Shepard	Reggie	Austin Colyer
Amy Spettigue	Susan Watson	Photographer's Assistants	Violetta Landek, Zebra Nevins
Wilkinson	Emory Bass		
Sir Francis Chesney	Ferdinand Hilt		

Band members: Rodd Barry, Dennis Cole, Gordon Cook, Jack Fletcher, Mario Maroze, Doug Spingler.

Dancers: Rodd Barry, Dennis Cole, Myron Curtis, Richard Denny, Jerry Kent, Don Lawrence, Mario Maroze, Richard Maxon, Stan Mazin, Doug Spingler, Clive Thompson, Cathy Conklin, Mickey Gunnersen, Beth Howland, Violetta Landek, Sara Letton, Sharron Miller, Zebra Nevins, Rande Rayburn, Alice Mary Riley, Skiles Ricketts, Toodie Wittmer.

Singers: Paul Adams, Austin Colyer, Gordon Cook, Stephen Everett, Jack Fletcher, William James, Konstantin Moskalenko, Hal Norman, Fred Osin, David Wilder, Laverne Burden, Jane Coleman, Renee Gorsey, Maria Hero, Nina Hirschfeld, Miriam Lawrence, Joyce McDonald, Betsy Norden, Mary Ann Ryszeski, Susan Stockwell, Elise Warner.

Standby: Mr. Hickman—Lee Goodman. Understudies: Miss Watson—Cathy Conklin; Mr. Smith—William James; Miss Shepard—Maria Hero; Mr. Hilt—Austin Colyer; Mr. Marshall—Emory Bass; Miss Steber—Laverne Burden; Mr. Bate—Jack Fletcher; Messrs. Barton, Bass—Stephen Everett.

Directed by Christopher Hewett; choreography, John Sharpe; musical director, Pembroke Davenport; ballet music adapted by Marvin Laird; costumes, Frank Thompson; lighting and additional settings, Peggy Clark; production stage manager, William Batchelder; stage manager, George Rondo.

Where's Charley? was produced at the St. James Theater, October 11, 1948, for 792 performances.

*Ivanov** (33). Revival of the play by Anton Chekhov; adapted by John Gielgud; based on the original translation by Ariadne Nicolaeff. The Tennent production presented by Alexander H. Cohen at the Sam S. Shubert Theater. Opened May 3, 1966.

Nikolai Alekseyevitch Ivanov ....John Gielgud	Pavel Kirilytch Lebedev ......Roland Culver
Mikhail Mikhailovitch Borkin ....Ronald Radd	Sasha ....Jennifer Hilary
Anna Petrovna ....Vivien Leigh	Guests at Lebedev's
Count Shabelsky ....Edward Atienza	1st Young Man ....Brooks Morton
Doctor Lvov ....John Merivale	2d Young Man ....Miller Lide
Zinaida Savishna ....Paula Laurence	3rd Young Man ....Tom Klunis
Marfa Yegorovna Babakina ....Helen Christie	Young Girls ..Esther Benson, Linda Geiser
Kossykh ....Dillon Evans	Old Lady ....Betty Sinclair
Avdotya Nazarovna ....Ethel Griffies	Butler ....Guy Spaull
	Maid ....Anna Minot
	Pyotr ....Michael Miller

Standbys: Mr. Gielgud—Tom Klunis; Misses Leigh, Christie—Esther Benson; Messrs. Culver, Atienza—Guy Spaull. Understudies: Miss Hilar—Linda Geiser; Miss Laurence—Betty Sinclair; Mr. Radd—Michael Miller, Brooks Morton; Mr. Merivale—Miller Lide; Mr. Evans—Michael Miller, Brooks Morton; Miss Griffies—Betty Sinclair; Misses Benson, Geiser—Anna Minot; Mr. Morton—Michael Miller.

Directed by John Gielgud; scenery and costumes, Rouben Ter-Arutunian; lighting, Jean Rosenthal; production associate, Hildy Parks; production manager, Jean Barrere; production stage manager, Harry Young; press, James D. Proctor, Robert W. Larkin.

Time: the end of the last century. Place: a district in Central Russia. Act I, Scene 1: The garden of Ivanov's estate, late summer. Scene 2: The drawing-room in Lebedev's house, later the same night. Act II, Scene 1: Ivanov's study, midday, a few weeks later. Scene 2: The Lebedev drawing room, about a year later, early summer.

The ideals of a middle-aged provincial landowner are frustrated and ineffectual; his wife is dying and his era is dying, too. This play was presented here in the Moscow Art Theater repertory of their second season's visit, 1923-24, and more recently off Broadway in a prizewinning revival under the direction of William Ball. This imported London production is Ivanov's first full-scale Broadway revival of record.

*A Time for Singing** (11). Musical based on Richard Llewellyn's novel *How Green Was My Valley;* book and lyrics by Gerald Freedman and John Morris; music by John Morris. Produced by Alexander H. Cohen at the Broadway Theater. Opened May 21, 1966.

David Griffith ....Ivor Emmanuel
Paymaster ....Jay Gregory
Dai Bando ....John Call
Cyfartha Lewis ....George Mathews
Gwillym Morgan
   (Dada) ....Laurence Naismith
Davey Morgan ....Gene Rupert
Ivor Morgan ....Brian Avery
Ianto Morgan ....George Hearn

Owen Morgan ....Harry Theyard
Evan Morgan ....Philip Proctor
Huw Morgan ....Frank Griso
Beth Morgan ....Tessie O'Shea
Angharad Morgan ....Shani Wallis
Bronwen Jenkins ....Elizabeth Hubbard
Mr. Evans ....John Malcolm
Iestyn Evans ....David O'Brien
School Teacher ....David Thomas

Singers: Robert Carle, Ed Eriksen, Jay Gregory, Marian Haraldson, Zona Kennedy, Reid Klein, Henry LeClair, Constance Moffit, Jack Murray, Mari Nettum, Joyce O'Neil, Michael Quinn, Maggie Task, Ann Tell, David Thomas, Maggie Worth.

Dancers: Bruce Becker, Steven Boockvor, Sandra Brewer, Roger Briant, Sterling Clark, Carolyn Dyer, Mary Ehara, Rodney Griffin, Patty Mount, Mimi Wallace.

Children: Paul Dwyer, Peter Falzone, Dewey Golkin, Laura Michaels, Janice Notaro.

Standbys: Miss O'Shea—Travis Hudson; Misses Wallis, Hubbard—Mari Nettum. Understudies: Mr. Emmanuel—George Hearn; Mr. Naismith—George Mathews; Messrs. Rupert, Avery—Harry Theyard; Mr. Theyard—Reid Klein; Mr. Proctor—Sterling Clark; Master Griso—Peter Falzone and Dewey Golkin; Messrs. Malcolm, Matthews—Mike Quinn; Mr. O'Brien—Jay Gregory; Mr. Call—David Thomas.

Directed by Gerald Freedman; choreography, Donald McKayle; scenery, Ming Cho Lee; costumes, Theoni V. Aldredge; lighting, Jean Rosenthal; musical direction, Jay Blackton; orchestrations, Don Walker; production associate, Hildy Parks; production supervisor, Jerry Adler; produced in association with Joseph Wishy; production stage managers, Jake Hamilton, George Thorn; press, James D. Proctor, Robert W. Larkin.

Time: about 1900. Place: in the memory of David Griffith, The Valley, The Town and The Morgan Home in South Wales. The family life, romances, union agitation against the mine owners and involvement in a tragic mine accident of the large Morgan family of Wales, as remembered fondly and sentimentally by their friend the village minister.

ACT I

"Come You Men" ....Male Singing Chorus
"How Green Was My Valley" ....Ivor Emmanuel and Chorus
"Old Long John" ....Male Singing Chorus
"Here Come Your Men" ....Male Singing Chorus
"What A Good Day Is Saturday" ....Tessie O'Shea, Laurence Naismith, Shani Wallis, Brothers and Company
"Peace Come to Every Heart" ....Company
"Someone Must Try" ....Emmanuel
"Oh, How I Adore Your Name" ....Miss Wallis
"That's What Young Ladies Do" ....Emmanuel
"When He Looks At Me" ....Miss Wallis
"Far From Home" ....Misses O'Shea, Wallis, Mr. Naismith, Brothers
"I Wonder If" ....Brothers
"What A Party" ....Messrs. Naismith, Emmanuel, Mathews, Call and Brothers
"Let Me Love You" ....Miss Wallis
"Why Would Anyone Want To Get Married" ....Frank Griso, Brothers, Miss O'Shea, Naismith
"A Time For Singing" ....Miss O'Shea and Company

ACT II

"When The Baby Comes" ....Company
"I'm Always Wrong" ....Miss Wallis
"There Is Beautiful You Are" ....Emmanuel
"Three Ships" ....Brian Avery, Misses Hubbard, O'Shea and Company
"Tell Her" ....Naismith, Master Griso
"There Is Beautiful You Are" (Reprise) ....Emmanuel
"Let Me Love You" (Reprise) ....Miss Wallis, Emmanuel
"And The Mountains Sing Back" ....Emmanuel

"Gone In Sorrow" ....Company
"How Green Was My Valley" (Reprise) ....Company

*Mame (9). Musical based on the novel by Patrick Dennis and the play by Jerome Lawrence and Robert E. Lee; book by Jerome Lawrence and Robert E. Lee; music and lyrics by Jerry Herman. Produced by Fryer, Carr and Harris at the Winter Garden Theater. Opened May 24, 1966.

Patrick Dennis, age 10	..... Frankie Michaels	Madame Branislowski	.... Charlotte Jones
Agnes Gooch	.... Jane Connell	Gregor	.... John Taliaferro
Vera Charles	.... Beatrice Arthur	Beauregard Jackson	
Mame Dennis	.... Angela Lansbury	Pickett Burnside	.... Charles Braswell
Ralph Devine	.... Ron Young	Cousin Fan	.... Ruth Ramsey
Bishop	.... Jack Davison	Uncle Jeff	.... Clifford Fearl
M. Lindsay Woolsey	.... George Coe	Sally Cato	.... Margaret Hall
Ito	.... Sab Shimono	Mother Burnside	.... Charlotte Jones
Doorman	.... Art Matthews	Junior Babcock	.... Randy Kirby
Elevator Boy	.... Stan Page	Patrick Dennis, aged 19-29	.... Jerry Lanning
Messenger	.... Bill Stanton	Gloria Upson	.... Diana Walker
Dwight Babcock	.... Willard Waterman	Mrs. Upson	.... Johanna Douglas
Art Model	.... Jo Tract	Mr. Upson	.... John C. Becher
Dance Teacher	.... Johanna Douglas	Pegeen Ryan	.... Diane Coupe
Leading Man	.... Jack Davison	Peter Dennis	.... Michael Maitland
Stage Manager	.... Art Matthews		

Mame's friends: Diana Baffa, Jack Blackton, David Chaney, Tommy Karaty, Pat Cummings, Jack Davison, Hilda Harris, Nicole Karol, Gene Kelton, Nancy Lynch, Art Matthews, Ross Miles, Stan Page, Ruth Ramsey, Betty Rosebrock, Scotty Salmon, Bella Shalom, Bill Stanton, John Taliaferro, Jo Tract, Jodi Williams, Kathy Wilson.

Standby: Miss Lansbury—Charlotte Fairchild. Understudies: Misses Connell, Ramsey, Douglas—Jodi Williams; Messrs. Waterman, Becher—Clifford Fearl; Mr. Braswell—Art Matthews; Mr. Lanning—Jack Blackton; Master Michaels—Michael Maitland; Misses Hall, Jones—Jo Tract; Mr. Coe—Jack Davison; Mr. Shimono—Hilda Harris; Miss Coupe—Betty Rosebrock; Miss Walker—Laurie Franks; Mr. Taliaferro—David Chaney; Mr. Fearl—Stan Page.

Directed by Gene Saks; dances and musical numbers staged by Onna White; scenery, William and Jean Eckart; costumes, Robert Mackintosh; lighting, Tharon Musser; musical direction and vocal arrangements, Donald Pippin; orchestrations, Philip J. Lang; dance music arrangements, Roger Adams; assistant choreographer, Tom Panko; hair styles, Ronald DeMann; associate producer, John Bowab; production stage manager, Terence Little; stage managers, Ralph Linn, Delmar Hendricks; press, David Lipsky, Lisa Lipsky.

Time: 1928 to 1946. Place: Mame's Beekman Place apartment and various locales in which she becomes involved.

In the musical as well as in the novel and the play, Mame describes the delightful eccentricities of a fun-loving New Yorker who takes her orphaned nephew into her effervescent life and brings him up through the roaring 1920s, the depression, into the affluent 1940s. Two of Mame's three producers, the Messrs Fryer and Carr, presented the straight comedy Auntie Mame on Broadway Oct. 31, 1956 at the Broadhurst Theater, for 639 performances.

ACT I

Scene 1: Somewhere in New York, 1928
   "St. Bridget" ....Jane Connell, Frankie Michaels
Scene 2: Mame's apartment
   "It's Today" ....Angela Lansbury and All
Scene 3: Hallway of Mame's apartment
Scene 4: Mame's bedroom
Scene 5: Mame's living room (and all around New York)
   "Open a New Window" ....Miss Lansbury and All
Scene 6: Mame's apartment
Scene 7: Shubert Theater—New Haven
   "The Man in the Moon" ....Beatrice Arthur, Miss Lansbury and All
   "My Best Girl" ....Michaels, Miss Lansbury

Scene 8: Salon Pour Messieurs
Scene 9: Mame's apartment
  "We Need a Little Christmas" ....Misses Lansbury, Connell, Mr. Shimono,
                                                        Charles Braswell, Master Michaels
Scene 10: Peckerwood
  "The Fox Hunt" ....Clifford Fearl, Master Michaels, Ruth Ramsey,
                                                        Charlotte Jones and Cousins
  "Mame" ....Braswell and All

ACT II

Scene 1: Prep school and college (and Singapore)
  "Mame" (Reprise) ....Master Michaels
  "My Best Girl" ....Master Michaels, Jerry Lanning
Scene 2: Mame's apartment
  "Bosom Buddies" ....Misses Lansbury, Arthur
Scene 3: Mame's apartment (six months later)
  "Gooch's Song" ....Miss Connell
Scene 4: Upson farm
  "That's How Young I Feel" ....Miss Lansbury and All
  "If He Walked Into My Life" ....Miss Lansbury
Scene 5: Mame's apartment
  "It's Today" (Reprise) ....Miss Lansbury and All
  "My Best Girl" (Reprise) ....Lanning
Scene 6: Mame's apartment (1946)
  "Open a New Window" (Reprise) ....Miss Lansbury

*Music Theater of Lincoln Center. Schedule of two musical revivals. *Annie Get
Your Gun (1). With book by Herbert and Dorothy Fields; music and lyrics by
Irving Berlin. Produced by Music Theater of Lincoln Center, Richard Rodgers
president and producing director, at the New York State Theater of Lincoln Center for the Performing Arts. Opened May 31, 1966. Annie Get Your Gun is scheduled to run until July 9, 1966, and to be followed by a revival of Show Boat on
July 19, 1966.

Little Boy; Indian Boy ....Jeffrey Scott
Little Girl ....Deanna Melody
Charlie Davenport ....Jerry Orbach
Dolly Tate ....Benay Venuta
Iron Tail ....Brynar Mehl
Yellow Foot ....Gary Jendell
Mac; Mr. Clay ....John Dorrin
Foster Wilson;
  Mr. Schuyler Adams ....Ronn Carroll
Frank Butler ....Bruce Yarnell
The Shy Girl ....Diana Banks
Annie Oakley ....Ethel Merman
Little Jake
  (Her Brother) ....David Manning
Nellie ....Donna Conforti
Jessie ....Jeanne Tanzy
Minnie ....Holly Sherwood
Col. William F. Cody ....Rufus Smith

Mrs. Little Horse;
  Mrs. Sylvia Potter-Porter ..Mary Falconer
Mrs. Black Tooth ....Jaclynn Villamil
Mrs. Yellow Foot ....Kuniko Narai
Conductor ....Jim Lynn
Porter ....Beno Foster
Waiter ....David Forssen
Major Gordon Lillie ....Jack Dabdoub
Chief Sitting Bull ....Harry Bellaver
The Wild Horse ....Jaime Rogers
Pawnee's Messenger;
  Mr. T. L. C. Keefer ....Walt Hunter
Major Domo ....Ben Laney
Mrs. Schuyler Adams ....Patricia Hall
Dr. Ferguson ....Marc Rowan
Mrs. Ferguson ....Bobbi Baird
Mr. Ernest Henderson ......Grant Spradling
Mrs. Ernest Henderson ....Lynn Carroll

Singers: Bobbi Baird, Vicki Belmonte, Chrysten Carroll, Lynn Carroll, Audrey Dearden,
Lynn Dovel, Mary Falconer, Patricia Hall, Florence Mercer, Susan Terry, Kenny Adams, Ronn
Carroll, John Dorrin, David Forssen, Beno Foster, Walter Hunter, Ben Laney, Jim Lynn, Marc
Rowan, Grant Spradling.

Dancers: Diana Banks, Joanne DiVito, Barbara Hancock, Ruth Lawrence, Kuniko Narai,
Eva Marie Sage, Rozann Ford, Evelyn Taylor, Jaclynn Villamil, Anne Wallace, Bjarne
Buchtrup, Tony Catanzaro, Frank Derbas, Ronn Forella, Marcelo Gamboa, Jeremy Ives, Gary
Jendell, Daniel Joel, Brynar Mehl, Gene Myers.

ETHEL MERMAN AND HARRY BELLAVER IN THE REVIVAL OF
"ANNIE GET YOUR GUN"

Standbys: Miss Merman—Eileen Rodgers; Mr. Yarnell—Jack Dabdoub.
Directed by Jack Sydow; choreography, Danny Daniels; musical director, Franz Allers; scenery, Paul McGuire; costumes, Frank Thompson; lighting, Peter Hunt; orchestrations, Robert Russell Bennett; dance arrangements, Richard De Benedictis; associate conductor, Jonathan Anderson; production stage manager, William Ross; press, Richard Maney.
Annie Get Your Gun was first produced May 16, 1946 at the Imperial Theater with Ethel Merman creating the role of Annie Oakley. It ran for 1,147 performances. It was last revived by the New York City Center Light Opera Company on February 19, 1958. For this Music Theater of Lincoln Center Revival, Irving Berlin added one new number to Act II—"Old Fashioned Wedding," sung by Miss Merman—and eliminated the number "Who Do You Love, I Hope." Minor book revision by Dorothy Fields included the elimination of a secondary romantic interest.

PLAYS PRODUCED OFF BROADWAY

Figures in parentheses following titles indicate number of performances. Plays marked with an asterisk (*) were still running on May 31, 1966, and their number of performances is figured from opening night through that date, not including previews or extra non-profit benefit performances.

HOLDOVERS FROM PREVIOUS SEASONS

Plays which were running on June 1, 1965 are listed below. More detailed information about them is to be found in previous Best Plays volumes of appropriate years. Important cast changes are recorded in a section in this volume.

* **The Fantasticks** (2,538). Musical suggested by the play *Les Romantiques* by Edmund Rostand; book and lyrics by Tom Jones; music by Harvey Schmidt. Opened May 3, 1960.

The Knack (685). By Ann Jellicoe. Opened May 27, 1964. (Closed January 9, 1966)

The Game Is Up (620). Cabaret revue conceived by Rod Warren. Opened September 29, 1964. New edition opened March 11, 1965. Third edition opened June 15, 1965 (see its entry in this volume). (Closed October 16, 1965)

Bits and Pieces XIV (426). Cabaret review conceived by Julius Monk. Opened October 6, 1964. (Closed June 5, 1965)

Othello (216). New York Shakespeare Festival revival of the play by William Shakespeare. Opened October 12, 1964. (Closed July 4, 1965) Joined in repertory May 6, 1965 by **Baal** (43). Revival of the play by Bertolt Brecht; adapted by Eric Bentley and Martin Esslin. (Closed July 3, 1965) *Baal* reopened September 7, 1965 for 15 more performances. (Closed September 18, 1965)

Association of Producing Artists at the Phoenix (281). Repertory of three plays. **Man and Superman** (100). Revival of the play by George Bernard Shaw. Opened December 6, 1964. **War and Peace** (102). Adapted by Alfred Neumann, Erwin Piscator and Guntram Prufer from the novel by Leo Tolstoy; English version by Robert David MacDonald. Opened January 11, 1965. **Judith** (79). By Jean Giraudoux, English version by John K. Savacool. Opened March 24, 1965. Repertory suspended performances June 27, 1965; resumed July 23, 1965. (Closed September 5, 1965).

The Room and **A Slight Ache** (343). Two one-act plays by Harold Pinter. Opened December 9, 1964. (Closed October 3, 1965)

* **A View From the Bridge** (557). Revival of the play by Arthur Miller. Opened January 28, 1965.

The Decline and Fall of the Entire World as Seen Through the Eyes of Cole Porter revisited (273). Cabaret revue assembled by Ben Bagley. Opened March 30,

1965. (Closed November 28, 1965) Second edition opened December 22, 1965 (see its entry in this volume).

The Wonderful World of Burlesque (211). A burlesque creation. Opened April 28, 1965. New edition opened May 24, 1965. (Closed June 30, 1965)

The Wives (33). By Lionel Abel. Opened May 17, 1965. (Closed June 13, 1965)

In White America (32). Return engagement of the dramatic reading selected and arranged by Martin Duberman. Opened May 18, 1965. (Closed June 13, 1965)

The American Savoyards (263). Repertory of six Gilbert & Sullivan operettas. **Iolanthe** (58) opened May 18, 1965. **H.M.S. Pinafore** (70) opened May 20, 1965; **The Mikado** (70) opened May 22, 1965; **The Gondoliers** (15) opened May 23, 1965. *The Yeomen of the Guard* and *Ruddigore* opened after May 31, 1965 (see their entries in this volume). Repertory closed January 2, 1966)

Square in the Eye (31). By Jack Gelber. Opened May 19, 1965. (Closed June 13, 1965)

The Exception and the Rule by Bertolt Brecht, adapted by Eric Bentley; and **The Prodigal Son** by Langston Hughes (141). Program of two one-act plays. Opened May 20, 1965. (Closed September 19, 1965)

PLAYS PRODUCED JUNE 1, 1965—MAY 31, 1966

Troubled Waters (5). By Ugo Betti, translated by Gino Rizzo and William Meriwether. Produced by Apex Productions in association with the Memphis State University at the Gate Theater. Opened June 3, 1965. (Closed June 6, 1965).

Directed by Eric Salmon; scenery, Mr. Salmon; lighting, Roger Morgan; press, Howard Atlee, Warren Pincus. With Sal Caruso, Raymond Purcell, William Countryman, Mary Ann Hoxworth, Harris Yulin, Yolanda Childress and Dina Paisner. About a man (a civil servant) who is in love with his own sister.

Live Like Pigs (128). By John Arden. Produced by Theodore Mann and Howard J. Zuker in association with Frank Cassidy at the Actors' Playhouse. Opened June 7, 1965. (Closed September 26, 1965).

Official	Stan Moore	Doreen	Roberta Collinge
Rachel	Josephine Lane	Mr. Jackson	Will Hare
Rosie Sawney	Naomi Thornton	Blackmouth	Robert Fields
Sally	Anne Gordon	Daffodil	Janet Lee Parker
Sailor Sawney	Paul Benedict	Old Croaker	Harriet Rogers
Col	Joseph Maher	Doctor	Betty Harmon
Mrs. Jackson	Audrey Ward	Policeman	Roger Hamilton

Directed by David Wheeler; scenery, Robert Allen; lighting, Neville Powers; music for the songs composed by Ervin Henning; press, Ben Kornzweig, Reginald Denenholz.
Time: the present. Place: a housing development in the North of England. An uninhibited family refuses to conform to the neighbors' way of life in a new lower-class English housing project.

Krapp's Last Tape, a revival of the play by Samuel Beckett, and **The Zoo Story,** a revival of the play by Edward Albee (168). Program of two one-act plays. Produced by Theater 1965 at the Cherry Lane Theater. Opened June 8, 1965. (Closed October 31, 1965)

KRAPP'S LAST TAPE

Krapp ....George Bartenieff

THE ZOO STORY

Jerry ....Ben Piazza   Peter ....George Bartenieff

Directed by Alan Schneider; design, William Ritman; stage manager, Charles Kindl; press, Howard Attlee, Warren Pincus.

KRAPP'S LAST TAPE—Time: in the future. Place: Krapp's den, a late evening. THE ZOO STORY—Time: the present, a Sunday afternoon. Place—Central Park, New York City. These two plays were first produced off Broadway by Theater 1960 on January 14, 1960. Then, as now, they made up a single program. This 1965 production was moved to the Village South Theater September 12, 1965.

New York Shakespeare Festival program of three plays at the Delacorte Theater in Central Park. **Love's Labor's Lost** opened June 9, 1965. **Coriolanus** opened July 7, 1965. **Troilus and Cressida** opened August 4, 1965. For details see their entries in the section on the Shakespeare festivals in this volume.

The Game Is Up (228). Third edition of the cabaret revue conceived by Rod Warren. Produced by Rod Warren and Downstairs at the Upstairs at Downstairs at the Upstairs. Opened June 15, 1965. (Closed October 16, 1965)

Betty Aberlin   Ruth Buzzi
Richard Blair   Linda Lavin
R.G. Brown

Directed by Sandra Devlin; singular piano, Daniel Strickland; stage manager, George Curley; press, Dorothy Ross. The first two editions of *The Game Is Up* played 392 performances, making a total for the three editions of 620 performances.

New sketches and musical numbers: ACT I—"Camp" (lyric and music by Rod Warren), "Counterpoint" (lyric and music by Alan Friedman), "I Like the Job" (lyric by Linda Ashton, music by Michael Cohen), "Suburbia Square Dance" (lyric by Michael McWhinney, music by Rod Warren).

ACT II—Resale Shop (by Rod Warren), "Lady Bird" (lyric and music by Lesley Davidson), American Express, Italian Style (by Kenny Solms and Gayle Parent), "The Day the Peace Action Broke Out" (lyric and music by Rod Warren), International Monopoly (by Rod Warren).

Mardi Gras! (68). Musical with book by Sig Herzig; music and lyrics by Carmen Lombardo and John Jacob Loeb. Produced by Guy Lombardo at the Jones Beach Marine Theater. Opened June 26, 1965. (Closed September 5, 1965)

John Laffity ....David Atkinson	Pierre ....Lloyd Harris
George Baxter ....Ralph Purdum	Vesta ....Barbara Ann Webb
Peggy Willard ....Karen Shepard	Katherine ....Juanita Hall
Caroline Willard ....Ruth Kobart	Captain Benedict Baxter .....Ralph Purdum
Louis Lamont ....Phil Leeds	Louis, the Guide ....Phil Leeds
Anne ....Gail Johnston	Anna ....Gail Johnston
Katie ....Juanita Hall	Meg ....Karen Shepard
Dan, her son ....James Kennon-Wilson	Wilbur de Paris ....Himself
Dominique You ....Phil Leeds	Lucky Laffity ....David Atkinson
Jean Laffite ....David Atkinson	Arnold Baxter ....Ralph Purdum
Marguerite de Villiers ....Karen Shepard	Carrie Nation ....Ruth Kobart
Madame de Villiers ....Ruth Kobart	Marie Le Veau ....Juanita Hall
Annette ....Gail Johnston	Lulu ....Jamie Simmons
Jacques ....Peter Gladke	Father Time ....Keith Connes

Understudies: Mr. Atkinson—Adam Petroski; Miss Shepard—Margaret Broderson; Miss Hall-Barbara Ann Webb; Mr. Leeds—Keith Connes; Miss Kobart—Maggie Worth; Mr. Purdum—Leslie Meadow; Miss Johnston—Sherry Lambert; Mr. Gladke—Lloyd Harris; Mr. Kennon-Wilson—Ted Goodridge; Miss Webb—Doris Galiber.

Singers: Katherine Barnes, Margaret Broderson, Doris Galiber, Joy Holly, Sherry Lambert, Carol Marraccini, Mary Ann Rydzeski, Jamie Simmons, Marsha Tamaroff, Betty Terrell, Elise Warner, Barbara Ann Webb, Maggie Worth, Gilbert Adkins, Eddie Carr, Peter Clark, Nino Galanti, Leslie Meadow, Donald Meyers, Richard Nieves, Adam Petroski, Herbert Pordum, Jerome Toti, Edmund Walenta, James Kennon-Wilson.

Dancers: Jean Adams, Kathie Dalton, Bonnie Dwyer, Mercedes Ellington, Mimi Funes, Peggy Marie Haug, Jane Karel, Joan Paige, Patti Palumbo, Carol Perry, Lucinda Ransom, Toni Reither, Renee Rose, Geri Spinner, Paula Tennyson, Patti Watson, Fred Benjamin, Donn Bonnell, Steven Boockvor, Henry Boyer, Bob Ellis, Ted Goodridge, Ralph Hoffman, Dennis Lynch, Myron Meljie, Ed Nolfi, Dick Prescott, Gary Ramback, Doug Spingler, Kip Watson, Ron Watson, Vernon Wendorf.

Entire production supervised by Arnold Spector; directed and choreographed by June Taylor; scenery and lighting, George Jenkins; costumes, Winn Morton; orchestrations, Philip J. Lang; production stage manager, Mortimer Halpern; dance arrangements, Milt Sherman; musical and vocal direction, Mitchell Ayres; stage managers, Norman Shelly, William Krot; press, Saul Richman.

Time: 1815, 1905 and 1965. Place: New Orleans. A New Orleans lawyer's society girl friend doesn't want to marry him because he isn't as romantic as his ancestors Jean Lafitte the pirate and Lucky Lafitty the gambler.

ACT I

Overture ....Conducted by Mitchell Ayres
"The Mardi Gras Waltz" ....Entire Ensemble
"I'd Know That Smile" ....John Laffity
"Mumbo Jumbo" ....Katie
"We're Wanted" ....Dominique You, Jean Laffite, Jacques, Pirates
"Ladies of the Ballet" ....Annette, Madame de Villiers, Ladies
"Pirate's Polka" ....Pirates, Ladies
"When I Take My Lady" ....Jean Laffite, Pirates
"When My Man Sails Home" ....Katherine
"We're Wanted" (Reprise) ....Dominique You, Pirates
"A Pirate's Lament" ....Dominique You, Annette
"Someone I Could Love" ....Marguerite de Villiers, Annette
"When I Take My Lady" (Reprise) ....Jean Laffite, Pirates
"I'd Know That Smile" (Reprise) ....Jean Laffite, Marguerite de Villiers
Finale ....Entire Company

ACT II

Entr'acte ....Conducted by Mitchell Ayres
"Come Along Down" ....Louis the Guide, Ensemble
"The Kind of a Girl" ....Lucky Laffity, Meg
"The Kind of a Girl" (Reprise) ....Arnold Baxter, Lucky Laffity, Meg
Wilbur de Paris and His New Orleans Jazz
"Down With Whiskey" ....Carrie Nation, Arnold Baxter, Ensemble
"The Kind of a Girl" (Reprise) ....Lucky Laffity
"We're Gonna See the Voodoo Queen" ....Marie Le Veau, Ensemble
"Someone I Could Love" (Reprise) ....Peggy Willard
"Mumbo Jumbo" (Reprise) ....Katie
Finale: ....Entire Company

Leonard Bernstein's Theater Songs (88). Program of songs with music by Leonard Bernstein from *On the Town, Trouble in Tahiti, Wonderful Town, Candide* and *West Side Story;* lyrics by various persons listed below. Produced by Judith Rutherford Marechal Productions, Inc., Josephine Forrestal Productions, Inc. and Seymour Litvinoff at the Theater de Lys. Opened June 28, 1965. (Closed September 12, 1965)

Trude Adams	Don Francks	Micki Grant

Conceived and directed by Will Holt; lighting, Jules Fisher; orchestrations, Fred Werner; presented by arrangement with Lucille Lortel Productions, Inc.; stage manager, Dale E. Whitt; press, Max Eisen, Samuel J. Friedman.

Will Holt replaced Dan Francks and Lee Beery replaced Trude Adams 8/17/65.

Musical numbers: ACT I—"Something's Coming" (lyrics, Stephen Sondheim); "Christopher Street," "Conversation Piece," "Wrong Note Rag," "What a Waste," "I Feel Like I'm Not Out of Bed Yet," "New York, New York" and "It's Love" (lyrics, Betty Comden and Adolph Green); "Glitter and Be Gay" (lyrics, Richard Wilbur); "Ohio" and "Quiet Girl" (lyrics, Betty Comden and Adolph Green); "America" (lyrics, Stephen Sondheim); "Best of All Possible Worlds" (lyrics, Richard Wilbur).

ACT II—"My Love" (lyrics, Richard Wilbur); "Tonight" (lyrics, Stephen Sondheim); "O Happy We" (lyrics, Richard Wilbur); "Morning Sun" and "Tahiti Duet" (lyrics, Leonard Bernstein); "It Must Be So" (lyrics, Richard Wilbur); "Eldorado" (lyrics, Lillian Hellman); "Trouble in Tahiti" (lyrics, Leonard Bernstein); "What's the Use" (lyrics, Richard Wilbur); "Gee, Officer Krupke" (lyrics, Stephen Sondheim); "It Must Be Me" (lyrics, Richard Wilbur); "Someday, Somewhere" (lyrics, Stephen Sondheim); "Make Our Garden Grow" (lyrics, Richard Wilbur) and "Some Other Time" (lyrics, Betty Comden and Adolph Green).

* **The American Savoyards. The Yeomen of the Guard** (22) and **Ruddigore** (28). Revivals of the operettas by Gilbert & Sullivan, presented in 1965 repertory with four other operettas which opened during the 1964-65 season: *Iolanthe, H.M.S. Pinafore, The Mikado* and *The Gondoliers*. Dorothy Raedler's productions, produced by Jeff G. Britton in association with M.J. Boyer at the Jan Hus Playhouse. *The Yeomen of the Guard* opened July 7, 1965; *Ruddigore* opened August 26, 1965. (Repertory closed January 2, 1966) * **The Pirates of Penzance** (2) and * **Princess Ida** (2). Revivals of the operettas by Gilbert & Sullivan presented in 1966 repertory with four other operettas scheduled to open during the 1966-67 season: *Trial by Jury, H.M.S. Pinafore, The Mikado* and *Utopia, Ltd.* Dorothy Raedler's productions, produced by American Gilbert & Sullivan Presentations, Inc., Jeff G. Britton, managing director, and Dorothy Raedler, artistic director, at the Jan Hus Playhouse. *The Pirates of Penzance* opened May 23, 1966. *Princess Ida* opened May 26, 1966.

1965 Repertory

PERFORMER	"THE YEOMEN OF THE GUARD"	"RUDDIGORE"
Bob Bellis	(Second Citizen)	
David Bennett	Sir Richard Cholmondeley	
John Campbell	Sergeant Meryll	Roderic Murgatroyd
David Damaska		Rupert Murgatroyd
Don Derrow	First Citizen	Jasper Murgatroyd
Richard Erbacher	(First Yeoman)	
Robert Fields	Jack Point	Old Adam Goodheart
Susan Geoppinger		Zorah
Donald Kaplan		Gilbert Murgatroyd
Dan Kingman	(Second Yeoman)	
Bruce Lawrence	Wilfred Shadbolt	Despard Murgatroyd
Dolores Leffingwell	Elsie Maynard	
Artis Lewis	Dame Carruthers	Dame Hannah
Jack Lines	Leonard Meryll	Lionel Murgatroyd
Tom Mook	(First Yeoman)	
Estella Munson	Kate	Rose Maybud
Craig Palmer		Conrad Murgatroyd
Frederick S. Roffman	(Second Citizen)	Ruthven Murgatroyd
Lauren Scott		Ruth
Ellen Shade	Phoebe Meryll	Mad Margaret
Edwin Sholz	Colonel Fairfax	Richard Dauntless
Jules Small	(Second Yeoman)	Mervyn Murgatroyd

(Parentheses indicate roles in which the actor alternates)

Chorus: Anne Bloch, Harriet Hops, Terry James, Elaine Kraut, Sylvia Lichtenstein, Rhonda Saunders, Yusef Bulos, Adrienne Fogler, Andrea Peters. Piano, Judith Somogi. Organ, Kenneth Bowen, Simon Sargon.

Directed by Dorothy Raedler; scenery, Henry Heyman; musical direction, Simon Sargon; associate producer, Ronald Bush; associate musical director, Judith Somogi; press, David Lipsky.

1966 Repertory

PERFORMER	"THE PIRATES OF PENZANCE"	"PRINCESS IDA"
Arden Anderson-Broecking	Edith	Melissa
Helen Andreu	Kate	Ada
Ron Armstrong	Sergeant of Police	Scynthius
Richard Best	The Pirate King	Arac
Robert Brink	Major-General Stanley	King Gama
Donald Chapman		Guron
William Copeland	Samuel	Florian
Donna Curtis		Princess Ida
Sandra Darling	Mabel	Lady Psyche
Nell Evans	Ruth	Lady Blanche
Don Junod		Cyril
Theodore Morrill	Frederick	Hilarion
Naomi Robin	Isabel	Chloe
Joyce Weibel		Sacharissa
Don Yule		King Hildebrand

Chorus: Dennis Carpenter, Dick Cerasani, Sheila Coleman, Bill Collins, Nina Gervais, Bill Gibbens, Carl John, Karl Patrick Krause, Dorothy Lancaster, Jack Lines, Regina Lynn, Craig Palmer, William Tost. Piano, Judith Somogi. Organ, Kenneth Bowen.

Directed by Dorothy Raedler; scenery, Henry Heyman; lighting, David Bamberger; musical director, Judith Somogi; associate producer, Dorothy Marie Robinson; assistant musical director, Kenneth Bowen; production stage manager, David Bamberger; press, Ben Kornzweig, Reginald Denenholz.

The Trojan Women (40). Return engagement of a revival of the play by Euripides; translated by Edith Hamilton. Produced by Circle in the Square and Theodore Mann at Circle in the Square. Opened September 3, 1965. (Closed October 9, 1965)

Hecuba	Carolyn Coates	Astyanax	Michael Maitland
Talthybius	Alan Mixon	Menelaus	Robert Mandan
Cassandra	Elaine Kerr	Helen	Dimitra Steris
Andromache	Joyce Ebert		

Trojan Women: Kay Chevalier, Tamara Daniel, Marilyn McKenna, Etain O'Malley, Anna Shaler, Lorraine Serabian, Ann Tarlov, Joanna Walton, Peggy White. Greek Soldiers: David Hutchison, Tony Cosenza. Voice of Poseidon recorded by Rod Steiger.

Directed by Michael Cacoyannis; music, Jean Prodromides; costumes, Theoni V. Aldredge; lighting, Jules Fisher; choreography, Michael Cacoyannis; chorus master, Elaine Kerr; production stage manager, Mark D. Healy; press, Ben Kornzweig, Reginald Denenholz.

Time: after the fall of Troy. Place: outside the walls of Troy. This production of *The Trojan Women* was staged at the Spoleto Festival of Two Worlds in Italy in 1963 and was presented off Broadway December 23, 1963 for 600 performances. In this return engagement, performances were suspended from 9/26 through 9/30.

Happy Days (30). Revival of the play by Samuel Beckett in two versions, French and English. Produced by Theater 1966 (Richard Barr, Clinton Wilder and Edward Albee) at the Cherry Lane Theater. French version (14) opened September 14, 1965. (Closed September 26, 1965) English version (16) opened September 28, 1965. (Closed October 10, 1965)

FRENCH VERSION

Winnie ....Madeleine Renaud   Willie ....Wyman Pendleton

ENGLISH VERSION

Winnie ....Ruth White   Willie ....John C. Becher

French version directed by Roger Blin; decor, Matias; stage manager Richard d'Anjou. English version directed by Alan Schneider; decor, Matias; stage manager, Charles Kindl; press, Howard Atlee, Robert Larkin, Michael Alpert, David Roggensack.

Time: the present. A wife, buried in the first act up to the waist and in the second up to the neck, prattles on and on about the past to her longsuffering and all but silent husband. *Happy Days* was first produced in New York by Theater 1962 off Broadway on September 17, 1961, for 28 performances. At the performance of 9/14/65 the role of Willie was played by Miss Renaud's husband, Jean-Louis Barrault.

Friends and Enemies (139). Program of two one-act plays by Arkady Leokum. Produced by The Red Barn Theater Limited at Theater East. Opened September 16, 1965. (Closed January 23, 1966)

ENEMIES

Gittleman ....Eli Mintz   Miller ....Jay Barney

FRIENDS

The Tutor ....Eli Mintz   A Delivery Boy ....David Roya
The Pupil ....Danny Fortus

Directed by William Hunt; scenery and lighting, DAFS, Inc.; costumes, Stephanie Kovanda; press, Public Relations Corporation of America.

ENEMIES—Time: 5 p.m. Place: a restaurant. A seemingly wealthy restaurant patron meets a waiter who makes good investments. FRIENDS—Time: shortly before 10 a.m. Place: the living room of a teacher's apartment overlooking a harbor. A penniless old scholar is badgered by his young student.

Swim Low Little Goldfish (1). By Ronald Collier. Produced by Al Jordan at the Forty-first Street Theater. Opened and closed at the evening performance, September 28, 1965.

Directed by Al Jordan; art direction, Howard Deutscher; lighting, James Dwyer; press, Richard Falk. With Jack Aaron, Carol Gutenberg, Peter George, JoAnn Hamilton, Eben Richards, Lisa Mayo. Comedy built around the subject of venereal disease.

The World of Ray Bradbury (5). Program of three one-act plays by Ray Bradbury: *The Pedestrian, The Veldt* and *To the Chicago Abyss*. The Claude Giroux-Orrin Christy Jr.-Frank Carrington production was produced by the Greater New York Chapter Inc. of American National Theater and Academy at the Orpheum Theater. Opened October 8, 1965. (Closed October 10, 1965)

Directed by Charles Rome Smith; scenery and lighting, Eldon Elder; costumes, Arnold Scaasi; press, John Springer Associates. With George Voskovec, Paul Sparer, Gretchen Kanne, Henry Madden, John Zizak, Denise Stevens, Stewart Bradley. Time: the 1990s. All three plays are science-fiction glimpses of an imaginary future. In THE PEDESTRIAN, two men go for a walk in the rain and become lawbreakers because such strolls are forbidden. In THE VELDT, a busy executive pacifies his children with an adventure machine which turns on its users and destroys them. In TO THE CHICAGO ABYSS, an old man reminisces sadly about the good old days before the holocaust.

The Trigon (70). By James Broom Lynne. Produced by Arthur Cantor at Stage 73. Opened October 9, 1965. (Closed December 5, 1965)

Arthur ....Jeremy Geidt   Mabel ....Veronica Castang
Basil ....Geoffrey Webb   Charles ....Michael Lipton

Standby for Miss Castang: Jessica Rains.

Directed by Arthur Cantor; designed by Richard Bianchi; associate producer, Carl A. Gottlieb; stage manager, David Rosenbaum; press, Artie Solomon, Donna Silberberg.

Time: early 1950s. Place: a top-floor flat in London. A triangular friendship of two roommates and a girl is disrupted by the intrusion of a stranger who seduces the girl and humiliates the two men. A foreign play previously produced in London.

An Evening's Frost (132). By Donald Hall. The University of Michigan Professional Theater Program production, produced by Judith Rutherford Marechal Productions, Inc. and Konrad Matthaei, in association with Jay Stanwyck, by arrangement with Lucille Lortel Productions, Inc., at Theater de Lys. Opened October 11, 1965. (Closed February 13, 1966)

Jacqueline Brookes	Will Geer
Donald Davis	John Randolph

Directed by Marcella Cisney; music, Richard Peaslee; scenery, Robin Wagner; lighting, Gary Harris; flutist, Margaret Strum; press, Dorothy Ross Associates.

A narrative describes Robert Frost's life from his birth in San Francisco to his final days of great public esteem after the Kennedy inauguration, and this word-picture of the poet is filled out with many selections from Frost's own prose, poetry and letters.

* Pick a Number XV (392). Cabaret revue conceived by Julius Monk. Produced by Thomas Hammond at the Plaza 9 Room, Hotel Plaza. Opened October 14, 1965.

Lee Beery	Liz Sheridan
Rex Robbins	John Keatts
Bill Hinnant	Elizabeth Wilson
Nancy Parell	John Svar

Directed by Julius Monk; choreography, Frank Wagner; musical direction and arrangements, Robert Colston, Frederick Silver; lighting, Chester Morss; stage manager, Robert P. Cohen; press, Paul Benson.

Sketches and musical numbers: "Pick a Number XV" (lyric and dialogue, by William F. Brown, music by Stanley Lebowsky); "The Good Old Days" (lyrics by David Finkle, music by Bill Weeden); Checkbooks and All That (by Ted James); "Happiness Is a Bird" (lyric and music by Claibe Richardson); "Pop Song" (lyric and music by Lesley Davison); Live From New York (by William F. Brown); "The New Menace" (lyric and music by June Reizner); "The Plaza's Going Native" (lyric by Fred Tobias, music by Stanley Lebowsky); "Coney Island" (lyric by Nelson Garringer, music by Fred Silver); Peyton Place Forever (by Tony Geiss); "On the Weekend" (lyric by Fred Tobias, music by Stanley Lebowsky); "New York Is a Summer Festival" (lyric by Tom Jones, music by Harvey Schmidt); "Love, Here I Am" (lyric and music by Walter Marks); The Kicker (by Robert Elliott); "Almost a Love Song" (lyric and music by Clark Gesner); "McNamara's Band" (lyric by Howard Liebling, music by Shamus O'Connor); "Signs of the Seasons" (lyric and music by June Reizner); Wonderland Revisited (by William F. Brown); "The Saga of Killer Joe" (lyric by Nelson Garringer, music by Fred Silver); "Societus Magnificat: An Oratorio" (lyric and music by Clark Gesner).

Play That on Your Old Piano (2). By Dan Blue. Produced by Gilbert Bledsoe and Maxwell Silverman at the Renata Theater. Opened October 14, 1965. (Closed October 15, 1965)

Directed by John Gerstad; scenery, William Ritman; costumes, Noel Taylor; lighting, Roger Johnson Jr.; choreographic consultant, Joan Gainer; stage manager, Andy Rasbury; press, David Rothenberg. With Richard Barrie, Alfred Dennis, Harold Herman, Gaylord C. Mason, Parker McCormick, Sylvia Miles, Martin Rudy, Viola Swayne, Dennis Scott and Sy Travers. Comedy about a teen-age boy pianist who wants to get on Major Bowes' radio program for amateurs.

Good Day by Emanuel Peluso and **The Exhaustion of Our Son's Love** by Jerome Max (64). Program of two one-act plays. Produced by Charles Gnys and Peter Harron at the Cherry Lane Theater. Opened October 18, 1965. (Closed December 12, 1965)

GOOD DAY

The Young Man ....Frank Langella   Bianco, a servant ....Joel Stuart
The Old Lady ....Nancy Marchand

THE EXHAUTION OF OUR
SON'S LOVE

Sara Calendar ....Clarice Blackburn   Sam Calendar ......Albert M. Ottenheimer
Celia ....Betty Lou Holland   Raymond Calendar ......Stephen Strimpell

Understudies: Jane Cronin and Joel Stuart.
Scenery, Peter Harvey; lighting, V. C. Fuqua; stage manager, Charles Kindl; press, Howard
Atlee, Michael Alpert, David Roggensack.
GOOD DAY directed by Ben Shaktman. Time: the present. Place: a room in a large house.
About a young man who falls into an old woman's power. THE EXHAUSTION OF OUR
SON'S LOVE directed by Walt Witcover. Time: a summer morning. Place: back porch in a
suburban Pennsylvania community on the way to Scranton. About a Jewish family awaiting a
phone call to verify whether their son has been killed in a service accident in Germany.

Woman (7). One-woman program of scenes from five plays; performed by Gale
Sondergaard. Produced by Dina and Alexander E. Racolin at the Gramercy Arts
Theater. Opened October 20, 1965. (Closed October 24, 1965)

Directed by Herbert Biberman; press, Max Eisen, Carl Samrock. Scenes from Congreve. Ibsen, Houghton, Martinez-Sierra and Corwin are chosen to dramatize "the emergence of
Woman into fuller status as a human being in relation to her man."

Kill the One-Eyed Man (8). By Herb Schapiro, based on the story *Diary of a
Madman* by Nikolai Gogol. Produced by Iliad-Europa Productions in association
with Russell Allen Jacobsen at the Provincetown Playhouse. Opened October 20,
1965. (Closed October 26, 1965)

Directed by Tom Competello; scenery, James Washington, Stephen Shea and E. Susan Reiner;
music, Gary Wm. Friedman; lighting, Earl Eidman; press, Ben Kornzweig, Reginald Denenholz. With Michael Twain, Rozanne Ritch, Hector Elizondo. A Russian civil servant maddened
by love believes himself to be the King of Spain.

Hotel Passionato (11). Musical with book by Jerome J. Schwartz; music by Philip
Springer; lyrics by Joan Javits. Produced by Slade Brown at the East Seventy-
fourth Street Theater. Opened October 22, 1965. (Closed October 31, 1965)

Directed by Michael Ross; scenery and lighting, Paul Barnes; costumes, Robert Mackintosh;
press, Shirley Herz. With Lee Cass, Roger Hamilton, the Kane Triplets, Linda Lavin, Phil
Leeds, Peter Maloney, Marian Mercer, Adam Petroski, Robert Rovin, Paul Sand, Art Wallace,
Ned Wertimer, Jo Anne Worley and Lois Zetter. About an attempted adultery in a hotel, complicated by the appearance at the hotel of various interested parties.

Hello Charlie (129). Musical in the Yiddish language; with music by Maurice
Rauch; lyrics by Jacob Jacobs; book by H. Kalmanowitch. Produced by Jacob
Jacobs at the Yiddish Anderson Theater. Opened October 23, 1965. (Closed Jan-
uary 6, 1966)

Benjamin Lichtenstein ....Leon Liebgold   Molly ....Chayele Rosental
Lilly ....Susan Walters   Miriam Rappaport ....Miriam Kressyn
Milton Kleinstein ....Rick Grayson   Frumeh ....Anna Jacobowitz
Jack ....Seymour Rexsite   Jeanette ....Thelma Mintz
Fanny ....Gita Galina   Ensemble of Dancers ....Michael Aubrey,
Chaim Ber Zeitlin ....Jacob Jacobs   Lisa Berg, Cathy Haas, Enid Hart,
Charlie Zeitlin ....Max Perlman   David DeMarie and David Marcus

Directed by Max Perlman; scenery, Arthur Aaronson; choreography, Michael Aubrey; stage
manager, Chaim Towber; press, Max Karper.

* Just for Openers (375). Cabaret revue conceived by Rod Warren. Produced by Rod Warren and Upstairs at the Downstairs at Upstairs at the Downstairs. Opened November 3, 1965.

Betty Aberlin	R.G. Brown
Richard Blair	Fannie Flagg
Stockton Brigel	Madeline Kahn

Directed by Sandra Devlin; musical direction, Michael Cohen; at the twin pianos, Michael Cohen, Edward Morris; lighting, Charles E. Hoefler, William J. McAnallen; stage manager, George Curley; press, Dorothy Ross, Richard O'Brien.

Sketches and musical numbers: ACT I—"Just for Openers" (lyric and music by Rod Warren); "The 'Dolly' Sisters" (lyric by Drey Shepperd, music by Ed Kresley); Hail, Columbia (by Rod Warren); "Anyone Who's Anyone" (lyric by David Finkle, music by Bill Weeden); "Where Did We Go Wrong?" (lyric by John Meyer, music by Stephen Lawrence); If the Crown Fits (by Kenny Solms and Gayle Parent); "America the Beautiful" (lyric by Michael McWhinney, music by Rod Warren); The Waitress (by Fannie Flagg); "New York Without Bob" (lyric and music by Alan Freidman); "The Telephone Hang-Up (by Bill Kaufman and Paul Korento); "Adaptations" (lyric by Ed Fearon, music by Lee Holdridge).

ACT II—"You're a Big Boy Now" (lyric and music by Rod Warren); The Second-Best Man (by Rod Warren); "The Matinee" (lyric by John Meyer, music by Stephen Lawrence); Fun in the Morning (by Fannie Flagg); "Mr. Know-it-all" (lyric by Larry Alexander, music by William Goldenberg); "Let's Abolish Holidays" (lyric and music by William Dyer and Don Parks); Space Age, (by Rod Warren); Finale: "Just for Openers."

Great Scot! (38). Musical with book by Mark Conradt and Gregory Dawson; music by Don McAfee; lyrics by Nancy Leeds. Produced by Scotia Productions in association with Edward H. Davis at Theater Four. Opened November 10, 1965. (Closed December 12, 1965).

Robert Burns	Allan Bruce	MacIntosh; Sailor;	
Jean Armour	Joleen Fodor	Town Elder	Charles Burks
McGurk; Creech	Jack Eddleman	Maggie; Mackerel; Lady Louise	
Heather; Duchess of Montrose;		Glenpatrick	Shirley Caballero
Fish Monger	Charlotte Jones	Agnes McGurk; Lady	
Gilbert; Rev. Dillingham;		Cynthia	Ginger Gerlach
Duke of Montrose	Cash Baxter	Allison; Lucy	Mary Jo Gillis
James Armour; Duffy	Charles Hudson	Clarinda	Anita Maye
Jamie	Arthur Whitfield	Lorna; Salmon	Lois Ann Saunders
MacCohen; Constable;		Jock; Town Elder	Dale Westerman
Bishop	Thomas Boyd	Jennie	Camelot Guinevere

Directed by Charles Tate; scenery, Herbert Senn, Helen Pond; costumes, Patton Campbell; musical direction, Joseph Raposo; orchestrations, Stephen Lawrence; lighting, Theda Taylor; additional orchestrations, Mr. Raposo, Gershon Kingsley; musical staging, Joyce Trisler; production stage manager, Fred Reinglas; press, David Rothenberg.

Time: 1783 and 1784. Place: Scotland. Based on the life of the Scottish poet Robert Burns.

ACT I

An evening in the life of Robert Burns—Fall, 1783

"You're The Only One" ....Robbie, Fathers, Ensemble
"Great Scot" ....Robbie, Fathers, Ensemble
The town square of Ayr—early the following morning
"I'll Find a Dream Somewhere" ....Robbie
Jean's bedroom—the same day
"He's Not For Me" ....Jean
The Poosie Nancy Tavern—immediately following
"She's Not For Me" (Reprise) ....Robbie, Jean, Ensemble
Outside the Armour house—the same day
The Highland Games—the next day
"Dance" ....Jamie, Ensemble
"That Special Day" ....Jean, Tom, Robbie, Ensemble

A street in Ayr—eight months later
The Burns cottage—immediately following
  "Brandy in Your Champagne" ....Heather, Creech
  "I'm Gonna Have A Baby" ....Robbie, Ensemble
A street in Ayr—immediately following
  "Original Sin" ....Armour, Elders
The Session Room of the Kirk—immediately following
  "I'll Still Love Jean" ....Robbie
Outside the Kirk—immediately following
  "Where Is That Rainbow" ....Robbie, Jean

ACT II

Princes' Street in Edinburgh—a few days later
  "Princes' Street" ....Ensemble
The ballroom—that night
  "You're The Only One" (Reprise) ....Robbie, Court
  "Happy New Year" ....Robbie, Court
Corridor of the ballroom
At the waterfront
  "That Big-bellied Bottle" ....Duffy, Fish Monger, Robbie, Ensemble
Jean's bedroom in Ayr—several months later
  "He Knows Where To Find Me" ....Jean
Robbie's apartment in Edinburgh (and other locations)—several months later
  "Where Does A Man Begin?" ....Robbie
Duchess' Garden
  "What A Shame" ....Court
  "I Left A Dream Somewhere" ....Robbie
The town square of Ayr—immediately following
  Finale: "We're Gonna Have a Wedding" ....Robbie, Jean, Ensemble

Miss Julie and **The Stronger** (11). Revival program of two one-act plays by August Strindberg. Produced by June Miller at the Provincetown Theater. Opened November 10, 1965. (Closed November 21, 1965)

MISS JULIE

Jean ....Leonard de Martino   Kristin ....Irene Kling
Julie ....Dianna Ballas

THE STRONGER

Mrs. X ....Irene Kling   Mrs. Y ....Dianna Ballas

Adapted and directed by Arthur Reel; lighting by Ed Smith; stage manager, June Miller; press, Mary Samford.

* Hogan's Goat (221). By William Alfred. Produced by The American Place Theater at St. Clements Church. Opened November 11, 1965.

Matthew Stanton ....Ralph Waite   Edward Quinn ....Tom Ahearne
Kathleen Stanton ....Faye Dunaway   James "Palsy" Murphy ....Conrad Bain
John "Black Jack" Haggerty ...Roland Wood   Bill ....Luke Wymbs
Petey Boyle ....Cliff Gorman   Ann Mulcahy ....Agnes Young
Bessie Legg ....Michaele Myers   Josephine Finn ....Tresa Hughes
Maria Haggerty ....Grania O'Malley   Boylan ....Tom Crane
Father Stanislaus Coyne ....Barnard Hughes   A doctor ....David Dawson
Father Maloney ....John Dorman

Constituents: Stan Sussman (piano), Eileen Fitzpatrick, Jack Fogarty, John Hoffmeister, Monica MacCormack, Michael Murray, Bruce Waite, Albert Shipley.

Directed by Frederick Rolf; scenery, lighting, costumes, Kert Lundell; production stage manager, Peter Galambos; press, Phillip Bloom.

Time: April 1890. Place: the City of Brooklyn. Act I, Scene 1: The parlor of Matthew Stanton's flat. Scene 2: Back room of Stanton's saloon. Scene 3: The all-night Printer's Church,

Lower Fulton Street. Scene 4: Back room of Fogarty's saloon. Scene 5: Haggerty's kitchen. Act II, Scene 1: Back room of Stanton's saloon. Scene 2: Stanton's parlor. Scene 3: The stern of a Coney Island steamer bound for Seagate. Scene 4: Stanton's parlor.

A rising young Irish-American politician subordinates everything to his ambition, which is finally thwarted after he causes his wife's death. *Hogan's Goat* closed 1/1/66 at the American Place Theater after 56 performances and reopened 1/7/66 at the East Seventy-fourth Street Theater for an extended run. *Hogan's Goat* played a week of subscription performances beginning 11/3/65 before its official opening.

Richard Mulligan replaced Ralph Waite 1/25/66-5/17/66. Kay Chevalier replaced Faye Dunaway 1/25/66. Caren McCrary replaced Miss Dunaway 5/17/66.

A Best Play; see page 169

The Fifth Commandment (60). By Edmund Morris; adapted by David Licht; translated into Yiddish by Slava Estrin and presented in the Yiddish language. Produced by the Folksbiene Company at the Folksbiene Theater. Opened November 12, 1965. (Closed March 6, 1966)

Clara Danielson .... Zipora Spaisman	Sam Yeager .... Joshua Zeldis
Bessie Glick .... Mina Kern	Sidney Danielson .... David Rogow
Leib Danielson .... Harry Rubin	Morris Danielson .... Sheftel Zak
Eddy Morison .... Michael Lux	Jennie .... Janet Ordinatsky
Susan Danielson .... Ruth Vool-Ellin	David Frostman .... Max Neiditch

Directed by David Licht; scenery and lighting, Harry Baum; technical director, Marvin Schwartz; press, Max Karper.

Time: today. Place: Phoenix, Arizona. *The Fifth Commandment* was originally produced on Broadway, in English, in 1955, under the title *The Wooden Dish*.

* **Happy Ending** and **Day of Absence** (225). Program of two one-act plays by Douglas Turner Ward. Produced by Robert Hooks, Inc. at the St. Marks Playhouse. Opened November 15, 1965.

HAPPY ENDING

Ellie .... Esther Rolle	Junie .... Robert Hooks
Vi .... Frances Foster	Arthur .... Douglas Turner

DAY OF ABSENCE

Clem; Second Citizen;	Third Operator .... Pamela Jones
Businessman .... Lonne Elder	Supervisor; Aide .... Frances Foster
Luke; Third Citizen;	Jackson .... Adolph Caesar
Mop Man .... Arthur French	Mayor; Clan .... Douglas Turner
John; Brush Man .... Robert Hooks	First Citizen; Industrialist;
Mary .... Barbara Ann Teer	Pious; Rastus .... Moses Gunn
First Operator; Doll	Clubwoman .... Esther Rolle
Woman .... Hattie Winston	Courier .... Bostic Van Felton
Second Operator .... Maxine Griffith	Announcer .... Mark Shapiro

Directed by Philip Meister; scenery and lighting, Richard Seger; costumes, Whitney Blausen; production stage manager, Hal De Windt; press, Howard Atlee and Michael Alpert.

HAPPY ENDING—Time: the present. Place: the kitchen in a Harlem tenement. About two sophisticated Negro domestics who have been mulcting their employers for years. DAY OF ABSENCE—Time: the present. Place: an unnamed Southern town. A small Southern community awakens to find all its Negroes have left—for one day.

Bugs and **Veronica** (75). Program of two one-act plays by John White. Produced by CAM Productions at the Pocket Theater. Opened November 18, 1965. (Closed February 6, 1966).

BUGS

Mrs. Rounce .... Alice Scudder	Mr. Rounce .... Jess Osuna
George Rounce .... Dylan Green	A Social Worker .... Lorraine Serabian
Millicent Marsh .... Joan Tyson	

VERONICA

Lou Long	Bernard Grant	Liz	Lorraine Serabian
Leo Lane	Ralph Bell	Freck	Jess Osuna
Plug	Dylan Green		

Directed by Anna Sokolow; designed by Koski-Long; original music, Teo Macero; production stage manager, Art Wolff; press, Arthur Cantor, Artie Solomon, Donna Silberberg.

BUGS—Time: the present. Place: living room of a tired frame house in industrial America. About a young man crazed by his fear of insects. VERONICA—Time: the present. Place: choice suite in a second-rate hotel on upper Broadway, New York City. About two Broadway song writers who are working against the pressure of repeated failures.

The Bernard Shaw Story (52). One-man program of Shavian writings and anecdotes compiled and performed by Bramwell Fletcher. Produced by Norman Kean at the East Seventy-fourth Street Theater. Opened November 18, 1965. (Closed January 2, 1966)

Adapted to this theater by Maury Tuckerman; lighting, Owen Ryan; production stage manager, Gary Peterson; press, Ben Kornzweig, Reginald Denenholz. *The Bernard Shaw Story* was previously staged by Hilton Edwards in Dublin at the Gate Theater in November, 1964, and in New York for one performance (ANTA matinee) at the Theater de Lys October 26, 1965.

An Impudent Wolf (13). By J. I. Rodale. Produced by The Theater of the Zanies at Theater 62. Opened November 19, 1965. (Closed November 28, 1965)

Directed by J. I. Rodale; scenery, J. I. Rodale; lighting, Norman Blumenfeld; press, Max Eisen. With Elaine Laurence, Barry Jay, Marcia Lewis, Liliane Simonet, Alvin Cohen, Ed Lauter, Antony Tenuta, Rusty Dore, Arthur Horn, Roseann Conte, Peter Freund. Comedy about the Little Red Riding Hood wolf brought to trial. Previously produced in experimental New York productions in 1964 and 1965.

Medea (77). Revival of the play by Robinson Jeffers. Produced by Judith Rutherford Marechal Productions, Inc., Paul Libin, Jay Stanwyck Productions, Inc. at the Martinique Theater. Opened November 28, 1965. (Closed February 13, 1966)

The Nurse	Helen Craig	Creon	David Hooks
The Tutor	Paul B. Price	Jason	Michael Higgins
The Children	Tony Di Caprio, Paul Rufo	Aegeus	Mervyn Williams
First Woman of Corinth	Rosemary Tory	Jason's Slave	Reno Roop
Second Woman of Corinth	Annette Hunt	Attendants to Medea	Frances Siegal,
Third Woman of Corinth	Brenda Lesley		Linda Simon
Medea	Gloria Foster	Soldier	Frank Savino

Standbys: Miss Craig—Rosemary Tory; Messrs. Hooks, Higgins—Frank Savino; Messrs. Williams, Price—Wil Albert.

Directed by Cyril Simon; scenery by David Mitchell; costumes by Clifford Capone; lighting by Roger Morgan; production stage manager, Charles Maryan; press, Ben Kornzweig, Reginald Denenholz, Anne Woll.

Medea has been played in New York by such performers as Matilda Heron (1866), Mrs. J.H. Hackett (1876), Januschek (1881) and Margaret Anglin (1918). The Robinson Jeffers version was produced on Broadway October 20, 1947, for 214 performances, with Judith Anderson in the title role.

The White Devil (152). Revival of the play by John Webster. Produced by Theodore Mann at Circle in the Square. Opened December 6, 1965. (Closed April 17, 1966)

Count Lodovico	Paul Vincent	Camillo	Frederic Warriner
Gasparo	Ed Rombola	Zanche	Terri Turner
Vittoria Corombona	Carrie Nye	Cornelia	Christine Pickles
The Duke of Brachiano	Paul Stevens	Francisco De Medicis	Robert Burr
Flamineo	Frank Langella	Cardinal Monticelso	Eric Berry

Isabella ....Maria Tucci	A Lawyer ....Ed Rombola
(Giovanni) ......Robert Benson Ross Burr	Matron ....Jacqueline Britton
Peter Miner	Carlo ....Michael Boccio
Marcello ....Peter Jacob	Hortensio ....Ralph Maurer
Doctor Julio ....Al Corbin	Silvio ....John Culjak

(Parentheses indicate role in which the actor alternates)

Directed by Jack Landau; scenery, Peter Wexler; lighting, Jules Fisher; costumes, Noel Taylor; music, Herbert Harris; production stage manager, Mark D. Healy; press, Merle Debuskey.

Time: Renaissance. Place: Rome and Padua. This Elizabethan horror drama of illicit love and murder was played in modern dress.

The Parasite (2). By Robert N. Summers. Produced by Al Jordan at the Renata Theater. Opened December 16, 1965. (Closed December 17, 1965)

Directed by Robert N. Summers and Al Jordan; art direction, Chester Delacruz; production stage manager, Lisa Mayo; press, Richard Falk. With Jay Barney, Sheila Gary, Ardyth Kaiser, Joan Kroschell, Carole Ann Lewis, Joseph R. Sicari, Peter Stuart, Louis Vuolo. Comedy about a parasitical promoter who preys on a young, wealthy woman.

New Cole Porter Revue (76). New edition of the revue conceived by Ben Bagley; with Cole Porter music. Produced by Square East at Square East. Opened December 22, 1965. (Closed February 27, 1966)

Dody Goodman	Carol Arthur
Bobby Short	Jane Manning
Danny Meehan	Virginia Vestoff

Material assembled and directed by Ben Bagley; choreography, Buddy Schwab; continuity, special vocal arrangements, grand finale, Bud McCreery; musical direction and arrangements, William Roy; percussionist, Dick Sheridan; collage paintings, Shirley Kaplan; projections, Wallace Litwin; costumes and gowns, Charles Fatone; lighting, Jules Fisher; stage manager, John Molthen; press, Merle Debuskey, Lawrence Belling.

* **The Pocket Watch** (168). By Alvin Aronson. Produced by The New Playwrights Productions Co., Inc. at Actors Playhouse. Opened January 5, 1966.

Rachel Goldman ....Rita Karin	Chaim Goldman ....Michael Gorrin
Freda Goldman ....Estelle Omens	Sam Schwartz ....Hy Anzell
Harold Schwartz ....Daniel T. Frankel	Irving Friedman ....C. M. Gampel
Sophie Schwartz ....Mimi Randolph	

Directed by Sherwood Arthur; scenery, Quinton Raines; lighting, Barbara Nollman; production stage manager, Quinton Raines; press, David Lipsky.

Time: summer of 1953. Place: Chaim Goldman's two-family house in a run-down neighborhood of a small suburb in Boston, Mass. About the squabbles of a lower middle class Jewish family.

* **The Mad Show** (201). Musical revue based on *Mad Magazine;* book by Larry Siegel and Stan Hart; lyrics by Marshall Barer, Larry Sigel and Steven Vinaver; music by Mary Rodgers. Produced by Ivor David Balding for the Establishment Theater Company, Inc., in association with Hitchcock-Balding Productions, Ltd., at the New Theater. Opened January 10, 1966.

Linda Lavin	Paul Sand
MacIntyre Dixon	Jo Anne Worley
Dick Libertini	

Devised and directed by Steven Vinaver; scenery and costumes, Peter Harvey; lighting, V. C. Fuqua; musical director, Sam Pottle; percussionist, Danny Epstein; press, John Springer Associates.

Sketches and musical numbers: ACT I—"Opening" (lyrics by Marshall Barer), Academy Awards, "You Never Can Tell" (lyric by Steven Vinaver), Interview, "Eccch" (lyric by Marshall Barer), Saboteurs, "The Real Thing" (lyric by Marshall Barer), Babysitter, "Misery Is" (lyric by Marshall Barer), Handle With Care, "Hey, Sweet Momma" (lyric by Steven Vinaver), Primers, "Well It Ain't" (lyric by Larry Siegel), Football in Depth, "Hate Song" (lyric by Steven Vinaver.)

Marcia Rodd replaced Linda Lavin 1/16/66; Marilyn Cooper replaced Joa Anne Worley 4/10/66; Reni Santoni replaced Paul Sand 4/10/66; David Steinberg replaced Reni Santoni 5/31/66.

ACT II—Kiddie T. V., "Looking for Someone" (lyric by Marshall Barer), Hollywood Surplus, "The Gift of Maggie (and others)" (lyric by Marshall Barer), T. V. Nik, Zoom, Snappy Answers, Getting to Know You, "The Boy From" (lyric by Norm Deploom), The Irving Irving Story.

Why Do I Deserve This? (12) *(Womit haben wir das verdient?)* Musical revue in the German language with sketches by Kay and Lore Lorentz, Eckart Hachfeld and Martin Morlock; music by Werner Kruse, Emil Schuchardt and Fritz Maldener; lyrics by Wolfgang Franke and Mischa Leinek. Produced by Gert von Gontard and Felix G. Gerstman in association with the Deutschen Theater, Inc. at the Barbizon-Plaza Theater. Opened January 18, 1966. (Closed January 29, 1966).

Lore Lorentz   Kay Lorentz
Karl-Heinz Gerdesmann   Werner Vielhaber
Ernst Hilbich

Directed by Kay Lorentz; scenery and costumes, Fritz Butz; lighting, Peter Frass-Wolfsburg; stage manager, Sally Cooke; press, Max Eisen. A foreign play previously produced in Dusseldorf, Germany.

Rooms (54). Program of two one-act plays by Stanley Mann: *Better Luck Next Time* and *A Walk in Dark Places*. Produced by Gene Persson, Edwin Wilson and Hy Silverman at the Cherry Lane Theater. Opened January 27, 1966. (Closed March 13, 1966)

BETTER LUCK NEXT TIME

Bellhop	Charles Davisson	Potter	Charles Davisson
William Foster	James Broderick	Miss Quincey	Irene Dailey
Jenny Zubitsky	Shirley Knight		

A WALK IN DARK PLACES

Dr. Robert Palmer	James Broderick	Mrs. Henry	Irene Dailey
Mrs. Levene	Dorothy Raymond	Helen Windsor	Shirley Knight

Directed by George Keathley; scenery and lighting, C. Murawski; associate producer, Margaret T. Barker; press, John Springer Associates.

BETTER LUCK NEXT TIME—Time: the present. Place: the 20th floor of a New York hotel suite. A discontented publisher keeps remarrying in order to find an uncomplicated mate. A WALK IN DARK PLACES—Time: the present. Place: the office of Dr. Robert Palmer, the 20th floor of a building in Manhattan. About a psychiatrist who probes the minds of a distraught mother and daughter.

Winterset (30). Revival of the drama by Maxwell Anderson. Produced by The American Revival Company (John Marqusee, Amnon Kabatchnik and Lewis Murray), at the Jan Hus Playhouse. Opened February 9, 1966. (Closed March 6, 1966.)

Man in Blue	Buck Anderson	Lucio	Dominic Chianese
Man in Gray	Michael Talcott	Piny	Virgilia Chew
Trock	Lester Rawlins	Garth	Nick Padula
Shadow	Robert Kya-Hill	Miriamne	Patricia McAneny

Esdras ....Sol Serlin	Carr ....Joel Stuart
The Hobo ....Leib Lensky	Herman ....James Adrian Cohen
Street Walker ....Caroline Faulkner	Sailor ....Tom Krichbaum
First Girl ....Carol Florence	Radical ....Kermit Brown, Jr.
Second Girl ....Joyce Lee	Policeman ....Irwin Rosen
Judge Gaunt ....Warren Wade	Sergeant ....Paul john Austin
Mio ....Joseph Hindy	

Directed by Amnon Kabatchnik; scenery, Richard Bianchi; lighting, Barbara Nollman; costumes, Dina Harris; production stage manager, Robert Stevenson; press, Howard Atlee.

Time: early 1930's. Place: on the bank of a river and a small cellar apartment. *Winterset* was originally produced on Broadway September 25, 1935 for 195 performances and was a Best Play of its season.

Phèdre (100). By William Packard; a new English version of the tragedy by Jean Racine. Produced by Institute for Advanced Studies in the Theater Arts (IASTA), at the Greenwich Mews Theater. Opened February 10, 1966. (Closed May 8, 1966)

Hippolyte ....Michael Durrell	Panope ....Marguerite Hunt
Theramene ....Sam Haigler Henry	Aricie ....Anne Draper
Oenone ....Mildred Dunnock	Theseus ....James Pritchett
Phedre ....Beatrice Straight	Ismene ....Valerie von Volz

Directed by Paul-Emile Deiber; costumes, Sylvia Kalegi; scenery, Geri Davis; lighting, David Arkin; music, Jean-Baptiste Moreau; press, Merle Debuskey. This version of the tragedy arising from a queen's incestuous love for her son was first staged in New York by IASTA as a workshop production.

Dorothy Sands replaced Mildred Dunnock 2/28/66. Jean Sullivan replaced Beatrice Straight 3/29/66-4/12/66.

The Deadly Game (105). Revival of the play by James Yaffe; adapted from the novel *Trapps* by Friedrich Duerrenmatt. Produced by Alton Wilkes and Jim Mendenhall Productions at the Provincetown Playhouse. Opened February 13, 1966. (Closed May 15, 1966)

Emile Carpeau ......Albert M. Ottenheimer	Howard Trapp ....Chet London
Bernard Laroque ....Rudolf Weiss	Gustave Kummer ....Roger De Koven
Joseph Pillet ....Lance Cunard	Pierre ....Michael O'Dowd
Nicole ....Jana Klenburg	A Visitor ....Paula Shaw

Directed by Alton Wilkes; scenery and lighting, Richard Jackson; executive technical director, Ben Wampler; stage manager, Jim Hall; press, David P. Rothenberg, Louise Weiner.

Time: a winter evening. Place: house of Emile Carpeau in the Swiss Alps. Three retired Swiss legal men stage a mock trial of an American business man who may have killed his boss. *The Deadly Game* was first produced on Broadway February 2, 1960 for 39 performances.

Jonah (13). By Paul Goodman. Produced by The American Place Theater at St. Clements Church. Opened February 15, 1966. (Closed February 26, 1966)

Angel ....Earle Hyman	Singer; Worm ....Yolande Bavan
Hephzibah; Cow ....Ruth Jaroslow	Courtier ....Jeff Rock
Jonah ....Sorrell Booke	Duchess ....Marcia Kurtz
Captain; Guide ....John A. Coe	Lady ....Gretchen MacLane
A Sailor; Duke ....Jamil Zakkai	King ....Robert Frink
Sailors ....Burt Supree, Jay Fletcher	Martial Singer ....Richard Frisch
Passengers ....Richard Frisch, William Shorr,	Coloratura ....Stephanie Turash
Stephanie Turash, Yolande Bavan	Heavenly Counselors ....Aileen Passloff,
Angel Helpers ....Larrio Ekson, Carl Wilson	Marcia Kurtz, Burt Supree,
Peasant ....William Shorr	Jay Fletcher, Gretchen MacLane
Ninevites ....Jay Fletcher, Carl Wilson,	
Pamela Jones, Larrio Ekson, Stephanie	
Turash, Richard Frisch	

Directed by Lawrence Kornfeld; scenery, costumes and choreography by Remy Charlip; music by Meyer Kupferman; lighting by Roger Morgan; production stage manager, Peter Galambos; harpsichord, Robert Shattuck; oboe and recorder, Cary Karp; press, John Springer Associates. A new version of the Old Testament tale, with Jonah speaking in a Yiddish accent and with a thesis that man must face up to his moral commitments. *Jonah* played 8 subscription performances, beginning 2/5/65 before its official opening.

The Coop (24). By Ralph S. Arzoomanian. Produced by Lyn Austin, Ann McIntosh and Janet Coleman at the Actors Playhouse. Opened March 1, 1966. (Closed March 20, 1966)

Danny	Clifton James	Toby	James Spruill
Bazakis	Andreas Voutsinas	Sylvester	William LeMassena
Chicken	Ron Van Lieu	Peggy	Patricia Fay

Directed by Martin Fried; scenery, Quinton Raines; lighting, Barbara Nollman; production manager, Charles Gray; press, Samuel Lurie, Stanley F. Kaminsky.
Time: the present. Place: prison. Performed without intermission. Five murderers serving life sentences occupy themselves with cruelty.

Laughwind (5). By Tom Waters. Produced by Cliff James at the Bouwerie Lane Theater. Opened March 2, 1966. (Closed March 6, 1966).

Directed by Mr. Waters; scenery, Elmon Webb; lighting, Carl Seltzer; press, Howard Atlee. With Vanda Barra, Donald Hylan, Walter Flanagan, Eugene Roche, Judith Younger. About a frustrated playwright who is anti-love and marriage.

Monopoly (49). Program of four one-act plays by Jerome Kass. Produced by The Establishment Theater Co., Inc. (Ivor David Balding, Peter Cook and Joseph E. Levine) at Stage 73. Opened March 5, 1966. (Closed April 17, 1966).

MAKE LIKE A DOG

Elvira Miller	Carolan Daniels	Stanley Miller	Jess Osuna

SUBURBAN TRAGEDY

Mr. Stein	John Karlen	Mrs. Goldman	Estelle Parsons
Barbara Lang	Deborah White		

PRINCESS REBECCA BIRNBAUM

Elsie	Francine Beers	Rebecca	Deborah White
Shirley	Estelle Parsons	Maury	Roy London
Helen	Carolan Daniels		

YOUNG MARRIEDS PLAY MONOPOLY

Ruth	Avra Petrides	Adam	Jess Osuna
Joe	John Karlen	Ava	Carolan Daniels

Standbys for Misses Daniels and Petrides—Kathy Shawn; for Messrs. Karlen and Osuna—John Mahon; for Miss White—Cara MacCormack.
Directed by Daniel Petrie; scenery, Alan Kimmel; lighting, Jules Fisher; costumes, Patricia Quinn Stuart; stage manager, Tom Iannicelli; press, Walter Alford, Louise Weiner, Paul Solomon.
In MAKE LIKE A DOG, a husband pretends to be a dog and is treated like one by his wife; in SUBURBAN TRAGEDY, a middle-aged woman discloses her love for a young teacher; in PRINCESS REBECCA BIRNBAUM, a young girl is dressed by her family for her first prom; in YOUNG MARRIEDS PLAY MONOPOLY, a quarrel over a game of Monopoly sets two couples to tearing away each other's defenses and exposing their unhappiness.

* **Serjeant Musgrave's Dance** (96). By John Arden. Produced by Ivor David Balding for the Establishment Theater Co. Inc. (Mr. Balding, Peter Cook, Joseph E.

Levine) by arrangement with Lucille Lortel Productions, Inc. at the Theater de Lys. Opened March 8, 1966.

Private Sparky	Terry Lomax	The Mayor	Dan Durning
Private Hurst	Roy R. Scheider	A Slow Collier	Simm Landres
Private Attercliffe	Leigh Wharton	A Pugnacious Collier	Paul Hecht
Bludgeon	David Doyle	Walsh	W. B. Brydon
Serjeant Musgrave	John Colicos	A Trooper of Dragoons	Walter Hadler
The Parson	Thomas Barbour	An Officer of Dragoons	Roger Hamilton
Mrs. Hitchcock	Charlotte Jones	Colliers	Guy Bon Giovanni, James
Annie	Jeanne Hepple		Davis, Jerry Hopkins
The Constable	John P. Ryan		

Directed by Stuart Burge; scenery, Ed Wittstein; costumes, Theoni V. Aldredge; lighting, Jules Fisher; music, Dudley Moore; dances, Rhoda Levine; production manager, Charles Maryan; associate producers, Peter L. Bellwood, Thomas Burrows, Jay Stanwyck; stage manager, Bernie Passeltiner; press, Walter Alford, Louise Weiner, Paul Solomon.

Time: winter, the middle of the last century. Place: a mining town in the north of England. Act I, Scene 1: A canal wharf, evening. Scene 2: The bar of a public house. Scene 3: The churchyard, sunset. Act II, Scene 1: The bar of the public house, night. Scene 2: A street, night. Scene 3: Interior of the pub (stable and bedroom), night. Act III, Scene 1: The market place, early morning. Scene 2: A prison cell.

A 19th century British army "serjeant" deserts with a few of his men and brings home the decaying corpse of a soldier killed in action to display it to the citizenry, in order to horrify the folks back home with the realities of war in the colonies.

W.B. Brydon replaced John Colicos 5/16/66.

Hooray! It's a Glorious Day . . . and all that (15). Musical with book by Maurice Teitelbaum and Charles Grodin; music by Arthur Gordon; lyrics by Ethel Bieber, Messrs. Teitelbaum and Grodin. Produced by Jeff Britton at Theater Four. Opened March 9, 1966. (Closed March 20, 1966)

Directed by Mr. Grodin; scenery and costumes, Peter Harvey; lighting, Jules Fisher; musical direction and vocal arrangements, Peter Fuchs; dance arrangements, Lannie Meyers; orchestrations, Gershon Kingsley; choreography, Sandra Devlin; production stage manager, Fred Reinglas; press, Frank Goodman, Martin Shwartz, Ruth Cage. With Raymond Allen, Laverne Burden, Louis Criscuolo, Lou David, Joan Eastman, Lois Holmes, Ronald Holgate, John Kane, Daniel Keyes, Mina Kolb, Joan Kroschell, Benny Smith.

Half Horse Half Alligator (32). One-man program of readings from American humorists performed by William Mooney. Produced by Yvette Schumer and Ronald Muchnick at the Players Theater. Opened March 13, 1966. (Closed April 10, 1966.)

Material arranged by Mr. Mooney; lighting, Roger Morgan; stage manager, John Swearingen; press, David Rothenberg.

Ludlow Fair and **The Madness of Lady Bright** (15). Program of two one-act plays by Lanford Wilson. Produced by Red Barn Theater, Ltd. at the Theater East. Opened March 22. (Closed April 3, 1966)

Directed by William Hunt; scenery and lighting, David F. Segal; costume supervision, Kapi Reith; press, Saul Richman. With Cris Alexander, Sasha von Scherler and Ann Wedgeworth.

LUDLOW FAIR is about two young women, roommates, confiding in each other the difficulties they have with men. THE MADNESS OF LADY BRIGHT is about an aging homosexual on the verge of insanity, distressed by his loss of looks.

6 From La Mama (16). Six one-act plays in two programs. First program: **Thank You, Miss Victoria** by William Hoffman; **This is the Rill Speaking** by Lanford Wilson; **Birdbath** by Leonard Melfi. Second program: **War** by Jean-Claude van

Itallie; **The Recluse** by Paul Foster; **Chicago** by Sam Shepard. Prdouced by Circle in the Square, Theodore Mann and Paul Libin at the Martinique Theater. First program opened April 11, 1966. Second program opened April 12, 1966. (Closed April 23, 1966)

THANK YOU, MISS VICTORIA

Harry Judson	Michael Warren Powell	Office Boy	Kevin O'Connor
Miss Genovese	Jacque Linn Colton	Second Office Boy	Victor LiPari

THIS IS THE RILL SPEAKING

Entire Company (in order   Michael Warren Powell, Mari-Claire
of speaking) ....Jacque Linn Colton,   Charba, Victor LiPari, Kevin O'Connor

BIRDBATH

Velma Sparrow ....Mari-Claire Charba   Frankie Basta ....Kevin O'Connor

WAR

Older Actor	Michael Warren Powell	The Lady	Mari-Claire Charba
Younger Actor	Kevin O'Connor		

THE RECLUSE

The Recluse ....Jacque Linn Colton   Jezebel ....Mari-Claire Charba

CHICAGO

Stu	Kevin O'Connor	Joe	Victor LiPari
Joy	Mari-Claire Charba	Sally	Stephanie Gordon
Myra	Jacque Linn Colton	Jim	Michael Warren Powell

All plays directed by Tom O'Horgan; lighting, Jose Sevilla; music, Mr. O'Horgan; press, Merle Debuskey.

In THANK YOU, MISS VICTORIA the dilettante son of a successful business-executive father, while loafing on the job in his first day at work, enters into a sado-masochistic relationship with a stranger on the telephone. THIS IS THE RILL SPEAKING is a picture of life in the author's native Ozark Mountains. BIRDBATH is a strange love affair between a writer and a waitress. In WAR a young actor and an old actor vie for the attentions of a woman symbolic of the muse of the theater. RECLUSE is about a woman living underground, alone, except for two dolls which she treats as people. CHICAGO is about a young man in a bathtub watching the world swirl around him.

The first program played one performance April 11; the second program played two performances April 12 and 13; then three plays—*Chicago, Birdbath* and *This Is the Rill Speaking* —were selected from the two programs and played the final 13 performances, April 15-23.

When We Dead Awaken (8). Revival of the play by Henrik Ibsen. Produced by Gregory Reardon at the Masque Theater. Opened April 18, 1966. (Closed April 24, 1966)

Directed by Henry Calvert; scenery, Edward Haynes; lighting, Fred Allison; press, David Lipsky, Marian Graham. With Peter Murphy, Jack Ramage, Roslyn Valero, Rosemary Tory, Pat McAndrew, George Axler. About the mysteries of life and death, of resurrection and immortality.

The Journey of the Fifth Horse (11). By Ronald Ribman; based, in part, on Ivan Turgenev's story *Diary of a Superfluous Man.* Produced by The American Place Theater at St. Clements Church. Opened April 21, 1966. (Closed April 30, 1966)

Terentievna	Mary Hayden	Miss Grubov (also Elizaveta	
Zoditch	Dustin Hoffman	Ozhogin)	Susan Anspach
Sergey	Christopher Strater	Pandalevski (also Bizmionkov)	Lee Wallace
Rubin (also Capt. Ivan		Katerina Prolomnaya	Catherine Gaffigan
Narvinsky)	William H. Bassett		

Nikolai Alexeevich	Anna Nikitishna
Chulkaturin .... Michael Tolan	Ozhogin .... Martha Greenhouse
Dr. Korvin .... Mark Hammer	Gregory .... Jack Aaron
Lawyer Levinov .... Harry Miller	Tania .... Jane Buchanan
Feathers (also Volbrina) ..... Susan Lipton	Lt. Zimin .... Jim Doerr
Kirilla Matveich Ozhogin .... Allan Rich	Officers .... Brian Turkington, Ron Seka

Directed by Larry Arrick; scenery and costumes, Kert Lundell; lighting, Roger Morgan; production stage manager, Peter Galambos; press, John Springer Associates.

Time: the late 19th century. Place: Petersburg, Russia. Act I, Scene 1: The Grubov Publishing House. Scene 2: The apartment of Mitkin Zoditch. Act II: The apartment of Mitkin Zodich.

The Journey of the Fifth Horse advances the idea that timid souls are apt to lead empty lives. It played 11 subscription performances starting 4/11/66 before its official opening.

The Return of Second City in "20,000 Frozen Grenadiers" (29). New edition of the Second City cabaret revue, with skits improvised by the performers. Produced by Bernard Sahlins at Square East. Opened April 21, 1966. (Closed May 15, 1966)

Sandra Caron	David Steinberg
Bob Klein	Fred Willard
Judy Graubart	

Directed by Sheldon Patinkin; musical director, William Mathieu; music, William Mathieu, Will Holt; press, Merle Debuskey, Lawrence Belling.

* The World of Günter Grass (41). Adaptation by Dennis Rosa of selections from Günter Grass' *The Tin Drum, Dog Years* and *Selected Poems;* based on an arrangement by Sandra Hochman; literary advisor, A. Leslie Willson. Produced by Arthur Cantor, Ninon Tallon Karlweis and Martin Rubin at the Pocket Theater. Opened April 26, 1966.

ACT I—THE FLOOD

The Poet .... Richard Morse	Point (A Rat) .... Charles Durning
Oskar (The Dwarf) .... Joe Servello	Pearl (A Rat) .... Judith Granite
Prinz (The Dog) .... Philip Baker Hall	

ACT II—AFTER THE FLOOD?

The Poet .... Richard Morse	The Assistant to the Chair .... Judith Granite
Oskar .... Joe Servello	The Topic Under
The Discussion Leader ...... Charles Durning	Discussion .... Philip Baker Hall

Directed by Dennis Rosa; original music, Ryan Edwards, based on Wagner themes; production designer, Richard Seger; lighting, Roger Morgan; graphics consultant, Shirley Kaplan; produced in association with Santa Fé Productions Inc.; production stage manager, Yon Koshi; press, Artie Solomon, Arthur Cantor, Irene Pinn.

Comments on Hitler and his aftermath, mostly in a key of sardonic humor, dramatized from the work of the German novelist-poet Günter Grass.

Bohikee Creek (30). Program of four one-act plays by Robert Unger. Produced by Patrick Baldauff, Frank Boone and Gillian Crowe at Stage 73. Opened April 28, 1966. (Closed May 22, 1966)

Folk Singer .... Richard Havens	Halfbeak .... Dennis Tate
I.	III.
Arnie .... James Earl Jones	Reba .... Billie Allen
Aunty Mom .... Georgia Burke	Coke .... Moses Gunn
Able .... Moses Gunn	IV.
II.	Bo .... James Earl Jones
Tinch .... Wayne Grice	Harold .... Julius Harris

Stage Crew: Don Blakely, Ed Daugherty, Ron Dizier, Frank Wilson.
Directed by Donald Moreland; scenery, Tad Gesek; music, Donald Moreland; stage manager, George Cavey; press, Max Eisen and Carl Samrock.
Time: the present. Place: South Carolina Islands. I: Sand bar at dawn. II: Clay mudbank, midnoon. III: Clearing at the water's edge, forenoon. IV: A wharf deep inland, dusk.
About the changing status of the Negro in the South.

Sunset (14). By Isaac Babel; translated by Mirra Ginsburg and Raymond Rosenthal. Produced by Transcenics, Inc., an Aldana Theater Production, at the Eighty-first Street Theater. Opened May 12, 1966. (Closed May 22, 1966)

Directed by Aldo Bruzzichelli; scenery, Kim Swados; costumes, Evelyn Thompson; lighting and sound, Gary Harris; music, Leo Smit; press, Dorothy Ross, Richard O'Brien. With Michael Wager, Martin Rudy, Sol Serlin, Richard Anders, Roberts Blossom, Madlyn Cates, Henry Ferrentino, Mel Haynes, Patricia Hyland, Sylvia Mann, Beatrice Pons, Don Potter, George Stauch, Geraldine Teagarden, Marc Victor, George Birimisa, Irene Grumman, Bill Knisely, Ralph Maurer, Chuck Pauley, Donna Pizzi, Beth Porter, John Ramsey, Ed Rombola, Bevya Rosen, Rick Rotante, David Somerset. About a struggle for dominance between an aging father and his 26-year-old son in Odessa in 1914. A foreign play previously produced in Russia.

Fitz and **Biscuit** (8). Program of two one-act plays by Maxime Furlaud. Produced by Eli Ask and Andy Blue at the Circle in the Square. Opened May 16, 1966. (Closed May 22, 1966)

Directed by Frank Corsaro; scenery by Eugene Lee; music and sound by Teiji Ito; press, Artie Solomon, Arthur Cantor. With Sam Waterston, Sally Kirkland, John Harkins, Jeff Siggins. FITZ is about a girl and boy shunning marriage because it represents conformity. BISCUIT is about a talking dog who persuades a boy to become a dog, too, and enjoy security and dependence on others.

Big Man (14). Program of two one-act plays by Lawrence Weinberg. Produced by Gene Persson at the Cherry Lane Theater. Opened May 19, 1966. (Closed May 29, 1966)

DUET FOR THREE directed by Anthony May. With Martin Priest, John P. Ryan, Maya Kenin. About a love affair in which the man has a homicidal Oedipus complex. BIG MAN directed by Alex Horn. With Rudy Bond, Lou Gilbert, Rue McClanahan, John McCurry, Barbara Hayes. About a self-made millionaire and a socialist confined to a mental hospital for treatment and sharing the same room. Both plays: scenery and lighting, C. Murawski; sound editor, John Batiste; press, David Rothenberg.

The Butterfly Dream (10). A Chinese classical comedy; English version by A.C. Scott. Produced by the Institute for Advanced Studies in the Theater Arts (IASTA) at Greenwich Mews Theater. Opened May 19, 1966. (Closed May 28, 1966)

Directed by Hu Hung-Yen; costumes, Fran Brassard; production design supervision, James Gore; press, Merle Debuskey, Violet Welles, Larry Belling. With Natalie Ross, Eric Tavares, Reid Shelton, Sam Haigler Henry, Tom Keo, Anne Draper, Michael Durrell. The play takes place outside the house of a Taoist scholar and sorcerer, in the living quarters of the house, and in the funeral chamber. Its time is the Sung Dynasty (988-1126), although it is based on a Ming Dynasty (1386-1644) novel. It is a comedy about a scholar who tests his wife's fidelity by feigning death; the butterfly of the title is symbolic of a returned soul.

Some Additional Productions Off Broadway

The American Place Theater. Subscription series of four plays produced by The American Place Theater at St. Clement's Church. *Hogan's Goat, Jonah, The Journey of the Fifth Horse* (see their individual entries in the off-Broadway list) and the following program presented to subscribers only:

DOUBLES AND OPPOSITES (17). Program of two one-act plays. *The Floor* by May Swenson, directed by Harvey Grossmann, with David Kaufman and Eddie Roll. *23 Pat O'Brien Movies* by Bruce Jay Friedman, directed by Gaby Rogers, with Ken Kercheval, Ted Beniades, Graham Jarvis. For both plays: scenery, costumes and lighting, Eugene Gurlitz. Opened May 11, 1966. (Closed May 25, 1966)

ANTA Matinee Theater Series. The Greater New York Chapter of ANTA's Matinee Theater Series, under the direction of Lucille Lortel, presented four afternoon programs at the Theater de Lys.

THE BERNARD SHAW STORY (1). One-man program of Shavian writings and anecdotes compiled and performed by Bramwell Fletcher (see its entry in the off-Broadway list). October 26, 1965.

THE ROPE and A WEEK FROM TODAY (1). Program of two plays by Norman Wexler. November 23, 1965. Directed by John Stix; lighting, Timmy Harris. With Nancy Cooperstein, Marian Hailey, Dennis Helfend, Gloria Hoye, Tony McGrath.

DARK FIRE and THE OWL ANSWERS (1). Program of two plays. December 14, 1965. *Dark Fire* is a one-woman performance by Vinie Burrows of selections from folk tales of Africa, with accompaniment on the drums by Lance Haven. *The Owl Answers* is a play by Adrienne Kennedy; directed by Michael Kahn; lighting, Timmy Harris. With Alex Giannini, Patrick Gorman, Ellen Holly, John Mintun, Bill Moor, Lew Skinner, Clarice Taylor, Robert Thirkield.

WILL GEER'S AMERICANA (1). Conceived by Will Geer; selections from the works of Robert Frost, Langston Hughes, Mark Twain and Walt Whitman. January 18, 1966. Lighting, Timmy Harris. With Jacqueline Brookes, Byron Fraser, Kate Geer, Larry Linville, Cleavon Little, Dwight Markfield, Brandwell Teuscher, Gil Turner, Melora Lou Turner, Marian Tanner, Tom Woodward.

Equity Theater (formerly Equity Library Theater). The following plays were produced by Equity Theater at the Master Theater.

A THURBER CARNIVAL (9). By James Thurber. October 1, 1965. Directed by Kenneth Harvey. With Arthur Anderson, Mary Betten, Thomas Carlin, Delphi Harrington, Holly Hill, Elliot Levine, Ruth Sanford, Bill Steele, Ted Story.

COME BACK, LITTLE SHEBA (9). By William Inge. October 22, 1965. Directed by Bernard Hiatt. With Kevin Bryan Conway, Eileen Dietz, Vincent Dowling, Frank Emerson, Henry Heffner, Joseph Jamrog, John Magill, Roger Mordern, Terry Schreiber, Ann Thomas, Ruth Thomas.

SAY, DARLING (15). Musical with book by Richard Bissell, Abe Burrows and Marian Bissell; songs by Betty Comden, Adolph Green and Jule Styne. November 12, 1965. Directed by Joseph Hardy. With Frank Andre, Ray Becker, Jerry Bell, Ruben Collazo, T. J. Escott, Douglas Fisher, Margot Head, Richard Houston, Elaine Hyman, Carl John, Marion Lauer, Diana Mathews, George Monk, Patricia O'Riordan, Christine Paget, Valerie Paul, David Rounds, Judi Rubin, Darrell Zwerling. Presented for an extra performance at the Brooklyn Academy of Music.

THE FIREBRAND (9). By Edwin Justus Mayer. December 10, 1965. Directed by Osvaldo Riofrancos. With Chris Assini, George Axler, Jay Bonnell, Elizabeth Brown, Stephen Douglass, Barbara Glidden, Jeska Hutchinson, Kendra Kerr, Marie-Antoinette, Donald Marlatt, Edward Stevlingson, John Toland.

ARMS AND THE MAN (10). By George Bernard Shaw. January 14, 1966. Directed by Tom Ellis. With Wallace Acton, Humbert Allen Astredo, Rod Bacon, Anne Gee Byrd, Maeve McGuire, Wayne E. Martens, Lee Sanders, Harris Yulin. Presented for an extra performance at the Brooklyn Academy of Music.

THE BOY FRIEND (17). Musical by Sandy Wilson. February 4, 1966. Directed by Richard France. With Yvonne Adrian, Christina Bartel, Richard Collum, Gordon Cook, Gerry Dalton, Lydia Franklin, Garold Gardner, Raymond George, Natasha Grishin, Yvonne Lynn, Richard Marr, Lesslie Nicol, Roseann Palma, Ted Richert, Marilyn Siskin, Fabian Stuart, Diane Tarleton, Ted Tiller. Presented for an extra performance at the Brooklyn Academy of Music.

WITNESS FOR THE PROSECUTION (9). By Agatha Christie. March 4, 1966. Directed by Paul Melton. With Jack Basic, Marilyn Beck, Margaret Brewster, Marietta R. Clarke, James Duncan, Arthur Foran, Mark Hammer, George Harris II, Howard Honig, Donald Hotton, Bill Hunt, Mitch Kessler, Trent S. Knepper, Thomas Kornylac, John Magill, Warren Miller, Robert Milton, Robert Molnar, James O'Connell, Albert Pickett, John Dannan Popovich, Peter Sheridan, Richard Smithies, Anton Sparr, Eva Stern, Elizabeth Swain, Sy Travers, Herman Karl Tuider, Catherine Ursillo, Leslie Wilkinson.

THE BEAUX' STRATAGEM (9). By George Farquhar. March 25, 1966. Directed by Edward Greer. With Terry Beasor, Judith Behringer, Raleigh Bond, Richard Branda, Michael Byrne, Susan Carr, Christopher Carrick, Veronica Castang, Frank Coleman, Joseph Daly, John Stephen Hrehovcik, Dan Leach, Sadie Long, David O'Neill, Pamela Rivers, Rose Roffman, Donald Somers, Tom Vail.

A TREE GROWS IN BROOKLYN (14). Musical with book by Betty Smith and George Abbott; music by Arthur Schwartz; lyrics by Dorothy Fields. April 15, 1966. Directed by Buff Shurr. With Ted Agress, Jeri Archer, Richard Collum, William J. Coppola, Alan Dellay, Dorothy Emmerson, Don Emmons, Isabelle Farrell, Cheri Jacobs, Mina Jo King, Mari Anne, Tom Mixon, Elizabeth Moore, Jeffrey Neal, Pamela Peadon, Lette Rehnolds, George Riddle, Harriet Slaughter, Ray Stewart, Herb Wilson.

HERE COME THE CLOWNS (9). By Philip Barry. May 13, 1966. Directed by Ben Hammer. With Michele Arthur, Robert Bernard, Gene R. Coleman, Joanne Dalsass, Daniel De Vito Jr., Lee H. Doyle, Gene Fanning, John Hallow, Henry Heffner, Joseph Jamrog, Seymour Penzer, Herb Reynolds, Judith Searle, Dorothy Tristan.

The Blackfriars' Guild. Two new plays produced by the Blackfriars' Guild (Rev. Thomas F. Carey, Moderator) at the Blackfriars' Guild.

MACKEY OF APPALACHIA (54). Musical with music, book, lyrics and direction by Walter Cool. October 6, 1965. Scenery and lighting, Allen Edward Klein; costumes, Alice Merrigal; musical numbers staged by Robert Charles. With James Batch, Frances Beck, John Beyer, James Bormann, Bob Charles, Frank Johnson, Kathryn Martin, Michael Murray, Mary W. O'Malley, Jacqueline Page, Kay Preston, Allister C. Whitman, Tish Yousef. About a poverty program which functioned in a little town in the Appalachian Mountains of West Virginia in 1900.

CONSIDER THE LILIES (82). By Rev. Edward A. Molloy. February 10, 1966. Directed by Walter Cool; scenery, T. Fabian; lighting, Marvin Gingold; costumes, Alice Merrigal. With Barbara Coggin, William H. Cox, Gerald Denning; Duke Houze, Joan Lake, Roy J. Lenahan, Christopher Smith, Karl E. Williams. About Catherine of Siena who convinced Pope Gregory XI to leave Avignon in France and return to Rome.

The New Theater Workshop. Monday Night Play Series of productions at the New Theater.

THE WATERS OF BABYLON (3). By John Arden. November 8, 15, 22, 1965. Directed by Stephen Aaron. With Michael Baseleon, Roscoe Lee Browne, Jan Farrand, Brendan Fay, Jonathan Frid, Michael Green, Leslie Hunt, Peter Nyberg, Leslye Rivers, Colgate Salsbury, James Lockhart.

TELEPHONE POLE (3). By Jean Reavey. November 29, December 6, 13, 1965. Directed by Dale Whitt. With Jordan Charney, Sally Kirkland, Joe Ponazecki, John Toland.

THEY GOT JACK (3). By Leo Rutman. January 17, 24, 31, 1966. Directed by Harold Stone. With Thomas Barbour, John Cazale, Philip Baker Hall, Alfonso Rosati, John P. Ryan, Eugene Wood.

CAPTAIN FANTASTIC MEETS THE ECTOMORPH and A SUBJECT OF SCANDAL AND CONCERN (3). By Barry Pritchard. March 7, 14, 21, 1966. *Captain Fantastic Meets the Ectomorph* directed by Edward Parone. With Joseph Chaikin and James Ray.

A Subject of Scandal and Concern directed by Stephen Aaron. With C. K. Alexander, George Gaynes, Leonard Hicks, Michael Higgins, Barnard Hughes, Janet Kapral, Michael Lombard, Colgate Salsbury.

THE BURIAL COMMITTEE (3). By Otway Crockett. April 4, 11, 18, 1966. Directed by Paul john Austin. With Bruce J. Comer, Michell Jason, Paul Olson, Garnett Smith, Jack Somack.

THE KITCHEN (3). By Arnold Wesker. May 9, 16, 23, 1966. Directed by Jack Gelber. With Lee Addoms, Conrad Bain, Booker T. Bradshaw Jr., David Clarke, Hortensia Colorado, Carol Corbett, Akila Couloumbis, Susan Dorlen, Morris Erby, Danny Frankel, Mari Gorman, John Granger, Mary Hara, James Harder, Joy Hatton, Nance R. Kass, John Kramer, Sylvia Miles, Albert M. Ottenheimer, Alek Primrose, Wells Richardson, Peter Rogan, Lee Roscoe, Colgate Salsbury, Jaime Sanchez, Pamela Saunders, Muni Seroff, Rip Torn, Helen Verbit, Joseph Wilson.

Institute for Advanced Studies in the Theater Arts (IASTA). Two workshop productions presented by IASTA at the Institute.

PHÈDRE (12). By Jean Racine; translated by William Packard. October 31, 1965. Directed by Paul-Émile Deiber; assistants to the director, Aida Alvarez, Armand Coullet; costumes, Sylvia Kalegi; scenery, Geri Davis; lighting, Gene Youtt. Cast (parantheses indicate actor alternates with preceding name): Michael Durrell, Sam Haigler Henry (Graham Jarvis), Mildred Dunnock (Maude Higgins; understudy, Dorothy Le Baker Hatch), Beatrice Straight (Jean Sullivan), Marguerite Hunt (Valerie von Volz), Anne Draper (Lupe Ferrer), Jeff David (Martin Waldron), Marguerite Hunt (Valerie von Volz). *Phedre* opened at the Greenwich Mews Theater 2/10/66; see its entry in the off-Broadway list.

THE DUCHESS OF MALFI (12). By John Webster. April 6, 1966. Directed by Desmond O'Donovan; associate director, Mary W. John; assistant to the director, Robert E. Will; costumes, Fran Brassard; scenic design consultant, William Pitkin; lighting, James Gore. Cast (parentheses indicate actor alternates with preceding name): Michael Twain (Michael Durrell), Richard Mangoode (Howard Roy), Charles Siebert, Reid Shelton (Martin Waldron), Alan Becker, Janine Cooper (Jo-Anne Jameson), Margaret Draper (Annette Hunt), Anne Draper (Delphi Harrington), Joseph Boley (Sam Haigler Henry), Max Brandt, Terry McNulty, April Gilmore (Lori Zarember).

Mobile Theater—New York Shakespeare Festival. Three mobile productions of plays by William Shakespeare: *King Henry V, The Taming of the Shrew* and *Romeo and Juliet,* the latter in the Spanish language. For details see their entries in the section on Shakespeare festivals in this volume.

Village Theater (282). Season of 40 short plays in the Yiddish language, each offered on a program filled out with variety entertainment, with the program changed weekly. Produced and directed by Ben Bonus at the Village Theater. Opened October 1, 1965. (Closed May 29, 1966)

CAST REPLACEMENTS AND TOURING COMPANIES

The following is a listing of some of the more important cast replacements in productions which opened in previous years, but which were still playing in New York during a substantial part of the 1965-66 season; or were still on a national tour; or opened in 1965-66 and cast a touring company in that same season. The name of the character is listed in italics beneath the title of the play in the first column, and in the second column appears the name of the actor who created the role and, immediately beneath, his subsequent replacements. The third column gives information about touring companies of these productions. Where there is more than one roadshow company (not including bus-truck troupes), #1, #2, and #3 appear before the name of the performer who created the role in those companies. Their subsequent replacements, if any, are listed beneath.

ABSENCE OF A CELLO

	NEW YORK COMPANY	TOURING COMPANIES
Andrew Pilgrim	Fred Clark 9/1/64	Hans Conried 1/4/66
Emma Littlewood	Ruth McDevitt 9/1/64	Ruth McDevitt 1/4/66
Otis Clifton	Murray Hamilton 9/1/64	Donald Buka 1/4/66

ANY WEDNESDAY

Ellen Gordon	Sandy Dennis 2/18/64	Monica Moran 9/9/64
	Barbara Cook 2/22/65	
	Sandy Smith 2/20/66	
John Cleves	Don Porter 2/18/64	Larry Parks 9/9/64
	George Gaynes 5/17/65	Jeffrey Lynn 5/24/65
	Jeffrey Lynn 8/2/65	Don Porter 6/28/65
	George Gaynes 9/6/65	

BAREFOOT IN THE PARK

Corie Bratter	Elizabeth Ashley 10/23/63	Joan Van Ark 7/28/64
	Penny Fuller 6/8/64	Christina Crawford 9/6/65
	Joan Van Ark 5/23/66	Beverly Penberthy 10/31/65
Paul Bratter	Robert Redford 10/23/63	Richard Benjamin 7/28/64
	Robert Reed 9/7/64	Philip Clark 9/6/65
	Anthony Roberts 4/5/65	
Mrs. Banks	Mildred Natwick 10/23/63	Myrna Loy 7/28/64
	Eileen Heckart 9/20/65	
	Ilka Chase 5/23/66	
Victor Velasco	Kurt Kasznar 10/23/63	Sandor Szabo 7/28/64
	Charles Korvin 9/20/65	
	Jules Munshin 2/21/66	

THE FANTASTICKS

The Narrator	Jerry Orbach 5/3/60	
	Gene Rupert	
	Bert Convy	
	John Cunningham	
	Don Stewart 1/8/63	
	David Cryer	
	Keith Charles	
	John Boni 1/13/65	
	Jack Mette 9/14/65	
	George Ogee	
	Keith Charles	

	NEW YORK COMPANY	TOURING COMPANIES
The Girl	Rita Gardner 5/3/60	
	Carla Huston	
	Liza Stuart	
	Eileen Fulton	
	Alice Cannon	
	Royce Lenelle	
	B.J. Ward 12/1/64	
	Leta Anderson 7/13/65	
The Boy	Kenneth Nelson 5/3/60	
	Gino Conforti	
	Jack Blackton	
	Paul Giovanni	
	Ty McConnell	
	Richard Rothbard	
	Gary Krawford	
	Bob Spencer 9/5/64	

FIDDLER ON THE ROOF

Tevye	Zero Mostel 9/22/64	Luther Adler 4/11/66
	Luther Adler 8/15/65	
	Herschel Bernardi 11/8/65	
Golde	Maria Karnilova 9/22/64	Dolores Wilson 4/11/66

FUNNY GIRL

Fanny Brice	Barbra Streisand 3/26/64	Marilyn Michaels 10/8/65
	Mimi Hines 12/27/65	
Nick Arnstein	Sydney Chaplin 3/26/64	Anthony George 10/8/65
	George Reeder	
	Johnny Desmond 7/5/65	
Eddie Ryan	Danny Meehan 3/26/64	
	Lee Allen	
	Phil Ford 12/27/65	

THE GLASS MENAGERIE (1965 revival)

The Mother	Maureen Stapleton 5/4/65
	Jo Van Fleet 7/22/65
Her Son	George Grizzard 5/4/65
	Farley Granger 8/18/65
Her Daughter	Piper Laurie 5/4/65
	Carol Rossen 8/18/65
The Gentleman Caller	Pat Hingle 5/4/65
	Hal Holbrook 8/18/65

HALF A SIXPENCE

Arthur Kipps	Tommy Steele 4/25/65
	Tony Tanner 3/21/66

HELLO, DOLLY!

Mrs. Dolly Gallagher Levi	Carol Channing 1/16/64	#1 Mary Martin 4/17/65
	Ginger Rogers 8/9/65	Dora Bryan 5/14/66
		#2 Carol Channing 9/6/65
		#3 Betty Grable 11/3/65
Horace Vandergelder	David Burns 1/16/64	#1 Loring Smith 4/17/65
		Replaced 5/14/66
		#2 Horace McMahon 9/6/65
		Milo Boulton
		#3 Max Showalter 11/3/65

THE OWL AND THE PUSSYCAT

F. Sherman	Alan Alda 11/18/64	Russell Nype 9/13/65
Doris W.	Diana Sands 11/18/64	Eartha Kitt 9/13/65

THE KNACK

	NEW YORK COMPANY	TOURING COMPANIES
Tom	Brian Bedford 5/27/64 Christopher Newton 5/25/65 Gerome Ragni 7/26/55	
Colin	Roddy Maude-Roxby 5/27/64 Sam Waterston 7/14/64 Skip Hinnant 6/13/65 Sam Waterston 8/24/65 Frederick Combs 10/5/65	
Tolen	George Segal 5/27/64 Brian Murray 6/9/64 Paul Savior 12/20/64 James Rado 6/13/65 Paul Savior 8/6/65	
Nancy	Alexandra Berlin 5/27/64 Margaret Ladd 12/13/64 Lee Lawson 12/29/64 Carol Booth 8/10/65	

LUV

Harry Berlin	Alan Arkin 11/11/64 Gabriel Dell 8/24/65	Herbert Edelman 9/6/65
Milt Manville	Eli Wallach 11/11/64 Larry Blyden 2/28/66	Tom Bosley 9/6/65
Ellen Manville	Anne Jackson 11/11/64 Barbara Bel Geddes 2/28/66	Dorothy Loudon 9/6/65

THE ODD COUPLE

Oscar Madison	Walter Matthau 3/10/65 Jack Klugman 11/8/65 Pat Hingle 2/28/66	Dan Dailey 12/27/65
Felix Ungar	Art Carney 3/10/65 Eddie Bracken 10/25/65	Richard Benjamin 12/27/65

OLIVER

Fagin	Clive Revill 1/6/63	#1 Robin Ramsay 11/15/64 #2 Jules Munshin
	Robin Ramsay Clive Revill 8/19/63 Robin Ramsay 10/14/63 Clive Revill 10/21/63 Robin Ramsay 9/25/65	
Oliver Twist	Bruce Prochnik 1/6/63 Ronnie Kroll 11/18/63 Victor Stiles 9/25/65	#1 Ronnie Kroll 11/15/64
Nancy	Georgia Brown 1/6/63 Maura K. Wedge 7/22/63 Judy Bruce Maura K. Wedge 9/25/65	#1 Judy Bruce 11/16/64 Maura K. Wedge #2 Joan Eastman

THE ROAR OF THE GREASEPAINT—THE SMELL OF THE CROWD

Cocky	Anthony Newley 5/16/65 Orson Bean 11/22/65	
Sir	Cyril Ritchard 5/16/65	

THE SUBJECT WAS ROSES

John Cleary	Jack Albertson 5/25/64 Chester Morris 9/7/65	Jack Albertson 9/13/65
Nettie Cleary	Irene Dailey 5/25/64 Martha Scott 7/5/65 Maureen O'Sullivan 9/7/65	Martha Scott 9/13/65
Timmy Cleary	Martin Sheen 5/25/64 Walter McGinn 9/7/65	Martin Sheen 9/13/65

A VIEW FROM THE BRIDGE

	NEW YORK COMPANY	TOURING COMPANIES
Eddie	Robert Duvall 1/28/65	
	Richard Castellano 6/8/65	
	Robert Duvall 9/14/65	
	Richard Catellano 10/19/65	
Beatrice	Jeanne Kaplan 1/28/65	
Rodolpho	Jon Voight 1/28/65	
	Wayne Geis 10/19/65	
Catherine	Susan Anspach 1/28/65	
	Susan Kapilow 8/31/65	

A SELECTED LIST OF PLAYS FIRST PRODUCED OUTSIDE NEW YORK CITY

Including plays produced for Broadway which closed during their tryout performances; their titles appear in **bold face italics**.

By George Freedley

ABUNDANTLY YOURS by Jerry Devine. Playhouse on the Mall, Paramus, N. J., July 6, 1965.

ANNE OF GREEN GABLES by Donald Harron; based on the novel by L. M. Montgomery; with songs by Norman Campbell. Charlottetown, Prince Edward Island, July, 1965.

BABY TALK by Manby Green and Edward Ferlbart; adapted from *Bichon* by Jean de Letnaz. Barn Theater, Augusta, Mich., August 11, 1965. Farce about a baby's parentage.

THE BERNARD SHAW STORY arranged by Bramwell Fletcher in monologue. White Barn Theater, Westport, Conn., August 15, 1965.

COME LIVE WITH ME by Lee Minoff and Stanley Price. Westport Country Playhouse, Westport, Conn., September 17, 1965. Comedy about an American screenwriter living in London.

THE CROSS AND THE SWORD by Paul Green. Amphitheater, St. Augustine, Fla., June-July 1965. Symphonic drama about the Spanish conquest and the story of St. Augustine, oldest city in U. S.

THE EMPLOYMENT AGENCY by Clifford Browder; EPHRAIM by Allan Kree; JO-ELLA by Judith Morley. Courtyard Theater, Oyster Bay, N. Y., August 13, 1965.

FAMILY THINGS, ETC. by William Inge (later appeared on Broadway as *Where's Daddy?*). Playhouse, Falmouth, Mass., July 12, 1965.

FIDELIO by Cherney Berg. Playhouse on the Mall, Paramus, N. J., July 20, 1965. Satire about musicians.

THE FROG POND by Georgette Scott. Ogunquit Playhouse, Ogunquit, Me., August 9, 1965. Love life of three bachelor girls in New York City.

THE GENIUS FARM, musical by Norman Rotchin and Hal Bonne. Mineola Playhouse, Mineola, N. Y., August 16, 1965. A college widow runs a school for male authors.

GNISTA by Harold W. Poe. University of Southwestern Louisiana, Lafayette, La., July 26, 1965.

GOODBYE, GHOST by Harold J. Kennedy. Coconut Grove Playhouse, Miami, Fla. March 1, 1966. With June Allyson, Hugh Marlowe.

THE GREAT WALTZ, musical revival with a new book by Jerome Chodorov; additional musical adaptation and lyrics by Robert Wright, George Forrest and Foreman Brown; music by Johann Strauss Sr. and Jr. arranged by Wolfgang Korngold. Music Center, Los Angeles, Calif., July 27, 1965.

Hot September, musical based on William Inge's *Picnic;* with book by Paul Osborn; music by Kenneth Jacobson; lyrics by Rhoda Roberts. Directed by Joshua Logan; choreography, Danny Daniels; scenery, Oliver Smith; costumes, Theoni V. Aldredge; lighting, Jean Rosenthal; musical staging, Joshua Logan and Danny Daniels; musical direction and vocal arrangements, Milton Rosenstock; orchestrations, Philip J. Lang; dance music and dance orchestrations, Robert Prince. Produced by Leland Hayward and David Merrick in a pre-Broadway tryout at the Shubert Theater in Boston, September 14, 1965. (Closed October 9, 1965)

With Lee Lawson, Richard Granat, Kathryn Hays, Patricia Roe, Sean Garrison, Paula Trueman, Lovelady Powell, John Stewart, Lada Edmund Jr., Ed Crowley, John Hallow,

Eddie Bracken, Evelyn Page, Betty Lester, Alice Evans. Singers: Darrell J. Askey, Brown Bradley, Connie Danese, Gay Edmond, Judie Elkins, Les Freed, Renee Gorsey, Gene Lindsey, Marilyne Mason, Diane McAfee, Charles McKenna, Richard Nieves. Dancers: Barbara Alexander, Gene Castle, Kay Cole, Barbara Douglas, Ronn Forella, Charles Kalan, Michele Karaty, Ray Morgan, Marie Patrice, Don Percassi, Michael Scotlin, Don Slaton, Geri Spinner, Anne Wallace.

Musical numbers: "Another Crummy Day/ Hey, Delilah," "Whistle of a Train," "Golden Moment," "Come on Strong," "Somethin' More," "Live," "What Do You Do?", "Tell Me the Truth," "Show Me Where the Good Times Are," "Frug," "This Town/A Guy Like Me," "Who Needs It?", "Hot September Dance," "Rosemary's Soliloquy," "Tell Me the Truth" (Reprise), "You," "I Got It Made," "Somethin' More" (Reprise), "Goodbye Girls," "I Blew It," "Golden Moment."

THE JOURNEY BACK by Janet Allen. Adelphi University, Garden City, N. Y., August 19, 1965.

THE LOVING COUCH by Ray Allen. American Theater, St. Louis, April, 1966 and subsequent tour of various cities. Directed by Ray Montgomery; with Virginia Mayo, Terry Phillips, Gene Shane, Sabrina, Reni Riano. Farce about romantic problems of a mother, who has a lover, and her son, who falls in love with a neurotic.

MADAME MOUSSE by Jean Pierre Aumont, American adaptation by Erich Segal. Westport Country Playhouse, Westport, Conn., August 16, 1965. Comedy about a meddling mother-in-law.

MAN OF LA MANCHA, musical based on *Don Quixote* and the life of Cervantes; with book by Dale Wasserman; music by Mitch Leigh; lyrics by Joe Darion. Goodspeed Opera House, East Haddam, Conn., July 24, 1965.

MINOR MIRACLE by Al Morgan. Coconut Grove Playhouse, Miami, Fla., September, 1965.

MRS. DALLY HAS A LOVER by James Hanley. Westport Country Playhouse, Westport, Conn., July 26, 1965. Full-length version of his one-act play.

NOTHING FOR ELIZABETH by Richard Ashley. Courtyard Theater, Oyster Bay, N. Y., August 20, 1965.

The Office by Maria Irene Fornes. See note at end of this section.

THE POKER SESSION by Hugh Leonard. Playhouse, Boothbay, Me., August 24, 1965.

The Porcelain Year by Reginald Rose. Directed by Alex Segal; scenery, Peter Larkin; lighting, John Gleason; costumes, Theoni V. Aldredge. Produced by Katzka-Berne in association with Defender Productions in a pre-Broadway tryout at the Locust Street Theater, Philadelphia, October 11, 1965. (Closed in New Haven, November 13, 1965). With Barbara Bel Geddes, Arthur Hill, Martin Balsam, Kim Darby, John Megna. Comedy about infidelity and recriminations in a marriage which has lasted 17 years.

PURPLE DUST, musical based on the play by Sean O'Casey; adapted by Ted Allan; lyrics by Sean O'Casey. Goodspeed Opera House, East Haddam, Conn., July 22, 1965.

THE RABBIT HABIT by Rex Carlton. Denver Auditorium, December 2, 1965. With Jayne Mansfield, Hugh Marlowe, Alex D'Arcy. Comedy about a dumb blonde married to a missile scientist.

A REMEDY FOR WINTER by Leonard Spigelgass. Westport Country Playhouse, Westport, Conn., August 9, 1965. Love triangle composed of author, actress and lady realtor.

REVERBERATIONS by Murray Schisgal. Green Mansions Theater, Warrensburg, N. Y., July, 1965.

SELL ME DOWN THE RIVER, DARLING by Theodore Apstein. Red Barn Theater, Augusta, Mich., July 6, 1965. Comedy about marital infidelity and racial segregation in New York's suburbs.

70 TIMES SEVEN by Warren Kliewer. Eaglesmere Playhouse, Eaglesmere, Pa., July 26, 1965.

THE SHAVIAN WOMEN IN LOVE AND MARRIAGE by George Bernard Shaw. Courtyard Theater, Oyster Bay, N. Y., August 6, 1965.

SO MUCH OF EARTH, SO MUCH OF HEAVEN by Henry Denker; based on a play by Ugo Betti. Westport Country Playhouse, Westport, Conn., August 30, 1965.

SOME WINTER GAMES by Robert Koesis. Red Barn Theater, Northport, N. Y., August 17, 1965.

TENNESSEE, U.S.A., musical with book, music and lyrics by Paul Crabtree. Cumberland County Playhouse, Crossville, Tenn., July, 1965. Fantasy of American history.

THERE'S AN ECHO, ECHO, ECHO IN THIS ROOM, ROOM, ROOM by Kenneth Pressman. Green Mansions Theater, Warrensburg, N. Y., July, 1965.

This Winter's Hobby by Jack Finney. Directed by Donald McWhinnie; scenery, Oliver Smith; costumes, Florence Klotz; lighting, Tharon Musser; associate producer, George Platt; production supervisor, Michael Thoma. Produced by Hillard Elkins in a pre-Broadway tryout at the Shubert Theater, New Haven, March 23, 1966. (Closed in Philadelphia April 9, 1966). With E. G. Marshall, Nan Martin, William Hickey, Michael Beckett, Norman Bly, Martha Bundy. Suspense drama about a mild-mannered husband who is victimized when he attempts to avoid the consequences of a fatal accident.

TOM JONES by David Rogers, based on the novel by Henry Fielding. Bucks County Playhouse, New Hope, Pa., July 26, 1965.

THE UNEXPECTED GUEST by Agatha Christie. Coconut Grove Playhouse, Miami, Fla., July 19, 1965.

Venus Is by Chester Erskine. See note at end of this section.

WHAT THIS COUNTRY NEEDS, musical with book by Ray Golden and Jack Marlowe; music and lyrics by Ray Golden. Music Box Theater, Hollywood, Calif., July 28, 1965. About computers and their errors.

WHEN THE WIND BLEW COOL AT

ROSIE'S PLACE by James De Felice. Tufts University, Medford, Mass., July 15, 1965.

THE WHOLE TRUTH by Philip Mackie. Playhouse, Boothbay, Me., July 13, 1965.

NOTE: The following two plays went into production in New York City for Broadway but closed during their tryout series of preview performances, never opening either in New York or on tour.

The Office by Maria Irene Fornes. Directed by Jerome Robbins; scenery, Ed Wittstein; costumes, Willa Kim; lighting, Jules Fisher; music, Robert Prince. Produced by Joseph E. Levine and Ivor David Balding in preview performances at Henry Miller's Theater, April 20, 1966. (Closed April 30, 1966). With Elaine May, Jack Weston, Ruth White, Doris Roberts, Tony Lo Bianco, Clifford Arashi, Bernard Passeltiner, Charles Welch, Marilyn Chris. About a novice secretary unused to office routine.

Venus Is by Chester Erskine. Directed by Word Baker; scenery and lighting, Jo Mielziner; costumes, Ramse Mostoller. Produced by Martin Lee in preview performances at the Billy Rose Theater, April 5, 1966. (Closed April 9, 1966) With George Bartenieff, Michael Baseleon, Ernest Graves, Diane Kagan, Lois Kibbee, Audra Lindley, Jonathan Moore, James Patterson, Lovelady Powell, Ann Shropshire, Jerry Strickler, Pamela Toll, Stratton Walling, Ed Zimmermann. Personal conflicts in a group of seaside-community people, on the day an exploratory robot is put on the planet Venus.

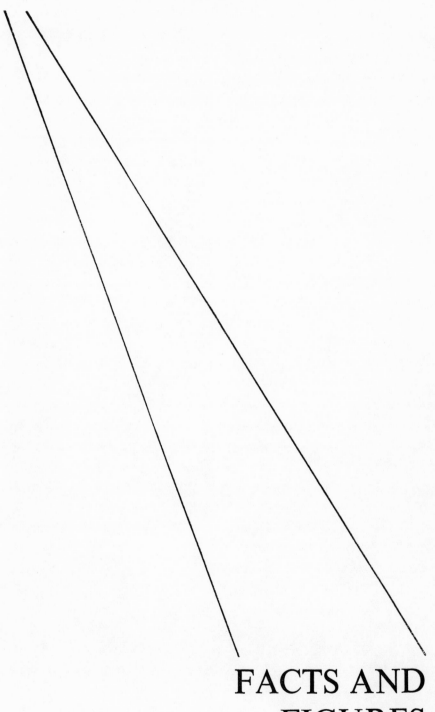

FACTS AND
FIGURES

LONG RUNS ON BROADWAY

THROUGH MAY 31, 1966

(PLAYS MARKED WITH ASTERISK WERE STILL PLAYING JUNE 1, 1966)

Plays	Number Performances	Plays	Number Performances
Life with Father	3,224	Hats Off to Ice	889
Tobacco Road	3,182	Fanny	888
My Fair Lady	2,717	*Funny Girl	885
Abie's Irish Rose	2,327	Follow the Girls	882
Oklahoma!	2,212	Camelot	873
Harvey	1,775	The Bat	867
South Pacific	1,694	My Sister Eileen	865
Born Yesterday	1,642	White Cargo	864
Mary, Mary	1,572	Song of Norway	860
The Voice of the Turtle	1,557	A Streetcar Named Desire	855
Arsenic and Old Lace	1,444	Comedy in Music	849
The Sound of Music	1,443	You Can't Take It With You	837
How to Succeed in Business		La Plume de Ma Tante	835
Without Really Trying	1,417	Three Men on a Horse	835
Hellzapoppin	1,404	The Subject Was Roses	832
The Music Man	1,375	Inherit the Wind	806
Angel Street	1,295	No Time for Sergeants	796
Lightnin'	1,291	Fiorello!	795
The King and I	1,246	Where's Charlie?	792
Guys and Dolls	1,200	The Ladder	789
Mister Roberts	1,157	Oliver	774
Annie Get Your Gun	1,147	State of the Union	765
The Seven Year Itch	1,141	The First Year	760
Pins and Needles	1,108	Two for the Seesaw	750
*Barefoot in the Park	1,084	Death of a Salesman	742
Kiss Me, Kate	1,070	Sons o' Fun	742
Pajama Game	1,063	Gentlemen Prefer Blondes	740
The Teahouse of the August		The Man Who Came to Dinner	739
Moon	1,027	Call Me Mister	734
Damn Yankees	1,019	West Side Story	732
Never Too Late	1,007	High Button Shoes	727
*Hello, Dolly!	989	Finian's Rainbow	725
A Funny Thing Happened on		Claudia	722
the Way to the Forum	964	The Gold Diggers	720
Anna Lucasta	957	Carnival	719
Kiss and Tell	957	The Diary of Anne Frank	717
*Any Wednesday	951	I Remember Mama	714
The Moon Is Blue	924	Tea and Sympathy	712
Bells Are Ringing	924	Junior Miss	710
Can-Can	892	Seventh Heaven	704
Carousel	890	*Fiddler on the Roof	702

449

Plays	*Number Performances*	*Plays*	*Number Performances*
Gypsy	702	Affairs of State	610
The Miracle Worker	700	Star and Garter	609
Cat on a Hot Tin Roof	694	The Student Prince	608
Li'l Abner	693	Bye Bye Birdie	607
Peg o' My Heart	692	Broadway	603
The Children's Hour	691	Adonis	603
Dead End	687	Street Scene	601
The Lion and the Mouse	686	Kiki	600
Dear Ruth	683	Flower Drum Song	600
East Is West	680	Wish You Were Here	598
Come Blow Your Horn	677	A Society Circus	596
The Most Happy Fella	676	Blossom Time	592
The Doughgirls	671	The Two Mrs. Carrols	585
Irene	670	Kismet	583
Boy Meets Girl	669	Detective Story	581
Beyond the Fringe	667	Brigadoon	581
Who's Afraid of Virginia Woolf?	664	No Strings	580
Blithe Spirit	657	Brother Rat	577
The Women	657	Show Boat	572
A Trip to Chinatown	657	The Show-Off	571
Bloomer Girl	654	Sally	570
The Fifth Season	654	Golden Boy	568
Rain	648	One Touch of Venus	567
*Luv	647	Happy Birthday	564
Witness for the Prosecution	645	Look Homeward, Angel	564
Call Me Madam	644	The Glass Menagerie	561
Janie	642	Wonderful Town	559
The Green Pastures	640	Rose Marie	557
Auntie Mame	639	Strictly Dishonorable	557
A Man for All Seasons	637	A Majority of One	556
The Fourposter	632	Toys in the Attic	556
The Tenth Man	623	Sunrise at Campobello	556
Is Zat So?	618	Jamaica	555
Anniversary Waltz	615	Stop the World—I Want to Get	
The Happy Time	614	Off	555
Separate Rooms	613		

LONG RUNS OFF BROADWAY

The Threepenny Opera	2,611	The Trojan Women	600
*The Fantasticks	2,538	The Crucible	571
The Blacks	1,408	The Iceman Cometh	565
Little Mary Sunshine	1,143	The Hostage	545
Leave It to Jane	928	Krapp's Last Tape and the Zoo	
The Boy Friend	763	Story	532
The Connection	722	Six Characters in Search of an	
The Knack	685	Author	529
The Balcony	672	The Boys From Syracuse	500

DRAMA CRITICS CIRCLE VOTING 1965-66

The New York Drama Critics Circle voted *Marat/Sade* the best play of the season by 21 points against 20 for *Philadelphia, Here I Come!*, 17 for *The Royal Hunt of the Sun*, 12 for *Inadmissible Evidence* and other points scattered among other plays. On a first ballot each critic voted his single best choice. In order to win on this ballot, a play had to receive a majority of votes cast, not a simple purality as in previous years. On subsequent ballots the critics voted in a point system listing a first choice (3 points), a second choice (2 points) and a third choice (1 point), with the play receiving the greatest number of points winning the award. The second ballot in the 1965-66 voting for best play was discounted owing to confusion, and results of the third ballot are detailed below.

Man of La Mancha was the Critics' choice as the year's best musical on the first ballot with eight out of a possible 14 votes, with two abstentions. A special citation was awarded to Hal Holbrook's one-man show *Mark Twain Tonight*. Two member critics—John McClain of the *Journal-American* and Whitney Bolton of the *Morning Telegraph*—were absent and not voting.

	THIRD BALLOT FOR BEST PLAY			FIRST BALLOT FOR
Critic	1st Choice (3)	2nd Choice (2)	3rd Choice (1)	BEST MUSICAL
John Chapman—*News*	The Royal Hunt of the Sun	Philadelphia, Here I Come!	Marat/Sade	Abstained
Ethel Colby—*Journal of Commerce*	Philadelphia	Marat/Sade	The Lion in Winter	Man of La Mancha
Richard Cooke—*Wall Street Journal*	Inadmissible Evidence	Philadelphia	Hogan's Goat	Man of La Mancha
Jack Gaver—UP	Royal Hunt	Philadelphia	Marat/Sade	Man of La Mancha
Richard Gilman—*Newsweek*	Serjeant Musgrave's Dance	Marat/Sade	Inadmissible	The Mad Show
William H. Glover—AP	Philadelphia	Entertaining Mr. Sloane	Royal Hunt	Man of La Mancha
Martin Gottfried—*Women's Wear Daily*	Entertaining Mr. Sloane	Marat/Sade	The Journey of the Fifth Horse	Marat/Sade
Henry Hewes—*Saturday Review*	Inadmissible	Royal Hunt	Marat/Sade	Man of La Mancha
Stanley Kauffmann—*Times*	The Caucasian Chalk Circle	The Condemned of Altona	Marat/Sade	"It's a Bird It's a Plane It's SUPERMAN"
Ted Kalem—*Time*	Inadmissible	Marat/Sade	Philadelphia	Mame
Walter Kerr—*Herald Tribune*	Philadelphia	Inadmissible	Hogan's Goat	Abstained
Emory Lewis—*Cue*	Marat/Sade	Happy Ending and Day of Absence	Royal Hunt	Man of La Mancha
John McCarten—*New Yorker*	Royal Hunt	Philadelphia	Abstained	Mame
Ward Morehouse—Newhouse Papers	Mark Twain Tonight	You Can't Take It With You	Chinatown Charlie	Mame
Norman Nadel—*World-Telegram & Sun*	Marat/Sade	Royal Hunt	Philadelphia	Man of La Mancha
Richard Watts Jr.—*Post*	Marat/Sade	Royal Hunt	Philadelphia	Man of La Mancha

Choices of some other critics:

	BEST PLAY	BEST MUSICAL
Whitney Bolton—*Morning Telegraph*	Philadelphia	Man of La Mancha
Robert Brustein—*New Republic*	Marat/Sade	Abstained
Judith Crist—*Today*	Philadelphia	Sweet Charity
Thomas P. Dash—*Show Business*	Marat/Sade	Man of La Mancha
George Freedley	The Lion in Winter	Wait a Minim!
John Gassner—*AETA Journal*	Marat/Sade	Mame
Leo Lerman—*Mademoiselle*	The Lion in Winter	Sweet Charity
John McClain—*Journal-American*	Philadelphia	Man of La Mancha
Hobe Morrison—*Variety*	Marat/Sade	Man of La Mancha
George Oppenheimer—*Newsday*	Marat/Sade	Man of La Mancha
Tom Prideaux—*Life*	Marat/Sade	Man of La Mancha
Michael Smith—*Village Voice*	The Journey of the Fifth Horse	A Beautiful Day

NEW YORK DRAMA CRITICS CIRCLE AWARDS

Listed below are the New York Drama Critics Circle Awards, given each season for (1) Best American Play, (2) Best Foreign Play, (3) Best Musical Production, (4) Best, regardless of category.

1935-36—(1) Winterset
1936-37—(1) High Tor
1937-38—(1) Of Mice and Men, (2) Shadow and Substance
1938-39—(1) No Award, (2) The White Steed
1939-40—(1) The Time of Your Life
1940-41—(1) Watch on the Rhine, (2) The Corn Is Green
1941-42—(1) No Award, (2) Blithe Spirit
1942-43—(1) The Patriots
1943-44—(1) No Award, (2) Jacobowsky and the Colonel
1944-45—(1) The Glass Menagerie
1945-46—(1) No Award, (2) No Award, (3) Carousel
1946-47—(1) All My Sons, (2) No Exit, (3) Brigadoon
1947-48—(1) A Streetcar Named Desire, (2) The Winslow Boy
1948-49—(1) Death of a Salesman, (2) The Madwoman of Chaillot, (3) South Pacific
1949-50—(1) The Member of the Wedding, (2) The Cocktail Party, (3) The Consul

1950-51—(1) Darkness at Noon, (2) The Lady's Not for Burning, (3) Guys and Dolls
1951-52—(1) I Am a Camera, (2) Venus Observed, (3) Pal Joey (Special citation to Don Juan in Hell)
1952-53—(1) Picnic, (2) The Love of Four Colonels, (3) Wonderful Town
1953-54—(1) The Teahouse of the August Moon, (2) Ondine, (3) The Golden Apple
1954-55—(1) Cat on a Hot Tin Roof, (2) Witness for the Prosecution, (3) The Saint of Bleecker Street
1955-56—(1) The Dairy of Anne Frank, (2) Tiger at the Gates, (3) My Fair Lady
1956-57—(1) Long Day's Journey Into Night, (2) Waltz of the Torreadors, (3) The Most Happy Fella
1957-58—(1) Look Homeward, Angel, (2) Look Back in Anger, (3) The Music Man
1958-59—(1) A Raisin in the Sun, (2) The Visit, (3) La Plume de Ma Tante

1959-60—(1) Toys in the Attic, (2) Five Finger Exercise, (3) Fiorello!
1960-61—(1) All the Way Home, (2) A Taste of Honey, (3) Carnival
1961-62—(1) The Night of the Iguana, (2) A Man for All Seasons, (3) How to Succeed in Business Without Really Trying
1962-63—(4) Who's Afraid of Virginia Woolf? (Special citation to Beyond the Fringe)

1963-64—(4) Luther, (3) Hello, Dolly! (Special citation to The Trojan Women)
1964-65—(4) The Subject Was Roses, (3) Fiddler on the Roof
1965-66—(4) The Persecution and Assassination of Marat as Performed by the Inmates of the Asylum of Charenton Under the Direction of the Marquis de Sade, (3) Man of La Mancha

PULITZER PRIZE WINNERS

1917-18—Why Marry?, by Jesse Lynch Williams
1918-19—No award.
1919-20—Beyond the Horizon, by Eugene O'Neill
1920-21—Miss Lulu Bett, by Zona Gale
1921-22—Anna Christie, by Eugene O'Neill
1922-23—Icebound, by Owen Davis
1923-24—Hell-bent for Heaven, by Hatcher Hughes
1924-25—They Knew What They Wanted, by Sidney Howard
1925-26—Craig's Wife, by George Kelly
1926-27—In Abraham's Bosom, by Paul Green
1927-28—Strange Interlude, by Eugene O'Neill
1928-29—Street Scene, by Elmer Rice
1929-30—The Green Pastures, by Marc Connelly
1930-31—Alison's House, by Susan Glaspell
1931-32—Of Thee I Sing, by George S. Kaufman, Morrie Ryskind, Ira and George Gershwin
1932-33—Both Your Houses, by Maxwell Anderson
1933-34—Men in White, by Sidney Kingsley
1934-35—The Old Maid, by Zoë Akins
1935-36—Idiot's Delight, by Robert E. Sherwood
1936-37—You Can't Take It with You, by Moss Hart and George S. Kaufman
1937-38—Our Town, by Thornton Wilder
1938-39—Abe Lincoln in Illinois, by Robert E. Sherwood
1939-40—The Time of Your Life, by William Saroyan
1940-41—There Shall Be No Night, by Robert E. Sherwood
1941-42—No award
1942-43—The Skin of Our Teeth, by Thornton Wilder

1943-44—No award
1944-45—Harvey, by Mary Chase
1945-46—State of the Union, by Howard Lindsay and Russel Crouse
1946-47—No award.
1947-48—A Streetcar Named Desire, by Tennessee Williams
1948-49—Death of a Salesman, by Arthur Miller
1949-50—South Pacific, by Richard Rodgers, Oscar Hammerstein II and Joshua Logan
1950-51—No award
1951-52—The Shrike, by Joseph Kramm
1952-53—Picnic, by William Inge
1953-54—The Teahouse of the August Moon, by John Patrick
1954-55—Cat on a Hot Tin Roof, by Tennessee Williams
1955-56—The Diary of Anne Frank, by Frances Goodrich and Albert Hackett
1956-57—Long Day's Journey into Night, by Eugene O'Neill
1957-58—Look Homeward, Angel, by Ketti Frings
1958-59—J. B., by Archibald MacLeish
1959-60—Fiorello!, by Jerome Weidman, George Abbott, Sheldon Harnick and Jerry Bock
1960-61—All the Way Home, by Tad Mosel
1961-62—How to Succeed in Business Without Really Trying, by Abe Burrows, Willie Gilbert, Jack Weinstock and Frank Loesser
1962-63—No award
1963-64—No award
1964-65—The Subject Was Roses, by Frank D. Gilroy
1965-66—No award

ADDITIONAL PRIZES AND AWARDS, 1965-66

The following is a list of major prizes and awards for theatrical achievement:

MARGO JONES AWARDS. The American Place Theater "for exploring the whole new area of poets, novelists and scholars and bringing their works to the living theater." A University Award to Professor Marston Stevens Balch and Tufts University Department of Speech and Drama.

KELCEY ALLEN AWARD. JOHN F. WHARTON, theatrical attorney and consultant-director of the Legitimate Theater Industry Exploratory Commission.

GEORGE JEAN NATHAN AWARD. GERALD WEALES for three articles in Drama Survey, a quarterly published by the Bolingbroke Society.

CLARENCE DERWENT AWARDS (for best non-featured performances). JEANNE HEPPLE in Serjeant Musgrave's Dance. CHRISTOPHER WALKEN in The Lion in Winter. Special commendation to Tom Ahearne in Hogan's Goat.

ANTA AWARD. DOROTHY BUFFUM CHANDLER, Los Angeles cultural leader.

DRAMA DESK-VERNON RICE AWARDS (for off-Broadway achievement). DOUGLAS TURNER WARD, author of Day of Absence and Happy Ending. WILLIAM ALFRED, author of Hogan's Goat. JOHN ARDEN, author of Serjeant Musgrave's Dance. KEVIN O'CONNOR for his performance in Six From La Mama. IRENE DAILEY for her performance in Rooms. The Living Theater for its work abroad.

BRANDEIS CREATIVE ARTS AWARD. EVA LE GALLIENNE

JOSEPH MAHARAM FOUNDATION AWARDS. HOWARD BAY, scene designer, for Man of La Mancha. Noel Taylor, costume designer, for Slapstick Tragedy (The Gnadiges Fraulein).

OBIE AWARDS for off-Broadway achievement. Best play: The Journey of the Fifth

Horse by Ronald Ribman. Best actor: DUSTIN HOFFMAN in The Journey of the Fifth Horse. Best actress: JANE WHITE in Coriolanus and Love's Labor's Lost. The following were cited for distinguished performances: CLARICE BLACKBURN in The Exhaustion of Our Son's Love, MARI-CLAIRE CHARBA in Birdbath, GLORIA FOSTER in Medea, SHARON GANS in Soon Jack November, FRANK LANGELLA in Good Day and The White Devil, MICHAEL LIPTON in The Trigon, KEVIN O'CONNOR in Chicago, JESS OSUNA in Bugs and Veronica, FLORENCE TARLOW in Istanbul, Red Cross and A Beautiful Day, DOUGLAS TURNER in Day of Absence. Distinguished playwrighting awards: EMANUEL PELUSO for Good Day and JACQUES LEVY for You're as Old as Your Arteries, Red Cross and The Next Thing. Distinguished design awards: LINDSEY DECKER for Red Cross and ED WITTSTEIN for Serjeant Musgrave's Dance. Special citations: JOSEPH H. DUNN for his production of The Automobile Graveyard; H.M. KOUTOUKAS, playwright; PETER SCHUMANN for his Bread and Puppet Theater; Theater for Ideas; Theater in the Street.

OUTER CIRCLE AWARDS. Man of La Mancha; Wait a Minim!; FRANK LOESSER for the revivals of his works at City Center; DAVID MERRICK for his contribution to the season; The Institute of Advanced Studies in the Theater Arts for its revival of Phèdre; GWEN VERDON for her performance in Sweet Charity; ANGELA LANSBURY and BEATRICE ARTHUR for their performances in Mame; DONAL DONNELLY and PATRICK BEDFORD for their performances in Philadelphia, Here I Come!; PETER BROOK for his direction of Marat/Sade.

LOLA D'ANNUNZIO AWARD. WILL GEER "for his long and continuous contribution to the off Broadway theater"; The Establishment Theater for its contribution to the off Broadway theater this year.

VARIETY'S POLL OF NEW YORK DRAMA CRITICS

Each year, representative first-string New York drama critics are polled by Variety to learn their choices for the bests in various categories. Fourteen critics participated in this year's balloting (Ethel Colby, Richard Cooke, Martin Gottfried, Stanley Kauffmann, Water Kerr, Ward Morehouse, Douglas Watt, Richard Watts Jr., Henry Hewes, Theodore Kalem, Emory Lewis, John

McCarten, Jack Gaver and William Glover). The results appear below. In each category there are listed every play and artist that received one vote or more, with the winner listed in **bold face type** (all winners in cases of ties).

ACTOR—Straight Play. **Nicol Williamson** in *Inadmissible Evidence*, HAL HOLBROOK in *Mark Twain Tonight!*, CHRISTOPHER PLUMMER in *The Royal Hunt of the Sun*, DONAL DONNELLY in *Philadelphia, Here I Come!*, PATRICK MAGEE in *Marat/Sade*, ROBERT PRESTON in *The Lion in Winter*.

ACTRESS—Straight Play. **Rosemary Harris** in *The Lion in Winter* and *You Can't Take It With You*, KATE REID in *Slapstick Tragedy*, GLENDA JACKSON in *Marat/Sade*.

ACTOR—Musical. **Richard Kiley** in *Man of La Mancha*, JOHN McMARTIN in *Sweet Charity*, JOHN CULLUM in *On a Clear Day You Can See Forever*.

ACTRESS—Musical. **Gwen Verdon** in *Sweet Charity*, BARBARA HARRIS in *On a Clear Day You Can See Forever*, ANGELA LANSBURY in *Mame*, JOAN DIENER in *Man of La Mancha*.

ACTOR—Supporting. **Eamon Kelly** in *Philadelphia, Here I Come!*, **Hiram Sherman** in *Where's Daddy?* **Robert Symonds** in *The Caucasian Chalk Circle*, BURT BRINCKERHOFF in *Cactus Flower*, DAVID CARRADINE in *The Royal Hunt of the Sun*, ROLAND CULVER in *Ivanov*, DONAL DONNELLY in *Philadelphia, Here I Come!*, LOUIS GOSSETT in *The Zulu and the Zayda*, GEOFFREY LUMSDEN in *Hostile Witness*, TED VAN GRIETHUYSEN in *Inadmissible Evidence* (plus one no-choice vote).

ACTRESS—Supporting. **Zoe Caldwell** in *Slapstick Tragedy*, BRENDA VACCARO in *Cactus Flower*, BEATRICE ARTHUR in *Mame*, CLARIBEL BAIRD in *You Can't Take It With You*, RUTH WHITE in *Malcolm* (plus one no-choice vote).

Actor—Most Promising. **Donal Donnelly** in *Philadelphia, Here I Come!*, Nicol Williamson in *Inadmissible Evidence*, FRANKIE MICHAELS in *Mame*, RANDY KIRBY in *Me and Thee*, CHRISTOPHER WALKEN in *The Lion in Winter* (plus four no-choice votes).

ACTRESS—Most Promising. **Glenda Jackson** in *Marat/Sade*, ZOE CALDWELL in *Slapstick Tragedy*, SARAH BADEL in *The Right Honour-*

able Gentleman, KAREN BLACK in *The Playroom*, SUZANNE GROSSMANN in *The Lion in Winter*, SHEILA HANCOCK in *Entertaining Mr. Sloane*, THELMA OLIVER in *Sweet Charity*, MAVIS VILLIERS in *Philadelphia, Here I Come!*, SHANI WALLIS in *A Time for Singing* (plus two no-choice votes).

DIRECTOR. **Peter Brook** for *Marat/Sade*, JOHN DEXTER for *The Royal Hunt of the Sun*, ELLIS RABB for *You Can't Take It With You*, GENE SAKS for *Mame*, NOEL WILLMAN for *The Lion in Winter*.

SCENE DESIGNER. **Howard Bay** for *Man of La Mancha*, WILLIAM and JEAN ECKART for *Mame*, DAVID HAYS for *Drat! The Cat!*, ROBERT RANDOLPH for *Anya* and *Skyscraper*, WILLIAM RITMAN for *Malcolm*.

COSTUMES DESIGNER. **Robert Mackintosh** for *Mame*, GUNILLA PALMSTIERNA-WEISS for *Marat/Sade*, JAMES HART STEARNS for *The Caucasian Chalk Circle* and *The Country Wife*, HOWARD BAY and PATTON CAMPBELL for *Man of La Mancha*, LOUDON SAINTHILL for *The Right Honourable Gentleman*, IRENE SHARAFF for *Sweet Charity*, NOEL TAYLOR for *Slapstick Tragedy*, FREDDY WITTOP for *On a Clear Day You Can See Forever*.

SCORE. **Mitch Leigh** for *Man of La Mancha*, JERRY HERMAN for *Mame*, CY COLEMAN for *Sweet Charity*, BURTON LANE for *On a Clear Day You Can See Forever*, MICHAEL LEONARD for *The Yearling*, RICHARD PEASLEE for *Marat/Sade*, MILTON SCHAFER for *Drat! The Cat!*, CHARLES STROUSE for *Superman*.

LYRICS: **Jerry Herman** for *Mame*, DOROTHY FIELDS for *Sweet Charity*, JOE DARION for *Man of La Mancha*, LEE ADAMS for *Superman*, IRA LEVIN for *Drat! The Cat!*

MOST PROMISING NEW BROADWAY PLAYWRIGHT. **Brian Friel** for *Philadelphia, Here I Come!*, PETER WEISS for *Marat/Sade*, JAMES GOLDMAN for *The Lion in Winter*, WILLIAM GOODHART for *Generation* (plus two no-choice votes).

THE TONY AWARDS

The Antoinette Perry (Tony) Awards are voted upon by members of the first and second night press lists, members of The League of New York Theaters, and the governing bodies of The Dramatists Guild, Actors Equity and the Society of Stage Directors and Choreographers. Below were the nominations in the various categories, made by a nominating committee composed of Judith Crist, drama critic of *Today* and film critic of the *Herald Tribune;* Donald Flamm, broadcasting executive; Lee Jordan, theater reviewer for CBS-TV; Edward Kook, president of Century Lighting Company; Norman Nadel, drama critic for the *World-Telegram and Sun,* and Tom Prideaux, reviewer for *Life.* The winner in each category appears in **bold-faced type.**

BEST PLAY (award goes to both producer and author). *Inadmissible Evidence,* produced by DAVID MERRICK ARTS FOUNDATION, written by JOHN OSBORNE. **Marat/Sade,** produced by **David Merrick Arts Foundation,** written by **Peter Weiss.** *Philadelphia, Here I Come!,* produced by DAVID MERRICK ARTS FOUNDATION, written by BRIAN FRIEL. *The Right Honourable Gentleman,* produced by PETER COOKSON, AMY LYNN and WALTER SCHWIMMER, written by MICHAEL DYNE.

BEST MUSICAL PLAY (award goes to both producer and author). *Mame,* produced by ROBERT FRYER, LAWRENCE CARR, SYLVIA HARRIS and JOSEPH HARRIS, written by JEROME LAWRENCE and ROBERT E. LEE. **Man of La Mancha,** produced by **Albert W. Selden** and **Hal James,** written by **Dale Wasserman.** *Skyscraper,* produced by CY FEUER and ERNEST H. MARTIN, written by PETER STONE. *Sweet Charity,* produced by ROBERT FRYER, LAWRENCE CARR, SYLVIA HARRIS and JOSEPH HARRIS, written by NEIL SIMON.

ACTOR—Dramatic Star. ROLAND CULVER in *Ivanov.* DONAL DONNELLY and PATRICK BEDFORD (one nomination) in *Philadelphia, Here I Come!.* **Hal Holbrook** in *Mark Twain Tonight!,* NICOL WILLIAMSON in *Inadmissible Evidence.*

ACTRESS—Dramatic Star. SHEILA HANCOCK in *Entertaining Mr. Sloane.* **Rosemary Harris** in *The Lion in Winter.* KATE REID in *Slapstick Tragedy.* LEE REMICK in *Wait Until Dark.*

ACTOR—Musical Star. JACK CASSIDY in *Superman.* JOHN CULLUM in *On a Clear Day You Can See Forever.* **Richard Kiley** in *Man of La Mancha.* HARRY SECOMBE in *Pickwick.*

ACTRESS—Musical Star. BARBARA HARRIS in *On a Clear Day You Can See Forever.* JULIE HARRIS in *Skyscraper.* **Angela Lansbury** in *Mame.* GWEN VERDON in *Sweet Charity.*

ACTOR—Dramatic Featured or Supporting. BURT BRINCKERHOFF in *Cactus Flower.* A. LARRY HAINES in *Generation.* EAMON KELLY in *Philadelphia, Here I Come!.* **Patrick Magee** in *Marat/Sade.*

ACTRESS—Dramatic Featured or Supporting. **Zoe Caldwell** in *Slapstick Tragedy.* GLENDA JACKSON in *Marat/Sade.* MAIRIN D. O'SULLIVAN in *Philadelphia, Here I Come!.* BRENDA VACCARO in *Cactus Flower.*

ACTOR—Musical Featured or Supporting. ROY CASTLE in *Pickwick.* JOHN MCMARTIN in *Sweet Charity.* **Frankie Michaels** in *Mame.* MICHAEL O'SULLIVAN in *Superman.*

ACTRESS—Musical Featured or Supporting. **Beatrice Arthur** in *Mame.* HELEN GALLAGHER in *Sweet Charity.* PATRICIA MARAND in *Superman.* CHARLOTTE RAE in *Pickwick.*

DIRECTOR—Play. **Peter Brook** for *Marat/Sade.* HILTON EDWARDS for *Philadelphia, Here I Come!.* ELLIS RABB for *You Can't Take It With You.* NOEL WILLMAN for *The Lion in Winter.*

DIRECTOR—Musical Play. CY FEUER for *Skyscraper.* BOB FOSSE for *Sweet Charity.* **Albert Marre** for *Man of La Mancha.* GENE SAKS for *Mame.*

COMPOSER AND LYRICIST—Musical Play. CY COLEMAN and DOROTHY FIELDS for *Sweet Charity.* JERRY HERMAN for *Mame.* **Mitch Leigh** and **Joe Darion** for *Man of La Mancha.* ALAN JAY LERNER and BURTON LANE for *On a Clear Day You Can See Forever.*

SCENIC DESIGNER. **Howard Bay** for *Man of La Mancha.* WILLIAM and JEAN ECKART for *Mame.* DAVID HAYS for *Drat! The Cat!.* ROBERT RANDOLPH for *Anya, Skyscraper* and *Sweet Charity.*

COSTUME DESIGNER. LOUDON SAINTHILL for *The Right Honourable Gentleman.* HOWARD BAY and PATTON CAMPBELL for *Man of La Mancha.* IRENE SHARAFF for *Sweet Charity.* **Gunilla Palmstierna-Weiss** for *Marat/Sade.*

CHOREOGRAPHER. JACK COLE for *Man of La Mancha.* **Bob Fosse** for *Sweet Charity.* MICHAEL KIDD for *Skyscraper.* ONNA WHITE for *Mame.*

1965-66 PUBLICATION OF RECENTLY-PRODUCED PLAYS

Baker Street. (Musical) Book by Jerome Coopersmith, adapted from stories by Sir Arthur Conan Doyle, music and lyrics by Marian Grudeff and Raymond Jessel. Doubleday. $3.95.

Ben Franklin in Paris. (Musical) Book and lyrics by Sidney Michaels, music by Mark Sandrich Jr. Random House. $3.95.

The Caucasian Chalk Circle. Bertolt Brecht, revised English version by Eric Bentley. Grove. $.95.

The Days Between. Robert Anderson. Random House. $1.95.

Do I Hear a Waltz? (Musical) Book by Arthur Laurents, based on his play *The Time of the Cuckoo,* music by Richard Rodgers, lyrics by Stephen Sondheim. Random House. $3.95.

Entertaining Mr. Sloane. Joe Orton. Grove. $1.45.

Fade Out—Fade In. (Musical) Book by Betty Comden and Adolph Green, music by Jule Styne. Random House. $3.95.

Generation. William Goodhart. Doubleday. $1.95.

Golden Boy. (Musical) Book by Clifford Odets and William Gibson, based on Mr. Odet's play, music by Charles Strouse, lyrics by Lee Adams. Atheneum. $3.95.

Hogan's Goat. William Alfred. Farrar, Straus and Giroux. $4.95.

Inadmissible Evidence. John Osborne. Grove. $3.95, $1.75.

Ivanov. Anton Chekhov, adaptation by John Gielgud. Theater Arts. $1.85.

Malcolm. Edward Albee, adapted from the novel by James Purdy. Atheneum. $4.95, $1.95.

The Old Glory. Robert Lowell. Atheneum. $4.95.

The Owl and the Pussycat. Bill Manhoff. Doubleday. $3.95, $1.95.

The Persecution and Assassination of Marat as Performed by the Inmates of the Asylum of Charenton Under the Direction of the Marquis de Sade. Peter Weiss. English version by Geoffrey Skelton, verse adaptation by Adrian Mitchell. Atheneum. $4.50, $1.95.

The Playroom. Mary Drayton. Random House. $3.95.

Poor Richard. Jean Kerr. Doubleday. $4.50.

The Right Honourable Gentleman. Michael Dyne. Random House. $3.95.

Romulus and *Romulus the Great.* Gore Vidal adaptation of Friedrich Duerrenmatt's play together with the original text. Grove. $6.00.

The Royal Hunt of the Sun. Peter Shaffer. Stein and Day. $3.95.

Serjeant Musgrave's Dance. John Arden. Grove. $1.75.

Square in the Eye. Jack Gelber. Grove. $1.95.

A SELECTED LIST OF OTHER PLAYS PUBLISHED IN 1965-1966

Acte. Lawrence Durrell. Dutton. $3.75.

Balm in Gilead and Other Plays. Lanford Wilson. Hill and Wang. $1.75.

Bertha and Other Plays. Kenneth Koch. Grove. $1.95.

Birthday Message. Tyrone Guthrie. Theater Arts. $.65.

The Complete Plays of D.H. Lawrence. Viking. $7.50.

Doctors of Philosophy. Muriel Spark. Knopf. $3.95.

Four New Yale Playwrights. John Gassner, editor. Crown. $4.95.

Fragments, Windows and Other Plays. Murray Schisgal. Coward-McCann. $4.95, $2.65.

Gentle Jack. Robert Bolt. Random House. $3.95.

The Inner Journey. James Hanley. Horizon. $4.50.

Lamp at Midnight. Barrie Stavis. Barnes. $4.95

Marching Song. John Whiting. Theater Arts. $1.75.

The Other Heart. James Forsyth. Theater Arts. $1.65.

A Patriot for Me. John Osborne. 13s 6d. Faber (British production).

A Penny for a Song. John Whiting. Theater Arts. $1.75.

Saint's Day. John Whiting. Theater Arts. $1.75.

Three Plays: The Young Disciple, Faustina, Jonah. Paul Goodman. Random House. $4.95.

The Waltz Invention. Vladimir Nabokov. Phaedra. $4.95.

457

ORIGINAL CAST ALBUMS OF
NEW YORK SHOWS

The following albums were issued during the 1965-66 season. The first number appearing after each title is the number of the monaural version, the second the number of the stereo version.

Anya. Mercury. 4133, 5133.
Bloomer Girl. Decca. 9126, 79126 (long playing reissue).
Carousel (revival). RCA Victor. LOC-1114, LSO-1114.
The Decline and Fall of the Entire World as Seen Through the Eyes of Cole Porter revisited. Columbia. OL-6410, OS-2810.
The Exception and the Rule. Folkways. 9849. (1964-1965 production)
Incident at Vichy. Mercury. OCM-2-2211, OCS-2-6211. (1964-1965 production)
"It's a Bird It's a Plane It's SUPERMAN." KOL-6570, KOS-2970
Ivanov. RCA Victor. VDM 109, VDS 109.
Kismet (revival). RCA Victor. LOC-1112, LSO-1112.
The Mad Show. Columbia. OL-6530, OS-2930.
Mame. Columbia. KOL-6600, KOS-3000.
Man of La Mancha. Kapp. 4505, S-4505.
On a Clear Day You Can See Forever. RCA Victor. LOCD-2006, LSOD-2006.
The Persecution and Assassination of Marat as Performed by the Inmates of the Asylum of Charenton Under the Direction of the Marquis de Sade. Caedmon. TRS 312-M (3), TRS 312-S (3).
Skyscraper. Capitol. VAS-2422, SVAS-2422.
Sweet Charity. Columbia. KOL-6500, KOS-2900.
A Time For Singing. Warner Brothers.
Wait a Minim! London. AM-58002, AMS-88002.
The Zulu and the Zayda. Columbia. KOL-6480, KOS-2880.

THE BEST PLAYS, 1894-1965

The following lists in alphabetical order all those plays that have appeared in previous volumes of the Best Plays Series. Opposite each title is given the volume in which the play appears, its opening date and its total number of performances, and those plays marked with asterisks were still playing on June 1, 1966. Adaptors and translators are indicated by (ad) and (tr), and the symbols (b), (m) and (l) stand for the author of book, music and lyrics in the case of musicals.

PLAY	VOLUME	OPENED	PERFS.
ABE LINCOLN IN ILLINOIS—Robert E. Sherwood	38-39	Oct. 15, 1938	472
ABRAHAM LINCOLN—John Drinkwater	19-20	Dec. 15, 1919	193
ACCENT ON YOUTH—Samson Raphaelson	34-35	Dec. 25, 1934	229
ADAM AND EVA—Guy Bolton, George Middleton	19-20	Sept. 13, 1919	312
AFFAIRS OF STATE—Louis Verneuil	50-51	Sept. 25, 1950	610
AFTER THE FALL—Arthur Miller	63-64	Jan. 23, 1964	208
AH, WILDERNESS!—Eugene O'Neill	33-34	Oct. 2, 1933	289
ALIEN CORN—Sidney Howard	32-33	Feb. 20, 1933	98
ALISON'S HOUSE—Susan Glaspell	30-31	Dec. 1, 1930	41
ALL MY SONS—Arthur Miller	46-47	Jan. 29, 1947	328
ALL THE WAY HOME—Tad Mosel, based on James Agee's novel *A Death in the Family*	60-61	Nov. 30, 1960	334
ALLEGRO—(b, 1) Oscar Hammerstein, II, (m) Richard Rodgers	47-48	Oct. 10, 1947	315
AMBUSH—Arthur Richman	21-22	Oct. 10, 1921	98
AMERICAN WAY, THE—George S. Kaufman, Moss Hart	38-39	Jan. 21, 1939	164
AMPHITRYON 38—Jean Giraudoux, (ad) S. N. Behrman	37-38	Nov. 1, 1937	153
ANDERSONVILLE TRIAL, THE—Saul Levitt	59-60	Dec. 29, 1959	179
ANDORRA—Max Frisch, (ad) George Tabori	62-63	Feb. 9, 1963	9
ANGEL STREET—Patrick Hamilton	41-42	Dec. 5, 1941	1,295
ANIMAL KINGDOM, THE—Philip Barry	31-32	Jan. 12, 1932	183
ANNA CHRISTIE—Eugene O'Neill	21-22	Nov. 2, 1921	177
ANNA LUCASTA—Philip Yordan	44-45	Aug. 30, 1944	957
ANNE OF THE THOUSAND DAYS—Maxwell Anderson	48-49	Dec. 8, 1948	286
ANOTHER LANGUAGE—Rose Franken	31-32	Apr. 25, 1932	344
ANOTHER PART OF THE FOREST—Lillian Hellman	46-47	Nov. 20, 1946	182
ANTIGONE—Jean Anouilh, (ad) Lewis Galantière	45-46	Feb. 18, 1946	64
ARSENIC AND OLD LACE—Joseph Kesselring	40-41	Jan. 10, 1941	1,444
AS HUSBANDS GO—Rachel Crothers	30-31	Mar. 5, 1931	148
AUTUMN GARDEN, THE—Lillian Hellman	50-51	Mar. 7, 1951	101
AWAKE AND SING—Clifford Odets	34-35	Feb. 19, 1935	209
BAD MAN, THE—Porter Emerson Browne	20-21	Aug. 30, 1920	350
BAD SEED—Maxwell Anderson, adapted from William March's novel	54-55	Dec. 8, 1954	332
BARBARA FRIETCHIE—Clyde Fitch	99-09	Oct. 23, 1899	83
BAREFOOT IN ATHENS—Maxwell Anderson	51-52	Oct. 31, 1951	30
* BAREFOOT IN THE PARK—Neil Simon	63-64	Oct. 23, 1963	1,084
BARRETTS OF WIMPOLE STREET, THE—Rudolf Besier	30-31	Feb. 9, 1931	370
BECKET—Jean Anouilh, (tr) Lucienne Hill	60-61	Oct. 5, 1960	193
BEGGAR ON HORSEBACK—George S. Kaufman, Marc Connelly	23-24	Feb. 12, 1924	224
BEHOLD THE BRIDEGROOM—George Kelly	27-28	Dec. 26, 1927	88
BELL, BOOK AND CANDLE—John van Druten	50-51	Nov. 14, 1950	233
BELL FOR ADANO, A—Paul Osborn, based on John Hersey's novel	44-45	Dec. 6, 1944	304
BERKELEY SQUARE—John L. Balderston	29-30	Nov. 4, 1929	229
BERNARDINE—Mary Coyle Chase	52-53	Oct. 16, 1952	157
BEST MAN, THE—Gore Vidal	59-60	Mar. 31, 1960	521

PLAY   VOLUME OPENED PERFS.

BEYOND THE HORIZON—Eugene O'Neill ....19-20..Feb. 2, 1920.. 160
BIG FISH, LITTLE FISH—Hugh Wheeler ....60-61..Mar. 15, 1961.. 101
BILL OF DIVORCEMENT, A—Clemence Dane ....21-22..Oct. 10, 1921.. 173
BILLY BUDD—Louis O. Coxe, Robert Chapman, based on Her-
  man Melville's novel ....50-51..Feb. 10, 1951.. 105
BIOGRAPHY—S. N. Behrman ....32-33..Dec. 12, 1932.. 267
BLITHE SPIRIT—Noel Coward ....41-42..Nov. 5, 1941.. 657
BORN YESTERDAY—Garson Kanin ....45-46..Feb. 4, 1946..1,642
BOTH YOUR HOUSES—Maxwell Anderson ....32-33..Mar. 6, 1933.. 104
BOY MEETS GIRL—Bella and Sam Spewack ....35-36..Nov. 27, 1935.. 669
BOY FRIEND, THE—(b, l, m) Sandy Wilson ....54-55..Sept. 30, 1954.. 485
BRIDE OF THE LAMB, THE—William Hurlbut ....25-26..Mar. 30, 1926.. 109
BRIEF MOMENT—S. N. Behrman ....31-32..Nov. 9, 1931.. 129
BRIGADOON—(b, l) Alan Jay Lerner, (m) Frederick Loewe ..46-47..Mar. 13, 1947.. 581
BROADWAY—Philip Dunning, George Abbott ....26-27..Sept. 16, 1926.. 322
BURLESQUE—George Manker Watters, Arthur Hopkins ....27-28..Sept. 1, 1927.. 372
BUS STOP—William Inge ....54-55..Mar. 2, 1955.. 478
BUTTER AND EGG MAN, THE—George S. Kaufman ....25-26..Sept. 23, 1925.. 243

CAINE MUTINY COURT-MARTIAL, THE—Herman Wouk, based on
  his novel ....53-54..Jan. 20, 1954.. 415
CALIGULA—Albert Camus, (ad) Justin O'Brien ....59-60..Feb. 19, 1960..   38
CALL IT A DAY—Dodie Smith ....35-36..Jan. 28, 1936.. 194
CANDIDE—(b) Lillian Hellman, based on Voltaire's satire (l)
  Richard Wilbur, John Latouche, Dorothy Parker, (m)
  Leonard Bernstein ....56-57..Dec. 1, 1956..   73
CANDLE IN THE WIND—Maxwell Anderson ....41-42..Oct. 22, 1941..   95
CARETAKER, THE—Harold Pinter ....61-62..Oct. 4, 1961.. 165
CASE OF REBELLIOUS SUSAN—Henry Arthur Jones ....94-99..Dec. 29, 1894..   80
CAT ON A HOT TIN ROOF—Tennessee Williams ....54-55..Mar. 24, 1955.. 694
CHALK GARDEN, THE—Enid Bagnold ....55-56..Oct. 26, 1955.. 182
CHANGELINGS, THE—Lee Wilson Dodd ....23-24..Sept. 17, 1923.. 128
CHICAGO—Maurine Watkins ....26-27..Dec. 30, 1926.. 172
CHICKEN FEED—Guy Bolton ....23-24..Sept. 24, 1923.. 144
CHILDREN'S HOUR, THE—Lillian Hellman ....34-35..Nov. 20, 1934.. 691
CHIPS WITH EVERYTHING—Arnold Wesker ....63-64..Oct. 1, 1963.. 149
CHRISTOPHER BLAKE—Moss Hart ....46-47..Nov. 30, 1946.. 114
CIRCLE, THE—W. Somerset Maugham ....21-22..Sept. 12, 1921.. 175
CLARENCE—Booth Tarkington ....19-20..Sept. 20, 1919.. 306
CLAUDIA—Rose Franken ....40-41..Feb. 12, 1941.. 722
CLEARING IN THE WOODS, A—Arthur Laurents ....56-57..Jan. 10, 1957..   36
CLIMATE OF EDEN, THE—Moss Hart, based on Edgar Mittlehol-
  zer's novel Shadows Move Among Them ....52-53..Nov. 13, 1952..   20
CLIMBERS, THE—Clyde Fitch ....99-09..Jan. 21, 1901.. 163
CLUTTERBUCK—Benn W. Levy ....49-50..Dec. 3, 1949.. 218
COCKTAIL PARTY, THE—T. S. Eliot ....49-50..Jan. 21, 1950.. 409
COLD WIND AND THE WARM, THE—S. N. Behrman ....58-59..Dec. 8, 1958.. 120
COLLECTION, THE—Harold Pinter ....62-63..Nov. 26, 1962.. 578
COME BACK, LITTLE SHEBA—William Inge ....49-50..Feb. 15, 1950.. 191
COMMAND DECISION—William Wister Haines ....47-48..Oct. 1, 1947.. 408
COMPLAISANT LOVER, THE—Graham Greene ....61-62..Nov. 1, 1961.. 101
CONFIDENTIAL CLERK, THE—T. S. Eliot ....53-54..Feb. 11, 1954.. 117
CONSTANT WIFE, THE—William Somerset Maugham ....26-27..Nov. 29, 1926.. 233
CONNECTION, THE—Jack Gelber (Not picked as one of Ten
  Best, but included as a supplementary play) ....60-61..Feb. 22, 1961.. 722
COQUETTE—George Abbott, Ann Preston Bridgers ....27-28..Nov. 8, 1927.. 366
CORN IS GREEN, THE—Emlyn Williams ....40-41..Nov. 26, 1940.. 477
COUNTRY GIRL, THE—Clifford Odets ....50-51..Nov. 10, 1950.. 235
COUNTY CHAIRMAN, THE—George Ade ....99-09..Nov. 24, 1903.. 222
CRADLE SONG, THE—Gregorio & Maria Martinez Sierra, (tr)
  John Garrett Underhill ....26-27..Nov. 2, 1926.. 108
CRAIG'S WIFE—George Kelly ....25-26..Oct. 12, 1925.. 360

PLAY   VOLUME OPENED PERFS.

CRIMINAL CODE, THE—Martin Flavin ....29-30..Oct. 2, 1929.. 173
CRUCIBLE, THE—Arthur Miller ....52-53—Jan. 22, 1953.. 197
CYNARA—H. M. Harwood, R. F. Gore-Browne ....31-32..Nov. 2, 1931.. 210

DAISY MAYME—George Kelly ....26-27..Oct. 25, 1926.. 112
DAMASK CHEEK, THE—John van Druten, Lloyd Morris ....42-43..Oct. 22, 1942..   93
DANCING MOTHERS—Edgar Selwyn, Ermund Goulding ....24-25..Aug. 11, 1924.. 312
DARK AT THE TOP OF THE STAIRS, THE—William Inge ....57-58..Dec. 5, 1957.. 468
DARK IS LIGHT ENOUGH, THE—Christopher Fry ....54-55..Feb. 23, 1955..   69
DARKNESS AT NOON—Sidney Kingsley, based on Arthur Koes-
    tler's novel ....50-51..Jan. 13, 1951.. 186
DARLING OF THE GODS, THE—David Belasco, John Luther Long ..99-09..Dec. 3, 1902.. 182
DAUGHTERS OF ATREUS—Robert Turney ....36-37..Oct. 14, 1936..   13
DEAD END—Sidney Kingsley ....35-36..Oct. 28, 1935.. 687
DEADLY GAME, THE—James Yaffe, based on Friedrich Duerren-
    matt's novel ....59-60..Feb. 2, 1960..   39
DEAR RUTH—Norman Krasna ....44-45..Dec. 13, 1944.. 683
DEATH OF A SALESMAN—Arthur Miller ....48-49..Feb. 10, 1949.. 742
DEATH TAKES A HOLIDAY—Alberto Casella, (ad) Walter Ferris .29-30..Dec. 26, 1929.. 180
DEBURAU—Sacha Guitry, (ad) H. Granville-Barker ....20-21..Dec. 23, 1920.. 189
DECISION—Edward Chodorov ....43-44..Feb. 2, 1944.. 160
DÉCLASSÉE—Zoë Akins ....19-20..Oct. 6, 1919.. 257
DEEP ARE THE ROOTS—Arnaud d'Usseau, James Gow ....45-46..Sept. 26, 1945.. 477
DEPUTY, THE—Rolf Hochhuth ....63-64..Feb. 26, 1964.. 109
DESIGN FOR LIVING—Noel Coward ....32-33..Jan. 24, 1933.. 135
DESIRE UNDER THE ELMS—Eugene O'Neill ....24-25..Nov. 11, 1924.. 208
DESPERATE HOURS, THE—Joseph Hayes, based on his novel .....54-55..Feb. 10, 1955.. 212
DETECTIVE STORY—Sidney Kingsley ....48-49..Mar. 23, 1949.. 581
DEVIL PASSES, THE—Benn W. Levy ....31-32..Jan. 4, 1932..   96
DEVIL'S ADVOCATE, THE—Dore Schary, based on Marris L.
    West's novel ....60-61..Mar. 9, 1961.. 116
DIAL "M" FOR MURDER—Frederick Knott ....52-53..Oct. 29, 1952.. 552
DIARY OF ANNE FRANK, THE—Frances Goodrich, Albert Hack-
    ett, based on Anne Frank's The Diary of a Young Girl ......55-56..Oct. 5, 1955.. 717
DINNER AT EIGHT—George S. Kaufman, Edna Ferber ....32-33..Oct. 22, 1932.. 232
DISENCHANTED, THE—Budd Schullberg, Harvey Breit, based on
    Mr. Schulberg's novel ....58-59..Dec. 3, 1958.. 189
DISRAELI—Louis N. Parker ....09-19..Sept. 18, 1911.. 280
DISTAFF SIDE, THE—John van Druten ....34-35..Sept. 25, 1934.. 177
DODSWORTH—Sidney Howard, based on Sinclair Lewis's novel ..33-34..Feb. 24, 1934.. 315
DOUGHGIRLS, THE—Joseph Fields ....42-43..Dec. 30, 1942.. 671
DOVER ROAD, THE—A. A. Milne ....21-22..Dec. 23, 1921.. 324
DREAM GIRL—Elmer Rice ....45-46..Dec. 14, 1945.. 348
DUEL OF ANGELS—Jean Giraudoux's "Pour Lucrèce," (ad)
    Christopher Fry ....59-60..Apr. 19, 1960..   51
DULCY—George S. Kaufman, Marc Connelly ....21-22..Aug. 13, 1921.. 246
DYBBUK, THE—S. Ansky, (ad) Henry G. Alsberg ....25-26..Dec. 15, 1925.. 120
DYLAN—Sidney Michaels ....63-64..Jan. 18, 1964.. 153

EASIEST WAY, THE—Eugene Walter ....09-19..Jan. 19, 1909.. 157
EASTWARD IN EDEN—Dorothy Gardner ....47-48..Nov. 18, 1947..   15
EDWARD, MY SON—Robert Morley, Noel Langley ....48-49..Sept. 30, 1948.. 260
EGG, THE—Felicien Marceau, (ad) Robert Schlitt ....61-62..Jau. 8, 1962..   8
ELIZABETH THE QUEEN—Maxwell Anderson ....30-31..Nov. 3, 1930.. 147
EMPEROR'S CLOTHES, THE—George Tabori ....52-53..Feb. 9, 1953..   16
EMPEROR JONES, THE—Eugene O'Neill ....20-21..Nov. 1, 1920.. 204
ENCHANTED, THE—Maurice Valency, adapted from Jean Girau-
    doux's play "Intermezzo" ....49-50..Jan. 18, 1950..   45
END OF SUMMER—S. N. Behrman ....35-36..Feb. 17, 1936.. 153
ENEMY, THE—Channing Pollock ....25-26..Oct. 20, 1925.. 203
ENTER MADAME—Gilda Varesi, Dolly Byrne ....20-21..Aug. 16, 1920.. 350
ENTERTAINER, THE—John Osborne ....57-58..Feb. 12, 1958..   97

PLAY   VOLUME OPENED PERFS.

EPITAPH FOR GEORGE DILLON—John Osborne, Anthony Creigh-
  ton ....58-59..Nov. 4, 1958..   23
ESCAPE—John Galsworthy ....27-28..Oct. 26, 1927.. 173
ETHAN FROME—Owen and Donald Davis, based on Edith Whar-
  ton's novel ....35-36..Jan. 21, 1936.. 120
EVE OF ST. MARK, THE—Maxwell Anderson ....42-43..Oct. 7, 1942.. 307
EXCURSION—Victor Wolfson ....36-37..Apr. 9, 1937.. 116

FALL GUY, THE—James Gleason, George Abbott ....24-25..Mar. 10, 1925.. 176
FAMILY PORTRAIT—Lenore Coffee, William Joyce Cowen ....38-39..May 8, 1939.. 111
FAMOUS MRS. FAIR, THE—James Forbes ....19-29..Dec. 22, 1919.. 344
FAR COUNTRY, A—Henry Denker ....60-61..Apr. 4, 1961.. 271
FARMER TAKES A WIFE, THE—Frank B. Elser, Marc Connelly,
  based on Walter Edmonds' novel Rome Haul ....34-35..Oct. 30, 1934.. 104
FATAL WEAKNESS, THE—George Kelly ....46-47..Nov. 19, 1946.. 119
*FIDDLER ON THE ROOF—(b) Joseph Stein, (1) Sheldon Har-
  nick, (m) Jerry Bock, based on Sholom Aleichem's stories ....64-65..Sept. 22, 1964.. 702
FIORELLO!—(b) Jerome Weidman, George Abbott, (1) Sheldon
  Harnick, (m) Jerry Bock ....59-60..Nov. 23, 1959.. 795
FIREBRAND, THE—Edwin Justus Mayer ....24-25..Oct. 15, 1924.. 269
FIRST LADY—Katharine Dayton, George S. Kaufman ....35-36..Nov. 26, 1935.. 246
FIRST MRS. FRASER, THE—St. John Ervine ....29-30..Dec. 28, 1929.. 352
FIRST YEAR, THE—Frank Craven ....20-21..Oct. 20, 1920.. 760
FIVE FINGER EXERCISE—Peter Shaffer ....59-60..Dec. 2, 1959.. 337
FIVE-STAR FINAL—Louis Weitzenkorn ....30-31..Dec. 30, 1930.. 175
FLIGHT TO THE WEST—Elmer Rice ....40-41..Dec. 30, 1940.. 136
FLOWERING PEACH, THE—Clifford Odets ....54-55..Dec. 28, 1954.. 135
FOOL, THE—Channing Pollock ....22-23..Oct. 23, 1922.. 373
FOOLISH NOTION—Philip Barry ....44-45..Mar. 3, 1945.. 104
FOURPOSTER, THE—Jan de Hartog ....51-52..Oct. 24, 1951.. 632
FRONT PAGE, THE—Ben Hecht, Charles MacArthur ....28-29..Aug. 14, 1928.. 276

GEORGE WASHINGTON SLEPT HERE—George S. Kaufman, Moss
  Hart ....40-41..Oct. 18, 1940.. 173
GIDEON—Paddy Chayefsky ....61-62..Nov. 9, 1961.. 234
GIGI—Anita Loos, based on Colette's novel ....51-52..Nov. 24, 1951.. 219
GIRL ON THE VIA FLAMINIA, THE—Alfred Hayes, based on his
  novel ....53-54..Feb. 9, 1954.. 111
GLASS MENAGERIE, THE—Tennessee Williams ....44-45..Mar. 31, 1945.. 561
GOLDEN APPLE, THE—(b, 1), John Latouche, (m) Jerome Mo-
  ross ....53-54..Apr. 20, 1954.. 125
GOLDEN BOY—Clifford Odets ....37-38..Nov. 4, 1937.. 250
GOOD GRACIOUS ANNABELLE—Clare Kummer ....09-19..Oct. 31, 1916.. 111
GOOSE HANGS HIGH, THE—Lewis Beach ....23-24..Jan. 29, 1924.. 183
GOODBYE, MY FANCY—Fay Kanin ....48-49..Nov. 17, 1948.. 446
GRAND HOTEL—Vicki Baum, (ad) W. A. Drake ....30-31..Nov. 13, 1930.. 459
GREAT DIVIDE, THE—William Vaughn Moody ....99-09..Oct. 3, 1906.. 238
GREAT GOD BROWN, THE—Eugene O'Neill ....25-26..Jan. 23, 1926.. 271
GREEN BAY TREE, THE—Mordaunt Shairp ....33-34..Oct. 20, 1933.. 166
GREEN GODDESS, THE—William Archer ....20-21..Jan. 18, 1921.. 440
GREEN GROW THE LILACS—Lynn Riggs ....30-31..Jan. 26, 1931..   64
GREEN HAT, THE—Michael Arlen ....25-26..Sept. 15, 1925.. 231
GREEN PASTURES, THE—Marc Connelly, adapted from Roark
  Bradford's Ol Man Adam and His Chillun ....29-30..Feb. 26, 1930.. 640
GUYS AND DOLLS—(b) Jo Swerling, Abe Burrows, based on a
  story and characters by Damon Runyon, (1, m) Frank Loesser..50-51..Nov. 24, 1950..1,200
GYPSY—Maxwell Anderson ....28-29..Jan. 14, 1929..   64

HAPPY TIME, THE—Samuel Taylor, based on Robert Fontaine's
  book ....49-50..Jan. 24, 1950.. 614
HARRIET—Florence Ryerson, Colin Clements ....42-43..Mar. 3, 1943.. 377

PLAY   VOLUME OPENED PERFS.

HARVEY—Mary Coyle Chase ....44-45..Nov. 1, 1944..1,775
HASTY HEART, THE—John Patrick ....44-45..Jan. 3, 1945.. 207
HE WHO GETS SLAPPED—Leonid Andreyev, (ad) Gregory Zil-
  boorg ....21-22..Jan. 9, 1922.. 308
HEART OF MARYLAND, THE—David Belasco ....94-99..Oct. 22, 1895.. 240
HEIRESS, THE—Ruth & Augustus Goetz, suggested by Henry
  James' novel *Washington Square* ....47-48..Sept. 29, 1947.. 410
HELL-BENT FER HEAVEN—Hatcher Hughes ....23-24..Jan. 4, 1924.. 122
* HELLO DOLLY!—(b) Michael Stewart, (1) (m) Jerry Herman,
  based on Thornton Wilder's *The Matchmaker* ....63-64..Jan. 16, 1964.. 989
HER MASTER'S VOICE—Clare Kummer ....33-34..Oct. 23, 1933.. 224
HERE COME THE CLOWNS—Philip Barry ....38-39..Dec. 7, 1938.. 88
HERO, THE—Gilbert Emery ....21-22..Sept. 5, 1921.. 80
HIGH TOR—Maxwell Anderson ....36-37..Jan. 9, 1937.. 171
HOLIDAY—Philip Barry ....28-29..Nov. 26, 1928.. 229
HOME OF THE BRAVE—Arthur Laurents ....45-46..Dec. 27, 1945.. 69
HOPE FOR A HARVEST—Sophie Treadwell ....41-42..Nov. 26, 1941.. 38
HOSTAGE, THE—Brendan Behan ....60-61..Sept. 20, 1960.. 127
HOUSE OF CONNELLY, THE—Paul Green ....31-32..Sept. 28, 1931.. 91
HOW TO SUCCEED IN BUSINESS WITHOUT REALLY TRYING—
  (b) Abe Burrows, Jack Weinstock, Willie Gilbert, based on
  Shepherd Mead's novel, (1, m) Frank Loesser ....61-62..Oct. 14, 1961..1,417

I AM A CAMERA—John van Druten, based on Christopher Ish-
  erwood's Berlin stories ....51-52..Nov. 28, 1951.. 214
IF I WERE KING—Justin Huntly McCarthy ....99-09..Oct. 14, 1901.. 56
I KNOW MY LOVE—S. N. Behrman, adapted from Marcel
  Achard's *Auprès de Ma Blonde* ....49-50..Nov. 2, 1949.. 246
I REMEMBER MAMA—John van Druten, based on Kathryn
  Forbes's book *Mama's Bank Account* ....44-45..Oct. 19, 1944.. 714
ICEBOUND—Owen Davis ....22-23..Feb. 10, 1923.. 171
ICEMAN COMETH, THE—Eugene O'Neill ....46-47..Oct. 9, 1946.. 136
IDIOT'S DELIGHT—Robert E. Sherwood ....35-36..Mar. 24, 1936.. 300
IMMORALIST, THE—Ruth and Augustus Goetz, based on André
  Gide's novel ....53-54..Feb. 8, 1954.. 96
IN ABRAHAM'S BOSOM—Paul Green ....26-27..Dec. 30, 1926.. 116
IN THE SUMMER HOUSE—Jane Bowles ....53-54..Dec. 29, 1953.. 55
IN TIME TO COME—Howard Koch, John Huston ....41-42..Dec. 28, 1941.. 40
INCIDENT AT VICHY—Arthur Miller ....64-65..Dec. 3, 1964.. 99
INHERIT THE WIND—Jerome Lawrence, Robert E. Lee ....54-55..Apr. 21, 1955.. 806
INNOCENTS, THE—William Archibald, based on Henry James'
  The Turn of the Screw ....49-50..Feb. 1, 1950.. 141
INNOCENT VOYAGE, THE—Paul Osborn, based on Richard
  Hughes's novel *High Wind in Jamaica* ....43-44..Nov. 15, 1943.. 40
INSPECTOR CALLS, AN—J. B. Priestley ....47-48..Oct. 21, 1947.. 95

J. B.—Archibald MacLeish ....58-59..Dec. 11, 1958.. 364
JACOBOWSKY AND THE COLONEL—S. N. Behrman, based on
  Franz Werfel's play ....43-44..Mar 14, 1944.. 417
JANE—S. N. Behrman, suggested by W. Somerset Maugham's
  story ....51-52..Feb. 1, 1952.. 100
JANE CLEGG—St. John Ervine ....19-20..Feb. 23, 1920.. 158
JASON—Samson Raphaelson ....41-42..Jan. 21, 1942.. 125
JEST, THE—Sem Benelli, (ad) Edward Sheldon ....19-20..Sept. 19, 1919.. 197
JOAN OF LORRAINE—Maxwell Anderson ....46-47..Nov. 18, 1946.. 199
JOHN FERGUSON—St. John Ervine ....09-19..May 13, 1919.. 177
JOHN LOVES MARY—Norman Krasna ....46-47..Feb. 4, 1947.. 423
JOHNNY JOHNSON—(b, 1) Paul Green, (m) Kurt Weill ......36-37..Nov. 19, 1936.. 68
JOURNEY'S END—R. C. Sherriff ....28-29..Mar. 22, 1929.. 485
JUNE MOON—Ring W. Lardner, George S. Kaufman ....29-30..Oct. 9, 1929.. 273
JUNIOR MISS—Jerome Chodorov, Joseph Fields ....41-42..Nov. 18, 1941.. 710

PLAY   VOLUME OPENED PERFS.

KATAKI—Shimon Wincelberg ....58-59..Apr. 9, 1959.. 20
KEY LARGO—Maxwell Anderson ....39-40..Nov. 27, 1939.. 105
KINGDOM OF GOD, THE—G. Martinez Sierra, (ad) Helen and
  Harley Granville-Barker ....28-29..Dec. 20, 1928.. 92
KISS AND TELL—F. Hugh Herbert ....42-43..Mar. 17, 1943.. 957
KISS THE BOYS GOOD-BYE—Clare Boothe ....38-39..Sept. 28, 1938.. 286

LADY IN THE DARK—(b) Moss Hart, (1) Ira Gershwin, (m)
  Kurt Weill ....40-41..Jan. 23, 1941.. 162
LARK, THE—Jean Anouilh, (ad) Lillian Hellman ....55-56..Nov. 17, 1955.. 229
LAST MILE, THE—John Wexley ....29-30..Feb. 13, 1930.. 289
LAST OF MRS. CHEYNEY, THE—Frederick Lonsdale ....25-26..Nov. 9, 1925.. 385
LATE CHRISTOPHER BEAN, THE—adapted by Sidney Howard from
  the French of René Fauchois ....32-33..Oct. 31, 1932.. 244
LATE GEORGE APLEY, THE—John P. Marquand, George S. Kauf-
  man, based on Mr. Marquand's book ....44-45..Nov. 23, 1944.. 385
LEAH KLESCHNA—C. M. S. McLellan ....99-09..Dec. 12, 1904.. 131
LEFT BANK, THE—Elmer Rice ....31-32..Oct. 5, 1931.. 242
LET US BE GAY—Rachel Crothers ....28-29..Feb. 19, 1929.. 132
LETTERS TO LUCERNE—Fritz Rotter, Allen Vincent ....41-42..Dec. 23, 1941.. 23
LIFE WITH FATHER—Howard Lindsay, Russel Crouse, based on
  Clarence Day's book ....39-40..Nov. 8, 1939..3,224
LIFE WITH MOTHER—Howard Lindsay, Russel Crouse, based on
  Clarence Day's book ....48-49..Oct. 20, 1948.. 265
LIGHT UP THE SKY—Moss Hart ....48-49..Nov. 18, 1948.. 216
LILIOM—Ferenc Molnar, (ad) Benjamin Glazer ....20-21..Apr. 20, 1921.. 300
LITTLE ACCIDENT—Floyd Dell, Thomas Mitchell ....28-29..Oct. 9, 1928.. 289
LITTLE FOXES, THE—Lillian Hellman ....38-39..Feb. 15, 1939.. 410
LITTLE MINISTER, THE—James M. Barrie ....94-99..Sept. 27, 1897.. 300
LIVING ROOM, THE—Graham Greene ....54-55..Nov. 17, 1954.. 22
LONG DAY'S JOURNEY INTO THE NIGHT—Eugene O'Neill ....56-57..Nov. 7, 1956.. 390
LOOK BACK IN ANGER—John Osborne ....57-58..Oct. 1, 1957.. 407
LOOK HOMEWARD, ANGEL—Ketti Frings, based on Thomas
  Wolfe's novel ....57-58..Nov. 28, 1957.. 564
LOST HORIZONS—Harry Segall, revised by John Hayden ....34-35..Oct. 15, 1934.. 56
LOST IN THE STARS—(b, 1) Maxwell Anderson, based on Alan
  Paton's novel Cry, The Beloved Country, (m) Kurt Weill .....49-50..Oct. 30, 1949.. 273
LOVE OF FOUR COLONELS, THE—Peter Ustinov ....52-53..Jan. 15, 1953.. 141
LOYALTIES—John Galsworthy ....22-23..Sept. 27, 1922.. 220
LUTE SONG—(b) Sidney Howard, Will Irwin, from the Chinese
  classic Pi-Pa-Ki, (1) Bernard Hanighen, (m) Raymond Scott ..44-45..Nov. 23, 1944.. 385
LUTHER—John Osborne ....63-64..Sept. 25, 1963.. 211
* LUV—Murray Schisgal ....64-65..Nov. 11, 1964.. 647

MACHINAL—Sophie Treadwell ....28-29..Sept. 7, 1928.. 91
MADWOMAN OF CHAILLOT, THE—Jean Giraudoux, (ad) Maurice
  Valency ....48-49..Dec. 27, 1948.. 368
MAGIC AND THE LOSS, THE—Julian Funt ....53-54..Apr. 9, 1954.. 27
MAGNIFICENT YANKEE, THE—Emmet Lavery ....45-46..Jan. 22, 1946.. 160
MALE ANIMAL, THE—James Thurber, Elliott Nugent ....39-40..Jan. 9, 1940.. 243
MAMMA'S AFFAIR—Rachel Barton Butler ....19-20..Jan. 19, 1920.. 98
MAN FOR ALL SEASONS, A—Robert Bolt ....61-62..Nov. 22, 1961.. 638
MAN FROM HOME, THE—Booth Tarkington, Harry Leon Wilson ..99-09..Aug. 17, 1908.. 406
MAN WHO CAME TO DINNER, THE—George S. Kaufman, Moss
  Hart ....39-40..Oct. 16, 1939.. 739
MARGIN FOR ERROR—Clare Boothe ....39-40..Nov. 3, 1939.. 264
MARY, MARY—Jean Kerr ....60-61..Mar. 8, 1961..1,572
MARY OF SCOTLAND—Maxwell Anderson ....33-34..Nov. 27, 1933.. 248
MARY ROSE—James M. Barrie ....20-21..Dec. 22, 1920.. 127
MARY THE 3RD—Rachel Crothers ....22-23..Feb. 5, 1923.. 162
MATCHMAKER, THE—Thornton Wilder, based on Johann Nes-
  troy's Einen Jux will es sich Machen, based on John Oxen-
  ford's A Day Well Spent ....55-56..Dec. 5, 1955.. 486

PLAY   VOLUME OPENED PERFS.

ME AND MOLLY—Gertrude Berg ....47-48..Feb. 26, 1948.. 156
MEMBER OF THE WEDDING, THE—Carson McCullers, adapted
  from her novel ....49-50..Jan. 5, 1950.. 501
MEN IN WHITE—Sidney S. Kingsley ....33-34..Sept. 26, 1933.. 351
MERRILY WE ROLL ALONG—George S. Kaufman, Moss Hart ....34-35..Sept. 29, 1934.. 155
MERTON OF THE MOVIES—George S. Kaufman, Marc Connelly,
  based on Harry Leon Wilson's novel ....22-23..Nov. 13, 1922.. 381
MICHAEL AND MARY—A. A. Milne ....29-30..Dec. 10, 1929.. 246
MILK TRAIN DOESN'T STOP HERE ANYMORE, THE—Tennessee
  Williams ....62-63..Jan. 16, 1963.. 69
MINICK—George S. Kaufman, Edna Ferber ....24-25..Sept. 24, 1924.. 141
MISTER ROBERTS—Thomas Heggen, Joshua Logan, based on
  Thomas Heggen's novel ....47-48..Feb. 18, 1948..1,157
MOON FOR THE MISBEGOTTEN, A—Eugene O'Neill ....56-57..May 2, 1957.. 68
MOON IS DOWN, THE—John Steinbeck ....41-42..Apr. 7, 1942.. 71
MORNING'S AT SEVEN—Paul Osborn ....39-40..Nov. 30, 1939.. 44
MOTHER COURAGE AND HER CHILDREN—Bertolt Brecht, (ad)
  Eric Bentley ....62-63..Mar. 28, 1963.. 52
MOURNING BECOMES ELECTRA—Eugene O'Neill ....31-32..Oct. 26, 1931.. 150
MR. AND MRS. NORTH—Owen Davis, based on Frances and Rich-
  ard Lockridge's stories ....40-41..Jan. 12, 1941.. 163
MRS. BUMSTEAD-LEIGH—Harry James Smith ....09-19..Apr. 3, 1911.. 64
MRS. MCTHING—Mary Coyle Chase ....51-52..Feb. 20, 1952.. 350
MRS. PARTRIDGE PRESENTS—Mary Kennedy, Ruth Hawthorne ....24-25..Jan. 5, 1925.. 144
MY FAIR LADY—(b, 1) Alan Jay Lerner, based on Bernard
  Shaw's Pygmalion, (m) Frederick Loewe ....55-56..Mar. 15, 1956..2,717
MY SISTER EILEEN—Joseph A. Fields, Jerome Chodorov, based
  on Ruth McKenney's stories ....40-41..Dec. 26, 1940.. 865
MY 3 ANGELS—Sam and Bella Spewack, based on Albert Hus-
  son's play La Cuisine des Anges ....52-53..Mar. 11, 1953.. 341

NATIVE SON—Paul Green, Richard Wright, based on Mr.
  Wright's novel ....40-41..Mar. 24, 1941.. 114
NEST, THE—Paul Geraldy, Grace George ....21-22..Jan. 28, 1922.. 152
NEXT TIME I'LL SING TO YOU—James Saunders ....63-64..Nov. 27, 1963.. 23
NICE PEOPLE—Rachel Crothers ....20-21..Mar. 2, 1921.. 247
NIGHT OF THE IGUANA, THE—Tennessee Williams ....61-62..Dec. 28, 1961.. 319
NO MORE LADIES—A. E. Thomas ....33-34..Jan. 23, 1934.. 162
NO TIME FOR COMEDY—S. N. Behrman ....38-39..Apr. 17, 1939.. 185
NO TIME FOR SERGEANTS—Ira Levin, adapted from Mac Hy-
  man's novel ....55-56..Oct. 20, 1955.. 796

O MISTRESS MINE—Terence Rattigan ....45-46..Jan. 23, 1946.. 452
* ODD COUPLE, THE—Neil Simon ....64-65..Mar. 10, 1965.. 510
OF MICE AND MEN—John Steinbeck ....37-38..Nov. 23, 1937.. 207
OF THEE I SING—(b) George S. Kaufman, Morrie Ryskind,
  (1) Ira Gershwin, (m) George Gershwin ....31-32..Dec. 26, 1931.. 441
OH DAD, POOR DAD, MAMMA'S HUNG YOU IN THE CLOSET AND
  I'M FEELIN' SO SAD—Arthur L. Kopit ....61-62..Feb. 26, 1962.. 454
OKLAHOMA!—(b, 1) Oscar Hammerstein, II, based on Lynn
  Riggs's play Green Grow the Lilacs, (m) Richard Rodgers ....42-43..Mar. 31, 1943..2,212
OLD MAID, THE—Zoë Akins, based on Edith Wharton's novel ....34-35..Jan. 7, 1935.. 305
OLD SOAK, THE—Don Marquis ....22-23..Aug. 22, 1922.. 423
ON BORROWED TIME—Paul Osborn, based on Lawrence Edward
  Watkin's novel ....37-38..Feb. 3, 1938.. 321
ON TRIAL—Elmer Rice ....09-19..Aug. 19, 1914.. 365
ONCE IN A LIFETIME—George S. Kaufman, Moss Hart ....63-64..Feb. 11, 1964.. 15
ONE SUNDAY AFTERNOON—James Hagen ....30-31..Sept. 24, 1930.. 406
ORPHEUS DESCENDING—Tennessee Williams ....32-33..Feb. 15, 1933.. 322
OUTRAGEOUS FORTUNE—Rose Franken ....56-57..Mar. 21, 1957.. 68
OUR TOWN—Thornton Wilder ....43-44..Nov. 3, 1943.. 77
OUTWARD BOUND—Sutton Vane ....37-38..Feb. 4, 1938.. 336

PLAY   VOLUME OPENED PERFS.

OVER 21—Ruth Gordon ....23-24..Jan.   7, 1924.. 144
OVERTURE—William Bolitho ....43-44..Jan.   3, 1944.. 221
                                        30-31..Dec.   5, 1930..   41

P.S. 193—David Rayfiel ....
PARIS BOUND—Philip Barry ....62-63..Oct. 30, 1962..   48
PASSION OF JOSEPH D, THE—Paddy Chayefsky ....27-28..Dec. 27, 1927.. 234
PATRIOTS, THE—Sidney Kingsley ....42-43..Jan. 29, 1943.. 173
PERIOD OF ADJUSTMENT—Tennessee Williams ....60-61..Nov. 10, 1960.. 132
PETRIFIED FOREST, THE—Robert E. Sherwood ....34-35..Jan.   7, 1935.. 197
PHILADELPHIA STORY, THE—Philip Barry ....38-39..Mar. 28, 1939.. 417
PHYSICISTS, THE—Friedrich Duerrenmatt, (ad) James Kirkup ...64-65..Oct. 13, 1964..   55
PICK-UP GIRL—Elsa Shelley ....43-44..May   3, 1944.. 198
PICNIC—William Inge ....52-53..Feb. 19, 1953.. 477
PIGEONS AND PEOPLE—George M. Cohan ....32-33..Jan. 16, 1933..   70
PLAY'S THE THING, THE—Ferenc Molnar, (ad) P. G. Wodehouse..26-27..Nov.   3, 1926.. 260
PLEASURE OF HIS COMPANY, THE—Samuel Taylor, Cornelia Otis
  Skinner ....58-59..Oct. 22, 1958.. 474
PLOUGH AND THE STARS, THE—Sean O'Casey ....27-28..Nov. 28, 1927..   32
POINT OF NO RETURN—Paul Osborn, based on John P. Mar-
  quand's novel ....51-52..Dec. 13, 1951.. 364
PONDER HEART, THE—Joseph Fields, Jerome Chodorov, adapted
  from Eudora Welty's story ....55-56..Feb. 16, 1956.. 149
POOR BITOS—Jean Anouilh, (tr) Lucienne Hill ....64-65..Nov. 14, 1964..   14
PORGY—DuBose Heyward ....27-28..Oct. 10, 1927.. 217
POTTING SHED, THE—Graham Greene ....56-57..Jan. 29, 1957.. 143
PRIDE AND PREJUDICE—Helen Jerome, based on Jane Austen's
  novel ....35-36..Nov.   5, 1935.. 219
PROLOGUE TO GLORY—E. P. Conkle ....37-38..Mar. 17, 1938..   70

R.U.R.—Karel Capek ....22-23..Oct.   9, 1922.. 184
RACKET, THE—Bartlett Cormack ....27-28..Nov. 22, 1927.. 119
RAIN—John Colton, Clemence Randolph, based on the story by
  W. Somerset Maughm ....22-23..Nov.   7, 1922.. 648
RAISIN IN THE SUN, A—Lorraine Hansberry ....58-59..Mar. 11, 1959.. 530
RATTLE OF A SIMPLE MAN—Charles Dyer ....62-63..Apr. 17, 1963..   94
REBOUND—Donald Ogden Stewart ....29-30..Feb.   3, 1930.. 114
REHEARSAL, THE—Jean Anouilh, (ad) Pamela Hansford Johnson
  and Kitty Black ....63-64..Sept. 23, 1963.. 110
REMAINS TO BE SEEN—Howard Lindsay, Russel Crouse ....51-52..Oct.   3, 1951.. 199
REQUIEM FOR A NUN—Ruth Ford, William Faulkner, adapted
  from Mr. Faulkner's novel ....58-59..Jan. 30, 1959..   43
REUNION IN VIENNA—Robert E. Sherwood ....31-32..Nov. 16, 1931.. 264
RHINOCEROS—Eugene Ionesco, (tr) Derek Prouse ....60-61..Jan.   9, 1961.. 240
ROAD TO ROME, THE—Robert E. Sherwood ....26-27..Jan. 31, 1927.. 392
ROCKET TO THE MOON—Clifford Odets ....38-39..Nov. 24, 1938.. 131
ROMANCE—Edward Sheldon ....09-19..Feb. 10, 1913.. 160
ROPE DANCERS, THE—Morton Wishengrad ....57-58..Nov. 20, 1957.. 189
ROSE TATTOO, THE—Tennessee Williams ....50-51..Feb.   3, 1951.. 306
ROYAL FAMILY, THE—George S. Kaufman, Edna Ferber .....27-28..Dec. 28, 1927.. 345
RUGGED PATH, THE—Robert E. Sherwood ....45-46..Nov. 10, 1945..   81

SATURDAY'S CHILDREN—Maxwell Anderson ....26-27..Jan. 26, 1927.. 315
SEARCHING WIND, THE—Lillian Hellman ....43-44..Apr. 12, 1944.. 318
SEASON IN THE SUN—Wolcott Gibbs ....50-51..Sept. 28, 1950.. 367
SECOND THRESHOLD—Philip Barry ....50-51..Jan.   2, 1951.. 126
SECRET SERVICE—William Gillette ....94-99..Oct.   5, 1896.. 176
SEPARATE TABLES—Terence Rattigan ....56-57..Oct. 25, 1956.. 332
SEVEN KEYS TO BALDPATE—George M. Cohan ....09-19..Sept. 22, 1913.. 320
SHADOW AND SUBSTANCE—Paul Vincent Carroll ....37-38..Jan. 26, 1938.. 274
SHADOW OF HEROES—Robert Ardrey, also called Stone and
  Star ....61-62..Dec.   5, 1961..   20
SHE LOVES ME—(b) Joe Masteroff, based on Miklos Laszlo's
  play Parfumerie, (1) Sheldon Harnick, (m) Jerry Block ......62-63..Apr. 23, 1963.. 302

PLAY

VOLUME OPENED PERFS.

SHINING HOUR, THE—Keith Winter ....33-34..Feb. 13, 1934.. 121
SHOW-OFF, THE—George Kelly ....23-24..Feb. 5, 1924.. 571
SHRIKE, THE—Joseph Kramm ....51-52..Jan. 15, 1952.. 161
SILVER CORD, THE—Sidney Howard ....26-27..Dec. 20, 1926.. 112
SILVER WHISTLE, THE—Robert E. McEnroe ....48-49..Nov. 24, 1948.. 219
SIX CYLINDER LOVE—William Anthony McGuire ....21-22..Aug. 25, 1921.. 430
SKIN GAME, THE—John Galsworthy ....20-21..Oct. 20, 1920.. 176
SKIN OF OUR TEETH, THE—Thornton Wilder ....42-43..Nov. 18, 1942.. 359
SKIPPER NEXT TO GOD—Jan de Hartog ....47-48..Jan. 4, 1948.. 69
SKYLARK—Samson Raphaelson ....39-40..Oct. 11, 1939.. 256
SLOW DANCE ON THE KILLING GROUND—William Hanley ......64-65..Nov. 30, 1964.. 88
SOLDIER'S WIFE—Rose Franken ....44-45..Oct. 4, 1944.. 253
SQUAW MAN, THE—Edwin Milton Royle ....99-09..Oct. 23, 1905.. 222
ST. HELENA—R. C. Sheriff, Jeanne de Casalis ....36-37..Oct. 6, 1936.. 63
STAGE DOOR—George S. Kaufman, Edna Ferber ....36-37..Oct. 22, 1936.. 169
STAR-WAGON, THE—Maxwell Anderson ....37-38..Sept. 29, 1937.. 223
STATE OF THE UNION—Howard Lindsay, Russel Crouse .....45-46..Nov. 14, 1945.. 765
STONE AND STAR—Robert Ardrey, also called Shadow of He-
  roes ....61-62..Dec. 5, 1961.. 20
STOP THE WORLD—I WANT TO GET OFF—(b, 1, m) Leslie Bri-
  cusse, Anthony Newley ....62-63..Oct. 3, 1962.. 555
STORM OPERATION—Maxwell Anderson ....43-44..Jan. 11, 1944.. 23
STORY OF MARY SURRATT, THE—John Patrick ....46-47..Feb. 8, 1947.. 11
STRANGE INTERLUDE—Eugene O'Neill ....27-28..Jan. 30, 1928.. 426
STREET SCENE—Elmer Rice ....28-29..Jan. 10, 1929.. 601
STREETCAR NAMED DESIRE, A—Tennessee Williams ....47-48..Dec. 3, 1947.. 855
STRICTLY DISHONORABLE—Preston Sturges ....29-30..Sept. 18, 1929.. 557
SUBJECT WAS ROSES, THE—Frank D. Gilroy ....64-65..May 25, 1964.. 832
SUMMER OF THE 17TH DOLL—Ray Lawler ....57-58..Jan. 22, 1958.. 29
SUNRISE AT CAMPOBELLO—Dore Schary ....57-58..Jan. 30, 1958.. 556
SUN-UP—Lula Vollmer ....22-23..May 25, 1923.. 356
SUSAN AND GOD—Rachel Crothers ....37-38..Oct. 7, 1937.. 288
SWAN, THE—Ferenc Molnar, (tr) Melville Baker ....23-24..Oct. 23, 1923.. 255
SWEET BIRD OF YOUTH—Tennessee Williams ....58-59..Mar. 10, 1959.. 375

TAKE A GIANT STEP—Louis Peterson ....53-54..Sept. 24, 1953.. 76
TARNISH—Gilbert Emery ....23-24..Oct. 1, 1923.. 248
TASTE OF HONEY, A—Shelagh Delaney ....60-61..Oct. 4, 1960.. 334
TCHIN-TCHIN—Sidney Michaels, based on François Billetdoux's
  play ....62-63..Oct. 25, 1962.. 222
TEA AND SYMPATHY—Robert Anderson ....53-54..Sept. 30, 1953.. 712
TEAHOUSE OF THE AUGUST MOON—John Patrick, based on Vern
  Sneider's novel ....53-54..Oct. 15, 1953..1,027
TENTH MAN, THE—Paddy Chayefsky ....59-60..Nov. 5, 1959.. 623
THERE SHALL BE NO NIGHT—Robert E. Sherwood ....39-40..Apr. 29, 1940.. 181
THEY KNEW WHAT THEY WANTED—Sidney Howard ....24-25..Nov. 24, 1924.. 414
THEY SHALL NOT DIE—John Wexley ....33-34..Feb. 21, 1934.. 62
THOUSAND CLOWNS, A—Herb Gardner ....61-62..Apr. 5, 1962.. 428
THURBER CARNIVAL, A—James Thurber ....59-60..Feb. 26, 1960.. 127
TIGER AT THE GATES—Jean Giraudoux's La Guerre de Troie
  n'aura pas lieu, (tr) Christopher Fry ....55-56..Oct. 3, 1955.. 217
TIME OF THE CUCKOO, THE—Arthur Laurents ....52-53..Oct. 15, 1952.. 263
TIME OF YOUR LIFE, THE—William Saroyan ....39-40..Oct. 25, 1939.. 185
TIME REMEMBERED—Jean Anouilh's Léocadia, (ad) Patricia
  Moyes ....57-58..Nov. 12, 1957.. 248
TINY ALICE—Edward Albee ....64-65..Dec. 29, 1964.. 167
TOILET, THE—LeRoi Jones ....64-65..Dec. 16, 1964.. 151
TOMORROW AND TOMORROW—Philip Barry ....30-31..Jan. 13, 1931.. 206
TOMORROW THE WORLD—James Gow, Arnaud d'Usseau ....42-43..Apr. 14, 1943.. 500
TOUCH OF THE POET, A—Eugene O'Neill ....58-59..Oct. 2, 1958.. 284
TOVARICH—Jacques Deval, (tr) Robert E. Sherwood ....36-37..Oct. 15, 1936.. 356
TOYS IN THE ATTIC—Lillian Hellman ....59-60..Feb. 25, 1960.. 556

PLAY	VOLUME	OPENED	PERFS.
TRELAWNY OF THE WELLS—Eugene W. Presbrey	94-99	Nov. 22, 1898	131
TWO BLIND MICE—Samuel Spewack	48-49	Mar. 2, 1949	163
UNCHASTENED WOMAN, THE—Louis Kaufman Anspacher	09-19	Oct. 9, 1915	193
UNCLE HARRY—Thomas Job	41-42	May 20, 1942	430
UNDER MILK WOOD—Dylan Thomas	57-58	Oct. 15, 1957	39
VALLEY FORGE—Maxwell Anderson	34-35	Dec. 10, 1934	58
VENUS OBSERVED—Christopher Fry	51-52	Feb. 13, 1952	86
VERY SPECIAL BABY, A—Robert Alan Aurthur	56-57	Nov. 14, 1956	5
VICTORIA REGINA—Laurence Housman	35-36	Dec. 26, 1935	203
VIEW FROM THE BRIDGE, A—Arthur Miller	55-56	Sept. 29, 1955	149
VISIT, THE—Friedrich Duerrenmatt, (ad) Maurice Valency	57-58	May 5, 1958	189
VISIT TO A SMALL PLANET—Gore Vidal	56-57	Feb. 7, 1957	388
VOICE OF THE TURTLE, THE—John van Druten	43-44	Dec. 8, 1943	1,557
WAITING FOR GODOT—Samuel Beckett	55-56	Apr. 19, 1956	59
WALTZ OF THE TOREADORS, THE—Jean Anouilh, (tr) Lucienne Hill	56-57	Jan. 17, 1957	132
WATCH ON THE RHINE—Lillian Hellman	40-41	Apr. 1, 1941	378
WE, THE PEOPLE—Elmer Rice	32-33	Jan. 21, 1933	49
WEDDING BELLS—Salisbury Field	19-20	Nov. 12, 1919	168
WEDNESDAY'S CHILD—Leopold Atlas	33-34	Jan. 16, 1934	56
WHAT A LIFE—Clifford Goldsmith	37-38	Apr. 13, 1938	538
WHAT PRICE GLORY?—Maxwell Anderson, Laurence Stallings	24-25	Sept. 5, 1924	433
WHEN LADIES MEET—Rachel Crothers	32-33	Oct. 6, 1932	191
WHITE STEED, THE—Paul Vincent Carroll	38-39	Jan. 10, 1939	136
WHO'S AFRAID OF VIRGINIA WOOLF?—Edward Albee	62-63	Oct. 13, 1962	664
WHY MARRY?—Jesse Lynch Williams	09-19	Dec. 25, 1917	120
WHY NOT?—Jesse Lynch Williams	22-23	Dec. 25, 1922	120
WITCHING HOUR, THE—Augustus Thomas	99-09	Nov. 18, 1907	212
WILD BIRDS—Dan Totheroh	24-25	Apr. 9, 1925	44
WINGED VICTORY—(b) Moss Hart, (m) Sgt. David Rose	43-44	Nov. 20, 1943	212
WINSLOW BOY, THE—Terence Rattigan	47-48	Oct. 29, 1947	215
WINGS OVER EUROPE—Robert Nichols, Maurice Browne	28-29	Dec. 10, 1928	90
WINTERSET—Maxwell Anderson	35-36	Sept. 25, 1935	195
WINTER SOLDIERS—Daniel Lewis James	42-43	Nov. 29, 1942	25
WISDOM TOOTH, THE—Marc Connelly	25-26	Feb. 15, 1926	160
WISTERIA TREES, THE—Joshua Logan, based on Anton Chekhov's The Cherry Orchard	49-50	Mar. 29, 1950	165
WITNESS FOR THE PROSECUTION—Agatha Christie	54-55	Dec. 16, 1954	645
WOMEN, THE—Clare Boothe	36-37	Dec. 26, 1936	657
WONDERFUL TOWN—(b) Joseph Fields, Jerome Chodorov, based on their play My Sister Eileen and Ruth McKenney's stories, (l) Betty Comden, Adolph Green, (m) Leonard Bernstein	52-53	Feb. 25, 1953	559
WORLD WE MAKE, THE—Sidney Kingsley, based on Millen Brand's novel	39-40	Nov. 20, 1939	80
YEARS AGO—Ruth Gordon	46-47	Dec. 3, 1946	206
YES, MY DARLING DAUGHTER—Mark Reed	36-37	Feb. 9, 1937	405
YOU AND I—Philip Barry	22-23	Feb. 19, 1923	178
YOU CAN'T TAKE IT WITH YOU—Moss Hart, George S. Kaufman	36-37	Dec. 14, 1936	837
YOUNG WOODLEY—John van Druten	25-26	Nov. 2, 1925	260
YOUNGEST, THE—Philip Barry	24-25	Dec. 22, 1924	104

NECROLOGY

JUNE 1, 1965—MAY 31, 1966

PERFORMERS

Albert F. (Ollie) Adams (82)—July 1, 1965
Peggy Allenby (65)—Mar. 23, 1966
Al Anger (65)—Mar. 13, 1966
George Armondos (64)—June 24, 1965
John Arnaut (65)—Oct. 6, 1965
Bill Bailey (80)—Mar. 10, 1966
Percy D. Barbat (82)—June 20, 1965
Nora Cunneen Barrett (65)—Oct. 3, 1965
Bessie Barriscale (81)—June 30, 1965
Reyner Barton—Feb. 10, 1966
Robert C. Battle (34)—Nov. 4, 1965
Nan Brennan Becker—July 21, 1965
Constance Bennett (59)—July 24, 1965
Lillian Blanchard (91)—May 1966
Mary Boland (83)—June 23, 1965
Harold E. Boyd (72)—Sept. 30, 1965
Irene Brown (72)—July 24, 1965
Ralph Bunker (77)—Apr. 28, 1966
Fairfax Burgher (70)—Sept. 20, 1965
Emmett Callahan (72)—Dec. 30, 1965
Victor Carreire (70)—Mar. 31, 1966
Nancy Carroll (60)—Aug. 6, 1965
Mathilde Casadesus (44)—Aug. 30, 1965
Sallie Marshall Chase (55)—Aug. 9, 1965
Elsie Clark (67)—Apr. 14, 1966
Neva West Clements—Oct. 5, 1965
Hallye Clogg (89)—July 6, 1965
Steve Cochran (48)—June 15, 1965
Maurice Cole (72)—June 6, 1965
Ray Collins (75)—July 11, 1965
Sheila Copelan (30)—April 20, 1966
Charles Corrigan (72)—April 4, 1966
Joseph Crehan (82)—Apr. 15, 1966
Lee Culmer—Oct. 1965
James Dealy (85)—Aug. 26, 1965
Frank M. Doorley (80)—Apr. 26, 1966
Jimmy Dwyer (72)—June 17, 1965
Donna Earl (63)—June 30, 1965
Neely Edwards (82)—July 10, 1965
Donald Falasco (38)—Aug. 24, 1965
Eddie Featherston—June 12, 1965
George N. Finkelstone (74)—Feb. 11, 1966
Consuelo Flowerton (65)—Dec. 21, 1965
Nony Franklin (40)—July 20, 1965
William Frawley (79)—March 3, 1966
Ralph Gamble (64)—Mar. 11, 1966
Ruth Gates (79)—May 23, 1966
Albie Gaye—Nov. 26, 1965
Archie Glen (77)—Apr. 8, 1966
Nina Gordani (64)—Jan 21, 1966

Gypsy Gould (64)—Feb. 1, 1966
Charity Grace (86)—Nov. 28, 1965
Joseph Granby (80)—Sept. 22, 1965
Eddie T. Gribbon (75)—Sept. 28, 1965
Alec Harland—June 11, 1965
William Harrigan (72)—Feb. 1, 1966
Pat Harrington Sr. (64)—Sept. 1965
Jonathan William (Pop) Hartman (90)—Oct. 19, 1965
Harry S. Hilliard—Apr. 21, 1966
Judy Holliday (42)—June 7, 1965
Nellie Hook (80)—Jan. 13, 1966
Hedda Hopper (75)—Feb 1, 1966
Kathryn Kunkel Horine (56)—Dec. 5, 1965
Eugene Howard (84)—Aug. 1, 1965
Kyra Deakin Hubbell (63)—Sept. 1, 1965
Gareth Hughes (71)—Oct. 1, 1965
Noel Hytown (66)—Nov. 25, 1965
Gail Kane (81)—Feb. 17, 1966
Nell Clark Keller (89)—Sept. 2, 1965
Renee Kelly (77)—Aug. 29, 1965
Irene Knight—Jan. 11, 1966
Florence Lamb (82)—May 9, 1966
Larri Lauria (64)—Dec. 23, 1965
Moe Lee (81)—Jan. 5, 1966
May Leslie (84)—July 21, 1965
Herman Lieb (93)—Mar. 9, 1966
William A. Loker (74)—Sept. 23, 1965
Edward Lowrie (72)—Sept. 1965
Rudd Lowry (73)—Dec. 15, 1965
Charles N. Lum (88)—Jan. 8, 1966
Angela McCall (90)—Aug. 20, 1965
Marie McDonald (42)—Oct. 21, 1965
Reginald Malcolm (82)—Jan. 20, 1966
Sam Mann (77)—June 18, 1965
Sid Marion (65)—June 29, 1965
Herbert Marshall (75)—Jan. 21, 1966
Helen Menken (64)—Mar. 28, 1966
Sully Michaels (49)—Jan. 4, 1966
Vic Milo (80)—Aug. 7, 1965
Pat Moran (64)—Aug. 9, 1965
Corinna Mura (55)—Aug. 1, 1965
Mary Nash (76)—June 28, 1965
Max Nesbitt (63)—Apr. 11, 1966
Joseph H. Niemeyer (78)—Sept. 27, 1965
Corinne F. North (69)—Jan. 5, 1966
Kathryn O'Connor (71)—Nov. 16, 1965
Pat O'Malley (75)—May 21, 1966
Catherine Dale Owen (62)—Sept. 7, 1965
Murray Parker (69)—Oct. 18, 1965
Barbara Parmalee (24)—Dec. 24, 1965
Charles Parmalee (37)—Dec. 24, 1965

Elizabeth Patterson (90)—Feb. 2, 1966
Alice Pearce—March 3, 1966
Vera Pearce (70)—Jan. 21, 1966
Harry H. Perry (84)—July 19, 1965
C. Mort Phinn (75)—July 1965
Harry S. Pimm (75)—Aug. 8, 1965
Sam Pinansky (77)—Mar. 12, 1966
Emily Pinter (65)—Aug. 23, 1965
Marie Polak (70)—Apr. 27, 1966
Hartley Power (71)—Jan. 29, 1966
Helen Ray (86)—Oct. 2, 1965
Naomi Ray (73)—Mar. 13, 1966
Helen Raymond (70)—Nov. 26, 1965
Gus Reed (85)—July 17, 1965
James Rennie (76)—July 31, 1965
Houston Richard (79)—Aug. 22, 1965
Al Ritz (62)—Dec. 22, 1965
Corinne Heath Sumner Ross (86)—June 22, 1965
Ronnie Ross (25)—Sept. 5, 1965
Johnny Sanna (64)—Dec. 30, 1965
Zachary Scott (51)—Oct. 3, 1965
Nance Shannon—Dec. 30, 1965
William J. Shepard (74)—July 24, 1965
Lisa Silbert (85)—Nov. 29, 1965
J. Anthony Smyche (80)—Mar. 20, 1966
Colette Southern (73)—Oct. 9, 1965
Sammy Spears—Mar. 24, 1966
Gase Stanley (75)—July 9, 1965
Edward Steel (68)—Oct. 18, 1965
Betty Stockfield (61)—Jan. 27, 1966
John Swor (87)—July 15, 1965
Robert Thorne (84)—July 3, 1965
Sophie Tucker (82)—Feb. 9, 1966
Charles Victor (69)—Dec. 23, 1965
June Walker (61)—Feb. 3, 1966
Gus Wally (62)—March 3, 1966
Vera Walton (74) Sept. 1, 1965
Mary Ward (78)—May 2, 1966
Allen H. Waterous (61)—Aug. 2, 1965
Minor Watson (75)—July 28, 1965
Constance Weiler (47)—Dec. 10, 1965
Buster West (64)—Mar. 18, 1966
Paul West (75)—Aug. 19, 1965
Lolita Ann Westman (65)—Nov. 14, 1965
Walter W. Whitfield (78)—Jan. 13, 1966
Mack Williams (58)—July 29, 1965
Muriel Window—Sept. 19, 1965
Lawrence Winters (50)—Sept. 24, 1965
Jack Wolf (56)—Nov. 14, 1965
William Worthington (69)—Mar. 9, 1966

PLAYWRIGHTS

James Allardice (46)—Feb. 15, 1966
Hugh Anderson (75)—Nov. 9, 1965
John G. Baragwanath (76)—June 27, 1965
Florence Ryerson Clements (70)—June 8, 1965
Russel Crouse (72)—Apr. 3, 1966
Irving Kaye Davis (65)—Nov. 8, 1965
Joseph Fields (71)—March 3, 1966
Charles Fue (80)—Aug. 20, 1965
James Edward Grant (61)—Feb. 19, 1966

Alfred Graham Jackson (72)—June 24, 1965
Randall Jarrell (51)—Oct. 14, 1965
Howard J. Green (72)—Sept. 2, 1965
William C. Lengel (77)—Oct. 11, 1965
Patrick F. MacManus (56)—Nov. 27, 1965
Norman Matson (72)—Oct. 18, 1965
W. Somerset Maugham (91)—Dec. 16, 1965
Hardwick Nevin (68)—July 10, 1965
Frank O'Connor (63)—Mar. 10, 1966
Carlos M. Ortega (80)—June 22, 1965
Leo F. Reardon (73)—Aug. 23, 1965
Robert Rossen (57)—Feb. 18, 1966
William Siegel (73)—May 23, 1966
Peggy Shane (69)—Aug. 2, 1965
H. G. Stoker (81)—Feb. 2, 1966
Nahum Stutchkoff (73)—Nov 6, 1965
Kenneth Webb (70)—Mar. 5, 1966

COMPOSERS AND LYRICISTS

Kenneth Casey (66)—Aug. 10, 1965
Will Dillon (89)—Feb. 10, 1966
Dave Ringle (71)—June 20, 1965

CRITICS

Gordon E. Armstrong (64)—Sept. 25, 1965
  New Haven *Register*
Maxine Keith (50)—Mar. 12, 1966
  Radio Station WNYC, N.Y.
Jacques LaRoche (66)—Aug. 20, 1965
  Montreal *La Presse*
James E. Lee (58)—July 28, 1965
  Worcester (Mass.) *Evening Gazette*
Louis L. Mace (71)—June 10, 1965
  Springfield (Mass.) *Union and Republican* (ret.)
Moore Raymond (62) June 13, 1965
  London *Daily Dispatch* (formerly)
Jack Thompson (59)—May 10, 1966
  New York *Journal-American*
Andrew J. Warner (81)—Oct. 24, 1965
  Rochester (N.Y.) *Times-Union*

PRODUCERS AND DIRECTORS

May Carey—Jan. 25, 1966
William Bridge-Adams (76)—Aug. 17, 1965
George Devine (55)—Jan. 20, 1966
Vincent J. Donehue (50)—Jan. 17, 1966
Mack C. Hilliard (89)—Dec. 19, 1965
Harry Hyams (84)—Dec. 20, 1965
Alexander Ince (70)—Jan. 24, 1966
Darrell D. Larsen (68)—July 24, 1965
Lester Meyer (91)—Nov. 14, 1965
Mortimer Offner (64)—Sept. 15, 1965
Erwin Piscator (72)—Mar. 30, 1966
Emmett Rogers (50)—Oct. 31, 1965
Billy Rose (66)—Feb. 10, 1966
David Ross (43)—Apr. 13, 1966
David O. Selznick (63)—June 22, 1965
Henry R. Stern (91)—Mar. 13, 1966
A. H. Van Buren (86)—Aug. 1, 1965
James B. Welch (54)—Nov. 21, 1965

CONDUCTORS

Ray Kavanaugh (69)—May 16, 1966
Robert Philpot (41)—July 19, 1965
Claude Thornhill—July 1, 1965

DESIGNERS

Cleon Throckmorton (68)—Oct. 24, 1965
Virginia Bolen Whitehead (49)—Oct. 12, 1965

OTHERS

Emma H. Aplin (48)—June 26, 1965
Head of Theater Guild-American Theater Society, Los Angeles office
Lucius Beebe (63)—Feb. 3, 1966
Journalist
John J. (Barney) Bowman (57)—Mar. 14, 1966
Assistant treasurer Henry Miller's Theater
Norbert Conway (76)—Sept. 6, 1965
Founder of Philadelphia ticket agency
Alfred D'Apolito (54)—Nov. 24, 1965
Vice president and director of *Playbill*
Edward H. Dodd (96)—June 19, 1965
Retired chairman of the board of Dodd, Mead & Co.
John S. Dudley (72)—May 1, 1966
Real estate lawyer and former counsel to ANTA and the Actors Studio
Bernie Ferber (59)—June 17, 1965
Former manager Shubert Theater, Washington
Kathryn Forbes (57)—May 15, 1966
Author
Harold Freedman (69)—Feb. 16, 1966
Literary agent
Cora Gibbs (65)—Jan. 23, 1966
Former assistant treasurer at Shubert Theater box office
Paul Vincent Gordon (45)—Oct. 6, 1965
Drama coach
Minnie Guggenheimer (83)—May 23, 1966
Sponsor of concerts at Lewisohn Stadium

Sophie Harris (65)—1966
A founder of Motley, costume designers
Helen Hoerle (65)—Feb. 2, 1966
Theatrical press agent
Emil Katzka (69)—Mar. 20, 1966
Backer of Broadway plays
Dorothy Kilgallen (52)—Nov. 8, 1965
Journalist
Herbert B. Langner (73)—Aug. 3, 1965
Patron of Stratford, Conn. Shakespeare Festival
Al Manuti (56)—Sept. 11, 1965
President of AFM Local 802
Louis Marino (75)—Aug. 3, 1965
Eaves Costume Company employee for 30 years
Louis Molitch (60)—Jan. 13, 1966
President of Clark Transfer, theatrical trucker
Newbold Morris—Mar. 31, 1966
President New York City Center
Harry Shumer—Sept. 19, 1965
Founder of theatrical hauling firm
Luise M. Sillcox (75)—June 28, 1965
Former executive secretary of The Authors League of America, Inc.
Charles G. Strakosch (82)—June 20, 1965
Assistant manager of the Metropolitan Opera House and former Broadway company manager
Paula Strasberg (55)—Apr. 29, 1966
Drama coach and instructor at the Actors Studio
James E. Stroock (73)—July 22, 1965
General manager Brooks-Van Horn Costume Company and collector of theatrical memorabilia
Florence Vandamm (83)—Mar. 15, 1966
Broadway photographer
Gertrude Clarke Whittall (97)—June 29, 1965
Benefactress of the Library of Congress, sponsor of an annual series of poetry readings, lectures and dramas

INDEX

Bold face page numbers refer to pages where Cast of Characters may be found.

Aaron, Jack, 421, 434
Aaron, Stephen, 437
Aarons, Dennis, 95
Abbott, George, 3, 40, 366, 388
Abbott, Philip, 79
Abbott, Ron, 83
Abel, Lionel, 416
Abels, Gregory, 85
Abelson, Hope, 382
Aberlin, Betty, 417, 424
Ableman, Paul, 110
Absence of a Cello, 72, 76, 117, 439
Abundantly Yours, 443
Accomplices, The, see Mit-schuldigen, Die
Ackerman, Michele, 75
Ackland, Joss, 113
Ackland, Rodney, 80
Ackland, Roger, 72
Act Without Words I, 73
Acte, 457
Acton, Tom, 436
Actors Equity Association, 44, 56, 57, 436
Actors Theater (Louisville, Ky.), 36
Actors Theater Repertory Company (Los Angeles, Calif.), 56
Actor's Workshop (San Francisco, Calif.), 26, 36, 42, 43, 65, 66, 86
Adair, Robin, 367
Adams, Albert F., 469
Adams, Jean, 418
Adams, Judith, 75, 76
Adams, Kenny, 393, 413
Adams, Lee, 18, 365, 405, 455
Adams, Paul, 408, 410
Adams, Tom, 412
Addoms, Lee, 437
Ades, Daniel, 87
Adkins, Gilbert, 418
Adler, Jerry, 375, 411
Adler, Luther, 440
Adrian, Yvonne, 436
Affleck, Timothy, 73, 74
Agnes Bernauer, 117
Agnese, Rita, 377, 367
Agress, Ted, 437
Ah, Wilderness!, 51, 52, 79, 87
Ahearne, Tom, 31, 425, 454
Ajoret, Danielle, 117
Albano, Gene, 408
Albarwild, 35
Albee, Edward, 3, 21, 32, 43, 70, 76, 78, 79, 80, 84, 394, 417

Albee-Barr-Wilder (Theater 1966) New Playwrights Unit Workshop, 35
Albert, Wil, 427
Albertson, Jack, 441
Albery, Donald, 370, 376
Albertson, Mabel, 383
Albery, Ian, 370
Albrecht, Jan, 72
Alda, Alan, 440
Aldana Theater Production, 435
Aldredge, Theoni V., 95, 97, 385, 389, 390, 394, 400, 403, 411, 420, 432, 457
Aldredge, Tom, 96, 394
Aldrich, Patricia, 407
Alelyunas, Paul, 64
Alexander, Barbara, 388
Alexander, C. K., 437
Alexander, Cris, 432
Alexander, Hugh, 71, 84, 85
Alexander, Jane, 89
Alexander, Jill, 373
Alexander, Larry, 424
Alfieri, 117
Alford, Walter, 431, 432
Alfred, William, 3, 29, 31-32, 169, 425, 454
Alibi For a Judge, 111
Allan, Ted, 444
Allardice, James, 470
Allen, Billie, 435
Allen, Corey, 56
Allen, Donald M., 88
Allen, Humbert, 436
Allen, Janet, 444
Allen, Jay Presson, 112
Allen, John, 388
Allen, Lee, 440
Allen, Mary, 393
Allen, Rae, 96
Allen, Raymond, 432
Allen, Robert, 73, 74, 416
Allenby, Peggy, 469
Allergy, 110
Allers, Franz, 368, 370, 414
Alley Theater (Houston, Tex.), 42, 51-52
Allio, René, 110
Allison, Fred, 433
Allinson, Michael, 398
Allio, René, 110
Allis, Frances, 74
Allman, Robert, 75, 76
All's Well that Ends Well, 88, 92
Alpert, Anita, 368
Alpert, Michael, 421, 423, 426
Alswang, Ralph, 40, 377, 398

Alu, Al, 71
Alvarez, Carmen, 390
Alvarez, Eddie, 97
Alycia, Marthe, 397
Amata, Carmie, 75
Amber, Michael, 373
Amen Corner, The, 366
American Conservatory Theater (Pittsburgh, Pa.), 36, 42, 84-85, 91-92
American Educational Theater Association, 36
American Gilbert & Sullivan Presentations, Inc., 419
American Musical Theater Club, 40
American National Theater and Academy, see ANTA
American P.E.N., 36
American Place Theater, The, 31-32, 425, 430, 433, 435-436, 454
American Revival Company, 429
American Savoyards, 28, 30, 34, 419-420
American Shakespeare Festival (Stratford, Conn.), 43, 92, 94-95
Ammon, Clifford, 89
Amorous Flea, The, 43, 50, 56, 75, 77
Amram, David, 95, 97
Anania, John, 384
Anatol, 81
Andersen, Duane, 74
Anderson, Arthur, 436
Anderson, Betty, 72
Anderson, Buck, 429
Anderson, David, 94
Anderson, Douglas, 394
Anderson, Eunice, 396
Anderson, Evelyne, 80
Anderson, George, 79
Anderson, Hugh, 470
Anderson, Jonathan, 414
Anderson, Judith, 56, 57
Anderson, Leta, 440
Anderson, Maxwell, 34, 429
Anderson, Robert, 72, 457
Anderson-Broecking, Arden, 420
Andre, Frank, 436
Andreu, Helen, 420
Andrews, Harry, 112
Andrews, Kip, 388
Androcles and the Lion, 86
Androsky, Carol, 88
Angelo, Dom, 403
Angelo, Don, 393

472

Angels Company, Theater 40 (Los Angeles, Calif.), 56-57
Anger, Al, 469
Anglin, Florence, 371
Anna Christie, 55
Annals, Michael, 9, 25, 382
Anne of Green Gables, 443
Annie Get Your Gun, 4, 28, 51, **413-414**
Anniversary, The, 110
Anouilh, Jean, 43, 60, 72, 73, 76, 80, 84, 89, 113
Ansara, Alan, 96
Anspach, Susan, 433, 442
ANTA (American National Theater and Academy), vii, 35, 36, 44
ANTA Award, 454
ANTA Washington Square Theater, 14, 25, 26
ANTA Matinee Theater Series, 436
Anthony, Joseph, 94, 370, 389, 403
Antigone, 65, 76, 84
Antonio, James, 96
Antony and Cleopatra, 80, 117
Any Wednesday, 112, 365, 439
Anya, 4, 5, 20, 25, **387-388**, 456, 458
Anzell, Hy, 428
APA—Phoenix, see Association of Producing Artists at the Phoenix
Apex Productions, 416
Aplin, Emma H., 471
Aplon, Boris, 388
Apollo of Bellac, The, 84
Applebaum, Louis, 93
Apstein, Theodore, 444
Aranson, Jack, 66
Arashi, Clifford, 445
Archambault, 73
Archer, Jeri, 437
Archer, William, 72, 78
Ardele, 72
Arden, Jane, 112
Arden, John, 33, 64, 110, 112, 416, 431-432
Ardouin, Jacques, 116
Ardrey, Molly, 394
Arena House (Harrisburg, Pa.), 43, 78
Arena Stage (Washington, D.C.), 42, 43, 63, 67-68
Argent, Maurice, 86
Aristedes, John, 386
Aristophanes, 118
Arizona Repertory Theater (Phoenix), 36
Arkin, Alan, 41
Arkin, David, 430
Armbruster, Richard, 366
Armistead, Horace, 372

Armondos, George, 469
Arms and the Man, 436
Armstrong, Gordon E., 470
Armstrong, Ron, 420
Armstrong, Will Steven, 14, 20, 22, 25, 94, 394, 400, 401, 404
Armstrong's Last Goodnight, 109, 110
Arnaud, François, 117
Arnaut, John, 469
Arndt, Jürgen, 407
Arnell, France, 392
Arnold, Diane, 408
Arnold, James, 96
Arnold, Victor, 394
Aronson, Alvin, 428
Arostegui, Diana, 97
Aronstein, Martin, 89, 95, 97, 376, 381, 382, 390, 399
Arquette, Michael, 374
Arrabel, Fernando, 118
Arrah-Na-Pogue, 85
Arrick, Larry, 434
Arsenic and Old Lace, 40, 112
Arthur, Beatrice, 18, 25, 412, 454, 455, 456
Arthur, Carol, 74, 428
Arthur, Louise, 83
Arthur, Michele, 437
Arthur, Sherwood, 428
Arthur, Sumner, 75, 78
Arzoomanian, Ralph S., 431
As You Like It, 59, 91, 111
Ashley, Elizabeth, 439
Ashley, Richard, 444
Ashworth, Susan, 111
Ask, Eli, 435
Askey, Darrel, 388
Asprey, Laurie, 101
Assassins Associés, Les, 116
Assini, Chris, 436
Association of Producing Artists at the Phoenix (APA-Phoenix), 13, 24, 27-29, 36, 40, 42, 43, 60, 71, 91, 415
Astin, John, 55
Astredo, Allen, 436
Astredo, Humbert Alan, 96
Atienza, Edward, 111, 410
Atkins, Eileen, 110
Atkins, Norman, 408
Atkinson, Clinton, 70-71
Atkinson, David, 417
Atkinson, Sarah, 401
Atlee, Howard, 394, 416, 417, 421, 423, 426, 430, 431
Attaway, Ruth, 379, 380, 381
Auberjonois, Rene, 71-72, 84, 85
Aubrey, Larry, 94
Aubrey, Michael, 423
Audiberti, Jacques, 115
Auerbach, S. Leonard, 84, 399-400

Aukerlund, Albin, 70-71
Aumont, Jean Pierre, 55, 444
Aurelia, Vincent, 94
Ausisi, Joseph, 385
Austin, Karen, 75
Austin, Lyn, 394, 431
Austin, Paul John, 430
Avery, Brian, 411
Avila, Doria, 408
Axler, George, 433, 436
Ayers, Ken, 367, 384
Ayers, Lemuel, 393, 368
Ayres, Mitchell, 418
Azenberg, Emanuel, 21, 400
Aznavour, Charles, 24, 377
Azova, Ludmilla, 371

Babbs, Donna, 371
Babcock, Jeannean, 85
Babel, Isaac, 33, 435
Baby Talk, 443
Baca, Bob, 50, 77
Bacall, Lauren, 12, 390
Baccala, Donna, 376
Backman, George, 79
Bacon, Karen, 70
Bacon, Rod, 436
Baddeley, Hermione, 55
Badel, Alan, 109, 112
Badel, Sarah, 378, 455
Baffa, Diana, 392, 412
Bagley, Ben, 66, 415-416, 428
Bailey, Bill, 469
Baillie, Lucille, 70-71
Bain, Conrad, 425, 437
Baines, Robert, 403
Baio, Joey, 370
Baird, Bobbi, 413
Baird, Claribel, 71, 387, 455
Bajour, 365
Baker, Anne, 383
Baker, Carroll, 55-56
Baker, David, 391
Baker, Henry, 368
Baker, Jim, 99
Baker, Joyce, 391
Baker, Keith, 96
Baker, Paul, 50, 76
Baker, Russell, 89
Baker, Ruth, 393
Baker Street, 457
Baker, Terri, 367
Baker, Word, 445
Balch, Marston Stevens, 454
Balcony, 78
Baldauff, Patrick, 434
Balding, Ivor David, 428, 445
Baldwin, James, 56, 366
Ball, Samuel, 87
Ball, William, 36, 42, 65, 71, 84, 91-92
Ballad of the Sad Cafe, 76, 80
Ballantyne, Paul, 81
Ballas, Dianna, 425
Ballew, Ryan, 74

Balm in Gilead and Other Plays, 457
Bamberger, David, 420
Banbury, Frith, 23, 378
Bancroft, Anne, 6, 23, 45, 385
Banke, Richard, 368
Banks, Diana, 368, 413
Banner, Blythe, 74
Bannerman, Guy, 94
Baragrey, John, 385
Baragwanath, John G., 470
Barbat, Percy D., 469
Barbour, Thomas, 432
Barcroft, Judith, 383
Bardi, Angelo, 116
Barefoot in the Park, 5, 16, 72, 102, 112, 365, 439
Barend, Robert, 399
Barer, Marshall, 403, 428
Barillet, Pierre, 12
Barker, Jean, 83
Barker, Katharine, 100
Barker, Margaret T., 429
Barlett, John, 72
Barnes, Katherine, 418
Barnes, Paul, 423
Barnett, Art, 408
Barnett, Barbara, 111
Barney, Jay, 421, 428
Barnhill, James O., 85
Baron, Andrew J., 96
Baron, Sandy, 374
Barr, Richard, 394
Barra, Vanda, 431
Barrard, John, 110
Barrault, Jean-Louis, 115, 421
Barrere, Jean, 386, 410
Barrett, John, 89
Barrett, Laurinda, 394
Barrett, Nancy, 373
Barrett, Nora Cunneen, 469
Barrie, Amanda, 112
Barrie, Barbara, 85, 403
Barrie, Sir James M., 77
Barrie, Richard, 422
Barriscale, Bessie, 469
Barrs, Norman, 384, 398
Barry, Michelle, 405
Barry, Philip, 437
Barry, Rodd, 390, 410
Barry, Roy, 390
Barry, Thomas, 368
Barsacq, André, 114, 117
Barshay, Don, 73
Bart, Lionel, 111
Bartel, Christine, 436
Bartenieff, George, 63, 417, 445
Barter Theater (Abingdon, Va.), 70-71
Bartlett, Peter, 75, 76
Barto, Jeri, 375
Barton, Donald, 409
Barton, John, 99
Barton, Reyner, 469

Bartrop, Sybil, 392
Bas Fonds de la Société, Les, 115
Baseleon, Michael, 437, 445
Basic, Jack, 436
Bass, Emory, 409
Bassett, William, 433
Bastug, Timothy, 75
Bastaille, Nicolas, 115
Batch, James, 437
Batchelder, William H., 378, 410
Bate, Tom, 409
Bates, Alan, 111
Bates, Michael, 113
Bates, Ronald, 403
Bateson, Timothy, 110
Baton, Pierre, 115
Battis, Emery, 85
Battle, Robert C., 469
Battles, Marjorie, 390
Battreall, Tommy, 370
Baum, Harry, 426
Bavan, Yolande, 430
Bavarian State Theater, 4, 28, 406-407
Baxley, Barbara, 49, 85
Baxter, Cash, 424
Baxter, Jane, 112
Baxter, Keith, 112
Bay, Howard, 15, 25, 367, 386, 454, 455, 456
Bayer, Frank, 379, 380, 381
Bayliss, Peter, 112
Beach, Albert A., 383
Bean, Orson, 441
Beattie, Herbert, 371
Beatty, Ned, 80
Beaumont, Ralph, 391, 409
Beautiful Day, A., 452
Beaux' Stratagem, The, 437
Becher, John C., 412, 421
Beck, Barbara, 367, 384
Beck, Marilyn, 436
Beck, Stanley, 379, 380, 381
Beck, William, 371
Becker, Bruce, 411
Becker, Edward, 408
Becker, Nan Brennan, 469
Becker, Ray, 436
Becket, 80
Beckett, Michael, 399, 445
Beckett, Samuel, 12, 29, 43, 70-71, 72, 80, 416, 417, 420
Beddoe, Don, 368
Bede, Claude, 93
Bedelia, Bonnie, 389
Bedford, Brian, 441
Bedford, Patrick, 398, 454, 456
Beebe, Lucius, 471
Beers, Francine, 431
Berry, Eric, 427
Beery, Lee, 422
Behan, Brendan, 82
Bel Geddes, Barbara, 441
Belack, Doris, 89, 399

Belial, 56
Bell, Jerry, 436
Bell, John, 100
Bell, Marie, 114, 116
Bell, Ralph, 427
Bell, Tom, 111
Bellaver, Harry, 413
Belling, Larry, 382, 384, 400, 428, 434, 435
Bellini, Cal, 382
Bellis, Bob, 419
Bellomo, Joe, 367
Bellon, Loleh, 116
Bellow Plays, The, 112
Bellow, Saul, 63, 84, 86
Bellwood, Peter L., 432
Belmonte, Viki, 393, 413
Ben Avram, Rachmael, 66
Ben Franklin in Paris, 457
Benedict, Paul, 73-74, 416
Benedict, Robert, 94
Benito Cereno, 31
Benjamin, Fred, 418
Benjamin, Richard, 439, 441
Benke, Kathleen, 77
Bennett, Alan, 71, 84
Bennett, Constance, 469
Bennett, David, 419
Bennett, Howard, 383
Bennett, Hywel, 111
Bennett, Jill, 110
Bennett, Lynette, 391
Bennett, Margot, 74
Bennett, Robert Russell, 414
Benrath, Martin, 407
Benson, Esther, 410
Benson, Paul, 422
Benson, Robert, 65, 86, 87, 96, 428
Bentley, Eric, 66, 79, 81, 85, 86, 88, 379, 415, 416
Benton, Robert, 3, 405
Berdeen, Robert, 382
Berg, Cherney, 443
Berg, Lisa, 423
Berg, Richard, 96
Berger, Peter, 82
Bergman, Alan, 379
Bergman, Harry, 376
Bergman, Ingmar, 113
Bergman, Ingrid, 113
Bergquist, Eleanor, 384
Berk, Jo Ann, 74
Berkshire Theater Festival (Stockbridge, Mass.), 43
Berlin, Alexandra, 96, 441
Berlin, Irving, 49, 51, 413
Berliner Ensemble Season, 113
Bernard, Joseph, 374
Bernard, Pierre, 114
Bernard, Robert, 437
Bernardi, Herschel, 399, 440
Bernard Shaw Story, The, 30, 427, 436
Bernay, Lynn, 390
Berney, William, 83

Bernstein, Karl, 383, 396
Bernstein, Stephen, 95
Berreby, Elie-Georges, 115
Berry, John, 400
Bertha and Other Plays, 457
Bertheau, Julien, 115
Bertil, Guy, 392
Bertin, Annie, 114
Bertin, Pierre, 115
Bertin, Roland, 115
Berwick, Arthur, 97
Besoyan, Rick, 82
Best, Richard, 420
Best Laid Plans, The, 4, 22, 64, 405
Bethea, Juanita, 72
Bethencourt, Francis, 378
Betten, Mary, 436
Better Luck Next Time, 429
Betti, Ugo, 33, 416
Bettis, Valerie, 404
Beyond the Fringe, 71, 84
Bianchi, Richard, 422, 430
Biberman, Herbert, 423
Bieber, Ethel, 432
Bier, Burt, 384
Bieri, Ramon, 98
Big Man, 30, 435
Bikel, Theodore, 6, 403
Billy Rose International Festival, 40-41
Billy Rose Theater, 40
Binchy, Kate, 110
Binns, Edward, 75
Birch, Charles, 382
Birch, Paul, 83
Bird, Joseph, 71, 387
Birdbath, 432
Birdwatcher, The, 113
Birney, David, 70
Birney, Jean, 70
Birrell, John, 82
Birthday Message, 457
Birthday Party, The, 43, 48, 50, 67, 72, 77, 89
Biscuit, 30, 435
Bishop, Casey, 56
Bishop, Ronald, 73
Bisoglio, Val, 396
Bissell, Marian, 436
Bissell, Richard, 436
Bits and Pieces, 415
Bittner, Jack, 371
Black, Bill, 373
Black, Karen, 389, 403, 455
Black, Michelle, 70-71
Black Comedy, 110
Blackburn, Bryan, 112
Blackburn, Charles, 85
Blackburn, Clarice, 423, 454
Blackfriars' Guild, The, 437
Blackman, Jack, 383
Blackmer, Sidney, 57
Blackton, Jack, 412, 440
Blackton, Jay, 411
Blair, Richard, 417, 424
Blake, Melvyn, 93

Blakeley, Colin, 112
Blakeley, Clyde W., 85
Blakely, Don, 435
Blanchar, Dominique, 116
Blanchard, Lillian, 469
Blanchard, Scott, 367
Blanco, Pascual, 97
Blankenship, Vicki, 394
Blass, Doris, 72
Blau, Herbert, 6, 26-27, 43-44, 65, 379, 381
Blausen, Whitney, 426
Blaxill, Peter, 70
Bledsoe, Gilbert, 422
Blin, Roger, 421
Blitzstein, Marc, 70
Bloch, Anne, 420
Bloch, Susan, 381
Blocher, Walter, 370
Block, Lawrence, 95
Block, Richard, 80
Bloecher, Ted, 370
Blood Knot, The, 43, 75
Bloom, Claire, 113
Bloom, Lee, 375
Bloom, Leo, 375
Bloom, Philip, 425
Bloomer Girl, 458
Bloomgarden, Kermit, 367, 389
Blossom, Roberts, 85
Blount, Helen, 78
Blue, Andy, 435
Blue, Dan, 422
Blues For Mister Charlie, 56
Blumenfeld, Norman, 427
Bly, Dan, 399
Bly, Norman, 445
Blyden, Larry, 441
Blyth, Ann, 51
Blythe, Peter, 111
Boccio, Michael, 428
Bock, Jerry, 365, 374
Bogan, Flair, 85
Bogert, William, 96
Bogin, Abba, 393, 409
Bohikee Creek, 30, *434-435*
Boland, Gene, 396
Boland, Joseph, 398
Boland, Mary, 469
Bolin, Shannon, 383
Bolt, Robert, 60, 74, 111, 457
Bolton, Guy, 387
Bolton, Whitney, 452
Bond, Edward, 110
Bond, Raleigh, 437
Bond, Sudie, 376
Bonem, Linda, 408
Bongiovanni, Guy, 70, 71, 432
Boni, John A., 408, 439
Bonus, Ben, 438
Bonne, Hal, 443
Bonnell, Donn, 418
Bonnell, Jay, 436

Bockvor, Steven, 388, 411, 418
Booke, Sorrell, 430
Bone, Frank, 434
Booth, Carol, 441
Booth, James, 111
Booth, Shirley, 57
Bordoff, Trudy, 394
Bormann, James, 437
Bosco, Philip, 94
Bosley, Tom, 441
Bostick, Carol B., 367
Boston, Ronald, 383
Boston University, 43
Botham, Richard, 385
Boucicault, Dion, 85
Boudoin, Dick, 72
Bouillette, Christian, 115
Bouley, Frank, 390
Boulton, Milo, 367, 440
Bouquet, Michel, 117
Bouquinistes, Les, 115
Bourdet, Edouard, 116
Bourdet, Micheline, 114, 116
Bourneuf, Philip, 79
Bousard, Joe, 78
Bova, Joseph, 96
Bovasso, Julie, 374
Bowab, John, 395
Bowan, Sibyl, 367
Bowden, Charles, 399
Bowen, Kenneth, 420
Bowman, John J. (Barney), 471
Bowman, Ross, 377
Bowmer, Angus L., 99
Box & Cox, 85
Boy Friend, The, 117, *436*
Boyd, Harold, 469
Boyd, Thomas, 424
Boyer, M. J., 419
Boyll, Lawrence, 388
Boyt, John, 74, 381
Bozinoff, Lillian, 375, 408
Bozzoni, Max, 115
Bracken, Eddie, 441
Bradbury, Ray, 32, 421
Braden, John, 85
Bradley, Brown, 393
Bradley, Maria, 393, 408
Bradley, Stewart, 74, 421
Bradshaw, Robert T., Jr., 400
Brady, Leo, 67
Brainard, Ella-Mae, 50, 77
Brand, Robert, 99
Brandeis Creative Arts Award, 454
Brandeis University, 48
Brandon, Billy, 370
Brassard, Fran, 435
Brasseur, Pierre, 116
Braswell, Charles, 390, 412
Braun, Martha, 75, 76
Braun, Carin, 407
Break-Up, 33
Brecher, Ellen, 85, 86
Brecher, Stuart, 86

Brecht, Bertolt, 46, 49, 66, 70, 73, 75, 81, 82, 85, 86, 87, 88, 113, 379, 415, 416
Breffort, Alexandre, 74
Brennan, Tom, 81
Brenner, Maurice, 374
Bresslaw, Bernard, 111
Breslin, Herbert, 386
Breuler, Robert, 99
Brewer, Sandra, 411
Brialy, Jean-Claude, 116
Briant, Roger, 411
Bricusse, Leslie, 78, 366, 372
Bridge-Adams, William, 470
Bridges, Beau, 400
Brigel, Stockton, 424
Briggs, Joel, 86
Brink, Robert, 420
Brinckerhoff, Burt, 390, 455, 456
Brisson, Frederick, 374
Britton, Barbara, 390
Britton, Ethel, 405
Britton, Jacqueline, 428
Britton, Jeff G., 419, 432
Broderick, James, 429
Broderson, Margaret, 418
Bromberg, Conrad, 89
Brook, Peter, 11, 25, 92, 393, 454, 455, 456
Brooke, Tom, 371
Brookes, Jacqueline, 85, 98, 422, 436
Brooks, Lawrence, 388
Brooks, Randall, 382
Brookwalter, DeVeren, 94
Brosset, Colette, 392
Brotherton, Joe, 86, 87
Broun, Heywood Hale, 383
Browder, Clifford, 443
Brower, Jay, 89
Brown, Arvin, 83
Brown, Elizabeth, 436
Brown, Foreman, 443
Brown, Georgia, 441
Brown, Graham, 81
Brown, Irene, 469
Brown, Joe, 111
Brown, Keith, 75
Brown, Kermit, Jr., 430
Brown, Lewis, 81
Brown, Linda, 79
Brown, Murray, 101
Brown, R. G., 417, 424
Brown, Robert, 79
Brown, Roger Alan, 393
Browne, Roscoe Lee, 75
Brown, Slade, 376, 423
Brown, Ted, 80
Brown, Walter P., 367, 384
Browne, Coral, 378
Browne, Lori, 405
Browne, Roscoe Lee, 379
Browne, Tad, 76
Browning, Susan, 79
Brubaker, Edward S., 98, 99
Bruce, Allan, 424

Bruce, Judy, 441
Brüdern, Gerd, 407
Bruneau, Philippe, 115
Brunjes, Hank, 399
Bruno, Eric, 385
Bruno, Michael, 396
Bruno, Pierette, 116
Brunsma, Donna, 82
Brush, Malcolm, 72
Bruckin, Perry, 390
Brustein, Robert, 37, 40, 43, 60, 452
Bruton, Mailie, 71
Bryan, Buddy, 368
Bryan, Dora, 440
Bryant, Ben, 403
Bryant, Mary, 383, 388, 406
Brydon, W. B., 432
Bryggman, Larry, 73
Buchanan, Jane, 434
Buchanan, Pilar, 97
Bucher, Doris, 72
Büchner (Buechner), Georg, 28, 378, 406-407
Buchner, Pamela, 101
Buchtrup, Bjarne, 413
Buecher, Nephele, 408
Bufman, Zev, 374
Bugbee, Geneva, 94
Bugs, 30, *426*
Buka, Donald, 439
Bull, Peter, 373
Bullard, Gene, 371
Bulos, Yusef, 420
Bumb, Frank E., Jr., 86
Bundy, Martha, 445
Bunker, Ralph, 469
Bunraku, 4, 28, *403*
Bunt, George, 405
Burden, Laverne, 410, 432
Burdick, William, 94
Burge, Stuart, 93, 432
Burgess, Robert, 96
Burgher, Fairfax, 469
Burial Committee, The, *437*
Burke, Alfred, 113
Burke, Brendan, 73
Burke, Georgia, 435
Burks, Charles, 424
Burland, Bob, 392
Burlingame, Lloyd, 378, 389
Burn, Jonathan, 393
Burnett, Carol, 50
Burnett, Connie, 408
Burns, Barry, 382
Burns, David, 440
Burns, Ralph, 395
Burns, Reese, 370, 408
Burr, Donald, 384
Burr, Robert, 96, 382
Burr, Ross, 427, 428
Burrows, Abe, 3, 12, 64, 80, 245, 390, 436
Burrows, Thomas, 432
Burrows, Vinnie, 436
Burrus, Bob, 77
Burton, Clyde, 382

Burton, Donald, 100
Bury, John, 99, 110
Bush, Geoffrey, 47, 73, 74
Bush, Ronald, 420
Bushnell, Scott, 72
Bushnell, William, 43, 44
Butler, Ann Marie, 73
Butler, Thomas J., 73
Butterfly Dream, The, 30, 33, *435*
Butz, Fritz, 429
Buzzi, Ruth, 395, 417
Bye Bye Birdie, 51
Byers, Jack A., 99
Byers, Ruth, 77
Byrne, Gaylea, 367
Byrne, Patsy, 100
Byrnes, Burke, 72, 96
Byrnes, Maureen, 392
Byrd, Ann Gee, 85, 436
Byrd, David, 85
Byrs, Henry, 377

Caballero, Shirley, 424
Caesar, Adolph, 426
Cache-Cache, 116
Cacoyannis, Michael, 23, 34, 420
Cactus Flower, 3, 4, 6, 7, 12, 14, 22, 24, 37, 64, 68, 245-268, *390*, 456
Caesar and Cleopatra, 72
Caffe Cino, 34
Cafe La Mama, 32, 34
Cage, Ruth, 375, 401, 432
Cage, The, 87
Cahill, James, 70
Cain, William, 86
Calbes, Eleanor A., 367
Calderón, Pedro, 118
Caldwell, Zoe, 81, 399, 455, 456
Calèche, La, 116
Calfa, Don, 383
Cali, Joseph, 394
California Arts Commission, 56
Call, Edward Payson, 72, 81
Call, John, 373, 411
Call Me Madam, 57
Callahan, Emmett, 469
Callahan, Kristina, 81
Callahan, Lee, 407
Callan, William, 394
Callinan, Richard, 393
Calvert, Henry, 433
Calvi, Gerard, 391
Calvin, Henry, 368
CAM Productions, 426
Cameron, Madge, 403, 404
Camp, Duane, 376
Camp, Hamilton, 377
Campano, Janet, 390
Campbell, Benedict, 94
Campbell, Douglas, 43, 59, 81, 93
Campbell, John, 419

Campbell, Judy, 112
Campbell, Norman, 443
Campbell, Patton, 15, 25, 386, 401, 424, 455, 456
Camus, Albert, 116
Canadian Shakespeare Festival (Stratford, Ontario), 93-94
Cancilla, Elaine, 395
Candida, 72, 85
Candide, 418
Canning, Heather, 393
Cannon, Alice, 75, 440
Cannon, Glenn, 88
Cannon, J. D., 383
Cantor, Arthur, 33, 40-41, 386, 392, 421, 422, 427, 434
Canvin, Rue, vii
Capodilupo, Tony, 382
Capone, Clifford, 427
Cappelletti, John, 81
Capshow, Gary, 87
Captain Fantastic Meets the Ectomorph, 437
Card, Bonnie Gene, 367
Carey, Mary, 470
Cargill, Patrick, 111
Carle, Robert, 411
Carlin, Thomas, 436
Carlo, Don, 371
Carlson, Les, 99
Carlton, Rex, 444
Carmichael, Ian, 111
Carnegie Tech, 42, 43, 65
Carney, Art, 441
Carney, Grace, 398
Carnovsky, Morris, 48, 49, 75, 94
Caron, Sandra, 434
Carousel, 4, 28, 64, 368-369, 458
Carow, Joseph, 367
Carpenter, Dennis, 420
Carpenter, John, 71, 94, 379, 381
Carr, Eddie, 418
Carr, Kenneth, 376
Carr, Lawrence, 412, 456
Carr, Susan, 385
Carradine, David, 9, 25, 382, 455
Carreire, Victor, 469
Carrington, Frank, 421
Carrol, Rhoda B., 70
Carroll, Beeson, 96
Carroll, Chrysten, 413
Carroll, Helena, 373
Carroll, Marie, 89
Carroll, Nancy, 469
Carroll, Ronn, 80, 413
Carron, Elizabeth, 371
Carson, Tom, 80
Carson, Trudy, 384
Carson, Wayne, 374
Carter, Dixie, 368
Carter, Henry, 77

Cartier, Deidre, 381
Cartier, Jacques, 78
Cartt, Susan, 373
Caruso, Barbara, 71, 85
Caruso, Sal, 416
Carved in Snow, 75
Cary, Christopher, 79
Casadesus, Mathilde, 469
Casarès, Maria, 114, 115
Cascio, Gigi, 400
Casey, Kenneth, 470
Cash, Rosalind, 394
Casile, Geneviève, 116, 397
Casler, Richard, 388
Cason, Barbara, 88
Cass, Lee, 408, 423
Cass, Leslie, 82, 83
Cassel, Jean-Pierre, 114
Cassidy, Frank, 74, 416
Cassidy, Jack, 18, 405, 456
Cassidy, Martin, 89
Casson, Lewis, 112
Castang, Veronica, 421
Castel, Nico, 371
Castellano, Richard, 442
Castle, John, 112
Castle, Roy, 373, 456
Cat on a Hot Tin Roof, 78
Catanzaro, Tony, 413
Catch Me If You Can, 366
Cathleen Ni Houlihan, 74
Catholic University Theater (Washington, D.C.), 67
Cattand, Gabriel, 114, 117, 118
Cau, Jean, 114
Caubisens, Henri, 404
Caucasian Chalk Circle, The, 4, 26, 27, 58, 81, 379, 451, 457
Causey, Sara Beth, 80
Cavern, The, 113
Cavey, George, 435
Caviar and Lentils, 117
Ce Soir À Samarcande, 116
Cecil, Henry, 111
Center Stage (Baltimore, Md.), 36, 43, 72
Cerasani, Dick, 420
Césaire, Aimé, 117
Chabeau, Ray, 384
Chabert, Pierre, 118
Chadwick, Tom, 72
Chagrin, Claude, 382
Chaikin, Joseph, 437
Chairs, The, 88
Chall, Steven, 381
Challenger, Rudy, 377
Challis, Ciya, 388
Challis, John, 101
Chamber Music, 64
Champion, Gower, 401
Chandler, Dorothy Buffum, 454
Chandler, Pat, 377
Chaney, David, 412
Changeling, The, 26, 117

Channing, Carol, 39, 48, 440
Chant Public Devant Deux Chaises Electriques, 114
Chapelle, Pola, 384
Chapin, Brian, 373
Chaplin, Sydney, 440
Chapman, Donald, 420
Chapman, John, 38, 451
Chapman, William, 371
Chappell, Fred, 72
Charba, Mari-Claire, 433, 454
Charisse, Rita, 392
Charlap, Mark, 77
Charles, Keith, 439
Charles, Marilyn, 384
Charles, Paul, 382
Charles Playhouse (Boston, Mass.), 36, 42, 46-47, 48, 73
Charles, Robert, 437
Charlie Girl, 111
Charlip, Remy, 431
Charney, Jordan, 399
Charny, Suzanne, 395
Charon, Jacques, 114, 397, 398
Chase, Ilka, 439
Chase, Jerry, 70-71
Chase, Sallie Marshall, 469
Chasman, Tanya, 376
Chastain, Don, 405
Chaste Maid at Cheapside, A, 112
Chaumette, François, 397
Chazel, Mireille, 392
Chekhov, Anton, 23, 63, 76, 83, 84, 87, 89, 93-94, 410
Cherry Lane Theater, 35
Cherry Orchard, The, 52, 58, 81, 93-94, 117
Chevalier, Kay, 420
Chew, Virgilia, 429
Cheyne, Peter, 94
Chianese, Dominic, 370, 429
Chicago, 433
Childress, Yolanda, 416
Childs, Donald, 86, 87
Chinese Wall, The, 72
Chodorov, Jerome, 3, 22, 365, 401
Chretien, Betty, 367
Chris, Marilyn, 74, 445
Christensen, Catherine, 371
Christian, David, 85
Christian, Kurt, 382
Christie, Agatha, 436
Christie, Helen, 410
Christmas, Eric, 93
Christy, Eileen, 368
Church, John, 382
Church, Peter, 79
Church, Tony, 100
Cicciarelli, Edward, 379, 380, 381
Ciceri, Leo, 74, 93
Cid, Le, 4, 28, 397-398

Cilento, Diane, 111
Cimino, Leonardo, 379, 381
Cioffi, Charles, 75, 81
Circle, The, 111
Circle-in-the-Square, 34, 420, 433
Cisney, Marcella, 422
City and a Painting on Wood, The, 113
City Theater (San Francisco, Calif.), 66
Claire, Ludi, 85, 400
Clarence Derwent Awards, 454
Claridge, Jessica, 101
Clark, Bryan E., 79-80
Clark, Elsie, 469
Clark, Fred, 439
Clark, Gordon, 85, 401
Clark, Harry, 385
Clark, John, 398, 399
Clark, Marc, 80
Clark, Oliver, 379, 381
Clark, Peggy, 367, 393, 405, 408, 409, 410
Clark, Peter, 393, 418
Clark, Philip, 439
Clark, Sterling, 411
Clarke, Gordon B., 390
Clary, Ray, 87, 88
Clausen, Howard, 83
Clavel, Maurice, 115
Clements, Florence Ryerson, 470
Clements, L. D., 371
Clements, Neva West, 469
Clermont, Elia, 115
Cleveland Play House, 36, 76
Clift, Jeanette, 79
Cliff, C. Morton, 85
Clogg, Hallye, 469
Cluchey, Rick, 87
Cludel, Paul, 114
Clugstone, John, 408
Clurman, Harold, 400
Coates, Carolyn, 379, 381, 420
Coburn, James, 53
Cochran, Steve, 469
Cocktail Party, The, 43, 49, 74, 80
Coco, James, 385
Coe, Fred, 383, 396
Coe, George, 412
Coe, John A., 75, 430
Coe, Peter, 370, 373
Coffey, Bud, 383
Coffey, Denise, 111
Coffey, Gordon, 87, 88
Cogan, Susan, 408
Cohan, George M., 72, 80
Cohen, Alexander H., 23, 45, 385, 410
Cohen, Alvin, 427
Cohen, James Adrian, 430
Cohen, Michael, 424
Cohen, Robert P., 422

Cohen, Steven, 71-72, 84
Colby, Barbara, 385
Colby, Ethel, 451, 454
Coldiron, Robert, 407
Cole, Charlotte, 76, 77
Cole, Dennis, 410
Cole, Elizabeth, 381
Cole, George, 111
Cole, Jack, 15, 25, 386, 456
Cole, Kay, 403, 408
Cole, Marta, 77
Cole, Maurice, 469
Cole, Olivia, 95
Cole Porter Theater (Los Angeles, Calif.), 40, 57
Coleman, Cy, 395, 455, 456
Coleman, Frank, 368
Coleman, Jane, 408, 410
Coleman, Janet, 431
Coleman, Shelia, 420
Coleridge, Sylvia, 113
Colicos, John, 33, 385, 432
Collard, Jack, 80
Collazo, Ruben, 436
Collection, The, 72, 89, 117
Collier, Ronald, 421
Collinge, Roberta, 416
Collins, Ann, 97
Collins, Bill, 420
Collins, Blanche, 377
Collins, Dorothy, 51
Collins, Paul, 374, 382
Collins, Ray, 469
Collins, Russell, 75
Collum, Richard, 436
Collyer, Eve, 378
Colombo, Pia, 114
Colonna, Robert J., 81, 98
Colorado, Hortensia, 437
Colson, C. David, 87
Colston, Robert, 422
Colton, Jacque Linn, 433
Colyer, Austin, 367, 408, 410
Combs, Frederick, 441
Comden, Betty, 77, 436
Come Back, Little Sheba, 57, 436
Come Live With Me, 443
Come Spy With Me, 112
Comédie Française, The, 4, 28, 68, 397-398
Comedy of Errors, The, 99-100
Comellas, Josine, 115
Comer, Bruce J., 437
Comic Illusion, The, 114, 116
Committee, The, 66
Competello, Tom, 423
Complete Plays of D. H. Lawrence, The, 457
Conaway, Charles, 404
Conchon, Georges, 115
Condell, Bruce, 101
Condemned of Altona, The, 4, 26, 27, 116, 379, 451
Condos, Dimo, 95

Conforti, Donna, 413
Conforti, Gino, 386, 440
Congdon, James, 396
Congreve, William, 81, 83
Conklin, Cathy, 393, 410
Conklin, John, 78
Connes, Keith, 417, 418
Connell, Jane, 18, 375, 412
Connolly, Thomas, 398
Connor, Jim, 373
Conolly, Patricia, 71, 387
Conrad, Barbara Smith, 381
Conrad, Joel, 403, 404
Conradt, Mark, 424
Conried, Hans, 439
Consider the Lilies, 437
Consul, The, 4, 28, 57, 371, 372
Conte, Henriette, 114
Conte, Louise, 116
Conte, Roseanne, 427
Conversation At Midnight, 53
Converse, Frank, 400
Convy, Bert, 376, 439
Conway, Kevin Bryan, 436
Conway, Norbert, 471
Cool, Walter, 437
Cook, Allen D., 82, 83
Cook, Barbara, 439
Cook, Gordon, 410
Cook, John, 93
Cook, Peter, 71, 84
Cooke, Richard, 451, 454
Cooke, Sally, 370, 429
Cookson, Peter, 378, 456
Cooney, Dennis, 400
Cooney, Ray, 111
Coop, The, 30, 431
Cooper, Anthony Kemble, 398
Cooper, Maury, 96
Cooper, Melville, 22, 398
Cooper, Peggy, 367
Coopersmith, Jerome, 366, 457
Cooperstein, Nancy, 436
Copains-Clopant, 115
Cope, Patricia, 408
Coppola, Anton, 367, 408
Coppola, Frank, 408
Coppola, William, 373
Copeland, William, 420
Copeland, Maurice, 75
Copelan, Shelia, 469
Coralian, Richard, 78
Corbett, Carol, 437
Corbett, Gretchen, 99
Corbin, Al, 428
Corbin, Clayton, 382
Corby, Joseph, 393
Corder, Paul, 371
Cordon, Michael, 376
Corigliano, John, 82
Corio, Ann, 366
Coriolanus, 30, 85, 92, 94-95, 96, 98, 417

Corneille, Pierre, 28, 116
Cornell University, 43
Coronet Theater (Los Angeles, Calif.), 56
Corrigan, Charles, 469
Corrigan, Elizabeth S., 381
Corrigan, Robert, 43
Corvin, John, 100
Coryell, Esther Jane, 383
Corzatte, Clayton, 71, 387
Cosenza, Tony, 420
Coslow, Jackie, 98
Coslow, Jacqueline, 95
Cosmonaute Agricole, Le, 115
Cosmos, Jean, 115
Costanza, Peter, 373
Costello, Mariclare, 75, 379, 380
Coster, Claudine, 116
Costigan, Ken, 79
Cotsworth, Staats, 96, 378
Couloumbis, Akila, 437
Coulouris, George, 379
Counsell, Marise, 370
Country Wife, The, 4, 27, 378, 379
Countryman, William, 416
Coupe, Diane, 392, 412
Courtois, Reine, 115
Coward, Noel, 43, 70, 72, 79, 83, 110
Cowl, Darry, 117
Cowles, Carolyn, 70
Cowles, Jack, 70-71
Cowles, Margaret, 82, 83, 89
Cowles, Matthew, 394
Cox, William, 74
Cozine, Ruthanne, 77
Crabtree, Don, 403
Crabtree, Paul, 444
Craig, Helen, 427
Craig, Wendy, 110
Crampton-Smith, Howard, 78
Crane, Dean, 393
Crane, Tom, 425
Crawford, Christina, 439
Crawford, Michael, 110
Crean, Patrick, 93
Creed, Kay, 371
Creep Past the Mountain Lion, 50, 77
Creeper, The, 111
Cregan, David, 111
Crehan, Joseph, 469
Creighton, Anthony, 118
Creighton, Georgia, 384
Crémieux, Henri, 118
Cremonini, Robert, 95
Cresta Run, The, 111
Crichton, Kyle, 70
Criscuolo, Louis, 432
Criss, Louis, 73
Crist, Judith, 452, 456
Critic, The, 63
Crockett, Otway, 437
Crofoot, Alan, 370, 399

Croft, Paddy, 75
Cromwell, James, 72
Cromwell, John, 81
Cronin, Jane, 383, 423
Cronyn, Hume, 57, 81
Crook, Mervin, 403
Crosley, Chase, 96
Cross, And the Sword, The, 443
Cross, Beverley, 366
Crosson, Joanna, 367, 393, 408
Croswell, Anne, 89
Crouse, Russel, 470
Crouzet, Roger, 118
Crowe, Gillian, 434
Crowley, Ed, 443
Crowther, John, 79, 400
Croydon, Joan, 85
Crucible, The, 85
Cruikshank, Andrew, 111
Crumpler, Suzanne, 367
Cryer, David, 85, 439
Cueto, Mario, R., 97
Cuka, Frances, 111, 112
Culjak, John, 428
Cullum, John, 377, 455, 456
Culman, Peter W., 70
Culmer, Lee, 469
Cultural Foundation of Boston, Inc., 48
Culver, Robin, 101
Culver, Roland, 410, 455, 456
Cumming, Patricia, 74
Cumming, Richard, 80, 81
Cummings, Elizabeth C., 70
Cummings, Pat, 412
Cummings, Robert, 6, 394
Cunard, Lance, 97, 430
Cunningham, John, 95, 439
Cunningham, Sarah, 383
Cunningham, Sean, 409
Cunningham, Zamah, 374
Curley, George, 417, 424
Curnock, Richard, 111
Currier, Terrence, 73
Curtis, Ann, 99
Curtis, Donna, 83, 420
Curtis, Keene, 71, 387
Curtis, Myron, 410
Cusack, Philip, 401
Cushing, Peter, 111
Cushman, Nancy, 384, 385
Cutell, Lou, 408
Cuthbertson, Ian, 109, 112
Cutts, Patricia, 79
Cypher, Jon, 386

Dabdoub, Jack, 388, 413, 414
Dabney, Augusta, 389
Dacqmine, Jacques, 117
DAFS, Inc., 421
Daguenet, André, 115
Dailey, Dan, 441
Dailey, Irene, 429, 441, 454
Daine, Lois, 389

Dallas Theater Center, 36, 42, 43, 49-51
Dalrymple, Jean, 386, 392, 407, 408
Dalsass, Joanne, 437
Dalton, Gerald, 393
Dalton, Kathie, 418
Daly, James, 74
Damaska, David, 419
D'Ambrosia, Angela, 78
Dame de Chez Maxim's, La, 116
Damien, Madeleine, 117
Damon, Catherine, 394
Damon, William, 89
Dana, Barbara, 400
Dance of Death, The, 59
Dandry, Evelyne, 116
Dandy Dick, 111
Daniel, Chuck, 387
Daniel, Tamara, 420
Daniels, Carolan, 390, 431
Daniels, Danny, 414
Daniels, Edgar, 398
Daniels, William, 377
D'Anjou, Richard, 421
Danner, Blythe, 73, 74
Dant, Edward J., 84
Danton's Death, 4, 25, 26, 378, 379
Doctors of Philosophy, 457
D'Apolito, Alfred, 471
Darbyshire, Michael, 373
D'Arcy, Sophia, 70
Dare, Danny, 57
Darian, Anita, 371
Darion, Joe, 15, 25, 195, 386, 455, 456
Darling, Sandra, 420
Dark Fire, 436
Dark of the Moon, 83
D'Arms, Ted, 89
Darrieux, Danielle, 116
Darrow, Henry, 83
Darwen, Timothy, 101
Dash, Thomas P., 452
Da Silva, Howard, 22, 49, 383
Daugherty, Ed, 435
Dauphin, Claude, 116
Davenport, Pembroke, 393, 410
David, Clifford, 377
David, Jeff, 380, 381
David, Lou, 432
David, Thayer, 382
Davidson, Gordon, 45, 54, 79
Davidson, Jeanne Shultz, 88
Davidson, John, 392
Davies, Ann, 373
Davis, Buster, 381
Davis, Carlos E., 97
Davis, Donald, 422
Davis, Edward H., 424
Davis, Geri, 430
Davis, Gwen, 405
Davis, Irving Kaye, 470
Davis, James, 432

Davis, Judith, 77
Davis, Michael, 395
Davis, Ossie, 383, 384
Davis, R. G., 66
Davis, Susan, 53
Davis, Sylvia, 383, 399
Davison, Jack, 75, 367, 412
Davisson, Charles, 429
Davisson, Tim, 94
Davy, René, 116
Dawson, David, 425
Dawson, Gregory, 424
Day, Frankie, 113
Day, Lynda, 385
Day of Absence, 30, 32 425, 451
Day of the Tortoise, The, 117
Days Between, The, 72, 457
Days in the Trees, 114
Deadly Game, The, 30, 34, 430
Dealy, James, 469
Dean, Jacque, 375, 408
DeAnda, Peter, 384
Dearden, Audrey, 413
Death of a Salesman, 80, 84
De Beer, Gerrit, 373
De Benedictis, Richard, 414
De Benning, Burris, 73
Debuskey, Merle, 97, 382, 384, 400, 428, 430, 433, 435
Deckard, Diane, 385
Decker, Lindsey, 454
Decker, Marceline, 386
Decline and Fall of the Entire World as Seen Through the Eyes of Cole Porter, The, 66, 415-416, 458
Dee, Ruby, 95
Defender Productions, 444
De Felice, James, 445
De Georgi, Marc, 115
De Ghelderode, Michel, 82
De Guy, Max, 398
DeHart, Jon, 389
Deiber, Paul-Emile, 397, 430
Dein, Joel, 383
Deirdre of the Sorows, 118
Dekker, Albert, 385
De Koven, Roger, 430
Delacruz, Chester, 428
Delamare, Lise, 397
De la Passardiere, Guy, 403
De Lappe, Gemze, 370, 393
Delerue, Georges, 397
Delfau, André, 397
Dell, Gabriel, 441
Dell, Georgia, 370
Della Sorte, Joseph, 74
Delli, Ceil, 384
Del Medico, Michael, 82
DeLon, Jack, 371, 408
Delorme, Danièle, 116
Deluc, Claire, 114, 115
Delson, Mary, 381

De Madina, Francisco, 97
DeMann, Ronald, 412
DeMarie, David, 423
DeMartino, Leonard, 425
Demas, Alexander, 96
Demas, Carole, 96
Demas, James G., 407
Demented Zarzuela, The, 77
De Mille, Agnes, 393
De Montherlant, Henri, 28
Dempsey, Jerome, 63
Denbeaux, Jacques, 83
Dench, Jeffrey, 100
Dendy, Mike, 50, 76
Denenholz, Reginald, 387, 416, 420, 423, 427
Dengel, Jake, 382
Denham, Reginald, 22, 398
Denner, Charles, 117
Dennis, Alfred, 422
Dennis, Sandy, 439
Dennison, George, 73
Denker, Henry, 444
Dennis, Sandy, 439
Denny, Richard, 408, 410
De Obaldia, René, 115
De Oca, Montes, 408
Deodato, Jo, 80
De Paris, Wilbur, 417
Deputy, The, 41, 45, 49, 54, 79
Derbas, Frank, 413
De Ré, Michael, 116
Derrow, Don, 419
Desailly, Jean, 114, 115
Desimone, B. J., 382
Des Jardins, Lance, 393, 408
Desmond, Johnny, 440
Destailles, Pierre, 116
Destoop, Jacques, 397
Deutscher, Howard, 421
Deutsches Theater, Inc., 406, 429
Deux Anges Sont Venues, 116
Deval, Jacques, 116
Devane, William, 96
De Vecchi, Antony, 386
Devereaux, John Drew, 401
Devil's Disciple, The, 51, 79, 83, 84
Devils, The, 4, 12, 23, 25, 45, 385-386
Devine, George, 110, 470
Devine, Jerry, 75, 77, 443
Devlin, John, 73, 379, 381
Devlin, Joyce, 78
Devlin, Sandra, 417, 424, 432
De Wilde, Frederic, 381, 394, 400
De Windt, Hal, 426
DeWitt, Fay, 66
Dewhurst, Colleen, 74
De Wolfe, Billy, 408
Dexter, Alan, 367
Dexter, John, 9, 382, 455

Dey, James Paul, 112
Dhéran, Bernard, 117
Dhery, Robert, 3, 20, 391
Dial M For Murder, 67
Diary of a Scoundrel, The, 80-81
Di Caprio, Tony, 427
Di Cenzo, George, 74
Dickens, Stafford, 398, 399
Dickerson, Betsy, 395
Diehl, Glenn O., 87, 88
Diener, Joan, 15, 386, 387, 455
Dietz, Eileen, 436
Diffen, Ray, 95, 378
Dillon, Brendan, 79
Dillon, Will, 470
Dilworth, Gordon, 377
Dine, Jim, 87
Divine Farce, 115
DiVito, Joanne, 368, 413
Dixon, Billie, 87
Dixon, MacIntyre, 383, 428
Dixon, Oliver, 96
Dizier, Ron, 435
D'Lugoff, Burton C., 382
Do I hear a Waltz?, 457
Doby, Kathryn, 395
Doctor Glass, 117
Doctor's Dilemma, The, 59
Dodd, Edward H., 471
Dodds, William, 373, 403
Dodge, Shirlee, 99
Doerr, Jim, 434
Doherty, Don, 389
Doll, Bill, 404
Doll's House, A, 80
Dolphin, Eileen, 380
Don Juan in Hell, 54, 86, 117
Donat, Peter, 93
Doney, Randy, 388
Donehue, Vincent J., 470
Donluca, Lise, 118
Donnelly, Donal, 398, 454, 455, 456
Donovan, Mary, 79
Doolittle, James A., 55
Doonan, Tony, 392
Doorley, Frank M., 469
Dore, Rusty, 427
Dorfman, Irvin, 372, 394
Dorfman, Nat, 372, 394
Dorlen, Susan, 437
Dorman, John, 425
Doro, Mariana, 375
Dorothy Ross Associates, 422
Dorothy Chandler Pavilion, 54
Dorrin, John, 368, 413
Dos Passos, John, 89
Dostoyevsky, Feodor, 60, 117
Dotson, Joyce, 83
Dotrice, Roy, 113
Doubleday, Kay, 87, 88
Doubles and Opposites, 32, 436

Douglas, Felicity, 111
Douglas, Johanna, 412
Douglass, Sally, 79-80
Douglass, Stephen, 436
Doumerg, Jo, 116
Dovel, Lynn, 413
Dowd, M'el, 378
Dowling, Vincent, 436
Downing, Robert, 396
Doyle, David, 432
Doyle, Lee H., 407
Doyle, Mary, 80, 81
Dox, Charles, Jr., 80, 81
Drake, Ervin, 365
Drama Desk–Vernon Rice
  Awards, 454
Dramatists Guild, The, vii
Drake, Alfred, 28, 368
Drake, Elton, 72
Draper, Anne, 430, 435
Draper, Don, 83
Draper, Michael, 82
Drat! The Cat!, 4, 5, 64,
  375, 456
Dratler, Jay, 50, 77
Drayton, Mary, 3, 22, 389
Dresdel, Sonia, 110, 111
Drexel, Todd, 95
Drexler, Rosalyn, 73
Drischell, Ralph, 85
Driscoll, Ann, 78
Driver, Don, 94
Drummond, Alice, 394
Drylie, Patricia, 388
Duberman, Martin, 84, 416
Du Bois, Raoul Pène, 367
Duby, Jacques, 116
Du Brock, Neal, 74
Ducaux, Annie, 115
Duchaussoy, Michel, 397
Duckworth, Dortha, 400
Dudley, John S., 471
Duel of Angels, 51, 79
Duell, William, 97
Duerrenmatt Friedrich, 49,
  50, 77, 86, 113, 430
Duet For Three, 435
Duffield, David, 111
Duffy, John, 85, 94
Dufilho, Jacques, 115
Dugan, Daniel, 98
Dukakis, Olympia, 74
Dukas, James, 379, 380, 381
Duke, Milton, 82
Dumesnil, Jacques, 117
Dumbwaiter, The, 72
Dunaway, Faye, 425
Duncan, Sandy, 367
Dunfee, Susan, 396
Dunford, Judith, 408
Dunn, Joseph H., 454
Dunning, Ruth, 111
Dunnock, Mildred, 83, 430
Duntiere, Victor, 366
Dupont, Jacques, 114, 392
Durand, Charles, 390
Durand, Juliette, 388

Durante, Vito, 391
Duras, Marguerite, 114, 115
Durning, Charles, 97, 375,
  403, 404
Durning, Dan, 96, 432
Durrell, Lawrence, 457
Durrell, Michael, 430, 435
Dutchess of Malfi, The, 438
Dutchman, 64, 117
Duvall, Robert, 13, 75, 396,
  442
Dwyer, Bonnie, 418
Dwyer, James, 421
Dwyer, Jimmy, 469
Dwyer, Paul, 370, 380, 411
Dyas, James, 79, 80
Dye, Lyle, Jr., 55
Dyer, Carolyn, 393, 411
Dyne, Michael, 23, 378
Dylan, 49, 56, 66, 76
Dyne, Michael, 378, 456
Dysart, Richard A., 85
Dysart, William, 101

Eaux et Forêts, Les, 114
Earl, Donna, 469
Eastman, Joan, 432
Easter, 74, 113
Easton, Michael, 373
Easton, Richard, 373
Ebb, Fred, 366
Ebeling, George, 89
Ebert, Joyce, 420
Ebner, Jacques, 392
Eccentricities of a Nightin-
  gale, 89
Echeverria, Pat, 70, 71, 85
Eckart, Jean, 18, 22, 25, 384,
  412, 455, 456
Eckart, William, 18, 22, 25,
  384, 412, 455, 456
Eddison, Robert, 110, 111,
  113
Eddleman, Jack, 424
Ede, George, 66
Edelman, Herbert, 441
Edmond, Gay, 405
Edmund, Lada, Jr., 443
Edmunds, Dallas, 405
Edouard et Agrippine, 115
Edward II, 66
Edwards, Ben, 382, 399, 400
Edwards, Eugene, 405
Edwards, Hilton, 10, 398, 456
Edwards, Neely, 469
Edwards, Ronnie Claire, 81
Edwards, Ryan, 434
Efron, Marshall, 87
Egan, Bill, 97
Egan, Jenny, 386
Eggleston, William, 89
Ehara, Mary, 411
Eichel, Paul, 377
Eidman, Earl, 423
Eisti, M. A., 89
Eikenbary, Anthony, 70
Einenkel, Robert, 71

Eire, Simon, 116
Eisen, Max, 377, 389, 400,
  423, 427, 429, 435
Eisler, Hanns, 75
Ekson, Larrio, 430
El Greco, 115
Elbertshagen, Frithjof, 407
Elcar, Dana, 67, 89
Elder, Eldon, 32, 383, 421
Elder, Lonne, 426
Eldridge, Elaine, 379, 380,
  381
Electra, 117
Elgar, Avril, 111, 112
Eliah, Drew, 82
Eliscu, David, 390
Elizondo, Hector, 423
Elkins, Flora, 63, 96
Elkins, Hillard, 405, 445
Elkins, Judie, 393
Eliot, Drew, 97
Eliot, T. S., 60, 74
Ellen, Sandy, 375
Ellington, Duke, 403
Ellington, Mercedes, 418
Elliot, Jane, 376
Elliott, Marianna, 89
Elliott, Michael, 110
Elliott, Patricia, 75, 76
Ellis, Larry, 399
Ellis, Tom, 436
Emeott, Robert D., 86
Emerson, Frank, 436
Emmanuel, Ivor, 411
Empire Builders, The, 87
Employment Agency, The,
  443
En Attendant Godot, 116
Encore Theater (San Fran-
  cisco, Calif.), 66, 87
Endgame, 72, 84
Endon, Anthony, 370, 391
Endon, Eugene, 370
Enemies, 30, 33, 421
Enemy of the People, An,
  85
Engel, Lehman, 392
Engel, Susan, 100, 112
Engineer, Zarin, 77
England, Hal, 53
Englehardt, Wallace, 396
English, Lisa, 72
English Stage Company, 389
Ensslen, Dick, 408, 409
Entertaining Mr. Sloane, 4,
  12, 21, 376, 451, 456, 457
Envoyé Spécial, Un, 115
Ephraim, 443
Epstein, Alvin, 49, 382
Epstein, Danny, 428
Epstein, Mark, 73
Erickson, Mitchell, 398
Establishment Theater, 454
Evening of Man vs. Woman
  or Woman vs. Man, An,
  70

Evening's Frost, An, 30, *422*
Equity Theater, 436
Equity Library Theater West, 57
Erbacher, Richard, 419
Erby, Morris, 96
Eriksen, Ed, 411
Erickson, Eddie, 377
Erickson, Mitchell, 398
Erikson, Philip, 371
Ernest in Love, 89
Erouk, René, 114, 115
Erskine, Chester, 445
Erskine, Dorothy, 78
Erskine, Howard, 374
Erwin, Bill, 83
Escande, Maurice, 398
Escoffier, Jean, 115
Escott, T. J., 436
Esslin, Martin, 415
Establishment Theater Company, Inc., 428, 431
Estey, Carol, 393
Estrin, Marc, 66, 87
Estrin, Slava, 426
Eternal Husband, The, 86
Euripides, 60, 83, 420
Euloge de Courdoue, 115
Evans, Alice, 395
Evans, Beverly, 371
Evans, Charles, 390
Evans, Dillon, 410
Evans, Gwyllum, 73, 368
Evans, Hugh C., 98
Evans, Jessie, 110
Evans, Lillian, 79
Evans, Maurice, 57
Evans, Michele, 368
Evans, Nell, 420
Evans, Terrence, 98
Evans, Tracy, 373
Evans-Leonard, Nancy, 74-75
Everett, Stephen, 410
Everhart, Rex, 95, 384, 385
Ewell, Tom, 6, 383
Ewing, Sherman, 70
Exception and the Rule, The, 416, 458
Exhaustion of Our Son's Love, The, 30, *422-423*
Eyser, Jacques, 115

Fabbri, Jacques, 114, 117
Faber, Erwin, 407
Fabian, T., 437
Fade Out–Fade In, 457
Faiola, Linda, 73
Fairchild, Charlotte, 412
Fairman, Michael, 390
Falasco, Donald, 469
Falconer, Mary, 413
Falk, Richard, 421, 428
Falkenhain, Patricia, 72
Falstaff, 93-94
Falzone, Peter, 390, 411
Family Things, Etc., 443

Fantasticks, The, 34, 43, 415, 439
Fanny's First Play, 111
Faulkner, Caroline, 430
Farewell, Farewell, Farewell, 72
Farmer, Elizabeth, 371
Farnworth, Ralph, 375
Farnsworth, Michael, 393
Farquhar, George, 437
Farrand, Jan, 83
Farrell, Mary, 394
Farrington, Kenneth, 110
Farwell, Jonathan, 87, 88
Father, The, 86-87
Fatone, Charles, 428
Fay, Patricia, 431
Faye, Tina, 405
Fear and Misery of The Third Reich, The, 73
Fearnley, John, 393
Fearl, Clifford, 412
Featherston, Eddie, 469
Feinstein, Martin, 398
Feit, Mona, 95
Fellows, Don, 374
Fels, Marion, 377
Felsenthal, Peter, 74
Ferber, Bernie, 471
Ferlbart, Edward, 443
Ferlinghetti, Lawrence, 73
Fernández, Félix E., 97
Fernandez, Rosita, 118
Fernald, Karin, 111
Ferraro, Edilio, 382
Ferrer, José, 386
Ferris, Barbara, 110, 112
Fersen, Christine, 397
Feuer, Cy, 385, 456
Feuillère, Edwige, 114
Feydeau, Alain, 397
Feydeau, Georges, 28, 113, 397
Ffrangcon-Davies, Gwen, 112
Fibiger, Don, 80
Fichandler, Thomas, 43
Fichandler, Zelda, 69, 89
Fichtner, Victor, 77
Fiddler on the Roof, 5, 365, 440
Fidelio, 443
Field, Betty, 6, 8
Field, Leonard S., 401
Field, Sylvia, 372
Fielding, Henry, 82
Fields, Dorothy, 395, 455, 456
Fields, Herbert, 413
Fields, Joseph, 470
Fields, Julius, 368
Fields, Robert, 416, 419
Fifth Commandment, The, 30, *426*
Fil à la Patte, Un, 4, 28, *397-398*
Fin du Monde, La, 116
Finlay, Frank, 112

Finley, Sue Sellors, 77
Finnegan, Edward, 73
Finnell, JoAnn, 76, 83
Finnerty, Warren, 73
Finney, Albert, 109, 110, 113
Finney, Douglas, 89
Finney, Jack, 445
Finkelstone, George N., 469
Firbank, Ann, 110
Firebrand, The, *436-437*
Firebugs, The, 43, 74
First One Asleep, Whistle, 4, 24, *400*
Fischer, Howard, 380, 381, 400
Fischoff, George, 390
Fischer, Barbara, 75
Fisher, Bob, 12
Fisher, Douglas, 436
Fisher, Gail, 379
Fisher, Harrison, 391
Fisher, Jules, 71, 84, 89, 373, 386, 391, 419, 420, 428, 431, 432, 445
Fisher, Lola, 79
Fisher, Nelle, 80
Fishing For Wives, 403
Fitz, 30, *435*
Fitzpatrick, Eileen, 425
Fitzgerald, Maureen, 73, 94
Fitzpatrick, Bettye, 78
Fixed Idea, The, 114, 115
Flacks, Niki, 81, 83
Flagg, Fanny, 424
Flamm, Donald, 456
Flanagan, Pauline, 87
Flanagan, Walter, 431
Flanders, Ed, 81
Flannigan, William, 394
Flatt, Robyn Baker, 76-77
Flea in Her Ear, A, 109
Fleetwood, Tom, 390
Fleming, Thomas T., 63
Flemming, Carol, 377
Flemyng, Robert, 49, 74
Fletcher, Allen, 84, 94
Fletcher, Bill, 97
Fletcher, Bramwell, 34, 427
Fletcher, Jack, 375, 410
Fletcher, Jay, 430
Fletcher, Mike, 94
Flon, Suzanne, 117
Floor, The, 436
Flora, The Red Menace, 366
Florence, Carol, 430
Flores, Antonio, 97
Flowerton, Consuelo, 469
Fiche, Nina, 79
Fodor, Joleen, 424
Fogarty, Jack, 425
Folger, Adrienne, 420
Foley, Michael, 408
Foley, Paul A., 370, 398
Foley, Robert, 70
Folle de Chaillot, La, 116
Folksbiene Company, 426

Fonda, Henry, 7, 45, 374
Foote, Gene, 395
Forbes, Brenda, 74
Forbes, Kathryn, 471
Force, Joan, 82
Ford, Constance, 394
Ford, David, 78
Ford, Paul, 6, 22
Ford, Phil, 440
Ford, Rozann, 413
Ford Foundation, 44, 48
Forella, Ronn, 367, 392, 413, 444
Fornes, Maria, 444
Forrest, George, 387, 443
Forster, Robert, 370
Forssen, David, 413
Forsyth, James, 457
Forsythe, Henderson, 378, 394
Fortus, Danny, 421
Forum Theater, 35
Fosse, Bob, 16, 395, 456
Foster, Beno, 413
Foster, Francis, 426
Foster, Gloria, 34, 427, 454
Foster, Paul, 433
Four New Yale Playwrights, 457
Four Seasons, The, 111
Four Thousand Brass Halfpennies, 110
Fournel, Max, 397
Fowler, Clement, 79, 85
Fowkes, Conard, 374
Fox, Frederick, 392
Fox, Jonathan, 385
Foxworth, Robert, 89
Fragments, Windows and Other Plays, 457
France, Richard, 392, 436
France, Suzanne, 384
Francine, Anne, 80, 81
Francis, Arlene, 5, 24, 370
Francisco, William, 84
Franck, Marcel, 116
Franck, Pierre, 397
Frank, Bernard, 388
Frank, Judy, 383
Frank, Maroussis, 393
Frank Merriwell's Last Race, 47-48, 73
Frank Productions, Inc., 401
Frank, Sherman, 404
Franke, Wolfgang, 429
Frankel, Daniel T., 428
Frankel, Kenneth, 81
Franklin, Hugh, 385
Franklin, Nancy, 403
Franklin, Nony, 469
Franks, Laurie, 367, 388, 412
Franzos, Leslie, 377
Fraser, Bryant, 391
Fraser, Byron, 436
Fraser, Ian, 373
Fraser, Ronald, 392
Frass-Wolfburg, Peter, 429

Franz, Eduard, 53
Frawley, Bernard, 88
Frawley, Maureen, 88
Frawley, William, 469
Frazier, Harry, 71, 85
Freda, Frank, 64
Frederick, Joel, 374
Frederics, Ron, 385
Freed, Les, 388, 405
Freedley, George, vii, 443, 452
Freedman, Gerald, 95
Freedman, Harold, 471
Freeman, Al, Jr., 96
Freeman, Arny, 390
Freeman, Stan, 365
Freiburger, Jim, 79
Freilich, Jo, 373
French, Arthur, 426
French, Valerie, 389
Fresnay, Pierre, 114, 115
Freund, Peter, 427
Frey, Jeanne, 393, 408
Fricke, Peter, 407
Frid, Jonathan, 437
Fried, Franklin, 382
Fried, Martin, 431
Friedlander, Mitzi, 80
Friedley, Aaron, Jr., 87
Friedman, Gary Wm., 423
Friedman, Phil, 385
Friel, Brian, 3, 10, 301, 398, 455, 456
Friend Indeed, A, 112
Friends, 30, 33, 421
Fries, Jerry, 408
Frink, Robert, 430
Frisch, Max, 72, 73, 83
Frisch, Richard, 430
Fritz, Richard, 381
Frizell, Cornelius T., 407
Frizzell, Lou, 74
Frog Pond, The, 443
Front Street Theater (Memphis, Tenn.), 36, 80
Frost, Robert, 34, 77
Fry, Ray, 379, 380, 381
Fryer, Robert, 412, 456
Fuchs, Peter, 432
Fue, Charles, 470
Fuerst, Tamara, 393
Fudge, Ann, 98
Fugard, Athol, 75
Fujikawa, Jerry, 405
Fujimoto, Haruki, 405
Fuller, Barry, 80
Fuller, Janice, 98
Fuller, Penny, 439
Fulton, Eileen, 440
Funes, Mimi, 418
Funny Girl, 112, 365, 440
Funny Thing Happened on the Way to the Forum, A, 40
Fuqua, V. C., 390, 404
Furlaud, Maxime, 32, 435
Furse, Roger, 373

Gabel, Martin, 370
Gabler, Carl, 77
Gaffigan, Catherine, 433
Gage, Gary, 86
Gage, Sara, 86
Gaiety of Nations, The, 113
Gaige, Truman, 368
Gainer, Joan, 422
Galambos, Peter, 425, 434
Galanti, Nino, 418
Galantière, Lewis, 76
Gale, Kenneth, 57
Galiber, Doris, 367, 418
Galileo, 43, 46, 49, 52, 63, 73, 75, 82, 87
Galina, Gita, 423
Gallagher, Bernard, 111
Gallagher, Helen, 395, 456
Gallenstein, Leo, 89
Gallery, James, 81, 98
Gam, Rita, 80
Gamble, Ralph, 469
Gamboa, Marcello, 392, 413
Game Is Up, The, 30, 34, 415
Game of Heroes, 23
Gammell, Robin, 71-72, 85
Gampel, C. M., 428
Gans, Sharon, 401, 454
Ganshaw, Bob, 404
Gantry, Donald, 98
Ganzemüller, Dieter, 407
García Lorca, Federíco, 50, 77, 83
Gardenia, Vincent, 86
Gardner, Claudette, 77
Gardner, Garold, 408
Gardner, Rita, 377, 440
Garfein, Jack, 55-56
Garfield, Kurt, 78
Garland, Geoff, 376
Garmston, Lynne, 407
Garrick Productions, 394
Garrison, Sean, 443
Garry, Ian, 375
Garvey, Joseph, 399
Gary, Sheila, 428
Gaskill, William, 110
Gaspar, Beatrice, 77
Gasparinetti, Luigi, 377
Gasper, Edd K., 70
Gasper, Eddie, 395
Gassett, Louis, 22
Gassman, Vittorio, 24
Gassner, Francis, 80
Gassner, John, 452, 457
Gates, Ruth, 469
Gatti, Armand, 114
Gaus, Robert, 73
Gauthron, Bernard, 392
Gaver, Jack, 451, 455
Gavin, Gene, 384
Gaye, Albie, 469
Gaynes, George, 437, 439
Geddis, Peter, 100
Geer, Ann, 72
Geer, Ellen, 81

Geer, William, 98, 422, 454
Geidt, Jeremy, 33, 421
Geiger, Milton, 75
Geis, Wayne, 442
Geiser, Linda, 410
Geisler, Linda, 385, 386
Gelb, James, 376
Gelber, Jack, 35, 416, 437
Gemignani, Rhoda, 86, 87
Gendel, Max, 386
General's Daughter, The, 403
Generation, 3, 4, 7-8, 14, 38, 45, 121-146, 374, 457
Genet, Jean, 78, 85, 115
Géniat, Gilberte, 118
Genius Farm, The, 443
Gensac, Claude, 116
Gentle Jack, 457
Gentry, Joseph, 405
Gentry, Michael, 405
Geoppinger, Susan, 419
George, Anthony, 440
George, George W., 396, 403
George, Hal, 94
George, Peter, 421
George Dillon, 118
George Jean Nathan Award, 454
George Washington University, 68
Georgetown University, 68
Gerdesmann, Karl-Heinz, 429
Gerety, Anne, 87, 88
Gerhart, Martha, 381
Gerlach, Ginger, 424
Gero, Frank, 388
Geroldo, Alfredo, 97
Gerringer, Robert, 379
Gerstad, John, 422
Gerstman, Felix G., 406, 429
Gerussi, Bruno, 93
Gervais, Nina, 420
Gesek, Tad, 435
Gianinni, Alex, 436
Gianino, Jack, 97
Giannini, Christina, 390
Gibbens, Bill, 420
Gibbons, June, 76
Gibbs, Cora, 471
Gibelli, Renato, 386
Gibson, David, 76-77
Gibson, William, 365
Gierasche, Stefan, 80, 81
Giese, Linda, 77
Gielgud, John, 23, 45, 68, 113
Giftos, Elaine, 404
Gilbert, E. A., 376
Gilbert, John, 87, 88
Gilbert, Willie, 366, 407
Gilbert, Yves-Marc, 118
Gilbert and Sullivan, 28, 83, 416
Gile, William, 73, 74
Gillespie, Helen, 398
Gillespie, Sean, 387

Gilliand, Mark, 94
Gillis, Mary Jo, 424
Gilman, Richard, 37, 451
Gilroy, Frank D., 72, 365
Gilstrap, Barbara, 77
Gingold, Hermione, 112
Gingold, Marvin, 437
Ginsburg, Mirra, 435
Giono, Jean, 116
Giovanni, Paul, 440
Girardot, Annie, 117
Girl From Maxim's, The, 114, 116
Giraudoux, Jean, 79, 84, 116, 415
Giroux-Orrin, Claude, 421
Gish, Lillian, 6, 95, 388
Gist, Robert, 53
Gladstone, Gabriel, 86
Gladke, Peter, 417
Glaeser, Gaye, 74
Glaser, Darel, 407
Glasgow, Bonnie, 368
Glass Menagerie, The, 28, 64, 75, 80, 81, 112, 366, 440
Glassman, William, 367
Gleason, John, 392
Glen, Archie, 469
Glenn, Charlotte, 85
Glenn, Scott, 376
Glick, Jacob, 381
Glidden, Barbara, 436
Glover, Bruce, 400
Glover, John, 71
Glover, Julian, 112
Glover, William H., 451, 455
Gluckman, Leon, 18, 401
Gnadiges Fraulen, The, 399
Gnista, 443
Gnys, Charles, 422
Gochman, Leo, 408
Goddard, Malcolm, 11, 25
Goddard, Michael, 393
Goddess, The, 56
Godfrey, Derek, 112
Goethe, Johann Wolfgang von, 28, 406
Gogol, Nikolai, 73, 113, 423
Gohl, James F., 381
Gold, David, 375, 395
Gold, Russell, 74, 80
Golden, Edward, Jr., 43
Golden, Ray, 445
Golden, Rita, 377
Golden Boy, 457
Golden Warriors, The, 50, 77
Goldman, Bernard, 110
Goldman, James, 3, 20, 324, 400, 455
Goldman, Jean, 63
Goldoni, Carlo, 43, 81, 84, 113, 117
Goldsby, Robert, 86
Golkin, Dewey, 411
Golonka, Arlene, 394

Gombrowicz, Witold, 117
Gondoliers, The, 416
Gonyaw, Anna, 76, 77
Good Day, 30, 422-423
Good Soldier Schweik, The, 118
Good Woman of Setzuan, The, 88
Goodbye, Ghost, 443
Goodhart, William, 3, 7, 121, 374, 455
Goodhue, John Scott, 99
Goodis, Marvin, 408
Goodman, Dody, 428
Goodman, Frank, 376, 400, 432
Goodman, Lee, 408, 410
Goodman, Michael, 88
Goodman, Paul, 32, 430, 457
Goodman Theater (Chicago, Ill.), 43, 48-49, 74-75
Goodridge, Ted, 418
Goodrow, Elaine, 79-80
Goodwin, Dan, 86
Goodwin, Russell, 367
Gordan, Mel, 367
Gordani, Nina, 469
Gordin, Al, 372
Gordon, Anne, 416
Gordon, Arthur, 432
Gordon, Guy, 393
Gordon, Lewis, 94
Gordon, Mark, 385
Gordon, Marvin, 404
Gordon, Mary McKenzie, 385
Gordon, Paul Vincent, 471
Gordon, Ruth, 5, 21, 372
Gordon, Stephanie, 433
Gore, Altovise, 404
Gore, James, 435
Gorelik, Mordecai, 83
Gorman, Cliff, 425
Gorman, Jo Firestone, 99
Gorman, Patrick, 97, 436
Gorrin, Michael, 428
Gorsey, Renee, 367, 408, 410
Gosling, Pat, 392
Goss, Bick, 405
Goss, Robert, 390
Gossett, Louis, 384, 455
Gottfried, Martin, 451, 454
Gottleib, Carl A., 422
Gould, Elliot, 375
Gould, Gordon, 71, 387
Gould, Gypsy, 469
Gould, Harold, 88
Gould, Michael, 393
Goulston, Andre, 398
Gouter des Généraux, Le, 114
Government Inspector, The, 109, 113
Gowers, Patrick, 393
Goyen, William, 51
Graber, Werner T., 407
Grable, Betty, 440

Graczyk, Edward, 78
Grace, Charity, 469
Graff, Ellen, 384
Grahal, Fernando, 386
Graham, Marian, 433
Graham, Ronny, 383
Graham-Jujan, James, 83
Granat, Frank, 396, 403
Granby, Joseph, 469
Grandi, Lois, 391
Grange, Robert, 101
Granger, Farley, 440
Granger, Michael, 379, 381
Granite, Judith, 385, 434
Granstrom, Allan, 87
Grant, Bernard, 427
Grant, James Edward, 470
Grant, Karen, 408
Grant, Sheila, 393
Granville-Barker, Harley, 112
Grasse, Jerry, 81
Graubart, Judy, 434
Graveley, George, 81
Graves, Ernest, 445
Gravet, Fernand, 116
Gray, Charles, 394, 431
Gray, Charles D., 23, 378
Gray, Christian, 384
Gray, Margery, 375
Gray, Stokely, 377
Grayson, Rick, 423
Great Ceremonial, The, 118
Great Indoors, The, 4, 24, 396
Great Scot!, 30, 34, 424
Great Waltz, The, 56, 443
Greco, El, 115
Gredy, Jean-Pierre, 12
Green, Adolph, 77, 436
Green, Del, 408
Green, Dylan, 426, 427
Green, Harriet, 371
Green, Howard, 82
Green, Howard J., 470
Green, Manby, 443
Green, Michael, 437
Green, Paul, 443
Green Julia, 110
Greenberg, Edward, 368, 370
Greene, Herbert, 367
Greene, James, 380, 387
Greengrocer's Daughter, The, 403
Greenhouse, Martha, 434
Greenidge, Terrence, 101
Greenspon, Muriel, 371
Greenwood, Jane, 71, 84
Greenwood, Jeremiah, 89
Greer, Edward, 398
Gregg, Nickerson, 367
Gregory, Andre, 63, 84
Gregory, Doris, 70
Gregory, Jay, 411
Gregory, Will, 390
Gresham, Edith, 379, 380, 381
Grey, Denise, 116

Gribbon, Eddie T., 469
Grice, Wayne, 435
Griffies, Ethel, 21, 372, 410
Griffin, Rodney, 411
Griffis, William, 398
Griffith, Maxine, 426
Grigas, John, 405
Grimaldi, Marion, 112
Grimes, Tammy, 55
Grinling, Amanda, 111
Gripari, Jacques, 115
Grishin, Natasha, 408
Griso, Frank, 411
Grizzard, George, 49, 440
Grodin, Charles, 432
Grom, Richard, 76, 80
Groseclose, Frank, 97
Gross, Charles, 89, 381
Gross, Gene, 63
Grosse Valise, La, 4, 5, 20, 391-392
Grossman, Harvey, 436
Grossman, Herbert, 375
Grossman, Lawrence, 383
Grossman, Norman, 382
Grossmann, Suzanne, 20, 400, 455
Grosso, Guy, 392
Grover, Edward, 83, 382
Grudeff, Marian, 366, 457
Gruenewald, Tom, 80, 86
Grundman, Clare, 375
Gudegast, Hans, 396
Guggenheimer, Minnie, 471
Guidote, Cecile, 77
Guilford, Carol, 396
Guinevere, Camelot, 424
Guinness, Alec, 109, 112
Guisol, Henri, 116
Guittard, Horace, 74, 388
Guitry, Sacha, 116
Gulliver, John, 101
Gulls, The, 113
Gunn, Bill, 96
Gunn, Moses, 426
Gunnerson, Mickey, 408, 410
Guss, Louis, 74
Gustafson, Karen L., 392
Gutenberg, Carol, 421
Guthrie, Sir Tyrone, 43, 58-59, 92, 457
Guys and Dolls, 28, 80

Haas, Cathy, 423
Haas, Nathan S., 98
Haber, André, 115
Hachfeld, Eckart, 429
Haddock, William, 379
Hadge, Michael, 376
Hadler, Walter, 432
Hager, David, 82, 83
Haigh, Kenneth, 111
Hailey, Marian, 383, 405, 436
Hailey, Oliver, 400
Haines, A. Larry, 8, 374, 456
Haire, James, 95
Hale, Randolph, 57

Halenke, Gustl, 407
Hales, Jonathan, 100
Half a Sixpence, 366, 440
Half Horse Half Alligator, 30, 432
Hall, Adrian, 81, 85, 86
Hall, Bruce, 78
Hall, Donald, 422
Hall, Ed, 384
Hall, Jim, 430
Hall, Juanita, 417
Hall, Margaret, 412
Hall, Patricia, 413
Hall, Peter, 92, 110, 112
Hall, Philip Baker, 434
Hall, Willis, 111
Hallhuber, Heino, 407
Halliwell, David, 111
Hallock, Carol, 368
Hallow, John, 401, 443
Halpern, Mortimer, 391, 418
Halverson, Richard, 75, 76
Hambleton, T. Edward, 387
Hamilton, Edith, 72, 83
Hamilton, Jake, 386, 411
Hamilton, JoAnn, 421
Hamilton, John, 95
Hamilton, Lynn, 97
Hamilton, Margaret, 394
Hamilton, Murray, 439
Hamilton, Rick, 99
Hamilton, Roger, 416, 423, 432
Hamlet, 87, 99-100, 110, 112
Hammack, Patricia, 385
Hammack, Warren, 50, 76-77
Hammer, Ben, 382, 437
Hammer, Mark, 434
Hammerstein, James, 367
Hammerstein, Oscar, 80, 392
Hammond, Dorothea, 89
Hammond, Thomas, 422
Hamparian, Peter, 404
Hancock, Barbara, 413
Hancock, John, 44, 65-66, 86, 87
Hancock, Sheila, 21, 376, 455, 456
Hancock, Stephan, 100
Hanft, Karl, 407
Hanley, James, 444, 457
Hanley, William, 3, 24, 76, 89, 370
Hanlon, Roy, 110, 113
Hannafin, Daniel P., 392
Hanning, Dorothy, 367
Hansen, Ronn, 399
Hanson, Philip, 75
Happiest Millionaire, The, 70
Happily Never After, 4, 22, 401
Happy Days, 29, 30, 420-421
Happy Days Are Here Again, 110
Happy Ending, 30, 32, 426, 451

Hara, Mary, 437
Haraldson, Marion, 375, 411
Harburg, E. Y., 89
Harden, Jacques, 115
Hardin, Jerry, 79
Hardwicke, Edward, 113
Hardy, Joseph, 73, 436
Hardy, Timothy, 393
Hardy, William, 51, 79
Hare, Will, 416
Harlan, Sheila, 80
Harland, Alec, 469
Harmon, Betty, 416
Harmon, Jennifer, 71, 387
Harmon, Lewis, 374, 378
Harmon, Myles, 79
Harnick, Jan, 84
Harnick, Sheldon, 86, 365
Harper Theater (Ill.), 49
Harrell, James Nelson, 77
Harrelson, Helen, 81
Harrington, Delphi, 436
Harrington, Pat, Sr., 469
Harrigan, William, 469
Harris, Barbara, 14, 16, 25,
  377, 455, 456
Harris, Cynthia, 405
Harris, Dina, 430
Harris, Gary, 422
Harris, Herbert, 382
Harris, Hilde, 412
Harris, Jeff, 75
Harris, Joseph, 412, 456
Harris, Julie, 15, 25, 384, 385,
  456
Harris, Julius, 435
Harris, Lee, 56
Harris, Lloyd, 417, 418
Harris, Robert H., 374, 383
Harris, Rosemary, 13, 14, 20,
  21, 25, 27, 71, 387, 455,
  456
Harris, Sam A., 387
Harris, Sylvia, 412, 456
Harris, Sophie, 471
Harris, Timmy, 436
Harron, Peter, 422
Hart, Enid, 423
Hart, Moss, 13, 28, 51, 70,
  71, 74, 76, 77, 79, 387
Hart, Stan, 33, 428
Hartford, Conn., Stage Com-
  pany, 36, 78
Hartman, David, 390
Hartman, Jonathan William,
  469
Harvey, 40
Harvey, John, 372, 383
Harvey, Kenneth, 436
Harvey, Peter, 423, 428, 432
Harwood, John, 393
Hasard du Coin du Feu, Le,
  114
Hasso, Signe, 56
Hastings, Harold, 388
Hastings, Michael, 110

Haswell, Robert, 380, 381
Hatet, Pierre, 115
Haug, Peggy Marie, 418
Hauptmann, Gerhart, 28, 113
Haven, Lance, 436
Havens, Richard, 434
Haviland, David, 398
Hawkes, John, 73, 88
Hawtrey, Nicholas, 113
Hay, Richard L., 88, 99
Hay Fever, 70, 72, 83
Hayden, Mary, 433
Hayes, Don, 80
Hayes, Helen, 60
Hayman, Barton, 87
Haynes, Edward, 433
Hays, Dan, 99
Hays, David, 375, 394, 455,
  456
Hayward, Leland, 367, 443
Haywood, Nancy, 373
Hazzard, Adrienne, 385
Head, Margot, 436
Heal, Joan, 111
Healy, Mark, D., 420, 428
Hearn, George, 411
Heartbreak House, 52, 87
Hebbel, Friedrich, 117
Hecht, Paul, 432
Heckart, Eileen, 439
Hedda Gabler, 72, 78
Heeley, Desmond, 93
Heffernan, John, 382, 394
Heffner, Henry, 436
Heflin, Kathleen, 87
Heilmann, Ursula, 407
Heim, Patrick, 395
Heiser, Catherine, 76
Helen Hayes Theater, 38
Helfend, Dennis, 436
Heller, Trude, 389
Hellman, Betty, 96
Hellman, Lillian, 74
Hello Charlie, 30
Hello Dolly!, 5, 35, 37, 39,
  48, 50, 102, 112, 365, 440
Helminiak, Jeanne, 80
Helmond, Katherine, 85, 86
Helmore, Tom, 389
Helou, Victor, 393
Helpmann, Max, 93
Helward, Dale, 79
Hely, Gerard, 112
Henderson, Don, 371
Henderson, Jo, 70
Hendricks, Delmar, 412
Heneker, David, 74, 366
Henning, Ervin, 416
Henrichs, Helmut, 407
Henriot, Rex, 86
Henriot, Zoaunne, 86
Henritze, Betty, 74
Henry, Martha, 93
Henry, Patrick, 75
Henry, Sam Haigler, 430, 435
Henry, Vincent, 368
Henson, Nicky, 111

Hepburn, Besty, 371
Hepple, Jeanne, 389, 432, 454
Herbert, Don, 382
Herbert, Fred, 374
Herbert, Jocelyn, 389
Herbert, John, 367
Herbert, Lila, 371
Here Come the Clowns, 437
Heriat, Philippe, 372
Herakles, 43, 71
Herman, Harold, 422
Herman, Jerry, 18, 365, 412,
  455, 456
Herrmann, Edward, 77
Hermany, Garda, 367
Hermany, Roma, 367
Hero, Maria, 367, 393, 408, 410
Herr, Sharon, 393
Herrod, Julie, 396
Hertzsch, Harry, 407
Herz, Shirley, 423
Herzig, Sig, 417
Hespen, Marti, 368
Heston, Charlton, 57
Hetherington, John, 96
Hewes, Henry, 451, 454
Hewett, Christopher, 410
Hewgill, Roland, 93
Hewitt, Robert, 384
Heyman, Barton, 65, 86, 87
Heymann, Henry, 82, 420
Hiatt, Bernard, 436
Hickey, William, 445
Hickman, Darryl, 409
Hicks, Leonard, 96, 437
Higgins, James, 383
Higgins, Jane, 72
Higgins, Michael, 83, 427
High Spirits, 51
Hiken, Gerald, 88
Hilary, Jennifer, 410
Hilbich, Ernst, 429
Hildner, Jeffrey, 72
Hilgenberg, Katherine, 368
Hill, Bennett, 377
Hill, Bruce, 78
Hill, Holly, 436
Hill, Jack, 66
Hill, Joseph, 398
Hill, Kenneth, 80
Hill, Lucienne, 72, 73
Hill, Ralston, 368
Hill, Thomas, 88
Hillerman, John, 67, 89
Hilliard, Harry S., 469
Hilliard, Marc C., 470
Hilt, Ferdinand, 409
Hindy, Joseph, 73, 74, 430
Hines, Mimi, 440
Hines, Patrick, 385
Hingle, Pat, 440, 441
Hinnant, Bill, 422
Hinnant, Skip, 441
Hirsch, John, 93
Hirsch, Robert, 114
Hirschfeld, Al, vii
Hirschfeld, Nina, vii, 410

Hirshhorn, Naomi Caryl, 79
Hitchcock, George, 86, 87
Hitchcock-Balding Productions, Inc., 428
Hjert, Gerald, 86
H.M.S. Pinafore, 416
Hoag, Mitzi, 79
Hobson, James, 408
Hochhuth, Rolf, 79
Hochman, Sandra, 434
Hoefler, Charles E., 424
Hoerle, Helen, 471
Hoff, Roger, 398
Hoffman, Dustin, 433, 454
Hoffman, Jane, 88
Hoffman, Patricia, 388
Hoffman, Theodore, 43
Hoffman, William, 432
Hoffmeister, John, 96, 425
Hogan's Goat, 3, 5, 6, 12, 14, 22, 25, 29-31, 169-194, 425-426, 435, 457
Hogg, Ian, 393
Hoiby, Lee, 399
Holbrook, Hal, 7, 85, 404-405, 440, 455, 456
Holbrook, Rudy, 85
Holden, Jan, 111
Holgate, Ronald, 432
Holiday, Bob, 17, 405
Holland, Anthony, 89, 399
Holland, Betty Lou, 423
Hollander, Jack, 376
Holliday, Judy, 469
Holliday, Polly, 80
Holly, Ellen, 97, 436
Holly, Joy, 418
Holm, Hanya, 388
Holm, Ian, 110
Holm, John Cecil, 383, 398
Holm, Jörg, 407
Holm, Klaus, 401
Holmes, Christine, 111
Holmes, Lois, 432
Holotik, Rosie, 408
Holsaert, Shai, 368
Holt, Will, 419
Home, William Douglas, 112
Homecoming, The, 110
Hong, Mae S., 400
Honig, Howard, 97
Hood, Curtis, 384
Hook, Nellie, 469
Hook, Walter, 370, 388, 408
Hooks, David, 75, 427
Hooks, Robert, 97, 426
Hooper, Susan, 99
Hooray! It's a Glorious Day . . . and all that, 30, 34, 432
Hoover, Bruce A., 387
Hoover, Richard, 65
Hope, Barry, 76, 77
Hops, Harriet, 420
Hopkins, Jerry, 432
Hopper, Hedda, 469
Horen, Robert, 374

Horine, Charles, 390
Horine, Kathryn Kunkel, 469
Horn, Arthur, 427
Horrigan, Patrick, 399
Horswill, James, 81
Horton, Edward Everett, 368
Hostage, The, 82
Hostile Witness, 4, 12, 22, 38, 68
Hot September, 24, 45, 443
Hotel Passionato, 30, 34, 423
Hotton, Donald, 394
Houdart, Dominique, 117
Houghton, Katharine, 372, 400
Houghton, Norris, 387
House, Eric, 46, 73
House of Bernarda Alba, The, 50, 74
Houseman, John, 55
Houston, Richard, 436
Houston, Tex., Music Theater, 40, 78
Houze, Duke, 437
Hovencamp, Henry, 93
How a Film Scenario Is Born, 118
How to Succeed in Business Without Really Trying, 4, 28, 407-408
Howard, Alan, 389
Howard, Celia, 78
Howard, Eleanor Harris, 383
Howard, Eugene, 469
Howard, James, 96
Howard, Richard, 113
Howard, Stuart, 78
Howard Ahmanson Theater (Los Angeles, Calif.), 54-55
Howarth, Donald, 110
Howarth, Susan, 73
Howell, Elizabeth, 388
Howey, William, 76
Howland, Beth, 375, 408, 410
How's the World Treating You?, 112
Hoxworth, Mary Ann, 416
Hoye, Gloria, 436
Hrehovcik, John Steven, 437
Hu Hung-Yen, 435
Hubbard, Elizabeth, 411
Hubbell, Kyra Deakin, 469
Hubeau, Catherine, 397
Hubert, Marcie, 96, 379, 381
Huddle, Elizabeth, 379, 380
Hudson, Charles, 424
Hudson, Travis, 403, 411
Hudson Theater, 24
Hughes, Barnard, 425
Hughes, Gareth, 469
Hughes, Langston, 416
Hughes, Tom, 50, 51
Hughes, Tresa, 425
Hull House's Parkway Community Theater, 49

Humphrey, Cavada, 387
Humphreys, Don, 77
Hunger and Thirst, 114
Hunt, Annette, 427
Hunt, Betty Lee, 395
Hunt, Doug, 408
Hunt, Lesley, 370, 398
Hunt, Marguerite, 430
Hunt, Peter, 78, 368, 370, 394, 414
Hunt, Ruth, 88
Hunt, William, 421, 432
Hurok, S., 397
Hurry, Leslie, 93
Hurst, David, 63, 85
Hurt, John, 111
Hussey, John, 393
Husson, Albert, 116
Huston, Carla, 440
Hutcheson, David, 112, 420
Hutchinson, Jeska, 436
Hutt, William, 93
Hyams, Barry, 381
Hyams, Harry, 470
Hylan, Donald, 431
Hyland, Frances, 93
Hylands, Scott, 85
Hyman, Earle, 430
Hyman, Elaine, 436
Hyman, Mitzi, 72
Hyman, Walter A., 21, 400
Hynes, Katherine, 398, 399
Hypothesis, The, 118
Hytown, Noel, 469

I Had A Ball, 365
I Rise in Flames, Cried the Phoenix, 79
I Want to See Myusov, 114, 117
Iannicelli, Tom, 431
IASTA, 35
Ibsen, Henrik, 34, 43, 71, 72, 78, 80, 83, 84, 85, 433, 443
Icarus's Mother, 73
Ideal Husband, An, 111
Idée Fixe, L', 115
Idiot, The, 114, 117
Idoles Les, 115
Iliad-Europa Productions, 423
Imaginary Invalid, The, 113
Imai, Masahiko, 403
Importance of Being Earnest, The, 52, 78, 79, 87
Impossible Years, The, 4, 7, 12-13, 45, 376
Impudent Wolf An, 30, 427
In White America, 43, 84, 416
Inadmissible Evidence, 3, 4, 7, 8, 9-10, 12, 14, 24, 25, 29, 64, 221-241, 389, 451, 456, 457
Ince, Alexander, 470

Incident At Vichy, 55, 103, 109, 112, 458
Indra-nila, 368
Infantry, The, 73
Inge, William, 3, 8, 60, 78, 400, 436
Ingham, Barrie, 112
Ingham, Rosemary, 82, 83, 85
Ingleson, Liz, 70, 80
Ingram, Rex, 50, 77
Inner Journey, The, 457
Inspector General, The, 73
Institute for Advanced Studies in the Theater Arts (IASTA), 430, 435, 454
Interplayers (San Francisco, Calif.), 66
Investigation, The, 73, 113
Iolanthe, 416
Ionesco, Eugène, 32, 43, 49, 74-75, 88, 89, 115
Ira Aldridge Theater (Washington, D.C.), 68
Irma La Douce, 74
Irving, Amy, 380
Irving Jules, 6, 26-27, 43-44, 65, 379, 381
Irving, George S., 371, 388
Ithaca Theater Festival, 43
Itkin, Bella, 74
"It's a Bird   It's a Plane It's SUPERMAN," 3, 4, 5, 14, 16-18, 25, 40, 63, 242-244, *405-406,* 451, 456, 458
Ivanov, 4, 7, 24, 45, 68, 109, 113, *410,* 456, 457, 458
Ives, Jeremy, 393, 413
Ivy Day, 74

Jackson, Alfred Graham, 470
Jackson, Anne, 55, 441
Jackson, Brian, 93
Jackson, Glenda, 100, 113, 455, 456
Jackson, Jack, 72
Jackson, Leonard, 96
Jackson, Nagle, 66, 99
Jackson, Richard, 430
Jacob, Peter, 96, 428
Jacobowitz, Anna, 423
Jacobs, Jacob, 423
Jacobs, Max, 75, 384
Jacobs, Sally, 393
Jacobsen, Russell Allen, 423
Jacobson, Irving, 386, 387
Jacobson, Kenneth, 443
Jacobson, Sol, 374, 378
Jaffrey, Saeed, 399
Jahn, Reinhard, 396
James, Cliff, 431
James, Dorothy, 398, 399
James, Eddie, 368
James, Hal, 15, 386, 456
James, Horace, 113
James, Ken, 94
James, Murphy, 405

James, Terry, 420
James, William, 410
Jameson, House, 396
Jampolis, Neil, 84
Jamrog, Joseph, 73, 436
Janney, Ben, 390
Jarmicki, Krysia, 94
Jaroslow, Ruth, 430
Jarrell, Randall, 470
Jason, Harvey, 398
Javits, Joan, 423
Jay, Barry, 427
Jay Stanwyck Productions, Inc., 427
Jeakins, Dorothy, 79
Jeanmarie, Zizi, 116
Jeffers, Robinson, 34, 427
Jefford, Barbara, 110
Jefford, Jacqueline, 116
Jeffreys, Anne, 368
Jelalian, Dennis, 89
Jellicoe, Ann, 70, 111
Jemma, Jean-Louis, 397
Jendell, Gary, 413
Jenkins, George, 8, 374, 382, 396, 418
Jenkins, Richard, 77
Jennings, John, 50, 77
Jennings, Mary, 371
Jens, Arnette, 63
Jens, Salome, 400
Jensen, Carol Leigh, 78
Jessel, Raymond, 366, 457
Jew of Malta, The, 99-100
Jewell, Martin, 368
Jillson, Joyce, 392
Jim Mendenhall Productions, 430
Joano, Clotilde, 382
Joel, Daniel, 413
Joella, 443
Johl, Peter, 404
Jolley, Scotter, 381
Jolviet, Pierre-Alain, 115
John, Carl, 420, 436
John, Mirian, 89
John F. Kennedy Center for the Performing Arts (Washington, D.C.), 40, 68
John Springer Associates, 428, 429, 431, 434
Johnson, Bari, 113
Johnson, Bernard, 377
Johnson, Dorothy, 80
Johnson, Eve, 85
Johnson, Frankie, 66
Johnson, Geoffrey, 370
Johnson, Gustave, 73
Johnson, Jack, 79-80
Johnson, Lyndon, 35
Johnson, Paul, 66
Johnson, Roger, Jr., 374, 401, 422
Johnson, Ronald, 96
Johnson, Scott, 86
Johnson, Van, 5-6, 383
Johnston, Barney, 375

Johnston, Gail, 417
Johnston, Justine, 408
Johnstone, Keith, 111
Jolivet, Pierre-Alain, 115
Jonah, 30, 31, 67, *430-431,* 435
Jones, Brooks, 72, 75
Jones, Charlotte, 412, 424, 432
Jones, Dale, 367
Jones, Dennis, 95
Jones, Eddie, 78
Jones, Freddie, 393
Jones, Griffith, 113
Jones, James Earl, 96, 379
Jones, John Randolph, 70-71, 383
Jones, Judd, 382
Jones, Lauren, 384
Jones, LeRoi, 32, 64, 117
Jones, Mark, 393
Jones, Marshall, 101
Jones, Mary Sue Fridge, 77
Jones, Pamela, 426
Jones, Preston, 76, 77
Jones, Roger, 101
Jones, Tom, 50, 75, 81, 415
Jones, William Stewart, 86
Jonns, Birl, 368
Jonson, Ben, 83
Joplin, Carol, 367
Jordan, Al, 421, 428
Jordan, Lee, 456
Jordan, Richard, 96, 374
Jordan, William, 396
Jory, Jon, 82, 83
Joseph Maharam Foundation Awards, 454
Josephine Forrestal Productions, Inc., 418
Journées Entières dans les Abres, Des, 114
Journey Back, The, 444
Journey of the Fifth Horse, The, 30, *433,* 435, 454
Joy, Holly, 377
Joyce, Stephen, 89, 95
Judith, 415
Judith Rutherford Marechal Productions, Inc., 418, 427
Judson Poets' Theater, 34
Juliani, J. C., 93
Julien, A. M., 114, 116
Julien, Edward, 391
Julius Caesar, 50, 52, 77, 87, 93-94
Jundelin, Robert, 376
Juno and the Paycock, 112
Junod, Don, 420
Jurgens, Curt, 6, 396
Just for Openers, 30, 34, *424*
Justes, Les, 116
Jutzi, Al, 87

Kabatchnik, Amnon, 429, 430

Kaetner, Hannes, 407
Kagan, Diane, 445
Kahl, Howard, 367, 388
Kahn, Madeline, 424
Kahn, Michael, 437
Kahn, Sammy, 384
Kaiser, Ardyth, 428
Kalegi, Sylvia, 430
Kalem, Theodore, 451, 454
Kalmanowitch, H., 423
Kalus, Hy, 74
Kaminsky, Stanley F., 394, 400, 431
Kamitses, Zoe, 99
Kamp, Irene, 396
Kampley, Linda, 95
Kander, John, 366
Kane, David, 101
Kane, Gail, 469
Kane, John, 100, 432
Kane Triplets, 423
Kanel, Françoise, 397
Kanin, Fay, 77, 78
Kanin, Garson, 21, 372
Kanin, Michael, 77, 78
Kanne, Gretchen, 421
Kapilow, Susan, 442
Kaplan, Abbott, 55
Kaplan, Donald, 419
Kaplan, Jeanne, 442
Kaplan, Shirley, 66, 428, 434
Karamu Players of Cleveland, 48
Karasevich, Joan, 94
Karaty, Tommy, 403, 404, 412
Karel, Jane, 418
Karin, Rita, 428
Karlen, John, 382, 431
Karlweis, Ninon Tallon, 434
Karm, Mickey, 366, 408
Karnilova, Maria, 440
Karol, 118
Karol, Nicole, 412
Karp, Cary, 431
Karper, Max, 423, 426
Karr, David, 383, 389
Karzen, Brooke, 80
Kash, Murray, 112
Kass, Jerome, 32, 431
Kass, Peter, 383, 399
Kastner, Peter, 389
Kasznar, Kurt, 439
Katayev, Valentin, 117
Kate, Marina, 78
Kates, Bernard, 385
Katselas, Milton, 74
Katzka, Emil, 471
Katzka-Berne, 444
Kauffmann, Stanley, 37-38, 51, 451, 454
Kaufman, David, 436
Kaufman, George S., 13, 28, 70, 71, 74, 76, 77, 79, 387
Kavanaugh, Clarence, 76
Kavanaugh, Ray, 471
Kawazoe, Hiroshi, 403

Kay, Arthur, 368
Kay, Charles, 100
Kay, Hershy, 375
Kay, Marlene, 367, 408
Kaye, Myrna, 76
Kazan, Elia, 26, 27, 60
Kazanoff, Ted, 73
Keach, Stacy, 379, 380, 381
Kealey, Kenneth, 376
Kean, Norman, 427
Kearsley, Barry, 86
Keathley, George, 429
Keating, Charles, 76
Keatts, John, 422
Keeler, John, 407
Keith, Lawrence, 405
Keith, Maxine, 470
Kelcey Allen Award, 454
Keller, Mary, 373
Keller, Nell Clark, 469
Kellner, Peggy, 98
Kelly, Eamon, 10, 398, 455, 456
Kelly, Eric, 74
Kelly, Renee, 469
Kelton, Gene, 384, 412
Kelton, Pert, 374
Kemp, Sally, 87
Kempner, Brenda, 393
Kennedy, Adrienne, 47, 73, 437
Kennedy, Harold J., 443
Kennedy, Madge, 372
Kennedy, Richard, 85, 86
Kennedy, Zona, 377, 411
Kennon-Wilson, James, 417, 418
Kenny, James, 89
Kenny, Sean, 370, 373
Kent, Enid, 99
Kent, Jerry, 408, 410
Kent, Sandra, 384
Kenting, Jodell Ann, 367, 371
Kenyon, Sandy, 53, 79
Keo, Tom, 435
Kercheval, Ken, 403
Kermoyan, Michael, 388
Kern, Mina, 426
Kernan, Sean, 82
Kerr, Elaine, 420
Kerr, Jean, 50, 75, 76, 78
Kerr, John, 56
Kerr, Kendra, 436
Kerr, Philip, 75
Kerr, Walter, 20-21, 36-37, 38, 451, 454
Kerrick, Maryann, 384
Kerry, Patricia, 111
Kershaw, James, 381
Ketel, Milan, 118
Keyes, Daniel, 432
Kibbee, Lois, 445
Kidd, Michael, 385, 456
Kiley, Richard, 15, 25, 386, 387, 455, 456
Kilgallen, Dorothy, 37-38, 471

Kill the One-Eyed Man, 30
Killing of Sister George, The, 109, 110
Kilpatrick, Lincoln, 379, 380
Kilty, Jerome, 49
Kim, Willa, 394, 445
Kimbrell, Marketa, 379
Kimbro, John, 370
Kimbrough, Charles, 78
Kimbrough, Clinton, 80, 81
Kimmel, Alan, 431
Kindl, Charles, 417, 421, 423
King, Alan, 12-13, 21, 45, 376, 400
King, Dennis, 374
King, John Michael, 388
King, Lila, 373, 396
King, Phil, 409
King and I, The, 51, 80
King Henry V, 97, 438
King Henry IV, Part 1, 81, 93-94
King Henry VI, Part 2, 98-99
King Henry VIII, 98
King Lear, 48, 64, 94-95
Kingman, Dan, 419
Kingsley, Eleanore, 368
Kingsley, Evelyn, 408
Kingsley, Gershon, 424, 432
Kinoy, Ernest, 365
Kipness, Joe, 391
Kipnis, Leonid, 81, 93
Kirby, Durward, 390
Kirby, Randy, 390, 412, 455
Kirchner, Ray, 384
Kiritake, Icho, 403
Kiritake, Kamematsu, 403
Kiritake, Kanjuro, 403
Kiritake, Moniuro, 403
Kiritake, Monya, 403
Kirkham, Sam, 367
Kirkland, Sally, 63
Kirkup, James, 77, 86
Kirkwood, James, 394
Kirsch, Carolyn, 392
Kismet, 4, 28, 64, 368, 458
Kiss Me Kate, 51
Kissinger, Charles, 80
Kissman, Lee, 73
Kitch, Ken, 43, 65-66, 87
Kitchen, The, 35, 437
Kitt, Eartha, 440
Kjeldsen, Ingeborg, 368
Klein, Allen Edward, 437
Klein, Bob, 434
Klein, I. W., 395
Klein, Nita, 118
Klein, Reid, 411
Klenburg, Jana, 97, 430
Kliewer, Warren, 444
Kling, Esther, 74
Kling, Irene, 425
Klotz, Florence, 383, 405, 445
Klugman, Jack, 441
Klunis, Tom, 385, 410

Knack, The, 43, 70, 415, 441
Knapp, Elanore, 386
Kneeland, Richard, 85, 86
Knepper, Trent S., 436
Knickerbocker, Paine, 65
Knight, Esmond, 110
Knight, Irene, 469
Knight, Shirley, 429
Knight of the Burning Pestle, The, 117
Knott, Frederick, 13, 22, 396
Kobart, Ruth, 371, 392, 417
Kobe, Gail, 79
Kobrin, Barry, 375, 377
Koelb, Clayton, 73
Koenig, Lee, 370
Koesis, Robert, 445
Kohler, Cherri, 83
Kohutek, Walter, 407
Kokich, Kazimir, 377
Kolb, Mina, 432
Kolouch, Fred H., 407
Koltai, Ralph, 99
Koob, Micki, 82
Kook, Edward, 456
Kooperman, Debby, 96
Kopit, Arthur, 50, 64, 76-77, 112
Kornfeld, Lawrence, 431
Kornzweig, Ben, 387, 416, 420, 423, 427
Korthaze, Richard, 384
Korvin, Charles, 439
Koski-Long, 427
Kosman, Louis, 377
Kott, Jan, 66
Kotto, Yaphet, 384
Koutoukas, H. M., 454
Kovanda, Stephanie, 421
Kozlik, Al, 93
Kraft, Beatrice, 368
Krahl, Robert, 87
Kramer, Joel, 71
Krantz, Ben, 389
Kranz, Ben D., 370
Krapp's Last Tape, 30, 416-417
Krause, Alvina, 49
Krause, Karl Patrick, 420
Krause, Mark, 73
Krause, Richard, 371
Kraut, Elaine, 420
Krawford, Gary, 403, 440
Krawitz, Seymour, 97
Kree, Allan, 443
Kress, Phyllis, 75, 76
Kressyn, Miriam, 423
Krichbaum, Tom, 430
Kroll, Ronnie, 441
Kroschell, Joan, 428, 432
Krot, William, 418
Kruger, Hardy, 382
Kruse, Werner, 429
Krysiak, Joseph J., 98
Kuluva, Will, 79
Kupferman, Meyer, 384, 431
Kurland, Ina, 408

Kursner, Christian, 115
Kurtz, Marcia, 430
Kuss, Richard, 95, 396
Kuzmany, Elfriede, 407
Kya-Hill, Robert, 429

Lacey, Franklin, 366
Lacombe, André, 117
LaCrosse, Bob, 390, 408
Lacune, La, 115
Lacy, Tom, 81
Ladd, Margaret, 396, 441
Lady Windermere's Fan, 85
Laerum, Ursula, 407
Lagos, Poppy, 85
Laird, Marvin, 385, 410
Lake, Joan, 437
Lamb, Florence, 469
Lambert, Sherry, 418
Lamberts, Heath, 93
Lamble, Lloyd, 113
Lamont, Michael, 382
Lamont, Robert, 368
Lamp At Midnight, 457
Lampert, Zohra, 399
Lancaster, Dorothy, 420
Lancaster, Joyce, 87
Landau, Jack, 34, 428
Landek, Violetta, 409
Landi, Mari, 405
Landis, Jeanette, 393
Landowski, Marcel, 397
Landres, Simm, 432
Landry, Paul, 88
Lane, Burton, 377, 455, 456
Lane, David Maverick, 80
Lane, Jody, 367
Lane, Josephine, 73, 416
Lane, Mara, 78
Laney, Ben, 367, 413
Lang, Harold, 66
Lang, Philip J., 412, 418
Lange, Bobbi, 368, 391
Lange, Greg, 370
Langella, Frank, 83, 423, 427, 454
Langham, Michael, 92
Langhorne, Nancy, 71
Langman, Betsy, 385
Langner, Herbert B., 471
Lanier, Sidney, 399
Lanning, Jerry, 412
Lansbury, Angela, 18, 412, 454, 455, 456
Lansbury, Bruce, 400
Lansbury, Edgar, 400
Lanti, Al, 375
Larabee, Louise, 378
Larken, Sheila, 80
Larkey, Joan, 86
Larkin, Bob, 78
Larkin, Peter, 55, 396, 403, 457
Larkin, Robert, 383, 400, 410, 411, 421
Larkins, Ellis, 403
Larkins, Grady, 83

La Rocco, Jody, 408
LaRoche, Jacques, 470
Larsen, Bart, 370
Larsen, Darrell D., 470
Larson, Suzanne, 75
La Rue, Danny, 112
Lary, Betty June, 77
Lascelles, Kendrew, 401
LaSelva, Vincent, 372
Last Analysis, The, 63, 84, 86
Latimer, Ken, 50, 76-77
Lauer, Marian, 436
Laughlin, Sharon, 72, 75
Laughton, Charles, 73, 87
Laughwind, 30, 431
Laura, Larri, 469
Laurence, Elaine, 427
Laurence, Paula, 410
Laurenson, James, 100
Laurents, Arthur, 366, 457
Laurents, Clyde, 373
Laurie, Piper, 440
Lauter, Ed, 427
L'Avare, 4, 28, 397-398
LaVigne, Robert, 86-87
Lavin, Linda, 405, 417, 423, 428
Lawler, Ray, 75
Lawless, James, 82
Lawless, Sue, 89
Lawrence, Bruce, 419
Lawrence, Don, 373, 410
Lawrence, Elizabeth, 78
Lawrence, Henry, 408
Lawrence, Jack, 365
Lawrence, Jerome, 18, 412
Lawrence, Miriam, 410
Lawrence, Ruth, 391, 413
Lawrence, Stephen, 424
Lawson, Kate Drain, 56
Lawson, Lee, 441
Lawton, Frank, 111
Lax, Francis, 114
Laye, Dilys, 111
Laye, Evelyn, 111
Layton, Joe, 375
Leabo, Loi, 392, 393
Leader of the Pack, 70
League of Resident Theaters, 43
Leake, Leon, 87
Leaming, Chet, 394
Leath, Ron, 78
Leatherman, Allen, 75, 76
Leatherman, Vaughn, 76
Leberfeld, Alfred, 65, 86, 87
LeBlanc, Whitney, 72
Lebor, Stanley, 100
Le Brun, Barbara, 77
LeClair, Henry, 411
Ledbetter, William, 371
Ledoux, Fernand, 114
Lee, Jack, 51
Lee, James E., 470
Lee, Joyce, 430
Lee, Martin, 394

Lee, Ming Cho, 95, 97
Lee, Moe, 469
Lee, Robert E., 18, 412
Lee, Sondra, 371
Leeds, Elissa, 400
Leeds, Nancy, 424
Leeds, Phil, 417, 423
Leeds, Sandy, 382
Lees, C. Lowell, 55, 83
Leffingwell, Dolores, 419
Left-Handed Liberty, 110
Le Gallienne, Eva, 64, 71, 454
Leggett, Gene, 77
Lehmann, Jo Ann, 404
Lehmeyer, John, 80, 81
Leibman, Ron, 63
Leigh, Carolyn, 77
Leigh, Jack, 385
Leigh, Mitch, 386, 455, 456
Leigh, Vivien, 23, 68, 410
Leighton, Margaret, 6, 24
Leinek, Mischa, 429
LeMassena, William, 431
Lemberger, Silvia, 407
Le Mottet, Alain, 115
Lenelle, Royce, 78, 440
Lenert, Marguerite, 85, 86
Lengel, William C., 470
Lennard, Maria, 79
Lennart, Isobel, 365
LeNoire, Rosetta, 396
Lensky, Leib, 430
Lenz, Rick, 383
Leokum, Arkady, 32, 33, 421
Leon, Felix, 22, 383
Leonard, Hugh, 67
Leonard, Lu, 375
Leonard, Michael, 390, 455
Leonard, Robert, 74-75
Leonard Bernstein's Theater Songs, 30, 34, *418*
Leontovich, Eugenie, 75
LePage, Roger, 373
LePelley, Lynn, 80
Le Person, Paul, 118
Le Poulain, Jean, 115
Lerman, Leo, 452
Lerner, Alan Jay, 3, 16, 377, 456
Le Sage, Alain-René, 113
Lesko, John, 385
Lesley, Brenda, 427
Leslie, May, 469
Lesser, Arthur, 391
Lesson, The, 89
Lester, Barbara, 389
Lester, Edwin, 56
Lester, Hugh E., 73
Lester, Seeleg, 56
Letchworth, Eileen, 372, 390
Letton, Sara, 410
Levasseur, André, 398
Levin, Bernard, 37
Levin, Dan, 394
Levin, Ira, 375, 455
Levin, Jane, 393

Levin, Michael, 382
Levine, Elliot, 436
Levine, Joseph, 445
Levine, Rhoda, 432
Levine, Sam, 6
Levinson, Nancy, 77
Levy, Jacques, 454
Levy, Richard, 380, 381
Lewin, John, 82
Lewis, Andy, 73
Lewis, Artis, 419
Lewis, Bobo, 66
Lewis, Bonda, 99
Lewis, Carol Ann, 428
Lewis, Dave, 73
Lewis, Emory, 451, 454
Lewis, Hal, 50, 77
Lewis, Lorna, 85
Lewis, Marcia, 427
Lewis, Michael, 377
Lewis, Ripple, 367
Lewis, Robert, 377
Lewis, Sammy, 57
Lewis, Teak, 408
Lewis, William, 371
Libertini, Dick, 428
Libin, Paul, 427, 433
Licht, David, 426
Lichtenstein, Sylvia, 420
Lide, Miller, 410
Lieb, Herman, 469
Liebgold, Leon, 423
Lietzau, Hans, 407
Life's A Dream, 118
Liff, Samuel, 389, 398
L'Illusion Comique, 116
Lilo, 403
Lily in Little India, A, 110
Lincoln Center Music Theater, *See* Music Theater of Lincoln Center
Lincoln Center Repertory Company, *See* Repertory Theater of Lincoln Center
Linden, Hal, 377
Linders, Diana, 71
Lindfors, Viveca, 382
Lindley, Audrey, 445
Lindsay, Joan, 367, 408
Lindy Opera House (Los Angeles, Calif.), 56
Linenthal, Michael, 87
Lines, Jack, 419, 420
Linkletter, Art, 57
Linn, Margaret, 96
Linn, Ralph, 412
Linton, Betty, 408
Linville, Larry, 85, 436
Lion in Winter, The, 3, 4, 13, 14, 20-21, 25, 324-347, *400-401*, 451, 452, 456
LiPari, Victor, 433
Lipsky, David, 390, 412, 420, 428, 433
Lipsky, Lisa, 412
Lipton, Michael, 421, 454
Lipton, Susan, 434

Lissek, Leon, 393
Lithgow, Arthur W., 85
Little, Cleavon, 436
Little, Terence, 412
Little Fox Theater (San Francisco, Calif.), 66
Little Foxes, The, 74
Little Malcolm and His Struggles with The Eunuchs, 111
Little Mary Sunshine, 43, 82-83
Little Pete, 66
Little Winter Love, A, 110
Littlefield, Nick, 368
Littlewood, Joan, 79
Litvinoff, Seymour, 418
Litwin, Wallace, 428
Live Like Pigs, 12, 30, 33, *416*
Living Theater, 454
Lloyd, Robert, 100, 393
Lo Bianco, Tony, 445
Locke, Bob, 99
Lockhart, James, 437
Lockwood, Margaret, 111
Loesser, Frank, 28, 80, 454
Loeb, John Jacob, 417
Logan, Joshua, 367, 443
Logan, Leroy, 98
Logan, Terrence, 376
Loker, William A., 469
Lokos, Allan, 373
Lola D'Annunzio Award, 454
Lomax, Terry, 385, 432
Lombard, Michael, 385
Lombard, Peter, 374
Lombardo, Carmen, 417
Lombardo, Guy, 417
London, Chet, 430
London, Judy, 73, 85
London, Roy, 431
Long, Sumner Arthur, 70
Long, Zola, 407
Long Day's Journey into Night, A, 48, 52, 83, 87
Long Wharf Theater (New Haven, Conn.), 36, 82-83
Longwell, Dennis, 78
Loper, Robert, 88
Lorca, *see* García Lorca
Lorentz, Kay, 429
Lorentz, Lore, 429
Los Angeles Civic Light Opera Company, 56
Lothar, Mark, 407
Loudon, Dorothy, 441
Louise, Mary, 395
Louw, Allan, 390
Love for Love, 83, 111
Lovejoy, Robin, 76
Lover, The, 79, 114, 117
Loverman, Celia, 63
Love's Labor's Lost, 30, 95-96, 99-100, *417*
Loving Couch, The, 444
Lowell, Robert, 31-32

Lowens, Curt, 382
Lowenstein, Sonia, 97
Lowrie, Edward, 469
Lowry, Jane, 70
Lowry, Judith, 83, 379
Lowry, Rudd, 469
Loy, Myrna, 439
Lozano, Roy, 382
Lu, Lisa, 66
Lubritsky, Fanny, 86
Lucas, Philip, 367, 408
Luckinbill, Lawrence, 85
Ludlow Fair, 30, *432*
Ludvinsky, Sholom, 384
Ludwig, Karen, 385
Ludwig, Salem, 70
Luisi, James, 395
Lum, Charles N., 469
Lumpkin, Elizabeth, 50, 76
Lumsden, Geoffrey, 398, 455
Lunch Hour, The, 73
Lund, Art, 394, 408
Lundell, Kert, 425, 434
Lupino, Richard, 83
Lurie, Samuel, 394, 400, 431
Lusby, Vernon, 367
Lustik, Marlena, 403, 404
Lutes, Betty, 74
Lutz, William, 375
Luv, 46, 68, 117, 365, 441
Lux, Michael, 426
Lyman, Libby, 70
Lynch, Hal, 79
Lynch, Nancy, 375, 412
Lynch, Richard, 78, 385
Lynn, Amy, 378, 456
Lynn, Ann, 112
Lynn, Anne, 78
Lynn, Jeffrey, 439
Lynn, Jim, 413
Lynn, Jonathan, 110
Lynn, Reginald, 420
Lynne, Gillian, 373
Lynne, James Broom, 33, 421
Lynne, Vincent, 405
Lyon, Eve, 70-71
Lysinger, Pat, 377

McAfee, Don, 424
McAnallen, William J., 424
McAndrew, Pat, 433
McAneny, Patricia, 429
McArthur, Susan, 75
Macaulay, Pauline, 111
McAcity, Helen, 383
McBride, Ora, 367
McBride, Vaughn, 76, 82
McCall, Angela, 469
McCallum, Sandy, 82, 86
McCarten, John, 451, 454-455
McCarter Theater (Princeton, N. J.), 85
McCarthy, Michael, 82
McClain, John, 37, 452
McClanahan, Ruth, 405
MacClay, Gina, 374

McClintock, Ernie, 97
McConnell, Ty, 75, 400, 440
MacCormack, Cara, 431
MacCormack, Monica, 425
McCormick, Michael, 370
McCormick, Parker, 401, 422
McCreery, Bud, 428
McCullers, Carson, 60
McDaniel, Tennent, 386
McDermott, Tom, 398, 399
McDevitt, Ruth, 439
McDonald, Dan, 93
MacDonald, Elizabeth, 87
McDonald, Jon Renn, 97
McDonald, Joyce, 368, 410
McDonald, Marie, 469
MacDonald, Norman, 97
McDonald, Pirie, 52, 87
MacDonald, Robert David, 415
MacDonald-Rouse, Heather, 401
McDorman, John, 72
McDowell, Malcolm, 101
McElroy, Evie, 82
McEnery, Peter, 100
McEnnis, Pat, 408
McFarland, Robert, 88
McGee, Patrick, 100
McGeorge, Nancy, 367
McGinn, Walter, 441
McGinness, Mary, 75, 76
McGonagill, Gerald E., 96
McGowan, Adair, 388
McGraith, Tony, 436
McGrath, Joe, 408
McGrath, Russell, 381
McGuire, Michael, 96
McGuire, Pat, 72
McGuire, Paul, 414
McIlwraith, Bill, 110
McInerney, Bernie, 86
McIntosh, Ann, 431
McKail, David, 110
McKay, Alex, 392
MacKay, John, 82
McKayle, Donald, 411
McKellen, Ian, 109, 110
McKenna, Marilyn, 420
McKenna, Siobhan, 113
McKereghan, William, 72
McKern, Leo, 111
Mackintosh, Robert, 18, 412, 423, 455
MacLane, Gretchen, 430
McLaughlin, Mac, 71
McLean, Bruce, 88
McLean, Douglas, 374
MacLeish, Archibald, 43, 71
MacLeod, Jane, 78
McLiam, John, 79
MacLiammoir, Michael, 74
MacMahon, Aline, 95
McMahon, Horace, 440
MacManus, Patricia F., 470
McMartin, John, 395, 455, 456
McMillan, Kenneth, 74

McMurdo, Judy, 408
McNamara, Dermot, 398
McNamara, Rosemary, 408
McNamee, Robert, 370
McNelis, Neil, 368
McQueen, Simon, 404
McQuiggan, John A., 81
McQuire, Michael, 87
MacRae, Duncan, 113
MacVeigh, Earle, 368
McWhinney, Donald, 445
McWhorter, George T., 408
Macbeth, 92, 99
Mace, Louis L., 470
Macero, Ted, 427
Machado, Maria, 118
Machiz, Herbert, 372
Mackey of Appalachia, *437*
Mackie, Philip, 445
Macri, Carlos, 367, 408
Mad Show, The, 30, 33, *428-429*, 451, 458
Madame Mousse, 444
Madame Princesse, 114, 116
Madden, Henry, 421
Maddox, Diana, 79
Madness of Lady Bright, The, 30, *432*
Madsen, Karen, 94
Madurga, Gonzolo, 97
Magee, Patrick, 113, 455, 456
Madwoman of Chaillot, The, 64, 116
Magidson, Herman, 404, 408
Magill, John, 436
Magre, Judith, 118
Mahar, Joseph, 74
Maher, Joseph, 416
Mahon, John, 431
Mahoney, Bill, 78
Mai, Fabiène, 118
Mairich, Max, 407
Maitland, Michael, 367, 412, 420
Major Barbara, 43, 73, 78, 85
Make Like a Dog, *431*
Malcolm, 4, 21, *394*, 457
Malcolm, John, 411
Malcolm, Reginald, 469
Maldener, Fritz, 429
Malekos, Nick, 395
Malin, Ella A., vii, 42
Malony, Peter, 423
Maloof, Gloria, 72
Mame, 4, 7, 16, 18, 25, 39, 45, *412*, 451, 452, 456, 458
Mamma, La, 116
Man and Superman, 75, 109, 112
Man Better Man, 113
Man for All Seasons, A, 57, 74
Man of La Mancha, 3, 4, 5, 6, 14-16, 25, 31, 195-220, *386-387*, 444, 451, 452, 454, 456, 458

Mandan, Robert, 420
Mandel, Loring, 43, 67, 89
Maney, Richard, 368, 370, 414
Manhoff, Bill, 365
Manikum, Philip, 110
Mankowitz, Wolf, 111
Manley, Beatrice, 379, 380
Mann, Gus, 72
Mann, Paul, 379
Mann, Sam, 469
Mann, Stanley, 32, 429
Mann, Stuart, 408
Mann, Theodore, 382, 383, 416, 420, 427, 433
Mann, Winifred, 65, 86, 87
Manning, David, 413
Manning, Jane, 428
Manning, Mary, 74
Manosalvas, Alfonso, 97
Man's a Man, A, 66
Mansfield, Jayne, 444
Manuti, Al, 471
Mapes, Leslie Ann, 373
Marand, Patricia, 405-406, 456
Marat/Sade, see Persecution and Assassination of Marat as Performed by the Inmates of the Asylum of Charenton Under the Direction of the Marquis de Sade, The
Marceau, Félicien, 116
Marcel Marceau, 4, 24, *386*
March, Iva, 404
Marchand, Corinne, 117
Marchand, Nancy, 401, 423
Marching Song, 457
Marc'O, 115
Marcus, David, 423
Marcus, Frank, 110
Marcus, Selma, 373
Marcy, George, 375
Marden, Adrienne, 56
Mardi Gras!, 30, *417-418*
Margo Jones Awards, 454
Margolin, Stuart, 83
Margolis, Ken, 87
Marguilies, David, 74, 85
Mari, Dolores, 371
Marian, Sid, 469
Marie, Rose, 51
Marie-Antoinette, 436
Marines Theater (San Francisco, Calif.), 66, 86-87
Marino, Louis, 471
Marivaux, Pierre de, 116
Mark, Donald, 408
Mark Taper Forum (Los Angeles, Calif.), 54
Mark Twain Tonight!, 4, 7, *404-405*, 451, 456
Markfield, Dwight, 436
Markham, Monte, 83
Markley, Carol, 88
Markley, Marilyn, 77

Marks, Alfred, 111
Marks, Walter, 365
Marlatt, Donald, 436
Marley, John, 72
Marlin-Jones, Davy, 67, 89
Marlowe, Arthur, 398, 399
Marlowe, Christopher, 60
Marlowe, Hugh, 444
Marlowe, Jack, 445
Maronek, James, 74-75
Maroze, Mario, 410
Marquis, Dixie, 396
Marqusee, John, 429
Marraccini, Carol, 418
Marr, Richard, 408
Marre, Albert, 14, 25, 386, 456
Marriage-Go-Round, The, 76
Marriage of Mr. Mississippi, The, 113
Mars, Kenneth, 405
Marsden, Betty, 112
Marshall, E. G., 445
Marshall, Herbert, 469
Marshall, Mary, 86
Marshall, Mort, 409
Marshall, Peter L., 384, 385
Marshall, Richard, 97
Martel, Michel, 401
Martin, Barry L., 392
Martin, Elliot, 383
Martin, Erin, 385
Martin, Herbert, 390
Martin, Lucy, 73
Martin, Mary, 37, 39, 50, 440
Martin, Michel, 397
Martin, Nan, 445
Martin, Nicholas, 80, 81, 98
Martinsen, Linda, 77
Marx, Arthur, 12
Mary, Mary, 40, 50, 52, 76
Maryan, Charles, 427, 432
Marye, Donald, 398
Mascolo, Joseph, 74
Maskin, Marc, 382
Mason, André, 114
Mason, Brewster, 100, 101, 112
Mason, Eric, 405
Mason, Gaylord C., 422
Mason, Ginia, 373
Mason, Linn, 394
Mason, Marilyne, 405
Masque of Dublin, The, 74
Massey, Anna, 112
Massie, Paul, 93
Masteroff, Joseph, 86
Masters, Marie, 83
Matchgirls, The, 112
Matheson, Murray, 79
Mathews, Carmen, 390
Mathews, Diana, 436
Mathews, George, 411
Mathews, Richard, 95
Matias, 421
Mathieu, William, 75, 434

Mating Dance, 4, 22, *383*
Matlovsky, Samuel, 79
Matsuda, Wackichi, 403
Matthau, Walter, 441
Matthews, Art, 377, 412
Matthews, Gerry, 377, 399
Matthews, William, 84
Mauban, Maria, 116, 117
Mauclair, Jacques, 397
Maude-Roxby, Roddy, 111, 441
Maugham, W. Somerset, 111, 470
Maunder, Wayne, 98
Maurer, Frederick, 407
Maurer, Ralph, 428
Maurette, Marcelle, 387
Max, Jerome, 422
Maxim, John, 392
Maxon, Richard, 410
Maxtone-Graham, John, 378
Maxwell, Paul, 110
Maxwell, Robert E., Jr., 408
May, Elaine, 445
Maye, Anita, 424
Mayer, Paul Avila, 84
Mayo, Lisa, 421, 428
Mayo, Nick, 57
Mayo, Virginia, 444
Mays, Kenneth, 394
Maza, Luis, 72
Mazen, Glenn, 379, 380
Mazin, Stan, 408, 410
Mazzone-Clementi, Carlo, 379, 380, 381
Mazzotti, Pascal, 118
Me and Thee, 4, 22, 64, *390*
Meadow, Leslie, 418
Mears, DeAnn, 71, 85
Measure for Measure, 47, 73, 92, 118
Mechanic Theater (Baltimore, Md.), 40
Medea, 30, 34, 56, 57, *427*
Meehan, Danny, 428, 440
Meeker, Ralph, 23, 370
Mehl, Brynnar, 393, 413
Mehl, Charles, 377
Mehring, Wolfgang, 118
Meister, Barbara, 408
Meister, Philip, 426
Melad, Alan A., 73, 74
Melfi, Leonard, 432
Mellor, James, 393
Melnick, Daniel, 382
Melody, Deanna, 413
Melton, Paul, 89
Melvin, Murray, 112
Menken, Helen, 469
Menotti, Gian Carlo, 371, 372
Mensching, Herbert, 407
Merande, Doro, 367
Mercado, Hector, 382
Mercer, Florence, 413
Mercer, Mabel, 371
Mercer, Marian, 423

Merchant, Vivien, 110
Merchant of Venice, The, 99-100
Meredith, Philip, 101
Merin, Eda Reiss, 83
Merivale, John, 410
Meriweather, William, 416
Merlis, Iris, 407
Merkey, Ryland, 50, 76, 79
Merman, Ethel, 28, 57, 413
Merrick, David, 7, 24-25, 28, 35, 36-39, 49, 63, 370, 389, 454, 456
Merrick, Jeannie Gibson, 377, 400
Merrigal, Alice, 437
Merry Wives of Windsor, The, 97-98
Mette, Jack, 439
Metropolitan Opera House, 40
Metropolus, Penny, 77
Metzger, Rita, 388
Metzler, Larry, 97
Meurisse, Paul, 117
Meyer, Lester, 470
Meyer, Lorraine, 79
Meyer, Michael, 86
Meyers, Donald, 418
Meyers, Jerry, 368
Meyers, Lannie, 432
Meyrand, Pierre, 114
Michael, Logan, 373
Michaels, Frankie, 412, 455, 456
Michaels, Lani, 373
Michaels, Laura, 411
Michaels, Marilyn, 440
Michaels, Sidney, 56, 76
Michaels, Sully, 469
Michel, Georges, 115
Middleton, Ray, 15, 366, 386, 387
Middleton, Thomas, 112
Midsummer Night's Dream, A, 66, 85, 87, 91, 117
Mielziner, Jo, 25, 26, 367, 381, 389, 409, 445
Migenes, Julia, 371
Mignal, Marie-France 117
Mihalyi Judith, 85
Mikado, The, 416, *419*
Miksak, Joseph, 87
Miles, Bernard, 110, 112
Miles, Hank, 390
Miles, Reginald, 74
Miles, Ross, 373, 412
Miles, Sylvia, 422
Milgrim, Lynn, 46, 73
Milk Train Doesn't Stop Here Anymore, The, 65, 87
Milland, Ray, 22, 398
Millar, Ronald, 112
Millay, Edna St. Vincent, 53
Miller, Arthur, 35, 43, 60, 80, 82, 84, 85, 415

Miller, Barbara, 85, 391
Miller, Betty, 71, 387
Miller, David, 399
Miller, Dick, 405
Miller, Fred, 370
Miller, Harold, 97
Miller, Harry, 434
Miller, Joe, 97
Miller, Jonathan, 71, 84
Miller, June, 425
Miller, Melinda, 89
Miller, Michael, 49, 410
Miller, Pat, 77
Miller, Richard, 370
Miller, Sharon, 408, 410
Milli, Robert, 82
Milligan, John, 385
Millikin, Paul, 73
Milner, Roger, 112
Milnes, Sherrill, 371
Milo, Vic, 469
Milwaukee Repertory Theater (Wisconsin), 80-81
Miner, Barbara, 78
Miner, Peter, 428
Minnesota Theater Company, 58-62
Minoff, Lee, 443
Minor, Philip, 81, 86, 98
Minor Miracle, 4, 22, *374,* 444
Minot, Anna, 410
Minto, John, 83
Mintun, John, 436
Mintz, Eli, 421
Mintz, Thelma, 423
Miracle Worker, The, 40
Misa, Ronnie, 379
Misanthrope, The, 49
Miser, The, 58, 73, 81, 82
Miss Julie, 30, 63, 85, 110, 113, 118, *425*
Mitchell, Adrian, 11, 269, 393
Mitchell, David, 427
Mitchell, Donald J., 405
Mitchell, Joseph, 365
Mitchell, Keven, 85
Mitchell, Ruth, 405
Mitschuldigen, Die, 4, 28, *406-407*
Mittelman, Minal, 79
Mixon, Alan, 385, 420
Mix, Richard, 79-80
Miyoshi, Shoraku, 403
Moak, Bob, 75-76
Moberly, Robert, 86
Mochizuki, Tatsuhachiro, 403
Modo, Michel, 392
Moe, Henry Allen, 35
Moerel, Jan, 85
Moes, Nicholas, 393
Moffat, David, 367
Moffat, Donald, 71, 85, 387
Moffatt, Sarah, 112
Moffit, Constance, 411
Mogck, David, 384

Moigne, Guy, 114
Moiseiwitsch, Tanya, 58, 81
Mole, Jean-Michel, 392
Molière, 28, 49, 70, 71, 73, 75, 78, 80, 84, 85, 86, 88, 113
Molitch, Louis, 471
Moller, Lindsay, 87
Molloy, Edward A., 437
Molnar, Robert, 436-437
Momma, Look at Bang Bang, 64
Mondy, Pierre, 114, 116
Monette, Bruce, 96
Monette, LaVergne, 408
Monette, Richard, 93
Monfort, Silvia, 117
Monk, George, 436
Monk, Julius, 34, 415, 422
Monkhouse, Bob, 113
Monnot, Marguerite, 74
Monod, Jacques, 115
Monopoly, 30, 32, *431*
Monsieur Alexandre, 115
Montague, Lee, 21, 376
Monte, Barbara, 377
Montel, Michael, 98
Montero, Germaine, 114
Montgomery, Bruce, 75
Montgomery, Earl, 380
Montgomery, Mann-Earl, 381
Montgomery, Ray, 444
Month, Christopher, 370
A Month in the Country, 109, 113
Montherlant, Henri de, 28
Mook, Tom, 419
Moon for the Misbegotten, A, 74
Mooney, William, 34, 432
Moor, Bill, 436
Moore, Charles, 384
Moore, Dudley, 71, 84, 432
Moore, Gary, 77
Moore, Gilda G., 83
Moore, James, 375
Moore, Jonathan, 445
Moore, Muriel, 72
Moore, Richard, 101
Moore, Robert, 390
Moore, Sandra, 77
Moore, Stan, 416
Moorehead, Agnes, 51
Moosholzer, A., 407
Morales, Carmen, 375, 395
Moran, Monica, 439
Moran, Pat, 469
Morand, Sylvester, 101
Mordern, Roger, 436
More, Julian, 74
Moreau, Jean-Baptiste, 430
Morehouse, Ward, 451, 454
Moreland, Donald, 435
Moretti, Michèle, 115
Morgan, Al, 374, 444
Morgan, Roger, 416, 427, 432, 434

Moriarty, Michael, 73, 96, 98
Morley, Judith, 443
Morley, Ruth, 383, 396
Morlock, Martin, 429
Morrill, Theodore, 420
Morris, Chester, 441
Morris, Edmund, 426
Morris, Edward, 424
Morris, Janet, 371
Morris, John, 95
Morris, Leslie, 371
Morris, Lynn, 374
Morris, Newbold, 471
Morris Repertory Theater, 81
Morris, Wendy, 371
Morrish, Ann, 111
Morrison, Hobe, vii, 452
Morrissey, Eamon, 398
Morrow, Karen, 392, 408
Morse, George, 385, 386
Morse, Richard, 95, 434
Morss, Chester, 422
Mortimer, John, 73
Morton, Brooks, 410
Morton, John Marison, 85
Morton, Winn, 418
Moskalenko, Konstantin, 393, 410
Mosley, Louise, 76
Mosley, Robert, 371
Moss, Larry, 375
Moss, Robert, 387
Moss, Stillman, 88
Most Happy Fella, The, 4, 28, *407-408*
Mostel, Zero, 440
Mostoller, Ramse, 445
Mother Courage, 81, 85
Motley, Robert, 74
Mounier, Henry, 115
Mount, Patty, 411
MPO Pictures, Inc., 406
Mr. Welk and Jersey Jim, 67, 89
Mrozek, Slawomir, 113, 118
Mrs. Dally, 4, 24, 37, 38, *370*, 444
Much Ado About Nothing, 98-99
Muchnick, Ronald, 432
Muldaur, Diana, 21, 372
Mulholland, Mary, 78
Mullen, Margaret, 388
Muller, Leo J., 408
Mulligan, Richard, 383
Munro, Alexis, 77
Munroe, Richard C., 72
Munsel, Patrice, 51
Munshin, Jules, 392, 439, 441
Munson, Estella, 419
Mura, Corinna, 469
Murawski, C., 429
Murch, Robert, 398
Murphy, Alec, 407
Murphy, Pamela, 376
Murphy, Peter, 433

Murray, Anne, 85
Murray, Brian, 441
Murray, Heidi, 372
Murray, Jack, 411
Murray, Janet, 94
Murray, Lewis, 429
Murray, Michael, 73, 425
Murzeau, Robert, 116
Musante, Tony, 66
Musants, Tony, 85
Music Box Theater (Los Angeles, Calif.), 56
Music Center (Los Angeles, Calif.), 54
Music Man, The, 4, 28, 40, 366, *367*
Music Theater of Lincoln Center (Lincoln Center Music Theater), 28, 413-414
Musica, La, 115
Musser, Tharon, 94, 374, 394, 396, 400-401, 412, 445
Muth, May, 390
Mutilated, The, 399
My Wife and I, 43, 78
Myers, Barbara, 389
Myers, Gene, 413
Myers, Michaele, 376, 425
Myers, William, 88
Mylroie, Jayme, 405

Nabokov, Vladimir, 457
Naccarato, John, 83
Nadder, Robert, 385
Nadel, Norman, 36, 451, 456
Naismith, Laurence, 411
Namiki, Senryu, 403
Napier, Alan, 79
Narai, Kuniko, 413
Nardone, Nikki, 407
Naselius, G. E., 74-75
Nash, Mary, 469
Nash, Roderick, 82
Nathan Weinstein, Mystic, Connecticut, 4, 22, *399-400*
National Council on the Arts, 44
National Endowment for the Arts, 35-36
National Endowment for the Humanities, 35-36
National Foundation on the Arts and Humanities, 35, 44
National Repertory Theater, 64
National Shakespeare Festival (San Diego National Shakespeare Festival; San Diego, California), 97-98
Natwick, Mildred, 439
Naughton, Bill, 111
Naughton, Harry, 375
Nazawa, Katsutaro, 403
Neag, Martha, 385
Neagle, Anna, 111

Neal, Sally, 368
Neary, William, 86
Nederlander, James, 40
Nederlander, Joseph, 40
Needles, William, 94
Negin, Mark, 84
Negri, Addi, 367
Negrin, Mark, 71
Negroni, Jean, 118
Neiditch, Max, 426
Neilson, Richard, 373
Nelson, Arvid, 79
Nelson, Barry, 390
Nelson, Gwen, 110
Nelson, Herbert, 96
Nelson, Joseph, 388
Nelson, Kenneth, 440
Nelson, Richard, 87, 381
Nelson, Ruth, 81
Nemiroff, Robert, 382
Neruda, Pablo, 97
Nesbitt, Max, 469
Nesor, Al, 403
Nettleton, Lois, 394
Nettum, Mari, 411
Nettum, Richard, 97
Netzel, Sally, 76, 77
Neumann, Alfred, 415
Neukum, Bob, 368
Never Too Late, 40, 70, 75, 78
Nevins, April, 405
Nevins, Claudette, 380
Nevin, Hardwick, 470
Nevins, Zerba, 409
New Cole Porter Review, 30, *428*
New Dramatists, 34
New Playwrights Productions Co., Inc., 428
New Theater Monday Night Play Series, The, 34-35
New Theater Workshop, The, 437
New York City Center, 397
New York City Light Opera Company, 28, 392
New York City Opera, 28
New York Drama Critics Circle, 7, 15
New York Shakespeare Festival, 30, 34, 91-93, 95-98, 417, 438
New York University, 43
Newark, N. J., State College Theater for the Performing Arts, 40
Neway, Patricia, 371
Newley, Anthony, 78, 366, 441
Newman, David, 3, 405
Newman, Judy, 405
Newman, Stephen D., 88, 98
Newman, William, 88
Newton, Christopher, 441
Newton, Ruth, 383
Nicaud, Philippe, 117

Nicholas, Carl, 408
Nichols, Thomas, 77
Nicholson, Terry, 408
Nicolaj, Aldo, 118
Niemeyer, Joseph H., 469
Nieves, Richard, 388, 418
Night of the Iguana, 72
Night-Train, The, 117
Nigro, Harry, 405
No Exit, 79
Noah, 84
Noble, Eulalie, 376
Noble, Sally, 82, 83
Noël, Denise, 117
Noel, Jacques, 114, 397
Nolfi, Ed, 418
Nollman, Barbara, 428, 430, 431
Norden, Betsy, 410
Norell, Michael, 70, 80
Norgate, Cliff, 101
Norman, Hal, 410, 403, 404
Norman, Monty, 74
Normington, John, 111
Norris, Christopher, 389
North, Alan, 366
North, Corinne F., 469
Norton, Elliot, 45
Nos Femmes, 115
Nossen, Bram, 370
Notara, Darrell, 384
Notaro, Janice, 411
Nothing For Elizabeth, 444
Noto, Lore, 390
Novak, Mark, 371
Novarro, Ken, 382
Nowak, Henry J., 96
Nozawa, Matsunosuke, 403
Nozawa, Katsuhei, 403
Numance (Numantia), 114
Nugent, Nelle, 396
Nunn, Trevor, 113
Nuss, Bill, 373
Nyberg, Peter, 437
Nye, Carrie, 372, 427
Nygaard, Ragnhild, 74
Nype, Russell, 57, 440

Oaks, J. Vernon, 388
Oberlin, Richard, 75, 76
Obey, Andre, 84
Obie Awards, 454
O'Brien, Adale, 83
O'Brien, Chester, 367
O'Brien, Chet, 393, 409
O'Brien, David, 411
O'Brien, Justin, 378
O'Brien, Richard, 376, 424
O'Brien, Sylvia, 378
O'Casey, Sean, 71, 83, 112, 118, 444
Ocasio, José, 97
O'Connell, James, 437
O'Connell, Patricia, 98
O'Connell, Richard L., 83
O'Connor, Frank, 470
O'Connor, Kathryn, 469

O'Connor, Kevin, 433, 454
O'Connor, Rita, 404, 408
Odets, Clifford, 60, 365
Odd Couple, The, 5, 12, 16, 366, 441
O'Dowd, Michael, 430
Oestreicher, Gerard, 382
Oeuf à la Coque, L', 116
Offenbach, Jacques, 81
Office, The, 5, 444
Offner, Mortimer, 470
Ogee, George, 439
Ogier, Bulle, 115
Oglesby, Ronda, 80
Oh Dad, Poor Dad, Etc., 43, 50, 76, 102, 112
Oh What a Lovely War, 68, 74, 79, 89
O'Horgan, Tom, 433
Oklahoma, 4, 28, 416
Old Dominion Foundation, 44
Old Glory, The, 31, 457
O'Leary, John, 74
Oliver, 4, 24, 102, 370, 441
Oliver, Henry, 399
Oliver, Larry, 372
Oliver, Rochelle, 403
Oliver, Thelma, 395, 455
Olivier, Sir Laurence, 111
Olney, Md., Theater, 36, 67-68
O'Loughlin, Gerald S., 403
Olrich, April, 401
Olson, Dale, 54
Olson, James, 399
Olson, Joyce, 393, 408
Olson, Uta, 74
O'Malley, Etain, 83, 420
O'Malley, Grania, 425
O'Malley, Pat, 469
Omens, Estelle, 428
On a Clear Day You Can See Forever, 4, 5, 14, 16, 377, 456, 458
On the High Seas, 118
On the Level, 110, 112
On the Town, 418
On the Wagon, 112
110 in the Shade, 51
O'Neil, Joyce, 411
O'Neill, Dick, 384, 385
O'Neill, Eugene, 43, 55, 60, 74, 79, 83, 87
Opéra du Monde, L', 115
Oppenheimer, George, 452
Orbach, Jerry, 368, 413, 439
Orchard, Julian, 373
Ordinatsky, Janet, 426
O'Reare, James, 79
O'Regan, Michael, 94
Oregon Shakespeare Festival (Ashland, Ore.), 43, 98-99
Orestes, 117
Orin, Renee, 399
O'Riordan, Patricia, 367, 436
Ornadel, Cyril, 372

Orson, Barbara, 85, 86
Ortega, Carlos M., 470
Orth, Elisabeth, 407
Orton, Joe, 21, 376
Osborn, Paul, 443
Osborne, John, 3, 9-10, 35, 64, 110, 118, 221, 389, 457
O'Shaughnessy, John, 74
O'Shea, Tessie, 19-20, 411
Osin, Fred, 410
Osterhouse, Garveth, 77
Ostermayer, Christine, 407
Ostrin, Arthur, 399
Ostrovsky, Alexander, 80
O'Sullivan, Mairin D., 10, 25, 398, 456
O'Sullivan, Maureen, 441
O'Sullivan, Michael, 17, 25, 50, 76, 85, 98, 405-406, 456
Osuna, Jess, 426, 427, 431, 454
Other Heart, The, 457
O'Toole, Peter, 109, 110
Ottenheimer, Albert M., 423, 430
Otto, Jeanne, 399
Our Town, 40, 76, 117
Out of Bounds, 118
Outcasts, The, 56
Outer Circle Awards, 454
Overdog, The, 112
Owen, Alun, 110
Owen, Bill, 112
Owen, Catherine Dale, 469
Owen, Edith, 75, 76
Owen, Paul, 78
Owens, Edwin, 95
Owl and the Pussycat, The, 365, 440, 457
Owl Answers, The, 436
Oyster, Jim, 370, 398, 399

Pabón, Ramón, 97
Pacitti, Joe, 75
Packard, William, 34, 430
Packer, Lyman, 71
Packer, Tina, 100
Padula, Nick, 429
Pagan, Norma Iris, 97
Pagan, Peter, 398, 399
Page, Anthony, 389
Page, Evelyn, 377
Page, Geneviève, 116
Page, Geraldine, 396
Page, Patti, 51
Page, Robert, 99
Page, Stan, 367, 412
Paget, Christine, 436
Pagnol, Marcel, 116
Paige, Joan, 418
Paisner, Dina, 416
Palace Theater (N.Y.C.), 40
Palmer, Betsy, 366
Palmer, Craig, 419, 420
Palmer, Lilli, 110
Palmieri, Joseph, 97

Palmstierna-Weiss, Gunilla, 11, 393, 455, 456
Palumbo, Patti, 418
Panko, Tom, 392, 412
Papa, Bruce, 371
Pape, David, 94
Papp, Joseph, 90, 95, 97
Pappas, Gretchen, 74-75
Pappas, William, 74-75
Parasite, The, 30, 428
Paravents, Les, 115
Pardoll, David, 372
Paré, Ronald, 375
Parédès, Jean, 116
Parell, Nancy, 422
Parella, Anthony, 399
Parichy, Dennis, 73
Paris, Lucile, 80
Parish, Michael, 95
Park, Richard, 371
Parke, Lawrence, 56
Parker, Betty, 89
Parker, James, 89
Parker, Janet Lee, 416
Parker, Murray, 469
Parks, Bert, 367
Parks, Caroline, 377
Parks, Hildy, 386, 410, 411
Parks, Larry, 439
Parmalee, Barbara, 469
Parmalee, Charles, 469
Parone, Edward, 74, 79, 437
Parrish, Elizabeth, 373
Parsons, Estelle, 21, 75, 394, 431
Pasadena Playhouse, 55, 83-84
Pasolli, Robert, 383, 388, 406
Passacaglia or The Great Society, 112
Passeltiner, Bernard, 432, 445
Passion Flower Hotel, 111
Passloff, Aileen, 430
Pasteau, Cathérine, 115, 118
Pastene, Robert, 82
Pastime of Monsieur Robert, The, 112
Patent Pending, 113
Paterson, William, 75, 76
Patinkin, Sheldon, 434
Patrice, Marie, 393
Patriot For Me, A, 110, 457
Patterson, Donald, 88
Patterson, Elizabeth, 470
Patterson, James, 10, 389, 445
Patton, Shirley, 99
Paul, Leslie, 72
Paul, Valerie, 436
Paull, Morgan, 74
Paulson, Arvid, 85
Paxton, Dorothy, 76
Paye, Virginia, 80-81
Payne, William, 79
Paynter, Eric, 367
Paynter, Jeanne, 88
Payton-Wright, Pamela, 81
Peabody, Alan, 86

Pearce, Alice, 470
Pearce, Vera, 470
Peaslee, Richard, 393, 422, 455
Peck, Allen, 368
Pecktal, Lynn, 70
Pedestrian, The, 421
Pedestrian in the Air, The, 43, 49
Pedi, Tom, 366
Peer Gynt, 83
Peerless, Donna, 94
Pegram, Nigel, 19, 401
Pellman, Art, 72
Peluso, Emanuel, 454
P.E.N., 36
Penberthy, Beverly, 439
Pendleton, Wyman, 394, 421
Pendulum, The, 118
Penn, Arthur, 396
Pennington, Michael, 100, 101
Penny for a Song, A, 457
Pentecost, George, 387
Penzner, Seymour, 96
Pepine, Arthur, 394
Pepsie, 116
Percival, Michael, 393
Performing Arts Center (La Jolla, Calif.), 40
Performing Giant, The, 111
Perkins, Don, 88
Perkuhn, Jackie, 370
Perlman, Max, 423
Perret, Lucille, 368
Perry, Carol, 418
Perry, Harry H., 470
Perry, Keith, 373
Perry, Mireille, 115
Persecution and Assassination of Marat as Performed by the Inmates of the Asylum of Charenton Under The Direction of the Marquis de Sade, The, 3, 4, 6, 7, 8, 9, 10-12, 14, 24, 25, 28, 29, 31, 269-300, 393, 451, 452, 456, 457, 458
Persky, Lester, 399
Persson, Gene, 429, 435
Pertzoff, Alexander, 73
Pertzoff, Olga, 73
Petchey, Briain, 94
Peter Pan, 77
Peters, Andrea, 420
Peters, Brock, 380
Peters, Gerald, 398
Peters, Lauri, 89
Peterson, Alan, 371
Peterson, Arthur, 83
Peterson, Wally, 383
Petina, Irra, 388
Peting, Moose, 370
Petrides, Avra, 73
Petrie, Daniel, 431
Petroski, Adam, 418, 423

Petrushka, Gina, 74
Pfeiffer, P. L., 385
Phalen, Robert, 380, 381
Phèdre, 30, 34, 430, 438
Philadelphia, Here I Come!, 3, 4, 8, 10, 12, 14, 24, 25, 29, 38, 45, 63, 301-323, 398, 451, 452, 456
Philanderer, The, 112
Phillips, Marc, 408
Phillips, Nelson, 382
Phillips, Paul, 395
Phillips, Randy, 384
Phillips, Sian, 110, 112
Philpot, Robert, 471
Phinn, C. Mort, 470
Phipps, John, 72
Phoenix Theater, see Association of Producing Artists at the Phoenix
Physicists, The, 49, 50, 77, 86
Piacentini, Vincent, 82
Piazza, Ben, 417
Pick a Number XV, 30, 422
Pickles, Christine, 427
Pickup, Ronald, 110, 111
Pickwick, 4, 7, 24, 372-373, 456
Picnic, 78
Pictures in the Hallway, 71
Pieran, Victor, 408
Pierre, Roger, 116
Pierson, Harold, 395
Pilhofer, Herbert, 81
Pillar, Gary, 394
Pimm, Harry S., 470
Pinansky, Sam, 470
Pincus, Warren, 416, 417
Pinero, Arthur Wing, 111
Pinget, Robert, 118
Pinkney, Lyn, 393
Pinn, Irene, 434
Pinnell, Ann, 76
Pinter, Emily, 470
Pinter, Harold, 12, 32, 48, 50, 67, 72, 73, 77, 89, 110, 117, 415
Pio-Ulsky, Konstantin, 388
Pippin, Donald, 412
Pirandello, Luigi, 49, 79, 84
Pirates of Penzance, The, 30, 83, 419-420
Piscator, Erwin, 415, 470
Pitkin, William, 94, 376
Pitot, Genevieve, 375
Pittsburgh Playhouse, 42, 65
Plater, Alan, 111
Platt, George, 405, 445
Play, 73
Play That On Your Old Piano, 30, 422-423
Playboy of the Western World, 86
Players Ring Gallery (Los Angeles, Calif.), 56

Playhouse, The (San Francisco, Calif.), 66
Playhouse in the Park (Cincinnati, Ohio), 75
Playroom, The, 4, 22, 25, *389, 457*
Playwrights Experimental Theater, 36
Plaza, 9, 34
Pleshette, John, 96, 383
Plotkin, Joel, 77
Plough and the Stars, The, 83
Plummer, Christopher, 9, 382, 455
Plutus, 118
Pocket Theater (Atlanta, Ga.), 72
Pocket Watch, The, 30, *428*
Poe, Harold, 443
Pogacar, Marco, 377
Pogue, Kenneth, 94
Poindexter, H. R., 51
Point Conception, 87
Pointer, Priscilla, 380, 381
Poker Season, The, 444
Polak, Marie, 470
Polan, Nina, 88
Ponazecki, Joe, 383, 401
Pond, Helen, 424
Pond, Ray Keith, 99
Poole, Ray, 95
Poor Bitos, 46, 63, 73, 84
Poor Richard, 75, 78, 457
Pope, Peggy, 73, 74
Popesco, Elvire, 116
Poppe, Herman, 99
Popwell, Albert, 367
Porcelain Year, The, 64, 444
Pordum, Herbert, 418
Porter, Cole, 34
Porter, Don, 439
Porter, Eric, 100
Porter, Hal, 113
Porter, Stephen, 71, 80, 85-86
Porter, Tom, 375
Porterfield, Robert, 70
Portman, Eric, 111
Postmark Zero, 4, 24, *382-383*
Pottle, Sam, 428
Potts, Nancy, 71, 89, 387
Poulos, Dorothy McConkey, 72
Poupart, Homer, 393, 408
Pourquoi Pas Vamos?, 115
Pousse-Café, 4, 5, *403-404*
Powell, Lovelady, 25, 445
Powell, Michael Warren, 433
Power, Hartley, 470
Powers, David, 391, 393, 403
Powers, James, 375
Powers, Mia, 388
Powers, Neville, 416
Powers, Renata, 384
Pownall, Leon, 94

Poynter, J. Thompson, 87
Pralon, Alain, 397
Prather, Tom, 78
Preble, Ed, 72
Prescott, Dick, 418
Presle, Micheline, 117
Pressman, Eugene, 374
Pressman, Kenneth, 445
Pressman, Lawrence, 46, 73
Preston, Edward, 377
Preston, Robert, 20, 400, 455
Pretzat, Anne, 371
Price, Dennis, 112
Price, Paul B., 427
Price, Sherill, 370
Pride, Malcolm, 110
Prideaux, Tom, 452, 456
Prigmore, James, 83
Prime of Miss Jean Brodie, The, 109, 112
Primrose, Alex, 83
Primus, Barry, 73, 74
Prince, Harold, 17, 57, 64, 405, 406
Prince, Julie, 385
Prince, Philippe, 115
Prince, Robert, 443
Prince Disguised, The, 114
Prince Travesti, Le, 116
Princess Ida, 30, *419-420*
Princess Rebecca Birnbaum, *431*
Priolo, Susan, 394
Pritchard, Barry, 43, 86, 437
Pritchard, Sally, 86
Pritchett, James, 430
Pritchett, Lizabeth, 391
Private Ear, The, 43, 71, 83
Private Lives, 79-80
Prochnik, Bruce, 441
Proctor, James D., 386, 389, 410, 411
Proctor, Phillip, 411
Prodigal Son, The, 416
Prodromides, Jean, 420
Professional Theater Program (University of Michigan), 24, 27-29, 36, 42, 43, 59
Professor, The, 113
Project Immortality, 43, 67, 89
Promenade du Dimanche, La, 115
Propper, Judith, 380, 381
Prosky, Robert, 89
Protero, Dodi, 370
Provincial Lady, The, 117
Prufer, Guntram, 415
Pryor, Matthew, 380
P.S. I Love You, 54
Public Eye, The, 43, 71, 79, 83
Public Relations Corporation of America, 421
Pueleo, Lisa, 407
Puleo, Robert, 407
Purcell, Raymond, 416

Purdum, Ralph, 417
Pugh, Ted, 83
Puntila, 113
Purnell, Louise, 110
Purple Dust, 118, 444
Pursley, David, 50, 76, 77
Pursley, Mona, 76
Pyatt, Jean, 83

Quam, Mylo, 382
Quayle, Anthony, 112
Questions, The, 88
Quick, George, 370
Quill, Gynter, 49
Quilter, David, 101
Quinn, Michael, 367, 388, 411
Quintero, José, 74
Quinton, Albert, 97
Quitak, Oscar, 373

Rabb, Ellis, 13, 27, 60, 71, 91, 387, 455, 456
Rabbit Habit, The, 444
Rabinovitch, Reuben, 384, 401
Raby, Roger Allan, 408
Racine, Jean, 34, 430
Racolin, Alexander E., 423
Racolin, Dina, 423
Rado, James, 400, 441
Rae, Charlotte, 373, 456
Raedler, Dorothy, 419, 420
Ragni, Gerome, 441
Raider-Wexler, Victor, 82
Rain, Douglas, 94
Raimbourg, Lucien, 116
Raines, Quinton, 428, 431
Rainmaker, The, 51
Rains, Jessica, 74
Raitt, John, 28, 368
Ramage, Jack, 433
Ramback, Gary, 418
Ramirez, Frank, 97
Ramsay, Robin, 370, 441
Ramsey, Logan, 396
Ramsey, Robin, 441
Ramsey, Ruth, 412
Randall, Tony, 6, 21, 394
Randolph, John, 422
Randolph, Mimi, 428
Randolph, Robert, 16, 25, 372, 374, 383, 388, 395, 406, 408, 455, 456
Rania, Estrellita, 66
Ransom, Lucinda, 418
Raphael, Gerrianne, 386
Raphel, Jerome, 74, 88, 98
Rapine, Betty Ann, 393
Raposo, Joseph, 424
Rasbury, Andy, 422
Rasey, Adelle, 399
Rash, Philip, 367
Rashomon, 50, 77, 78
Rat's Mass, A, 47, 73
Ratten, Die, 4, 28, *406-407*
Rattle of a Simple Man, 55
Rauch, Maurice, 423

Rawlins, Lester, 74, 429
Rawls, Eugenia, 75
Ray, Helen, 470
Ray, James, 96, 437
Ray, Naomi, 470
Ray, Sandra, 367
Rayburn, Rande, 393, 410
Rayfiel, David, 399
Raymon, Lourette, 388
Raymond, Dorothy, 429
Raymond, Gary, 111
Raymond, Helen, 470
Raymond, Moore, 470
Rea, Oliver, 58
Reams, Lee Roy, 395
Reardon, Gregory, 433
Reardon, Leo F., 470
Reardon, Nancy, 70, 96, 378
Raymont, Carol, 393
Reavy, Jean, 437
Recluse, The, *433*
Red Barn Theater Limited,
    421, 432
Redfield, Liza, 367
Redford, Robert, 439
Redgrave, Lynn, 111
Redgrave, Michael, 109, 113
Redgrave, Vanessa, 109, 112
Redman, Joyce, 112
Reed, Alex, 398-399
Reed, Gus, 470
Reed, Robbie, 385
Reed, Robert, 439
Reed, Taylor, 373
Reeder, George, 440
Reedy, Marvin, 95
Reel, Arthur, 425
Reeves, Nancy, 377
Reggiani, Serge, 116
Rehearsal, The, 72
Reich, John, 49, 74
Reid, Beryl, 109, 110
Reid, Gregory, 94
Reid, Kate, 23, 94, 455, 456
Reilly, Charles Nelson, 384,
    385
Reilly, William, 377
Reine Morte, La, 4, 28, *397-398*
Reinecker, Herbert, 117
Reiner, E. Susan, 423
Reiner, Hanne Marie, 377
Reinglas, Fred, 424, 432
Reinhardt, Ray, 71, 85
Reinholt, George, 89
Reinke, Gary, 86
Reis, Curt, 80
Reith, Kapi, 432
Reither, Toni, 418
Rembach, Frank, 18, 401
Remedy For Winter, A, 444
Remick, Lee, 13, 396, 456
Remington, Barbara, 377
Renaud, Madeleine, 29, 114,
    115, 421
Rendle, Adrian, 111
Rennie, James, 470

Renoir, Rita, 114
Renton, Donna, 75
Repertory Theater of Lincoln
    Center (Lincoln Center
    Repertory), 26-27, 29, 44,
    59-60, 61, 378-381
**Repos du Septième Jour,
    Le,** 114
Resin, Dan, 367, 377
Resnik, Muriel, 365
Rétoré, Guy, 114
Return of Second City, 30,
    433
**Revenge of the Forty-Seven
    Ronin, The,** *403*
Reverberations, 444
Revill, Clive, 441
Rexsite, Seymour, 423
Reynolds, Mell, 407
Reynolds, Paulene, 82
Rhodes, Jan, 376
Rhodes, Walter, 82
Riano, Reni, 444
Ribman, Ronald, 32, 433
Rice, Adnia, 367
Rice, Jack, 95
Rice, Peter, 373
Rice, Philip, 393
Rich, Allen, 434
Rich, Doris, 380, 394
Richard, Houston, 470
Richard II, 86
Richard, III, 58, 81, 83, 92
Richards, Angela, 112
Richards, Dal, 405
Richards, Doreen, 376
Richards, Eben, 421
Richards, Gerald, 74
Richards, Joe, 373
Richards, Jon, 372, 401
Richards, Ken, 377
Richards, Lisa, 73
Richards, Lloyd, 391
Richards, Paul E., 88
Richardson, Douglas, 99
Richardson, Howard, 83
Richardson, Ian, 11, 100, 393
Richardson, Jack, 3, 24, 64,
    383
Richardson, Lee, 81
Richardson, Ralph, 109, 112
Richardson, Wells, 437
Richman, Mark, 79
Richman, Saul, 418, 432
Ricketts, Skiles, 410
Riddle, Gladys, 97
Ride a Cock Horse, 109, 110
Riggs, Seth, 372
**Right Honourable Gentle-
    man, The,** 4, 12, 23, *378,*
    456, 457
**Right You Are If You
    Think You Are,** 51, 79
Riley, Alive Mary, 367, 410
Riley, Drexel H., 76
Ringle, Dave, 470
Ringwood, Susan, 94

Riofrancos, Osvaldo, 97, **436**
Riordan, John, 71
Riquier, Georges, 116
Risso, Richard D., 98, 99
Ritch, Rozanne, 423
Ritchard, Cyril, 441
Ritchie, June, 110, 111
Ritchie, Sharon, 395
Ritman, William, 14, 25, 376,
    394, 417, 422, 455
Rittman, Trude, 377
Rittmaster, Janice, 86
Ritter, Ilse, 407
Ritter, Thelma, 394
Ritz, Al, 470
Riva, Emmanuèle, 115
Rivalry, The, 56
Rivals, The, 50, 64, 76, 83
Rivera, Walter, 407
Rivers, Elizabeth, vii
Rivers, Leslye, 437
Riverwind, 43, 50, 77
Rizzo, Francis, 372
Rizzo, Gino, 416
Road, The, 113
**Roar of the Greasepaint—
    The Smell of the Crowd,
    The,** 4, 13, 37, 366, 441
Robards, Jason, Jr., 6, 23,
    385
Robbins, Jerome, 36
Robbins, Rex, 422
Robert, Yves, 118
Robert Frost, 79
Robert Hooks, Inc., 426
Roberts, Anthony, 439
Roberts, Doris, 394, 445
Roberts, Elizabeth, 399
Roberts, William D., 73, 99
Robertson, Allen, 77
Robey, Wilson, 408
Robin, Naomi, 420
Robinson, David, 112
Robinson, Dorothy Marie,
    420
Robinson, Roger, 95
Robinson, Terry, 370
Rocca, Danielle, 118
Rocco, Sonny, 370
Roche, Eugene, 431
Rochefort, Jean, 117
Rock, Jeff, 430
Rockefeller Foundation, 44,
    47
Rodale, J. I., 427
Rodgers, Anton, 7, 373
Rodgers, Eileen, 414
Rodgers, Margaret, 51
Rodgers, Mark, 72
Rodgers, Mary, 33, 428
Rodgers, Paul, 75, 76
Rodgers, Richard, 28, 80,
    366, 392, 413
Rodgers, Shev, 386
Rodogune, 116
Rodríguez, María-Rosa, 116
Roerick, William, 378

Roffey, Jack, 22, 398
Roffman, Frederick S., 407, 419
Rogan, Peter, 437
Rogers, David, 445
Rogers, Emmett, 470
Rogers, Eric, 370, 373
Rogers, Gil, 80
Rogers, Ginger, 39, 440
Rogers, Harriet, 416
Rogers, Jaime, 413
Rogers, Paul, 100, 101, 110, 113
Roggensack, David, 394, 421, 423
Rogow, David, 426
Roland, Tom, 86
Rolf, Frederick, 425
Roll, Eddie, 386, 436
Rollason, Mic, 113
Rolle, Esther, 426
Rombola, Ed, 427, 428
Rome, Harold, 22, 383, 391
Romeo and Jeanette, 89
Romeo and Juliet, 82, 94-95, 97
Romulus and Romulus the Great, 457
Ronde, La, 50, 77
Room, The, 415
Rooms, 30, 429
Roop, Reno, 427
Roos, Casper, 384
Rope, The, 436
Rosa, Dennis, 33, 434
Rose, Billy, 40, 470
Rose, Clifford, 393
Rose, George, 9, 382
Rose, Jürgen, 407
Rose, Philip, 399
Rose, Reginald, 64, 444
Rose, Renée, 418
Rose Tattoo, The, 74, 84
Rosebaum, Richard, 422
Rosebrock, Betty, 412
Rosemont, Norman, 375
Rosen, Abigail, 400
Rosen, Irwin, 430
Rosen, Jonathan, 96
Rosen, Paul Lani, 96
Rosenberg, James, 72
Rosenstock, Milton, 443
Rosental, Chayele, 423
Rosenthal, Jean, 381, 403
Rosenthal, Lawrence, 367
Rosenthal, Raymond, 434
Rosenthal, Ricky, 370
Rosqui, Tom, 380, 381
Ross, Bill, 368, 370, 389
Ross, Corinne Health Sumner, 470
Ross, David, 470
Ross, Dorothy, 376, 417, 424
Ross, Herbert, 377
Ross, J. A., 403
Ross, Jamie, 74
Ross, Martin, 391

Ross, Marty, 404
Ross, Michael, 423
Ross, Natalie, 435
Ross, Ronnie, 470
Ross, William, 414
Rossen, Carol, 85, 440
Rossen, Robert, 470
Rossmann, Erna, 407
Rotchin, Norman, 443
Roth, Ann, 94, 370, 394
Roth, Nancy, 368
Rothbard, Richard, 440
Rothenberg, David, 399, 422, 424, 430, 432
Rothenberg, Jerome, 79
Rothstein, Norman, 383
Rounds, David, 436
Rounseville, Robert, 15, 386, 387
Rousseau, Gene, 85, 86
Roussilon, Jean-Paul, 117
Roussin, André, 116
Routledge, Patricia, 112
Rouvel, Cathérine, 114
Rovin, Robert, 403, 423
Rowan, Marc, 413
Rowe, Earl, 390
Rowles, Polly, 405
Rowley, Frank, 385, 386
Roy, Will, 408
Roy, William, 428
Roya, David, 421
Royal Hunt of the Sun, The, 3, 4, 8, 9, 12, 14, 25, 146-168, 382, 451, 457
Royal Shakespeare Company (Stratford-on-Avon, England), 11, 28, 92, 99-100
Rozakis, Gregory, 382
Ruben, Paul, 71
Rubin, Judi, 436
Rubin, Harry, 426
Rubin, Martin, 434
Rubin, Sally, 74
Rubino, Joseph A., 79
Rubinstein, Carol, 84
Ruddigore, 30, 419
Rude, Roberta, 77
Rudney, Edward, 94
Rudy, Martin, 422
Rufo, Paul, 427
Ruisinger, Thomas, 95
Rupert, Gene, 411, 439
Ruskin, Joseph, 79
Russell, Douglas, 98
Russell, Douglas A., 88
Russell, Jay, 398
Russell, Robert, 366
Russell, Rosalind, 18
Russell, Scott, 78
Rust, John, 56
Ruta, Ken, 81
Ruth, Thea, 82
Rutman, Leo, 437
Rux, Macksene, 83
Ryan, Charlene, 395
Ryan, Chris, 367

Ryan, John P., 432
Ryan, Mitchell, 96, 396
Ryan, Owen, 427
Rydell, Stephen John, 393
Ryder, Alfred, 79
Rydzeski, Mary Ann, 418
Ryland, Jack, 96, 372
Rynning, Jim, 86, 87
Ryszeski, Ann, 410
Ryther, Georgia, 72

Saatan, Barbara, 404
Saarinen, Eero, 26
Sabin, David, 70, 390, 391
Sabinson, Harvey B., 37, 370, 373, 374, 390, 391, 392, 396, 398, 399, 403, 405
Sabol, Dick, 401
Sabrina, 444
Sachs, Evelyn, 372
Sachleben, Horst, 407
Sackler, Howard, 66, 112
Sacristain Bossu, Le, 115
Safina, Anthony, 372
Sage, Clifford, 50, 77
Sage, David R., 74
Sage, Eve Marie, 413
Sahlins, Bernard, 434
Saidenberg, Theodore, 377
Saint-Denis, Michael, 92
St. Jean, André, 368
Saint Joan, 68, 80, 82, 89
Saint of Bleecker Street, The, 4, 28, 371
Sainthill, Loudon, 378, 455, 456
Saint's Day, 457
Saks, Gene, 374, 412, 455
Salinaro, Dom, 408
Sallis, Peter, 389
Salmi, Albert, 55
Salmon, Scotty, 404, 412
Salsbury, Baker, 99
Salsbury, Colgate, 437
Salve, Juleste, 405
Samaret, N. J., Performing Arts Center, 40
Samford, Mary, 425
Samie, Catherine, 397
Sampson, George, 382
Samrock, Carl, 389, 423, 435
Samrock, Victor, 374
San Francisco Mime Troop, 66
Sanchez, Jaime, 437
Sand, Paul, 423, 428
Sanders, Donna, 392
Sanders, Herbert, 391
Sanders, Honey, 366
Sanders, Steve, 390
Sanders, Susan, 368
Sandifur, Virginia, 370
Sands, Diana, 440
Sands, Dorothy, 430
Sanford, Beth, 79
Sanford, Ruth, 436

Sanna, Johnny, 470
Sappington, Fay, 390
Sarcey, Martine, 117
Sargent, Meryl, 80
Sargon, Simon, 420
Sarky, Daniel, 115
Sarlatte, Celeste, 87
Sarno, Janet, 89
Saroyan, William, 81, 82
Sartre, Jean-Paul, 49, 79, 116, 378
Satacroce, Dan, 72
Sato, Reiko, 368
Satur, Claudio Garcia, 97
Saturday Night and Sunday Morning, 111
Saunders, Lanna, 398
Saunders, Lois Ann, 424
Saunders, Peter, 398
Saunders, Rhonda, 420
Saussen, Edmund, 407
Sauter, Eddie, 406
Sauvaneix, Hélène, 115
Savacool, John K., 415
Saved, 110
Savidge, Mary, 94
Savino, Frank, 427
Savior, Paul, 441
Say, Darling, 436
Say Who You Are, 111
Saxon, Wanda, 368
Scaasi, Arnold, 421
Scammell, Terence, 95
Scales, 113
Scanlan, John, 75
Scardino, Don, 389
Schaefer, Anna Paul, 50, 76, 77
Schaefer, Frank, 76, 77
Schaefer, George, 396
Schafer, Milton, 375, 455
Schapiro, Herb, 423
Schary, Dore, 22, 383, 384
Schary, Jeb, 384
Scheider, Roy R., 432
Schell, Maximilien, 110
Scherkenbach, Bob, 405
Schier, Ernest, 63
Schiltz, Maryvonne, 117
Schirmer, Gus, 408
Schirmer, Gus, Jr., 367
Schisgal, Murray, 43, 46, 55, 67, 73, 77, 78, 79, 86, 89, 365
Schlegel, Jeanne, 367
Schlesinger, John, 99
Schley, Karl Maria, 407
Schmid, Helmut, 407
Schmidt, Douglas W., 72, 75
Schmidt, Harvey, 50, 75, 415
Schneider, Alan, 71, 376, 394, 399, 417, 421
Schnabel, Stefan, 372
Schnitzler, Arthur, 50, 77
Schofield, Frank, 96
School for Wives, 80
Schreiber, Terry, 436

Schrock, Gladden, 83
Schuchardt, Emil, 429
Schuck, John, 72
Schuelein, Rainer, 393
Schulberg, Budd, 365
Schulberg, Stuart, 365
Schultze-Westrum, Edith, 407
Schumann, Peter, 454
Schumer, Yvette, 432
Schütt, Bertil, 117
Schwab, Buddy, 428
Schwartz, Jerome J., 423
Schwartz, Martin, 401
Schwartz, Marvin, 426
Schwarzkopf, Klaus, 407
Schweiger, Heinrich, 407
Schwimmer, Walter, 378, 456
Scimonelli, Glenn, 374
Schofield, Paul, 100, 101, 109, 113
Scotford, Sybil, 66, 373
Scotia Productions, 424
Scotlin, Michael, 367
Scott, A. C., 435
Scott, Bette, 368
Scott, Bruce, 400
Scott, Dennis, 367, 422
Scott, Georgette, 443
Scott, Jeffrey, 413
Scott, Lauren, 419
Scott, Marc, 408
Scott, Martha, 441
Scott, Michael, 86
Scott, Zachary, 470
Scott Theater (Ft. Worth, Tex.), 40, 74
Screens, The, 114, 115
Scruggs, Lang, 70
Scudder, Alice, 426
Seale, Douglas, 43, 75
Seattle Repertory Theater, 36, 43, 52, 87, 91
Secombe, Harry, 5, 7, 373, 456
Secretissimo, 116
Segal, David F., 432
Segal, George, 441
Seger, Richard, 33, 426, 434
Seibert, Jeannette, 367, 377
Seigner, Louis, 116
Seitz, John, 79-80
Seka, Ron, 434
Selden, Albert W., 15, 386, 456
Sell Me Down The River, Darling, 444
Sellars, Elizabeth, 112
Sellers, Cathérine, 117
Seltzer, Carl, 431
Selznick, David O., 470
Senn, Herbert, 424
Sense and Nonsense, 77
Sequestres d'Altona, Les, 116
Serabian, Lorraine, 420, 426, 427
Serio, Joy, 367, 408

Serjeant Musgrave's Dance, 12, 30, 33, 68, 89, 109, 112, 431-432, 451, 457
Serlin, Sol, 430
Sermonin, David, 80
Seroff, Muni, 437
Serrault, Michel, 118
Serres, Jacques, 116
Serva, David, 386
Servant of Two Masters, The, 81, 84
Servants of the People, 73
Servello, Joe, 434
Service for Joseph Axminster, The, 73
Setrakian, Ed, 96
70 Times Seven, 444
Sevilla, Jose, 433
Sewell, Danny, 370
Seyler, Athene, 112
Seyrig, Delphine, 114
Shade, Ellen, 419
Shaff, Monty, 404
Shaffer, Louise, 400
Shaffer, Peter, 3, 9, 71, 79, 83, 146, 382
Shakespeare, William, 43, 50, 60, 70, 72, 73, 76, 77, 78, 80, 81-82, 83, 84, 85, 86, 87-88, 90-101, 112, 115, 117, 438
Shaktman, Ben, 423
Shaler, Anna, 385, 386, 399, 420
Shalet, Diane, 380
Shalom, Bella, 391, 412
Shane, Lisa, 112
Shane, Peggy, 470
Shannon, Nance, 470
Shapiro, Herman, 367, 393, 408
Shapiro, Mark, 426
Shapiro, Mel, 78, 88, 97-98
Sharaff, Irene, 395, 455, 456
Sharma, Barbara, 395
Sharp, Robert, 388
Sharp, William, 88
Sharpe, John, 51, 395, 410
Shattuck, Robert, 431
Shaver, David, 74
Shaver, Leslie, 74
Shavian Women In Love And Marriage, 444
Shaw, Barnett, 76, 77
Shaw, George Bernard, 43, 60, 70, 72, 73, 75, 76, 78, 80, 82, 83, 84, 85, 86, 87, 89, 110, 111, 112, 415, 444
Shaw, Joseph, 94
Shaw, Lavonia, 76
Shaw, Margery, 82
Shaw, Paula, 430
Shaw, Sebastian, 110, 111, 112
Shawhan, April, 401
Shawn, Kathy, 431
She Loves Me, 86

Shea, Al, 367
Shea, Stephen, 423
Sheehan, Grant, 80
Sheen, Martin, 441
Sheffield, D. Hudson, 75, 84
Shelley, 111
Shelley, Mary, 75-76
Shelton, Reid, 368, 435
Shelly, Norman, 399, 400, 418
Shenar, Paul, 71, 85
Shepard, Karen, 388, 409, 417
Shepard, Sam, 73, 433
Shephard, William, 99
Shepard, William J., 470
Sheppard, Julie, 382
Sheppard, Morgan, 393
Sheridan, Dick, 428
Sheridan, Liz, 422
Sheridan, Richard Brinsley, 50, 76, 81, 83
Sherin, Edwin, 89
Sherman, George, 63
Sherman, Milt, 418
Sherman, Hiram, 6, 8, 400, 455
Sherwood, Holly, 413
Sherwood, Madeleine, 389
Shimizu, Dana, 366
Shimizu, Keenan, 366
Shimono, Sab, 366, 412
Shipley, Albert, 425
Shoemaker's Prodigious Wife, The, 83
Sholz, Edwin, 419
Shookoff, David, 99
Shorr, William, 430
Short, Bobby, 428
Shove, Dawna, 370
Showalter, Max, 440
Shropshire, Ann, 445
Shuman, Roy, 97
Shumer, Harry, 471
Shumlin, Herman, 46, 59
Shurr, Buff, 437
Shust, William, 80
Shyre, Paul, 79, 89
Schwartz, Martin, 376, 432
Sicari, Joseph R., 428
Sidney, P. Jay, 389
Sidney, Susan, 393
Siebert, Charles, 71, 85
Siegal, Frances, 427
Siegel, Larry, 33, 428
Siegel, Morton, 85
Siegel, William, 470
Siggins, Jeff, 376, 403
Sign in Sidney Brustein's Window, The, 64
Sigrist, Susan, 368, 408
Silber, Don, 382
Silberberg, Donna, 422, 427
Silbert, Lisa, 470
Siler, Cinda, 76, 77
Siletti, Mario, 85
Sillcox, Luise M., 471

Silveira, Ruth, 88
Silver, Frederick, 422
Silver, Joe, 383
Silverman, Hy, 429
Silverman, Maxwell, 422
Silverman, Stanley, 381
Silverman, Steve, 382
Sim, Alistair, 111
Simmonds, Stanley, 373
Simmons, Ashley, 77
Simmons, Jamie, 417, 418
Simmons, Lucretia, 385, 386
Simmons, Nat, 71, 387
Simmons, Stanley, 367, 370, 393
Simon, 77
Simon, Chantal, 115
Simon, Cyril, 427
Simon, Linda, 427
Simon, Michel, 114
Simon, Neil, 3, 5, 16, 72, 365, 366, 394, 456
Simonet, Liliane, 427
Simonini, Pierre, 397
Simpson, N. F., 111
Sinclair, Betty, 410
Sinclair, Michael, 395
Singer, Gail, 84
Singer, Jane, 89
Singer, Jordan, 72
Sinnott, Patricia, 407
Sinor, Matthew Raymond, 98
Siretta, Dan, 375
Sisk, Michael, 82
Six Characters in Search of an Author, 49, 65, 84
6 From La Mama, 30, 433
Skelton, Geoffrey, 11, 269, 393
Skin of Our Teeth, The, 59, 75, 88, 89
Skinner, Lew, 436
Skulnik, Menasha, 22, 383, 384
Skundberg, Robert, 86, 87
Skyscraper, 4, 16, 25, 37, 384-385, 456, 458
Slapstick Tragedy, 4, 24, 399, 456
Slater, Thomas, 82
Slight Ache, A, 415
Slocum, Richard, 77
Slow Dance on the Killing Ground, 53, 67, 76, 89
Slowik, Joseph, 75
Small, Jules, 419
Small, Mary E., 367
Small, Neva, 376
Smart, Lisa, 407
Smashing Day, A, 111
Smiley, Brett, 370
Smiley, Donnie, 370
Smith, Anthony, 66, 86
Smith, Archie, 88
Smith, Benny, 432
Smith, Buddy, 77
Smith, Byron, 98

Smith, Charles Rome, 83, 421
Smith, David, 372, 409
Smith, Ed, 425
Smith, Haydon, 373
Smith, Ivan, 407
Smith, Jack, 88
Smith, Lois, 63
Smith, Loring, 440
Smith, Maggie, 113
Smith, Malcolm, 372
Smith, Michael, 452
Smith, Myles, 85
Smith, Nick, 95
Smith, Oliver, 372, 377, 390, 405, 445
Smith, Roger, 51
Smith, Roy, 405
Smith, Rufus, 401, 413
Smith, Sammy, 392
Smith, Sandy, 439
Smith, Steven, 75
Smolko, John, 405
Smyche, J. Anthony, 470
Snider, Barry, 79
Snook, Robert, 76, 83
Snyder, Tom, 37
So Much of Earth, So Much of Heaven, 444
Soares, Silvia, 85
Soble, Stanley, 95
Soboloff, Arnold, 395
Society Hill Playhouse (Philadelphia, Pa.), 64
Soif et La Faim, La, 115
Sokolow, Anna, 427
Solari, Rudy, 56
Solin, Harvey, 73
Solomon, Artie, 386, 392, 422, 427
Solomon, Paul, 432
Solters, Lee, 370, 373, 374, 390, 391, 392, 396, 398, 399, 403, 405
Somack, Jack, 437
Some Winter Games, 444
Something Nasty in the Woodshed, 111
Sommer, Josef, 95
Sommers, Barbara, 116
Somogi, Judith, 420
Sondergaard, Gale, 34, 423
Sondheim, Stephen, 366
Sophocles, 117
Sorbello, Charmian, 78
Sorbello, Rosalind, 78
Sorel, Theodore, 95
Sorian, Jack, 376
Sorvino, Paul, 383, 384
Soule, Robert, 79-80
Sound of Music, The, 40
South Pacific, 4, 28, 366
Southern, Colette, 470
Soyinka, Wole, 113
Spaisman, Zipora, 426
Sparer, Paul, 421
Spark, Bonnie Ellen, 368
Spark, Muriel, 457

Spaull, Guy, 410
Spears, Sammy, 470
Spector, Arnold, 418
Spencer, Bob, 440
Spencer, Bud, 393
Spencer, Christine, 384
Spencer, T. J., 67
Speyer, David, 380
Speyer, Lara, 380
Spielberg, David, 83
Spindelman, Alfred, 375
Spinetti, Victor, 5, 392
Spingler, Doug, 410, 418
Spinner, Geri, 418
Spittel, Dick, 404
Spivakowsky, Michael, 384
Sponono, 49
Spradling, Grant, 368, 413
Sprague, Ted, 391
Spread Eagle, 67, 89
Spriggs, Elizabeth, 100, 101, 112
Spring and Port Wine, 111
Springer, John, 421
Springer, Philip, 423
Spruill, James, 73, 431
Square East, 428
Square in the Eye, 416, 457
Squire, William, 100, 101, 112
Squires, Patricia, 80
Staff, Frank, 401
Stafford, Ed, 72
Stage Society Theater (Los Angeles, Calif.), 56
Stahl, Mara, 99
Stanford Repertory Theater, 88
Stanley, Alvah, 82
Stanwyck, Jay, 432
Stambusky, Alan, 98
Stanley, Gase, 470
Stanton, Barbara, 74
Stanton, Bill, 412
Stapleton, Maureen, 440
Stark, Bruce W., 394
Starr, Bill, 375, 384, 405
Starr, Pall, 101
Stattle, Robert, 380, 381
Stauch, George, 97
Stavis, Barrie, 457
Stearns, James Hart, 27, 381, 455
Steber, Eleanor, 409
Steckl, Jane, 87
Steel, Edward, 470
Steele, Bill, 436
Steele, Tommy, 440
Stein, Gertrude, 60
Stefan, Bronia, 73
Steffe, Ed, 388
Steffens, Roger M., 81
Stehli, Edgar, 385
Steiger, Rod, 420
Stein, Joseph, 365
Stein, Julian, 391
Steinberg, David, 434

Steiner, John, 393
Steiner, Sigfrit, 407
Stephen D, 67-68
Stephens, Robert, 109, 110, 113
Steris, Dmitri, 83, 420
Sterling, Clark, 377
Stern, Henry R., 470
Stern, Leo, 399
Stern, Joseph, 70
Stern, Peter, 373
Sternhagen, Frances, 378
Stevens, Denise, 421
Stevens, Fran, 404, 408
Stevens, Leslie, 76
Stevens, Nancy, 373
Stevens, Paul, 96, 427
Stevens, Roger L., 35, 36
Stevens, Van, 367
Stevenson, Margot, 398
Stevenson, Robert, 430
Stevelingson, Edward, 85, 436
Stewart, Carl W., 407
Stewart, Christine, 395
Stewart, David J., 380
Stewart, Dixie, 377
Stewart, Don, 439
Stewart, Gordon, 83
Stewart, Lesley, 384, 385
Stewart, Michael, 365
Stewart, Patricia, 79-80
Stewart, Robert W., 74
Stiers, David O., 86, 87
Stiles, Victor, 370, 441
Stirling, Susan, 76
Stix, John, 436
Stockfield, Betty, 470
Stockwell, Susan, 410
Stoker, H. G., 470
Stone, Harold, 84, 437
Stop the World—I Want to Get Off, 78
Storch, Arthur, 376, 405
Storm, James, 98
Stotter, Vivienne, 75
Story, Ted, 436
Straight, Beatrice, 430
Strait, Ralph, 89
Strakosch, Charles G., 471
Strasberg, John, 74
Strasberg, Paula, 471
Strasfogel, Ian, 86
Strasser, Robin, 85
Strater, Christopher, 433
Stratton, John, 395
Stratton, Ronald, 367
Strauss, Johann, Jr., 443
Street Scene, 4, 28, *371-372*
Streicher, M. M., 96
Streisand, Barbara, 112, 440
Strickland, Daniel, 417
Strickler, Jerry, 445
Stride, John, 111
Strimpell, Stephen, 423
Strindberg, August, 34, 85, 86, 110, 113, 117, 118, 425

Strip-Tease, 118
Strobach, Ben, 386, 406
Strom, Myrna, 391
Strong, Don, 373
Stronger, The, 30, 63, 84, 118, *425*
Stroock, James E., 471
Strouse, Charles, 18, 365, 405, 455
Strudwick, Shepperd, 23, 385
Strum, Margaret, 422
Struthers, Thomas P., 84
Stuart, Joel, 423, 430
Stuart, Lisa, 440
Stuart, Patricia Quinn, 431
Stuart, Peter, 428
Stubbs, Ray, 97
Student Prince, The, 56
Studio Arena Theater (Buffalo, N. Y.), 40
Sturner, Lynda, 370
Stutchkoff, Nabum, 470
Suart, Fabian, 393
Subject of Scandal and Concern, A, 35
Subject Was Roses, The, 8, 46, 68, 72, 365, 441
Subotnick, Morton, 381
Suburban Tragedy, *431*
Sudrow, Irving, 398
Suga, Sensuke, 403
Sugimoto, Kazuo, 403
Suite in Three Keys, 109, 110
Sullivan, Brad, 96
Sullivan, David, 380, 381
Sullivan, Hugh, 393
Sullivan, Jean, 430
Sullivan, Kate, 96
Sullivan, Sheila, 408
Sullivan, Susan, 75, 76
Sulmonetti, Julius, 95
Summer Musicals (Dallas, Tex.), 50
Summer of the Seventeenth Doll, 75
Summers, Caley, 75
Summers, Robert, 70, 428
Sumner, Marnel, 386
Sunset, 30, 33, *435*
Superman, see "It's a Bird It's a Plane It's SUPERMAN"
Supree, Burt, 430
Surface, Herbert, 392, 393
Susa, Conrad, 94, 98
Susskind, David, 382
Sussman, Stan, 425
Sutton, Dudley, 21, 376
Suzman, Janet, 100, 101, 112
Svar, John, 422
Swados, Kim, 74
Swayne, Viola, 422
Swearington, John, 432
Sweeley, Michael, 398
Sweet, Dolph, 396
Sweet Charity, 4, 5, 7, 16,

25, 40, 64, *394-395*, 452, 456, 458
Swenson, Max, 436
Swerling, Jo, 80
Swetland, William, 82, 83
Swim Low Little Goldfish, 30, *421*
Swor, John, 470
Sydow, Jack, 414
Sylbert, Paul, 372
Symington, Donald, 72, 75
Synge, J. M., 86, 118
Symonds, Barry, 380, 381
Symonds, David, 380
Symonds, Robert, 381, 455
Symonds, Victoria, 380
Symposon, Tony, 373
Syse, Glenna, 48
Szabo, Sandor, 439
Szilard, Paul, 403
Szogyi, Alex, 63, 84

Tabard, Pierre, 117
Tabor, Susan, 389
Taffin, Toni, 117
Tahmin, Mary, 78
Tahse, Martin, 40
Take Her, She's Mine, 40
Takeda, Izumo, 403
Takemoto, Harukodayu, 403
Takemoto, Mojidayu, 403
Takemoto, Oritayu, 403
Takemoto, Tsudaiyu, 403
Takesawa, Danroku, 403
Takezawa, Yasshichi, 403
Talcott, Michael, 429
Tale of the Morning Glory, The, 403
Taliaferro, John, 388, 412
Tallman, Randolph, 50, 76, 77
Talyor, Holland, 385, 386
Tamaroff, Marsha, 418
Taming of the Shrew, The, 94-95, 97
Tandy, Jessica, 57, 81
Tango, 113
Tani, Yoko, 113
Tanner, Marian, 436
Tanner, Tony, 440
Tanzy, Jeanne, 372, 413
Tarleton, Diane, 388
Tarlov, Ann, 420
Tarlow, Florence, 454
Tarpey, Tom, 86
Tarrant, Barry, 76
Tartuffe, 42, 64, 68, 70, 72, 75, 78, 84, 85
Tarver, Milton, 99
Task, Maggie, 388, 411
Tate, Charles, 424
Tate, Dennis, 435
Taubenhaus, Marjorie, 74
Taubman, Howard, 37
Tavares, Eric, 435
Tavern, The, 72, 80
Taylor, Cecil P., 110

Taylor, Clarence, 436
Taylor, Evelyn, 413
Taylor, John Russell, 102
Taylor, June, 418
Taylor, Malcolm, 385
Taylor, Maxine, 367, 382
Taylor, Noel, 396, 399, 422, 428, 454, 455
Taylor, Ross, 111
Taylor, Simon Watson, 87
Taylor, Theda, 424
Taylor-Young, Leigh, 401
Tchor, Ludmilla, 407
Teague, Anthony, 71, 85
Teer, Barbara Ann, 400, 426
Teijelo, Gerald M., Jr., 96, 377
Teitel, Carol, 85
Teitelbaum, Maurice, 432
Telephone Pole, *437*
Tell, Ann, 373, 411
Tempest, The, 50
Temps Difficiles, Les, 116
Tennessee, U.S.A., 444
Tennyson, Paula, 418
Tenuta, Antony, 427
Ter-Arutunian, Rouben, 23, 25, 386
Terrell, Betty, 418
Terri, Salli, 79
Terry, Susan, 413
Teuscher, Brandwell, 436
Teuscher, Robert, 98
Thank You, Miss Victoria, *432*
Thark, 111
That Scoundrel Scapin, 88
Theater Atlanta (Ga.), 40
Theater Collection, vii
Theater Company of Boston, Inc., 36, 46-47, 73-74
Theater Group, 41
Theater Group (Los Angeles, Calif.), 40, 45, 54-55, 79
Theater of Nations Season, 117
Theater of the Living Arts (Philadelphia, Pa.), 36, 63
Theater of the Zanies, The, 427
Theater St. Paul (Minn.), 43, 86
Theatre du Nouveau Monde, 113
Their Very Own and Golden City, 109, 110
Theobald, Julie, 393
There's An Echo, Echo, Echo, In This Room, Room, Room, 445
They, 63, 84
They Got Jack, *437*
Theyard, Harry, 372, 386, 411
Thibault, Jean-Marc, 116
Thierrée, Jean-Baptiste, 117
Thirkield, Robert, 436

This is the Rill Speaking, *432*
This Property is Condemned, 112
This Was Burlesque, 366
This Winter's Hobby, 64, 445
Thoma, Michael, 405, 445
Thomas, Ann, 436
Thomas, Cambell, 77
Thomas, Charles, 100, 101
Thomas, David, 377, 411
Thomas, Debbie, 372
Thomas, Dylan, 82
Thomas, Henry, 78
Thomas, Jacque, 77
Thomas, Kent, 384
Thomas, Louis, 386
Thomas, Madoline, 100
Thomas, Powys, 94
Thomas, R. Scott, 73
Thomas, Richard, 389
Thomas, Robert, 116
Thomas, Ruth, 436
Thompson, Anne, 88
Thompson, Clive, 410
Thompson, David, 95
Thompson, Ella, 384
Thompson, Frank, 368, 384, 409, 410, 414
Thompson, Jack, 470
Thompson, Sada, 81, 85
Thomson, Gordon, 94
Thomson, Walter, 398, 399
Thor, Sigrid, 76
Thorent, André, 114
Thorn, George, 375, 411
Thorne, Raymond, 89
Thorne, Robert, 470
Thorne, Worley, 52
Thornhill, Claude, 471
Thornton, Angela, 398
Thornton, Naomi, 73, 74, 416
3 Bags Full, 4, 13, 14, 22, 25, 64, *401*
Three Plays: The Young Disciple, Faustina, Jonah, 457
Three Sisters, The, 89
Threepenny Opera, The, 70
Throckmorton, Cleon, 471
Thurber Carnival, A, *436*
Thurber, James, 436
Thurman, Elizabeth, 72
Thwarting of Baron Bolligrew, The, 111
Tigar, Kenneth, 73
Tiger, The, 42, 46, 55, 67, 73, 77, 78, 86, 89
Tilden, Beau, 367
Tilton, James, 71, 80, 387
Time for Singing, A, 4, 19-20, 25, 39, *411*, 458
Time of Your Life, The, 81, 82
Timon of Athens, 99-100
Tiny Alice, 8, 12, 56, 65, 72, 84

Tionco, Maureen, 366
To the Chicago Abyss, 421
Tobias, Fred, 403
Todd, Richard, 111
Toigo, Alfred, 368
Toilet, The, 32
Toja, Jacques, 116, 397
Tolan, Michael, 434
Toland, John, 436
Toll, Pamela, 445
Tolkan, James, 396
Tom Jones, 445
Tomlin, Gillian, 83
Tomlinson, David, 112
Tomlinson, Kate, 374
Tone, Richard, 372, 403
Toner, Tom, 79, 82
Tony Awards, 455-456
Too Good To Be True, 49, 111
Topaze, 114, 116
Torn, Rip, 437
Torrens, Tania, 117
Tory, Rosemary, 427, 433
Toser, David, 71-72, 84
Tost, William, 420
Toti, Jerome, 418
Touliatos, George, 80
Tovatt, Ellen Darrel, 72, 75
Towber, Chaim, 423
Towers, Constance, 388
Townsend, Jill, 389
Toyomatsu, Seitjuro, 403
Toyotake, Tsubamedayu, 403
Tracey, Andrew, 19, 401
Tracey, Paul, 19, 401
Tract, Jo, 412
Tracy, Lee, 5, 374
Tracy, Matt, 77
Tragedy of King Cristophe, The, 117
Tragedy of Tragedies, The, 82
Trammell, Lynn, 76
Transcending, 111
Transcenics, Inc., 435
Travail, Maurice, 115
Travanty, Don, 403
Travers, Ben, 111
Travers, Sy, 422
Travis, Michael, 79
Travis, Warren, 87, 88
Tree Grows in Brooklyn, A, 437
Tregre, George, 367, 392
Tréjean, Guy, 116
Trelawney of the Wells, 111
Trenkle, Tom, 367
Tribush, Nancy, 403
Trigg, Zenaide, 72
Trigon, The, 12, 30, 33, 421
Trilling, Ossia, vii, 109
Trinity Square Playhouse of Providence, R.I., 48, 85
Tripp, James, 85
Trisler, Joyce, 424

Troilus and Cressida, 30, 92, 95-96, 417
Trojan Woman, The, 30, 34, 64, 72, 83, 420
Trouble in Tahiti, 418
Troubled Waters, 30, 33, 416
Trowell, Stanford, 393
Trueman, Paula, 74, 367, 443
Truex, Ernest, 21, 372
Tucci, Maria, 95, 428
Tucker, Alan, 101
Tucker, Sophie, 470
Tuckerman, Maury, 427
Tudal, Antoine, 115
Tudor, Jennifer, 393
Tugend, Harry, 394
Tufts University, 454
Tumarin, Boris, 380, 381
Turash, Stephanie, 430
Turenne, Louis, 385
Turgeon, Peter, 372
Turgenev, Ivan, 113
Turn a Deaf Ear, 86
Turner, Bonnie, 373
Turner, Douglas, 96, 420, 454
Turner, Gil, 436
Turner, George, 21, 376
Turner, Holly, 374
Turner, Jerry, 77
Turner, Melora Lou, 436
Turner, Nadine, 73
Turner, Terri, 97, 427
Turner, Vickery, 112
Turkington, Brian, 434
Turpin, Jean, 115
Turque, Michael, 386
Turque, Mimi, 386, 387
Tschudin, Michael, 85, 86
Tsuji, Midori, 404
Twain, Michael, 423
Twang, 111
Twelfth Night, 42, 70, 76, 78, 85-86, 87
Two Fables in Perversity, 83
Two Venetian Twins, The, 117
Tyndall, David, 73
Typists, The, 42, 46, 55, 67, 73, 77, 78, 86, 89
Tyranos, John, 97
Tyrone Guthrie Theater (Minneapolis, Minn.), 43, 47-48, 57-60, 81-82, 91-92
Tyson, Joan, 426

Ullman, Robert, 37, 370, 374, 390
Uncle Vanya, 63, 76, 82, 83, 84
Under Milk Wood, 82
Unexpected Guest, The, 445
Unger, Robert, 32, 434
Urbont, Jacques, 396
U.S.A., 89
UTBU, 4, 21, 37, 64, 394

Va et Vient, 115
Vaccaro, Brenda, 390, 455, 456
Vail, Tom, 437
Valadin, Brigitte, 392
Vale, Michael, 376
Valentine, Ted, 101
Valère, Simone, 117
Valero, Roslyn, 433
Valery, Dana, 401
Valéry, Paul, 115
Van Aken, Gretchen, 370
Van Ark, Joan, 439
Van Bridge, Tony, 73, 94
Van Buren, A. H., 470
Vance, Nina, 51, 79
Vandamm, Florence, 471
Vandervort, Philip, 383
Vandis, Titos, 377
Vaneck, Pierre, 116
Van Felton, Bostic, 426
Van Fleet, Jo, 440
Van Griethuysen, Ted, 389, 455
Van Heusen, James, 384
Van Hooten, Robert, 85, 86
Vanier, Phyllis, 78
Van Itallie, Jean-Claude, 432
Van Leer, Winn, 113
Van Lieu, Ron, 431
Van Nuys, Ed, 78
Van Patten, Dick, 372
Van Patten, Joyce, 79
Van Zandt, Porter, 383
Vari, John, 72
Varona, Jose, 97
Varrato, Edmund, 373
Varrone, Gene, 375
Varte, Rosy, 117
Vaughan, Gladys, 95
Vaughan, Stuart, 43, 52, 87, 88, 91
Vega, Jose, 401
Vega, Leslie, 400
Veglia, Paul, 368
Vejar, Rudy, 368
Veldt, The, 421
Venora, Lee, 368
Vent dans les Branches de Sassafras, Du, 114
Ventura, Clyde, 372
Venture, Richard, 89
Venus Is, 5, 445
Venuta, Benay, 368, 413
Verbit, Helen, 437
Verdon, Gwen, 16, 64, 395, 454, 455, 456
Vernon, John, 96, 382
Veronica, 30, 426-427
Very Rich Woman, A, 4, 13, 21-22, 38, 372
Vesey, Desmond, 75
Vest, Bud, 395
Vestoff, Virginia, 428
Vialle, Max, 392
Vian, Boris, 87, 114
Victor, Charles, 470

Victor, Dee, 71, 387
Vidette, John, 96
Vielhaber, Werner, 429
View From the Bridge, A, 415, 442
Vigoda, Abe, 65, 86, 87
Viharo, Robert, 394
Vilar, Dominique, 117
Vilar, Jean, 114
Village Theater, 438
Villamil, Jaclynn, 413
Villiers, Mavis, 398, 455
Vilsen, Luc, 115
Vinaver, Steven, 33, 428
Vincent, Paul, 427
Vincent, Yves, 117
Vines, William, 95
Visions of Sugar Plums, 86
Vitold, Michel, 115
Vivian Beaumont Theater (Lincoln Center), 5, 25-27, 35, 40, 44
Voelpel, Fred, 375
Vogel, George, 88
Voight, Jon, 89, 442
Volpone, 48, 83
Von Gontard, Gert, 406, 429
Von Koss, Doug, 66
Von Rahau, Lee, 66
Von Scherier, Sasha, 432
Von Volz, Valerie, 430
Vool-Ellin, Ruth, 426
Vos, Eric, 88
Voskovec, George, 421
Voutsinas, Andreas, 431
Voysey Inheritance, The, 112
Vulo, Louis, 428
Vye, Murvyn, 366, 380

Wade, Warren, 430
Wager, Michael, 400
Wagner, Frank, 422
Wagner, Robin, 89, 381, 422
Wagner, Shirley Jac, 380, 381
Wagner, Thomas, 401
Wait, Robert R., 78
Wait a Minim!, 4, 12, 18-19, 401-403, 452, 454, 458
Wait Until Dark, 4, 7, 13, 22, 396, 456
Waite, Bruce, 425
Waite, Ralph, 399, 425
Waiting for Godot, 68, 70-71, 80
Wakatake, Fuemi, 403
Wakefield Circle of Mystery Plays, 82
Walberg, Betty, 377, 406
Walburn, Raymond, 21, 372
Walenta, Edmund, 418
Wales, Gary, 367
Walk in Dark Places, A, 429
Walken, Christopher, 20, 400, 454, 455
Walker, Arlene, 394

Walker, Charles, 72
Walker, Diana, 412
Walker, Donald, 367, 388, 411
Walker, June, 470
Walker, Lillias, 113
Walker, Nancy, 394
Walker, Robert, 101
Walker, Rudolph, 113
Walker, Sydney, 71, 387
Walker, Zena, 112
Wall, William J., 70
Wallace, Anne, 413
Wallace, Art, 367, 423
Wallace, George, 51
Wallace, Lee, 85, 433
Wallace, Marie, 378, 395
Wallace, Mimi, 391, 411
Wallace, Ron, 83
Wallace, Trudy, 391
Wallach, Eli, 55, 441
Wallach, Ira, 72, 76
Waller, David, 100, 101
Walling, Stratton, 445
Wallis, Shani, 411, 455
Wally, Gus, 470
Walsh, Alexandria, 399
Walston, Victor, 99
Walter, Meg, 375
Walters, Paulette, 387
Walters, Susan, 423
Walton, Joanna, 420
Walton, Vera, 470
Waltz Invention, The, 457
Waltzer, Jack, 380
Wamen, James, 368
Wampler, Ben, 430
War, 432-433
War and Peace, 415
Ward, Audrey, 79, 416
Ward, B. J., 440
Ward, Douglas Turner, 32, 426, 454
Ward, Janet, 376
Ward, Mary, 374, 378, 470
Ward, Timothy, 380, 381
Ward, Wayne, 367
Wardwell, John, 399
Warfield, David, 72
Waring, James, 68
Warner, Andrew J., 470
Warner, David, 100, 101, 109, 112
Warner, Elise, 410, 418
Warner, Neil, 386
Warner, Sunny B., 85, 86
Warren, Joseph, 398
Warren, Lesley Ann, 375
Warren, Rod, 34, 415
Warrick, Ruth, 56
Warriner, Frederic, 95, 427
Warwick, Margaretta, 75
Washbourne, Mona, 110
Washington, James, 423
Washington Opera Society, 68
Washington Theater Club, 67

Wasserman, Dale, 16, 195, 386, 456
Waterhouse, Keith, 111
Waterman, Willard, 412
Waterous, Allen H., 470
Waters, Mira, 387
Waters, Paulette, 71
Waters, Tom, 431
Waters of Babylon, The, 35, 64, 437
Waterson, Sam, 400
Waterson, Stan, 441
Wathen, Peggy, 367
Watkyn, Arthur, 118
Watson, Donald, 74
Watson, Kip, 418
Watson, Minor, 470
Watson, Patti, 418
Watson, Paul, 80
Watson, Ron, 418
Watson, Susan, 368, 392, 409
Watson, Thomas, 74
Watt, Douglas, 454
Watts, Gwendolyn, 111
Watts, John, 101
Watts, Richard, Jr., 37, 38, 451, 454
Watt, Stan, 389
Wax Museum, The, 73
Way Out of the Way In, The, 74
Way of the World, The, 58, 81
Wayland, Newton, 73
Wayne, David, 6, 390
Wayward Stork, The, 4, 22, 64, 394
We Comrades Three, 28
Weales, Gerald, 454
Webb, Alan, 394
Webb, Alyce Elizabeth, 372
Webb, Barbara Ann, 417, 418
Webb, Elmon, 431
Webb, Geoffrey, 421
Webb, Kenneth, 470
Weber, Anthony, 97
Webster, Byron, 377
Webster, Hugh, 111
Webster, John, 34, 427
Wedge, Maura K., 370, 441
Wedgeworth, Ann, 432
Week From Today, A, 436
Weibel, Joyce, 420
Weidman, Jerome, 3
Weidner, Paul, 78
Weigel, Hans, 117
Weiler, Constance, 470
Weill, Kurt, 70, 371
Weinberg, Lawrence, 435
Weinberg, Tobi, 96
Weiner, Louise, 386, 389, 430, 432
Weinstein, Arnold, 63
Weinstock, Jack, 366, 407
Weir, Helen, 101
Weiss, Peter, 3, 10-11, 113, 269, 393, 455, 456

Weiss, Rudolph, 430
Welch, Charles, 445
Welch, James B., 470
Welles, Violet, 382, 384, 400, 435
Welty Revisited, 77
Wendell, Lynn, 367
Wendorf, Vernon, 418
Wendt, William C., 367
Werner, Fred, 385, 395
Wernicke, Annemarie, 407
Wertimer, Ned, 423
Wesker, Arnold, 35, 110, 111, 437
West, Bernie, 394
West, Buster, 470
West, Donald, 82
West, Jennifer, 394
West, Madge, 80
West, Paul, 470
West, Timothy, 100, 101
West Side Story, 418
Westerman, Dale, 408, 424
Westman, Lolita Ann, 470
Weston, Jack, 445
Weston, Jim, 86
Weterick, Fred, 383, 395
Wetmore, Joan, 372, 396
Wettstein, Norton, 95
Wexler, Norman, 436
Wexler, Peter, 79, 428
Weyand, Ronald, 380, 381
Wharton, John F., 6, 39-40, 454
Wharton, Leigh, 432
What This Country Needs, 56, 445
What's-His-Name the Ana-lyst, 64
Wheeler, David, 73, 74, 416
Wheeler, John, 395
Wheeler, Kathryn, 79
When the Wind Blew Cool At Rosie's Place, 445
When We Dead Awaken, 30, *433*
Where's Charley?, 4, 28, *407-408*
Where's Daddy?, 4, 8, *400*
White, Deborah, 431
White, Jane, 96, 454
White, John, 32, *426-427*
White, Onna, 412, 456
White, Peggy, 420
White, Ruth, 21, 29, 394, 421, 445, 455
White Devil, The, 30, 34, *427-428*
Whitehead, Robert, 26, 27, 60, 400
Whitehead, Virginia Bolen, 471
Whiteley, Larry, 373
Whiteside, Ann, 75, 82
Whitfield, Arthur, 367, 424
Whitfield, Howard, 374
Whitfield, Walter W., 470

Whiting, Gordon, 110, 113
Whiting, John, 23, 45, 385, 457
Whitman, Alice C., 437
Whitmore, James, 55
Whitney, Iris, 401
Whitt, Dale, 437
Whittall, Gertrude Clarke, 471
Whole Truth, The, *445*
Who's Afraid of Virginia Woolf?, 40, 43, 56, 70, 76, 78, 79
Who's Got the Pot?, 77
Why Do I Deserve This?, 30, *429*
Wicks, Frank, 83
Wickwire, Nancy, 82
Widdoes, Kathleen, 387
Widney, Stone, 377
Wiensko, Robert H., 383
Wilbur, Richard, 70, 72, 75, 85
Wilcox, Larry, 391
Wilcox, Nina, 400
Wilcox, Patti O'Donnell, 76, 77
Wilcox, Richard, 80
Wilcox, Roger Kent, 74-75
Wilcox, Ronald, 76, 77
Wild Duck, The, 71
Wilde, Oscar, 78, 79, 85, 87
Wilder, Clinton, 394
Wilder, David, 410
Wilder, Ian, 82
Wilder, Thornton, 43, 60, 75, 76, 88
Wilhelm, Kurt, 75
Wilkes, Alton, 430
Wilkinson, Kate, 72, 380
Wilkinson, Leslie, 437
Wilkinson, Marc, 382
Will Greer's Americana, *436*
Willard, Fred, 434
Williams, Angela, 78
Williams, Billy Dee, 89
Williams, Clarence, III, 396
Williams, Clifford, 99
Williams, Clyde, 394
Williams, Hugh, 111
Williams, Jodi, 412
Williams, Mack, 470
Williams, Margaret, 111
Williams, Mervyn, 427
Williams, Michael, 100, 393
Williams, Misha, 99
Williams, Ralph, 81
Williams, Tennessee, 3, 24, 28, 65, 72, 74, 75, 78, 79, 80, 81, 84, 87, 89, 366, 399
Williams, Valdo, 394
Williamson, Laird, 99
Williamson, Nicol, 10, 25, 389, 455, 456
Williamson, Sandra, 74
Williamson, Susan, 393

Willis, Kirk, 75, 76
Willman, Noel, 20, 400, 455, 456
Willson, A. Leslie, 434
Willson, Meredith, 366
Wilson, Carl, 430
Wilson, Charles, 372
Wilson, Dolores, 390, 440
Wilson, Edwin, 429
Wilson, Elizabeth, 422
Wilson, Frank, 435
Wilson, Georges, 114, 116
Wilson, Joseph, 437
Wilson, Kathy, 412
Wilson, Lanford, 32, 432, 457
Wilson, Sandy, 117
Wilson, Wayne, 97
Wily Widow, The, 113
Wimmer, Maria, 407
Winblad, Bjorn, 50, 76
Wind in the Sassafras Trees, 114
Window, Muriel, 470
Windows, 79
Windsor, Barbara, 111
Windt, W. Bernard, 99
Wing, Lee, 89
Wingate, Peter, 82
Winston, Hattie, 426
Winston, Helene, 79
Winston, Paul, 408
Winter, Edward, 380, 381
Winter's Tale, A, 49, 74, 98-99
Winters, Lawrence, 470
Winters, Marian, 383
Winterset, 30, 34, *429-430*
Winwood, Estelle, 399
Wiseman, Joseph, 55
Wishy, Joseph, 411
Witcover, Walt, 423
Withers, Iva, 51
Witness For the Prosecu-tion, *436*
Wittman, Ellen, 383, 396
Wittmer, Toodie, 393, 410
Wittop, Freddy, 21, 377, 401, 455
Wittstein, Ed, 391, 432, 445, 454
Wives, The, 416
Wolf, Jack, 470
Wolf, Peter, 51
Wolff, Art, 427
Wolff, Beverly, 372
Woll, Anne, 387, 427
Wolsk, Eugene V., 21, 400
Wolsky, Albert, 374, 404
Woman, 30
Woman Horse, The, 117
Womble, Andre, 75, 76
Wonderful Town, 418
Wonderful World of Bur-lesque, The, 415
Wood, Angela, 380
Wood, Bert, 367

Wood, Eugene R., 74, 385, 386
Wood, Jonathon, 75
Wood, Peggy, 50, 77
Wood, Roland, 425
Woodman, William, 75, 80
Woods, Arline, 74
Woods, Richard, 71, 387
Woodward, Tom, 436
Woolf, Henry, 393
Woolman, Claude, 83
Workman, Jenny, 368
World of Charles Aznavour, The, 4, 7, *377*
World of Gunter Grass, The, 30, 33, 39, *433*
World of Ray Bradbury, The, 30, 32, *421*
World Theater Season, 113
World's Baby, The, 110
Worley, Jo Anne, 423, 428
Worth, Carl, 87
Worth, Coley, 403
Worth, Irene, 109, 110
Worth, Maggie, 393
Worthington, William, 470
Woyzeck, 4, 28, *406-407*
Wright, Mark, 376, 394, 399
Wright, Marshall, 98
Wright, Robert, 387, 443
Wulf, Richard, 370
Wurtzel, Stuart, 71, 84
Wycherley, William, 378
Wyckham, John, 99, 370
Wylie, John, 79
Wylton, Tim, 100, 101
Wyman, Stephen, 71
Wymark, Patrick, 110
Wymbs Luke, 425

Xmas in Las Vegas, 4, 24, 64, *383*

Yale Drama School, 40, 43
Yaffe, James, 34, 430
Yamada, Kagashi, 403
Yarnell, Bruce, 413
Yearling, The, 4, 5, *390*
Yeats, W. B., 74, 79
Yeats & Company, 79
Yeoman of the Guard, The, 30, *419*
Yes is For a Very Young Man, 73
Yohn, Erica, 380
Yoo, Duk Hyung, 50, 77
Yorke, Alan, 394
Yoshida, Bunjaku, 403
Yoshida, Bunsho, 403
Yoshida, Eliza, 403
Yoshida, Minosuke, 403
Yoshida, Peter, 96
Yoshida, Tamako, 403
Yoshida, Tamao, 403
Yoshida, Tamasho, 403
You Can't Take It With You, 4, 7, 13, 27-28, 40, 42, 50, 51, 70, 71, 77, 79, *387*, 451, 456
You Never Can Tell, 109, 112
Young, Agnes, 425
Young, Frederick, 378
Young, Harry, 384
Young, Janis, 85
Young, Ron, 412
Young, Stark, 89
Young, William W., 83

Young Marrieds Play Monopoly, *431*
Younger, Beverly, 75
Younger, Judith, 431
Youngstein, Max, 389
Yousef, Tish, 437
Yule, Chris, 407
Yule, Don, 367, 372, 420
Yulin, Harris, 416
Yvonne, Princess of Burgundy, 117

Zahn, Mary, 375, 392
Zak, Sheftel, 426
Zakkai, Jamil, 430
Zang, Edward, 46, 73
Zavattini, Cesare, 118
Zeisler, Peter, 43, 44, 58-59
Zeldis, Joshua, 426
Zerbe, Anthony, 63, 98
Zetter, Lois, 423
Zierk, David, 74
Zimmermann, Ed, 378, 445
Zimmerman, Rachael Ann, 99
Zimmet, Marya, 400
Zipprodt, Patricia, 388, 404
Zizak, John, 421
Zoo Story, The, 30, *416-417*
Zorich, Louis, 380
Zucchelli, Rosette, 115
Zuckerman, Ira, 70
Zuker, Howard J., 416
Zulu and the Zayda, The, 4, 22, *383*, 458
Zweig, Stefan, 83
Zwerling, Darrell, 436
Zwetkoff, Peter, 407
Zykovs, The, 117